St George & the Dragon, Church of St Cross, Winchester

The Spine of Albion

An Exploration of Earth Energies
and Landscape Mysteries
along the Belinus Line

Gary Biltcliffe
Caroline Hoare

Sacred Lands Publishing

Published by
Sacred Lands Publishing
P O Box 7737
Weymouth
Dorset DT4 4FZ
UK
www.belinusline.com

First published 2012 by Sacred Lands Publishing
Reprinted with revisions and amendments 2017

ISBN: 978-0-9572382-0-6

British Library Cataloguing in Publication Data
A catalogue record for this book is available from the British Library

Artwork and photographs by Gary Biltcliffe and Caroline Hoare unless otherwise stated
Cover design by Yuri Leitch

Set in Minion Pro 11/12.5pt by Beamreach (www.beamreachuk.co.uk)
Printed and bound by Beamreach (www.beamreachuk.co.uk)

Contents

Preface and Acknowledgements

Over the past four years since first publication, Caroline and I have received much acclaim for The Spine of Albion, including an award from the British Society of Dowsers; to which we are most grateful. We have toured the UK promoting the book with talks and walks at key sacred sites, major cities and towns featured in the book and made many friends along the way. Most gratifying are the emails we have received from many inspired individuals who have made their own pilgrimage along this sacred spine of Britain. Furthermore, many dowsers and sensitives have informed us that long before our book was published they were aware of the powerful serpent or dragon energies, we call Elen and Belinus, in their native areas and at sacred places including Uffington White Horse and the Rollright Stones. Others were so inspired by some of the places visited by Elen and Belinus that it literally 'changed their life'.

Our intention when writing this book was to inspire people to connect with this ancient land, once collectively called Albion, and walk its ancient paths with the awareness of its legends and folklore to lift the veils of materialism and receive the beauty, wisdom and love that Albion offers. This the second print is a refined version of the former with additional maps and pictures.

I am grateful to all those who have helped and encouraged me over the years, particularly in the late 90s when the enormity of the task nearly forced me to give it up and hand the work on to others. I wish to give special thanks to Yana Nilsson, a healer and holistic therapist and recognise the late John Beasley a dowser and mystic, who both assisted me in the early years of my research of the Belinus Line. I would also like to thank members of the Wessex, Hampshire, Sussex, Dorset and Wyvern Dowsers, including Dave Swan and Bob Sephton, and in particular, Sandy McKenzie, Paul Craddock, Pat Law and Paul Barnett who supported my findings on St Catherine's Hill and other places, which gave me the confidence to continue. My gratitude also goes out to the late John Michell for pointing out the significance of the place-name Meon on the Belinus Line.

I am also indebted to those who helped my dowsing skills, including Jim Longton back in 1990 in Lancashire, the late Dennis Wheatley, a great man who believed in my quest, and the late Hamish Miller who tutored me back in the 90s and also encouraged me to keep going and finish the book. I am also grateful to the psychics whose insights were invaluable to the research including Marie Field, Mary Kingston, Darrell Harrison and Theolyn Cortens.

Other contributors I wish to thank are Frank Zweers for donating his amazing photographs of special places along the Spine of Albion, Yuri Leitch for his artwork and insights for the cover, Paul Weston for his continual support, Brian Cowper for guiding us to a sacred cave in Cumbria, Paul Broadhurst for his insights, support and friendship over the years, and Ba Miller, Maria Wheatley and Peter Knight for their encouragement, help, advice and continued support from the early days.

Finally, I have to thank the one person who has helped to bring it all together, my partner and co-author Caroline Hoare, whose insights and invaluable skills in the research and making of this book has made it a reality.

Picture Credits

The Isle of Wight. © Will Glover, Clarence House Holiday Apartments Ventnor (www. iowholidayapartments.co.uk).

The Nostrils at Culver Cliff, Isle of Wight. Courtesy of Andrew Butler.

View of St Catherine's Hill, Winchester. Courtesy of Dr Jim Champion.

The Great Hall of Winchester Castle. A watercolour by Francis Grose c.1780. © Society of Antiquaries of London.

Carving of the 'Three Disgraces' at St John the Baptist Church, Burford. Courtesy of the Vicar and Church Wardens of Burford Church.

The Creation window depicting a swan at its centre at Aston Church. Courtesy of Aston Church.

Diagram showing the geological strata of Barr Beacon. Courtesy of GeoConservationUK and the Black County Geodiversity Partnership.

Ruins of Chartley Castle. Courtesy of Martin Handley.

Big Fenton Farmhouse. Courtesy of Andrew Moss.

Carving of the head of the giant Tarquin on the ceiling of the Audit Room in Chetham's Library. Courtesy of the Governors of Chetham's Hospital and Library.

Stained-glass window of the legendary King Arthur and *Roman altar stone of the horned god Mars inside Whalley Church.* Courtesy of the vicar of Whalley Church.

View of Clitheroe by Mathias Read c.1715. Courtesy of Burnley Borough Council, Townley Hall Art Gallery & Museums.

Artist's rendition of a Sarmatian cavalryman with a 'dragon' wind-sock standard taken from an image engraved on a stone found at Ribchester. From the research by Dr Dan Robinson, Keeper of Archaeology at the Grosvenor Museum, Chester.

Norman pillar carved with a Green Man inside St Mary's Church, Kirkby Lonsdale. Courtesy of the Rector and Wardens of St Mary's Church.

Aerial view of Brougham Hall. Courtesy of Simon Ledingham.

Large boulder with cup and ring marks in Carlisle Museum that once stood above Ninekirks at Honeypot Farm. Courtesy of Tullie House Museum and Art Gallery Trust.

Carlisle Cathedral with its once extensive buildings from an engraving by Sir Charles Nicholson dated 1906 and *Carving of a pair of kissing male and female dragons on a capital of a pillar in the choir of Carlisle Cathedral.* Courtesy of the Dean and Chapter of Carlisle.

Carving of the head of the giant Tarquin on the ceiling of the Audit Room in Chetham's Library. Reproduced courtesy of the Governors of Chetham's Hospital and Library.

'A true picture of one Pict' and *Pictish Woman by John White.* Illustrated in Thomas Heriot's *'A brief and True report of the New Found Land of Virginia', dated 1588.* © Wilson Special Collections Library, University of North Carolina Chapel Hill.

Interior of the north aisle of Stobo Kirk and *Window showing Merlin with St Kentigern, Stobo Kirk.* Courtesy of the Parishes of the Upper Tweed (www.uppertweedale.org.uk).

The Forteviot Arch. © National Museums Scotland.

Painted ceiling inside St Mary's Church, Grandtully. Courtesy of Historic Scotland.

Map of Roman England based on Jones & Mattingly's Atlas of Roman Britain (ISBN 978-1-84217-06700, 1990, reprinted 2007).

Geological Map of Great Britain attributed to AlexD

Photographs by Frank Zweers p.98/99, 124/125, 162, 218/219, 232/233 (Cloud End), 286/287, 366/367, 376/377 (Buddhist Centre), 418/419 (Loch Leven Island), 424, 430/431, 468/469, View of Balnakeil Church.

About the Authors

Gary Biltcliffe was born in 1960 and brought up in Lancashire. He has dedicated the last 30 years to historical research and investigation of earth mysteries, dowsing ancient sites, uncovering lost knowledge and early folklore. He has appeared on radio and television and has lectured widely in the UK and North America. Gary has also led International groups around Britain's sacred sites and written articles for journals and magazines. He moved to Dorset in 1993 and researched much of its ancient history culminating in his first publication *The Spirit of Portland, Revelations of a Sacred Isle* in 2009.

Caroline Hoare was born in 1958 and brought up on a farm in the heart of the Dart Valley in South Devon. She started her working life in a Fine Art auction house and later transferred to the world of publishing and book selling. Caroline moved from London to Dorset in 2003 and trained as a Geomancer, Feng Shui Consultant and Holistic Interior Designer. She has also spent the last thirteen years alongside Gary travelling to lost cities around the world, researching history and ancient civilisations and has a keen interest in the mythology and folklore of Britain.

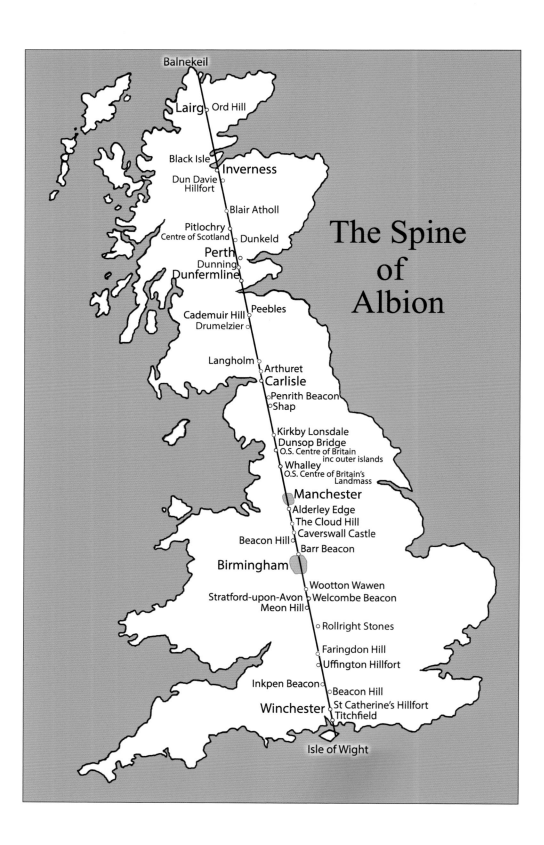

Balnekeil

Lairg Ord Hill

Black Isle
Inverness
Dun Davie
Hillfort

Blair Atholl

Pitlochry
Centre of Scotland Dunkeld
Perth
Dunning
Dunfermline

Peebles
Cademuir Hill
Drumelzier

Langholm
Arthuret
Carlisle
Penrith Beacon
Shap

Kirkby Lonsdale
Dunsop Bridge
O.S. Centre of Britain
inc outer islands
Whalley
O.S. Centre of Britain's
Landmass

Manchester
Alderley Edge
The Cloud Hill
Caverswall Castle
Beacon Hill
Barr Beacon

Birmingham

Wootton Wawen
Stratford-upon-Avon Welcombe Beacon
Meon Hill

Rollright Stones

Faringdon Hill
Uffington Hillfort

Inkpen Beacon
Beacon Hill

Winchester St Catherine's Hillfort
Titchfield

Isle of Wight

The Spine

of

Albion

The Discovery

The Dragon Force

One of the greatest unexplained and controversial mysteries of our time is the many alignments that link together sacred sites all over the UK and Europe called 'leys' or 'ley lines'. The history surrounding this subject has many landmarks, beginning with Alfred Watkins in 1921. He was the first to propose that certain landscape features such as prehistoric earthworks and churches seem to fall on visible alignments. He named them leys due to the frequency with which the word ley appeared in the many place names on the lines, such as Crossley, Endley and Longley. His controversial theory arose in a moment of vision while out riding his horse in Herefordshire. In a flash, he perceived the existence of a system of glowing lines intersecting at hills, churches and other sacred places. His research and findings published in *The Old Straight Track* in 1925 concludes with the revelation that prehistoric man constructed a system of aligned sites for the purpose of travel.

Investigators of this phenomenon have a rule that alignments or leys are only genuine if they pass through more than four mark points. These include hilltops, churches, megalithic stones, holy wells, unusual rock formations, crossroads, prehistoric camps and hillforts. The ley theory proposed by Watkins was criticised by many archaeologists at the time, who pointed out that given the high density of prehistoric monuments in Britain, a line drawn through any part of the country would inevitably clip a number of sites, especially large earthworks such as hillforts, henges and sculptured hills. They also ridiculed him for failing to explain why many of the trackways go over hills and mountains rather than around them. As a result, his work was unrecognised by the academic world.

Watkins' research, however, was not confined solely to map work, for he mentions that 'Experience and practice brings an insight, which quickly spots a ley. Often one can be first seen on the map, but I more often see it out of doors in "the lay of the land" itself, and this before the mark points are found'.

In the 1960s and '70s, several New Age researchers changed the perspective of the ley mystery suggesting that rather than trackways these lines, in the words of Professor Elliot Smith, were 'a concrete expression of the divine power of life-giving energy'. In 1969, John Michell published the most influential and inspiring book *View Over Atlantis*, later revised as *The New View Over Atlantis* in 1983. His articulate writings on the subject of ley lines gave an almost academic acceptability to the New Age and he continued to enliven the debate further by likening the British ley system to the *dragon lines* of ancient Chinese tradition. His theories changed people's conception of the land as a living, breathing entity. He wrote: 'It was recognised that certain powerful currents, lines of magnetism, run invisible over the surface of the Earth. The task of the geomancer was to detect these currents and interpret their influence on the land over which they passed'.

The Chinese geomancers were trained in the art of astrology and the divination of the land, and were skilled in finding the most auspicious place to build shrines and temples for the emperors. They understood the life-giving qualities of the earth serpents or dragons and in certain places shaped their landscape to harness their energy, inducing spiritual harmony and aiding fertility within the land. The emperor's palaces and tombs were the only structures permitted on the dragon paths, thus ensuring the imperial leader power in life and death and the future success of his dynasty.

For the Chinese, the dragon or *lung mei* was a symbol of this divine force, containing either male (*yang*) or female (*yin*) properties. The male current or White Tiger followed the high places such as mountaintops across the country, whilst the female current or Blue Dragon visited lakes, rivers and springs deep in the valleys. With the aid of divining rods, a compass and a vast knowledge of the celestial influences, the Chinese geomancer detected these paths of the dragon, constructing buildings so as not to interfere or block their natural flow. The sole purpose of this practice of *feng shui* was to bring order and beauty to the landscape. The geomancers were also skilled in channelling and directing the natural streams of earth energy to the imperial seat of the Emperor.

Many of the well-known leys travel only a few kilometres and often begin at landscape features such as mounds or sculptured hills. Longer leys that stretch over many kilometres are rare and if plotted on maps often suffer from inaccuracies.

The St Michael Line, first noticed by John Michell, is the most famous long-distance ley in Britain. It courses from Land's End in Cornwall to Hopton-on-Sea on the Norfolk coast, marked by numerous prehistoric sites and hilltop churches dedicated to St Michael. Standing on one particular hill called the Mump near Burrowbridge in Somerset, Michell noticed its elongated shape points to the Tor a prominent hill in Glastonbury 16 km (10 miles) away. On a map, he discovered that this line extends eastwards to pass through the great southern entrance stones of the Avebury stone circle in Wiltshire.

Numerous churches dedicated to St Michael and St Mary stand along the whole length of the line, with many constructed either side of it, as if the builders of these sanctuaries were aware of a sacred corridor hidden within the landscape. This alignment of sacred centres and places of power also has a solar influence, for it is aligned to the Beltane sunrise and forms the longest east–west through-route in Britain.

Earth Mysteries researcher David Furlong, using Google Earth computer mapping, has since determined the accuracy of the St Michael Line. Furlong has given some thought to how the ancients surveyed this alignment, suggesting that they must have aligned it to the high points in the landscape. He says, 'Setting out long distance alignments is not so difficult providing there is a sufficient number of workers and care is taken in the sighting of the alignment. The most obvious way to do this would be by sighting to the rising or setting of a specific star' (www.davidfurlong.co.uk).

Together with John Michell, many authors proposed that the Neolithic and Bronze Age peoples in Europe built their stone temples, earthworks and barrows similar to the principles of the Chinese. They too had diviners to locate these hidden pathways, marking their route with standing stones, dolmans, stone circles, long barrows and tumuli. As astronomers and astrologers, the Celts and their priesthood, the Druids, continued this tradition of tracing the emergence of the dragon force, manipulating and animating its fertilising power required in the land. Ceremonial processions along these dragon paths created straight tracks, similar to those walked by later pilgrims visiting holy shrines. Michell refers to the St Michael Line as having the 'appearance of a "via sacra", a sacred pathway between ritual centres which is a feature of ancient landscapes throughout the world, and is supported by records of pilgrimage routes between places on the alignment".

The Michael and Mary Serpents

During the late 1980s, Hamish Miller and Paul Broadhurst further explored the enigma of the St Michael Line. Hamish had a great gift for dowsing energy currents, a sensitivity that evolved from a near-death experience. Together with Paul's articulate writing skills and meticulous research, they produced an account of their journey dowsing the line, starting on the coast of Cornwall near Land's End.

However, instead of finding a straight line, Hamish detected a sinuous path of energy that weaved across the landscape visiting prehistoric sites and Christian sanctuaries either side of the straight alignment. Hamish also discovered that at certain secret places of power the line narrowed down to a point in the ground and reappeared a little further away in precisely the same manner. He realised that this unusual behaviour was the result of another line of energy crossing with it to form what Hamish called a *Node*. He found himself having to de-tune to follow this new line effectively for, although similar in width and strength, it had a gentler and softer nature. This they concluded was a feminine current of energy.

They soon discovered that two currents, one male the other female, like the Chinese White Tiger and Blue Dragon, followed the ley for the whole length of its course. Hamish also discovered that the currents form a Node at various prehistoric sites including Iron Age hillforts, mounds and stone circles, some located in medieval churches and others unmarked in the middle of a field.

Over the centuries, those initiated into the underground stream of esoteric knowledge were aware of these secret Nodes, regarding them as fortuitous places of yin and yang power and, like the Chinese, built their temples and churches over them. In the course of dowsing the Michael and Mary lines of the St Michael alignment, Miller and Broadhurst uncovered evidence that our ancestors had at one time manipulated these currents or lines of dragon force, in order to exert greater control or authority over certain places of power. Their research was published in the book *The Sun and the Serpent* in 1989. Their discoveries have since motivated generations of Earth Mystery enthusiasts around the world to rediscover and re-examine their own sacred sites.

Modern researchers claim that these long-distance alignments are linked to a grid or network of lines that circumnavigate the Earth and that their crossing places or Node points were utilised by man as their centres of religious practice. Today the realm of science is drawing ever closer to realising that metaphysics can explain some of the mysteries of the Earth, and that our planet is a living entity; this is known as the Gaia principle. Often people make the comparison that the electromagnetic life force around the human body is similar in essence to that of the Earth's, the Nodes relating to the acupuncture points of our own human body.

In Chinese acupuncture, a chart of the life force or *chi* around the human body depicts twelve lines or meridians in the form of invisible channels under the skin, each paired with another linking the main organs. The acupuncture points are the Node points of each meridian, considered to be the entrance and exit points for the vital energy surging within our body. The insertion of a needle into one of these Nodes affects the corresponding part of the body through which the meridian travels; this helps the energy to freely flow throughout the body.

Chi consists of the opposite as well as the complementary forces of yin and yang: yin representing the feminine elements (watery, dark, negative) and yang the masculine elements (airy, light, positive). If the positive and negative forces are in balance, chi will flow smoothly around the body, whereas imbalance will create sickness and ill health. This concept also applies to the Earth; its sickness is termed by geomancers as 'geopathic stress', which comes from the Greek *geo* meaning 'of the earth' and *pathos* meaning 'suffering' or 'disease'. It relates to irregularities in the earth's magnetic field, which can be aggravated by a variety of natural and manmade features.

Like the human body, many researchers believe that there are key crossing points of the earth energy meridians at different places around our planet, and that our ancient ancestors marked these Nodes with stone or earth monuments.

Dowsers around the world, like Miller, have detected similar dragon currents and found that they are generally a few metres wide and avoid a dead straight course. The name dragon derives from the Latin *Draconem* and the Greek *Drakon* meaning 'serpent'. Throughout the world, folklore and legend refer to dragons and serpents as mysterious reptilian creatures that haunt the countryside and protect treasure in a 'dragon's den'. They would repeatedly terrorise the local population from their lair, often located in curious shaped hills, mounds, lakes or springs. In British legends, the dragon consumed

virgin maidens offered by the locals to appease its hunger or wrath until a brave knight rescues her by slaying the dragon. The earliest example of this depiction comes from the ancient Greek tale of Perseus rescuing Andromeda from the sea dragon. In many cultures, the dragon represents God's wrath or the destructive force of nature. In the Americas, the ancient tribes of the Toltecs and Aztecs sacrificed their people to the earth serpent in order to regenerate the fertility in the land.

Unlike European societies, Eastern cultures still view the dragon as having great spiritual significance, corresponding to the primal forces of nature and possessing great supernatural powers. In Chinese mythology, only a hero with a pure heart can tame or destroy the dragon. Dragon slayer legends are worldwide and date back to Mesopotamia and Ancient Greece. According to British folklore St George, England's national hero and patron saint, saved the people of Uffington in Berkshire and Wormingford in Essex from a monstrous dragon.

An Indian Hoysala sculpture of a Naga couple

J.E. Hanauer in *Folklore of the Holy Land* (2003) refers to an early rendition of this medieval tale in Palestine where a dragon had taken hold of a city's water supply at a fountain, refusing anyone water unless a maiden or youth was offered as a sacrifice. The locals, unable to destroy the serpent, were obliged to comply with his wishes or die of thirst. When all the youths had perished, it became the turn of the king's daughter and as she was about to be devoured, *Mar Jiryis* or St George appeared on a white horse and speared the monster between the eyes. Such allegorical tales as this have hidden meaning, for the knight may characterise the new Christian doctrine destroying the old serpent wisdom. There are many stories that recall the ancient practice of worshipping the earth serpent whose power determined the success of the harvest or even the cleanliness of drinking water.

Further examples are found in many folk plays around the world, which link dragons with the fertility of the land. In Bavaria the midsummer ritual of St George slaying the dragon reaches its climax when the knight pierces a bladder of blood carried inside the effigy. Spectators then mop up the blood and spread it over the flax fields to animate the harvest. In Sicily two loaves were carried in procession with the dragon effigy on St George's Day and were later broken into little pieces for farmers to bury in their fields to ensure the fertility of their crops.

The Sumerian deity Ningizzida with two Griffins, dated to 2000 BC

Beltane is a Celtic festival celebrated on 1 May, which marks the beginning of spring. In towns and villages across Europe, Beltane festivals parade the effigy of a dragon through the streets to welcome or draw the fertility force into their environs to precipitate a good harvest. The slaying of the dragon was not the killing of the beast but the fixing of its fertile qualities at a sacred place when it rises to its full power in the spring. There are many images of the dragon slayers St George and St Michael around the world, which depict them pinning the dragon to the ground without piercing it.

However, when the dragon force is out of balance the negative energy can be detrimental to our health. The practice of driving a stake in the ground to cure imbalanced earth energies, called by dowsers 'black streams', is a modern version of the dragon-slaying act. In the story of *Ludd and Llefelys* in the old Welsh myths collectively called *The Mabinogion*, the whole country suffers from the effects of two dragons fighting at the centre of England, and by fixing the problem at the omphalos, either by removal or by staking to the ground, peace and harmony is restored once more.

However, many of these tales and festivals suggest a spiritual aspect to the serpent or dragon force. Patrick MacManaway, former chairman of the British Society of Dowsers, asserts that 'dragon lines are the pathways of connection in the universal matrix of consciousness, connecting people, places and events, past, present and future, carrying the dynamic flow of life force between and around all things'.

In the early 1980s Colin Bloy, a master dowser and healer, researched these unseen undulating currents of energy and became aware of the different qualities within them. He detected they were associated with certain frequencies that were either beneficial or detrimental to life, causing illness and disease. Where such energy lines impinged on a person's quality of life, he applied various healing techniques usually on the nearest crossing point, which Bloy discovered reversed the negative effects. Copper rods inserted at specific points in the ground can neutralise the negative charge in the ground and certain crystals have the ability to heal and cleanse an environment.

The frequencies referred to by Colin Bloy are often difficult to detect, especially within the dragon lines, as they vibrate outside of human physical sensory perception. Consequently, the individual needs to spend time tuning into the landscape to become sensitive to these hidden energies. Those with a natural psychic ability and a strong connection with the landscape find it easier than most at identifying the paths of the serpent. Birds and animals follow the dragon currents during the migration season because they are naturally in tune with the innate earth forces, just as our ancient ancestors once were.

Over time, Bloy realised that visualisation was perhaps the most effective form of healing, a practice used by priests and magicians throughout the ages. There are plenty of instances where the power of the mind has proved to affect all sorts of healing and change, including the use of prayer. For it is the heartfelt intention that accompanies the thought processes involved with visualisation that influences the outcome. Important to this process is that one must be strongly aware of the beneficial powers provided by the Universe, which can be channelled through intentioned thought to the troubled area by a shaft of pure healing light which is then envisioned to flood and dissolve the harmful influences, restoring harmony to the body or land.

Bloy founded the Fountain Group in 1981 to help heal communities disturbed by such problems as violence and discordance. Using his spiritual healing techniques a network of groups made a real and positive difference to the lives of inhabitants living in the affected communities. Healers and dowsers would gather to send healing and loving thoughts to a focal point of the town or omphalos, such as a fountain or market cross. Often this healing would continue daily, revealing observable results such as reduced crime rate and a more positive mood amongst the people of the town. Dowsers also discovered that the energy field of the area had expanded and changed in frequency.

Colin Bloy and Roger Brown, founder of the Fountain Group in Australia, discovered that 'when one is in a meditative state the brain produces alpha rhythms, a frequency of around 8 Hz, which is the same as the pulse of the Earth, its heartbeat and a rate associated with a feeling of unconditional love'. Visualising a surge of pure energy towards a certain area apparently alters the vibration of the ambient energy field, increasing a sense of well-being (Broadhurst and Miller 2000).

Earth Mystery author Paul Devereux attempted to investigate these invisible energies in the 1980s at the Rollright Stone Circle near Chipping Norton in Oxfordshire, with the use of sophisticated equipment for a research-based venture called the 'Dragon Project'. However, the results, even though controversial, proved inconclusive.

Like the St Michael alignment, many leys are orientated to certain solar, lunar and stellar risings and settings, but some have no trace of dowsable energy; their sole purpose appears to mark a sacred route or direction. Several Earth Mystery investigators however, have detected straight paths of energy dispersing from a build-up of earth forces at certain sacred sites, such as stone circles and prehistoric mounds. I also had an experience of this many years ago.

Orgone and the Swinside Experience

In 1992, on the summer solstice, I decided to visit Swinside Stone Circle near Broughton-in-Furness, one of the most remote and intact prehistoric monuments in Cumbria, to record any unusual events between sunrise to sunset. I arrived early on a warm sunny morning with a couple of friends and settled down for the day. Sometimes we would just meander among the stones, observing their shape, or explore the surrounding landscape. During the day, visitors would come and go, some like us would spend time sitting by the stones whilst others simply wished to capture the scene on their camera. However, it was towards the end of the day that the most curious event occurred.

Shortly after 5 pm, we noticed that many of the cows from the surrounding fields had gathered around the stone circle for about twenty minutes, some venturing inside as if drawn by some unseen force. Later, just before the sun set into the notch of a distant hill, I sensed an electrically charged atmosphere emanating from the circle that started to grow in intensity. Then as I was taking photographs, I suddenly noticed a line scorched in the grass a few inches wide, leading out from a gap in the northeast quadrant of the circle. We followed the strange discoloured line in the grass to a dry-stone wall 50 metres away and from there it continued through the fields beyond. The line, which was orientated to the east, also passed over the largest stone of a group just poking out of the ground, possibly the remains of a cairn. The scorch line seemed to have appeared after I had sensed a build-up of energy at the circle. Perhaps the release of accumulating energy within the circle created the line.

After developing my photos a few days later, I was delighted to see that the line had

Scorched line captured at Swinside Stone Circle, Cumbria

been captured as a streak of light across the grass. However, when I returned to the stone circle a few weeks later, the scorch mark had virtually disappeared although I was still able to detect it with my dowsing rods. Did ancient man create these monuments to accumulate and release some unknown form of energy and mark their course across the landscape, becoming the straight tracks later proposed by Watkins?

I discovered that these strange discoloured lines in the grass are acknowledged in many parts of Britain, particularly in the West Country of England where they are called *trods*. According to Nigel Pennick in *The Ancient Science of Geomancy*, 'People seeking relief from rheumatism will walk a trod, though animals are reputed to avoid them'. Such lines are also known as fairy paths and disaster will befall anyone who constructs a house upon them.

Having witnessed this remarkable path of energy from the stone circle, I wondered if there was any truth in the theory that stone circles are accumulators and releasers of some unknown force. Many others have experienced this type of power accumulation inside stone circles with side effects such as nausea and dizziness. Those who ignored the sensations and remained inside the circle during the moment of discharge developed flu-like symptoms or were physically sick.

In *Needles of Stone* (1978), Tom Graves describes how he suffered a strong migraine caused by a discharge of energy when he touched a certain stone at the Rollright Stone Circle. John Day, during his involvement with the Dragon Project, could psychically see a build-up of light inside the stone circle over a period of several days, resulting in the discharge of a laser-like beam into the landscape from a gap between two stones, which seems reminiscent of my experience at Swinside Stone Circle.

Author and researcher Andrew Collins has worked with psychics at sacred sites in the British landscape for many years and has written extensively on their experiences in his journal *Earthquest News*. Some recounted unusual events at stone circles, mounds and hillforts where they saw bands of coloured light and heard sounds such as clicking, buzzing and humming, phenomena they perceived as 'accumulating' energies – they could even predict when the site would overload and discharge. Other examples of energy release witnessed by the Earthquest team were sudden winds, rain and storms. There are countless 19th century tales of inexplicable bursts of rain and hail showers when excavators dug into the earth barrows or mounds, some so violent that they ran in fear for their lives.

However, the question as to what type of energy is accumulating at these sacred sites is a mystery. Perhaps it is a form of *orgone* energy, first referred to in the late 1930s by the exiled Austrian scientist Wilhelm Reich, who carried out numerous experiments in America. Orgone is a form of subtle radiation or wave emission produced by a particle known as *bion*, which is biological ether, created through the interaction of sunlight with all living organisms. Orgone becomes concentrated when caught by strong electromagnetic bands in the upper atmosphere and by geomagnetic fields upon the Earth's surface. Reich believed that orgone allies to the concept of cosmological ether of space and the hidden life force that regulates the planet and its weather system. Cultures such as the Chinese would associate orgone with the life force they call chi, the Japanese *ki* and the Asian Indian *prana*.

Reich eventually developed a device that stored this energy called an 'orgone accumulator', a chamber lined with alternating layers of organic and inorganic material to attract and focus this 'life force'. He built accumulators large enough to contain a person and claimed noticeable healing results when curing mental disorders and cancer. In spite of all the positive results, investigations by the government claimed Reich's accumulators a sham and orgone energy non-existent. A judge ordered an injunction for the destruction of all accumulators and for research on orgone energy to cease. Two years later Reich died in prison just before his release, having served a sentence for contempt of court.

John Michell believed that during prehistoric times man understood and controlled orgone. The great long barrows and tumuli with internal chambers were megalithic orgone accumulators containing layers within the mound that were carefully built up of organic and inorganic substances such as earth, chalk, clay and stone. Perhaps the greatest of these is the prehistoric Silbury Hill, situated within the Avebury Stone Circle complex in Wiltshire. Excavations have revealed that this magnificent artificial cone-shaped pyramid consists of alternate layers of chalk, stones and earth.

Except for the Dragon Project, science has spent little time exploring earth energies, never mind ley lines, which to some extent has allowed it to remain the topic of ridicule outside the Earth Mystery community. Dowsing has only become an acceptable practice for locating underground sources of water; the use of a Y-shaped stick or angled rod to detect fluids is as old as humanity and still used by modern industries to search for oil and gas. Because the human body consists of ninety-five per cent fluids, we are naturally attuned to finding it. Earth energies are easier to detect if the dowser is naturally sensitive to the higher vibratory force within the landscape. However, as dowsing is a spiritual exercise and its success dependent on the divine state of mind, it requires a certain amount of practise, concentration and visualisation to achieve good results.

The Pilgrimage

Greatly inspired by *The Sun and the Serpent*, I decided to take a couple of weeks off work during April 1991 and travel to the South West of England from Lancashire to visit for the first time some of the places featured on the St Michael Line such as St Michael's Mount, Glastonbury and Avebury. My pilgrimage began at Land's End, where I dowsed the Michael and Mary currents entering the country at a granite rock formation overlooking the Atlantic called Carn Les Boul.

After following the serpents for many days, I was able to refine my dowsing skills to differentiate between the male and female currents. There are obvious differences between the two; the feminine current seems to weave about the countryside with more mobility than the male, preferring to course through valleys, springs, holy wells and lakes. The male flow appears drawn to high places such as hills, mounds and rocks, radiating a certain power and rigidity in comparison to the gentle and serene nature of his counterpart. I dowsed these currents to be large circular beams as tall as they are wide. Perhaps this is why they are known as serpents or dragons because they appear like large worms wriggling across the landscape.

During my stay in Cornwall, I visited several sites that feature on another dragon line through Cornwall, later researched by Miller and Broadhurst, called the Apollo/

St Michael Axis. Beginning at Skellig Michael in Southern Ireland, the alignment goes through St Michael's Mount in Cornwall, Mont Saint-Michel in France, and Sacre di San Michele in the Italian Alps. This corridor of sanctuaries continues through Greece and her islands, where it connects with many sites sacred to Apollo, all the way to Israel. Their aim was to dowse its corresponding male and female serpents, which they named Apollo and Athena; their remarkable quest is recorded in *The Dance of the Dragon*, published in 2000.

My fascination for King Arthur and his knights since childhood influenced my decision to take a detour off the St Michael Line to visit the coastal town of Tintagel in Cornwall, Arthur's reputed birthplace. After ambling through the town, I was drawn to Merlin's Cave beneath the ruined Tintagel Castle. As I sat on the damp rocks inside the cave's shadowy interior with the waves thundering around me, something stirred deep within, heightening my senses and leaving me with the anticipation of something significant to come. I later discovered that many people have received inspiration after visiting this cave, possibly due to the friction of energy created by the force of the sea charging up the numerous quartz seams that run through the rock, or perhaps the invisible force of the dragon whose lair according to folklore is found within caves all over the world.

Under certain conditions, an energetic environment of this kind can induce one to higher states of consciousness, which may explain the reverence attached to so many caves around Britain by our ancient ancestors. Perhaps this is due to the presence of orgone energy, which according to Reich is naturally drawn to caves. The shamans and hermits of old regarded these deep caverns as places of initiation and I had a strong sense that my pilgrimage along the St Michael Line was part of a personal initiation.

I journeyed on through Devon visiting many of the sites along the St Michael Line to Somerset, soon arriving at Glastonbury. I instantly made my way to the famous Tor, a conical-shaped terraced hill to the east of the town topped by the tower of the old St Michael's Church. As I sat wistfully enjoying Glastonbury's ethereal landscape, my thoughts turned to the St Michael Line, the longest east–west ley line in Britain and wondered whether there was a north–south equivalent.

After a while, I descended the Tor and ventured into the town to explore the many shops selling New Age books. Browsing the shelves, I noticed a book called *Brigantia: A Mysteriography* by Guy Ragland Phillips, published in 1976. By coincidence, Brigantia was the early Celtic name for the region of northern England that included my home county of Lancashire. To my amazement, the book fell open at the page illustrating an outline plan of Britain with a north–south alignment all the way from the Isle of Wight to the top of Scotland called the Belinus Line.

The projection of this alignment instantly impressed me, for it appeared to form the longest north–south land-route avoiding the sea. This seemed the perfect counterpart to the St Michael Line I had envisioned earlier. Phillips stated that the line is born out of Brigantia, which began as a divinity or political unit as far back as the Bronze Age, and possibly earlier. Its territory included the counties of Cumbria, Lancashire and part of Cheshire. Phillips also stated that the name Brigantia was derived from the Pre-Celtic goddess 'Bride', a cult figure known variously as Brid or Brigid, later Christianised as St Bridget.

Phillips' discovery began with the research of a whole grid network of ley lines in Brigantia, including north–south parallel lines 19 km (12 miles) apart from the west coast to the east. He stated that these lines were 4 degrees west of magnetic north, which in 1974 was 9.5 degrees west of true north. He noted that the most impressive of these lines formed the best through-route in Britain, which seemed pivotal to this whole system of lines in Brigantia. Starting from Lee-on-the-Solent on the south coast of Hampshire, he projected this line through the cities of Winchester, Birmingham, Manchester and Carlisle, crossing the largest body of water at the Firth of Forth via the Forth Railway Bridge. It then continues to the old prehistoric centre at Lairg and the tiny hamlet of Hope on the north coast of Scotland. Interestingly, the Saxon monk Nennius mentions in the *Historia Brittonum*, written in around AD 828, that Winchester, Manchester and Carlisle were principal cities of the early British and Romans and important political centres.

Phillips named this alignment the Belinus Line after a legendary Iron Age King of Britain who was also a renowned road builder. According to *The History of the Kings of Britain*, written by the 12th century historian and monk Geoffrey of Monmouth, King Belinus ruled the kingdoms of Cornwall, Kambria (Wales) and Loegria (England) from *c.* 380–363 BC. During his reign, he 'summoned workmen from all over the island and ordered them to construct a road of stones and mortar which would bisect the island longitudinally from the Cornish Sea to the shore of Caithness and should lead in a straight line to each of the cities on route'.

Belinus decreed that all temples on these roads were to become safe sanctuaries for travellers whether they were in fear of attack or arrest. Every citizen must respect a Highway Code of laws first enforced by his father King Molmutius. Some historians have mistaken Belinus for a later king called Heli or Beli Mawr, son of Mynogan, who reigned around 113 BC. This confusion may have arisen due to the adoption of his name by many later Iron Age kings due its association with the pagan sun god Bel.

Monmouth mentions that Belinus, along with his brother Brennius, sacked Rome after his reign in 390 BC, recorded by Roman historians as an invasion by the northern Celtic barbarians. On either side of the old 14th century St John's Gate in the city of Bristol are the only known statues of these famous brothers. The mystery of why they were displayed here stems from an old local legend that attributes Brennius with enlarging and improving the city. Although archaeologists and historians have relegated these kings to myth and legend, the memory of them remained

Statue of King Belinus at St John's Gate, Bristol

11

within the psyche of the British race right up until the Middle Ages.

It is quite possible that many of the sites where prehistoric cultures worshipped the principal sun god Belinus became confused over time with this Iron Age king. Belinus as a sun god derives from the Assyrian and Phoenician god Beli, also named as Bel or Baal synonymous with Apollo of the Greeks and Horus of the Egyptians. According to the Dutch classical scholar Vossius (1577–1649), Apollo had many shrines around Europe with the twin Apollo/Belinus dedication. William Camden, a 17th century antiquarian, remarks that 'the Britons worshipped Apollo under the name Belus or Belinus'. The Celtic fire festival of Beltane, celebrated on 1 May, possibly derives from this deity, as the lighting of Beltane fires on certain hills was a ceremonial act to encourage the sun's warmth at the beginning of spring and as a form of purification. Farmers would herd their cattle between the fires before letting them loose on the new spring pastures. Beli, like Apollo, is associated with fire and the sun's restorative powers, but originally he served as a pastoral deity of cattle, sheep and crops.

The offerings of clay horse figurines discovered at the Belenos Sainte-Sabine shrine in Burgundy indicate that Belinus was also associated with the horse, his principal role being God of death and King of the Underworld. His link to several hilltop shrines including Glastonbury Tor seems appropriate, as the lighting of balefires on Beltane and Samhain on these hills lasted up until the time of Oliver Cromwell (1640–60). Many still retain the name Beacon Hill and mark the Belinus alignment at places where the ancient tribes worshipped the sun back in the mists of time.

Celtic traditions say that *Belisama* was the consort of Belinus, a goddess worshipped in Gaul and Britain associated with lakes, rivers, fire, crafts and light. The Latin inscription *Minervae Belisamae sacrum*, found in the town of Saint-Lizier in the department of Ariège, France, equates her with Minerva, a goddess associated with both Brigit and Sulis, a deity worshipped in the ancient city of Bath in England. This may simply be another name or title for Bride or Bridget, who is also associated with fire, craft and blacksmithing. In Lancashire, formerly part of the Kingdom of Brigantia, the name given to the River Ribble in Roman times was the Belisama. Ptolemy, the Greek geographer (AD 90–168), recorded a Belisama estuary, which corresponds to the area around the mouth of the Ribble near Preston. According to local folklore, she was also the goddess of the River Mersey.

Having researched the different aspects of Belinus, I felt that the ancient sun god so revered by the early Britons seemed more befitting to the character of the alignment than the Iron Age king proposed by Phillips.

Calculating alignments over a long distance, particularly when using maps, has its drawbacks because it fails to account for the curvature of the Earth. In fact, the further the line is from a north–south latitude or east–west longitude the more inaccurate it becomes. Phillips' map-drawn alignment between Cumbria and Cheshire demonstrates this as he projects the line to Winchester and Lee-on-the-Solent on the south coast of England.

Therefore, to determine a more accurate alignment, I used modern computer programs such as Google Earth. However, before I had the means and technology to do this, I had already undertaken several years of walking and dowsing the paths of the energy currents between the Isle of Wight and the north coast of Scotland. This gave me a much clearer indication of the true route of the alignment through the positioning of the Node points and a feel for the 'lay of the land', noting that certain hills and river valleys marked the axis. My newly plotted line differs slightly to Phillips' by 0.8 km (0.5 miles) through Brigantia, but straying further to the west as it travels north, particularly in Scotland where it leaves the country at a Node on Faraid Head near Durness, 6 km (3.7 miles) west of the village of Hope on Phillips' line.

Phillips suggested that because the movement of the magnetic pole is cyclical swinging either side of grid north, the Belinus Line may have fallen exactly on magnetic north in the distant past, which the prehistoric priests determined by the use of some form of ancient compass. Magnetic north is unreliable as a fixed direction because it varies over a period of years due to changes in the Earth's core. At the present time, it is located in northern Canada and is rapidly moving towards Siberia in Russia. In Britain, the magnetic pole appears to be moving eastwards towards true north. My revised version of the Belinus Line, which corresponds with the Node points and the experience of walking the land, is aligned 345.5 or 14.5 degrees west of grid north, represented by the vertical grid lines on an Ordnance Survey map. In 1966, magnetic north was 7.5 degrees east of grid north, but today it is estimated to be around 2 degrees west of grid north. True north is the direction along the surface of the Earth towards the geographic North Pole. There is also an astronomical true north, which is marked in the skies by the north celestial pole, about one degree off the position of Polaris, the present Pole Star.

If the Belinus line was aligned to magnetic north in the Iron Age as Phillips proposed, then perhaps the early geomancers marked the line in the landscape with their earth and stone monuments one section at a time, using prominent hills to guide them. Perhaps they used the beacon hills, as Furlong suggests, which regularly appear on or close to the Belinus alignment. Because of the constantly changing cyclical movement of the magnetic pole, even over the span of a year, the priests would have needed to complete this line within a short time scale.

My newly calculated line connects the old centres of government, kingship and religion in England and Scotland, for it now passes through Winchester, Carlisle and Dunfermline, the ancient capital of Scotland before Edinburgh. In Dunfermline the line is marked by the Abbey, which together with Winchester Cathedral links the two great Saxon and early Norman Christian centres of Britain. The alignment also clips Inverness, the capital of the Highlands. Moreover, rather than the modern centres, it is the oldest districts of the cities of Birmingham and Manchester that fall on this line. Although these places would have appeared relatively insignificant in medieval times in comparison with Winchester and Carlisle, they grew to become internationally renowned centres of trade and manufacture during the Industrial Revolution. These physical centres of power relate to the spiritual beliefs of the ancient indigenous tribes of the world in that east–west lines carry spiritual energy and north–south lines hold physical power.

I believe that one of the reasons why Britain became such a 'great' nation is because of its unique geology, composed of many different types of rocks, sands, clays and minerals. Almost everything Britain produced during the Industrial Revolution in Victorian times, a period that turned the country into one of the most powerful nations in the world, came out of its mines and quarries. The unique and diverse arrangement of rocks that form the British Isles is unlike that of any other country in the world. Its many geological fault lines have been the focus of numerous reports of paranormal activity, which has given Britain the reputation as the world's most haunted island.

Map of Great Britain showing its unique and diverse geology

Furthermore, where many of these fault lines merge, we find places of power and many of these fall on the Belinus Line and the path of the male and female serpents associated with it.

Groundbreaking research by the American Dr Philip Callahan on the subtle influences emitted by certain types of geology is included in his remarkable book *Ancient Mysteries, Modern Visions*, first published in 1984. He discovered that certain rocks have inherent magnetic qualities and that all substances are either *diamagnetic*, meaning 'repelled by a magnetic field', or *paramagnetic*, meaning 'attracted to a magnetic field'. Organic material such as plants, water and rocks formed from the same matter such as chalk and pure limestone are diamagnetic. Sandstone, granite, and metals, such as ironstone and slate, however, are paramagnetic due to their quartz silica content. Organic soil, with a high concentration of iron-rich clay, is highly fertile due to its balanced consistency of both diamagnetic and paramagnetic ingredients, a quality akin to the chi of the Chinese, having the correct balance of yin and yang.

During his wartime posting to Ireland, Callahan noticed two types of limestone. One highly paramagnetic variety is found in the mountainous rim of the country, its high crystalline content having been formed by the extreme pressures beneath the Earth exposed millions of years later to become the weather-resisting rocks we see today in places such as the Burren in County Clare. The other is the softer diamagnetic type, found in the subsoil bedrock that underlies the great plains of central Ireland, with fewer impurities. Callahan further discovered that the Irish Celts built their dwellings with insulating diamagnetic limestone and their temples with the paramagnetic variety. All over Ireland there are many enigmatic round towers standing like obelisks in the landscape, considered by the locals to be sacred monuments older than the churches built next to them. When Callahan, tested these monuments, he found to his surprise that even on the plains of central Ireland the towers were made of the highly paramagnetic type of limestone found in the mountains. Callahan hypothesised that the hollow-tube towers with pointed caps were 'antennas' to collect and store electromagnetic waves of energy, although it is my opinion that they were also orgone accumulators.

Callahan believed that the Neolithic or Bronze Age builders and the later Celts utilised certain stones because of their magnetic qualities, which perhaps explains why the highly paramagnetic blue stones, found only in the Welsh Preseli Mountains, were used in the construction of Stonehenge, Britain's greatest megalithic monument. Perhaps the quartz-bearing standing stones in many of Britain's prehistoric sites were deliberately shaped in such a way to attract orgone like an aerial picks up radio waves.

The Axis Mundi and Centres of Albion

During the first decade of the new millennium, I travelled to various sacred sites around the world and became fascinated by the reverence given by their ancient cultures to the celestial north, a direction they considered to be the realm of the ancestors or the afterlife. Many of their most sacred sites consisted of a 'road of the dead' leading north linking together sacred temples. I began to wonder if the ancient tribes of Britain honoured this sacred direction, perhaps along a middle route through their country. Was this the Belinus Line?

In *Twelve Tribe Nations* by John Michell and Christine Rhone, Michell refers to a north–south corridor of great sanctuaries through the Holy Land, comparable to the Apollo/St Michael Axis across Europe, which includes places of vision mentioned in the Old and New Testaments of the Bible. Israel's 'Axis of Vision' is a wide line following the north–south spine of hills from Bethlehem in the south to Mount Lebanon in the north, featuring Jerusalem, Bethel, Shilon, Jacob's Well and Mount Tabor. Michell discovered that the geomantic centre of the Holy Land lies somewhere in the region of Jacob's Well on the axis, and suggests a place nearby called Meonenim, a plain near Sheshem. I also noticed that the Meonenim is mentioned in various translations of the Bible in connection with the 'Oak of the Soothsayers', 'Oak of the Diviners' or 'Oak of the Wizards' (*Judges* 9:37). Perhaps this sacred oak represents the *axis mundi* of the Holy Land.

In ancient mythology, the axis mundi or 'world axis' lies at the centre of the world, connecting heaven and earth:

> 'As the celestial pole and geographic pole, it expresses a point of connection between sky and earth where the four compass directions meet. At this point travel and correspondence is made between higher and lower realms. Communication from lower realms may ascend to higher ones and blessings from higher realms may descend to lower ones and be disseminated to all.' (Eliade 1961)

The location of the axis mundi symbolically functions as the *omphalos* or *navel* of a region or country, the point of its origin.

It has been the quest of many Earth Mystery researchers over the years to seek the hidden centres of power within the British landscape. Finding the centre is important to people, for it is from the centre that we receive nourishment. In the womb, the umbilical cord feeds us through the centre of our body, the 'navel', and connects us to our mother. This fundamental experience transfers symbolically to our existence on the Earth plane, hence our natural propensity to locate our 'centre'. According to Nigel Pennick in *The Ancient Science of Geomancy*, 'The individual's spirit is centralised in the body and the body has a physical location, so the world's spirit was thought of as centralised at a fixed point'.

Centre points can be found in all parts of the world, in every culture, landscape, city, town, even the smallest village. The ancient Greeks determined the centre of the world to be at Delphi, the Incas of South America believed it was Cuzco. In the creation myths of the Ancient Egyptians, the 'primordial mound' or 'island of creation' that rose from the floodwaters was the centre of the world.

In the British Isles, members of the New Age Movement believe that the largest stone circle in Europe at Avebury and the Tor near Glastonbury are centres of spiritual power. These sites, along with The Hurlers Stone Circle and St Michael's Mount in Cornwall and Bury St Edmunds in Suffolk, mark the St Michael Line, an east–west axis mundi of centres across southern Britain.

The Belinus Line begins its journey on the south coast of mainland Britain at Saltern Park near Hill Head in Hampshire, close to the Meon Estuary. We later encounter the name Meon at the centre of England in Warwickshire where the line passes by Meon Hill. *Meon* is the ancient British word for 'middle', similar to Meonenim in the Holy Land. Michell refers to other related names at the centre of other countries, such as Myon in France, Milan in Italy, anciently known as Mediolanum, and Midhe or Meath, the central province of Ireland.

In the north of England, the proximity of the alignment, within metres of the geographical centre of Britain, further substantiates this line as a middle axis. According to Ordnance Survey, the small Lancashire town of Whalley is at the centre of Britain when surveyed without its outer islands. The carvings on the ancient crosses in the churchyard also allude to the axis mundi.

Remarkably, only 18 km (11 miles) NNW of Whalley, the alignment passes near 'Middle Knoll' just north of the tiny village of Dunsop Bridge, which is the nearest natural feature to the exact centre of Britain if you include her 401 offshore islands. In Scotland, the alignment passes through Pitlochry in Perthshire, the most geographically central town in Scotland, Inverness, the capital of the Highlands, and Lairg, the centre of Sutherland. Therefore, I believe the Belinus Line is Britain's north–south axis mundi of centres.

Dowsing the Currents

In spring of 1993, having just moved to Dorset, I began to research the alignment using maps and visited libraries to study the history, archaeology and folklore of some of the places on the line. It was only after noticing some remarkable links that I started to record my findings. Having honed my dowsing skills over many years of detecting energy currents in Cumbria and the serpent energies of the St Michael Line, I decided to investigate whether similar serpents existed at any of the sites on the Belinus Line. My first challenge was to choose a specific location to begin this investigation.

The Belinus Line passes through St Catherine's Hill, an Iron Age hillfort on the outskirts of Winchester. This seemed to be the perfect site to begin my research, especially as dowers regard it as 'a hub of ley lines'. This enigmatic hill is also a renowned ancient place of gathering and features on its summit a turf-cut labyrinth; this reminded me of Glastonbury Tor, which has a labyrinthine path cut into its slopes. My first visit here was in 1994, but it was only after several trips over many years that I fully understood the true nature of this mystical place.

Standing on the summit with a group of friends, I took out my dowsing rods and scanned the area for earth energy lines. At the centre of the hillfort there is a circular enclosure of trees and just to the northeast of there is the labyrinth. Here I detected a band of powerful energy, its frequency similar to the Michael/Mary serpent lines, approximately 2 m (6½ ft) wide, which I followed to a raised mound inside the enclosure of trees.

Using a dowsing colour chart I detected the female serpent by asking the dowsing rod to point to the colour that vibrates through her flow and violet was indicated. I applied the same question to the male current and I dowsed pale yellow.

After dowsing these terrestrial energy currents in more detail, I found that each consisted of twelve individual bands of alternate positive and negative energy. One of the currents was more powerful than the other and its course straighter. Its quality seemed to reflect a solar power, which I soon determined to be masculine. Its counterpart was feminine having a gentler quality to its flow as it weaves and glides through the landscape. Michell described these invisible channels of energy as consisting of a creative and fertilising force, which carries 'manifestations of spirit', their quality waxing and waning with the seasons and the positions of the celestial bodies (Miller & Broadhurst 1989).

Many dowsers such as Tom Graves, Hamish Miller, Sig Lonegren and Dennis Wheatley, to name but a few, have described the technique of dowsing in detail and help to make sense of the intricacies involved in the detection of earth energies.

After many visits to Winchester dowsing the currents around the hill, I discovered that their width varies according to the time of year and the phases of the sun and moon, the terrain, and their passage through certain buildings. I have occasionally dowsed the currents at over 6 m (20 ft) wide, especially in open countryside. This expansion reflects the *auric* or magnetic field of the current reacting to certain environments, although their core strength always remains the same at around 1.5–2 m (4–6 ft) wide.

After my initial dowsing experience on St Catherine's Hill, it was necessary to restart the investigation where the currents and alignment enter the British Isles on the south coast of the Isle of Wight. First, however, I thought it necessary to apply a name to these earthly currents that would best reflect the spirit within them.

Elen and Belinus

In *The Sun and the Serpent*, the authors observed that the male energy visited many hilltop shrines dedicated to the Christianised sun god St Michael, whereas the female energy connects with holy wells, springs, lakes and river valleys, sites associated with the divine goddess within the land in her Christianised form of St Mary. As for the Belinus Line, I felt the name of the pagan sun god Belinus best represented the male current, for throughout Western Europe *Bel*, whose name means 'shining one', was the most popular Celtic god of hilltop sanctuaries, which were subsequently rededicated to St Michael upon the arrival of Christianity.

The name Elen for the feminine energy seemed to present itself as I was dowsing her flow at certain places along the alignment. Elen was a British goddess associated with the Earth's energy matrix, an earlier archetype of the Virgin Mary, serving both its lunar and solar qualities. In *The Mabinogion*, there is mention of 'Elen of the Hosts', a daughter of King Cole, who built the highways from one fortress to another across the length and width of Britain similar to King Belinus. Many believe that the long straight roads in Britain are Roman, but in Wales, ancient tracks are still referred to as *Sarn Elen*, meaning 'road of Elen'. Some historians believe that the Romans merely paved over these old roads to better aid their infantry and, in doing so, hampered the British chariots that relied on earthen tracks.

The name Elen derives from the root *El* or *Elle*, which has Hebrew origins, meaning 'light' or 'illuminated'. As already mentioned, many of these ancient tracks were thought by historians to follow ley lines that linked hillforts, burial mounds, stone circles and long barrows. Goddess expert Caroline Wise researched the origins of this ancient deity and found that, like Belinus, Elen is associated with the sun, shining bright and sitting on a red-gold throne, charging up the wells and springs as she travels through the Isle of Albion.

According to the medieval historian and monk Geoffrey of Monmouth, St Helen became Elen's Christian counterpart, with many wells and springs across Britain rededicated to her. In the 4th century, St Helen reputedly found remnants of the true cross in the Holy Land and paraded it around England and Wales.

During the early years of investigating the Belinus Line, I was surprised to discover that other researchers had mentioned some of the key sites not just on the alignment but also on the path of the serpents. Andrew Collins mentioned the Belinus Line in his revolutionary book *The Circlemakers* published in 1992. He observed that many of the mysterious crop formations appeared close to prehistoric sites especially those associated with both the St Michael Line and the Belinus Line. Collins also refers to Guy Raglan Phillips' book *Brigantia* and noted that a number of formations occurred around St Catherine's Hill in Winchester on what he called 'Britain's second most important corridor of sanctity – the so-called Belinus Line'. He also mentions that upon its course are renowned places of power such as the Rollright Stones in Oxfordshire and Long Meg and her Daughters stone circle near Penrith in Cumbria. Intriguingly, the latter two sites mentioned by Collins lie several miles away from the Belinus Line calculated by Phillips and myself.

Many psychics and Earth Mystery enthusiasts have also associated Uffington White Horse and Stratford-upon-Avon with the Belinus Line, as well as those sites mentioned by Collins. Remarkably, as the dowsing research progressed they proved to be accurate insights.

From the very beginning of my research of the line, I have been supported by close friends who provided invaluable insights. In 2002, I was introduced to Caroline Hoare, who at the time was working in publishing in London. She had already embarked on her own spiritual journey and showed a keen interest in Earth Mysteries. I soon realised that destiny had played its hand when, having accompanied me to many of the Belinus Line sites, Caroline displayed a natural ability to detect earth energies and more specifically those of Elen and Belinus. In the summer of 2003, she gave up her job and came to live with me in Dorset, and since then has accompanied me on this amazing journey, dowsing and researching the history and folklore of every site along the Belinus Line. Her personal revelations have also contributed greatly to the book, particularly her insights into the ancient tribes of Britain. Caroline has also trained as a geomancer and holistic healer, using her skills to assist me to heal and realign many of the sites on the alignment and currents. Together we provided a balanced understanding of the subtle nature of the male and female serpents and in so doing found ourselves working in perfect unison.

The Sacred North and the Cygnus Connection

Unlike the St Michael Line, which targets the Beltane sunrise in the east, the Belinus Line has no solar orientation. Although its trajectory south appears to be angled towards the midday sun on the summer solstice, the exact time between sunrise and sunset, it is a couple of degrees out. However, after consulting David Furlong's work, I soon realised that its orientation may have more of a cosmic significance. Furlong discovered that the St Michael Line was probably surveyed using high points in the landscape, towards the setting of a particular star, perhaps using beacon fires. He discovered that it was one star in the constellation of Orion and states:

'The star in question is Mintaka which would have reached its extinction point on the alignment, which has an approximate azimuth of 242°, around 2800 BCE. The process is quite simple. Watch on a hilltop position on a clear night for the setting of Mintaka and mark that position. In daylight the alignment to another hilltop can be marked. Proceed to the next hilltop and repeat the observation, marking the sites en route.' (www.davidfurlong.co.uk/michael_alignment.htm)

I discovered with the help of Stella computer programs such as Skyglobe that the Belinus Line, orientated at 346 degrees, targets the setting of the bright star Deneb in the constellation of Cygnus during the reign of the historical King Belinus around 500 BC. Moreover, it was during this period that the Iron Age tribes constructed the hillforts along the Belinus Line. Another bright star called Vega, in the constellation of Lyra the Harp, also seemed significant to the alignment for it leads or escorts Deneb to its setting on the northern horizon. Perhaps, as Furlong discovered with the St Michael Line, the ancient geomancers used these bright stars as markers to set out the Belinus alignment from hilltop to hilltop using the beacon fires.

Further celestial influences were revealed at key nodal points on the Belinus Line, many of them on beacon hills or escarpments. More significantly, these sites all have aspects to the northern horizon, which seemed integral to their ritual function. In addition, some of the key hills that highlight the alignment point towards the NNW, as if to deliberately mark its course. This also occurs on the St Michael Line, with the shape of Burrow Mump and Glastonbury Tor pointing in the direction of the alignment towards Avebury.

I soon discovered that those observing the northern skies at sites on the Belinus Line in the south would have seen Deneb setting into the horizon right up until the Dark

Ages. This appears less evident as you move further north along the line, because the star gradually becomes circumpolar, although strategically placed hills and mountains would still give one the illusion of Deneb setting into the horizon.

Interestingly the stars of Cygnus, also known as the Northern Cross, were considered sacred to the early Christians who believed they represented the Calvary Cross or *Crux Cum St Helena*, the Cross of St Helen. They saw in these stars the embodiment of Christ and Mary, perhaps revering the site into which the cross set.

However, it was author Andrew Collins, with his groundbreaking book *The Cygnus Mystery*, who alerted me to its true significance. He noted that many important prehistoric sites in Britain align in some way to the rising or setting stars of the Cygnus constellation, particularly its brightest star Deneb. Furthermore, these stars fall within a dark split in the Milky Way caused by dust clouds called the 'Great Rift' or 'Dark Rift'. The rift extends from Cygnus to Aquila and then broadens out to Sagittarius, where it obscures the Galactic Centre. This unusual feature of the Milky Way was revered by ancient religious cultures around the world who believed it to be representative of a magical pathway to the heavens or afterlife and rebirth. Collins found that many shamanic cultures around the world saw the stars of Cygnus as representing a cosmic bird of first creation and aligned many of their stone monuments and temples to them as if to absorb their influence. Certain European cultures depicted the constellation as a celestial swan flying along the Milky Way.

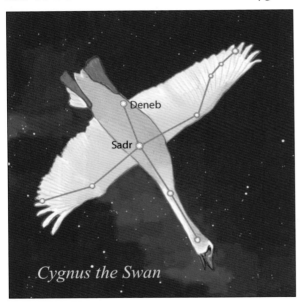

Cygnus the Swan

North American tribes such as the Blackfoot believed that the 'skyworld' was not just a destination for the soul to pass into the afterlife but also inhabited by sentient beings, which could travel to Earth through a portal in the Milky Way or the sky pole. The shamans believed that these sky beings provided them with knowledge from the ancestors, in the form of ancient wisdom and advice on how to live a more spiritual life on Earth. Perhaps as they walked north along the well-trodden paths of the Belinus Line, between the stone monuments and earthen shrines, the ancient Britons envisioned this celestial swan swooping down before them carrying its brightest star Deneb.

Collins refers to earlier surveys that calculated the main axis of Avebury, which is a line through the centre of its two inner circles, to have an azimuth of 339.2 degrees, which aligns to the setting of Deneb around 2600 BC. In addition, Callanish on the Isle of Lewis in Scotland, with its great northern stone avenue, aligns with the rising of

Sadr, lying at the centre of the cross of Cygnus. Many temples around the world also align with this sacred constellation, including the great pyramids. Collins (2006) states that:

'Around the world, Cygnus was once seen as the entrance and exit to the sky-world, making it a candidate for the original location of heaven, which before the rise of Christianity was often seen as existing in the extreme north, and accessed via the Pole Star and north–south meridian line, which splits the heavens in two along its longitudinal zenith.'

Science too has realised the significance of this constellation when, in the 1980s, deep underground particle detectors at many locations around the world simultaneously recorded an unexpected and important discovery. Powerful cosmic rays were found to penetrate 304 m (1000 ft) of solid rock above the underground facilities. At the time, this was thought to be impossible, but equipment repeatedly picked up a unique signal from the decaying cosmic particles. The source was identified as coming from Cygnus X3, a binary star system within the Cygnus constellation and these unique cosmic particles were soon dubbed *cygnets*, meaning 'children of the swan' (Collins 2006).

What is most interesting is that this cosmic ray generator, over 37,000 light years distant from Earth, is the only one in the galaxy targeting us. Science writer and astronomer Carl Sagan proposed that cosmic rays reaching Earth from a neutron star, which Cygnus X3 probably is, are responsible for sudden leaps in human development. More recently, scientists have gone further and speculated that high bursts of cosmic rays might have altered our DNA sequences.

Since 1993, I have visited and researched hundreds of crop circles and during that time witnessed remarkable events that made me a firm believer in their authenticity as an otherworldly phenomenon, despite contrary claims by the circlemakers and TV documentaries. Although some of them are manmade, the incredibly large and sophisticated formations seem impossible to create in just a few hours in the dead of night. I believe the true circlemakers are non-physical cosmic intelligences linked to human consciousness. In fact, certain formations, referred to later, have appeared exactly on the Belinus currents at a time when their hidden paths were only known to Caroline and I. This occurred so frequently that we believed the circlemakers were playing with us.

Southern England and in particular Avebury, has been the epicentre of the world's crop circles since they started to appear there in the 1980s. As a dowser and psychic, travelling to numerous sacred sites around the world, I have found that the earth energy matrix of other countries differs to that of England, because the lines of power are much further apart and fewer in number. If we compare this to the human body with its veins and arteries, then England behaves like the heart, pumping earth energy into the global grid. Perhaps this is why historically this little island has influenced so much of the world. It is interesting too that the core of the spiritual New Age movement and the crop circles phenomenon is rooted at the very heart of the world's energy matrix, within a triangle of sites formed by Winchester, Glastonbury and Avebury in the south of England.

The Three King Arthurs of Albion

Throughout our adventures following the alignment and dowsing the male and female serpents, we encountered many places associated with King Arthur. Historians generally agree that there was a British warrior or 'battle-leader' living in the early part of the 6th century, who fought twelve major conflicts against the Anglo-Saxons and halted their invasion of England for 50 years. There is also the Arthur of the Norman romances, referred to in a number of ballads and poems, who held court at

Stained-glass window of the legendary King Arthur, Whalley Church.

different places around Britain and, inspired by the highest principles, set out with his knights on a series of adventures and quests. Some of the stories of Arthur, such as the throwing of his magical sword Excalibur into a lake, reflect the beliefs and practices of the Celtic Iron Age. After an epic battle, his body was spirited away by nine maidens in a boat to the mystical Isle of Avalon to receive healing for his wounds. The Celtic Arthur is alive in many prehistoric and natural features in the British landscape, including mountains, hills and caves where he sleeps with his knights until he is called upon to rescue Britain in her hour of need.

Merlin, the wizard and prophet who predicted the fate of Arthur, is also featured along the Spine of Albion. Like Arthur, he is both mythical and historical and features in medieval ballads and poems.

This book is not just the recordings of two dowsers following invisible lines along a supposed axis of Britain, for it has a wider significance for those who wish to understand the mysteries of the British landscape. At numerous sites along this route, we have peeled back the many layers of hidden history, integrating folklore, legend, archaeology and geology, especially significant where the male and female serpents cross. This has provided us with a greater insight as to why these sites were considered holy or special and why certain powerful individuals continued to be drawn to them. In addition, our historical discoveries embody a wealth of information that may prove these commanding characters had certain knowledge relating to the Belinus Line as a hidden cosmic axis of Britain and the restorative and the inspiring serpentine energies associated with it. Certain fictional and legendary characters also feature prominently along our journey as if acting as guardians or spirits of this enigmatic north–south axis, which we have come to acknowledge as the 'Spine of Albion'.

Michell wrote that 'the serpent represents the mercurial currents of the earth spirit, gliding in serpentine channels through the Earth's crust'. The age-old symbol of the Caduceus includes the rod of Mercury, also called the staff of Hermes, entwined by two snakes or serpents and crowned by the wings of a large bird, said by some researchers to be those of a swan. One of Mercury's roles was as a 'divine conduit' or conductor of solar consciousness. I believe the Belinus Line is a perfect representation of Mercury's rod, a cosmic axis that receives the celestial consciousness from the constellation of Cygnus, awakening and revitalising the DNA within the terrestrial strands of the serpent energies that weave along it.

Although science helps to rationalise the incredible and provides our work with validity, it lacks any notion of heart or spirituality. The most important aspect of our quest is to connect with Mother Earth and her landscape through the heart to understand how she can enrich our lives. If we put aside archaeological thinking and scientific explanations, we can start to fully realise the wonder, beauty and intelligence of nature as we walk the old trackways and pilgrim routes.

> 'there is no requirement to know that the Iron Age followed the Bronze Age; all that is necessary is a love of the countryside, an ability to observe, a willingness to consider the incredible, a huge reserve of perseverance and tolerance when inspiration seems lacking, and above all determination to find the truth …. He who believes in the reality of the ley system is engaged in a quest. His aim is to further his knowledge of a mysterious force and its many manifestations and incredible implications. He will become footsore, his head will burst with ideas, he will be coming to terms with himself and learning about spiritual truths rather than material falsities.' (Screeton 1974)

The following chapters reveal the sacred places marking the alignment and the path of the serpents, uncovering their secrets and demonstrating how the celestial influences have shaped them today. As we take you on this fascinating and enthralling journey, we hope you will be as inspired and captivated as we have been by many of the long-forgotten sites, which we have taken to our hearts.

Winged Caduceus

Chapter 1

The Isle of the Dragon
The Secret Power of the Isle of Wight

The Isle of Wight is a large island in the English Channel, situated at the base of England and separated from the mainland by a strait called the Solent. This unique diamond-shaped land mass, loved by British holidaymakers, is today famous for its sandy beaches, holiday camps and music festivals.

The Isle has gained a reputation amongst writers as 'Britain's Magical Island' because of its long history of paranormal events, which include ghostly encounters, time-slips, occult practices and its legendary association with the mysterious Druids. Long ago, the island had many names; the Druids called it the land of *Guitt* or *Gwitt* and the

The Isle of Wight. (© Will Glover)

Welsh knew it as *Ynys Weir*. The Romans named it *Vectis* and it was the *Wiht-land* of the Saxon Jutes. The invincible General Vespasian, who later became Emperor of Rome, invaded and captured the island in AD 43 and it was from here that he surveyed the country in preparation for the invasion of Britain. Many local historians believe that during the Roman occupation, the island became a base for the mysterious cult of Mithras practised by the Roman elite.

When the Romans left to defend their homeland, the Saxon Jutes arrived on the island, forming an independent pagan kingdom until Wulfere, King of Mercia, forcibly converted them to Christianity in AD 616. Wulfere's own kingdom was centred on Stone in Staffordshire, also associated with the Belinus Line, so it seems mysterious that he travelled so far south through enemy territory to convert these Jutes, especially after he had, according to legend, just murdered his own sons for practising Christianity. The 'old ways' must have resurfaced for in AD 685 another king of uncertain origin called Caedwalla, angered by the pagan practices of the Isle of Wight Jutes, invaded and massacred over half the population. Those who survived were still undeterred by this act of genocide, for St Wilfred made a further attempt

to Christianise the island two years later. The flame of the old religion still flickers today, for there are many reports of witchcraft on the island stretching back over hundreds of years.

Britain is reputed to be the world's most haunted country because it has the most recorded paranormal events. According to local author Gay Baldwin, the Isle of Wight is the world's most haunted island. Its reputation stems from the great number of unexplained phenomena that have taken place all over the island, observed by both locals and visitors alike. People have witnessed phantom Roman soldiers marching across Brading Down and marauding Vikings carrying flaming torches. Some of the unique incidences experienced by tourists and locals include the appearance of ghost buildings. When a couple attempted to revisit a particular pub where they had enjoyed a drink on a previous outing, they found that it had vanished with no record of it ever having existed, and people have seen the ghostly appearances of villages and streets in areas of open countryside.

There is no doubt that this island is a unique and mystical place where I believe the veil between the worlds of spirit and matter is especially thin. I have often found that certain places made famous by their stories of haunting are located on or near unusual geology such as fault lines. A fault is a fissure between two landmasses and when seismic activity takes place, the friction between the rocks creates energy. Under certain conditions, this energy will release in the form of balls of light or as a strong magnetic field. If this field is subjected to additional forces such as the gravitational force of the full moon or solar particles from high 'sun spot' activity, it may cause a rip in our dimensional time and space.

The geology of the Isle of Wight is particularly remarkable because of its unusual layering of sedimentary rocks that has gradually formed over a period of 140 million years. Some of the layers tilt almost vertically, created when immense pressures within

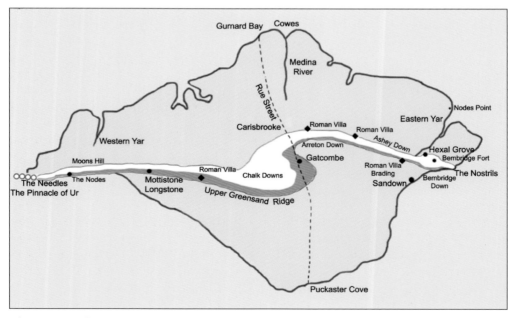

The serpent ridge

the Earth's crust formed the European Alps. Visitors flock to Alum Bay at the western side of the island to see the spectacular multicoloured cliffs made up of at least twelve different types of coloured sand.

Brian Innes, writing in a monthly magazine called *The Unexplained* back in the 1970s, stated that the unusual S-shaped east–west ridge of hills that form the geological backbone of the island might provide a vital clue to the many Isle of Wight mysteries. The ridge, also a geological fault, runs all the way from the high eminence of Bembridge Down on the east coast near the town of Brading, to the chalk stacks called the Needles on the extreme west coast. Situated on this ridge are Ashey, Arreton Down and Carisbrooke, where the stratum curves to the southeast to Gatcombe at the centre of the island. From here it swings back to the west through Chillerton Down and Mottistone before it reaches the Needles. Innes further remarks that a geological layer of Upper Greensand best defines this serpent-shaped ridge, consisting of hard crystalline iron-bearing sandstone, otherwise known as Firestone because of its fiery colour.

Innes also mentions some of the unusual place names associated with this ridge. Above the head of the serpent at Bembridge is 'Nodes Point' and near its tail at the Needles is 'The Nodes'. In astronomy, the Nodes mark the position where the path of the moon crosses the ecliptic or path of the sun. When the moon moves about the Earth, its path across the ecliptic creates a flattened S-shape, and interestingly on the tail of the Isle of Wight serpent is Moons Hill. Astronomers called the north Node of the moon *Caput Draconis* or Dragon's Head and the south Node *Cauda Draconis* or Dragon's Tail.

According to local folklore, the mysterious Druids, administrators of religion to the ancient Britons, resided at three sacred sanctuaries on the Isle of Wight – the Needles, the Longstone at Mottistone, and Hexal Grove near Brading on the east coast. The Archdruid, the head of this ancient religious order, resided on one of the natural rock stacks of the Needles called 'The Pinnacle of Ur', claimed by the sea long ago. The Longstone is a large megalith by the side of a recumbent fallen stone, part of a Neolithic long barrow later used by the Druids to tether their white bulls for sacrifice. This megalithic site situated on the Firestone layer is directly linked through its folklore to St Catherine's Hill near Winchester where my journey first began. The 4 m (13 ft) tall Longstone made of Upper Greensand was in legend thrown here by a giant standing on St Catherine's Hill. Perhaps this alludes to some kind of energetic connection between the two sites. On the slopes of Bembridge Down, at the edge of Brading Haven, stood the Druids' most sacred Grove and holy well, now lost to the ravages of time.

As great astronomers, the Druids could not have failed to notice that the backbone of the island mirrors the moon's dragon path. For them the construction of a specific place of worship was unnecessary as the whole island represented a sacred moon temple. Some of the island's most haunted places are on the Firestone layer that forms the back of this serpent. Knighton Gorges, for instance, was once the grandest house on the Isle dating back to Norman times, which received notoriety during the 18th century for its lavish and raucous New Year's Eve parties. However, nothing visible remains of it today, due to its complete dismantlement during the Victorian period. Nevertheless, over the years many have seen the house reappear on New Year's Eve, and the ghostly apparitions of its former occupants (Baldwin 2004).

I believe the combination of its position on the Firestone ridge, the springs that surround it and the emotionally charged events at the house during its long and fraught history have created a 'loop recording' or rip in time, which only psychic people can see. Scottish historian Archie McKerracher of the Society of Antiquaries of Scotland claims the Earth's magnetic field can retain the memory of an 'emotional or violent event' that recurs and haunts the area, with generated wavelengths of electromagnetic energy bearing the resemblance of a persistent bad dream.

Another unique and strange aspect of the island is its coastal outline. From above it resembles a diamond that is remarkably symmetrical, one side being the mirror image of the other. A north–south river called the Medina divides the island, flowing from the northern tip of the diamond at Cowes through the town of Newport; even the northern estuaries are equidistant from the centre of the island, including the rivers of the Eastern and Western Yar.

The Binstead Idol

Arriving at the ferry terminal in Yarmouth one warm summer morning, Caroline and I decided to first take a stroll through the quaint little harbour town. The cobbled streets with period houses and shops gave us the impression of stepping back in time. Although this was not my first visit to the island, I was looking forward to discovering some of its hidden pathways. Dowsing is one of many levels of investigation, but as we later discovered it proved to be a vital way of making sense of the historical, mythological and cosmic connections between the sites.

When I first projected the alignment through the Isle of Wight, there appeared to be nothing of significance directly on its path. There are no important churches or prehistoric sites, only some earthworks at East Ashey Manor Farm and a curious mount called Kemp Hill at Upton. The Victorian resort of Sandown marks the alignment on the south coast and on its northern shores it falls between the little Victorian church at Binstead and the medieval ruins of Quarr Abbey. We decided to begin our investigations at the beach near Binstead where I dowsed the male current near an old jetty. I then followed him inland to Binstead Hall and beyond to a small Victorian church dedicated to the Holy Cross. Hoping to find an ancient site to mark the current, I was initially disappointed to discover such a late structure. However as I entered the churchyard by the south gate, I noticed a grotesque stone figure covered in lichen set into the keystone of the arch.

Described as a 'Sheela-na-gig', the ancient carving depicts a female with a large head or beard displaying her genitals while seated upon the head of a beast. Its origin is a mystery, but it may have survived from an earlier church. Information from the local library indicated that generations of local people have given reverence to this stone figure and still cherish it today. According to Adrian Searle in *Isle of Wight Folklore*, it is Binstead's oldest resident known as 'The Saxon Idol' and locals regard it as their protector. During the 18th century, church authorities considered the figure offensive and had it removed, but due to a massive public outcry they were forced to reinstall it. This certainly implies that the old pagan beliefs continued to survive on the island up until Victorian times.

Sheela-na-gig carvings, found on many churches around Britain and Ireland, are remnants of their pagan past, said to represent the fertility of the Earth goddess.

The addition of the beard on the Binstead idol may be a representation of both a male and a female deity. Writers have variously described the beast on which the figure sits as a ram, a horse or a bear. It also wears a muzzle and grasps its snout, a feature resembling other examples of bear carvings in Norman churches. The constellation called Ursula Major, the Great Bear, also known as the Big Dipper, the Plough and King Arthur's Chariot, rotates around the Pole Star playing the role of protector. Therefore, the bear represents in cosmology the guardian of the gateway to the afterlife.

The Binstead idol at Binstead Church

I later discovered that a spate of Victorian renovation on many of the island's churches removed most of the early pagan carvings, so the Sheela-na-gig at Binstead is exceptionally rare. It appears to be Romanesque in style and may have originated from either an earlier Norman church that preceded the Victorian rebuilding or the nearby Quarr Abbey, removed after the Dissolution of the Monasteries by Henry VIII between 1536 and 1541 during the period of the English Reformation. The herringbone masonry in the chancel wall, however, may be a remnant of a Saxon church.

The building is permanently locked except for services, so we arranged a viewing with one of the churchwardens the following day. Inside I noticed an original Norman chancel, early 14th century windows and beautiful quatrefoil panelling. The stalls once belonged to the chapel at Winchester College, also a site on the Belinus alignment. Its medieval bell once hung in the tower at Quarr Abbey and a carving of a 'Green Man' stares down from the chancel ceiling. Many churches around Britain display the Green Man with foliage issuing out of his nose and mouth. He represents the fruitfulness of the Earth, symbolic of fertility in the form of the death and rebirth of the Green God. He also embodies the power of nature, further characterised by Jack in the Green, Green George, the Old Man of the Woods, the Corn or Barley God, the Green Knight and Robin Hood.

We found more curious and mystical carvings in keeping with the island's occult traditions on the exterior of the west gable. Below the bell turret is the grinning face of a man with curling foliage issuing from his chin. To the right of this is an upside down creature, possibly a horse or dragon, biting its tail and to the left is the stylised carving of a griffin.

The serpent biting its own tail is known as an *ouroboros* and represents eternity in occult tradition but very seldom is it depicted as a four legged beast. It has its roots in ancient Greece and symbolises the cyclic nature of time, the endless round of existence and the eternal cycle of renewal. Christians believe it represents the opposing force

Carving of the ouroboros or dragon biting its tail at Binstead Church

of evil and pagans regard it as a guardian of nature. The ouroboros is rarely depicted in churches and perhaps its presence here represents the serpentine earth current in the form of Belinus.

The griffin too with its body of a lion and the head and wings of an eagle embodies the formidable qualities of Earth. Some traditions say that the male griffin has no wings, which possibly signifies that Binstead's winged version is female, seen as a guardian of gold and treasure. From the time of Dante, the figure became a symbol of the dual nature of Jesus Christ, the divine and the physical, precisely because of its mastery of earth and sky. The griffin also became the adversary of serpents and basilisks, both of which were embodiments of satanic demons.

In 1844, Sir Thomas Hellyer, a local Isle of Wight mason, restored the church in the early English style selecting some of the earlier features such as the dragon and griffin carvings from an old Norman arch. Perhaps Hellyer's intention was to arrange the occult carvings to provide some symbolic message, purporting to the balance of the elements; the solar griffin represents earth and air while the ouroboros embodies fire and water. The large grinning head of a man set between the two may represent the 'creator' who controls the dual forces of light and dark. The griffin and the ouroboros are also opposing symbols of order and chaos used in occult practices and secret societies.

Moving further around the outside of the church, I noticed above the main porch an ancient carving of a dove, a Christian symbol of the Holy Spirit. Yet another interesting feature at Binstead Church is the grave of a giant. The vicar informed me that a local inhabitant named Samuel Landon was buried here in 1844, said to have been the 'biggest man in the world'. He then remarked that in those days the islanders thought the world was their island. Many locals believe the name Wight refers to an ancient race of magical beings of great strength. In the old Gaelic language, it means 'magical' or 'mysterious'. According to Geoffrey of Monmouth, ancient Britain was the abode of giants who survived the biblical flood. Over the centuries, the incoming Celtic tribes forced them to retreat to remote areas of the country. Folklore and myth present us with numerous tales of giants appearing throughout Britain; perhaps Samuel Landon was a genetic throwback from this mythical race of men who once settled on the island.

The medieval Cistercian monks from the nearby Quarr Abbey built a church on this site for the workers who quarried stone in the surrounding woods to keep them from 'troubling the abbey'. The Normans incorporated the local limestone into many of their most famous buildings including the Norman White Tower of London and Winchester Cathedral. Both of these buildings were a powerful statement of a 'new order' founded by William the Conqueror after his defeat of the Saxon dynasty at the Battle of Hastings in 1066. The surrounding woods are full of grassy pits from where the white limestone was quarried centuries ago.

Although limestone is a popular building stone, selected for its ease of cutting and durability, many cultures around the world consider it sacred encompassing 'the spirit of the Earth'. It is formed over tens of thousands of years from layers of sediments at the bottom of shallow seas containing within its deposits information of its environment and therefore recording some of Earth's history. The island's long-standing reputation as a sacred isle may have enticed the Normans to use the Isle of Wight stone to construct their new centres of power in order to make a symbolic statement, proclaiming their spiritual and sovereign authority over the land.

Behind the church on the male current is Binstead Hall where, according to a local, its owner sensed something otherworldly about the place and felt the presence of a ley line. Belinus enters the church in a north–south direction through the pulpit, departing the churchyard very close to the Sheela-na-gig carving. Finding the male current at this fascinating little church turned out to be more intriguing than first expected. Never before have I encountered so many symbols of the old religion at one site – a Green Man, Sheela-na-gig, griffin, ouroboros and a giant's grave to boot. This was certainly a fascinating start to our journey on this enigmatic island and it turned out to be just a taste of what was to come.

Quarr Abbey and Eleanor of Aquitaine

As we continued to dowse the area around Binstead, the female current remained elusive, so we decided to take a moment to pendulum dowse over the OS map to find her location. The pendulum started to swing over a place called Quarr Abbey, just over a kilometre west of Binstead. On our way to the abbey, along an ancient leafy footpath between Binstead and Fishbourne, we passed through the 'Poetry Gate' where passers-by are encouraged to leave poems in a box. Soon after, we arrived at a clearing where suddenly the rods swung, indicating the presence of Elen. Close by we noticed an information board that referred to the ruins of a medieval Cistercian abbey immediately in the field to our right. All that remains today is a parapet, a bell-cot with lancet windows and a stretch of ruined wall. In 1132, Henry of Blois, Bishop of Winchester, consecrated the abbey to Our Lady of the Quarry. Henry later proved to be a significant character on our quest through Hampshire.

A plan on the information board showed that the main body of the abbey once stood parallel to the footpath. This building was the only monastic house on the island and one of the first Cistercian abbeys in England. Little is known of its history, except that in 1131 Baldwin de Redvers, fourth lord of the Isle of Wight and later Earl of Devon (whose family crest is the griffin), was granted some land in the parish of Binstead. Baldwin appealed to Abbot Gervase of Savigny in France to send some of his monks to establish an abbey on this piece of land. Gervase was also well acquainted with King Henry I (1100–35) having granted him funds to build many abbeys around England. His grave, discovered by archaeologists near the High Altar, contained bones of an abnormally large man, 2.1 m (6 ft 9 in) tall, a giant in his day. During its dissolution, the abbey was dismantled and much of the stone was taken and used locally to build defences.

We followed Elen north into the field and after a few paces she suddenly turns west at the site of the High Altar and continues as if still connecting with the old nave. As we absorbed the energy of the site, we both felt a strange atmosphere, a heady mix of serenity, a secret past and otherworldliness.

Elen continues through a farmhouse, constructed from the abbey stone, towards an unusual large red-brick edifice built in the Moorish style that became the new Quarr Abbey in 1908. The French Benedictine Abbot Don Paul Bellot founded the new abbey, bringing with him one hundred of his order from France. One story tells of how he fled with the monks from Solesmes Abbey near Le Mans at the turn of the century due to persecution.

During the time, the medieval Quarr Abbey House, the summer residence for visiting royalty and aristocracy, was extended using stone from the old abbey. The Elen current passes through the nave of the abbey church by the altar and continues through the main entrance towards a carved limestone statue of a crowned female figure holding a baby, perhaps the Madonna and Child to whom the old abbey was dedicated. We wondered if it was divine inspiration that led to its placement on the female current. From here, Elen turns north through the exhibition room of the abbey stable block towards the island's northern shores and across the Solent. Today the abbey is a monastic dwelling for a dwindling community of Benedictine monks.

Statue of the Madonna and Child at Quarr Abbey

Near the point where Elen meets the Solent on the north coast, archaeologists excavated the remains of a Neolithic road that once crossed the strait. Around 2000 years ago the Solent was much narrower than at present, giving the appearance of a wide river which was fordable at low tide.

After enjoying a hearty lunch at the abbey café, we retraced our steps to the lane that passes through the site of the old abbey ruins. From here, Elen's path runs south, across the main road to Ryde, into a field just to the east of a copse. According to the map, this dense woodland has the enticing name *Elenors Grove*, formerly called Queen Eleanor's Grove before its recent corruption. A curious tradition from island folklore informs us that Henry II exiled his dynamic queen Eleanor of Aquitaine to Quarr Abbey in 1173. Apparently, she spent many happy hours wandering through the enchanting woods opposite the abbey and, having become fond of the place, requested her grave should lie 'beneath the shade of the melancholy boughs'. The tradition even claims that beneath the woodland her body is contained in a golden coffin, behind a golden door at the end of an underground passage bound by a magic spell. However, records show that she died in France in 1204 and was buried alongside her estranged husband at Fontevraud Abbey. Who knows; perhaps those close to her fulfilled her dying wish by secretly returning her remains to this enchanting place.

Long ago, the Grove incorporated the whole field through which the Elen current now passes, so it is more likely that the legend is a *geomythic* clue as to the location of this feminine energy. Geomythic refers to symbolic truths expressed through stories concerning natural features in the surrounding rural area or landscape.

Alternatively, Eleanor may have sensed the powerful female serpent and deliberately walked her path during her prolonged captivity. Unless, of course, it is just one of those synchronistic occurrences that by chance leaves us a clue to the hidden mysteries of the landscape. However, many local people claim to have seen Queen Eleanor's ghost walking from the old abbey ruins towards the woods.

Greatly inspired by this magical area of Binstead, we decided to continue on the path of Elen through the hinterland of the island, leaving any further exploration of the male current to the following day. In the field beside Elenors Grove, the current passes through a very gnarled old oak tree, possibly a remnant of the old grove. Soon we were entering woodland curiously named Puckers Copse, at the centre of which is an atmospheric pool.

Puck is a mischievous woodland elemental or pixie that often appears as a ball of light, which if followed could prove perilous. Such events can be explained through the biological process of organic decay that under the right conditions creates gases such as phosphine and methane, the oxidation of which can produce a glowing light. The name Puck is quite common throughout the island, with place names such as Puckaster Cove on the south coast and Puckpool Point near Ryde. As we strolled beneath the majestic trees, I could almost sense the mischievous elementals observing us, perhaps discussing the exploits of this curious couple waving metal rods around. As we imbued ourselves with the invigorating and inspiring energy of Elen, I felt sure we left them happy in the knowledge that the female serpent is at last recognised and honoured.

Entering open fields near Newham Farm, we could see ancient earthworks ahead of us, said to be the remains of a medieval dam ingeniously built by the monks of Quarr to force the stream to flow at a higher level in order to provide water for the abbey. After disappearing through private land, we find the current again flowing along Green Lane near Upton. This was once an ancient track that ran between Quarr Abbey and the old port of Brading. She appears again at Kemphill Farm crossing the alignment over

Old tinner's track near Upton

Kemp Hill. 'Kemp' is a Saxon name for warrior but also derives from the Roman word *campus*, meaning 'battleground'. We took a footpath to its summit where we found spectacular views of almost the entire island. Its name Kemp or Warrior may point to an ancient place of gathering or contest where warriors from different tribes would demonstrate their skill and strength as they trained for battle.

Just south of the hill the current passes through a remote cemetery near Little Upton Farm surrounded by Scots pine trees. Discovering that it had only recently become sanctified ground, I wondered if perhaps those involved in its planning were subconsciously aware of the feminine energy. At the village of Ashey close to the alignment, the current led us to a spring-fed pool next to Deacons Lane. Long ago, these sites were revered as sacred sanctuaries of the Earth goddess, many named after a local feminine deity, later Christianised to St Mary, St Anne or St Helen. We took a moment to honour this long-forgotten sacred spring and the rejuvenating qualities of the female serpent that resides there.

As we headed towards the central chain of hills that make up the sacred backbone of the island, we saw the billowing white smoke of a steam train that carries passengers between Ryde and Wootton Common. We crossed the railway track at a charming little station south of Ashey where another group of Scots pines mark the current. Like the oak, these trees were sacred to the Druids, connecting the overground and underground earth energies as their roots penetrate deep within the Earth seeking out watercourses.

Close to the alignment at East Ashey Manor Farm, Elen passes through curious earthworks bordered by a wood. Further research informed us that this site was once a nunnery founded in the 13th century by the nuns of Wherwell Abbey near Winchester. However, there may have been a nunnery at Ashey during Saxon times, for the Domesday Book records the area as the manor of Nonelle, which later became Nunwell. Nearby, possibly on the site of the farm, once stood the medieval Nunwell Manor, the original home of the Oglanders, before they built Nunwell House near Brading in 1522. East Ashey had its own local government called a Court Leet, controlling a large area of the island including Ryde. Richard d'Oglander acquired the manor, having fought alongside William the Conqueror at the Battle of Hastings.

The name Oglander is interesting as the word *Og* is an old British name found throughout England and Wales, such as the Ogbourne River near Avebury and the Ogmore River in Glamorgan. I also researched that Og is the earlier form of St George and is linked to Britain's prehistoric giants Gog and Magog referred to by Geoffrey of Monmouth. They may have been one of the many British noble families returning to reclaim their land after leaving England during a period of great pestilence known as the 'yellow peril', which decimated the population of southern England during the 6th century. During this turbulent time, many of these families, particularly those with wealth, moved north or emigrated across the Channel to Gaul. In *The Life of St Samson of Dol*, the biographer refers to the Welsh saint leaving the country after a pestilence to join a British colony called 'New Britain' or Brittany, set up as a refuge by a King of Gaul (France).

Historical records also inform us that this area has pagan associations, for during the reign of Elizabeth I a woman from Ashey was burnt at the stake having been found guilty of practising witchcraft. Its position on the alignment highlights the significance of this religious site with its neighbouring sacred spring.

Beneath Ashey Down we dowsed the female current passing through a wooded area called Bloodstone Copse. A notice board nearby alerted us to the presence of a spring called the Bloodstone Well. The name derives from the reddish algae that cling to the stones in the stream, giving the appearance of a trail of blood.

The spring also marks the alignment and, like the pool at Ashey, now lies neglected and hidden. The water authorities have disguised its source by placing pipes here to divert its waters to a modern pump house above. However, the Elen current pointed the way for us, and where she crosses the stream I placed one of my sacred stones in the water to honour the source of this once revered spring.

Interestingly, Elen avoids the notoriously haunted Knighton Gorges estate, about a kilometre northeast of the alignment. Instead, she prefers to flow along the old green track that leads to the side gates of Nunwell House, the later home of the Oglanders. Thankfully, we had picked one of the rare occasions when the house was open to the public and entered the grounds at the admission gate to continue tracking her path. Weary from our long walk across the island in the midday summer heat, we paid for the later tour and settled on the lawn with a guidebook.

As Commanders of the Home Guard from 1295–1945, the Oglanders were the chief protectors of the island. They were devoted Royalists and during the Civil War Sir John Oglander, the 17th century diarist, found himself imprisoned for supporting King Charles I. Nunwell House became the King's last refuge, before his capture and imprisonment by the Parliamentarians. In 1982, the house was sold to the Aylmer family who by tradition are descendants of Alfred the Great.

I dowsed Elen passing through a large oak tree in the grounds before ascending Brading Down through dense woodland. On top of the Down, the current targets a large grassy knoll called the Devil's Punchbowl, now hidden by trees next to the road that cuts through Brading Down. The mound dates from the early Bronze Age and previous excavations have left a deep depression on its summit.

I have frequently read folktales that refer to these curious landscape features as the work of the devil or haunt of evil spirits. Strangely, this tumulus is just one of many on the island, but the only one named after the devil. The later Christian missionaries often assigned this title to sites of pagan worship, in order to discourage people from connecting with the healing and nourishing energy of the earth serpents.

Earth Lights or Plasma Balls

Brading Down is a hotspot for strange light activity and ghostly Roman armies marching across fields. The light balls seen on the Downs might be plasma emissions from the great fault line that runs beneath. I too have witnessed mysterious balls of light on many occasions throughout my life, but the most remarkable was during a school trip to the Forest of Dean by the River Wye in 1976.

One evening our teacher took nine of us down river to the tiny village of Symonds Yat so he could visit the local pub. While he enjoyed a pint of beer inside, we stood outside on the balcony chatting and sipping soft drinks. The warm spring evening gave us a clear view of the spectacular scenery of the Wye Valley. Around 9 pm, as we were gazing at the stars in the clear night sky, someone suddenly spotted a slow moving light. We followed the luminous ball with our eyes as it travelled south to north, but then to our surprise it stopped dead. I mentioned rather sarcastically that I had never seen a shooting star stop before and then suddenly to our amazement it started to move rapidly towards us, growing larger and larger until it hovered about 9 m (30 ft) above us. Not knowing what to do next, we just stood and stared in wonderment at the hovering ball. It appeared to resemble a miniature sun with no hard edges and almost gaseous in substance. I looked around at my friends, who were all open-mouthed, unable to comprehend this alien experience. Then, as quickly as it had arrived, it shot off down the valley at an incredible speed, like the Starship Enterprise engaging warp drive. Incredibly, nobody inside the pub noticed this strange incident.

In contrast to the excitement and joviality of the walk to the pub, the return journey was one of eerie silence after witnessing such a mind-numbing event. Although amused by our story, the teacher was puzzled by the fact that all nine of us had witnessed it. I can barely remember what happened later that night back in the wooden cabins within the dark pine forest, but some of my friends displayed unusual or bizarre behaviour and one had to be physically restrained.

For many years I believed it was a UFO sighting, but I now know that this is a natural phenomenon seen by many people around the world at certain places of power. I believe that this ball of light was plasma, possibly released by some local geological fault under pressure. Plasma is the fourth state of matter after liquids, solids and gases, its atoms having divided into free-floating 'negative' electrons and 'positive' ions – an atom that has lost its electron(s). At least 99 per cent of the known universe including the sun is in fact matter in its plasma state. Plasma is a unique substance because it is electrically conductive and responds to magnetic fields. Gases under such huge subterranean pressures from the Earth's crust or fault lines may evolve into plasma and move to the surface through fissures.

Plasma emits strong magnetic fields that affect the human brain and can give us varying degrees of physiological disturbances including hallucinatory or visionary experiences. In *Space Time Transients and Unusual Events* (1977), the authors Dr Michael Persinger and Gyslaine Lafreniere scientifically demonstrate a correlation between areas of unusual paranormal events such as strange creatures, UFOs and time slips, and geological anomalies that produce plasma, such as fault lines.

People often relate fault lines with earthquakes, but when seismic activity occurs the energy disperses evenly and efficiently, whereas balls of plasma release when the stresses are focused in one place, where the rocks cannot move or fold over each other. I later discovered that a major fault line runs through the Wye Valley, a renowned hotspot for so-called UFO activity.

Ancient Brading

From the Punchbowl, Elen changes direction to flow east towards the town of Brading, reputably founded by King Alfred in the 9th century. Tourists often miss the splendours of this ancient town as they make their way from the ferry at Ryde to the golden beaches of Sandown. Centuries ago, Brading was an important trading port situated on the Eastern Yar, then a wide estuary. In Victorian times, the area known as Brading Haven diminished when the river reduced to a stream. We located Elen passing through St Mary's Church, allegedly built on the earliest Christian site on the island established by St Wilfred.

Wilfred was born into a Northumbrian noble family in AD 633, entering a religious life as a teenager and becoming a student at Lindisfarne Abbey. Under orders from the Pope and King Caedwalla, he sailed into Brading Harbour in AD 687 to convert the islanders. On a mound overlooking the harbour, now the church of St Mary, the saint preached against the practices of the old Celtic church and baptised twelve hundred families to the new faith. He then built the island's first Catholic Christian church on the mound and dedicated it to St Mary the Virgin, for which the King awarded him a quarter of the island.

According to *The Tales and Legends of the Isle of Wight* by Abraham Elder, the churchyard of St Mary's is of great antiquity, being the burial place of some of the 'rude forefathers of the isle' prior to the coming of Christianity. Curiously, some of the human bones found in the churchyard were of a greater size than normal, leading to stories that the earliest occupants of the Isle were giants (Searle 1998). The unusual entrance to St Mary's Church is located directly beneath the tower, designed as an open porch, similar to only four other churches in England. Elen bisects the church at an angle from the northwest, passing through the Oglander Chapel and their elaborate tombs that show all the trappings of their former wealth and power. Near the High Altar

is a most unusual sight; a Saxon stone stoup decorated with pagan symbols including spirals and an inverted pentagram. The inverted pentagram, or five-pointed star, is a potent symbol said to represent 'occult magic' and the subservience of matter over spirit. According to the church guide, this stoup probably came from the earlier Saxon church on this site, perhaps introduced here after St Wilfred left the island. Its miraculous survival is probably due to the islanders' continued tolerance of such pagan symbols in their churches. Elen also passes through a cloisonné enamel plaque in a niche depicting St Mary holding a rose in her right hand, the rose being the emblem of Brading.

Stone font carved with a pentagram in Brading Church

We follow the current to an ancient preaching cross in the churchyard with steps so worn that it may mark the site where St Wilfred first preached. It continues to a red-brick enclosure known as The Pound, the old prison for the Court Leet.

We lingered in this ancient town for a while longer, visiting the museum next to the church attended by a local woman. She informed us of an ancient tradition that the Phoenicians settled on the island and used the old green lane that now runs to Quarr

Abbey as a 'tinner's track'. As renowned traders, the Phoenicians visited the island to market tin, copper and lead from the southern counties of England for export to Europe. The Phoenicians also used Puckaster Cove to transport tin by boat from their main trading base at the village of Niton.

The ancient Greek writer Diodorus mentions an island called *Ictis* off the south coast of Britain that was fordable at low tide and a tin trading centre for the Phoenicians. Many believe this name refers to St Michael's Mount in Cornwall, as it too is fordable at low tide even today and close to several tin mines. However, I believe that the Isle of Wight is also a contender for the legendary Ictis, due to its similarity to the island's Roman name Vectis, also fordable at low tide during Roman times. Centuries later, the Cistercian monks of Quarr Abbey would re-use the old tinner's track as they journeyed to Brading.

On re-examining the map, I could actually make out this old route marked by roads and footpaths, which remarkably coincide with the path of Elen in many places. Perhaps the sanctity of this route lures the female current as she follows in the footsteps of the old white monks travelling to Brading to visit the first Christian shrine built by St Wilfred.

The Druid Grove

We continued across fields, reclaimed from the old estuary, towards the imposing prominence of Bembridge Down. Early maps show that the Isle of Wight was divided into three separate islands. The western island called Freshwater Isle was separated from the main island by the Western Yar, whilst the eastern island called Binbridge Isle, now Bembridge Down, was separated by the Eastern Yar. Each of these islands had a Druid sanctuary – the Pinnacle of Ur on Freshwater Isle, the Longstone on the main island and the Grove of Hexal on Binbridge Isle. Three islands within one landmass were undoubtedly significant to the Druids as the number three was considered sacred. The Grove was said to be the most sacred of these sites and contained a holy well and an ancient stone. When an attempt was made to drain the estuary in 1620, a stone-lined well, probably the Druids' well, was uncovered, although its exact location is unknown today.

Looking across the area of the old estuary, I could imagine great trading ships sailing towards the port of Brading, bringing with them goods from Europe or the Middle East in exchange for Britain's valuable metals such as tin, lead, iron and copper. Beyond the estuary we stood on what must have been the shore of the Isle of Binbridge, before entering dense woodland curiously named 'Centurions Copse'. This place is steeped in legend and seems to have parallels with the Druidic myth of the sacred Hexal Grove.

According to island folklore, the earthworks within Centurions Copse are the remains of the drowned coastal city of Wolverton, named after Wulfere, the Saxon King of Mercia, who built a settlement here. Somewhere nearby, a standing stone was said to have existed marking a holy well, possibly the old Druids' well. An early prophecy foretold that 'Wolverton would thrive so long as the well was untainted and disaster would come if the clear waters were marred'. According to legend a trickster hermit, having gained the trust of the locals, prophesied that a stranger wearing a grey cowl would one day come and poison the well. When a man arrived at the well matching the hermit's description and kneeled down to touch the waters, the locals stoned him to death only to discover he was just a simple monk collecting holy water. His blood spilt into the well and tainted the waters forever. The prophecy seemed to ring true because a short time later the town was destroyed by fire. The ghost of the murdered monk is said to still haunt these lonely woods. As we wandered gingerly through the dense woodland, not even the twitter of a bird broke the eerie silence. The earthworks are in fact the remains of Wolverton Manor and a chapel dedicated to St Urian. The name Centurion may be a misinterpretation by Sir John Oglander in the 17th century when trying to make sense of the obscure St Urian.

Elen then begins to climb the slopes of Centurion's Hill to the summit of Bembridge Down on the head of the Firestone serpent that forms the central ridge of the island. On the highest part of the Down, corresponding to the 'eye' of the serpent, is a concrete hexagonal building set into the ground. Bembridge Fort was built during the Victorian period as part of the national defences against a French invasion. Until recently, a private communication company occupied it but today it is preserved by the National Trust.

Elen passes through the fort and continues east following the road to a huge obelisk made of Cornish granite. According to a plaque on the monument, the obelisk once stood on the highest point of the Down before the building of the fort forced its removal to its present position. The obelisk commemorates the life of Charles Anderson-Pelham, better known as Baron Yarborough and Baron Worsley of Appuldurcombe House. He was the first Commodore of the Royal Navy and died in 1846. As we stood at the base of the immense quartz granite obelisk, we could feel it emanating a powerful energy and soon started to feel giddy, as if the structure was somehow interfering with our own energy fields.

At the end of the track on Culver Down, Elen passes through Culver Point, Culver being a Saxon word for 'dove'. During the 19th century, it was the site of a wartime battery and some of the old gun emplacements are still visible today.

Elen disappears out to sea at White Cliff Ledge, marking the end of her journey through the island. Below are two caves called 'The Nostrils', so named because they resemble the openings of a nose when viewed from the sea. The caves are difficult and dangerous to visit and can only be accessed over slippery rocks at certain times of the year when the tide is low. In fact, the caves

The Nostrils at Culver Cliff, Isle of Wight

are the very first place of connection for Elen in the British Isles, a hidden sanctuary where, like the knights of Arthur seeking the Grail, only a brave individual who risks life and limb from sudden tides can enter. Like many caves throughout the country, this surely is a place of initiation; worthy perhaps of the mysterious cult of Mithras purportedly practised on the island in Roman times.

As we watched the sun set, we reflected on our discoveries and began to understand the energetic importance of Bembridge and Culver Down, although, as we were to discover later, it had another secret to reveal.

All Saints' Church and Swanmore

The following day we returned to the church at Binstead to begin our investigation of the male serpent. Curiously, he took us east along a path called Ladies Walk towards a large church, its spire dominating the skyline on the northern outskirts of the seaside town of Ryde. Referred to as 'the cathedral of the island', All Saints' Church stands as a great landmark on top of the highest hill overlooking the Solent. Constructed in 1869, this grand Gothic building was the design of the famous Victorian architect and Freemason Sir George Gilbert Scott (1811–78). It was reportedly his finest work. Scott was also responsible for the design of the Albert Memorial and the renovation of Westminster Abbey.

Inside the church, we were amazed at the quality of workmanship and the materials used. Scott also designed the marble and alabaster font, but his finest work is the pulpit made of Derbyshire alabaster on polished marble columns, which Scott earlier designed for the Great Exhibition of 1852 and won first prize. Another remarkable feature is its altar, made from olive wood brought over from the Holy Land.

The male current flows under the massive 56 m (186 ft) bell tower, taking in the pulpit and leaving by the High Altar. As we stood beneath the huge tower looking up, I sensed that this enormous structure was acting as an aerial, drawing orgone and other cosmic energies down into the church. This energy seemed to be interacting with Belinus because his flow had widened significantly after passing beneath the tower. As an initiate into the Mystery School, Scott incorporated sacred geometry within the architecture of many of the churches he designed around the country, including mystical carvings and stone features such as the labyrinth under the tower of Ely Cathedral.

Belinus then curves in a southerly direction, passing through housing estates to another hilltop church at Swanmore. Part of the diocese of Winchester, the church guide describes St Michael and All Angels as 'a little gem'. Built in 1862, the style of its interior resembles that of churches found in the Rouen area of France. From its square tower one can see panoramic views over the island and across the Solent to Portsmouth. Although appearing typically Victorian from the outside, its interior is extraordinary, with its unique coloured brickwork and splendid carved choir screen decorated with the twelve apostles. The walls, constructed from multicoloured bricks, present an alchemical mix of pale yellow, red, black and grey, signifying earth, air, fire and water. According to the guidebook, the church still practises an early form of Catholicism. We found Belinus entering the north wall through the screen under the tower to the Lady Chapel with its beautifully painted ceiling of St Michael surrounded by choirs of angels. At the entrance to this chapel is another fine representation of St Michael slaying the dragon.

The Devil's Punchbowl

South of here, we follow the current to the Nunwell estate passing Whitefield Farm. Belinus flows just east of his counterpart through the garden before he ascends Brading Down. As we followed him to the summit, we soon realised he was making his way towards Elen at the Devil's Punchbowl. On top of the mound both Belinus and Elen shrink into its centre to a point in the ground and re-emerge a little further on at right angles to each other, forming the shape of a Maltese cross.

As this was a quiet location, I had the opportunity to dowse what Hamish Miller called the Earth signature of the Node. He discovered that the Nodes of the St Michael Line project an image of a warped five-pointed star that he was able to dowse around or near the crossing point. At this Node, a precise six-pointed star manifested, which Caroline marked in the grass with string as I dowsed. Although the significance of these shapes is still a mystery, I believe it is an expression of resonance, perhaps even a musical tone.

Node signature dowsed at the Devil's Punchbowl

We then settled ourselves on the mound to absorb its energy and allow any impressions of the site to enter our minds. Caroline and I both picked up that long ago this site was a focus for ceremony used by the Bronze Age peoples and the later Druids on the highest point of the Down, where locals have seen the ghosts of Roman soldiers. This sacred mound represents a major power point or junction box of earth energy; the powerful natural forces building up from the geological fault beneath our feet focus at this point through the

The Devil's Punchbowl, Brading Down

mound. The Druids understood this natural phenomenon and utilised this energy to regenerate the land and cleanse it of any negative forces, similar to the work of modern geomancers who heal areas affected by geopathic stress.

The ridge on which the Devil's Punchbowl resides is part of a much greater geological fault visible in satellite photographs. From the Needles, the fault line stretches across the water to the chalk stacks called the Harry Rocks on the Purbeck coast in Dorset and across the rest of the county to Lyme Regis. Part of this fault is the South Dorset Ridgeway, which has a great number of Bronze Age tumuli along its course.

Archaeologists believe that all tumuli are burial places; however, many bear no signs of interment dating from the period of construction. This has led some researchers to believe that these Bronze Age mounds originally had a different function. Archaeology has revealed that many of the larger mounds are made of layers of organic and inorganic materials such as earth and chalk. Scientist Wilhelm Reich discovered that raising a mound formed of such layering attracts a cosmic energy he called orgone. This energy, according to Reich, exists in all living things and accumulates in the upper atmosphere. He suggested that the ancient races around the world who built these mounds knew how to amass this energy and use it to create a healthier and harmonious living environment.

You will see such mounds all over the country, many on top of hills in close proximity to fault lines and ridgeways, such as on the chalk downs of Wiltshire, Sussex, Hampshire and Dorset. I believe that when the geological fault produces energy, the layering acts as a condenser that stores it within the tumuli. Eventually the mound reaches a point of discharge and releases the energy, creating cloud and rain. Although this theory may seem beyond the realms of logic, many archaeologists past and present have experienced sudden rainstorms whilst excavating tumuli. I believe that disturbing the delicate structuring of these mounds triggers a massive discharge, which manifests as clouds. Reich discovered during his 'cloud busting' experiments in the 1930s that he could manipulate orgone to change the weather.

This being the case, why would the Bronze Age culture need to bring rain to a country that has its fair share? However, data recovered from deep soil samples indicates that during the Bronze Age, Britain had a much warmer climate on a par with the Mediterranean today and experienced long periods of sunshine and drought. By cleverly constructing and regulating these mounds, the Bronze Age peoples could produce as much rain as they needed at just the right time to irrigate their crops.

Other dowsers have discovered that many of these ancient grassy mounds are the focus of earth energies and ley lines. Alfred Watkins believed they were erected to mark the passage of ley lines across the country. Could it be that the mounds had another function, to boost the flow of the local energy grid? Perhaps the Devil's Punchbowl is a conduit to focus the two serpents to connect with the great fault line. Alternatively, the serpent energies might just be seeking out these mounds to draw from their power. The Bronze Age peoples may have created a grid network of earth energy lines across Britain, using natural features and manufactured mounds resembling the National Electricity Grid, which uses power stations and pylons to circulate the electricity. If this was indeed true then our ancient ancestors must have had superior knowledge of the Earth's energy system, using it to fine-tune their landscape to create the perfect environment for their crops and their people to thrive.

I also discovered that other major energy lines and leys in England connect with the Isle of Wight, one of which is the famous 'Avebury ley', discovered by Watkins. In the sacred prehistoric landscape of Avebury, very close to the largest stone circle in the Europe, is Knoll Down, an eminence said to be the terminus of the destroyed Beckhampton Stone Avenue or tail of the Avebury serpent. The ley runs all the way from Knoll Down to a point in the sea just west of the Needles connecting the tail of the Avebury serpent with the tail of the Isle of Wight serpent. Also on this alignment are many important historical sites including the largest henge in England at Marden, Stonehenge, Old Sarum, Salisbury Cathedral, Clearbury Ring and Godshill in Hampshire.

Glastonbury and Shaftsbury are both on a ley that runs to the eastern shore of Bembridge Isle, starting from Glastonbury Tor through Castle Hill and the ancient Priory at Shaftsbury to Bembridge. Significantly, for the Isle of Wight, both these leys connect the two great sanctuaries of Avebury and Glastonbury on the St Michael Line.

The Romans also recognised that the island had an important connection with the rest of Britain. Innes (1981) quotes G.B. Berry who wrote in 1967 that the great Roman general Vespasian, having captured the island in AD 43, used it as a base to survey a series of roads that would run northwest, in order to mark the successive stages of his invasion of Britain. One of these roads is Rue Street, which stretches from Puckaster Cove on the south coast to Gurnard Head on the north shore, passing through Gatcombe and Carisbrooke.

A few years ago, we made the acquaintance of two local independent Earth Mysteries researchers on the island who informed us of a lost megalith in a wood just to the west of the Devil's Punchbowl. Old maps show that it may be a lone survivor of a group of three, which stood in the adjacent field on top of the fault line. We circled around the edge of the wood just above Nunwell House until we noticed the megalith poking through the brambles. From a certain angle the stone resembles a crouched dragon with its wings held tight to its side. Now heavily worn, it appears to be made of Upper Greensand, the same geology that forms the serpent ridge. When I touched the stone, I could sense it still had power, although it no longer stands in its original position, having been removed by farmers from the middle of the field long ago. Whether it formed part of a megalithic monument such as a dolmen is hard to tell. This area of the ridge marks the neck of the serpent so perhaps the three stones that once stood here were part of a bigger sacred complex that included the Devil's Punchbowl.

Before trees obscured the view north, there would have been a spectacular outlook standing on the Punchbowl. Turning my thoughts to the northern skies, I realised that the hilltop church of St Michael and All Angels at Swanmore was significant. According to the map, the church marks the exact angle where Deneb the brightest star in the Cygnus constellation would have set into the horizon in 500 BC. As mentioned in the introductory chapter, from this latitude in pre-Christian times, Deneb set below the horizon but as you travel further north along the alignment the star gradually becomes circumpolar.

The Cult Centre of Mithras

Looking south from Brading Down, we could just make out the seaside town of Sandown where the alignment enters the island. Here, according to legend, St Paul landed in the 1st century AD with several Christians during his visit to Britain. The early apostle evidently preached to the island Druids before crossing over to Hampshire. Although this seems unlikely, there are many legends of him visiting England including the site of St Paul's Cathedral in London. Perhaps it is more than a coincidence that a place on the Hampshire coast adjacent to the Isle of Wight is called Paul's Grove.

We followed the Belinus current along a footpath through Adgestone Vineyard leading to a large Roman villa on the outskirts of Brading, first discovered in 1879. Soon after, the Oglanders from Nunwell House purchased the site and organised the first official excavations. Now open to the public, this fine villa began as a simple timbered structure and then expanded to a complex of buildings around a central courtyard that you see today. Many of the superb mosaics discovered during excavation depict mythical subjects symbolic of the Mithras religion, an ancient pagan mystery religion best known for its associations with the Roman Empire. Author Brian Innes, amongst others, suggests that the island was a base for this mysterious cult, but the Mithraeum, an underground ceremonial crypt, has yet to be found. However, from the size of the site, it appears reminiscent of a settlement or camp rather than a villa. In fact, recent evidence suggests that the site was far more extensive than we see today and therefore any future excavations may reveal the elusive subterranean Roman sanctuary.

At its height, the emperors and the elite of Rome aspired to the religion and it was widely practised by the Roman legions. Initiates would endure ceremonies involving a symbolic death and rebirth. Inside the Mithraeum, seven grades of initiation took place. The initial induction begins by leading an initiate through a maze of underground

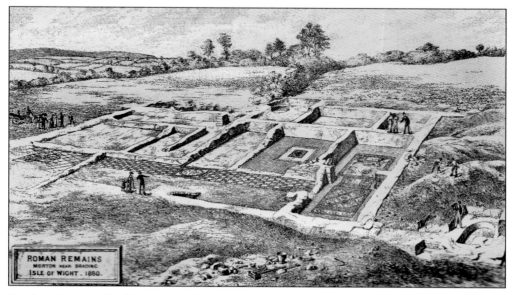

Brading Roman villa. (From A Guide to the Roman Villa recently discovered by John E. Price and F.G. Hilton-Price, dated 1881, Dryden Press, London)

passages to a crypt. Once inside, they are showered with blood from a sacrificial bull, poured through a grid above. Like Belinus, Mithras is a god associated with the sun, one of his ancient titles being 'The Light of the World'. He is often portrayed slaying a bull, hence the use of bull sacrifice as part of the initiation.

Vectis, the Roman name for the island, has been translated as 'lever' referring to the island's unusual stratum that extends vertically. However, it could also have been a corruption of the word 'Invictus', another title for the Roman sun god Mithra. During the 1st century AD, Mithras was the leading religion in Europe, so perhaps St Paul and his missionaries specifically landed at Sandown to visit the Roman villa, the cult centre of Mithras, to preach the new faith.

I dowsed the male current crossing the car park to a structure, which the guide refers to as Building 36. Archaeologists are mystified as to its purpose but suggest that it could have been a furnace or bathhouse. We continued to a garden feature and a 24 m (79 ft) deep well that when first excavated contained human and animal remains and offerings. As we stood by the garden feature, I started to feel a strong and vital energy emanating from the ground. A few paces south of Building 36 we had a strong dowsing reaction to something beneath the ground. Could this be the site of the elusive Mithraeum?

Either by accident or design, the situation of this Roman complex on the Belinus current may have helped the Latin invaders to manipulate Britain and the psyche of the people. Perhaps during a Mithras ritual, the priests invoked the vital solar influence of the male current and, through focused intention, the serpent's power becomes amplified, affecting everything in its path as it snaked its way through the British Isles.

Outside the ancient town hall of Brading, there is a large iron ring set into the pavement, once used for tethering bulls. Here the cruel tradition of using dogs to bait bulls took place long ago. Apparently, the adrenalin of the suffering bull makes the meat tastier; at one time, it was against the law to eat unbaited meat. As we called into the nearby pub for some refreshment to reflect upon our findings, its name 'The Bugle' and the pub sign depicting a bull intrigued me. On enquiry, a local told us that 'Bugle' is an island name given to young bulls and at one time there were several pubs with this name around the Isle of Wight. The island's connection with the bull is intriguing. Although folklore says that they were sacrificed here by the followers of Mithras and the Druids, some of the place names such as Cowes, Apes Heath and Apse Down, which derive from the Memphis Bull god Apis, suggest a Phoenician or Egyptian connection. In ancient times, the northern part of the island, either side of Cowes, would appear to have looked like horns; curiously, the right horn today bears the name Egypt Point.

The lure of Bembridge Down, the head of the serpent, also seems to draw the Belinus current. However, instead of climbing the hill to meet with Elen, he swings south to connect with a little Norman church at Yaverland. Over the entrance arch is another of those grinning faces, reminiscent of Binstead church at the north of the island where we started our journey; I was amused by its knowing but cheeky expression, an acknowledgement perhaps of the many mysterious encounters and places we had experienced on our journey through the island.

Inside the church there is a splendid Norman chancel arch built by the original builders in AD 1150. The Norman de Aula family built it originally as a private chapel on the grounds of their manor house, which still stands close by. Local folklore informs us that the church once stood in Centurions Copse, formerly the city of Wolverton, which we encountered earlier on the feminine current. It was later transported to Yaverland Manor on rollers after the disastrous flooding of Brading Harbour, transferring from the female serpent to the male.

The church, now dedicated to St John the Baptist, is one of four on the Isle of Wight assigned to this popular saint. This may suggest that the medieval order of the Knights Templar had a connection with the island, as they revered this saint above all others. The Cistercian order, who built the abbey at Quarr, also had a close association with the Knights and according to Worsley in his *History of the Isle of Wight*, written in 1781, the Templars owned the manor of Uggeton, the lands in Kern just south of Ashey Downs and the haunted estate of Knighton Gorges.

The mighty eminence of Bembridge Down and its surrounding lands once formed the ancient Binbridge Isle before the draining of the harbour. In medieval times the parish of Yaverland was called *Evreland* and later *Yaverlond*, this may have been an earlier name for this little isle reminiscent of Avalon. Curiously, old maps show that the outline of the island once resembled a human foetus, a symbolic figure that both currents are drawn to connect with as they enter the coast of Britain. Perhaps the serpents chose this island as the perfect place to birth their journey at the base of the Spine of Albion; even the diamond outline of today's Isle of Wight mirrors the shape of the human coccyx, a small triangular bone attached to the sacrum at the base of the spinal column.

The base of the spine also houses the *kundalini* of Eastern mystical tradition, a hidden coiled force of energy envisioned as a sleeping serpent that when awakened produces spiritual enlightenment. The body has seven centres of power called *chakras*

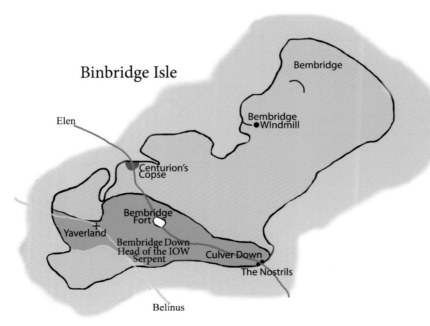

Binbridge Isle before the draining of the harbour shaped like a foetus

and the kundalini resides in the Base Chakra. I believe the sleeping serpent resides within the strata of the Isle of Wight at the base of Britain in the form of the serpent ridge, the island's own secret kundalini force.

Belinus reaches the southern coast over the Red Cliffs, close to a holiday centre east of Sandown. We sat by the edge of the soft red sandstone looking across the sea and contemplated the significance of the path taken by these two great serpent energies. Each current flowed through sites associated with their gender. Belinus connects with churches dedicated to male saints such as St Michael and St John and the phallic tower of All Saints at Ryde as well as a possible centre of Roman solar worship at the villa at Brading. In contrast, the path of Elen flows through Quarr Abbey dedicated to Our Lady of the Quarry and follows the path taken by Eleanor of Aquitaine, queen of Henry II. She then passes through the site of a Nunnery at Ashey, through a holy well called the Bloodstone Spring, to St Mary's Church at Brading, the possible site of a Druid well in Brading Haven and finally to the secret caves at the Nostrils below Culver Down.

Sandown and the Root of the Alignment

Our final task was to seek out the place where the alignment enters Britain on the south coast of the Isle of Wight. Using Google Earth and detailed maps, we determined that the exact location is a point just to the west of Sandown Pier below the high cliffs, where we found the Sea Scouts hut, the tiny West Winds Cottage and the Inshore Lifeboat building. On the clifftop directly above is Battery Gardens, where defensive buildings still exist from Napoleonic times.

The alignment has been marked in modern times by a straight path leading from the cliffs through the gardens, along Grange Road to Beachfield Road. At this junction stands the most remarkable sight, a modern-built representation of a Celtic church. The Roman Catholic Church of St Patrick is complete with an Irish Round Tower that stands right on the alignment. In the Irish landscape, the enigmatic stone-built round towers with their pointed caps are a magnificent sight, standing like giant pencils or obelisks pointing to the heavens. Their history has been the subject of much speculation for historians, both ancient and modern, and even today there is still no satisfactory answer to their true purpose and function.

Similar to Egyptian obelisks, megalithic standing stones and church spires, these mysterious towers served to attract cosmic energies or amplify earth energies. Buildings that have been shaped and exactly proportioned in this way can draw upon natural energies such as orgone in the upper atmosphere, as demonstrated by Wilhelm Reich's experiments. This secret knowledge, passed down through the various Mystery Schools, dates back to the pyramid builders of Ancient Egypt. Based on this principle, St Patrick's round tower placed here at the foot of the alignment in Sandown must also help to heighten the power of the Spine of Albion.

Almost opposite St Patrick's, also on the alignment, is Christ Church, the first Church of England built on the island. Constructed in Victorian times, it has its High Altar positioned north, which is rare in English churches, perhaps a remnant of an old pagan practice.

As we made our way back to the mainland on the ferry, I sat and considered all the

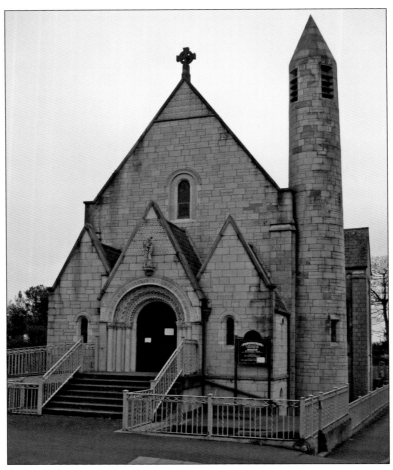

St Patrick's Church, Sandown

stories I had heard and read concerning the Phoenicians, Egyptians and Druids. Did the Phoenicians deliberately carve out the old tinner's track to connect with or attract the hidden feminine force? Were the Druids in touch with the potent telluric power that lay within the Firestone ridge that mirrored the path of the moon? Perhaps the stonemason who carved the dragon biting its own tail at Binstead knew something of the island's great and mysterious power. In *The Return of the Serpents of Wisdom*, author Mark Amaru Pinkham states:

> 'Either Stonehenge, Avebury and/or one of the sacred isles, the headquarters of the Arch Druids, could have served as Control Centrals of this northern grid [network of leys in the British Isles]. Perhaps the pivotal vortex [energy centre or hub] was the Isle of Wight, anciently known as 'The Dragon's Isle' having been recognised as a natural fount of serpent power for thousands of years.'

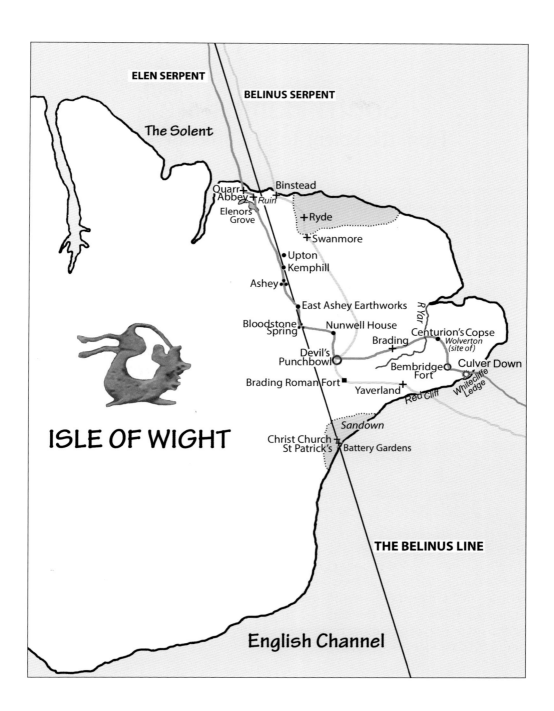

ELEN SERPENT

BELINUS SERPENT

The Solent

Quarr Abbey
Binstead
+ Ruin
Elenors Grove
+ Ryde
+ Swanmore
• Upton
• Kemphill
Ashey •
• East Ashey Earthworks
Bloodstone Spring
Nunwell House
Centurion's Copse
Brading
• Wolverton (site of)
Devil's Punchbowl
Bembridge Fort
Culver Down
Brading Roman Fort
Yaverland
Red Cliff
Whitecliffe Ledge
R Yar

ISLE OF WIGHT

Sandown
Christ Church St Patrick's
Battery Gardens

THE BELINUS LINE

English Channel

Chapter 2

South Hampshire
From the Solent to St Catherine's Hill

Over a thousand years ago, Hampshire was an important area within the Saxon realm of Wessex, a kingdom in southern England that stretched from Kent to Cornwall bordered by the River Thames and the Severn Estuary. During the 9th century, its ruler was King Alfred the Great, a wise and powerful warrior who became overlord of England after winning many decisive battles against the Danes. At the centre of his kingdom was Winchester, which in AD 848 became the religious and economic capital of his new

View of St Catherine's Hill, Winchester.

nation. After the Norman Conquest of Saxon England in 1066, William the Conqueror arrived in Winchester and built his royal palace and a new cathedral, making it joint capital with London. From the time of King Alfred, the Bishops of Winchester were the most powerful and wealthiest men in the kingdom and custodians of a landscape steeped in myth and legend, including stories of King Arthur and the Grail.

From the Isle of Wight, the alignment enters Hampshire close to where the River Meon enters the Solent next to the residential area of Hill Head. It actually passes through Monks Hill, a raised elongated mound on the seafront now topped by select residences, which may have been the site of a medieval lodging close to the landing place for the monks of Quarr Abbey who lived on the opposite shore. Both Hill Head and its neighbour, Lee-on-the-Solent, have little historical importance before Victorian times, being merely small settlements on a marshy extension of the Meon Estuary. As mentioned earlier, meon is an old English word meaning 'middle', alluding to this area as a geographical centre. Indeed, in ancient times, before Portsmouth came

into existence, the Meon was the most central river and port along the south coast of England. Was this ancient name recording for prosperity the existence of a central cosmic axis, the very point where the Belinus Line begins its journeys through the 'middle' of Britain?

We started our journey by driving along the seafront road in Lee-on-the-Solent to locate the male and female serpents, but found no sign of them until I had a dowsing reaction at the Alver River Nature Reserve just north of Browndown Point. After parking the car, we performed some rigorous dowsing checks to ensure that it was a serpent line associated with our alignment. We determined it to be Belinus after measuring its width and inner bands and asking yes or no questions as to whether it was male or female.

Although recognised as a nature reserve, there appeared to be no sign of any wildlife enthusiasts, except for the odd dog walker. Access to this area is now through a new housing development, where we followed a sign to a 17th century farmhouse. In fact, the area felt strangely eerie and, after parking next to Grange Farm, we had to rely on the dowsing rods to show us the direction we needed to take to locate Belinus. Suddenly, hidden amongst trees we came upon a large manmade mound and earthworks known as a 'motte and bailey'. These were defensive structures, containing a high lookout mound called a motte and an inner enclosure called a bailey. Known as the Alverstoke Mound, the graffiti-strewn information board informed us that the Normans built it shortly after their invasion in 1066 to defend an important crossing point of the River Alver. The rather overgrown and unkempt mound is a scheduled ancient monument, said to be the oldest surviving defensive earthwork in the Gosport area. Having found the Belinus current passing through the mound, I questioned whether its original purpose was for defence.

Alverstoke motte and bailey

Excavations of a number of motte and baileys around the country have indicated that the high mounds were earlier structures that the Normans refortified. According to E.O. Gordon in *Prehistoric London*, many of these mounds were meeting places of the Druids called *Gorsedds*, often located close to rivers or near the coast for easy access for foreign traders and missionaries. Many dowsers have discovered ley lines and energy currents connecting with these so-called motte and baileys, suggesting that they serve a more mysterious function. I believe that this particular motte here in the Alver Valley is a perfect example of a Bronze Age mound later fortified because of its position near the coast, its original function now forgotten and its presence in the landscape ignored.

Following the current north, Belinus took us to a large field. A later visit to the nearby Heritage Centre revealed that it was once the site of a large Saxon village. The very proximity of this village to the motte reinforced my belief that the mound existed before the Norman invasion and was probably re-used by the Saxons.

Looking at the map, we could see that if the Belinus current continues on this present course, he would almost certainly pass through the ancient town of Titchfield after skirting the modern residential area of Stubbington. We made the decision to ignore the modern town and head for the more historic Titchfield. However, it was not until much later that a local dowser alerted us to a site of historical importance hidden amongst Stubbington's residential housing estates.

Crofton Old Church

Looking at the OS map again, I could just make out the little cross that marks a church at the very northern end of Stubbington. We arranged to meet the local dowser there who had luckily provided us with good directions, as the church is difficult to find.

Crofton Old Church was once the parish church of the ancient district of Crofton and dedicated to St Edmund, King and Martyr, in 1331. It seemed most fitting that the first mainland church visited by the male current is dedicated to a king. According to the church guidebook, its foundation began in AD 878, perhaps the property of the Benedictine monks of Winchester. After the Norman invasion, the church and manor of Crofton fell into the ownership of Count Man of Brittany, who fought with William the Conqueror. The Domesday Book refers to the church as Crofton Church of the Holy Rood, perhaps because Count Man rebuilt the earlier church in the shape of a cross. According to early records, the Bishops of Winchester later regained ownership of the church, handing the chapel to the mother church at Titchfield, founded by the Premonstratensians of Titchfield Abbey in 1232.

I dowsed the male current entering the church from the southeast through the pulpit, which has a sarsen stone beneath disguised by whitewash. Outside by the north wall, I encountered the rector who was observing me with a keen eye. As my rods swung towards the exact point where Belinus exits the church, he came over and excitedly pointed out three more sarsen stones in the foundations of the north wall and added that inside the church I had dowsed over the site of the original Saxon altar next to the pulpit. The name *sarsen* is a corruption of Saracen, meaning 'something foreign'. Within the width of his flow is another sarsen stone in the northwest corner of

Sarsen stones in the north wall of Crofton Old Church, Stubbington

the churchyard and the remains of a window arch possibly from the Saxon Holy Rood Church. As we explored the site further, I noticed faint traces of a circular henge, which led us to believe that Crofton Old Church was built over a prehistoric site, possibly a stone circle. It is well-known that Christian missionaries sent from Rome during the 6th and 7th centuries targeted pagan ceremonial sites in order to assert their authority over the population.

Our exploits also caught the attention of a group of flower arrangers who enquired what we were doing. When we explained that a powerful line of earth energy flowed through their church, one woman exclaimed 'no wonder it feels so serene and beautiful here'. The famous 18th century diarist Samuel Pepys noted on his way through Crofton that the graves in the churchyard were 'accustomed to being sown with sage', a herb revered for thousands of years for its healing properties, earning it the old title of 'herb of immortality'. Perhaps this herb was grown here because the church stands on a renowned site of healing; a therapeutic force that still permeates the building with an atmosphere of serene beauty felt by the flower arrangers.

Crofton Old Church proved to be a most interesting place and only 0.6 km (0.3 miles) from the alignment, and to think that we almost missed this church, the first on the mainland visited by the male dragon.

Titchfield

Just 3 km (1.9 miles) north of the coast is the small market town of Titchfield and the first place of historical importance on the mainland. The ancient High Street orientated north–south actually marks the path of the alignment, a clear indication that there must be something quite special hidden in this quiet little Hampshire town. As we walked along the narrow cobbled streets admiring its ancient half-timbered houses, we could immediately sense its historical importance. The purchase of a book on the history of Titchfield at one of the little period shops reinforced this initial impression.

Titchfield was once part of a royal estate and a major port for over a thousand years, first mentioned in a Saxon charter issued by King Ethelred as having a religious house at 'Ticccfelda'. Just off the High Street is the parish church, one of the oldest in Britain still in use. It was first established as a minster, which provided for a very large area. Just under a kilometre away to the north is the ruin of an old Premonstratensian abbey, where the monks provided accommodation for many kings and queens before they embarked to France. During the medieval period, the port thrived and the market increased along with the town's population.

In AD 681, St Wilfred reputedly founded one of the first stone-built churches here, a year after establishing the first church on the Isle of Wight at Brading. Like Brading, Titchfield was an important port that later became a market town and also has a pub called the Bugle.

As we approached the parish church dedicated to St Peter, I first noticed that the churchyard is a circular raised area of ground, suggesting a pre-Christian sanctuary. The church is also close to the river like many of the Saxon churches in the country.

I started to walk around the graveyard in search of the Belinus current and found him passing through the southeast corner of the church and leaving northwest towards the marketplace. Walking further around the church, I dowsed another energy line, but this time female, flowing in a north–south direction through the centre of the church and, after checking it further, I discovered the current to be Elen. Interestingly, a small sarsen stone marks the exact spot where she enters the building. Upon closer inspection, this was the only stone around the outside of the church that appeared to have no other purpose than to mark something; perhaps we were not the first to locate this powerful energy line.

Inside, the currents form a Node on the steps where the nave meets the chancel. According to a Saxon plan of the church, this was the original position of the High Altar of the first church built by St Wilfred. Perhaps St Wilfred was aware of this secret place of power where two serpent energies meet for the first time on the mainland of Britain and confined them within his stone sanctuary.

St Wilfred built his church at Brading over an earlier pagan site, so it is possible he continued this practice here at Titchfield. In AD 595, Pope Gregory sent a missionary to Britain almost a hundred years before Wilfred called Augustine to convert the pagan kings. According to the Venerable Bede (AD 672–735) in *Bede: Ecclesiastical History of the English People* (Dumville 2003), Pope Gregory ordered that:

'The temples of the idols in that nation ought not to be destroyed; but let the idols that are in them be destroyed; let holy water be made and sprinkled in the said temples, let altars be erected, and relics placed. For if those temples are well built it is requisite that they be converted from the worship of devils to the service of the true God.'

The church is dedicated to St Peter whose feast day is 1 August, the old Celtic festival of Lughnasa or Lammas. Perhaps Wilfred's church was built over a site where the old Celtic tribes celebrated the first harvesting of their crops. The festival, named after the sun god Lugh, started at sundown on 3 July and ended at sundown on 1 August. People sometimes lit bonfires because of Lugh's association with the power of the sun and light. One local website states that the earliest church at Titchfield stood next to 'an ancient pagan site by an old tree'. Together with his allies the Benedictine Bishops of Winchester, Wilfred sought to eradicate paganism from Hampshire and caused the destruction of many prehistoric sites.

Remnants of the Saxon church built by St Wilfred still survive at Titchfield in the 8th century tower, the outer walls and the interior window, the architectural style is similar to Northumbrian churches also founded by Wilfred. The tower also displays with its outer masonry a remarkable course of red bricks reused from the Roman period, evidence perhaps that a Roman building or temple stood on this site before the time of the Saxons. The existence of the Saxon minster suggests that they were continuing the tradition of honouring this ancient place of power, which eventually grew into one of the most important early Christian centres along the south coast of England.

According to some historians, the River Meon that passes by the church takes its name from a tribe of Saxon Jutes called the Meonwara. Although *wara* is Saxon for 'tribe', Meon is an ancient British name, so it is more likely that the Jutes took their name from the river. Around this time in the 6th century, many of the villages and towns adopted new names after they were abandoned during a time of terrible pestilence in the 5th century.

King William Rufus inherited the lands at Titchfield from his father William the Conqueror, eventually passing them to Payn de Gisors, a Norman nobleman linked with the Knights Templar. His descendant Jean de Gisors acquired the land in 1180. According to the best-selling book *The Holy Blood and the Holy Grail*, Jean de Gisors was the first Grand Master of the esoteric secret society called the 'Prieure de Sion' between 1188 and 1220. He was also vassal to Henry II and his son Richard the Lionheart. This secret order was said to have been established by a group of knights that separated from the Knights Templar (Baigent *et al.* 1982).

Due to the silting and decline of the port at Titchfield, Jean de Gisors instructed the building of a new larger port further east at Portsmouth. He also rebuilt the ancient sanctuary of St Peter's Church and the fine western doorway including the strange and curious medieval carving of a Green Man with six curling foliate stems spouting from his mouth. Images of the Green Man can be seen in many churches around Britain, and often in the most obscure places. However, the Titchfield carving that greets you at the main entrance is a blatant reminder of the pagan origins of this sanctuary. The

Carving of a Green Man at St Peter's Church, Titchfield

stonemason responsible for this particular version of the Green Man may have been in touch with the telluric energies here, as the long curling stems of foliage remind me of the separate bands I had dowsed within the male and female serpents.

Belinus enters through the South Chapel built in the first half of the 14th century by the Abbot of Titchfield. Although now incorporated into the body of the church, the chapel was originally separate to the rest of the building. A curious weathered Purbeck marble grave slab with the worn effigy of a knight lying on the flow of Belinus might be that of William de Pageham, a Knights Templar who died in 1305, a possible descendant of an earlier William de Pageham recorded as Lord of the Manor of 'Ticcefield' in *c.* 1056.

The South Chapel or Southampton Chapel takes its name from the Earls of Southampton whose magnificent 16th century marble and alabaster monument dominates this part of the church. The Wriothesley family, pronounced 'Risley', included some of the most wealthy and influential men in Tudor and Elizabethan times. Thomas Wriothesley (1505–50) served both Henry VIII and Thomas Cromwell and had a key role in the annulment of the marriage between the Tudor king and his first wife Catherine of Aragon, which led to England breaking from the Church of Rome. Wriothesley soon became a Knight of the Honourable Order of the Garter for his services and by 1542 governed over almost everything in England; he even sought to bring about an alliance between England and Spain. In 1544, he received the title Baron Wriothesley of Titchfield just before becoming Lord Chancellor of England, and in 1547 he was awarded the title Earl of Southampton. After the Dissolution of the Monasteries Thomas persuaded King Henry to award him the lands of Quarr Abbey on the Isle of Wight, Titchfield and Hyde Abbey in Winchester. Perhaps it is more than a coincidence that the serpent currents of the Spine of Albion visit all three places, including his own burial vault.

Tomb of the Earls of Southampton, Titchfield Church

The monument is certainly one of the grandest I had ever encountered; far more elaborate than many of the royal tombs in Westminster Abbey. This imposing monument made of various coloured marble and alabaster is raised on two tiers surmounted by an elevated rectangular tomb with black crowned bulls and beautifully carved obelisks at each corner. The vault beneath also contains his grandson Henry Wriothesley, Third Earl of Southampton, a well-known patron of the famous English playwright William Shakespeare.

Lighting up the tomb is a stained-glass window above showing St Michael slaying a dragon, often thought to be a symbol of Christianity subduing the heathen or pagan faith, represented by the dragon. Michell states that the missionaries from Rome became the new dragon slayers; St Wilfred's mission to subdue the pagan faith was by way of controlling the natural force within the land, which the ancients had honoured for thousands of years.

I first introduced my partner Caroline to the Belinus Line in 2003, with a visit to Titchfield Church. Inside she was surprised and a little disconcerted to see her namesake, a member of the local Hornby family who died in 1891, commemorated in one of the stained-glass windows overlooking the Southampton monument. We later realised the synchronicity of this, an acknowledgement perhaps of the role Caroline was about to play on this long journey ahead. The window depicts both a female angel and St George slaying the dragon. This was the first of many encounters with St George along the Spine of Albion.

Before heading north on the trail of the serpents, we first had to establish where Elen enters mainland Britain on the south coast. We found her just to the west of the Meon Estuary beyond a group of houses called the Meon Shore Chalets at Meon Spit, where Mesolithic artefacts were uncovered. She continues through the tiny hamlet of Meon, once a settlement of the Meonwara mentioned in the Domesday Book, and a farmhouse, formerly Great Posbrook House.

From Titchfield Church, Elen stays close to the Meon River, whereas Belinus passes through the old market area of the town. Both were now heading towards the ruined abbey north of the village. The alignment is also marked in Titchfield by three curious, large sarsen stones in a wooded open space at the centre of the town on West Street, moved here from a site further west of the town during the building of a relief road.

The Abbey and the Bard

Titchfield Abbey, built in 1232 by Peter des Roches, then Bishop of Winchester, has within its fabric the finest limestone, shipped from the quarries of Binstead on the Isle of Wight and Caen in France. The Bishop invited a French monastic order of Premonstratensians known as the White Canons, so-called because they wore white robes, to establish a new community at the abbey and provide respectable accommodation for the elite of Britain before embarkation to and from France. Saint Norbert and his thirteen companions founded the Canons in northeast France at Premontre. Norbert was a close friend of Bernard de Clairvaux who masterminded the Knights Templar.

According to Paul Hindle, author of *Medieval Roads and Tracks*, this religious order built a network of roads that radiated out from Titchfield to their other establishments around the country. This included Shap Abbey in Cumbria, close to a site that was once a prehistoric serpent temple almost on the scale of Avebury that proved to be a very significant site on the Spine of Albion. Their efforts established Titchfield as one of the most important towns in England during medieval times.

During the Dissolution of the Monasteries in 1537, Thomas Wriothesley the First Earl of Southampton converted the abbey into a private mansion, adding four castellated towers to create the splendour of a Gothic Tudor castle, renaming it 'Place House'. After his death, his son Henry succeeded to

Place House, formerly Titchfield Abbey

the title and played host to Edward VI and his young sister, the future Queen Elizabeth. However, due to his involvement in a number of Catholic plots against the Queen, he spent several years imprisoned in the Tower of London.

His son, also called Henry, was only seven when he became the Third Earl and was placed under the guardianship of the powerful Elizabethan minister Lord Burghley. He later became the patron of many writers including Shakespeare, but due to his friendship and involvement with the Catholic sympathiser the Earl of Essex, he landed himself in the Tower of London, like his father and grandfather before him. Eventually released by James I, he began a career as a politician, becoming an active member of the House of Lords as well as Captain of the Isle of Wight. He soon resumed his associations with the stage and in 1603 entertained Queen Anne with a performance of Shakespeare's *Love's Labour's Lost* at Southampton House in London. Shakespeare dedicated his poem *Venus and Adonis* to the Earl, having been a frequent visitor at Place House. Henry also socialised with many mystics during his lifetime including Sir Francis Bacon and the famous astrologers and alchemists Dr John Dee and Edward Kelly.

After turning down Elizabeth De Vere, daughter of the Seventeenth Earl of Oxford, he married Elizabeth Vernon while she was 'already highly pregnant'. According to Graham Phillips in his fascinating book *The Search for the Grail*, her father Robert Vernon found a relic that may have been associated with the Grail. He was obsessed with tracing his mother's lineage to one Owain Dgantgwyn who died in AD 520. He was of British royal descent, ruling over the Kingdom of Powys during the age of King Arthur, and may have been a legendary warrior himself. Phillips also believes Owain's descendant Fulk Fitz Warine, a member of the Peveril family, born around 1175, was the guardian of a little alabaster cup also called the Marion Chalice, which was handed down through subsequent generations. Did Henry Wriothesley choose to marry a Vernon because they were descended from Arthur and guardians of the Grail? Interestingly their daughter Penelope married William, Second Baron Spencer, and instituted the line of Princess Diana.

An 18th century plan of Place House indicates the existence of a 'play-house room' on the second floor, suggesting that Shakespeare might have performed there. Local history states that Shakespeare produced and acted in some of his plays for the first time in the nearby abbey barn and attended a school built by Henry opposite the abbey. The old tannery, across the fields from the abbey next to a cemetery, is the supposed inspiration for *Hamlet*, one of his most famous plays.

According to Atasha Fyfe in her article *Shakespeare and Hermetic Magic* (2010), many of Shakespeare's plays contain hidden symbolism and an in-depth knowledge of occult matters according to Hermetic principles. Hermeticism originates from the Greek text *Corpus Hermeticum* based on the philosophy, teachings and ritual magic practices of the Ancient Egyptian God Thoth, also called Hermes. Cosmo Medici, Grand Duke of Tuscany, introduced Hermeticism to the Western world in 1460, but the Knights Templar practised it long before. It later found its way into the court of Elizabeth I, especially amongst the circles frequented by Dr John Dee and Francis Bacon.

Hermetic principles were also the mainstay of a select group of people, possibly a secret society called 'The School of Night', also called 'The School of Atheism'. This group included Henry Wriothesley, Christopher Marlowe, Francis Bacon, John Dee,

Sir Walter Raleigh and many other notable Elizabethans who met together at Raleigh's estate in Sherborne in Dorset. Some authorities claim that this nocturnal group were pagans who studied and worshipped the old gods. Others say they were either Rosicrucians or forerunners of the Royal Society.

Driving along the narrow country lane leading to the abbey, we could see the grand towers rising above the trees in the distance. Parking in the driveway, we stood and marvelled at the turreted gatehouse built in the unusual style of Elizabethan Gothic, the perfect venue for a horror movie. The site, now owned and preserved by the Department of the Environment, has free admission and is surprisingly devoid of the usual 'tourist' regalia. The freshly mown grass and pruned apple trees are visible signs that the abbey is still being cared for. The building is now just a shell and all that remains are its exterior walls, the fireplaces and windows. To the east you can see where the Premonstratensian abbey and cloisters once stood, indicated by an outline of stones in the grass. As I wandered through the grounds, a sudden chill came over me, as if being watched; later other people who accompanied us to the abbey, including local dowsing groups, had a similar experience.

Elen flows down the east–west axis of the old abbey from the site of the High Altar and into the nave between the four towers. Belinus passes through the main door, crossing with Elen within the four central towers adorned with stone dragons. As we followed the male current across the site of the cloisters, we questioned why the Node point was not at the old site of the High Altar. The Premonstratensians unusually dedicated their abbey to both St Mary and St John the Evangelist, as if they were honouring both the male and female energies here. Standing on the power point I looked up to see a fireplace marking an upper room where King Charles I is said to have spent his last night of freedom, similar to the story at Nunwell House on the Isle of Wight. I could imagine Shakespeare and Wriothesley meeting here with other members of the School of Night, discussing the old Hermetic teachings as they huddled around the fire, perhaps advising Shakespeare on the themes of his plays.

These hallowed walls have certainly witnessed some remarkable events and overseen many famous visitors including a long line of British Kings and Queens such as Richard II and his Queen Anne of Bohemia, Henry V and Henry VI, who used the abbey as the venue for his marriage to Margaret, daughter of René of Anjou, titular King of Jerusalem. Edward VI, the young Queen Elizabeth I, Charles I and his wife Queen Henrietta Maria, Charles II and Queen Anne were also guests of the abbey at one time or another.

As the Belinus current approaches from the south, it passes close to the medieval barn where Shakespeare reputedly performed some of his plays. Elen meanwhile arrives at the abbey having crossed the ancient Anjou Bridge over the River Meon. The presence of two Nodes at Titchfield perhaps marks two sacred sanctuaries that were once part of a larger prehistoric complex. Both crossing points were later Christianised and manipulated for reasons we can only speculate. Certainly, the serpents may have heightened the influence of the Premonstratensians at Titchfield, aided by their abbey lying at the hub of a network of roads that linked them to all their other establishments across the whole country.

A local man informed me that long ago an ancient road passed by the abbey that linked the port of Titchfield to Winchester. This also marks the route of the Spine of Albion all the way from the coast to ancient Winchester.

Botley Old Church and the Twyford Stones

The little hamlet of Curbridge, just north of the abbey, also stands upon this ancient route to Winchester and here we find the perfect spot to ponder our next move, an idyllic country pub called the Horse and Jockey overlooking the River Hamble. Sitting outside we noticed a field across the river that, according to a local history guide, is the site of a Roman temple and port. As we watched a group of revellers mooring their motorboat alongside the little wooden jetty by the pub, we imagined boatloads of Roman soldiers gliding up the river and embarking at the same spot.

At this point, due to inaccessibility of the area, we decided to dowse our OS map with a pendulum to locate the path of the currents. I dowsed Elen to the west about 1.5 km away, passing through a group of buildings called Manor Farm and then north to a church in the town of Botley. Caroline located Belinus over 2 km to the east heading towards the small town of Bishop's Waltham.

Botley has the usual rural Hampshire blend of half-timbered buildings and Georgian houses with an attractive market square. The Victorian politician William Cobbet described it as 'the most delightful in the world'. Arriving at All Saints' Church, we were surprised to see a modern Victorian building with a mock Tudor roof and windows. Upon entering, we encountered the vicar sat at his computer in an adjacent office. Having invited us in to view the church, we were instantly drawn to the magnificent Norman font. Noticing our interest, the vicar informed us with some pride that the font had come from the earlier parish church situated 1.5 km down the road, abandoned after suffering severe damage when a tree fell on its roof in 1835. The parishioners decided to build a new larger church closer to the modern village, the old settlement having long since vanished. The vicar then returned to his computer and we continued to look around the church.

I dowsed Elen passing through the font, clearly happy to connect with the new church. Picking up the church guide, I was intrigued by a statement that described the earlier church as having 'great antiquity'. Thanking the Vicar we set off down an extremely narrow lane, still called Church Lane, until we reached the Historical Farm Tourist Centre.

We soon found the old Botley church, secreted away behind farm buildings half hidden by trees. At first glance it reminded me of the many Celtic Christian churches that I had seen in Ireland; it even had a classic dogtooth Norman arch above the main door. Dowsing around the ancient walls in the early evening light, I tracked Elen flowing down the axis of the church to the altar, which was unusually orientated northeast, the direction of the solstice sunrise. This implies that this charming little church,

St Bartholomew's Church, Botley

dedicated to St Bartholomew, is on the site of a pre-Christian temple.

The map indicated that the church is part of the Manor Farm estate, which I had located earlier at Curbridge when dowsing over the map with the pendulum. We felt reassured that our map dowsing had been accurate and by locating the serpents in this way proved we had become accustomed to their unique vibration. It is possible that the female current's attachment to the old font has ensured her presence in the new church. Alternatively, the current may have followed the congregation there, attracted by the energy of prayer.

Elen meanders northwest across fields towards the Itchen Valley to Bishopstoke. We were surprised to find her passing through a curious raised grassy platform on recreation ground near the river, in the middle of which was a grave slab. At its western end is the brick outline of a tower, and inside is a plaque that records a little history of old St Mary's Church and reminding us that 'the place thou standeth is holy ground'. The town and this church date back to Saxon times when King Edred gave the lands to the Bishop of Winchester in AD 946. Records show that the Danes destroyed a church on this site around 1001, but it continued as a place of worship up until Victorian times when the increased population demanded a larger building and burial ground.

Early Christian symbol on masonry at St Mary's Church, Twyford

Further along the River Itchen is the ancient village of Twyford, known as 'the place of two fords'. Elen visits the church of St Mary built high on a ridge passing first through an ancient yew tree in the churchyard, said to be the oldest in the country. The Norman church with Saxon origins has some fascinating features. During a Victorian renovation, builders discovered a piece of masonry carved with the early Christian symbol of a cross within a circle, now incorporated into the wall of the porch. The Victorian architect Alfred Waterhouse designed the rebuild, keeping some of its Norman pillars. Another impressive feature is the beautiful Pre-Raphaelite paintings on the altar screen and wall of the chancel. Elen also connects with the font as she sweeps diagonally through the church and tower.

Intriguingly, the Twyford parish website records, 'There is an unusual concentration in the village of sarsen stones, including a ring of twelve which form the foundations on which the towers of both the present

Two of the sarsen stones lying near St Mary's Church, Twyford

church and of its medieval predecessor were built .... According to local folklore, the twelve stones originally stood as an upright circle on a mound near the site of the church.'

Old stones placed at the foot of the tower could be the megaliths from this circle. While continuing to follow Elen, we came across two further sarsen stones next to a path that leads from the church to the river. The Itchen, known as the 'Queen of Rivers', was once of great importance to the prehistoric peoples of this area for transportation and food.

Hospital of St Cross

Hospital of St Cross, Winchester

On the outskirts of the city of Winchester, Elen meanders through the water meadows by the Itchen Valley to Hospital of St Cross, which has England's oldest continuing and most enduring almshouses. While dowsing the currents on St Catherine's Hill on a previous visit, I detected her ascending from this group of monastic buildings, which are clearly visible in the valley below. Hospital of St Cross has a long tradition of providing hospitality for the local poor and hungry traveller, which continues today. Upon arrival at the Porters Lodge, pilgrims or travellers still have a right to demand bread and beer, known as the Wayfarer's Dole.

At the age of 28, Henry of Blois, Bishop of Winchester, founded the Hospital in 1136, inspired by a vision. The story relates that whilst taking a stroll across the water meadows by the River Itchen, the Bishop came across a young maiden holding a child in her arms and carrying a pail of milk on her head. She stopped him and begged assistance for her people living nearby who had been left to starve after the disastrous

Carving of an owl on the tree of life, Hospital of St Cross, Winchester

civil war between King Stephen and his cousin Empress Matilda. Seeing her as a parallel to the Virgin Mary and Child, he took it to be a sign from God. Only a short distance away, on the site of a ruined church destroyed by the Danes, he decided to construct a new community, designed to house thirteen men, three pensioners, a master and nine poor brethren to help the needy.

Many assume the word 'Hospital' derives from Hospitality, but it may have taken the name from the order of the Knights Hospitallers who administered here from 1136–85. The earlier name for St Cross was *Seynt Croys*, perhaps a mistranslation of Holy Cross for there is no record of an actual saint by that name. However, the history of the Hospital may also invoke a Knights Templar connection, through the housing of 'nine poor brethren'. The Hospitallers were a brother order of the mystical Knights, also founded by nine poor brethren, and both shared the emblem of the Holy Cross. Henry of Blois had close associations with this order, for his father was a Knights Templar and his uncle Hugh de Payens was one of their founders.

St Cross is surrounded by the most stunning landscape, set in the water meadows of the River Itchen at the foot of St Catherine's Hill. My first impression as we entered the Hospital grounds through the courtyard was a sense of timelessness. Passing through the old courtyard and medieval gate, we glimpsed the magnificent church, with its typically Norman squat tower. Built *c.* 1135, it has the privilege of being one of the finest examples of Transitional Norman churches in the country.

In the courtyard, I noticed a stone carving of an owl set into the wall on top of what appeared to be a 'tree of life' or axis mundi. In Welsh mythology, the owl is a totem of Gwyn, the warrior protector god of Britain. Interestingly, the monument stands with its back to St Catherine's Hill as if the stonemason responsible for this carving was hinting at the energetic connection between these two sites.

Elen approaches the church through its southwest corner, flowing down the length of the building, beneath the tower and out through its northwest corner where we find a magnificent bronze of St George slaying the dragon. Carved into a pillar in the north aisle is what appears to be a Templar-style cross. Its deliberate positioning allows it to receive light on only two days of the year, 3 May and 14 September, from a particular window on the eastern side of the north transept set at an unusual angle. According to the church calendar, 3 May represents the 'Invention of the Cross', and 14 September, Holy Cross Day. Both days commemorate a visit made by Helen, the mother of the Christian Roman Emperor Constantine, to the Holy Land from AD 326–28 for the sole purpose of locating the places and relics of Christ. On 3 May, Helena found the sacred wood of the Holy Cross and having discovered what she believed to be the site of the Crucifixion and Christ's burial place on the hill of Golgotha in Jerusalem, she built the Church of the Holy Sepulchre there, dedicating it on 14 September AD 335. This day became a time to honour the Cross as a symbol of triumph, of Christ's victory over death.

As I looked around this splendid building, every style of Norman architecture is on display, including the rich chevron carvings on the arches, doorways, windows and the ribbed vaulting. Glorious stained-glass windows from the 15th century depict St Catherine, St Swithun, St John and the Madonna. I later discovered that the church possesses its own Holy Grail, a solid gold chalice decorated with a diamond-encrusted cross.

The east window appears orientated towards St Catherine's Hill and, after checking with Google Earth, I discovered that the church is indeed set along a direct axis towards the Node point on the summit of the hill. Henry probably understood the energetic significance of the hill and orientated his church to align with its power point and draw from its energy.

As I dowsed the current flowing across the Hospital's enchanting gardens towards St Catherine's Hill, I gazed across at the idyllic water meadows and remembered that this very scene inspired the great English poets Keats and Trollope. The medieval atmosphere of the Hospital and refectory hall still echoes with the memories of over a thousand years of pilgrims eating, drinking and sharing tales of their travels to Canterbury. Perhaps they witnessed Crusader Knights resting here before setting sail from Southampton on their long journey to the Holy Land. Many of them may have ascended St Catherine's Hill at first light to walk the labyrinth and worship at the chapel in preparation for their journey. Although St Catherine's Hill was calling for us to further investigate its hidden mysteries, we first had to retrace our steps to explore the path of the male current as he makes his way north from Titchfield Abbey.

Wickham and Shedfield

The male current follows the Meon Valley northeast of Titchfield towards the town of Wickham, where on the outskirts of the town he enters the parish church of St Nicholas next to the River Meon. Wickham has seen a thriving market here since medieval times and was a major centre of trade since the time of the Meonwara, due to its situation by the crossroads of two Roman highways. The church stands upon a raised knoll, said to be a Saxon place of burial but more likely a prehistoric mound revered long before, as Bronze Age artefacts have been unearthed in the vicinity. The Normans built a church here in 1120 over the site of an earlier one founded by St Wilfred before AD 670, when

Wessex King Wulfere controlled the region.

Luckily, the Victorian architects who rebuilt much of the church left us with a splendid Norman doorway with its fine chevron carving and a figure of a centaur with his outstretched bow, representing the astrological sign of Sagittarius.

Wickham is also famous as the birthplace of another Bishop of Winchester called William of Wykeham (1324–1404), and a display in the church commemorates his life. Interestingly, we encountered this historical character at many places as we journeyed through Hampshire along the Belinus Line. He was a man from humble beginnings who some believe was given patronage by the local Lord of the Manor, Nicholas Uvedale, whose family tomb lies on the

Figure of a centaur carved on the Norman doorway of St Nicholas' Church, Wickham

male current in the church. This enabled Wykeham to be educated at the nearby Priory School of St Swithun before taking employment as a stonecutter, to which his great skills earned him the attention of Edward III who recruited him as Clerk of the Works. Three years later, he had risen to Chief Warden and Surveyor of the royal castles. His well-mannered countenance and skill continued to earn him favours with the King who consulted him on nearly all civil as well as military matters.

In 1367, at the age of 43, he became Bishop of Winchester, a position elevating him, like Henry of Blois before him, to one of the most powerful and wealthiest men in England. However, this meteoric rise presented him with his fair share of critics, including the king's son John of Gaunt, who accused him of embezzlement and 'simony' (the buying and selling of ecclesiastical privileges). This led to Wykeham's impeachment and removal from his position as Lord High Chancellor, although later restored to him by King Richard II.

Further north is the handsome Victorian church of St John the Baptist at Shedfield, built on land given to the parish by the Bishop of Winchester. Superbly decorated with variously coloured bricks, it replaced a smaller chapel of ease built in 1828 that still exists as a ruin in the graveyard beyond, standing for only 40 years due to poor workmanship. Today the ruined tower is a home for bats and owls. The Victorian stonemasons clearly continued the old medieval styles of carving as they adorned

Dragon carving at St John the Baptist Church, Shedfield

the new church tower with numerous winged dragons and Celtic-style heads. Halfway down the tower is a huge carving of a dragon menacingly crawling headfirst towards the ground as if preparing to pounce.

I wondered whether both architects who designed the 19th century churches were aware of the male serpent flowing through here. As we continued north towards Bishop's Waltham I picked up the current by a pub called the Black Dog, a spectral creature often associated with ley lines.

Bishop's Waltham and Owlesbury

Belinus enters the delightful historic town of Bishop's Waltham, visiting the ruins of a palace belonging to the Bishops of Winchester. In 1134, Henry of Blois designed a stone castle close to lakes in a thousand acre parkland that eventually became the residence of some of the wealthiest and most powerful noblemen in Britain.

It was here that Henry II (1154–89) called upon Henry of Blois for supplies for the Crusade, and Richard the Lionheart, son of Henry II, used the castle to entertain his guests after he was proclaimed King of England. Margaret of Anjou, wife of Henry VI, slept here in a bed of 'blue and gold'. Other notable guests were Emperor Charles V of the Holy Roman Empire and King Henry VIII, who met here in 1522 after both declaring war on France. The following century saw Bishop William of Wykeham overseeing a major rebuilding scheme, and a wall, which formed part of his new Great Hall, still survives complete with five large windows and embattled transoms. Bishop Langton carried out the final alterations in the late 15th century, creating a grand stately home.

Ruins of the Bishop's Palace, Bishop's Waltham

The ruins of the palace, now maintained by English Heritage, are secluded within a tranquil setting of well-kept lawns and huge beech trees surrounded by a medieval moat. We detected the male current entering from the south through the remains of the Great Hall and followed him to the ruined chapel with its sunken crypt. Here he crosses with another unknown male energy that enters through the West Tower.

As we sat on the grass looking down at this former sanctuary built by Henry, we thought about his ambition to become the most powerful man in England. Did he control the serpents like a Chinese geomancer to allow him greater influence and power over others, or was it pure intuition that guided him? I wonder if he used divinatory instruments to locate these places of power, which he enhanced through the building of his great Norman stone edifices.

We continued to follow the current into the town across the roundabout through a pub called the Barley Corn Inn, where they once sold Green King beer, and a Methodist chapel in Basingwell Road. We then dowsed him crossing Bank Close near Dodds Alley to St Peter's Church at the highest point of the town. According to Alfred Watkins, the name *dodd* is often associated with ley lines and derives from the name of an ancient surveyor who, in time-honoured fashion, sighted straight lines with the aid of two wooden staves called a Dod-man. The church guide informed us that a Saxon minster stood in the vicinity dating from AD 700. Moreover, St Boniface (St Wynfrith), whom we encountered on the Isle of Wight, travelled here in 715 to receive a blessing before he journeyed overseas. An unusual granite font, now in the church, is the only remnant of this time, found in a garden in Basingwell Road in 1933 built into a rockery. A place of worship on the site of St Peter's is recorded as far back as 1001, but the Danes burnt down this wooden edifice. Henry of Blois built the first stone church here in 1136 during his time as Bishop of Winchester. As well as the Saxon font, the church retains other early features such as the porch built by William of Wykeham and a tall rounded 16th century turret on the tower. One of the stained-glass windows depicts St George standing on the dragon as if pinning him to the ground rather than spearing him.

The trail continues to St Andrew's Church at Owslebury by an old Roman road. The village is the second highest in the county and its name derives from a fortification or stronghold frequented by the 'Ousel', an Old English word derived from Saxon for the blackbird. King Edgar granted the land of 'Oselbyng' to the Bishops of Winchester in AD 964 and it remained in their possession until 1551, when Sir Henry Seymour of nearby Marwell Hall acquired it. Belinus passes through a stained-glass window showing the figures of a knight, a bishop (possibly Henry of Blois) and St Michael.

Henry's College of Prayer and Morestead

The route of the alignment is of interest here, as it passes through Marwell Manor Farm just to the west of old Marwell Hall, now a Zoological Park. The farm stands over the site of a medieval ecclesiastical college built by Henry of Blois to house four secular priests. Their sole purpose was to pray continually for the King of England, the Bishops of Winchester and other important benefactors of the state. The college contained a church or chapel dedicated to four Saints, Stephen, Lawrence, Vincent and Quintin, with houses and other buildings nearby serving the priests. As we walked along a footpath at the side of the farm, we peered through trees at the deep entrenchment of a moat. The great earthwork now surrounds a farm but once protected a unique building that Henry may have deliberately built on the alignment near the base of Britain to manipulate the energy of the Spine of Albion. He may have directed this power through perpetual prayer to exert his authority over key places or people, including the King himself.

Sir Henry Seymour (1503–78) was an English politician who first acquired the manor of Marwell after the Reformation when the college was in ruins, and soon arranged for the building of a new grander residence nearby. According to legend, the new hall witnessed the private wedding ceremony of Henry VIII and Lady Jane Seymour, Henry Seymour's daughter. Their future son Edward VI also visited Marwell Hall and carved his initials E.R. over the stone porch. Jane Seymour reputedly haunts the corridors and Anne Boleyn, Henry VIII's previous wife, walks the Yew Walk in the grounds planning her revenge on Jane. The hall also has the legend of the Mistletoe Bride attached to it, which is found at several other country houses throughout England, such as Minster Lovell near Witney in Oxfordshire.

From Owslebury, we follow Belinus north along a very narrow sunken lane lined with yew trees, one of the many delightful old British roads so often mistaken for

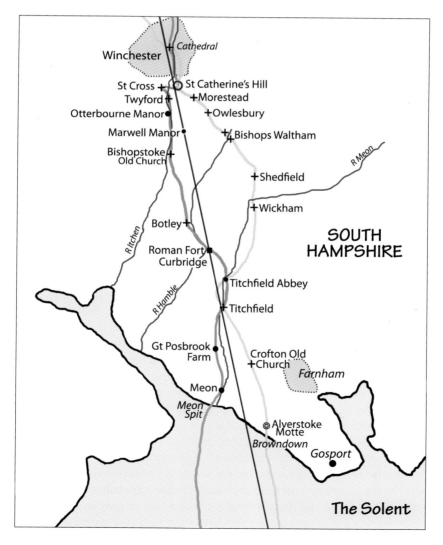

those built by the Romans, though judging by the height of the banks it may date as far back as the Iron Age. Almost hidden by hedgerows along a sweeping bend in the road we encounter the little church at Morestead. After parking the car in a lay-by, we risked life and limb walking along the narrow busy lane to reach the gate to the church situated close to a blind bend. However, as we entered the churchyard it felt as if we had stepped into another world. Set in a delightful garden, this plain but modest little Norman church, with no known dedication, was part of the estate of the Bishops of Winchester and is reputed to be Saxon in origin.

Belinus crosses the Pilgrims' Trail and the M3 motorway, which has created a great scar in this ancient landscape separating St Catherine's Hill from the Downs. Even though the currents seem relatively unaffected by this monstrous defacing, this massive severing of the Belinus and Elen currents must have left them at the time weakened and distorted. However, I know that there are geomancers and healers out there who actively work with their local energy matrix affected by such scars in the land.

St Catherine's Hill

One of my first discoveries on the Belinus Line was the Node of the male and female serpents on St Catherine's Hill and, like Titchfield, these findings were made all the more significant by the presence of the alignment. However, unlike Titchfield, this particular site is a renowned sacred sanctuary, having fascinated historians, archaeologists and Earth Mysteries researchers for decades. Ley hunters and dowsers have discovered that major lines and energy currents intersect on the hill, some recorded by well-known authors such as Paul Devereux. The hill has also drawn many psychics over the years, some referring to it as the hub of a wheel or the centre of a spider's web of energy that radiates straight lines of telluric energy to other major sacred sites across the country.

Interesting comparisons can be made between St Catherine's Hill and St Michael's Mount in Cornwall. Both are major hubs of intersecting serpent energies, both have folklore of a giant throwing stones, and both are a similar distance from the beginning of their alignments in the south. The giant on St Catherine's Hill hurled a large megalith from here that fell on the downs above Mottistone to become the Longstone. This story is probably an allegory of an energetic link between the hill and the powerful Firestone ridge.

E.O. Gordon refers to St Catherine's Hill as a Gorsedd, a place of civil and religious administration under the Druids. During the reign of King Canute (1017–35), the hill was known as the 'Great Seat of the Winton'. Winton, believed to be the early name of Winchester, derives from the old Welsh and Cornish name *wyn* or *whit*, meaning 'holy'; *ton* means 'mound' or 'hill'. Canute presented the hill as a gift to the Benedictine monks of St Swithun's Priory in Winchester.

However, in *The Quest for the Omphalos*, Bob Trubshaw suggests that most cultures marked a 'holy hill' as their omphalos, and St Catherine's Hill marked by the Spine of Albion is one such hill. The unusual dedication to St Catherine rather than St Michael may be due to the symbolism of her wheel and spindle representing the axis mundi.

The information board by the parking area informed us that Iron Age roads called 'Dongas' criss-cross the downs around St Catherine's Hill and are thought to date from the time of the construction of the hillfort around 500 BC. Earlier we had driven along some of these hollow-ways between Morestead and Owslebury, one following the alignment for a short distance.

A well-trodden footpath worn by pilgrims past and present leads to the summit of St Catherine's Hill, passing to the left of two large trees that form a symbolic gateway to the hill. As you arrive at a large ditch and bank earthwork containing ancient beech trees, the path takes you in a sun-wise direction for a short distance before entering the levelled summit of the hill. At its centre is a circular copse that conceals a raised area or mound on which apparently stood a 12th century chapel, its dedication having given the hill its name.

Positioned just outside this inner sanctum to the northwest is a turf-cut miz-maze or labyrinth. Its date of origin is uncertain, due to centuries of re-cutting and restoration work. Between the labyrinth and the inner sanctum within the copse are yet more earthworks that are only discernible in winter when the vegetation is low. This raised rectangular bank is orientated east–west and has a neighbouring earthwork to the west. It is more likely that this is the site of the early chapel than the proposed site within the copse. The round earthwork to the west may have been the footings of a separate Saxon tower.

As I stood gazing at the twisting curves of the labyrinth at the entrance, I remembered a vivid dream I had had two weeks before. While floating above a labyrinth cut into the grass on a hill very like this one, a soft voice whispered 'this is a place of initiation where you can receive knowledge'. With the dream in mind, I started to walk the labyrinth, slowly treading the extremely narrow and worn path continuously towards its centre. As you walk through this ancient potent figure carved into the turf, a shift in consciousness occurs; the meandering path as it twists back and forth allows you to perform 180-degree turns as you enter each quadrant, which seems to have the effect of shifting your awareness from the right brain to the left.

Drawing of St Catherine's Hill labyrinth

When I reached the centre, I began to meditate and soon experienced a strong surge of energy rippling through my body, making me feel extremely light-headed. In some subtle way the 'spirit of place' seemed to permeate my consciousness, for after leaving the labyrinth I felt that the experience had somehow sharpened my dowsing skills in preparation for locating the hidden paths of the serpents.

When I first dowsed the currents here in 1994, I found that they merged together for a few metres as if becoming one androgynous flow, then separated without actually crossing over each other. This behaviour seemed curious, but I was reminded in *The Sun and the Serpent* that Miller and Broadhurst found a similar occurrence on the St Michael Line at the ruined abbey at Bury St Edmunds, which they explained as a sacred marriage between the Mary and Michael serpents. Both Caroline and I dowsed this phenomenon several times at St Catherine's Hill, and after leaving their meeting place on the mound they each flow though the labyrinth, Elen to the left and Belinus to the right. However, we always felt uneasy with our findings, and we had a nagging feeling that they were out of place. Back in the 1990s, a friend of mine informed me that St Catherine's Hill was being used as a centre for dark occult practices and he personally found evidence of it on the hill.

Andrew Collins confirmed this in his book *The Second Coming*, which details information received from psychics that St Catherine's Hill was the centre of occult activity used by shadowy groups working in the south of England. They acted out a corrupt form of Greco Roman ritual magic using the negative aspect of St Catherine, her spiked wheel symbolically representing a dark or negative web of energy lines, in order to subdue the network of British ley lines.

One of the greatest writers of all time on the occult was Dion Fortune (1890-1946). During her lifetime she explored many of Britain's sacred sites and understood the power of these places and that man could manipulate them. In *Aspects of Occultism* published in 1962 she wrote:

> 'Whenever a place has had prayers and concentrated desires directed towards it, it forms an electrical vortex that gathers to itself a force, and it is for a time a coherent body that can be felt and used by man. It is round these bodies of force that shrines, temples, and in later days churches are built; they are the Cups that receive the Cosmic downporings focused on each particular place.'

After completing the investigation of the currents and the Nodes along the Spine of Albion in 2011, we came to realise that the unusual behaviour of the currents on St Catherine's Hill might be the result of the negative ceremonies performed here during the past two decades. After carrying out a number of healing ceremonies on the hill accompanied by other healers and psychics, we discovered that the currents had changed course to form not one but two Nodes, one on the mound and one at the centre of the labyrinth, possibly their original pattern.

The male current approaches the inner sanctum from the south over the charred remains of a bonfire. He continues towards the central mound and now shrinks to form a Node with Elen, crossing the western end of the rectangular earthwork, possibly the site of the chapel. He then enters the west side of the labyrinth, shrinking again to form another Node with Elen at its centre.

The female current, having ascended the hill from Hospital of St Cross, enters the inner sanctum from the west to the Node, then turns sharply to the northeast, passing

Node point within the inner sanctum of St Catherine's Hill, Winchester

over the eastern end of the chapel site and into the east side of the labyrinth, crossing again with Belinus at its centre. She had clearly benefited from our healing, as her current was now much wider and stronger than before. From the newly discovered Node in the labyrinth, she curves across the plateau of the hill before descending to the city of Winchester. Belinus meanwhile leaves the hill to the northwest, also heading for the city.

Labyrinth marking the second Node at St Catherine's Hill, Winchester

A plan of the new arrangement of the currents shows that they now form a *Vesica Pisces* between the two Nodes. Its name derives from Latin meaning 'bladder of the fish', because its shape literally resembles a fish bladder when inflated. However, its origins are shrouded in mystery; many believe that Pythagoras of Ancient Greece first discovered the sacred properties of this figure in his study of sacred geometry, making it an important part of his teachings. In esoteric lore the shape, formed by two overlapping circles, was symbolic of the merging of the two different polarities, male and female or spirit and matter. John Michell describes the Vesica Pisces as representing a state of perfect equilibrium between two equal forces. Henry of Blois may have built the chapel deliberately between these two Nodes to receive and possibly manipulate their power.

After restoring balance to this ancient sanctuary, just one thing remained that still puzzled us. We noticed that Hospital of St Cross diverts the flow of Elen from a relatively straight course between the church at Twyford and St Catherine's Hill. Did Henry of Blois deliberately lure the female serpent off course to enter his church? It is also possible that Henry cut the first labyrinth on the hill, for its design is almost identical to one inside Chartres Cathedral in France, purportedly built by the Knights Templar. This mystical order incorporated labyrinths into many of

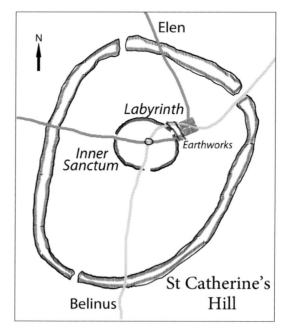

their buildings across Europe in the form of stone carvings, paintings and floor tiles. They also adopted St Catherine as patron of their order. Henry of Blois held the title Count of Chartres and had strong ties with the order through his father and uncle, Hugh de Payens.

My labyrinth experience also included the strong impression that it was long ago a place of initiation for the preparation of a spiritual ritual on this hill. It begins with walking the labyrinth to achieve balance and to connect with the Node of serpents at its centre, before proceeding to the chapel to honour the goddess personified as St Catherine. The climax of the ritual culminates on the mound inside the inner sanctum of trees to embody the power of the serpents once more through meditation. My feeling was that Bishop Henry had an immense understanding of the nature of these dragons through the art of geomancy.

Henry of Blois, the Old Wizard of Winchester

Henry of Blois holding a jewelled ring

Henry of Blois was born *c.* 1101 at Blois Castle overlooking the River Loire. He was the son of Count Stephen of Blois, a Knights Templar, and came from a great dynasty that owned most of northern France. His mother Adela, daughter of William the Conqueror, favoured the most beautiful Benedictine monastery of Cluny in Burgundy to educate her son. Patronised by several of Henry's wealthy relatives, it was the largest and most influential religious establishment in Europe and the crossing place of two powerful Earth currents called Apollo and Athena.

Soon after Miller and Broadhurst had dowsed and researched the St Michael Line, they found themselves walking through the town of Blois following an even longer line of power. The Apollo/St Michael Axis, first referred to by Lucien Richter, connects many St Michael and Apollo sanctuaries along a southeast axis from Ireland across Europe to Israel. Miller and Broadhurst dowsed male and female serpents along the whole length of this alignment similar to Michael and Mary, but named these Apollo and Athena and recorded their findings in *The Dance of the Dragon*.

The male current or Apollo passes straight through the town of Blois where Henry was born and through the site of his christening, the Benedictine abbey of St Laumer. At Cluny, both currents Node at an unmarked spot on the lawns that later proved to be the site of the old church. Cluny was the great European centre of the Benedictine movement, an order far more Gnostic in their teachings than the later Cistercians. At Cluny Henry was initiated into the Mystery School teachings, which included astronomy, astrology, alchemy and metallurgy, architecture and engineering, herbal medicine, as well as Gnostic, Arabic, Greek and early Christian doctrines. We have experienced a great number of Benedictine houses on dragon lines, which implies that they must have been aware of this potent force. Perhaps Cluny schooled Henry to become not only one of the most powerful Bishops in Europe but also a master geomancer of the dragon force.

At the age of 29, Henry achieved through royal patronage the prestigious appointment of Abbot of Glastonbury, one of the holiest places in Britain at that time. He soon changed the fortunes of this ancient but poorly neglected and badly managed abbey with its 30,000 acres of land. Henry's single-minded tenacity was to enlarge and enrich Glastonbury Abbey for centuries to come by overseeing a massive rebuilding programme. He used his substantial inheritance to introduce many fine furnishings, objects and relics, including a precious sapphire altar found by Henry in one of the porches of the Lady Chapel at the west end of the abbey.

Hank Harrison provides us with a wealth of knowledge regarding the personal life of Henry of Blois in *Crown of Stars: The Grail in the Troubadour World* (2009) and states that Henry was obsessed with collecting relics and jewels. How he acquired so many precious items is a mystery, perhaps it was due to his influence with the Pope and the Knights Templar. The only portrait of Henry depicts him holding a large jewelled gold ring while pointing to heaven. He also channelled large sums of money into grand building programmes including roads, ponds, wells and canals as well as his palaces, and churches, those at Bishop's Waltham, Marwell, Hyde Abbey, Wolvesey and the Church and Hospital of St Cross in Winchester.

Henry must have learned a great deal from the books in the ancient library at Glastonbury having had many of them copied including the *Book of Enoch*, the works of Bede and the Welsh *Mabinogion*, which was one of the first to mention the tales of King Arthur and the Knights of the Round Table. Henry also had access to the fine books in the vast library of Cluny Abbey, including those of an esoteric and Gnostic nature. Beyond scripture, he had a great aptitude as a draftsman and for architecture and it is almost certain that he learned the art of sacred geometry.

Henry knew his cousin Eleanor of Aquitaine well and met with her on many occasions. Both Eleanor and her husband King Henry II had a fascination with Arthurian legends and were probably involved with the dig at Glastonbury Abbey to find the bones of Arthur and Guinevere. The new tomb used to house the newly discovered bones was made from Purbeck marble, a stone first introduced to church architecture by Bishop Henry. He also supplied Purbeck marble for the building of the Temple Church in London, the main seat of the Knights Templar in England.

Henry of Blois' fascination with King Arthur and the Grail mysteries inspired him to carry out his own personal quest for the Holy Grail. He knew such contemporaries as Geoffrey of Monmouth and William of Malmesbury and became the patron of Chretien de Troyes, author of *Percival*. This was one of the first books to mention Arthur's search for the Holy Grail and strongly linked with Geoffrey of Monmouth whose *History of the Kings of Britain* also contained this story.

Harrison believes Henry of Blois may have been the original author of *Perlesvaus*, later known as *The High History of the Holy Grail*, a Grail quest in a landscape filled with megalithic temples, fairy mounds and sacred rituals. Through allegory, Henry could express his knowledge of ancient occult and esoteric practices anonymously. A plaque in the British Museum depicts Henry offering a gift to God along with angels, one of which is holding a bowl or chalice. It has the inscription: 'the donor might follow the offering to heaven; but not immediately, lest England weep, for war and peace, turmoil or tranquillity, depend on him'.

The Cistercian Abbot Bernard of Clairvaux (1090–1153), the instigator of the failed Second Crusade, called Henry the 'Old Wizard of Winchester'. Bernard preached against intellectualism, art, music, decorated architecture and even leisure activities, in fact everything that Henry, his troubadour family and the Benedictine monks of Cluny and Glastonbury stood for. The troubadours sprung from Bardism and like the Druids came from royal families to join the monastic orders. The Benedictines were free thinkers following a form of worship that was more akin to the early Celtic church and used memory techniques and other elements of Druidism within their Christian practice and passed them on to the troubadours. Bernard of Clairvaux regarded this form of worship as too liberal and far too supportive of occult and esoteric practices (Harrison 2009).

During King Stephen's reign, his brother Henry of Blois became his chief advisor and showed that he also had a keen tactical mind during times of war. After Stephen's death in 1154, Matilda's son Henry of Anjou invaded England and took the throne as Henry II. By then Bishop Henry was hugely wealthy and had control over most of southern England, possessing six castles including Winchester and Southampton. After befriending and supporting Thomas à Becket, the Archbishop of Canterbury, during his trial, Henry's relationship with the new King Henry II broke down. As a result, the King destroyed or confiscated many of the Bishop's castles and palaces in Winchester. At the end of his life, Henry was infirm and blind and when the King thought it necessary to pay him a visit, he rebuked him 'predicting that the King would suffer much adversity for his persecution of Becket' (Harrison 2009).

Two days later on 8 August 1171, Henry of Blois died at Wolvesey Palace in Winchester and with him the power of the Benedictine order. He was enshrined at Glastonbury Abbey until the fire of 1184, when his remains transferred to the church of St Mary at Ivinghoe. They are now residing in a tomb in front of the High Altar of Winchester Cathedral.

Ivinghoe was close to Henry's heart, and he established a convent there in 1135, known variously as the Priory of St Margaret's in the Wood. He often visited the area, living in nearby Berrystead or Becrysted House. Ivinghoe is situated at the most eastern end of the sacred prehistoric ridgeway that runs from the south coast of Devon to the Norfolk coast. Nearby, the Mary current of the St Michael Line passes through the church and the Beacon at Ivinghoe.

Henry is certainly a fascinating and intriguing character, his ancestral connections and esoteric upbringing gave him the opportunity to be a master of occult knowledge, influenced by the Gnostics.

The Cygnus Connection

Before we leave St Catherine's Hill there is one more discovery to disclose, something highly relevant to the whole quest. Whilst monitoring the currents on a recent winter visit to St Catherine's Hill, I observed that from the central mound looking NNW through the trees you can plainly see two distinct hills on the northern horizon; landscape features that can only be seen on a clear day. I also noticed that Winchester

College, the Cathedral and St Bartholomew's Church north of the city align to this cusp or cup between these two hills. I later realised from looking at the map that these distant hills are Beacon Hill and Sidown Hill, 29 km (18 miles) north on the edge of Highclere estate.

As mentioned in the introductory chapter, the Belinus alignment targets the setting of Deneb, the brightest star in the constellation of Cygnus, also known as the Northern Cross before it became circumpolar around the time of Christ's birth. Having checked with the Skyglobe program, I discovered that around 500 BC the British tribe who built the ramparts and inner enclosure on St Catherine's Hill, would have seen these two hills on the horizon as significant. Standing on the central mound observers would see Deneb drop towards the northern horizon like a diving swan and disappear into the side of Sidown Hill, only to reappear again in the gap between both hills, disappear once more behind Beacon Hill and later reappear. It then occurred to me that this event must only take place when both the hills and the stars are visible. Checking once more with Skyglobe, I discovered that during the same century BC, around the March equinox, Deneb set at dusk and at the September equinox at dawn. However, at the winter solstice, the lighting of a beacon on both Beacon Hill and Sidown Hill would provide a spectacular backdrop for the setting of Deneb (see p 504).

At the time that Henry of Blois arrived in Winchester, Deneb had become circumpolar, in other words, it no longer set into the horizon but merely skimmed a few degrees above at the point of true north.

As mentioned earlier, the policy of the early Roman Catholic missionaries was to convert the pagan communities and rededicate their old shrines to Christian saints, choosing one that most resembles the pagan deity of a particular temple. St Catherine chapels, particularly those along the southern coast of England, may have once been dedicated to Aphrodite or Astarte as in mythology they are both linked with the sea and more importantly with swans. For instance, St Catherine's Chapel in Abbotsbury, Dorset, stands above an ancient swannery belonging to the sovereign of England. Swans also frequent the River Itchen at the base of St Catherine's Hill in Winchester.

Was the hillfort and chapel dedicated to St Catherine because of its association with Cygnus or was it simply because the circular rampart resembles a wheel, a symbol of this saint? We could also assume that the Knights Templar adopted St Catherine as their patron saint because her spiked wheel symbolically represents a 'sun wheel', a round table for solar or cosmic worship observing the rising and settings of the sun, moon and major constellations, a role for which the hill is perfectly suited.

The legend of the 'Wyntun Dragon' is also associated with this Iron Age hill. The dragon is a landscape figure that stretches 27 km (17 miles) from Old Winchester Hill to St Catherine's Hill. St Catherine's Hill represents the dragon's head and snout and its tail coils around Old Winchester Hill. It seems appropriate that we have two Node points of the great earth serpents of Belinus and Elen at the head of a landscape dragon overlooking the ancient capital of a lost kingdom.

Chapter 3

Winchester, the Ancient Capital of England

'The birthplace of our existence as a nation'[1]

Geographically, Winchester lies in a favourable location, situated on the east slope of a hill that falls gently down to the River Itchen. The surrounding chalk downs, free of dense forests since Neolithic times, has allowed an extensive road network to connect the city with important towns and ports all over the south of England. In the early days, the nearest port on the River Itchen for the transport of goods to and from Winchester would have been either at Bitterne Manor or at a point close to St Mary's Church at South Stoneham in the suburbs of Southampton, 14.5 km (9 miles) away. Such a distance from the sea was deliberate, for this gave the military forces in the city time to muster their troops to meet invaders from the coast.

1 George William Kitchin, Dean of Winchester (1827–1912)

The unique situation of the city is an indication of its illustrious history and mythological origins that stretch back into the mists of time, glimpsed only through faint fragments of folklore and legend. The modern view presented by historians is that the Romans were responsible for the establishment of all British towns and civilisation, as we know it, although many alternative historians present a very different interpretation of our ancient past. Ignored are the local oral traditions and the old Welsh records, some of which are so ancient they are now veiled as myth.

Within the British Isles, certain cities and towns, such as Winchester, Oxford, Stratford-upon-Avon and Glastonbury, share a mythical heritage, which define them as sacred centres of old Albion. *The British Chronicles*, copied from old Welsh documents into Latin by the 9th century Welsh monk Nennius, refer to Winchester as a city established 3000 years ago. Nennius states that the original builder of Winchester or *Kaerguenit*, as it was anciently known, was King Rud Hud or Lud Hudibras, son of King Leil. *Kaerguenit* or *Kaer Gwent* means a 'white' or 'holy' fortified enclosure. According to Geoffrey of Monmouth, Hudibras reigned for 39 years from 968–929 BC, restoring peace to the country after the hapless rule of his father Leil.

Local traditions say that King Dunvallo Molmutius the Law Giver (434–394 BC) later rebuilt and enlarged Winchester. E.O. Gordon (1932) refers to Winchester as Winton and 'the supreme seat of civil government in Britain under Molmutius, a king recognised as sovereign paramount by the voice of the British people'. During his 39-year reign, he created the 'Molmutine Laws', a code of laws which King Alfred the

Winchester Cathedral

Great translated and according to Geoffrey of Monmouth were still adhered to in the 12th century.

Probert's *Ancient Laws of Cambria*, translated in 1823, contains the *Institutional Triads of Dunvallo Molmutius*, the laws of ancient Britain. Bill Cooper in *After the Flood* comments on these laws:

> 'During Dunvallo's reign, crimes of violence were virtually unheard of in his kingdom; such was the severity of punishment meted out to such criminals while he was on the throne. The laws reveal a level of culture and literacy amongst the early Britons that is quite unlike the popular image that has been cultivated in recent years by the modernist treatment of British history. It also speaks volumes for the existence of a king whom modernists have always said was a mythical figure, and it reveals our ancestors to have been a highly cultivated and civilised people, and not the illiterate painted savages of popular fame.'

Shakespeare also knew of the laws of Molmutius, for in his play *Cymbeline*, the main character, speaks these words:

> 'Say then to Caesar,
> Our ancestor was that Molmutius which
> Ordained our laws, whose use the sword of Caesar
> Hath too much mangled; whose repair and franchise
> Shall by the power we hold, be our good deed.
> Though Rome be therefore angry; Molmutius made our laws,
> Who was the first of Britain which did put
> His brows within a golden crown and called Himself a king.'
> (Act III, Scene I)

In the chronological records of Wales, Molmutius was 'One of the Three Wise Kings of Britain' and the first to establish municipal government. In fact he was, as Shakespeare reminds us, the first true king to wear a crown, for his predecessors were only 'Chiefs and Rulers'.

John Michell wrote: 'several prehistoric tracks and roads either made or repaved by the Romans point towards Winchester, and the fact that they go to different centres in the city indicates that it was a large place in very early times'. Gordon also states 'As a road maker we have his [Molmutius's] work in the seven converging roads like the spokes of a wheel in the old White City'. This great network of roads may in fact have radiated out from Winchester rather than towards Winchester, possibly completed by his son King Belinus, also a renowned road builder. Today, Molmutius stands immortalised as part of a series of statues on the façade of Winchester Town Hall. His burial place is traditionally the White Mound

Statue of King Molmutius, Winchester Town Hall

on which William the Conqueror built the Tower of London.

By 150 BC, Winchester had become a great trading centre established within the confines of the Iron Age settlement around Oram's Arbour, the high ground above the castle. When the Romans arrived in AD 70, they recognised the importance of the area and refortified the already existing town, making Winchester their *civitas* or regional capital. Close to where the cathedral stands today were two temples, built for the solar and lunar worship of their Roman gods. They also laid out the city using a grid system of streets lined with shops and public buildings with a *forum* or market place at its centre, constructing public baths and fine houses with glass windows and mosaic floors. They renamed the British settlement *Venta Belgarum*, meaning 'capital of the Belgares', an ancient Celtic tribe who occupied the area during the time of the Roman invasion.

The Belgares or Belgae tribe were a sea-faring race that controlled many ports and trading places along the various coasts of northern Europe. The name Belgares may suggest they were followers of Bel, similar to the Phoenicians who worshipped the sun god Bel or Baal. Along the south coast of England, including the Isle of Wight, there are many legends that refer to Phoenician traders settling around ports and estuaries close to tin mines and trading places.

Wykeham's College of St Mary

At the foot of St Catherine's Hill we followed the path of Elen across the water meadows by the River Itchen to Winchester College. Public access to the college is limited to guided tours and luckily as we arrived there was one about to commence from the main entrance. Our guide informed us that the college is the oldest school in the country founded in 1382 and has been in continuous use ever since. As mentioned previously, William of Wykeham was born in the Hampshire town of Wickham and died at Bishop's Waltham Palace, both places visited by the male current south of here. Researching Wykeham's life was fascinating, but unlike Henry of Blois his meteoric rise was not due to his noble birth but through his genius as a stonemason and politician.

Although William's parents were poor, their family lineage was creditable in the eyes of his patron Nicholas Uvedale, Lord of the Manor of Wykeham (Wickham) and at the time Governor of Winchester Castle. Uvedale's influence helped steer the young man to find his vocation as an architect and surveyor, at which, like Henry of Blois, he excelled. His skills were soon noticed by King Edward III, who instructed William to enclose the ancient Druid Gorsedd at Windsor with a round stone-built tower. This became the base for the British Order of the Round Table assemblies and also accommodated the annual meetings of the Knights of the Order of St George and the Garter.

It is thought that Wykeham also influenced Edward III to revive the Arthurian rites in an effort to unite the British against foreign influence and papal control. William later became one of the richest and most powerful men in the country, having been ordained Bishop of Winchester in 1366 and Lord Chancellor of England in 1367. Froissart records from this period that, 'Wykeham was so much in favour with the King of England, that everything was done by him, and nothing was done without him'.

Due to the disastrous plague known as the Black Death that swept through most of southern England in the 14th century, William realised that there was a grave shortage of learned priests. To remedy this he developed a scheme that would oversee a student's education right to the very end of his schooling and built Winchester College for this very purpose. He later founded New College, Oxford, for those who wished to continue their scholarly career.

As we followed the guide through the main gate, I noticed an ancient stone statue above the entrance dedicated to the Blessed Virgin Mary of Winchester, also known as St Mary de Winton. It dates from the time of the college's foundation; its dedication chosen by William having been inspired in the cathedral during masses said to the Blessed Virgin Mary.

We continued to the outer courtyard, the service area of the college, and through the Middle Gate to the Chamber Court. Here we gazed at the impressive Gothic chapel and the Great Hall, both faced with white limestone. I discreetly dowsed Elen flowing through a gap known as the Crimea Passage, between the chapel and the hall, and passing beneath the tower of the chapel to the cloisters. Her width seeps into both the west end of the chapel and east end of Wykeham's old hall now called the Seventh Chamber. Inside the chapel, her flow includes an exquisite medieval window, formerly the old east window before its removal for restoration in 1820. The guide informed us that the dishonest restorers swapped and replaced the windows with replicas without the college realising; selling pieces of it to collectors around the world. Fortunately for the college, wealthy benefactors managed to track down most of the pieces, reconstructing the window in its present position. One interesting window shows William of Wykeham paying homage to the Virgin and Child. Gordon says that Bishop Wykeham's love of Celtic traditions shows in the design of this chapel, which is shaped like a *Tau* cross, a T-shaped cross that originated in Egypt, said to be the cross of Moses and used in the initiation of a Pharaoh.

From the Crimea Passage we entered the ancient cloisters, completed in 1400, which encompass a consecrated burial ground where many of Wykeham's students lie. This area now features a small but handsome Gothic chapel called Fromond's Chantry built in 1440 and now used for Holy Communion and christenings. Our guide marvelled at how the stonemasons were able to carry the huge stone blocks needed to build the chantry through the narrow openings of the old cloisters.

Our dowsing indicates that the chantry lies on the feminine current, her presence heralded by a magnificent carved dragon on the exterior of this jewel of a building. Inside she passes through the width of the High Altar where coffins of old scholars lay before burial. Two statues also fall upon her path: St George slaying a large dragon, and a curious female statue whose identity is a mystery. She has a lily in one hand and two fingers held aloft in the other; some say she is St Agnes, whilst others call her St Gabriel.

Standing just outside the chantry, we could clearly see St Catherine's Hill dominating the skyline and interestingly the female saint features in two of the windows. It seemed befitting that Wykeham built the chapel and chantry on the female current, two perfect places to contemplate and honour the dead.

As we walked around the cloistered courtyard, we became aware of a potent atmosphere, one so nourishing and serene that we almost unconsciously drifted into a meditative state. Nearby and marking the alignment is the eloquent Georgian schoolhouse, built in 1687 to replace the hall built by Wykeham next to the chapel, said at the time of its building to be the finest and largest in England. This may come as no surprise if you accept the oral tradition that its designer was the great architect Sir Christopher Wren. Although there is no written proof of this story, it certainly exudes his architectural style and it is widely known in these quarters that he visited Winchester at the time of its construction whilst working on the Bishop's Palace nearby.

Wykeham regularly walked up St Catherine's Hill from the college, having acquired the land as part of the college estates. According to Gordon, Wykeham ordained that from the college his students should walk up St Catherine's Hill twice a day and walk the labyrinth on its summit, chanting as they went. A poem by Lord Selborne mentioned by Gordon (1932) alludes to this unusual ritual:

'Four hundred years and fifty their rolling course had sped
Since the first serge-clad scholar to Wykeham's feet was led:
And still his seventy faithful boys, in these presumptuous days,
Learn the olde truths, speak the old words, tread in the ancient ways,
Still for their daily orisons resounds the matin chime:
Still linked in bands of brotherhood St Catherine's steep they climb.'

Engraving entitled The 'Win Ton', St Katherine's Hill. Going to Hilles'

Gordon also includes in *Prehistoric London* an engraving entitled *The 'Win Ton', St Katherine's Hill. Going to Hilles*. This depicts a line of scholars following a clear path to St Catherine's Hill from the college. Although this path has since disappeared, the female current may well follow the route taken by the young boys all those centuries before. According to the guide, students of Winchester College still continue this tradition once a year, although they are more likely to run and shout their way up rather than walk and chant!

More recently, we discovered that from St Catherine's Hill the sighting line to the point on the horizon where the star Deneb sets (which I shall now refer to as 'the Deneb

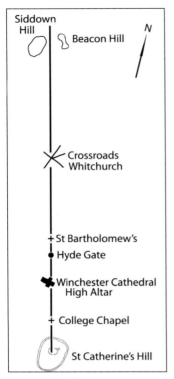

Siddown Hill
Beacon Hill
N

Crossroads
Whitchurch

+ St Bartholomew's
• Hyde Gate
Winchester Cathedral
High Altar

+ College Chapel

St Catherine's Hill

The Deneb Line

Line') includes the college chapel and the chantry. As mentioned before, this particular star was important to observe and mark with certain features and temples, for ancient cultures believed its setting point where it touched the Earth, represented the opening of a doorway or road for souls to journey to the afterlife. As the owner of St Catherine's Hill, Wykeham presumably visited the hill often with his scholars and perhaps noticed that the cathedral and St Bartholomew's Church aligns with the cusp between the two hills. Was it by pure coincidence that Wykeham built his chapel on this 'road of the dead' or was it a conscious act to capture the celestial power of the heavens?

Furthermore, did Wykeham dedicate the college to St Mary of Winton inspired by the Virgin Mary or the divine feminine spirit of Elen, having attuned to her frequency during his devotion to prayer at the High Altar of the cathedral? He may have sensed her path during the many walks taken to and from St Catherine's Hill, hoping that the scholars too would benefit from the effects of her energy.

It was becoming apparent to us that either Wykeham had extraordinary intuitive powers or he had access to information of an esoteric nature, even knowledge of the dragon energies, like his predecessor Henry of Blois. Although Freemasonry did not exist officially until 1717, this fraternity was almost certainly born out of the medieval lodges of operative stonemasonry. I have no doubt that Wykeham, being a surveyor and architect of so many important historical buildings, was a member of an early Lodge. I also discovered that the present Masonic Lodge in Winchester is named after him.

From the college, we find Elen crossing College Walk and passing through private houses and gardens that belong to the historic Cathedral Close. Instead of following her into the cathedral, I had a strong feeling at this point to look for the male current, which I sensed was not far away. Walking east along College Walk, I soon picked up Belinus crossing the road from the direction of St Catherine's Hill into the grounds of Wolvesey Castle, maintained by English Heritage.

Wolvesey Castle

As we entered through the gate, the scale of the imposing ruins and freshly mown lawns that surround it impressed us. Even though many refer to it as a castle, it was in fact an important residence of the wealthy and powerful Bishops of Winchester for over 1500 years since Anglo-Saxon times. The ruins we see today chiefly date from the time of the Normans to late medieval times.

William Gifford, the second Norman Bishop of Winchester, decided to build a new palace on the site around 1110. Henry of Blois expanded, beautified and fortified the building at the time of the civil war fought between his brother King Stephen and cousin Matilda. It was from here that Matilda fled in humiliation after her failed attempt to secure Winchester during the civil war in 1141. Thomas à Becket also stayed here after returning to England from exile while facing charges for treason. In 1680, stonemasons built a new baroque palace alongside the old, incorporating Henry of Blois' ancient chapel, leaving the remaining buildings to gradually fall into ruins.

Surprisingly, Belinus changes his course in the grounds, avoiding the main section of the ruins built by Blois, preferring instead the private chapel of the present Bishops of Winchester and the 12th century walls of the West Hall built by Gifford. I felt frustrated that we were unable to visit this chapel behind the high walls, especially having discovered that it stands on the foundations of the church built by Henry of Blois. Later we found it to be aligned exactly true north with the central mound on St Catherine's Hill. Today it seems only the present Bishops of Winchester can enjoy the serpent power that dwells within this place.

As we walked towards Cathedral Close through the old city gate with its tiny St Swithun-upon-Kingsgate Church, we could not help but be in awe of such historic surroundings. A cobbled lane took us past the Old Court House, an attractive half-timbered house now called Cheyney Court through which the alignment passes. Gordon refers to the late Dean Stephens who believed the Old Court House stands over the site of a Druidic circle or Cor (henge or circle) where 'the Arch-Druid held his justice in "the face of the sun – the eye of Light" within the precincts of the open-air cor, court, or circle' (Gordon 1932). The sarsen stone that lies beneath the old city gate is just one of many found around Winchester not native to the area – perhaps this is a remnant of the alleged stone circle.

We located Elen passing through the Pilgrims School and some ruins in a garden opposite the north transept of the cathedral called the Deanery, the site of the Old Priors Hall. She then enters the cathedral just east of the south transept through a solitary grave.

The Cathedral

Stepping through the great west doors, I was overwhelmed with the awe-inspiring power of this majestic cathedral, radiating a beauty frozen in stone. As the organ played, the harmonious sacred proportions of the stone structure, fine-tuned over the centuries by highly skilled stonemasons, seemed to vibrate the very fabric of the building. As the sun streamed through the ancient stained-glass windows, it created a strange play of coloured light, which danced delicately on the pillars and Gothic arches.

In 1079, Bishop Walkelin felled a local forest of beeches to make a foundation raft to support his giant building on what was then a water meadow, in the hope of deterring the waters from destabilising it. Over the centuries, as these trees inevitably began to sink and rot, the walls began to subside and crack. It was not until the early part of the 20th century that concrete underpinning, undertaken by a brave diver, saved the cathedral from imminent collapse. John Michell suggests that the ground on which the cathedral stands was long ago 'an unknown form of prehistoric site, possibly a stone circle'.

According to Holinshed's *Chronicles of England, Scotland and Ireland*, King Lucius, the great grandson of the British King Caractacus, 'followed in the footsteps of the apostles' by building the first minster at Winchester on the site of a stone circle, transferring the Druidic rites and teachings to the maintenance of the Christian clergy. This is very likely, as the early missionaries from Rome suppressed the 'old practices' by Christianising many important Druidic sites. The Druidical circle that Dean Stephens believed stood on the site of the Old Court House may have been part of a larger megalithic complex. Large megaliths lying in a corner of the Abbey Gardens just to the east of here may belong to these circles.

When the Romans arrived, they transformed the already large and thriving town into a *civitas* or regional capital. The cathedral guidebook suggests that the stones set into the monolith pillars in the transepts are from the ruins of a Roman temple that stood on or near this site. However, a plan of Roman Winchester shows that the *Forum* and *Basilica* were a little west of the cathedral.

Excavations in the 1960s unearthed the remains of the city's first church, built in stone by King Cenwalh of Wessex and St Birinus in AD 648 on the site of the present cathedral. This building known as the Old Minster was originally a simple cross-shaped structure enlarged over the centuries to become both monastery and cathedral church. In 901, Edward the Elder, son of King Alfred, built New Minster alongside it to the north. The close proximity to the Old Minster caused much confusion for the congregation, as they could not differentiate one choir from another. In 970 the Old Minster was enlarged and beautified by the Benedictines in competition with the English monks of the New Minster.

To the east of New Minster, near the present Guildhall, stood another monastery called Nunnaminster, built by the wife of King Alfred in 903. This vast nunnery, later renamed St Mary's Abbey, became one of the most important centres of arts and learning in England. In 964 all three religious buildings were brought within one great walled enclosure to isolate them from the expanding city. When William the Conqueror arrived in Winchester soon after the Battle Hastings, he realised that this crowded site was totally unsuitable for his new palace. He charged Bishop Walkelin in 1079 to pull down the Old Minster and build a brand new Romanesque-style Norman cathedral. In 1107, superstitious locals blamed the collapse of Walkelin's central tower on the unpopular King William II or Rufus, whose tomb lay underneath. However, poor workmanship and sinking foundations were the most likely cause.

Alfred's New Minster with its relics of the old kings, queens, and saints was another casualty of this Norman reorganisation of Cathedral Close. Henry I ordered its removal to a new site outside the city walls to the north, known as Hyde Mead. It was renamed Hyde Abbey, receiving the bones of King Alfred, his wife Ealhswith and son King Edward the Elder with great ceremony in 1110.

Henry of Blois later added much finery to the Norman cathedral and redesigned the area behind the High Altar to house the relics of St Swithun. Unfortunately, after the destruction of his shrine in 1538 at the hands of Henry VIII's officers, his bones along with those of other saints, kings and queens were unceremoniously scattered around the cathedral floor. Whilst walking towards the High Altar of the cathedral, I remembered reading in an old guidebook that:

'twenty kings of the royal line are buried here, and thirty-five made Winchester their capital .... It was built to be to Norman England what the Temple had been to the Jews – the central expression of a nation's faith, the place dedicated to the concentrated worship of the conquering race.'

Nearby is the finely decorated choir screen carved with serpents, dragons and images of the Green Man, designed by Sir George Gilbert Scott whose work we had seen earlier in All Saints' Church at Ryde. In the south transept, I dowsed Elen entering through the southeast corner into the Fishermen's Chapel with its watery themes and an altar decorated with spirals designed to resemble a tree trunk. Interestingly, St Catherine's Hill is depicted here in one of the stained-glass windows.

In the corridor outside the Presbytery, a few metres east of the south transept, Elen passes through the only two stained-glass windows in the south wall. One depicts St Michael slaying the dragon along with St Urial, St Gabriel and St Raphael, and the other shows a typical scene from the life of St George, saving a princess by killing the dragon. I failed to notice the significance of this window at the time, but the further north we travelled along the Belinus alignment the more we began to regard St George as a guiding spirit. Elen then passes under the mortuary chests containing the bones of Saxon kings, queens and bishops, placed here in 1544, across the front of the High Altar and leaves through the north wall.

From Wolvesey Palace, the male current enters the cathedral's east end through the small side chapel of Bishop Thomas Langton, once the shrine to St Birinus, who converted many Saxon kings and directed the building of the first minster at Winchester. Interestingly, in the 7th century, the former capital or religious centre of Wessex was on the St Michael Line at Dorchester-on-Thames. Therefore, it would seem that Birinus was directly responsible for moving the spiritual centre of Wessex from the St Michael Line to the Belinus Line.

From the Langton Chapel the male current passes through the modern shrine of St Swithun behind the High Altar. Here its width increases and I could physically feel the power radiating from this hallowed spot.

The Saxon monk St Swithun is often associated with the weather. Born in Winchester around AD 800, he became advisor to King Aethelwulf during one of England's most turbulent periods in history. In 852, he became Bishop of Winchester, which even then was one of the most powerful positions in England.

There are many legends that surround this man that refer to certain accomplishments not altogether ecclesiastical. One was overseeing the construction of a bridge at the east gate of the city that survived up until quite recently. Another was of a more magical nature. While standing on the same bridge one day he noticed a woman in distress having broken all her eggs after accidentally dropping her basket. He promptly walked over, lifted the basket from the ground, and handed it back to her. To her surprise, all the eggs appeared restored to their natural state. It is interesting that these tales of miracles are often associated with papal missionaries, as if they were superhuman – or perhaps it was simply a form of medieval propaganda.

St Swithun also preferred the freedom of the surrounding landscape to the confinement of churches and monasteries, often choosing to attend to the business of his diocese at night. This also applied to his final resting place; for he requested his tomb should lie outside under the eaves so that rainwater would fall upon his grave. The monks of

Winchester buried him in AD 862 according to his wishes but decided later to move his bones inside the church so that pilgrims had better access. During the exhumation, a violent storm erupted followed by 40 days of constant rain, hence the legend and the well-known saying: 'If it rains on St Swithun's Day it will rain for 40 days and 40 nights'. His new shrine became a focus for pilgrims when miracles started to occur, becoming the second most popular place of pilgrimage in medieval England.

The male current passes through an unusually small door beneath a compartment at the back of the High Altar called the Feretory. A guide, unperturbed by the occasional flash of my dowsing rod, informed us that above the door on a platform behind the screen were once located the bones of St Swithun and many Saxon kings and queens of England, having been moved there by Henry of Blois from the crypt. Belinus flows through a narrow passage called the Holy Hole leading from this small door, where pilgrims would crawl in the belief that they would receive healing from the bones of St Swithun above. He continues to the Presbytery, where he crosses with Elen at the High Altar and where kings were crowned, the precise spot over which travels the Deneb Line. Overlooking the Node behind the altar is the breathtaking stone *reredos* that contains many carved statues of historical kings, saints and angels. Commissioned by Cardinal Beaufort in the 15th century, the description 'being as magnificent as this or any other nation can exhibit' perfectly conveys this grand display.

Just below the crossing, the male current is marked by the tomb of Henry of Blois, originally the final resting place of King William II or Rufus, son of William the Conqueror. One of the most controversial mysteries continually debated today is the death of the young King William Rufus, apparently accidentally shot with an arrow whilst out hunting in the New Forest. Even more curious was his rushed burial in the cathedral without proper royal ceremony. Mysteriously his older brother, Richard, Duke of Beorn, was killed in exactly the same manner as Rufus, his bones lying in a lead coffin in the walls under the screen on the south side of the Presbytery.

Belinus continues between the choir stalls with their wonderful carvings of dragons and serpents, through the screen designed by Sir George Gilbert Scott and into the great nave. The pillars of the nave seem to mark his outer width as he heads for the great west door, brushing past Bishop William of Wykeham's chantry and the magnificent Norman Tournai font made of black marble.

Before following Belinus out through the large west doorway, I noticed the crypt was open to visitors. In the winter months, this is normally closed because it floods naturally due to the rise in the water table. This was the perfect opportunity to dowse beneath the High Altar, as the currents can be detected above or below ground level. As we reached the foot of the stone stairs, we found the atmosphere of the Norman pillared crypt with its fine Romanesque arches to be most enchanting. Many people wonder why the old stonemasons went to so much effort to build the grandest cathedral in the Western world on a flood plain. No doubt they were attracted by the powerful telluric energies that exist at this site. With discreetly hidden dowsing rods, I found the crossing point of Elen and Belinus at a well that lies directly under the High Altar. According to John Michell, this well dates back to the time of the Druids who worshipped their god in three forms similar to the Christian trinity.

The well may have been dug according to an ancient Etruscan cosmological principle of building cities. The priest geomancer would first survey the land, determined by the position of the stars and planets, and then divine a spot perhaps using visible signs

Holy Well or Roman 'mundus' under the High Altar marking the Node in the crypt of Winchester Cathedral. (From a postcard dated 1912)

in nature and portents or omens such as lightning strikes. Then a north–south axis would be marked out, which they called *cardo,* together with an east–west line called *decumanus.* This was followed by the digging of a deep shaft called a *mundus* at the centre point of the new town in order to connect the surface world of the living to the powers of the 'underworld' and offerings were dropped in the well, including soil from the native land of the new settlers (Keller 1975). The Romans later adopted this ritual from the Etruscans and probably used it in the building of many towns and cities in England, including Winchester.

I believe the Norman architects and stonemasons deliberately chose the site on which the cathedral stands because it was the mundus of the Romans, the exact centre of the old city. Moreover, the waxing and waning of the water levels issuing from this well animates the immense telluric power at this place where the serpents cross. Let us hope that the great volume of water beneath the city is not the cause of a catastrophe mentioned in the 'Prophesies of Merlin'. The 12th century poem, attributed to the prophet Merlin and based on a lost manuscript in the Cornish language, says that 'Three springs shall burst forth in the town of Winchester, and the streams which run from them will divide the island into three parts'.

The Church of St Lawrence

From the site of the stone circle at Cheyney Court, the alignment almost touches the west end of the cathedral and runs parallel with the tree-lined avenue to the Old Square next to the museum. As we walked along the pedestrian street that connects

89

Path marking the alignment between Winchester Cathedral and St Lawrence's Church

the Square to the High Street, we entered a small church dedicated to St Lawrence tucked away between shops and cafés, the only historic building that remains to mark the alignment. Just south of here, where Minster Lane joins Symonds Street, once stood the High School of Winchester until the time of the Reformation, where King Aethelwulf and Alfred the Great were educated and much later William of Wykeham (Warren 1932).

Also known as the Church of St Lawrence in the Square, it is curiously the Mother Church of Winchester, supposedly because it is the only surviving parish church of Norman foundation within the city walls. It is also unusual because of its almost square design with no separate chancel. More importantly, it was built over the foundations of the Royal Chapel within William of Conqueror's palace, which Henry of Blois rebuilt after it was devastated by fire during King Stephen and Matilda's civil war. Further restorations followed and a stained-glass window now marks the spot where the alignment enters the church depicting four great bishops of Winchester: St Swithun, William of Wykeham, William of Waynflete (1395–1486), holding aloft the chapel he founded at Magdalene College, Oxford, and Lancelot Andrews (1555–1626). Bishop Henry of Blois is curiously absent from this window, perhaps because of his Gnostic Christian beliefs.

Since 1660, a curious custom has been staged at this little church, whereby every new Bishop of Winchester before enthronement had to enter the church alone for private prayer and then change into his Episcopal robe in the presence of the Archdeacon of Canterbury. After ringing the church bell, the Rector presents the new Bishop to the Mayor and citizens of the city in the Square in front of the church before parading to the cathedral for the enthronement service.

Unfortunately, the alignment suffered the negative effects of public execution in the Square during Cromwell's time. Staging this act of barbarity on a powerful alignment must have had a detrimental effect on the city and the surrounding area. Grahame Gardner writing in *Dowsing Today* (2008) believes that the intense emotional trauma that this type of event can invoke imprints itself onto a site, which then transmits along the alignment 'inducing a similar resonance at other points on the ley'.

From the west entrance of the cathedral, we followed the male current leaving the precinct by Minster Lane into St Thomas's Passage. Here on the corner we noticed a small megalith or sarsen stone just to our right similar to those found in Abbey Gardens. He then passes through the church of St Thomas, with its impressively tall spire and carved dragons, built over the site of a medieval church dedicated to St Petroc, a 6th century Celtic Christian saint famous for his missions around the West Country. Today the council runs the church as a community centre and youth club.

The Great Hall and Arthur's Round Table

Belinus then ascends the steep hill behind the church to the gardens of the old Peninsular Barracks, the former site of one of the most famous castles in the nation. William the Conqueror's victory march through the gates of Winchester as the newly crowned Norman King was a ceremonial act to capture the principal city of the Saxons and take its royal treasure and most importantly the government records. These records, dating back hundreds of years, were a key part of the Domesday survey that William used to acquire land from many Saxon nobles and farmers. William decreed that they could keep their lands only if they provided some form of written proof of ownership. This cunning act compromised the Saxons who previously secured their lands through verbal agreements due to the high levels of illiteracy.

A year later, William ordered the building of a castle to house his military commander to ensure the security of the region. During the course of the next century, the castle became the seat of the new Anglo-Norman government, which continued as England's ceremonial centre of chivalry; then in the late 12th century this power base shifted to Westminster. The walls of William the Conqueror's castle were not the first defences built in Winchester, as according to archaeologists the Romans constructed walls of stone to such quality that they lasted right up to the Anglo-Saxon period.

The Great Hall of Winchester Castle. (A watercolour by Francis Grose c. 1780,
© Society of Antiquaries of London)

Unfortunately, Cromwell's armies dismantled almost the entire castle in the 17th century, including its great walls, leaving very little for us to see today.

Belinus turns north by a fountain and heads to a tranquil garden dedicated to Eleanor, wife of Henry III, behind a medieval building called the Great Hall. On entering the pillared hall through the south door, I could see that its proportions were similar to the nave of a church, with its ancient Purbeck marble pillars forming two aisles shimmering with the light from the Gothic windows. A musty smell now pervades the atmosphere here, once the main seat of government before London. It has witnessed many great occasions over its long history and been the scene of high drama. Henry VIII chose this hall to entertain Charles V, Emperor of the Holy Roman Empire, and Sir Walter Raleigh was tried here for treason on the orders of Elizabeth I before being beheaded in the Tower of London.

A chapel built by William the Conqueror for holding council once partially stood on the site of the Great Hall. Henry II rebuilt the Norman castle and installed royal apartments for his queen Eleanor of Aquitaine. Their grandson Henry III (1207–72), who was born at the castle, later rebuilt the Great Hall.

Hanging on the west wall is a huge circular painted wood table said to be Arthur's Round Table with 24 segments representing Arthur and his Knights. In 1520, Henry VIII instructed artists to repaint the table with a Tudor rose at the centre, representing the red rose of the House of Lancaster, of which his grandmother Margaret Beaufort was the last remaining member. It also included an image of King Arthur in Henry's own likeness as a young man. For many years its origins were unknown, but few academics believed that it was from the period of King Arthur. The latest expert analysis of Arthur's Round Table using carbon dating and dendrochronology (tree ring dating) shows that the table was almost certainly made during the latter part of the 13th century during the reign of either Henry III or his son Edward I. Perhaps its presence here is a symbol of King Arthur's connection with the city, written in the Norman romances introduced by Henry of Blois and Eleanor of Aquitaine.

Arthur's Round Table in the Great Hall, Winchester

For over a thousand years, the very name of King Arthur would conjure up visions of a national hero who fought for the freedom and independence of the British. Historically, he was a 5th century war leader who successfully stemmed the growing tide of Saxon influence in a series of great battles. Sir Thomas Malory, author of *Le Morte d'Arthur*, published in 1485, believed Camelot was at Winchester 'where Arthur held court at a round table with twenty-four places for his knights'. Layamon, author of *Brut*, dated around 1200, refers to Winchester as the place besieged by Mordred:

'The evil Mordred while Arthur was abroad on a campaign besieged Winchester and persuaded the locals to support him on offer of great riches. Arthur on hearing this attacked the city, meanwhile Mordred escaped leaving the locals to the wrath of Arthur who killed everyone and destroyed the city and its walls.' (Madden 1847)

The first writer to introduce the concept of the 'Round Table' to the Arthurian story was the Norman poet Master Robert Wace. Interestingly he dedicated his romances to the French Court of Eleanor of Aquitaine, wife of Henry II. Her daughter Marie de Champagne was patron to Chrétien de Troyes, the principal composer of the Arthurian romances. Modern writers believe that Eleanor's experience during her first marriage to Louis XII was the inspiration for the character Guinevere in the later romances. After a great fire destroyed Glastonbury Abbey in 1184, King Henry II took great interest in its rebuilding and the search for the supposed grave of Arthur and Guinevere.

Henry II and Eleanor apparently modelled themselves on this fabled couple, perhaps redesigning Winchester Castle to resemble the romantic image of Camelot. Henry II's grandson was born at Winchester Castle in 1207 and christened at the cathedral, eventually becoming Henry III. One of his first tasks as king was to rebuild the castle following severe damage after a French invasion. In 1222, work began under the guidance of Peter des Roches, who also built Titchfield Abbey, and fashionable round towers with conical roofs, reminiscent of Arthur's Camelot, replaced the square Norman towers. Throughout its long and celebrated history, the Great Hall has been a place for administering justice, first as a parliament house when Winchester was capital of England and then becoming a court of law in recent times.

Edward I (1239–1307) came to the throne at the height of a new age of chivalry. His interest in Arthur began in 1278 when he and his wife Eleanor attended a second reopening of the supposed tomb of Arthur and Guinevere at Glastonbury Abbey. The King carried the relics of Arthur in solemn state while Eleanor bore those of Guinevere to a splendid new tomb of black Purbeck marble.

Many historians now believe that the table was made for a great tournament organised by Edward I in 1290, in meadows near Winchester, to celebrate the marriage of one of his children. According to a written account of the event, the theme was very Arthurian in nature with Edward taking a leading role, presumably that of Arthur, whilst others were dressed as the Knights of the Round Table as they re-enacted the Grail romances. This curious re-enactment of such Arthurian themes perhaps stemmed from a belief by Edward that Winchester was the legendary Camelot. As a young prince, he was possibly educated to accept that this great city was once a national centre of sovereignty, a ritual ceremonial place of kingship stretching back to the very dawn of British history.

The Tudor kings would later claim a descent from the Welsh kings and Arthur himself. King Henry VII groomed his first son to be King Arthur II, who was born at the Royal Court in Winchester, which Malory also believed was the legendary Camelot. The young prince was baptised at Winchester Cathedral. According to Geoffrey Ashe in *The Quest for Arthur's Britain* (1968), a tapestry displaying the coat of arms of the legendary Iron Age King Belinus was woven especially for the occasion, which eventually became a floor mat in the Warden's bedroom at Winchester College. Was this an attempt by the Tudor monarch to display their bloodline link to this once great British king? If this was indeed the case then why did they not choose the coat of arms of the first British king Brutus? I can only assume that the tapestry eludes to a known link between King Belinus, the legendary road builder, and this city. Sadly, Prince Arthur's premature death prevented him from ever emulating the legendary saviour of Britain, curtailing the plan to herald in a new age of enlightenment and independence from European papal control. This, of course, became the role of his brother Henry and the rest as they say is history.

As well as its mythical associations, the design of Arthur's Round Table could be an allegory of the circular enclosure on St Catherine's Hill, a round table representing the stars, presided over by the female saint who represents the solar wheel.

Before leaving the castle grounds, the male current flows over the foundations of the western tower built by Henry II on a mound just north of the Great Hall. Another larger mound existed at the southern end of the castle complex on which William the Conqueror built his main residence. Archaeologists were inconclusive with their dating of the palace mound, which suggests it may have been much older. England's new Norman king was renowned for building castles on sacred mounds of the Britons, such as Cardiff Castle in Wales, the Tower of London on the 'White Mound', and Totnes Castle. He also constructed Windsor Castle on an earlier manufactured hill later called the Round Table Mound, where William of Wykeham built the round tower that dominates the castle today. The construction of castles upon these holy mounds was a permanent reminder of their imperial power, firmly supplanted over the former ceremonial sites of the ancient British. Remains of motte and baileys litter the landscape of England, mostly attributed to the Normans. Now, however, recent excavations have shown them to be much older and merely strengthened and heightened by the invaders, hiding any archaeological evidence of earlier occupation.

Belinus further connects with the medieval West Gate at the top of the High Street, an impressive monument adorned with fine carvings and the royal coat of arms of Winchester. He then travels north through a block of modern flats called 'Baeltarum', which stands on part of the Iron Age settlement of Oram's Arbour. Recent work by archaeologists has revealed an ancient enclosure, dating between 600 and 300 BC, which extends eastwards from Oram's Arbour Park above Clifton Terrace to St Peter's Street in the centre of the city. This implies that the settlement covered an area of over 50 acres, making it one of the largest Iron Age settlements in England. The remains of a large round house were also discovered in 2002, which may have been the royal residence of King Molmutius, the legendary king who rebuilt and enlarged the city of Winchester around 400 BC.

Hyde Abbey and King Alfred the Great

The Theatre Royal on Jewry Street also marks the male current as he heads north along Staples Gardens, as well as Hyde House, once part of a mansion within the grounds of the old Hyde Abbey. As we rounded the corner, Hyde Abbey Gate came into view, the only surviving part of the original abbey.

During the 9th century, Winchester was the royal seat of King Alfred the Great (AD 849–899), who revived the old Roman town by rebuilding the streets to a grid pattern.

He translated the old British laws of King Molmutius and incorporated them into his own. Saxon Winchester thrived under Alfred's rule, reviving it once more as a great centre of religious worship and education.

The relics of King Alfred and his wife Queen Ealhswith and son Edward the Elder were transferred to the new abbey along with those of St Barnabas, which soon enhanced its reputation as a site of pilgrimage. In its glory days the abbey estate covered a considerable area and contained cloisters, a chapter house, monks' dormitory, two churches, mills and stables. It was completely demolished in 1538 during the Reformation, leaving St Bartholomew's Church and Hyde Gate as our only reminder of this historic area. In 1788, Bridewell Prison took over the site of the Abbey Church but it was demolished in 1869 and later covered by a residential housing estate.

Belinus flows through the 15th century Hyde Abbey Gate, rebuilt several times over the centuries, to the eastern end of St Bartholomew's Church, constructed at the same time as Hyde Abbey for the workers. After the Reformation, it continued as a parish church, with a new tower constructed from stones taken from the ruined abbey.

The site of this church may have been of greater significance long ago as its High Altar lies directly on the 'road of the dead' or Deneb Line, between St Catherine's Hill and the cusp between Sidown Hill and Beacon Hill.

As I entered the churchyard by the south gate, I noticed a large stone lying on its side on the path of Belinus. I recognised it to be another of the many megalithic sarsen stones found at strategic places around the city. The church possibly stands over a prehistoric sanctuary, for the area around Hyde was a well-known burial ground during the Roman occupation. Ancient cultures often buried their deceased outside the northern walls of their settlement, the north being the direction of the Celtic realm of the dead. An unidentified grave slab opposite the east end of the church directly behind the High Altar marks the alleged secret burial place of King Alfred the Great. The width of the male current encompasses both the High Altar and the grave. During the Reformation, many sacred relics, including the bones of kings, queens and saints, were either completely destroyed or scattered indiscriminately. A local tradition maintains that during this turbulent time, the monks surreptitiously recovered Alfred's bones and reburied them at St Bartholomew's Church. Inside the church is a stained-glass window showing King Alfred holding a model of Hyde Abbey, with an old carved stone head of the king beneath; a remnant from Hyde Abbey perhaps.

The reverence shown towards King Alfred is understandable when you read of his remarkable achievements during his reign. He was born in Wantage in Oxfordshire in AD 849, the fifth son of King Aethelwulf of Wessex and Mercia and Queen Osburgh of the Isle of Wight Jutes. At the

Hyde Abbey Gate, Winchester

Old Minster in Winchester his tutoring was overseen by St Swithun, who groomed him to become a well-cultured and learned man. At the age of 22 he succeeded his brother Ethelred to the throne and ruled from AD 871–899, during which time he defended Anglo-Saxon England from Danish raids. He exhibited great military skill and innovation, establishing England's first Royal Navy.

His practical support of religion, personal scholarship and the promotion of education were high on his agenda. He made two pilgrimages to Rome and remained a committed Christian. These great qualities reminded me of the legendary King Arthur of whom Alfred would have been aware. The great statue of Alfred in the Broadway, at the bottom of the High Street, depicts him holding up a great sword by the blade, like a Christian cross or possibly the sword of truth, a symbol of Arthur's *Excalibur*. Today the whereabouts of Alfred's final resting place, like that of King Arthur, is still a mystery and a continuing quest for archaeologists.

From here, Belinus leaves this great city, so we backtracked to the cathedral to find Elen's path crossing the inaccessible Cathedral Green from its north wall towards the High Street. I noticed on the Green a line of poles sticking out of the grass, which I soon discovered belonged to a group of archaeologists from the University of Southampton. They were using geophysics, or ground radar, to map the foundations of New Minster first built by King Alfred and finished by his son Edward. From the position of these poles we could determine that Elen passes through the site of the High Altar.

Nearby Elen visits the medieval tower of St Maurice's Church tucked away between Market Lane and High Street, its main body dismantled in the late 1950s. Its original foundations are Saxon, however, built by the northern entrance to the cathedral precinct. In a room beneath the tower, there are information boards that trace some of the city's fascinating history.

The female current continues through the Brooks Shopping Centre, the site of a Roman bathhouse, before crossing North Walls Park towards the River Park Leisure Centre. Here she follows a tributary of the Itchen to the eastern end of Hyde Abbey. A newly developed garden now commemorates this once great shrine to King Alfred, the outline of the east end of the old abbey church walls and the position of the High Altar now marked by stones and holly bushes, including the supposed graves of Alfred, his wife and son.

Having dowsed Elen across the old abbey garden through the site of the High Altar, I was reminded of its original dedication to St Mary. Looking west the squat tower of St Bartholomew's Church can be clearly seen; the two serpents now 150 metres from each other.

After its dissolution in 1539, Hyde Abbey and its lands were granted to Sir Thomas Wriothesley, First Earl of Southampton, of Titchfield Abbey. He reduced the abbey and church to rubble, selling off anything of value. Perhaps he purchased it in the hope of finding the precious relics of Alfred or some other hidden treasure.

As we departed Winchester, I wondered why this once great capital of England and spiritual centre of an entire nation declined so rapidly. Some say Winchester suffered from the corruption of its most eminent inhabitants and a writer of the time penned this solemn statement: 'Our ancestors knew Winchester sometimes a goodly town, in treasure rich and plentiful, in name, of great renown. But now, for hunger after gold our men so greedy are; that even such Cities excellent, they know not how to spare'.

I reflected on the famous characters who made Winchester great and their connection to the Belinus Line: King Molmutius, the Law Giver, and his son Belinus, the surveyor of roads, King Arthur, Alfred the Great, St Swithun, Henry of Blois and William of Wykeham. I believe they all had one thing in common – a belief in the ancient code of chivalry, justice and the quest for knowledge and truth.

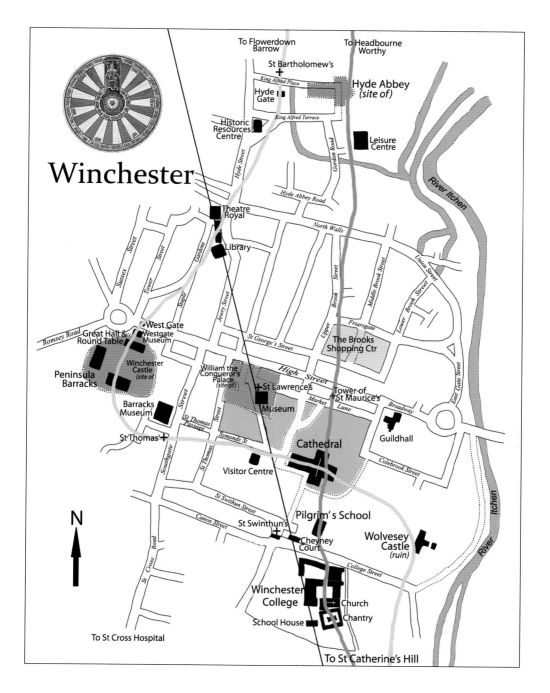

Chapter 4

North Hampshire to Oxfordshire
From the White City to the White Dragon

The trail of the male serpent continues through the outskirts of the city of Winchester across a rural landscape of fertile fields to the village of Littleton. At the highest point of the village next to Littleton Road lies a secluded Bronze Age cemetery called Flowerdown Barrows. The site, maintained by English Heritage, consists of three barrows, including two small early Bronze Age 'bowl' barrows near to the entrance and a late Bronze Age 'disc' barrow a little further east.

Dating from 2400–1500 BC, the disc barrow is particularly impressive, measuring 61 m (200 ft) in diameter, said to be the largest of its type in Hampshire. As we approached this atmospheric monument shrouded in the early morning mist, the surrounding bank and ditch reminded us of the prehistoric henge-like structures found in many parts of the country. At its centre is a small raised mound that once housed a burial. We dowsed Belinus crossing diagonally through the barrow towards the northwest, intersected by several other lines of energy also radiating out from its centre. However, Belinus appears not to interact with these lines, preferring to remain energetically independent of them as he passes through the monument.

Given the size of the disc barrow, it may have been the grave of a local tribal leader from the Bronze Age, perhaps even a king. Alternatively, its true function could be that of a junction box of earth power, a meeting place of energy lines at this high point tapping into a subterranean fault.

Ashdown House, Lord Craven's Temple for the Winter Queen

A Templar Church and the Jesus Stone

Further north along the main road is Littleton's parish church dedicated to St Catherine of Alexandria, Virgin and Martyr, with a fascinating history. The Domesday records show that in AD 635, Cynegils, King of Wessex, bestowed this chapel upon Winchester's Old Minster. Although extensively restored, the foundations of the present church date from the 11th century when Henry of Blois gifted the little Norman church to the Knights Templar or Knights of Jerusalem. The Order used it to accommodate their personal guests and pilgrims on route to the shrine of St Swithun in Winchester. The church's earlier dedication was to St Mary Magdalene, a saint once venerated by the Knights Templar.

An elaborately carved Purbeck marble font, similar to the unusual black Tournai font that stands in Winchester Cathedral, attracts the male current as he flows through the church to the High Altar. Henry of Blois introduced the use of Dorset's Purbeck marble to English stonemasons as well as importing black marble Tournai fonts from Belgium. The current also visits a house called 'Monks Rest', once attached to the church as a rest house for sick monks from St Swithun's Priory in Winchester.

Located in the Test Valley, the pretty village of Barton Stacey boasts one of the most historic churches in Hampshire and one of the oldest sites of continuous Christian worship in England. Belinus seeks out an ancient yew in the churchyard before entering the tower of All Saints' Church founded by the Mortimer family in 1074. The Domesday Book records its rare dedication to St Victor at Bertune. Having acquired the manor of Barton Stacey, Ralph de Mortimer brought French Benedictine monks with him from the Normandy Abbey of St Victor-en-Caux in Seine-Maritime, France. His family continued to hold the land and church until 1444.

A Saxon altar stone in the south transept may be the only remnant from the earliest church here. Unfortunately, any carvings the stone may have had are no longer visible and during restoration in the 1900s, builders placed it upside down in the floor. Two

The Templar Church of St Catherine at Littleton, Hampshire

pillars remain from a Norman church, restored many times over the centuries. The 12th century font of Purbeck marble is similar in style to the one in Littleton Church.

To the east of here the alignment passes very close to the Norman church of St Michael, by the River Dever at Bullington. The splendid avenue of lime trees leading to the church entrance is worthy of a detour off the busy A34 between Winchester and Newbury.

Also east of the alignment is Tidbury Ring, an Iron Age earthwork that lies on the path of a well-known ley line called the Winchester Ley, researched by Paul Devereux. Its course runs SSE from Tidbury through the city to the labyrinth on St Catherine's Hill, marked by St Bartholomew's Church, Hyde Gate, Winchester Cathedral and Wykeham's Collegiate Church. The angle of the Winchester Ley differs only slightly from the Deneb Line, which starts from the mound on St Catherine's Hill rather than the labyrinth.

We encountered another tiny ancient church at Tufton next to the River Test, the site of a Saxon church founded in AD 986 by Elfrida, widow of King Edgar in 'expiation of her crimes'. Its setting is so typical of rural farming communities in Hampshire, the pretty red-brick thatched houses and timber barns being a unique feature of the county. Upon entering this church dedicated to St Mary, we noticed the ancient chancel arch that apparently dates from the 12th century.

Crossing the busy A34, the current guided us to the intriguingly named town of Whitchurch, next to a major fording place on the River Test where three ancient roads meet: the Harroway or Hoary Way (*hoar* being a Saxon word meaning 'ancient', 'aged' or 'white haired'), Portway, a Roman thoroughfare that once linked London to Weymouth, and the old route between Winchester and Oxford that bisects both these roads and the Deneb Line. Although some historians believe Whitchurch is the site of the elusive Roman town of *Vindomis*, its name actually derives from the Saxon *Whit* meaning 'white' or 'holy', a descriptive word often used for a chapel constructed of white limestone or chalk.

The church of All Hallows is a restored Norman building which has some unique and interesting features. Inside I dowsed Belinus passing through the 'Mary Maze', a small mosaic of a maze conceived by a local designer and blessed by the vicar. Placed in the church in 1993, it depicts the Mother Mary with the Christ Child on her lap as Joseph looks on from behind. This particular labyrinth encourages you to take two paths, but only one leads you to the centre, representing the journey through life to find salvation.

Another feature of this church is an ancient stone carving previously discovered embedded in the north wall during Victorian restoration. The stone portrays Jesus clean-shaven with a halo and cross behind his head holding the gospels in his left hand and raising his right in blessing. This carving is unique to this part of the country but similar in style to the Romano-Christian stones found around Hadrian's Wall depicting early representations of Christ. Its Latin inscription dating from the Saxon period translates as 'Here the body of Frithburga lies buried in peace'. The builders of the early White Church probably reused the early Christian stone as a gravestone or epitaph for this Saxon princess.

Romano-British carving of Jesus at All Hallows Church, Whitchurch

The Egbury Mystery and the Seven Barrows

Belinus curves slightly to the northwest to visit the remains of an unusual Iron Age banked enclosure surrounded by low-lying farmland near the hamlet of Egbury. Its tree-lined banks still survive to the south and west bordering a crop field. When we last visited the area tracking the male current, we failed to notice this well-hidden prehistoric enclosure; even its location was unclear on our map. However, it came to my attention again about a year or so later during a vivid dream.

In addition to the practice of dowsing, I have at times allowed psychic information, intuition and dreams to play a part in the Belinus Line quest. Of course, most dreams are the play of the subconscious, and information obtained through psychic means can often lead one astray. Nevertheless, every now and then they provide names and places previously unknown. This particular dream was interesting because it gave not only a specific place but also a message.

The dream sequence involved a beautiful auburn-haired woman who alerted me to an object left at Egbury, causing harmful disruption to the energy matrix of Britain. At first I dismissed this rather bizarre warning, but Caroline was sure that it was a site on one of the currents in Hampshire. After consulting her notes Egbury hillfort was one of the sites on the male current she had highlighted to revisit.

Around the time of the Celtic festival of Imbolc, when nature starts to experience the first flourishing of life, we set off early one morning to revisit Egbury accompanied by a psychic friend who was familiar with the Belinus quest. After seeking permission from the local farmer to visit the site, we finally had clear directions as to its whereabouts. Parking our car in a muddy lay-by, we walked to the gate of the field where we could just make out the tall banks obscured by leafless trees. Before long, the psychic sensed the importance of two large dominant ash trees nearby, which she felt were somehow acting as guardians of the site.

After meditating by the trees, she was suddenly drawn to explore around their roots and, before long, pulled out an unusual stone. It was a cube-shaped piece of pale granite of the type native to Cornwall or Devon. Although there was no marking upon it, I had a strong intuition that this foreign object symbolically represented an egg, covertly deposited here to draw the vital energies of the site, to be later retrieved to empower some other place. We had no idea how long the granite cube had been at the site but we sensed its presence was having a detrimental effect on the site's energies, just as my dream had foretold, and more significantly was directly restricting the flow of Belinus who passes straight through the remains of the fort. After submerging the object in a nearby river to ground its negative intentions, we carried out a cleansing ritual to restore balance and harmony to this ancient site. We were relieved to dowse that the current's life force had become stronger and its width had increased to over 3 m through the site. Often the vital energy of the Earth responds to its suffering and communicates its distress to sensitive individuals, particularly those who work with the healing of the landscape.

Although we are experienced in the use of visualisation to help heal these sites, many people prefer to use invocation or ceremony to direct the healing. I believe from experience that one of the most powerful and most effectual prayers is 'the Great Invocation', a 'World' prayer released in 1945 by Alice Bailey and the Tibetan monk Djwhal Khul.

'From the point of Light within the Mind of God
Let light stream forth into the minds of men
Let Light descend on Earth

From the point of Love within the Heart of God
Let love stream forth into the hearts of men
May Christ return to Earth

From the centre where the Will of God is known
Let purpose guide the little wills of men
The purpose which the Masters know and serve

From the centre which we call the race of men
Let the Plan of Love and Light work out
And may it seal the door where evil dwells

Let Light and Love and Power restore the Plan on Earth.'

Just below Watership Down, made famous by author Richard Adams, is the village of Litchfield located near the A34. Its church is dedicated to St James the Less, the son of Alphaeus and one of the apostles of Christ. The male current focuses on the raised mound on which the church resides, perhaps built in the prehistoric age and later adopted by the Saxons as their place of worship. Charles I slept here during the Civil War in 1644 before moving north to face Cromwell's army at the second Battle of Newbury.

Three kilometres west of Litchfield, an ancient ford to the south of the village of St Mary Bourne marks the Spine of Albion. Long ago, the Roman Portway crossed this ancient ford of the River Bourne with other prehistoric tracks. At that time, the river was much wider; it is now reduced to a small brook trickling through a flat plain in an open field. In the village, just outside the south entrance of St Peter's Church, is a yew hollowed with age believed to be over a thousand years old. The main attraction, however, is another connection with Henry of Blois, for here inside the church stands one of the mysterious seven magnificent black Tournai fonts that Henry brought from Belgium. Made from a soft black marble, the font has fine symbolic carvings on all four sides; in particular, the north side shows seven pillars each surmounted with a fleur-de-lis that reminded me of the seven initiatory steps of the Mithras cult.

Just north of Litchfield, Belinus passes through another prehistoric site called the Seven Barrows. Unfortunately, the A34 and a railway line cuts straight through the Bronze Age cemetery, making it difficult to appreciate this sacred place. The site consists of both 'bowl' and 'disc' barrows, five located on the west side of the dual carriageway and three on the east. The barrows on the east side of the road are impossible to access so our dowsing was limited to the five on the west side, where we found no sign of the current. Much later, heading back south along the dual carriageway, the dowsing rod indicated that the male current was passing through one of the barrows amongst the eastern group.

Whilst standing on one of the tallest mounds, I noticed that Beacon Hill, one of the two hills to mark the setting of Deneb, stands just 2 km directly north of here. In the northern sky, the two most prominent constellations are Ursula Major and Draco, having commanded this position over many millennia. They continually circle around the celestial pole, which today is marked by the star Polaris. Our ancient ancestors regarded the Pole Star, which defines true north, as the gateway to the afterlife. They also believed that the neighbouring constellations of Ursula Major and Ursula Minor, the Great and Little Bears, both consisting of seven stars, were its guardians.

The site of Seven Barrows next to the A34, with Beacon Hill beyond

Although this site is called Seven Barrows, this was an extensive burial ground with numerous tumuli; the name may therefore refer to one of the Bear constellations. Using the Skyglobe computer program, I noticed that between the Bronze and Iron Ages the seven stars of Ursula Major or the Plough, as it is also known, were much lower in the sky; its lowest star would have been seen to touch Beacon Hill if viewed from the barrows at the winter solstice. The Plough in legend was the chariot to the afterlife, and in the case of Beacon Hill the chariot collects the souls at the winter solstice, when the Solar King dies and is reborn.

Beacon Hill, 261 m (856 ft) high, is a north–south orientated ridge with the most unusual shaped fortifications on its northern summit, resembling an hourglass or a four-pointed star. Following Belinus, we climbed up to the summit of the hill, where to our astonishment we discovered a Node with his counterpart Elen at a mysterious grave.

The Saxon Church and the Octagonal Nave

St Swithun's Church, Headbourne Worthy

The journey of Elen from the northern outskirts of Winchester to Beacon Hill, takes us first to the pretty village of Headbourne Worthy. Its secluded church dedicated to St Swithun is shrouded by majestic willows in a hollow by the River Itchen next to the B304, once a pilgrim route to and from the city. We dowsed Elen flowing along a footpath leading to the church lined with yew trees and crossing over a tiny footbridge. The unusual church has a separate tower with Saxon masonry adjoining the nave, set on an island bordered by bubbling brooks. Elen seemed to delight in these surroundings, as I dowsed her through the entrance of the church just clipping the tower.

The surrounding lands have been in the possession of the kings and queens of England and the Bishops of Winchester for centuries. A church has frequented this site since the time of King Canute (AD 994–1035), built out of stone quarried at Binstead on the Isle of Wight. Another feature of note is the 11th century large crucifix or rood above the door of the vestry, now badly weathered.

The village of Micheldever to the northwest of here has a long history of settlement dating back to prehistoric times, with signs of both Roman and Saxon occupation. Alfred the Great and his son Edward the Elder, who held the lands, gave the village and its church to the Abbot and monks of Hyde Abbey in AD 903. After the Dissolution of the Monasteries, Thomas Wriothesley, First Earl of Southampton (of Titchfield

Abbey), acquired the manor along with Hyde Abbey and built a house here, although there are no traces of it today.

Elen visits the medieval parish church of St Mary's with its unusual octagonal nave built in 1808 by the unorthodox architect George Dance Jr. As I dowsed the current partly through the bell tower into the nave, we noticed various mystical symbols carved into the masonry above a window. Having demolished Hyde Abbey, Wriothesley used some of its stone to restore St Mary's medieval tower in 1544. The rather abstract appearance of the church is due to the marrying of the large octagonal nave with a late 19th century semicircular chancel and medieval tower.

Inside, Elen connects with the font and the very elaborate marble monuments of the powerful Baring family, who became the Earls of Northbrook. We could not help but wonder if Dance was inspired by the Elen current to build this most unusual and unique nave, its shape seeming to benefit her flow as it suddenly widens through the church.

Just north of here within Laverstoke Park, Elen visits the prehistoric cemetery of Abra Barrow on the brow of a hill next to crop fields near the village of Freefolk. She also connects with the ruins of St Mary's Church on the grounds of Laverstoke House, once the site of a medieval village. Hyde Abbey held these lands and its church from early times up until the Reformation. In 1798, Joseph Portal acquired the Manor and built Laverstoke House, making use of the nearby St Mary's Church as a family vault. The Portal family built paper mills here that supplied banknotes for the Bank of England until quite recently. We were rather saddened that visitors can no longer access this delightful shrine.

Soon we were climbing the chalk downs to a curious hillfort on Ladle Hill. Archaeologists believe that this Iron Age enclosure, built on the site of an earlier Bronze Age settlement, is unfinished due to the abandoned piles of building spoil and the incomplete defensive circuit. Almost rectangular, this 7-acre hillfort has a large disc barrow to the north through which Elen passes. The circular ditched earthwork is almost identical to Flowerdown Barrow at Littleton visited earlier. Looking across the valley, we could see her next destination – the impressive earthen banks of Beacon Hill.

Beacon Hill

Beacon Hill, one of the most famous Iron Age hillforts in England, is located about 8 km (5 miles) south of Newbury overlooking the Highclere estate. Its name derives from the ancient practice of lighting fires on its summit to signal the threat of invasion and celebrate solar festivals. It was part of a long chain of beacons from St Catherine's Hill in Winchester to Uffington Castle in Berkshire located on the prehistoric Ridgeway. Crop circle enthusiasts often visit this site to view the mysterious crop formations that appear on its slopes. Unusual lights have been seen hovering over its summit and dowsers and ley hunters have discovered several paths of energy that radiate out from the hill to different parts of the country.

It was a warm summers evening when we returned to this enigmatic hill. After the exertion of the steep climb, a magnificent panoramic view over four counties greeted us. The hillfort has only one rampart outlining its unusual hourglass shape. Elen approaches the site from the direction of Ladle Hill, passing through the triangulation marker on the highest point of the summit towards the western side of the hillfort, where a most unusual sight confronted us, a grave on a mound surrounded by iron railings.

The Node is marked by the final resting place of George Edward Stanhope Molyneux Herbert (1866–1923), the famous Fifth Earl of Carnarvon of Highclere Castle, who financed the discovery of the tomb of Egyptian Pharaoh Tutankhamun made by renowned Egyptologist Howard Carter in 1922.

Lord Carnarvon, like so many of the aristocracy of that period, became interested in the occult and held many séances in the East Anglia Room at Highclere Castle. The Earl died in Egypt in 1923, after developing septicaemia from a mosquito bite shortly after the official opening of the burial chamber. Some say that his premature death was the result of an ancient curse associated with the Pharaoh's tomb. In fact the Earl disregarded a warning letter sent to him in December 1922 by a famous psychic who strongly advised him not to get involved with the tomb or 'death would claim him in Egypt'. Various stories tell that at the very moment of his passing, all the lights went out in Cairo, the clocks stopped in the castle and the Earl's pet dog keeled over and died. Under the conditions of the Earl's will, his body was placed in a coffin made from Highclere oak and buried on Beacon Hill, said to be his favourite spot overlooking his ancestral home.

As we dowsed around Carnarvon's final resting place, we soon detected the point where the two serpents crossed. The male current approaches the hillfort from Seven Barrows in the south, continues along the northerly axis of the hill, through the fort's southern entrance and then veers off in a westerly direction to join Elen near the grave. Was Lord Carnarvon emulating the ancient Chinese Emperors, whose tombs were located on the crossing of two dragon currents?

As we stood pondering over our dowsing results, I suddenly realised that the position of the Node and the grave is on the side of the hill where along with Sidown Hill the star Deneb would have appeared to skim when viewed from St Catherine's Hill around 500 BC. Was Carnarvon aware of this celestial event, choosing this place in the knowledge that it was a symbolic gateway to the afterlife? Standing on the sacred spot, we could certainly appreciate the view that Carnarvon loved so much, enhanced by the magnificent sight of Highclere Castle in the valley below with its wonderful collection of ancient and exotic trees.

Elen sweeps down from Beacon Hill and across to the wooded Sidown Hill, one of the highest hills in Hampshire. As noted earlier, it was almost certain that Sidown was revered long ago in connection with the stars of Cygnus, particularly during the period when the Iron Age hillforts were built and later during the time of Henry of Blois. There are signs of early occupation on the hill including prehistoric terracing on its slopes.

On my very first visit here in 1995, I was curious to know why this Node was so far from the alignment, over 4 km (2.5 miles) to the west. However, having recently discovered its powerful connection with St Catherine's Hill, I now understand why.

Highclere and the Wyverns

Highclere Castle is the traditional home of the Earls of Carnarvon. The Fourth Earl, better known as Lord Porchester, was a prominent Freemason who from 1833–1849 was a leading member of the Conservative party, becoming Secretary of State and a key player during the development of the British Empire. In recent times, the Seventh Earl was horseracing manager to the Queen. Today the house is famous as the setting for the hit TV drama series *Downton Abbey*.

Highclere Castle, Hampshire

During a guided tour of the castle, we were informed that an avenue of beech trees leading from the old south entrance marked a straight path that ascended Sidown Hill to a folly on its south side called 'Heaven's Gate'. Caroline and I looked at each other wide-eyed, realising the significance of this name, which alludes to this hill as a gateway to the afterlife. Interestingly, Elen visits both the 18th century folly and the castle. The guide continued to say that in earlier times family members and their guests would often walk up the grove to drink tea in the stucco-walled room inside the folly. It was first built in 1731 but collapsed shortly afterwards. All that remains today is a brick building consisting of a central arch flanked by two smaller arches either side. The design may be symbolic of the twin pillars of Freemasonry represented in many classical monuments and follies in the grounds of numerous stately homes around England.

Thomas Barry, the architect of the Houses of Parliament, built the house you see today out of Bath stone between 1838 and 1850. He transformed the old brick and freestone house into a grand Classical mansion. As we toured the interior, a statement made by the guide caused our jaws to drop, as Highclere was built over the site of a palace of the Bishops of Winchester, owners of this parish since AD 749. The earliest building recorded here was a hunting lodge, adopted by the Bishops as their summer residence in the 12th century during the time of Henry of Blois. This incredible piece of information gave us a greater insight into the knowledge held by the Benedictine monks of Winchester, which afforded them a deeper understanding of the hidden mysteries of this extraordinary landscape, including its serpent energies and its connection with the celestial bodies. Perhaps it is of no coincidence that these religious leaders chose to build their palace behind Sidown Hill.

The guide, beginning to notice our gaping mouths, further remarked that a later Bishop of Winchester, William of Wykeham, rebuilt the palace at Highclere around 1370, visiting it during his many journeys to and from his colleges of Winchester and

New College Oxford. Unfortunately, all that remains today of the medieval house is the 'Monk's Garden' where the Winchester monks grew their herbs and vegetables. Several small sarsen stones lie around the grounds close to the house, possible remnants of an important prehistoric site usurped by the Saxon Bishops of Winchester.

After the Dissolution of the Monasteries, the Bishops lost their valuable estate at Highclere to William Fitzwilliam and then to Sir Richard Kingsmill in 1572, who redesigned their palace as an Elizabethan brick mansion. Sir Robert Sawyer, attorney general to Charles II and James II, purchased the property in 1679, and eventually it passed through marriage to the Herbert family, known then as the Earls of Pembroke. Henry Herbert became the First Earl of Carnarvon in 1793, having inherited Highclere from his uncle in 1769.

The interior of the house has many carvings of winged dragons with scaly legs and a tail called Wyverns, a creature represented in the heraldic shield of the Carnarvon family. Perhaps they identified with it because according to ancient British tradition it is a symbol of strength, power and endurance. However, it is more notorious as a sign of the devil and often portrayed as hateful and loveless. In one grisly tale, the Wyvern befriends a human until it gets the taste for their blood. However, there may be a lighter angle to this story in that the Wyvern could also represent the blood of the Earth that flows through the veins or serpent lines that reside here.

Carving of wyverns on the exterior of Highclere Castle

As we surreptitiously dowsed Elen through the centre of the house, we noticed two dragons standing with their wings outstretched looking down upon her flow. She passes through the drawing room and two libraries, leaving at the northeast side of the house towards the north lawn, where according to a Hampshire archaeologist the old palace of the Bishops once stood.

Following a path through the grounds, we arrived at the splendid Cemetery Chapel built in 1855 by Sir Thomas Allom at the request of the Third Countess of Carnarvon. The interior contains richly carved pews and floor tiles each decorated with the Carnarvon crest. Our attention, however, was drawn to the curious depiction of three Grail cups featured in the finely decorated windows.

On the edge of the estate, Elen visits the parish church of St Michael and All Angels at the village of Highclere, built by Sir George Gilbert Scott in 1870 for the Fourth Earl, whose memorial is marked by two windows depicting a choir of angels. Scott also designed All Saints Church on the Isle of Wight and restored the choir screen at Winchester Cathedral.

The chalk downs are interrupted at Highclere by a Firestone or Upper Greensand ridge, which runs beneath the estate, emanating a paramagnetic force similar to the

Isle of Wight. The park has an enormous 21 km circumference and is one of Capability Brown's masterpieces. During his extensive redesign of the estate from 1774–77, the old village of Highclere was relocated.

The male current also enters the park from Beacon Hill through a prehistoric bowl barrow hidden in a plantation on the east side of the estate to visit a folly called the Temple, also known as the Rotunda. This fine piece of classical architecture stands isolated, high on the Firestone ridge surrounded by oak trees, perhaps remnants of a larger oak forest that once grew in the area. This spectacular circular sixteen-pillared domed structure dates from 1760, later modified by Barry in 1838.

The folly called the Temple in the grounds of Highclere Castle

The Temple once featured in a regular Christian festival, where members of the Herbert family and local parishioners of Highclere Church would gather after the service on Whit Sunday, which literally means 'white' or 'holy' Sunday, to walk in procession to the Temple. It was quite an occasion, when girls wore white dresses and flower-adorned hats, as was the old pagan custom. They would then meet for luncheon at the Carnarvon Arms before returning to the Temple for their festivities. It was also a meeting place for wealthy members of the Temple Club, which became the first 'Thrift Club' in Hampshire. Traditionally Thrift Clubs were a way of saving money to meet income tax bills, sharing the interest earned amongst its members.

Southwest of Highclere, the church of St James at the village of Ashmansworth stands close to the alignment, reputed to be the oldest church in Hampshire. Some believe it was the original site of a Roman building, as artefacts and pottery from that period were unearthed during excavations of the church in 1899. However, given its proximity to the old prehistoric route, it may have been a significant sacred place certainly since the Iron Age. The Bishops of Winchester held the church and manor on several occasions from 909 until 1645, eventually becoming part of Highclere Castle estate in the late 18th century. The Saxon doorway and several medieval wall paintings are of further interest.

Walbury Beacon

Elen travels west, crossing the county border of Berkshire and the ancient Wayfarer's Walk, which follows the South Hants Ridgeway, to connect with the highest chalk hill in the country capped by Walbury hillfort. Standing at 290 m (954 ft) above sea level, its outstanding views across the Kennet Valley to the north are breathtaking. The Iron Age ditch and bank enclosure is a tremendous feat of engineering by the Celtic peoples of the area. Walbury Hill, also known as Inkpen Beacon, is another link in the chain of beacons from St Catherine's Hill to Uffington hillfort further north. In 1588, a bonfire on the summit warned London of the imminent Spanish invasion, and in 1992, a

Combe Gibbet on a prehistoric long barrow

similar event here celebrated the Queen's 40th anniversary of her accession to the throne.

In order to trace the Elen current, from the east car park we walked along the track known as Wayfarer's Way, which divides the hillfort into two sections. We were aware of Elen's flow just to our right passing through the enclosure to the remains of a Neolithic long barrow, on top of which is Combe Gibbet, a 7.6 m (25 ft) high wooden hanging cross. In the 17th century, a man and his lover murdered his wife and son while they were crossing the downs. A local witnessed the ghastly deed, which resulted in the arrest of these murderers and a death sentence. Their bodies were seen hanging from the gibbet for several months afterwards as a deterrent to others.

As Elen approaches the long barrow and gibbet, her flow suddenly splits to pass either side of the mound and then returns to a single flow, as if to avoid the gruesome structure. We were convinced that before the erection of the gibbet, Elen's flow through this long barrow would have been unhindered. This was the first occasion we had witnessed a splitting of a current; a similar division occurs on the Mary current dowsed by Hamish Miller through Glastonbury Abbey in Somerset. Here she separates to avoid or encompass something not apparent on the ground surface. The violent act of death by hanging at this megalithic place of power has obviously left a detrimental stain at this site. The gibbet may have been a deterrent for criminals long ago, but its continued presence here provides a constant reminder of its gruesome function, the dark memory kept alive by radiating negative energy across the landscape.

In a field to the northwest of the hillfort, a magnificent crop formation of a serpent appeared on the 29 July 2011. Some believe the 213 m (700 ft) image represents Quetzalcoatl, the 'feathered serpent', god of ancient Central America, or the yin and yang serpent. We had a sense that its location was significant, set below Walbury in the nearest suitable crop field to the flow of the female serpent. To us, it appears to represent the balance of the male and female dragon energies symbolised by the crescent-moon-shaped head and the sun in its tail. Perhaps this symbol of balance is a sign of the energetic requirements of the

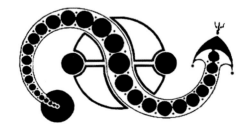

Crop formation that appeared in a field below Walbury hillfort, July 2011

site, now distorted by the gibbet, on an ancient sanctuary of the goddess.

In open farmland below the hillfort, now in the county of Berkshire, we followed Elen to a long mound, once part of the great earthwork known as Wansdyke, constructed by the Saxons around the 5th or 6th century. It once stretched all the way to the Bristol Channel, having formed a border or barrier to defend newly acquired land from the Britons. It is quite possible that one of the great battles fought by the warrior Arthur against the Saxons occurred in the vicinity of this earthwork border.

Many hilltop churches dedicated to St Michael were built over pagan places of worship marking the dragon force. St Michael's at Inkpen in the Kennet Valley is no exception. Roger de Ingpen, a Knights Templar, built the little church on a raised platform of land here in 1220. Two images of St Michael slaying the dragon overlook the path of Elen as she passes through the church. In the sanctuary are two Templar grave slabs. One is an extremely worn stone effigy lying next to the High Altar, the resting

place of Sir Roger de Ingpen. He is dressed in the typical Knights Templar chainmail and surcoat, holding a shield in one hand and grasping his sword in the other. As we explored the churchyard, we found a piece of a standing stone and another portion of a Templar grave slab. The mystical order of the Knights Templar held several acres of land in this region and possibly planted the purple crocuses in a nearby field that still bloom in spring today.

The alignment passes close to two churches within sight of Walbury hillfort, one dedicated to St Lawrence of Canterbury at West Woodhay and the other to St Martin at East Woodhay. From medieval times, a fair held at Woodhay took place on the first three days of February to celebrate the feast day of St Lawrence. The 14th century church at West Woodhay contains several handsome windows produced by William Morris's company, including the east window of the Crucifixion designed by Edward Burne-Jones. This great Pre-Raphaelite artist is renowned for his mystical allegorical themes of the Celtic King Arthur and the Grail and here the cross represents a tree, symbolic of the world tree.

East Woodhay has a long history of settlement and, according to local tradition, was the site of yet another palace of the Bishops of Winchester. Although the church is a Victorian brick restoration, there has been a place of worship here since the 12th century. The Hospital of St Cross near Winchester acquired the church from this time up until the Reformation. Henry of Blois may have founded the original church here and built the Bishop's palace on a site just north of the church near Heath End. Archaeological surveys have been unable to reveal the true purpose of this site; however, foundations of extensive buildings and a road were found. Inside the church we noticed a stained-glass window of Bishop William Wykeham and a modern window with a magnificent depiction of St George and the Dragon.

The 12th century St Mary's Church at Kintbury is also close to the alignment on the site of a Saxon abbey. Written records imply that it was 'a holy place' but it seems to have disappeared after the Norman invasion.

Another church of St Lawrence perches on the banks of the Kennet River in the town of Hungerford. When the 12th century church collapsed in 1816, restoration changed its design from Norman to Georgian Gothic using Bath stone. Elen flows north–south through the semicircular apse of the church across the High Altar. Her path is marked in the churchyard on the south side by a curious piece of ironstone possibly placed there to fix the current after the later restoration. Before the Reformation, a chantry chapel once stood on this spot built in 1325 by Sir Robert de Hungerford in memory of his wife Geva, his mutilated stone effigy still lies within the church.

As we strolled around the town, I recalled the dreadful events that happened here a few years ago. The massacre at the hands of a crazed gunman sent shock waves through the community and would certainly have affected the Elen current at the time.

In the county of Wiltshire, 2.4 km (1.5 miles) northwest of Hungerford, Elen visits a gigantic 450-year-old London plane tree in the delightfully rustic village of Chilton Foliat, a hybrid of one that grew in the streets of England's capital. Close by is the old church of St Mary, dating from Saxon times and restored by the Gothic Revivalist Benjamin Ferrey in 1845. We nicknamed St Mary's 'the Church of Angels' because of its numerous carved winged figures around the walls, their gentle gaze seemed to follow us as we dowsed Elen through the chancel and a stone effigy of a knight.

Membury Camp, another large Iron Age enclosure, has an interior covering an impressive 34 acres. Its date of construction is uncertain, due to its partial excavation, although several Mesolithic and Neolithic finds uncovered here indicate a site of great antiquity. Elen enters the southern entrance, passing through a pool before leaving through the northwest corner.

It was only recently that I discovered that a crop circle had appeared in 2002 on the path of Elen between Chilton Foliat and Membury, in a field near the village of Crooked Soley. The formation measured around 91 m (300 ft), its design consisting of 1296 curved squares of which 504 were left standing upright. Experts believe it represents the human mitochondrial DNA and secrets of sacred measure described by Plato as the 'Heavenly Measure'.

The book *Crooked Soley: A Crop Circle Revelation* by Harpur *et al.* (2005) explores all aspects of this formation and its implications as regards the crop circle phenomenon. The authors suggest that:

'Behind the crop circle phenomenon is an evident purpose. Some intelligence, human, alien, or spiritual, is in the process of communication. It is exposing us to a course of re-education, beginning with the symbols of sacred knowledge and wisdom. The most striking evidence for this is the amazing formation that appeared at Crooked Soley in Wiltshire on 27 August 2002. Clearly expressed in its design are certain numerical symbols that are known esoterically as the "Keys to Creation". They are also keys to that universal science associated with the Holy Grail.'

The Battle of Badon Hill

Elen's brief incursion into Wiltshire takes her through the valley below the hilltop village of Baydon, an Old English name meaning 'hill of blackberries'. The village is the second highest in Wiltshire at 230 m (754 ft) above sea level and evolved from an ancient settlement next to the Roman road called Ermine Street. A 6th century wrist clasp excavated here implies that this ancient thoroughfare continued into Saxon times.

According to the 9th century Welsh monk Nennius in his *Historia Brittonum*, the warrior Arthur fought his most decisive battle on Badon Hill against the Saxons:

'The twelfth battle was on Badon Hill and in it nine hundred and sixty men fell in one day, from a single charge of Arthur's and no one laid them low save he alone; and he was victorious in all his campaigns.'

The Welsh Annals from the *Harleian MS 3859* (Phillimore 1888) cite:

'The battle of Badon, in which Arthur carried the cross of our Lord Jesus Christ for three days and three nights on his shoulders and the Britons were the victors.'

Gildas, the prophet of the British people, wrote in *Ruin of Britain*, published in AD 540, that the victory at Badon Hill took place in AD 498. There is no doubt that the Britons retain a strong memory of a conflict between Arthur's forces and the Saxons at a site then called Badon Hill around the beginning of the 6th century. If this is the case then

Arthur's victory at Badon Hill must have been decisive, for the *Anglo-Saxon Chronicle* records that for the next 50 years there were no Saxon victories in Britain.

The real location of Badon Hill remains a mystery, for the site and the memory of the battle has drifted into myth and legend. Certainly, the conquering Saxons would wish to forget this humiliating defeat and avoid recording its true location. Today, Arthurian researchers suggest various sites for this battle, including Solsbury Hill near Bath in Somerset, Baedon Hill near Margam Park in Glamorgan, Badbury Rings near Wimborne in Dorset and Badbury Hill near Liddington Castle in Wiltshire. The generally accepted view is that the battle had to be somewhere along the natural defensive barrier of the prehistoric ridgeway between Dorset and Cambridge, making Badbury Hill in Wiltshire the most likely candidate. However, historians have frequently overlooked this site despite being less than 3.2 km (2 miles) from the Ridgeway in Wiltshire. Furthermore, it is next to a major Roman road that was still in use after the Romans departed. Perhaps evidence for this battle lies hidden in the remnants of ditches on the slopes of the hill, said to be part of ancient fortifications.

Lord Craven's Temple of Diana

Along the ancient track known today as the Oxfordshire Circular Walk, we followed the female dragon to the extraordinarily beautiful Ashdown Park, once the historical seat of the Craven family. Elen veers off from her north–south course on the edge of the estate to visit a most unusual house designed in the Dutch style. The First Earl of Craven, a loyal supporter of Charles I, built this three-storey building as a hunting lodge in the mid-17th century for his beloved Princess Elizabeth of Bohemia. Elizabeth was the granddaughter of Mary Queen of Scots and sister to Charles I. We noticed on the map that this rather lonely romantic building is set within an ancient ritual landscape that includes several Bronze Age barrows and an Iron Age hillfort called Alfred's Castle. Some historians believe Ashdown House was designed and built by a pupil of Inigo Jones, whilst others suggest that it was Sir Balthazar Gerbier and William Winde who had previously designed Lord Craven's other homes at Hamstead Marshall in Berkshire and Coombe Abbey near Coventry.

Dowsing Elen around the exterior of the house revealed some surprising results. She enters the building from the southwest and leaves through the northwest corner, having made a 90-degree turn somewhere inside the house, but what had led to this strange behaviour had yet to be uncovered.

To access Ashdown House we joined a large group for a guided tour. Although this made dowsing its interior almost impossible, it was most informative. The guide mentioned that the estate was originally a deer park called Aysham created by the Abbot of Glastonbury in medieval times. After the Dissolution of the Monasteries, the Essex family acquired the lands and a hunting lodge. The Craven family bought the estate in 1625 with monies amassed by Sir William Craven, the father of the First Earl, having risen from a humble Yorkshire cloth trader to become Lord Mayor of London in 1610.

In 1661, during the time of the Great Plague in London, William is said to have left the city on horseback barely escaping with his life, having ridden across the country slumped in his saddle until he reached his Ashdown estate. Impressed with his inherited lands, he decided to build a house over the site of the earlier hunting lodge for Princess Elizabeth. Unfortunately, she died of smallpox before its completion.

Lord Craven first met and fell in love with Princess Elizabeth when he led an English army supporting her husband Frederick V of Bohemia in a bid to regain the lost lands of Palatinate. According to Frances Yates in *The Rosicrucian Enlightenment*, 'a culture was forming in the Palatinate which came straight out of the Renaissance but with more recent trends added … a Rosicrucian State with its court centred on Heidelberg'. Frederick was soon persuaded by anonymous Rosicrucians to take the throne from the ousted Catholic Ferdinand of Austria in 1618. He and Elizabeth were known as the 'Winter King and Queen' because of their extraordinarily short rule. Their failed attempt to secure the throne of Bohemia led to more conflict in Europe, which eventually evolved into the Thirty Years War.

After Frederick's premature death, Craven remained loyal to Elizabeth and provided financial support for her and her family whilst in exile at the court of William of Orange. Her brother Charles I meanwhile was embroiled in the Civil War against Cromwell. After the restoration of Charles II in 1660, Elizabeth returned to England where Lord Craven ran her household and acted as her chaperone, leading to a story that they had secretly married. Although there is no evidence to support this, she did bequeath most of her estate to him, including her paintings. Although the tour is restricted to the three-storey staircase, several of the family portraits inherited by Lord Craven lined the walls. We were drawn to one particular painting called 'Star of the North' portraying Elizabeth's daughter, also called Elizabeth, who, rather than being dressed for a pageant as the guide suggested, was attired in what we felt was ceremonial apparel more akin to that of a priestess.

We also noticed a 19th century engraving of the house standing within an oak forest showing tree-lined avenues radiating out in all four cardinal directions. The deliberate placing of these avenues and the layout of the house with its roof capped with a golden dome, seemed to us a symbolic representation of a temple to Diana, a Roman goddess associated with woodland groves and the hunt.

According to some authorities, the First Earl Craven was also a member of the mystical Rosicrucian order whose plan was to groom the young Elizabeth to be the future Protestant European queen and rule over a new Golden Age of Enlightenment. However, the Catholic Gunpowder Plotters, who failed to blow up the Houses of Parliament in 1605, planned to kidnap Elizabeth and crown her as the Stuart Queen of the Catholics. An omen of this 'New Age' was the appearance at the time of two new stars in the constellations of Cygnus and Serpentarius.

Elen sweeps across the grounds to visit Alfred's Castle, a bank and ditch earthwork enclosing over 2.5 acres of land. This is a rare example of an Iron Age domestic fortified dwelling reused by the Romans who built a villa here. Its name is an 18th century addition, initiated by local antiquarians in an attempt to associate the site with the famous Battle of Ashdown, fought between the Saxons and the Danes in AD 871. King Alfred, whose capital was Winchester, mustered his Saxon troops here prior to battle, which he won decisively, placing him firmly on the throne of England. Recent Saxon finds including swords, spearheads and javelins may substantiate the claim made by early antiquarians.

Standing on the earthwork, bathed in the warmth of the summer sun, we lingered for a while mesmerised by the splendid views of the house below and the surrounding cornfields. At its centre, Elen crosses over an earthwork, possibly the remains of a building, and then heads north towards the famous prehistoric Ridgeway, the oldest thoroughfare in England. During later research of this site, I learned that its stones were used to provide the foundations of the original hunting lodge built by the monks of Glastonbury. This may provide the answer of what lured the female serpent away from her usual north–south flow.

Many of the fields to the east of Ashdown House are littered with ancient weathered stones, many of them sarsen. Local folklore says that after the nearby battle of Badon Hill, possibly the village of Baydon referred to earlier, Merlin pursued his Saxon enemies through the valley and, having caught up with them, used his magic to transform them into stone. Local farmers believed that the stones floated to the surface, because when they returned to a field they had recently ploughed, they found that huge boulders had appeared where there was none before. Perhaps Lord Craven knew that the power of these mysterious stones would enhance his mystical Temple of Diana, no doubt further improved by the proximity of the St Michael alignment just south of here at Fognam Farm.

Elen continues north towards the Ridgeway and targets one of the most famous Neolithic long barrows in the country, set close to the Uffington prehistoric sanctuary, which includes Dragon Hill and the oldest chalk-cut figure in Britain.

A Palace for the Winter Queen

Leaving the Uffington complex for later scrutiny, we retraced our journey back to the Temple at Highclere. We detected the male current entering Great Pen Wood, on the border of Berkshire, to the village of Enborne and the church of St Michael and All Angels.

The church stands on an elevated position above the Highclere estate with extensive views to the south, its earliest masonry dating from the mid-12th century. A place of worship has existed here since Saxon times when the manor was in the ownership of Edward the Confessor (1042–66). Belinus passes through the stone font with its finely carved heads, said to be Saxon, and two rare 14th century wall paintings decorating the chancel, one depicting the annunciation.

Hamstead Marshall, the former 300 acre estate of the Earls of Craven, nestles in the picturesque Kennet Valley. The presence of three large mounds located at the northern end of this great parkland, said to be the remains of motte and bailey castles, emphasises its historical importance. The two mounds closest to the church of St Mary near the old Bath to London road are all that remains of the Marshall family estate created in Norman times; the other is half a mile to the east, standing near the Saxon fishponds. The path of Belinus connects with all three of the mounds, which for some reason remain unexcavated. This leaves us to surmise that they may have been prehistoric mounds later utilised by the Marshalls for their motte and bailey castles. During the Civil War John Marshall held the estate for Empress Matilda when she was fighting her cousin King Stephen for the throne of England.

Stephen, the brother of Henry of Blois, besieged the castle here for two months in

One of the mounds at Hamstead Marshall

1153 until Marshall surrendered it by force to the King's troops. He also handed over his eldest son William as a hostage to ensure loyalty. Many times, Stephen threatened to kill poor William, suggesting various gruesome methods. Through sheer courage and determination, William survived this common ordeal to become the Earl of Pembroke and Protector of England after the death of King John; his descendants are the Herbert family, who later became the Earls of Carnarvon of Highclere.

William Marshall also fought in the Crusades in the Holy Land alongside the Knights Templar, promising to end his days amongst them. Some believe he was inducted into the mystical order on his deathbed; an effigy of him can be seen in the famous Temple Church in London. By the 14th century, the estate had transferred to the Crown and Edward III used it as a Christmas retreat in the 1350s.

In Tudor times, the manor passed to Sir Thomas Parry, as a reward for his loyal service to Queen Elizabeth I, having supported her while under house arrest, ordered by her sister Queen Mary. He built a fine Tudor mansion at Hamstead Marshall, and according to an old tale, young Elizabeth often visited to enjoy its hunting grounds.

In a book called *Kennet Country*, Fred S. Thacker describes how Hamstead Marshall became the scene of a grisly sacrifice or murder in 1575. A midwife assisted in a mysterious delivery there: 'A healthy baby girl was born and then, to the midwife's horror, cast upon the fire. The midwife was first paid and then poisoned. She died six days later, but on her deathbed she told her dreadful tale, naming Queen Elizabeth I as the mother' (Thacker 1932). Although it is unlikely that Elizabeth would have given birth at the age of 45, it is not impossible and, if exposed, this certainly would have tarnished her reputation as England's Virgin Queen.

The Elizabethan house eventually became a ruin probably at the hands of Parliamentarian troops stationed in the area during the Battle of Newbury. In 1620, the widowed mother of the First Lord Craven bought the estate for him and, soon after, he began the mammoth task of building a grand palace here for Elizabeth, Empress of Bohemia. Interestingly her famous son Prince Rupert and his cavaliers fought in the Battle of Newbury against the Parliamentarians on the edge of the estate close to the church at Enborne (Stokes 1996). Perhaps the strange and rather eerie atmosphere we felt here is due to the great number of lives lost on the battlefield, the stain of battle having left a residual energy within the land.

Craven commissioned the eccentric Dutch architect Sir Balthasar Gerbier to design it as a miniature version of Heidelberg Castle, Princess Elizabeth's old home and the Rosicrucian centre in the Palatine. Although Elizabeth died of smallpox before construction work had even started, the Earl still continued with the project and by 1663 began to erect the building as a monument to her memory. After the death of Gerbier, Captain William Winde became the overseer of the project, taking another 35 years to build it, although the new mansion looked nothing like Elizabeth's former castle now in Germany.

The second Lord Craven preferred the family's Warwickshire estates, but his son William returned to Hamstead only to see the great mansion destroyed by fire in 1718. He dreamed of rebuilding it and engaged James Gibbs to undertake the work, but by the time of his death in 1739 the house remained unfinished. The fate of the house suffered a further blow when his brother Fulwar favoured the adjoining lodge, rebuilding it as a small mansion. Today the gateposts are all that survive from Lord Craven's grand gesture to Princess Elizabeth; the most easily accessible are those viewed from the churchyard.

The Belinus current connects with two of the mysterious mottes or mounds now standing in a private garden, rather than the site of the mansion and the church. Intriguingly, Lord Craven built both Ashdown House on the female current and Hamstead Marshall next to the male current as a memorial to Princess Elizabeth. Did his association with the mystical Rosicrucian order provide him with the knowledge of the serpent power existing at these sites, or is it just divine coincidence?

The existence of three motte and bailey sites so close together is an enigma. However, the presence of the male serpent may indicate their original purpose as ritual monuments serving the environment. They all stand close to a major fault, where the diamagnetic chalk downs to the south and the paramagnetic clay landscape to the north clash to form the Kennet Valley. Fault lines produce subtle energies, as mentioned previously, and the prehistoric mounds constructed on these faults were accumulators of the terrestrial energy that released orgone across the landscape to help fertilise the soil at significant times of the solar year.

The Wickham Beacon and the Shroud Crop Circles

North of Hamstead Marshall on a hill overlooking the village of Wickham is a curious church dedicated to St Swithun of Winchester, built over a Roman camp and beacon site. Ceadwalla, the Saxon King of Wessex, granted Wickham to the monastery at

Abingdon in AD 686, its monks building a chapel of ease there. The chapel has thick walls of flint and mortar with a Saxon tower built apart from the nave, considered the oldest in Berkshire. Although restored in Victorian times, many parts of the tower retain original stonework. The male current seems to enjoy connecting with beacon sites and hilltop towers and here he passes through at a 45-degree angle. The Saxon builders reused many Roman tiles in the fabric, but the site may date from an earlier period indicated by Iron Age pottery finds nearby.

Numerous treasures adorn its interior, including eight impressive papier-mâché elephants brought here from the Paris Exhibition in 1862 by William Nicholson. Sir Giles Gilbert Scott, grandson of Sir George Gilbert Scott, designed two ornate pew ends in the centre aisle. The fabulous elaborate font cover is also a priceless piece of design, displayed at the famous Crystal Palace Exhibition in 1862. By the door on the path of the current is a mysterious ancient stone said to be a stonemason's reject. This reminded me of a biblical Freemasonic tale, where a large cumbersome stone, rejected by the builders of the Temple of Solomon, eventually becomes its main cornerstone. Perhaps this strange stone of an uncertain date had significance for the local stonemasons who placed it here as the cornerstone of St Swithun's Church and its ancient tower.

Belinus passes through isolated fields either side of the M4 where two mysterious crop formations appeared in July 2010 called the Shroud Crop Circles. They materialised literally a couple of days after we had visited the area while dowsing the male current. Both depict one-half of a stylised or digitalised face of a man with a beard. When placed one on top of the other, they seem to represent the face of Christ, similar to that of the Turin Shroud, hence their name. Why they appeared so close to a busy motorway in an area never visited by the circle-makers before is unusual to say the least. Was the power of the male Belinus current directly involved with the manifestation of the crop circles? The Field Reports indicate that this beautifully crafted formation was far too sophisticated to have been manmade. However, if human circle-makers were responsible for this creation, why did they choose these particular fields? Was it divine inspiration or was the male serpent subconsciously communicating with them?

In Wiltshire, many crop formations have appeared over the years on both the Michael

St Mary's Church, Great Shefford

and Mary currents as well as on the alignment, although I later discovered that just as many have appeared on the Belinus alignment and currents in Hampshire since the 1980s.

Standing in the grounds of East Shefford House by the River Lambourn, the tiny redundant church of St Thomas has attracted Christian worshippers since 1100. Belinus visits this tiny building, which contains a Norman font and medieval wall paintings. Continuing along the Lambourn Valley, Belinus enters the tower of St Mary's Church on the banks of the river at Great Shefford.

The tower, with its unusual tubular flint design and octagonal parapet, similar to an Irish Round Tower, is attached to a fine Transitional Norman church.

An avenue of lime trees, of which 19 remain of the original 24, flanks the path towards the entrance of the church. According to the official village website, there have been settlers here since AD 400 and an early Saxon graveyard discovered in 1890 contained 95 burials. St Mary's retains many of its 13th century features including a carved foliated font.

At East Garston, the current visits All Saints' Church on the outskirts of the village. Positioned close to the alignment, it stands on land once held by Edward the Confessor. The Victorian building that replaced an earlier chapel retains the 12th century doorways and many pieces of fine masonry including a relief carving of a St Lorraine Cross below a medieval head.

Positioned precisely on the alignment south of here is Templars Farm at Shefford Woodlands. A number of Knights Templar churches appear on or very close to the alignment, but they established this particular building as a pilgrim's rest house.

Ancient Lambourn and the Megaliths

Belinus visits yet another ancient church in the Lambourn Valley, although this one was a Saxon minster built over a pagan sanctuary. The Michael or male current dowsed by Hamish Miller passes just south of Lambourn, between the church of St Michael at Aldbourne and the two tumuli near South Fawley. The actual St Michael alignment passes just northwest of the town through Upper Lambourn 2.4 km (1.5 miles) away. As the Belinus alignment is only 2.9 km (1.8 miles) northeast of Lambourn, it is the nearest town and settlement to the crossing of these two great alignments next to a large complex of burial mounds called Seven Barrows.

The church of St Michael and All Angels in the middle of the town of Lambourn is said to have one of the greatest 12th century naves in England, although it may date back to the 9th century, as King Alfred mentions Lambourn in his last will and testament. By 1032, it had become the local minster, serving several villages in the area under charter from King Canute. The land was later granted to the Dean of St Paul's Cathedral in London who remained its patron until 1836. The present parish church is mostly of Norman cruciform design dating from about 1180 and features fine carvings of foliated heads and winged dragons on the capitals of the tower arches and in the north aisle.

Whilst tracking the male current outside the church, I came across many ancient uncut sarsen stones, probably prehistoric, both in the boundary wall of the churchyard and in the church's foundations. The circular shape of the original churchyard is still apparent on the north side and may be the remains of a prehistoric site such as a stone circle. Many St Michael churches superseded those of early pagan temples, as Miller and Broadhurst found on their journey along the St Michael alignment.

Belinus enters from the east, marked by a sarsen stone, and continues along the length of the church close to a pillar under the tower carved with a wonderful Green Man.

He leaves through the magnificent Norman doorway at the west end carved in the Celtic style with its worn serpent heads and gruesome human faces, reminiscent of carvings found at Kilpeck Church near Hereford. Perhaps the stonemasons were alluding to the serpent energy here. One of the foundation stones, possibly from the stone circle, lies at the north corner of the west wall to the left of the Norman doorway. The church also includes a fine stained-glass window of St Michael slaying the dragon.

After chatting to a parishioner during one of our visits, we discovered that the church had attracted several incidences of negative activity. The residents, frustrated by the excessive drinking and drug-taking by local youths congregating

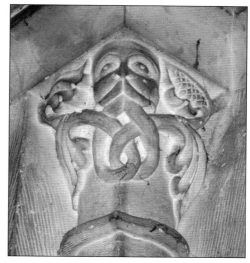

Green Man inside St Michael and All Angels Church, Lambourn

around a laurel tree in the churchyard, cut down the tree to stop any further problems. To make matters worse thieves stole an early stone-carved head from the church, having deliberately cut it from its mounting. Incredibly, it was a divine moment of

Megalithic corner stone at St Michael and All Angels Church, possibly from a stone circle

good fortune that a Lambourn resident spotted the head for sale on a market stall at Portobello in London and it now resides once more in the church, safely installed in its old location. Unfortunately, like so many churches these days, entry is now only possible for a few minutes after services.

Just to the north of the church Belinus passes through a residential estate, once the site of Lambourn Place, a large Tudor mansion owned by Sir Thomas Essex who died in 1558, said to be the site of King Alfred the Great's Palace. If this early tradition is true, then Alfred built his palace close to the crossing of the St Michael Line and the Belinus Line. Perhaps his success at becoming overall king of the Saxons in England was due to his esoteric knowledge of the land and its places of power.

Belinus continues across the downs along an ancient track heading for the curiously named Hangman's Stone. According to local folklore, this upright megalith is associated with a sheep stealer who while resting on the stone accidentally strangled himself, having tethered himself to his sheep by placing a cord around his neck; his ghost is still said to haunt the area.

The high banks of the lane leading to and from the megalith indicate an ancient route worn over millennia by horses and travelling pilgrims. Perhaps they used this track to travel between the stone circle at Lambourn, now St Michael and All Angels Church, and the Uffington White Horse, passing the Hangman's Stone, which acted as a prehistoric marker.

One and a half kilometres northwest of the Hangman's Stone, near a cluster of Bronze Age mounds called the Seven Barrows, is the crossing of the Belinus alignment and the St Michael alignment. This prehistoric cemetery has at least twenty-six barrows of different types and aerial photographs have captured shadows of many more in the neighbouring fields. Excavations of the mounds uncovered a ceremonial battle-axe, a mace-head made of antler horns and gold and amber jewellery. The site is similar to the barrow field just south of Highclere Castle and interestingly shares the same name. This may be allegorical, for within occult circles seven is a magical number. Perhaps in the case of these burials, seven represents the number of initiatory levels, the mastering of which allows one to gain entry to the afterlife, crucial to both the worshippers of Mithras, or Baal-Astarte associated with the Sumerian god Bel, and Christian religion. Where better to have such a place than the crossing point of the pagan north–south Belinus alignment and the Christianised St Michael Line.

Just as significant to this site however, are the seven stars in the constellation of Draco, the Dragon, and the Plough or Ursula Major. During the Bronze Age these particular stars, which symbolically guard the Pole star, appeared lower in the sky skimming the hills to the north of here.

Belinus passes through a Bronze Age mound called Idlebush Barrow or Wade's Barrow, named after the giant said to be the father of the legendary Wayland, a Norse blacksmith god. We now realised that both currents were drawing together as they approach the great prehistoric centre of Uffington, which includes Uffington Castle hillfort, a highly stylised chalk-cut figure of a horse and most curious of all, Dragon Hill.

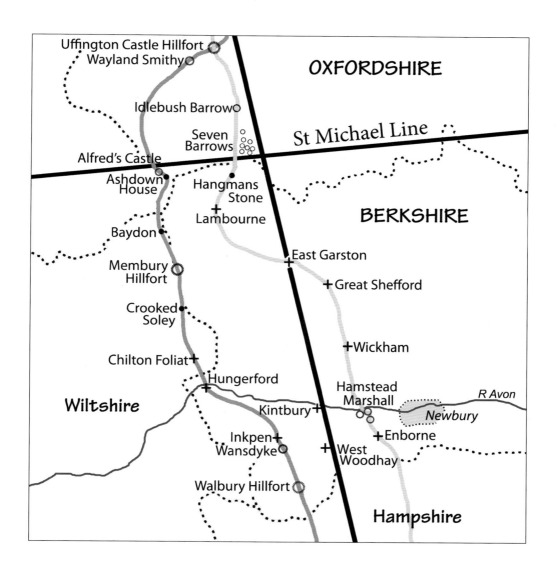

OXFORDSHIRE

St Michael Line

BERKSHIRE

Uffington Castle Hillfort
Wayland Smithy

Idlebush Barrow

Seven
Barrows

Alfred's Castle

Ashdown
House

Hangmans
Stone

Lambourne

Baydon

Membury
Hillfort

East Garston

Great Shefford

Crooked
Soley

Chilton Foliat

Wickham

Hungerford

Wiltshire

Kintbury

Hamstead
Marshall

R Avon

Newbury

Inkpen
Wansdyke

Enborne

Walbury Hillfort

West
Woodhay

Hampshire

Chapter 5

The Oxfordshire Spirit Path
Knights, Dragons and Elves

Uffington, a Prehistoric Ritual Centre

'Walk here as a pilgrim, for this is holy ground.'
(G.K. Chesterton 1911)

The Vale of the White Horse has scattered landmarks of earth and stone, silent sentinels that have survived for thousands of years as vestiges of a great civilisation. This complex of prehistoric monuments has been a mystery to archaeologists and historians for centuries. Could the dowsing of Elen and Belinus here help to uncover some of its secrets?

In May 1989, Hamish Miller and Paul Broadhurst were tracking the Mary current through the Vale, hopeful that she would lead them to either Dragon Hill or the chalk-cut prehistoric figure. Instead, Mary curved around the complex to the parish church of Uffington 2.4 km (1.5 miles) to the north. The Michael current also avoids the sacred area, passing 9.5 km (6 miles) to the south between the villages of Aldbourne and South Fawley. Miller and Broadhurst found the behaviour of the currents intriguing, as if they were deliberately avoiding the prehistoric centre and yet enclosing it at the same time (see p 503).

Our research of the Uffington complex has been complied over many years of careful exploration, but my first ever visit to this beautiful area of the Berkshire Downs was on a cool spring morning in 1994. As I was driving west along the narrow road

View looking along the 'Oxfordshire Spirit Path'
from Uffington White Horse

from Kingston Lisle to the White Horse, I started to focus my senses on detecting the dragon currents of the Belinus alignment. Passing below the chalk figure, I immediately sensed something powerful that sent a shiver through my body. I stopped the car and with dowsing rods confirmed it was the Belinus current. After leaving the car in the parking area, I continued to follow him towards a distinctive flat-topped cone-shaped eminence called Dragon Hill.

Approaching the steep-sided mound from the south, its shape seemed reminiscent of Silbury Hill in the prehistoric complex of Avebury in Wiltshire, although considerably smaller and carved out of the landscape rather than constructed. The serpents of the Belinus line have visited many large mounds so far on this journey, both natural and manmade, but this one seems impressive. Geologists refer to it as a natural chalk mound that man has sculptured in ancient times to give it a level summit.

After climbing up the chalk-cut steps on its south side to the level platform, I walked across to the bare patch of chalk, where according to legend the dragon spilled its blood. Close to the spot where grass never grows, I found a Node of Elen and Belinus. The dowsing rods detected a pattern or signature of a six-pointed star, as well as a vortex of spiralling energy radiating out from the Node to the edge of the mound.

The Bronze Age peoples who developed the Uffington complex obviously levelled the summit of Dragon Hill for a specific purpose. It reminded me of an Aztec or Toltec pyramid I had visited in Mexico. The top of the pyramids have a levelled summit for the high priests to perform ceremony, including gruesome sacrifices where the spilling of blood was vital to appease the gods, who controlled the weather and therefore the harvest.

Above the hill, cut into the turf on the side of the downs is the elegant yet simple chalk figure of a creature in full gallop with an overly long body and tail measuring 110 m (374 ft). Although many refer to it as a horse, it has an extremely long neck with a small almost rounded head and a beak, giving it the appearance of a dragon.

According to legend, St George killed a dragon here and in honour of this heroic deed the locals carved its effigy into the chalk hillside. Another legend informs us that Uther Pendragon, emperor of Britain and father of the King Arthur of the medieval

romances, died here and was buried with great ceremony under Dragon Hill. Local folklore says that the horse was cut to celebrate King Arthur's most famous battle at Badon Hill, possibly fought a few miles south of here at Baydon Hill, visited earlier in Wiltshire. Another local tale attributes the horse to King Alfred's victory over the Danes in AD 871, said to have been fought nearby at Ashdown Park, whilst others believe it marks a victory for Hengist, the Saxon king, in the 5th century.

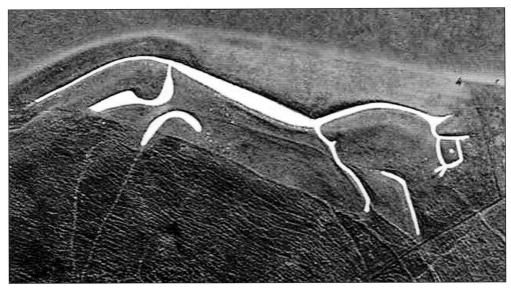

'Before the Gods that made the Gods, Had seen their sunrise pass. The White Horse of the White Horse veil was cut out of the grass.' (G.K. Chesterton 1911)

The latest dating techniques carried out at the figure in the 1990s gave a much earlier date than many historians and archaeologists expected. Optical stimulated luminescence (OSL) dating, which measures when minerals were last exposed to sunlight, was used to test the area between the lower layers of the chalk trenches that form the outline of the horse. Results gave dates ranging from 1400–600 BC, suggesting its origin dates back to the late Bronze Age, making it the oldest hill figure in Britain. Perhaps the tales of the famous kings cutting the horse after a great victory refer to the re-cutting or scouring of the figure as part of a national celebration.

Many historians and researchers are convinced that the chalk-cut figure at Uffington is a horse. However, given that the new dating of the figure is earlier than most people had previously thought, did the Bronze Age peoples idolise the horse to such a degree that they would carve it into a hillside?

Up until the Romans introduced the Arab breed of horse into Britain, the native variety were the Exmoor and the Welsh Mountain Ponies standing no higher than 11–13 hands high, bred mainly for meat and carrying heavy burdens. After 1066, the Normans introduced to Britain the war horse or charger, bred specifically for the purpose of carrying men wearing heavy armour, and it is from these breeds that our heavy horse derives. During the time of Charles II, crossbreeding continued in this country to refine the riding horse, creating the thoroughbred that became fashionable when those in high society wanted to be seen riding out in parks on fine horses.

The White Dragon

Given the late arrival of the large horse to this country and the unlikely probability that the Bronze Age people would honour their pack pony in this manner, perhaps the creature portrayed across the chalk downs really is a dragon. Over the centuries, locals have maintained that the Uffington figure was a portrait of the dragon slain by St George on nearby Dragon Hill.

Although similar reptilian creatures to a dragon existed during the dinosaur age, they died out millions of years ago. They do survive, however, as potent symbols in many prehistoric aboriginal and Eastern cultures. The Chinese and Japanese revered the dragon, or *lung*, as a creature that represents fertility and the four elements – earth, wind, fire and water. It was a symbol of imperial and supernatural power associated with rain-making. In esoteric teachings, it represents the path to enlightenment and hidden knowledge.

Unlike Western traditions, which regard the dragon as evil, the Eastern dragons are wise, sacred and beneficial. Temples and shrines were built to honour them as they controlled the forces of nature, nourishing the earth with rainwater and the warmth from the sun. There are nine major Chinese dragons, but the most powerful is the horned dragon, which has the ability to produce rain in parched lands. The Uffington dragon also has horns and was first cut during a period when the south of England experienced a warmer and drier climate at the end of the Bronze Age. Perhaps the pre-Celtic population of Berkshire had a similar reverence to the symbolic dragon of the Chinese, carving its image into the landscape to invoke rain.

The dragon is common in British folklore in many parts of the country, their lair found at mounds, caves and lakes, all places that attract orgone. Interestingly, the hill figure lies next to the great southern ridge of chalk that stretches across England between the coasts of Devon and Norfolk called 'The Ridgeway'. Along its course, especially in the region between Avebury and Uffington, is another fault of Firestone or 'Dragon's Food', properly called Upper Greensand. As mentioned in Chapter 1, the Upper Greensand fault along the backbone of the Isle of Wight may be responsible for the many supernatural events recorded on the island, particularly around the tumuli or burial mounds that attract orgone energy from the upper atmosphere and draw telluric energy from below to produce rain. At Uffington, we have a rain-making dragon in close proximity to the Firestone fault, in a region littered with prehistoric mounds.

Another aspect of dragon legends is that they menace the local population until a brave knight comes to their rescue by killing it. John Michell reminds us of the numerous stories of dragon slaying found in many cultures around the world. Its true origins, however, lie within the principles of fertility. As an annual process, the Chinese saw the dragon as being produced from a seed born from the Earth, fertilised by the union of yin and yang within the elements of sky, wind and water. The dragon, nourished by the celestial influences, reanimates the landscape until its life force wanes at the end of the cycle. As the dragon grows stronger, it devours the land until it dies at the hands of one who is initiated into the ways of the Earth.

Whether it be a horse or dragon, it is incredible to think that this white chalk figure has survived and been maintained for over 3000 years. However, its likeness to a horse may be the reason it survived. When the Celts arrived in southern England during the Iron Age, they must have viewed this white shining figure on the Uffington hillside as a representation of their white mare goddess Rhiannon. The Romans called her Epona, a goddess who represented the spirit of the land and brought fertility to the crops.

Climbing the steep White Horse Hill, I dowsed Elen travelling along the tail and spine of the horse to the head and through its open eye and beak. Legend says that anyone who stands on the eye of the Uffington White Horse and turns around three times clockwise whilst making a wish will have that wish fulfilled. The eye must be a place of power, as the feminine current shrinks to encompass the 0.6 m (2 ft) wide circular patch of chalk, then returns to its normal width a little further on. The strange shrinking might be due to the blind spring beneath, first detected by the renowned water dowser Guy Underwood. *Encyclopaedia Britannica* informs us that the word 'dragon' is derived from the French and Latin form of the Greek *draku*, linked with *derkomai* meaning 'to see' or 'sharp-sighted'. The behaviour of the current here is curious; perhaps the eye is a key point in this sacred landscape.

It seems appropriate that Elen connects with the chalk figure, symbolised by the Celts as their goddess. Belinus too is associated with white horses. In France, for instance, the Celtic god Belinos carries the sun across the sky in a horse-drawn chariot; a Celtic model of a horse and wagon carrying a gilded sun-disc was found at Trundholm in Denmark. Excavations of a Belinos shrine in Sainte-Sabine, Burgundy, revealed large numbers of small clay horse figurines that were offerings to this solar deity.

St George also rides a white horse, as did the kings of Europe. At St George's Well in Llan San Sior near Abergele in Clwyd, Wales, horses were regularly sacrificed until relatively recent times. St George and St Michael were considered the heavenly twins, the protectors of mankind, to be called upon in troubled times. Michael is the ruler of the heavens whilst George is his earthly counterpart – the guardian of the earth energy matrix perhaps. Another local legend says that King Arthur sleeps at Uffington protected by St George and St Michael.

The Celestial Pole Marker

As I was standing on the creature's head looking down at its long elegant stylised form, I remembered that the author and presenter Graham Hancock proposed that the horned figure represents the Taurus constellation. However, it occurred to me that from the chalk-cut figure there are uninterrupted views to the northern horizon, so perhaps the creature might characterise a constellation synonymous with the northern skies. Due to the magnificence of the view from the hill, I had a sense that the ancients built the complex here specifically to view the northern stars, particularly the setting of bright stars such as Vega and Deneb. After consulting the Skyglobe program, the secrets of this site started to unfold

From Dragon Hill I could see on the northern horizon a distinctive hill which according to my compass lies exactly true north, directly below the celestial pole. This I discovered was Faringdon Hill or Folly Hill, which marks a true north ley line discovered by Roy Cooper called by some the 'Oxfordshire Spirit Path'. It runs from the Uffington White Horse through Folly Hill, Lyneham Long Barrow, the Rollright

Stone Circle, Stourton Church and Brailes Hill. I discovered this line even extends to Guy Cliffe, home of the legendary Saxon hero Guy of Warwick, who some equate with King Arthur. This made me wonder if the prehistoric builders chose this particular location along the Ridgeway because of its true north alignment with Folly Hill and the other sites.

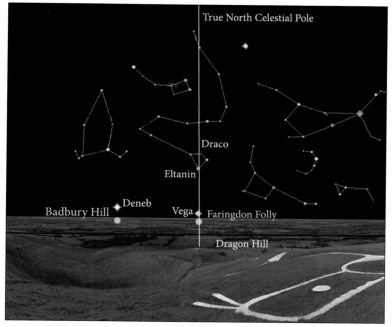

The constellation of Draco aligning with Vega over Folly Hill marking the celestial pole, seen from Uffington White Horse c.1600–1300 BC

Skyglobe indicated that from 1600–1300 BC, when Deneb hovered over Badbury Hill to the west of Faringdon, 'Eltanin' the main star at the head of Draco aligned with Vega over Folly Hill, the brightest star in the constellation of Lyra and the celestial pole marker. Moreover, the constellation of Draco stood vertical to the celestial pole and wound around it like a caduceus. The program revealed that this celestial alignment with Folly Hill is more in evidence from Uffington at dusk, when both the hill and the stars are visible during the March or September equinoxes. At the winter solstice the conjunction occurs around midnight, making it necessary to light a beacon on Folly Hill for observers on Dragon Hill.

In 1500 BC, there was no star in the celestial pole position; instead two stars of Ursula Minor, the Little Bear Kochab and its neighbour Pherkad, encircled it. These two stars, sometimes referred to as the Guardians of the Pole, served as the Earth's pole stars from 1500 BC until AD 500. Thus, the ancients had to find fixed markers for calculating true north using rising and setting stars and local landscape features. Interestingly, the White Horse is orientated north–south, with its head pointing south and its tail north, mimicking the Draco constellation in the heavens, encircling the north pole like the world serpent winds around the cosmic axis. In Roman legend, Draco, also known as *Serpens*, was a dragon killed by the goddess Minerva and tossed into the sky upon its defeat. The Bronze Age tribes travelling along the Ridgeway must have noticed this alignment and built a ceremonial centre to honour it, carving a level viewing platform into a natural chalk hill and an effigy to represent the heavens in the form of Draco.

During the 10th century, locals called Dragon Hill *Eccles Beorh* or 'church barrow', alluding to some early religious practice. The legend of Uther Pendragon lying buried beneath Dragon Hill may also be an allegory of the worship of Draco. Pendragon means 'head of the dragon' and true north was determined by the conjunction of Eltanin, the star on the head of Draco, Vega and Folly Hill. Moreover, the formation of the stars at the head of Draco forms an irregular four-sided figure similar to the head of the Uffington chalk-cut figure.

Elen continues up the hill from the eye of the dragon across the scant remains of a Neolithic long barrow and enclosure. Archaeologists have found early British burials here, containing 46 skeletons, some minus their heads; the local guidebook says the Victorians removed them for anatomy experiments.

The great number of prehistoric burials around the hill figure gives one the impression that the ancients revered this area as a sacred place of the dead. Perhaps the ancient tribes believed that the great stellar dragon or horse during the time of the Celts conveyed the souls of the dead to the heavenly realms at the celestial pole. Today, archaeologists live in hope of finding a shrine or a ritual centre here to explain the great number of Neolithic Bronze Age and Iron Age burials. The answer could be staring them in the face!

Elen enters the massive single bank and ditch hillfort called Uffington Castle through its north entrance, where she heads for the centre to form a second Node with the Belinus current. From here, she gently swings around to leave on the southern side of the west entrance. Belinus meanwhile enters the hillfort through its entrance in the south coming from Idlebush Barrow. This Node also exhibits, like the others, a spiralling vortex and the signature of a six-pointed star.

Uffington Castle stands on the highest point in Oxfordshire, built around the same time as St Catherine's Hill. Evidence from excavations carried out in the 1850s revealed a settlement of the Iron Age *Dobunni* tribe, who fortified the site by erecting timber walls faced with sarsen stones over the ditches. However, archaeological finds within the hillfort inform us that no battles or intensive occupation took place. Instead, it was utilised for seasonal ceremonial practices, only later becoming a fort during turbulent times. The very fact that the male and female serpent currents cross at the centre of the hillfort further convinced me that this was originally a site designed for sacred ceremony and seasonal festivals.

It is also likely that the fort was a key place on a chain of beacon hills running north from the Isle of Wight to warn of invasions that included St Catherine's Hill, Beacon Hill and Walbury Hill. Did the ancients use these beacon hills to survey this section of the Spine of Albion?

Wayland and Sleeping Arthur

Elen's path continues west from the hillfort towards Wayland Smithy Long Barrow along the ancient Ridgeway. Here, hidden amongst trees, we find a 56 m (185 ft) long

Neolithic long barrow, built around 3500 BC, which predates all the other monuments at Uffington. The south-facing façade consists of gigantic sarsen stones over 3 m (10 ft) tall, truly a megalithic monument, albeit a slightly smaller and younger version of West Kennet Long Barrow situated within the Avebury complex.

However, its orientation is unlike that of West Kennet and many others around the British Isles in that it targets the horizon in the NNW. According to Professor John North, Wayland Smithy was orientated to the setting of Deneb at the time of its construction (Collins 2006). The barrow had two phases of building, in 3700 BC and 3400 BC. During the second phase, a long trapezoid-shaped mound of chalk was added to the earlier monument with 63 m (260 ft) tall blocking slabs placed at the southern face. This covered a passage to a central chamber that opened into three stone-lined cubicles forming a cross or cruciform shape, which interestingly mirrors the stars of Cygnus, called the Northern Cross.

Wayland Smithy long barrow

The barrow takes its name from a legend that Wayland, the Norse God of blacksmithing, inhabited this site. According to tradition, when a horse had lost its shoe, the rider would leave it and some money on the capstone of the barrow. When returning the next day, the horse was shod and the money gone. Every hundred years the Uffington Horse would gallop across the sky to be reshod by Wayland at his smithy. Apparently, this last occurred in around 1920, so he will be due again in 2020!

Collins reminds us in *The Cygnus Mystery* that Wayland is the divine Smith in Germanic and Norse tradition who attained astral flight by adorning himself with the feathers from the wings of a swan. Wayland supposedly flew over long distances, eventually crossing the North Sea to rest in Britain. He lands on the high downs in Berkshire, where he discovers an ancient chambered tomb, making it his home. It was also here, folklorists says, that Merlin commissioned Wayland to make the great sword Excalibur for King Arthur and a secret passage links the monument to the White Horse at Uffington. Was this an allegory for the path of Elen?

Elen swings into the barrow to flow NNW along the whole length of the monument, including the 6 m (20 ft) long passage and the sarsen stone entrance. From the Node in the hillfort, Belinus heads north across the ramparts to a thorn tree beside a dried-up spring. The erosion of the banks at this point is evidence that a substantial flow of water issued forth from this spot long ago. Given the proximity of the monuments to this spring, the site would have had great relevance to the prehistoric tribes and the Celts, as the Swallowhead Spring was to the Avebury complex.

Belinus then continues down the hill towards Dragon Hill, where he crosses with Elen. From this Node, Elen meanders down the steep-sided contoured valley called the Manger. This natural amphitheatre, formed from the melting of ice after the last Ice Age, has an extraordinary feature along its steep slopes in the form of large earthen strips known as 'Giant Stairs' or 'Dragon Stairs'. The natural, semi-bowl-shaped feature is renowned for its remarkable acoustic effects, carrying sound like a whispering gallery or Roman amphitheatre.

The ancient tradition of Cheese Rolling took place down the side of the Manger during the scouring of the White Horse. Obviously, the scouring has continued since ancient times, but it was only recorded in the Victorian era when, every seven years, the chalk-cut figure was cleaned and new chalk added 'under jurisdiction of the local lord'. With it came festivities such as wrestling and horseracing at the hillfort. Today English Heritage supervises the maintenance.

During the summer of 2000, I visited Uffington to investigate a crop formation in the shape of a dragonfly that appeared in a field directly below the White Horse. That evening I slept under Dragon Hill and had a remarkable dream. I could see white-robed figures standing on the hill and at other locations around the Uffington complex, having gathered there for some important ritual. From amongst the crowd on Dragon Hill, an aged white-haired man stepped forward holding a sword. He stood for a moment until a horn blew, resounding around the complex. He shouted at the northern stars in an unknown language and then stabbed the sword into the ground. Then a flash of lightning struck the hillfort above and thunder shook the ground.

I awoke with the impression that the white-haired man standing on Dragon Hill was a high priest ceremonially closing down the site's energies to stop an impending evil from misusing the dragon force. I sensed that the whole area was some sort of trig point where, using the right 'key', the local energy matrix could be 'adjusted' to a higher or lower frequency. Legend tells us that a dragon was killed here, but I wonder if they were really referring to the closing down of the dragon currents.

The Celtic King Arthur and his Knights sleep within many places of power in England, Scotland and France, either beneath a hill or in a cave, but always waiting for a call to rescue their country in its hour of need. The legend at Uffington is more specific, for when Arthur awakes from his perpetual sleep, the Uffington Horse will rise up and dance on nearby Dragon Hill. Over the years, I have begun to realise that Arthur's name in some instances is a code word for a place of power where the earth energies lie dormant or sleeping. Another legend mentioned earlier says that Arthur sleeps at Uffington protected by the heavenly twins of St Michael and St George. Perhaps when a positive new age of greater understanding arrives, the energy at these places will come alive once more and, like the Grail stories, reanimate the land and its people.

The figure of the White Dragon may represent a totem animal or an emblem of a lost race. The Dobunni had their capital at Cirencester a few miles to the west. However, the identity of the indigenous race that carved the landscape figure before them and buried their dead here in great numbers is unknown.

The Loegrians

The earliest British name for the territory of England bordered by the rivers Severn and Humber was *Lloegyr*, Latinised as 'Loegria'. Legend says that the King of Loegria was Locrinus (1137–1127 BC), son of Brutus. Despite many theories that the Loegrians were a Saxon tribe, it is more likely that they were descendants of a Bronze Age culture responsible for the turf-cut dragon, who eventually became absorbed by the invading tribes of the later Celts, and completely deleted from memory by the Romans and Saxons. Holinshed's *Chronicles* (1587) record another King of Loegria called Pinar, joint ruler of Britain from 482–434 BC.

I believe the White Horse complex was the scene of great regional assemblies during the Bronze Age. The vast natural amphitheatre of the Manger would seat a large number of gathering tribes while their elders spoke in the valley below. They may have assembled here to discuss the threat to their culture from the incoming tide of Celtic foreigners. The Loegrians were unlike the short dark-haired Iron Age Celts for they were tall, with pale skin, fair hair and blue eyes.

The battle standard of the Indo-European-speaking *Cymri* or Cambrian Celts, who settled in Wales, was the red dragon. Geoffrey of Monmouth writing in *The History of the Kings of Britain* (1136) tells of the prophecy of Myrddin (or Merlin) in which a battle rages between a red and white dragon, symbolising the historical struggle between the Welsh and the English – or perhaps the Loegrians. In Chinese tradition, the emperors considered themselves descendants of the dragons and wore the insignia of a red dragon with five toes, a symbol of strength and power, while the white dragon represented a virtuous and pure king. Was the white dragon an emblem of the Loegrians?

Archaeology reveals that a great cultural change took place during the Iron Age in southern Britain, when many previously peaceful communities took to living together in defensive settlements and increased the manufacture of weapons, as if in fear of some great impending force. This was a dark period in British history, perhaps immortalised by Tolkien in *The Lord of the Rings*.

The Loegrians may have fought a great battle in the area against the Iron Age Celts from Europe. This invading force, unlike the Loegrians, were fierce warriors with sturdier iron weaponry that easily pierced bronze armour and shattered inferior bronze swords. Given that the old border between Lloegyr and the Cymry lands is just north of Berkshire, where Gaelic place names are hard to find, it seems likely that the Loegrians may have actually succeeded in keeping the Indo-European-speaking Celts from overtaking their lands.

Berkshire is the ancient realm of battles, for many key conflicts, both real and legendary, took place within its boundaries. A great number of well-worn ancient routes pass through the county from many parts of England that gave easy access for invading armies. I believe that several key battles took place at certain sacred places of power to influence one side or the other, which had a reverberating effect on the local earth energy matrix. Uffington is a good example of this, featuring Arthur against the Saxons and King Alfred against the Danes. Perhaps the Loegrians and the later warrior kings understood the geographical and energetic significance of the Uffington complex, positioned at a point along the Ridgeway where the telluric and serpent energies focus together to receive the celestial influences from the heavens.

Recent evidence of occult practices in the Uffington area indicates a conflict of another type, albeit on a more subtle level that still takes place here. Considering the legendary and historical importance of the pre-historic complex, where the St Michael Line and its serpents embrace with those of the Belinus Line, it is likely that certain groups might take advantage of this powerful union. During 19th century excavations of a barrow above the head of the White Horse, archaeologists found the copy of a book called *Demonology and Witchcraft* by Sir Walter Scott published in 1831, deliberately buried with the inscription 'Demon De Uffing' inside. Often people leave artefacts at a site to honour the place, but many others use them to influence the site to fulfil a specific negative agenda. Although the average reader will know nothing of these occult practices and probably dismiss them out of hand, you might want to read of the real-life harrowing experiences of Andrew Collins and his colleagues in his fascinating books *The Black Alchemist* (1981) and *The Second Coming* (1993).

During a visit to the site in the late 1990s, I dowsed that the male and female currents had switched polarity between the hillfort and Dragon Hill. As a result, the male travelled down the White Dragon instead of the female. This peculiar switching has not since occurred and is still a mystery to me, but it may have been the result of a specific form of human interaction causing a detrimental effect upon the serpent energies.

After many visits to Uffington, I started to become aware that the surrounding monuments are part of a great energy centre or chakra. The energy accumulated from the great Ridgeway fault seems to focus here, emphasised by the extraordinary valley called the Manger.

A short distance to the east of the Uffington White Horse, the alignment passes close to the little village of Kingston Lisle. Here in the front garden of a cottage, enclosed by a fence designed for public access, is a sarsen stone potted with numerous holes called the 'Blowing Stone'. An ancient and sacred thorn tree once grew next

to the stone known as 'King Alfred's Thorn'; unfortunately, it blew down in the devastating hurricane of 1987. Legend informs us that King Alfred blew through one of the holes in this stone on either White Horse Hill or Blowingstone Hill on the Ridgeway above, to summon his troops for battle. Although there are several holes in the stone, one in particular when blown into creates a low-pitched tone similar to a horn. As I tried this out for myself, I too managed to create a fantastic resonant sound that seemed to echo across the valley.

The Blowing Stone, Kingston Lisle

I wondered if the stone originally stood below the Manger for the acoustics there would certainly amplify its sound for many miles around. Cooper King in *A History of Berkshire* suggested in 1887 that it might have been a sacred Celtic stone used by the local Iron Age tribe to summon a gathering. Perhaps for the Loegrians, the sound produced from the stone was a way of summoning assemblies to honour the dead, to warn of invasion or to signal certain celestial events such as the dragon's head aligning with the celestial pole, marking the opening of the gates to heaven.

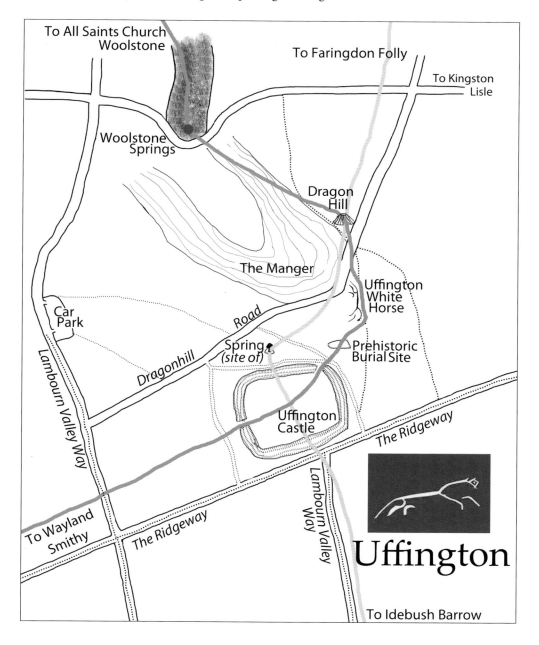

The Path of Elen to the Cotswolds

Below Dragon Hill, Elen crosses the main road into dense woodland where the sacred Woolstone Springs trickle softly in idyllic surroundings. A number of wells surface here from underneath the Uffington complex creating several pools that flow into a stream, which eventually feeds the River Thames. There is some interesting folklore attached to this site, suggesting that the pools were formed by the hoofprints of the White Horse and her foal. The White Horse figure, said to be a mare, has an invisible foal beside her and on moonlit nights they come alive, graze in the Manger and drink at the nearby Woolstone Springs. Perhaps this story is a link with moon worship, as wells and springs are associated with the lunar goddess. Another legend says that Wayland the Smith drinks from the springs before shoeing the horse at the Smithy or long barrow on the Ridgeway also on the female current. This site must have been an important part of the prehistoric complex, as Swallowhead Spring is to the Avebury complex. Sadly it is now on private land and inaccessible to the public.

Not far from the springs is a tiny church concealed amongst trees dedicated to All Saints on the edge of the village of Woolstone with a remarkable story. Here we experienced another of those strange coincidences that have regularly greeted us on this journey, for inside the church we read in a guidebook that the Bishops of Winchester once owned the manor of Woolstone from Saxon times until the Dissolution of the Monasteries, including the Woolstone Springs. The church, built by the Benedictine monks of St Swithun's Priory in Winchester, dates from 1195 and the Bishops kept a granary in the village. In 1327, one particular Bishop came into conflict with the Abbot of Abingdon who owned the adjoining village of Uffington. The disagreement concerned some pastureland called Summerlease and the only way they could resolve it was by combat! Unfortunately, the Bishop's man lost and before long the Black Death decimated the village.

Surprisingly, inside this tiny church, rebuilt in the 13th century, there are three carved Green Men, one staring down at you from a ceiling boss. Elen passes through the south transept, dedicated to the Virgin Mary, and the gaze of a stone head looks upon her as she enters the church. Two of the leaded windows depict symbols of sacred geometry and another remarkable feature is an exquisite lead font, one of only three in the county. There may have been an earlier church on the site when Henry of Blois supervised the running of the estate.

At the road junction, a short distance from All Saints, Elen passes through what appears to be an ancient megalithic stone, possibly placed there long ago to mark her path. A short distance away is the majestic 13th century church of St Mary in the village of Uffington, known as the 'Cathedral of the Vale'. The church, with Norman foundations, has at its old south door a statue of St George pinning the dragon to the ground, no doubt to alert the visitor to the silent and invisible paths of the female serpent energies that reside here. Miller and Broadhurst dowsed the Mary current through this church, which I eventually located flowing through its east–west axis. Caroline followed the flow of Elen from the south transept near the present entrance 'crossing over' Mary under the tower. Interestingly, there was no sign of a Node, and we detected hardly any acknowledgement between them, as if the two serpents were operating at different frequencies; the Christianised energy that Mary conveys seems to differ with the more pagan and arcane energy of the Elen current.

Curiously, the flow of each current is marked by a font, their positioning in the middle of each aisle seeming awkward, almost hindering the parishioners as they quietly walk to their pews. Elen passes through the corner of the north transept through the Mothers' Union Chapel, formerly the Chapel of St Michael and All Angels. Several stone dragons reside in the church and outside Elen connects with a very early yew tree minus one of its boughs.

The sleepy village of Fernham to the north of St Mary's was once a thriving community and here Elen avoids the little church to connect with the nearby village pump with its recently restored shelter. The 2.4 m (8 ft) deep stone-lined bottle well is of uncertain date, but an early worn stone trough displayed beside it may be evidence of its antiquity.

By Onetree Hill to the north of the village, now the private land of Ringdale Manor, Elen connects with a bank and ditch earthwork known as Lower Coxwell Camp. The church of St Mary at Little Coxwell nestles on the Midvale Ridge just 3.2 km (2 miles) southwest of the large market town of Faringdon, hidden at the end of a narrow footpath with quaint cottages either side. The Cistercian monks of Beaulieu Abbey in Hampshire built it in the 12th century as a chapel of ease and some of its masonry still survives in the walls by the High Altar. We dowsed Elen approaching the church through a walled garden abundant with summer blooms before entering the old chancel.

The Wooden Cathedral and Badbury Camp

The picturesque village of Great Coxwell is famous for its 13th century barn, which served as a grain store for the Cistercian monks of Beaulieu Abbey. This massive wooden structure with a stone-lined roof stands as a monument to the incredible skills of the Gothic carpenters, now preserved by the National Trust. William Morris, the 19th century Pre-Raphaelite artist and designer, described the barn as the finest piece of architecture in England, 'unapproachable in its dignity, as beautiful as a cathedral, yet no ostentation of the builder's art'. Morris lived a short distance away at Kelmscott Manor and regularly escorted his guests to visit the barn.

By analysing the roof timbers, experts give the date of construction at around 1300. However, the walls are more difficult to date and may be earlier. As we wandered through this majestic barn, the sense of

Thirteenth century barn at Great Coxwell

complete harmony and sacredness enveloped us, a similar experience to that of many cathedrals we had visited over the years. The Cistercians, who were master masons, knew how to design their buildings using the art of sacred geometry. Indeed, their efforts have rewarded us with a masterpiece of design, which lures Elen's flow as she passes diagonally through the building towards a wooded hill in the northwest.

Shortly we arrived at a small car park on the side of Badbury Hill, the wooded eminence seen from the barn. Here we read on the information board that inside the trees on the summit is an Iron Age hillfort called Badbury Camp. We realised that this clump of trees has a connection to the Uffington complex and Deneb, which hovers over this hill when Vega and the head of Draco align to mark the celestial pole. Its name has given Arthurian researchers another likely candidate for the elusive site of the famous battle of Badon Hill where Arthur had a decisive win against the Saxons. The interior of this Iron Age hillfort is thick with trees, locally known as Badbury Clump, curiously bisected by two clear paths seen as an equal-armed cross from the air. As we walked through the interior following the route of Elen, we could sense a tension in the atmosphere. This strategic site is close to the ancient fording place of the River Thames at Radcot and a crossing of a network of old roads, one connecting London to Bristol. Due to its strategic location, it is possible that many battles took place in the area, inevitably tarnishing the landscape with the traumatic memory of events full of bloodshed.

The Meadows of Kelmscott

Soon we crossed the Thames to the picturesque region of the Cotswolds where we found Elen gliding through the water meadows close to Kelmscott Manor. A local guide describes the manor as the 'loveliest haunt of ancient peace'. Victorian artists William Morris and Gabriel Rossetti, members of the celebrated Pre-Raphaelite brotherhood, were once joint tenants of this 17th century farmhouse. As we walked towards the manor through the village, lined with delightful period buildings, the dowsing rods twitched indicating Elen's path through one particular cottage.

Above the front door is a woodcut relief carved with the figure of William Morris reclining in the water meadows, perhaps mesmerised by the female current that haunts the area. Certainly, Kelmscott has a timeless feel, no doubt aided by the preservation of the village from modern development.

On the northern edge of the village, Elen enters the graveyard of the parish church appropriately dedicated to St George where she takes us straight to the grave of William Morris. As we rested on the grass and discussed the implications of our findings, we wondered if Morris'

Woodcut carving of William Morris above the door of a cottage in Kelmscott connection with Elen was unconscious. However, reading the Kelmscott Manor visitor guide, we discovered that Morris had a fascination with the occult. This and the position of his grave left us in no doubt that he must have known something of the hidden serpent pathway of Elen, perhaps inspiring his extraordinary creativity.

On entering the 12th century church, we immediately noticed the pagan carving of a two-headed Janus over the door, an image quite rare for a village church. There were also sword-cut markings on the door jambs made by knights before departing for the Crusades. It was the custom upon their return to cut across their line to form a cross; judging from the lack of crosses it seems that very few returned. Inside, marking the current is an impressive and rare medieval stained-glass window depicting St George slaying the dragon. Medieval wall paintings of the Old and New Testaments in red ochre and a Green Man add to the splendour of this lovely church. The church guide describes a curious tale concerning the consecration of the churchyard from the *History of St George* by Peter Heylyn written in 1633:

'There is a chapel dedicated to St George in a small village of my County of Oxfordshire: which here I mention for a special rarity that concerns it. For when the churchyard there was to be consecrated, the people thereabouts were invited to that ceremony by a public instrument, under the hands and seals of all the Bishops then in England: and forty days' indulgencies promised unto them, that either then repaired thither, or should in after times observe the Festival of St George, in the foresaid Chapel.'

This curious tradition implies that this church stands on a site of great antiquity somehow connected to St George.

The Treasures of Langford

Continuing north, Elen visits three fine churches in close proximity. The early church at Langford with its rare Saxon tower and stone carving of the Crucifixion proved to be another of those old Celtic Christian shrines on the path of Elen. This tiny almost hidden village of Langford was once in the manor of the Saxon Earl of Mercia who may have built a priory or minster here. During the 11th century, it passed to King Harold II, the fateful last Saxon king of England who fell at the Battle of Hastings. Aelfsige of Faringdon built the present building using skilled masons around the year 1080. The church dedicated to St Matthew had an earlier dedication to St Mary, Elen's Christian counterpart.

Glimpses of the original Saxon minster can be seen around the church including the north wall of the porch. On one of the upper levels of the tower is an ancient low-relief carving inserted into the plaster depicting two bearded men wearing kilts and with a sundial placed on each of their heads. Above the entrance door is a carved relief of Christ on the cross dating from 1020–40, flanked by the figures of Our Lady the Virgin and St John who are strangely placed looking away from Christ. One explanation for this is that they were re-installed the wrong way round. In the tower is the superb limestone carving of a headless rood, a figure wearing a long tunic carved in the shape of a cross, thought to be that of Christ. The guidebook says it is typical of those found in northern France in AD 700, and it is certainly rare in England.

A short distance away, the church of St Peter and St Paul at Broadwell rewarded us with yet more historical treasures. Elen passes through the tower of this exquisite Norman church with its fine Saxon font and stained-glass window of St George dressed in red, green and gold finery. Curiously, the orientation of the church is not the usual east–west but 50 degrees east of north, the pagan direction of the summer solstice sunrise.

The little village of Kencot has a church dedicated to St George and a splendid carved medieval tympanum above the door illustrating a classical myth showing the great figure of a centaur or Sagittarius shooting an arrow into the mouth of a mighty dragon. Sagittarius is the zodiacal sign that appears when the sun dies at mid-winter, so this carving may represent the symbolic slaying of the Earth dragon at the winter solstice. We see

Medieval tympanum above the door of St George's Church, Kencot, showing a centaur or Sagittarius shooting an arrow into the mouth of a dragon

the depiction again on a painted wooden post on the Green just before the church gate. Elen is marked in this church by a carving of a Green Man.

Just to the west, the alignment passes through RAF Brize Norton, which has taken over the role of receiving the dead and injured from the Afghanistan conflict.

Burford, the Priory and the Dragon

Burford is steeped in unspoiled riches of the past, including a church built using cathedral-like proportions. The ancient Cotswold market town lies at the junction of two old roads next to a natural fording of the Windrush River, strategically placed for the transport of merchandise to all points of the compass. In Norman times, the town was granted a charter to form a merchant Guild, and it was the first to hold a market in the Cotswolds, collecting tolls from anyone wishing to trade. Its many imposing buildings along the High Street are a sign of its prosperous and illustrious past.

To the west of the High Street, we located Elen entering the private grounds of the ancient Burford Priory, made famous as the love nest of Nell Gwyn and King Charles II. Marking the positions where she enters and leaves the grounds, we found that Elen avoids the main building by making a curious swing to the east to flow along the lawn in front of the main entrance. This strange behaviour is often an indication that Elen is still lured by a sacred building or temple that stood there in the past.

Around 1585, Lord and Lady Tanfield rebuilt the priory as a private house, entertaining James I there in 1603. However, their aggressive and underhand ways made them unpopular with the locals, having completely taken over their small town. Even after death the townspeople enjoyed no respite from this wicked pair as the Tanfields continued to haunt the streets by driving their fiery carriage precariously, terrorising the neighbourhood. It was not until a ghost-busting group of seven clergymen using 'bell, book and candle' scooped up the spirits in a bottle and threw it under Burford Bridge, trapping them inside forever.

From 1949, the house was the residence of a community of nuns, followed by Benedictine monks in the 1980s. In 2008, it was sold to Elizabeth Murdoch and her husband, the daughter of the globally powerful and controversial media tycoon Rupert Murdoch. A recent summer party held there saw the likes of David Cameron, Peter Mandelson and many other leading members of the government. According to The Mail Online, 'The party guest list paints a telling picture of the powerful web of influence that the couple had spun before the hacking crisis erupted. It reads like a roll call of the modern establishment – with the Murdochs and other News International executives at the hub'. This elite group, dubbed the Chipping Norton Set, have homes within a few miles of the Priory.

The house also received media attention in 2009, when the hit TV series *Time Team* spent three days uncovering a Saxon settlement in the vegetable garden at the back and a 12th century hospital that one stood on the site of the priory. We watched the programme with great interest and were astonished when they uncovered the footings of a chapel on the front lawn belonging to the hospital of St John the Evangelist exactly where the feminine current makes its surprising turn.

From the priory, the path of Elen took us straight to the enormous church of John the Baptist situated next to the banks of the River Windrush. Here the current passes through the northwest corner of the west window, visiting a finely carved 14th century font with numerous figures, including Mary and St John the Evangelist standing either side of Christ on the cross. Another carving shows a worn figure of a noblewoman holding what appears to be a Grail cup. Elen's width expands to over 3 m (10 ft) wide as she travels under the tower and through the High Altar, watched by a Green Man carved on a corbel.

Although described as one of the largest and finest Christian churches in the country, for us its main attraction is a curious pagan carving set high up in the turret wall in the south aisle. Its origins are uncertain, with some authorities believing it to be Romano-British whilst others suggest it may be as late as the 11th or 12th century.

Carving of the 'Three Disgraces' at St John the Baptist Church, Burford

Its position in the church makes it difficult to appreciate the detail of the figures, which Christians say represent the Holy Family on their flight to Egypt. The worn figure on the right appears to be that of a seated figure on a horse or a centaur, perhaps the sign of Sagittarius, similar to those seen at many other churches on the path of the currents. But as the creature has a gaping mouth and teeth, it reminds me of a dragon. On the left, a female seems to be showing her vulva, carved as a large inverted V, while being groped by the figure of a man with his 'manhood' poking down from beneath his skirt, now defaced. The sexual content of the imagery must have posed a dilemma for the church for it is clearly a pagan fertility carving, like the Sheela-na-gig at Binstead Church on the Isle of Wight. Some researchers believe it is a pagan mockery of the Holy Family, but the style of the figures suggests a Celtic origin. Another theory proposes that the centaur is the horse goddess Epona accompanied by her attendants.

A more likely explanation is that the Three Disgraces represent a local fertility ritual honouring the dragon force within the land. Burford has an ancient custom of holding a dragon procession on the longest day of the year still performed today. Although this celebration reputedly commemorates the success of Ethelbald, King of Wessex, after winning the Battle of Burford in AD 752, I believe the dragon parade is a distant memory of harnessing the fertilising attributes of the female dragon, which passes through the town, church and Burford Priory, the love nest of King Charles II.

Just to the east of Burford, the alignment passes through a little church built over a Roman villa at Widford, dedicated to St Oswald of Worcester, Archbishop of York from AD 972–992. This tiny remote chapel nestles in an idyllic spot by the river in a field surrounded by earthworks indicating evidence of a lost village. Now curving towards the northeast, Elen's flow continues to a barrow near the village of Shipton-under-Wychwood. The prehistoric mound is now in the middle of a crop field but visible from the road. It would have once stood on the edge of the ancient Wychwood Forest, which covered much of this region up until Saxon times.

Also on her path lies Shipton Court, one of the finest Elizabethan houses in the country, and the nearby 13th century village church dedicated to St Mary the Virgin situated on the bend of the River Evenlode. The church guide confirms evidence of a Saxon minster on this site, replaced by a Norman church in 1100. The current connects with a font displaying a Green Man and a shield of the Earls of Warwick, showing a bear straddling a staff. She also flows through the William Morris window in the tower depicting St Michael slaying the dragon.

Lying close to the alignment is the 18th century Bruern Abbey, one of the most beautiful houses in the Cotswolds, now a private school. A dissolved Cistercian abbey once stood on this site founded in 1147 with an unusual dedication to St Mary de Brueria Tretone.

Driving through the village of Churchill, we expected to find Elen at Churchill's elevated parish church as its boundary walls incorporate megalithic stones, indicating a possible site of a stone circle. Instead, she visits the Heritage Centre on the northern outskirts of the village, where we located her at one end of the ruined nave of Churchill's earliest church. Its foundations stretch beneath the graveyard, which indicate the true extent of this religious site. Earthworks of a medieval village are still visible in the neighbouring fields where over the years many Roman and Saxon artefacts have been uncovered, substantiating the local belief that a Saxon church once stood on this site.

Before entering the Rollright prehistoric complex, Elen visits another St Mary's Church in the village of Salford, passing through the circular 12th century font and

Tympanum carved with a Maltese Cross, a rampant lion and a centaur at St Mary's Church, Salford

north doorway decorated with an unusual tympanum carved with a Maltese cross, a rampant lion, serpent heads and yet another centaur or Sagittarius. The centaurs seem to mark our journey through the Cotswolds as if the firing of the arrow represents a ley line, the Belinus Line perhaps.

Faringdon Folly and the Oxfordshire Spirit Path

Meanwhile the male current leaves Dragon Hill across fields to the east of the village of Uffington, to target Folly Hill, also known as Faringdon Clump and at one time called Cromwell's Battery. This high place is of great historical significance for in ancient times the nearby market town of Faringdon commanded the old ford as it crossed the Thames along the old route from London to Bristol.

In 1144, Robert Earl of Gloucester built a castle on the summit of the hill to defend the Thames Valley against Royalist attacks during the civil war between Empress Matilda and King Stephen; this was destroyed soon after. Now an unusual folly stands on the hill built in 1935 by Lord Berners of Faringdon House as an observation tower. During its construction, excavations of the site found skeletons in the encompassing ditch attributed to those who fell during the siege of the castle in 1145. There are also remains of a ring of defensive ditches on Folly Hill that may date from the Iron Age. We followed the well-marked path to the summit and found ourselves looking up at Berners' hideous 42 m (140 ft) brick tower. The eccentric composer and writer

Faringdon Folly

commissioned his friend Lord Wellesley to build a Gothic folly knowing he detested that particular style of architecture. Unsurprisingly, there was huge opposition from the locals after its erection.

The hill lies on the Oxfordshire Spirit Path discovered by Roy Cooper, a true north–south line from Uffington White Horse to Brailes Hill in Warwickshire. Belinus passes through the tower, crossing with another unidentified current, which we discovered connects with Faringdon's ancient parish church of All Saints.

Some research at the local library also revealed that according to Rapin in *Saxon Annals*, Folly Hill was the site of the royal palace of King Alfred. Recently, historians dispute this, claiming it to be at Faringdon-on-Dee in Cheshire. Having encountered many of King Alfred's sites on both the male and female serpents at Winchester, Lambourn, Ashdown House and Uffington, it is quite likely that this town was also of strategic interest to him, as it overlooks an ancient ford in the Thames Valley. Perhaps he also knew that the hill was significant due to its position on a spirit path that targets the celestial pole.

According to some authorities, the 13th century Radcot Bridge, just north of Faringdon, is the oldest bridge across the Thames and the site of many battles. The Belinus alignment passes close to this ancient ford, which further supports our belief that it follows a physical route through Britain.

Bampton and the Morris Men

The town of Bampton, just a few miles north of Faringdon, is reputed to be a national centre of traditional folk-culture. The origins of the town possibly go back to the time of the Celts, as its earliest written name ends with the Indo-European word *tune* similar to the Gaelic *toon*, rather than the Saxon *ton*.

The town grew around a Saxon minster built around AD 950, within a large Saxon royal manor. According to written records, the ancient tradition of Morris dancing in the town dates from at least the 14th century and takes place every Spring Bank Holiday. On Christmas Eve, there are performances of Mummers' Plays in pubs and private houses until late into the evening.

Exploring the history of the term 'Morris', Richard Freeman believes it may derive from 'Moorish', which explains why many of the dancers blacken their faces. The Morris dancers would also perform at fairs held at Beltane or May Day, further substantiating the dance as an old pagan form of ritual worship, the bells and ribbons worn by them apparently representing fertility within the land.

The Belinus current passes through Ham Court, a farmhouse in the village incorporating the gatehouse of a castle built in 1315, as well as being attracted by the tall 13th century spire of St Mary's Church. Formerly dedicated to a male saint called Beornwald, the grand church has two, although somewhat worn, images of the Green Man, which mark the male serpent's passage through the south doorway towards the tower and north chapel. Here we noticed what appears to be a Knights Templar grave slab mounted on the wall with the badly worn effigy of Sir Gilbert Talbot, who lived at Bampton Castle. He died during the Battle of Agincourt in France fighting alongside Henry V. The exterior of the church has many fascinating carvings and gargoyles including winged dragons and a hairy creature just by its entrance.

A tumulus near Lew and the remains of a moat at Caswell Farm near Curbridge are all that define the male current until we reach Minster Lovell Hall. The alignment passes through the 12th century church of St Faith at Shellingford that has a splendid Norman arch over the entrance with typical chevron decoration and a serpent's head. According to local tradition, a motte and bailey castle once stood next to the church. Also on the alignment is the Victorian church of the Holy Ascension at Littleworth.

The Legends of Minster Lovell Hall

Here in the heart of Oxfordshire we arrived at the romantic ruin of Minster Lovell Hall, once described as one of the finest houses in the county. Set amongst willow trees by the River Windrush, there is a long history of settlement here from the Neolithic era in a region that was once part of the ancient Wychwood Forest. Discovered close to the house was a fine Saxon enamelled and filigreed gold jewel, similar in style to the Alfred Jewel discovered in Somerset, both now displayed in the Ashmolean Museum in Oxford. The Domesday survey records a 'Minstre' here or monastery; the name Lovell was added in 1226. Although disputed by many historians, this may suggest that a Saxon monastery once stood on this site.

William Lovell built the first house and church here in 1122. His widow Maud then passed it to the Benedictine Abbey of Ivry and soon after a small priory was added, dedicated to St John. The Benedictines owned many sites along the Belinus Line and generally adhered to a form of Gnostic teaching and, like Henry of Blois, had knowledge of the Earth's subtle energies. The present house, now managed by English Heritage, dates from 1435, built by the Seventh Baron of Lovell after he demolished the earlier house and priory. In 1747, its final resident was Thomas Coke who soon abandoned the house, allowing it to fall into decay.

Close by on a raised knoll or platform is St Kenelm's Church, rededicated by the Seventh Baron. Its unusual cruciform shape defines the older Priory of St John over which it was constructed. St Kenelm was a friend of St Chad who we later discovered was a holy man very closely connected with the Belinus currents in the Midlands.

Ruins of Minster Lovell Hall

Upon entering the churchyard from the north gate, Belinus targets a mound thought to be a Saxon grave. Inside the church, he connects with a medieval stone stoup set into the wall of the Lady Chapel and leaves through a buttress carved with two wonderful examples of a scratch dial, perhaps left there by the stonemasons to mark the path of the male current.

In the early afternoon sunshine, families were settling down on the grass in the grounds of the hall preparing their picnics. As we discreetly dowsed around them, we detected the male current passing through the Northwest building and the West Wing connecting with a well in the courtyard now filled with rubble. Inside the Northwest building, we dowsed an unidentified female current crossing with Belinus, her flow also encompassing part of the old great hall and chapel.

I noticed that the architecture of this once stately mansion resembles a monastic building, with its early stone arches, roof bosses and a cloister-like courtyard. I read the impressive list of its previous occupants and visiting monarchs, including Lord Francis, the First Viscount Lovell, one of the most powerful men in England in 1468. He became Lord High-Chamberlain, Chief Butler of England and Most Honourable Member of the Privy Council to King Richard III as well as Knight of the Most Noble Order of the Garter, one of an elite group of twenty-four knights of St George. An old rhyme said to celebrate him states: 'The catte, the ratte, and Lovel our dogge rule all England under the hogge'; the 'catte' was Sir William Catesby, the 'ratte' Sir Richard Ratcliffe and the 'hogge' Richard III, due to the image of a wild boar on his coat of arms. Unfortunately, for Francis, his power was short-lived when Richard III died at the hands of the Lancastrians at Bosworth Field, hailing in the reign of the Tudors. He fled to Flanders after the battle but disappeared two years later whilst fighting overseas.

According to a local legend, upon his return from Europe to Minster Lovell Hall, he hid with his faithful dog in an underground room known only to his servant. The servant kept him safely locked in, loyally bringing him food each day. However, the servant suddenly stopped visiting his lord, having either died or been bribed, leaving Lord Francis to starve. Over two centuries later in 1708, the new owners discovered a vaulted room whilst laying a new chimney. As workers peered inside, they saw a skeleton sitting upright in a chair with a pen in his hand. Unfortunately, as far as we know, there is no underground room and the story is pure myth.

After the disappearance of Lord Francis, Henry VI confiscated Minster Lovell, which later came into the possession of Henry VIII in 1509. Thereafter, it became the home of many prominent families including Sir John Harrington, godson of Elizabeth I, and Attorney General Sir Edward Coke, who signed Sir Walter Raleigh's execution papers. After its demolition, many of the villagers took its stone to build or repair their own cottages.

Minster Lovell Hall is also associated with another macabre legend recalled in the old poem *The Legend of the Mistletoe Bough*. On the eve of the wedding of one of the young Lovells, the bride organises a game of hide and seek. Unfortunately, she chooses as her hiding place a self-locking heavy oak trunk. Despite her stifled cries for help, her body remained undiscovered for many years. This event is similar to the death of Ginerva, a daughter of the Orsini family of Medina in Italy. Many believe that the author of the poem used the Italian story to create a legend around Minster Lovell. But why? Having one macabre story is strange enough, but two is bizarre! Was the mystery of a trapped female in the attic and an incarcerated male in the cellar an allegory alluding to the male and female earth energy currents here?

As we sat observing the many children and dogs running around the ruins in the hazy afternoon sun by the gently flowing river, we sensed that, despite its dramatic history, this enchanted site felt quite magical.

A Forest of Goblins and Chipping Norton

The Royal Forest of Wychwood is the largest area of ancient woodland in Oxfordshire and has within its sacred boundaries the remains of Neolithic long barrows and Bronze Age burial mounds. Wychwood derives from the Saxon name *Hwiccewudu* after the Hwicce tribe who lived in the area. The forest, however, has also been the hunting ground of British kings long before the Saxons arrived. On the edge of the forest is the village of Leafield where Belinus visits the impressive Victorian church of St Michael and All Angels, designed by the famous Gothic revivalist Sir George Gilbert Scott. Two earlier chapels existed on this site but the earliest church stood just south of here, built for the Kings' Foresters of Wychwood in 1364, now converted into cottages in Purrants Lane. This was also the site of a hermitage occupied by Ernald and later handed over to St John's Hospital at Lechlade in 1270. The male current passes through one of the cottages, its walls showing obvious signs of medieval masonry from the chapel.

Just north of St Michael's Church, Belinus took us to a sealed-up well next to a stone cross with a Saxon base. A mound in a field beyond, known to be at one time the highest point in Oxfordshire, was also on his flow.

Many people who visit the forest today often remark how quiet and eerie it is and devoid of bird song. Over many centuries, there have been stories of strange lights floating around the trees and ghost sightings. Some people have experienced unusual snowstorms, which suddenly whip up, as they made their way through the forest.

Many of the forest's elementals have inspired the names of the beers brewed today by the famous Wychwood Brewery such as King Goblin, Hobgoblin and Brownies. These tiny mythical creatures are the 'guardian fairies' that protect the forest and its trees. As I stopped to take a photograph, I sensed something approaching from the woodland, and when I studied my photo later, I found that I had captured a pale blue light hovering on the left of the picture.

An unusual deviation from the male currents usual north–south course took us to the hamlet of Shorthampton and the tiny 13th century church of All Saints with its exquisite medieval wall paintings lovingly restored.

Now heading for the town of Chipping Norton, Belinus took us along a narrow country lane to a mysterious enclosure called Knollbury. This rectangular ditch and bank fort dates to the Neolithic age, later used during the Iron Age. The archaeological finds uncovered here from this Neolithic culture bore no evidence of conflict or warfare, suggesting that the enclosure may have been used for ritual or ceremonial purposes.

Chipping Norton is the highest town in Oxfordshire, but its church, said to be the largest in the Cotswolds, is set at the bottom of a hill by the banks of the river. The parish

Orb caught on camera in Wychwood Forest, Oxfordshire

church of St Mary the Virgin, originally dedicated to St Nicholas and later Thomas à Becket, is a grand awe-inspiring affair which, like the church at Burford, has high vaulted ceilings. The old stonemason's art of sacred proportion almost overwhelms you as you enter, our senses stirred by its richly moulded geometric panels and delicate tracery around the windows. A beautiful stained-glass window in the north aisle, which came from Bruern Abbey next to the alignment, represents stars from the heavens and symbols of sacred geometry.

Undeterred by the local flower arrangers, we dowsed Belinus passing through the medieval Guild Chapel funded by the local wool merchants in the 18th century, which once housed a High Altar of St Katherine. We soon got chatting to a woman who was particularly fascinated by our dowsing. She had a wealth of knowledge about the church's history and informed us that there was once a Norman Castle located on a mound nearby, now in a private garden, although little remains of it today. As we walked up Spring Hill, we realised that this mound also on the current, was probably another important sacred site of the Iron Age or Celtic race, now long forgotten from the annals of history.

The town received a charter in 1205 that raised its status as a major trading centre and it continued to prosper from the profits of the lucrative wool trade up to the 15th century. Many of the old houses were rebuilt in the 18th century to give the town a more fashionable Georgian appeal. Chipping Norton is another of those most haunted places in England. One of its famous ghosts is a shadowy figure known as the Stowfair Man who roams the town at night and makes things disappear. A local priest, who hanged himself from the tower of the church, also haunts the town. The Crown and Cushion Hotel in the High Street is home to the ghosts of the conspirators of the Gunpowder Plot, for it was here that Robert Catesby originally hatched his unsuccessful plan to blow up the Houses of Parliament in 1605. There is a mysterious network of tunnels under the town apparently built by the monks to aid their many secret visits to the local taverns.

We soon found ourselves on the outskirts of the famous megalithic Rollright Stones, where we last dowsed the female current. Clearly both were attracted to yet another fascinating place of hidden power.

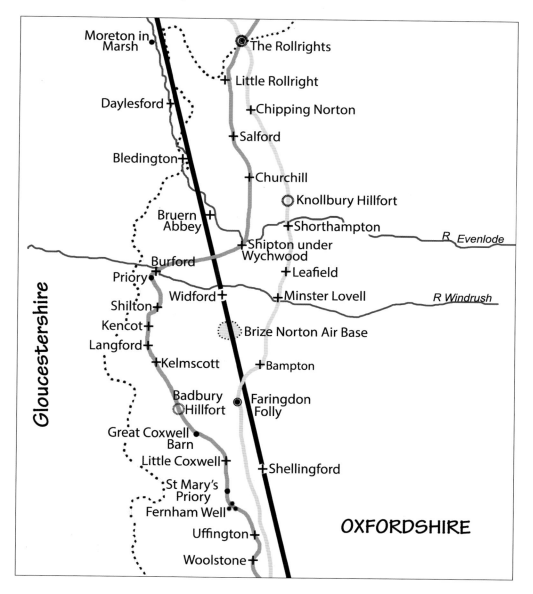

Chapter 6

The Warwickshire Trail
Witches, Devils and the Bard

Gnarled Stones and Sleeping Knights

Within the environs of the Rollright Stones is the tiny hamlet of Little Rollright with its church tucked beneath the rolling hills of the Ridgeway, known as the Jurassic Way. When I first arrived here in 1995, I dowsed Elen disappearing into a clump of trees near a farm, just missing the church. After seeking permission from the farmer, I discovered that the woods shelter a large pond fed by a spring called the Rollright Spinney, another of those hidden places of the goddess enchanted by the presence of the female serpent. From here, Elen continues up the hill across crop fields towards another clump of trees that conceals the familiar gnarled megaliths of the enigmatic Rollright Stone Circle.

This ancient monument lies alongside a country road that forms the boundary between Warwickshire and Oxfordshire and is accompanied by a standing stone 2.4 m (8 ft) tall, called the King Stone. This strangely shaped megalith relates to the circle as an outlier or marker on the Warwickshire side of the road. Also within a short distance are the Whispering Knights, a cluster of four tall standing stones and a collapsed capstone once part of a Neolithic chambered barrow or dolmen.

Rollright Stone Circle, also known as the King's Men

The near-perfect circle of stones, also referred to as the King's Men, measures 31.6 m (104 ft) across and has approximately 77 weathered stones, most of which are about a metre tall. All the megaliths are natural blocks of unhewn oolitic limestone, erected possibly during the late Neolithic period or early Bronze Age.

The Rollright Stones became the subject of a scientific field-based research venture called the 'Dragon Project', founded by author and Earth Mysteries researcher Paul Devereux, who published his findings in *Places of Power* in 1990. Sensitive equipment registered unusual anomalies at the stone circle, King Stone and Whispering Knights, particularly in the higher-frequency spectrum range of ultrasound and infrared. At the Whispering Knights in particular, humming and ticking sounds were recorded during the phase of the full moon and infrared photography picked out a glow of light radiating from the King Stone. Also registered at the King Stone was a strange ultrasonic pulsing that only occurred at sunrise, a phenomenon that later experiments would show reoccurring over many months.

The Rollright monuments seem to provoke varying responses from visitors, some leaving mystified or troubled and others totally enchanted. Several great dowsers have explored and written extensively about this site, including the late Dennis Wheatley in *A New View of the Rollright Ring* (1998), a man who for many years influenced my understanding of sacred sites and greatly encouraged me to pursue the research of the Belinus Line.

Without allowing the dowsing results of others to cloud my judgement, I focused all my senses on the task of plotting the male and female serpents. First, I detected Elen arriving from the direction of the Spinney at Little Rollright to the south. As she approaches the stone circle, her path shrinks in width to just less than 0.6 m (2 ft), as if some kind of communication is silently occurring between the current and the stones. Instead of entering the circle as I anticipated, she merely skims the megaliths in the

southeast quadrant. Despite having checked and rechecked Elen's flow, I obtained the same results every time. Maria Wheatley, the daughter of the late Dennis Wheatley, observed that this particular section of the circle aligns to the moon. Its feminine force may have impregnated the stones in this quadrant, attracting the female serpent to unite with the celestial goddess.

Elen then passes through the site of the old admittance hut and across the road towards the King Stone. Having negotiated the stile, I followed the current towards the solitary megalith enshrined within iron railings. My expectations rose as I approached the gnarled stone, but again Elen surprised me by veering to the west, missing the megalith by a metre to connect with a ridge or long mound, on top of which are a couple of small stones. I questioned why Elen avoided the King Stone and even wondered if I was having a bad dowsing day.

At this point, I decided to take a break for refreshments at the nearby garden centre café to recharge my batteries. Once revived, I felt it necessary to return to follow the path of the male current from Chipping Norton. After a few miles, I suddenly realised that I had been driving in completely the wrong direction. Ever since I was a child, I have always had a good sense of direction, as if I had an inbuilt compass. However, the Rollright landscape seemed to distort or scramble this natural sense. I later learned that several other visitors to the site have experienced the same disorientation. I believe this is due to a strong magnetic field peculiar to the area that upsets one's sense of direction, possibly connected with the fault that follows the Jurassic Way close to the megalithic site.

The Whispering Knights

Belinus approaches the Rollright complex across the fields from the southeast to the Whispering Knights, a group of huddled upright stones of a Neolithic portal tomb dating from 3800 BC. According to legend, they were once knights turned to stone by a witch. Examining them more closely, I could just make out the eerie outline of their petrified faces illuminated by the low afternoon sun. For many centuries, the local witches revered these stones like an oracle, placing their ears against them to listen for words of guidance. The male current makes an unusual 90-degree turn as he enters the monument and then heads off towards the King Stone. However, this curious deflection had me baffled as if something within the tomb was causing a deliberate change in his course.

Belinus then crosses the road, passing straight through the King Stone, and to my surprise formed a Node with Elen at a spot marked by a small circle of stones on top of the ridge. The King Stone is supposedly a surviving megalith from the entrance of another chambered tomb that once stood on the ridge slightly to the north. According to Christine Bloxham in *Folklore of Oxfordshire* (2005), this megalith has a wealth of folklore, including the tale of the arrival in the area of a new king with his knights and men. As the leader walked towards the ridge a witch, also the landowner, meets with him and declares:

'Seven Long strides shalt thou take, and
If Long Compton thou canst see,
King of England thou shalt be.'

The King replied:

'Stick stock stone,
As King of England I shall be known.'

The King proceeded to step forward, but before he could take his seventh stride, the ridge magically rose up preventing him from seeing the village of Long Compton below. The witch cackled:

'As Long Compton thou canst not see
King of England thou shalt not be
Rise up, stick, and stand still, stone,
For King of England thou shalt be none;
Thou and thy men hoar stones shall be
And I myself an eldern tree.'

Another version given by A.J. Evans in 1895 reads:

'Said the Danish General
If Long Compton thou cou'd see
Then King of England I shou'd be.
But replied the British General
Then rise up Hill and stand fast stone
For King of England thou'lt be none.'

It seems on this occasion the power of the king was no match for the pagan magic of the witch and thereafter the standing stone, stone circle and dolman were known as the King Stone, King's Men and Whispering Knights (Grinsell 1977).

Curiously, all the poems refer to the ridge that magically rises in order to deny the king his view of Long Compton. The village lies in the valley below, believed to have been the abode of witches for centuries; one story states, 'There are enough witches in Long Compton to drag a wagon load of hay up Long Compton Hill'. Relevant to the legend is the fact that the ridge stands on the ancient boundary that separated the territories of a British and Danish tribe.

The Node lies on a spur that was reportedly a long barrow housing the burial of an Archdruid, but archaeological excavations have failed to reveal any evidence for such a monument. Curiously, when I first discovered this Node there were just two insignificant stones here. Now other visitors have been adding to them, forming

The Node near the King Stone

a complete circle either to make a campfire or to construct a focal point for ceremony. Deliberating over my findings here, I wondered what other researchers would make of this. I imagine most people would assume that the currents would either cross in the stone circle or at the King Stone, or perhaps even within the Whispering Knights. This unmarked area of the ridge was a mystery; and I needed to make sense of it.

It was only until much later that I came to understand the real significance of my initial findings whilst researching the geology and exploring the wealth of Rollright folklore for its allegorical and geomythic meanings. I determined that from the King Stone, the village of Long Compton is impossible to see until you stand on the ridge. Folklore tells us that the ridge magically rose preventing the king from seeing the village and ruling over all of England. This strongly indicates that the ridge is an integral part of the Rollright complex. Furthermore, William Stukeley, the famous 18th century antiquarian, recorded a local custom celebrated on midsummer's day when young men and women enjoyed cakes and ale on a square or oblong piece of ground near the King Stone. He believed that this festival provoked a memory of their ancient ancestors, who constructed the Archdruid's barrow and stone circle, which Stukeley in 1725 referred to as a temple. The Archdruid was the pagan equivalent to a Christian Archbishop.

I believe the Node marks a place of ceremonial kingship on or near the long barrow where the new sovereign could survey all the lands he was about to rule. The Archdruid would preside over the ceremony just as the Archbishop once crowned kings over the Node in Winchester Cathedral.

Folklore also refers to fairies here, seen to emerge out of a hole in the ridge and dance around the King Stone at night. The local children would often place a flat stone over this hole to prevent the fairies from reappearing. However, when they returned the next day the stones had been mysteriously removed (Evans 1895). Furthermore, the last fairy in Oxfordshire was said to have descended into the ground near the King Stone. I also discovered that the ridge not only is a section of an ancient boundary but also forms part of a regional geological fault. Balls of light or plasma released from a fault line are often mistaken as fairies.

The King Stone is also said to have curative and protective properties for in the 19th century various people would chip off a piece of the stone for protection, including soldiers before battle. As with many ancient sites, stories of an underground tunnel are often allegories of an energetic connection and here, according to tradition, a tunnel links the King Stone to the King's Men stone circle. Evans also mentions a story of a cave beneath the King Stone where the king and his warriors lie sleeping and will awake to defend England against its enemies and rule over the land once more. This tale is identical to several sleeping warrior traditions around Britain generally associated with Celtic King Arthur and his Knights, including Uffington. Superstitions and folklore can play an important part here, leaving clues for us yet shielding the uninitiated from their true meaning.

Another legend states that on a moonlit night the King Stone ventures down to the Little Rollright Spinney for a drink when he hears the midnight bell at Long Compton. This may allude to the interaction of the yin and yang energies at the site.

The stones of the Rollright complex are carved from oolitic limestone; oolites are small rounded particles or grains so named because they look like fish eggs, commonly formed by layers of material, usually calcite, that have been deposited around tiny particles such as quartz, sand or fossil fragments through the rolling motion of the tide in shallow waters. Dr Phillip Callahan believes that the prehistoric races, and the Celts, who built many of their religious structures from this type of stone, recognised the exceptional qualities of oolitic limestone. He further explains that the traces of iron captured in the sediments create a weak magnetic field that somehow benefits nature and wildlife.

Tom Graves, the famous dowser, also recognised the beneficial effects of oolitic stone while investigating the Rollright Stones as part of the Dragon Project. He believes that the quartz seeds within the stone act as the accumulator for a type of static electromagnetic energy generated by water streams beneath the stones. When these seeds become overcharged, the released energy takes the form of balls of light (Biltcliffe 2009). In my previous book *The Spirit of Portland: Revelations of a Sacred Isle*, I discovered that the Dorset Isle is a hotbed of paranormal events and light-ball phenomena, and I believe the oolitic limestone of which the Isle is formed, is partly responsible.

Cracks or fissures allow underground water streams to surface and many of these natural springs bubble up along these faults, such as on the prehistoric Ridgeway at Uffington and the serpent ridge on the Isle of Wight.

It occurred to me that the reason the currents cross on the ridge rather than the stone circle, as one might expect, is that the geological fault lures the ying and yang forces to connect with the telluric energies deep within the Earth, as they do at Uffington Castle, the Devil's Punchbowl on the Isle of Wight and Portland. I suggest that the King's Men stone circle was deliberately constructed to amplify the energy tapped from the fault to feed the local earth grid, similar to an electrical alternator, spreading the beneficial energy out into the surrounding crop fields. In fact, I started to view this complex as a sophisticated orgone energy-making machine that releases its energy through the aid of human interaction. Folklore provides us with a clue from the many stories attached to stone circles around the country, such as dancing maidens turned to stone. Perhaps this alludes to a similar act associated with this circle of megaliths, where people are required to dance clockwise around the stones, particularly at the spring festival of Beltane (1 May) or Midsummer's Day, to release or amplify the charge of energy that has built up during the day.

The Celestial Connection

Another aspect of this site only revealed itself recently while I was standing at the Node point on the ridge. Like the Uffington prehistoric centre, there is a magnificent sightline to the northern horizon marked by Brailes Hill, a pointer for true north. Most impressive is the view to the NNW that dips down into the plains of Warwickshire. Again, this seemed significant, for this is where the stars of Cygnus and the Great Rift in the Milky Way set. In the distance, Brailes Hill, which lies on the cosmic axis from Uffington and marks true north, particularly stands out due to a distinctive clump of trees on its summit. Using Skyglobe, I calculated that Draco aligned with Vega exactly above Brailes Hill in the late Neolithic and early Bronze Age, between 1600 and 1300 BC. Here the bright star Deneb appeared to hover at 340 degrees over two distant hills, which I calculated was somewhere around Stratford-upon-Avon. The exact location of these hills was a mystery at the time but I felt certain that eventually we would identify them.

Long Compton Church and Harrow Hill also fall upon this sighting line. I then started to realise the significance of this prehistoric complex. Like St Catherine's Hill and Uffington, I believe it was another cult centre for the worship of the Pole Star and possibly the constellation of Cygnus, the gateway to the afterlife and a portal for sentient beings to provide the shamans with ancient wisdom.

In *Stars, Stones and Scholars*, the author Andis Kaulins believes that the quirky shape of the King Stone is not the result of the chippings taken by Victorian souvenir hunters; rather it was deliberately carved to resemble the head of a goose looking skyward. Equally, the head could be that of a swan or a hawk if viewed from a different angle. Both images are representations of the cosmic bird and the goose could be the head of a swan, the carrier of souls to the afterlife.

View of the King Stone carved as the head of a goose or swan

View of the King Stone carved as a hawk

Vega is in the constellation of Lyra, or *Lyre*. In Greek mythology, the lyre is the musical instrument of Orpheus killed by the Bacchantes. After his death, his lyre was abandoned in a river until Zeus sent an eagle to retrieve it, ordering both the eagle and the lyre to be placed in the sky. The Ancient Egyptians and Greeks associated the hawk or eagle with the Lyre constellation, as did the Celtic peoples of Europe. Therefore, it is also possible that the British Neolithic or Bronze Age builders knew of these animal associations with the stars, as Lyra was also known as King Arthur's Harp. Thus, the hawk image portrayed by the King Stone might allude to the star Vega and mark a viewing point to observe this star aligning with Draco and the celestial pole above Brailes Hill.

Both the famous astronomer Norman Lockyer (1906) and the great surveyor of megalithic sites Alexander Thom (1967) have suggested that the King Stone was an astronomical marker that may relate to ceremonies undertaken at the stone circle. Their theories, however, failed to provoke serious debate, due to the lack of any conclusive evidence of a significant astronomical alignment between the stone and the circle. However, I believe the hawk-shaped stone marks the viewing point for the stars Vega and Deneb, both linked to the afterlife. The Rollright site is on a true north cosmic axis to the Pole Star between Uffington and Brailes Hill and may have been a funerary site like Uffington to prepare the dead. Moreover, the Bronze Age culture probably timed the ceremonies to coincide with Deneb and the Great Rift in the Milky Way as it passes behind Brailes Hill, symbolically opening the gate to heaven.

The Rollright complex has one other phenomenon in common with Uffington, St Catherine's Hill and the Isle of Wight, through its association with the occult and witchcraft. Although many peaceful earth-loving people visit the stones today, there has been evidence over the years of more sinister practices, particularly around the time of Halloween, including animal sacrifice. Unfortunately, a remote place of power such as this is open to abuse. However, witchcraft of this nature is rare and 'white magic' was the general practice used by witches for good purposes. It was the Catholic Church that taught that both black and white magic were essentially evil and false due to their associations with paganism and 'because it involved an appeal to powers beyond those of God, a presumptuous attempt to compel by human arts benefits which could be granted or denied only by the Divine Will' (Hole 1977). Interestingly many early saints such as St Ninian (Carruthers 1979) and St Columba (Oram 2001) were believed to be powerful magicians.

The more I investigated the Rollright complex, the more insights I received related to the Belinus alignment and its serpent energies. Here we have another key Node over a geological fault with tales of sleeping knights and a prehistoric celestial viewing point to observe true north. Perhaps, like Uffington, the story of the sleeping knights under the ridge is an allegory for sleeping energy, referring to a chakra point, similar to Uffington and the Isle of Wight.

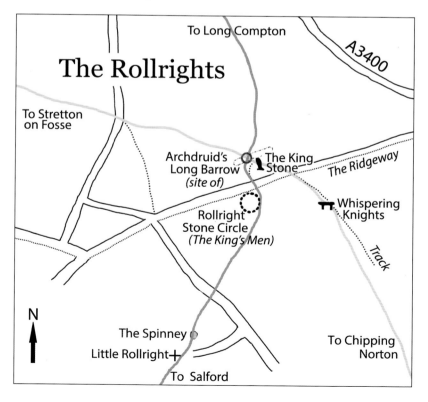

The Goddess Trail to Stratford

Before we journey deep into middle England and the heart of Warwickshire, Elen visits the village of Long Compton, famous for its tales of witches. Its long main street of period cottages leads to the fascinating parish church dedicated to St Peter and St Paul. In Dugdale's *History of Warwickshire* (1656), St Augustine, the first Archbishop of Canterbury, visited here around AD 598 and performed a miracle by raising a man from the grave. The deceased man revealed to St Augustine that he had been a patron of the place in the days of the Britons 150 years before. This act of necromancy seemed appropriate to the folklore of the village. Several carvings inside the church, including that of a woman with a horned headdress, attest to the occult mystery that surrounds this village. The female current passes through the east side of the church, through the High Altar and into a field beyond, which I later discovered was once the site of a stone circle.

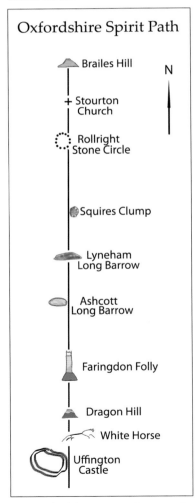

Oxfordshire Spirit Path

N

- Brailes Hill
- + Stourton Church
- Rollright Stone Circle
- Squires Clump
- Lyneham Long Barrow
- Ashcott Long Barrow
- Faringdon Folly
- Dragon Hill
- White Horse
- Uffington Castle

The Oxfordshire Ley or Spirit Path discovered by Roy Cooper

Just north of here, Elen crosses over Harrow Hill which, according to Bob Trubshaw (2011), is the name of a number of hills found in different areas of the country said to derive from the Anglo-Saxon word *Hearg* and associated with well-established sacred places for the worship of pagan deities. In 1997, the man in charge of the Rollright admittance hut informed me that the witches no longer use these stones at night, preferring instead the slopes of Harrow Hill to perform their ritual magic.

We followed Elen to the earthworks of an ancient moated manor house by the River Stour, just south of Sutton under Brailes, in the shadow of Brailes Hill. This is the last point on the Oxfordshire true north ley, another high promontory steeped in folklore crowned with a wooded spinney where according to Earth Mystery researchers many other ley lines converge with the Oxfordshire Spirit Path. Interestingly, in *The Truth Will Set You Free*, David Icke describes a journey he took initiated by a psychic to heal a line of energy through England. The line included three chakras connected with the Spine of Albion – the Isle of Wight, Uffington Castle and Brailes Hill.

However, Elen does the unexpected and avoids the majestic hilltop, winding her way instead around its western slope to visit springs almost hidden amongst the trees at its base.

Following the Stour Valley, we arrived at All Saints' Church at Honnington, mentioned in the Domesday Book as *Hunitone*, 'The homestead where honey is produced'. The Benedictine Priory of Coventry owned the manor here until its dissolution, and in 1668 it came under the ownership of a rich merchant called Sir Henry Parker, who rebuilt the church. Although the tower is 13th century, the remainder embraces the classical 17th century Baroque design. Certainly, the church reflected the wealth and power of its new owner at the time, with its elaborate semicircular chancel, circular domed nave and Wedgwood blue and white painted interior. Flowing north–south through the church, Elen takes in the extravagant Baroque and Rococo-styled sculptured marble monuments of the Parker and Townsend families.

Situated on a bend of the River Stour, the Saxon church in the village of Tredington stands close to an ancient pre-Roman road called the Fosse Way. Dedicated to St Gregory the Great in the 14th century, it has the tallest spire in Warwickshire and its circular churchyard, bordered by what appears to be a ditch and bank, is an indication of its great antiquity. Its foundations may well be associated with the earliest period of Christian worship but the oldest remnant is a Norman arch.

Elen passes diagonally through the church and a side chapel, dedicated to St Mary the Virgin and St Michael, to an unusual font near the tower with a stepped base. On the pedestal of the font is the unique feature of two large metal staples set into the stone. According to the church guide, this was to help 'ground' the priest whilst performing baptisms and to ward off evil spirits and witches. I also wondered if these grounding rods also acted to either reduce or enhance the effects of the powerful female serpent energy that courses through this sanctuary connecting with the underground water streams.

Elen continues to follow the Stour to the medieval church of St Mary at Halford, where the ancient Fosse Way between Exeter and Lincoln crosses a ford. The church is certainly worth a visit for it has a marvellous carved tympanum over the door depicting the Archangel Gabriel holding the message of Annunciation. Sir Nicholas Pevsner described it as 'the best piece of Norman sculpture in the county'. Carvings on the internal pillars may date back to the Saxon period.

The Haunting of Ettington

Soon we arrived at a magnificent Gothic house and ruined chapel set in beautiful grounds with a fascinating history. Ettington Hall, now an exclusive five-star hotel, was the home of the Shirley family from before the Norman Conquest right up until the 20th century. However, the importance of the site goes further back, for according to recent archaeological finds a Roman villa occupied the site. The name Ettington, originally spelt *Eatendon* and later *Eatington*, is a Saxon word for 'ground' or 'meadow by the water', referring in this case to the River Stour. The land was held by Saswalo or Sawallis, a Saxon Thane or Lord, under Henry de Feriers, whose descendants took the name de Shirley around 1200.

The de Shirleys are one of the oldest families in Britain, having contributed to several important military events throughout history. Sir Ralph fought alongside Edward I against Sir William Wallace of Scotland, made famous in the movie *Braveheart*. Sir Thomas Shirley fought in the Crusades around 1340 and returned with the head of a Saracen commander he killed in combat, its image proudly displayed in their family crest.

William Shakespeare, the great English playwright, was very much part of the social scene at Ettington, having been a close friend of the Underhill family, who leased the property for a 100 years during the 16th century. Shakespeare, evidently intrigued by the Shirley family history and their connection to several historic battles, used their exploits to inspire many of his plays. Sir Hugh Shirley, killed in the Battle of Shrewsbury in 1403, was immortalised in his play *Henry IV*. Sir Ralph fought beside Henry V at the Battle of Agincourt in France. The relationship with the Underhills must have been a close one, as they helped Shakespeare to purchase the house in which he lived for much of his life in Stratford and where he eventually died in 1616, called New Place House.

From 1641, when the Shirley family moved back into their family home, Ettington Hall saw many improvements and alterations throughout the ensuing centuries, creating a grand mansion with an eclectic mix of architectural styles.

After Sewallis Shirley died in 1912, the Hall had several leaseholders until it became a nursing home in 1935. During the Second World War it functioned as

Ettington Hall, Warwickshire

a prisoner of war camp for Italian soldiers and, much later, it became a nightclub. A great fire engulfed the house in 1979 causing considerable damage, after which it remained locked up and derelict for three years. Fortunately, in 1983 a hotel chain rescued the building and restored it to its former glory.

Film buffs may recognise the exterior of Ettington Hall from Robert Wise's 1963 classic *The Haunting*. Indeed, the whole location looks like it has stepped straight out from the pages of a ghost story, with its imposing Gothic façade and turreted towers. Ettington's resident ghosts are in no way imaginary or fictional, as many guests and members of staff over the years can testify. In fact, the AA named it the 'Most Haunted Hotel in the UK' and it is often the venue for various companies to host their ghost-hunting events.

Close to the house is the ruin of a 12th century chapel, showing Saxon foundations in the tower. According to the Domesday survey, its original dedication was to the Holy Trinity, but after further rebuilding during medieval times it was rededicated to St Thomas à Becket. The present chapel incorporates some of the Saxon walls and the mortuary chapel of the Shirley family.

We dowsed Elen passing diagonally through the corner of the ruined tower to the Shirley Chapel, restored by the hotel to use for wedding ceremonies. To our surprise the guidebook mentions that a sculptured stone head in the chancel arch is that of William of Wykeham, a former Bishop of Winchester and founder of Winchester College in the late 14th century. Two stained-glass windows contain fragments of the original 'Jesse'

Ettington Hall Chapel

window, commissioned by Wykeham for his chapel at Winchester College, where we also dowsed the female serpent. As we stood before his stone face looming out at us from the chapel wall, we wondered what his connection was to this place, 120 km (74 miles) away from Winchester.

Elen also passes through the northwest end of the house, taking in the Great Drawing Room and Long Gallery on the upper floor, both heavily haunted according to the guidebook, later confirmed by our photographs, which captured numerous orbs.

A Culdee Shrine

A little further north, the church at Alderminster, dedicated to St Mary and the Holy Cross, stands on the site of an early Celtic shrine. Around AD 530, a small religious community led by St Aegis, possibly a Celtic Christian monastic sect called the Culdees, which originated from Ireland and Scotland, departed the hallowed grounds of Glastonbury Abbey to establish a church here next to the River Stour. After St Aegis' death in AD 582, his shrine became a place of pilgrimage until suppressed in 673 by the Archbishop of Canterbury. A Culdee shrine such as this would have been an annoyance to the emerging Roman Catholic Church. Moreover, during this same period, the papal power of Rome working through the missionary St Augustine changed the course of British history by abolishing the Celtic church completely. Why this early Christian community settled here is a mystery; perhaps they took over a site revered by the early Druids, or, like us, they may have sensed the miraculous power of the feminine serpent energy here.

The building of a Norman church obliterated any remnants of this early Christian sanctuary, with many more constructed over the following years. Elen passes through its southeast side, once the site of an early Chapel of the Holy Cross built by the powerful medieval fraternity called the Guild of the Holy Cross, which lasted up until the Reformation.

On the opposite bank of the Stour stands a remote church by a farm; its close proximity to St Mary's is unusual and a medieval village called Whitchurch once surrounded it. The Saxons built a thatched wooden church here under the direction of the monks of Deerhurst near Tewkesbury. Having made a detour to find the little church, we discovered Elen flowing down its axis.

Further along the banks of the Stour is the small village of Clifford Chambers just south of Stratford-upon-Avon. Here Elen visits the church of St Helen, her Christianised counterpart. The building has splendid Norman artistry throughout including foliated lion heads and a dragon gargoyle on the exterior, which mark the current as it passes through in a north–south direction.

Soon we were entering the famous town of Stratford-upon-Avon along a footpath that follows the River Avon. In the distance we could see the spire of the parish church, which would reveal a hidden secret. However, for now, we must return to the male current at the Rollright Stones.

The Belinus Journey and Meon Hill

From the Node at the Rollrights, Belinus guides us to St Michael and All Angels Church at Great Wolford. An avenue of six lime trees, representing the twelve apostles, welcomed us as we strolled towards the church entrance. The present Victorian edifice replaces one dating back to the 12th century, but ancient earthworks in the churchyard may suggest a much earlier place of worship. Today, the most remarkable feature is the rather grotesque and even menacing stone faces that stare down at you from the exterior of the nave; two of the ugliest mark the path of the current.

At the highest point in Warwickshire, next to the Fosse Way, stands the Victorian church of St Peter in the picturesque village of Stretton-on-Fosse. Its origins go back to Saxon times but only until the 16th century were the dead buried here. A 13th century stone cross marks the Belinus current, found originally in the nearby vicarage grounds.

Standing at the northern end of the Cotswold chain of hills is Meon Hill, a visible landmark for many miles around and another hillfort on the Spine of Albion. More precisely, the alignment passes through its lower eastern slopes while the male serpent, coming across Ilmington Downs, heads straight for the summit of the hillfort. The same mysterious Iron Age tribes that changed the contours of St Catherine's Hill, Beacon Hill and Walbury Hill carved the bank and ditch fortifications here. This is also another place of power, which yet again is associated with strange legends of witchcraft, occult and 'devilish deeds'.

In the 8th century, according to local folklore, the devil standing on Meon Hill kicked a stone at the newly founded Evesham Abbey. The prayers of the goodly

Meon Hill, Warwickshire

people at the abbey, however, caused his satanic majesty to miss, and the stone fell instead on Cleeve Hill near Cheltenham, where it was carved with a cross. Another version of this strange tale says the devil threw a large clod of earth to smother the newly built abbey. However, the Bishop of Worcester saw the fiend in time and with the power of prayer caused him to miss his target, the load falling instead at this spot to form Meon Hill.

These stories seem to refer to Meon Hill as an unwanted pagan presence in the landscape that overlooks a new Christian shrine. Another allegorical tale suggests a link with the dead, for the Celtic King Arawyn, the lord of departed spirits, goes on a hunt around the hill at night, gathering souls whilst riding his pale steed accompanied by his phantom white red-eared hounds. For many years, locals have seen phantom black dogs around the hill, a portent of death to anyone who crosses their path.

On an even more gruesome note, the discovery in 1945 of a murdered farm worker impaled by a pitchfork on the hill and marked with pagan symbols shocked the region. Many of the locals believed that witchcraft was responsible and a police investigation failed to uncover a suspect. Interestingly, a story revealed that the witches of Meon Hill and Long Compton were blood relations and frequently travelled between the two sites.

The male current visits many pagan hilltop shrines linked with the dead on its journey along the Spine of Albion. Long before Christianity, the worship of Bel or Belinos, the pagan sun god, took place on hills in northern Europe and the British Isles. Meon Hill also has a solar connection with Nottington hillfort, 2.9 km (1.8 miles) north of Cleeve Hill. Gerald Fawley observed that from its summit at sunrise on the summer solstice the sun appears to roll up the western side of Meon Hill. The same phenomenon occurs at Glastonbury Tor from a viewpoint on St Edmund's Hill where the sun rolls up the slopes of the contoured conical hill at the winter solstice sunrise (Mann & Glasson 2010).

As mentioned previously, the name Meon is significant to the Belinus Line, having encountered the Meon Estuary on the southern shores of mainland Britain right at the beginning of this journey. Its meaning is intriguing and John Michell believes it refers to an Old English word for 'middle'. Even though geographically it is not central to the landmass of England today, it is in the central county of Warwickshire and ancient

tribes may have regarded it as an *omphalos* or 'middle hill' of their kingdom. The omphalos, from the Greek word meaning 'navel', embodies harmonious placement beneficial to the landscape, man and the cosmos, usually defined on the Earth's surface by a marker stone or *gnomon*, which links heaven to earth, invoking a cosmic axis.

Further research of the name Meon revealed some interesting results; the middle string of an ancient five-string lyre, an instrument played by the sun god Apollo, is the 'Meon' string. Hypothetically, one could liken the Spine of Albion with the middle string of Britain, plucked by the sun god Apollo or in this case Belinus. The inclusion of Meon names along the alignment reiterates my belief that this line marks the central axis of Britain. As originally determined, the Belinus Line almost aligns with the midsummer sun at its highest zenith in the solar year.

The male current heads north from the hillfort towards the spire of a distant church. Later we arrived in the village of Lower Quinton and its parish church dedicated to St Swithun of Winchester. In AD 871, St Edith, the daughter of King Egbert, founded a nunnery on this site. The name Quinton derives from *Queanstun*, *Quean* being the Saxon word for 'woman'. St Swithun was the tutor of St Edith's son, hence the rather out of place dedication.

Inside the church, Belinus passes through St Anne's Chapel and a beautiful window depicting his Christian counterpart St George. An unusual feature is a 'Sedilla', a triple-arched stone priest's seat, and a double piscine set into the wall. Either side of the current stands the tombs of Sir William and Lady Clopton, once great landowners in Warwickshire and Wales. The Cloptons later proved to be a significant family associated with the Belinus Line and their illustrious descendants used secret occult knowledge to harness the Elen and Belinus serpent energies.

Ludd's Town

Dowsing around the quaint village of Luddington, we found the male current avoiding the church and crossing the main street to an unusual old cottage. Luck was on our side as we spotted the owner coming out of the front door, so I quickly approached her and asked if she knew anything about the history of her home. 'Well, it was a blacksmith's forge for a time,' she replied, 'but before this it was a chapel built in Norman times'. The old woman invited us into her little home and mentioned that the interior has exactly the same dimensions as the old smithy, built over the foundations of the old chapel. I was just managing to hold my excitement at bay when she added, 'Legend says Shakespeare married Ann Hathaway here'. Remarkably, the guidebook at the Victorian All Saints' parish church, built to replace the old chapel, confirmed her story. More intriguing was Shakespeare's connection with this old chapel.

The presence of ancient earthworks in the village is evidence of prolonged settlement over millennia. Of particular interest is the name of the village and its possible connection with the legendary King Ludd, who founded London or 'Lud's Town' before the time of the Romans. According to the earliest surviving records of British history, transmitted orally from Welsh and English sources, King Ludd reigned in 72 BC and built walls of lime and stone around London, adding to it a western tower and entrance called Ludgate, which survived until 1760. A story in the Welsh *Mabinogion* relates that certain troubles in his kingdom were the result of two fighting dragons at its centre or omphalos. The King summoned all the wise men to determine the whereabouts of this centre, which they curiously found to be Oxford.

Is it a coincidence then that Ludd, a name associated with the search for an omphalos, also appears in the name of a village beneath Meon (middle) Hill?

Over the years, I have become proficient at dowsing the currents whilst being a passenger in a car. On one occasion in the late 1990s, I dowsed the male current whilst being driven from Luddington to Stratford-upon-Avon. As the evening light began to fade, his snaking route took us along a narrow street of terraced houses on the outskirts of the town. As we rounded a sharp bend, the rods swung towards the dark silhouette of a large church with a tall spire. Unfortunately, due to the late hour, the church was locked, so I made a note of its name to investigate another day.

Work commitments soon took my attention away from the Belinus Line and several months went by until an article in a newsletter inspired me to return. A group called the Centre for Advanced Education, Research and Studies in Divine Intelligence, or 'Caer Sidi' for short, published the newsletter and its author proposed the construction of a new establishment for this group where two major lines of earth energy, the St Michael Line and the Belinus Line, cross near Uffington. Theolyn Cortens describes how she intuitively located the route of the Belinus Line through Britain before discovering it in the book *Brigantia* by Guy Raglan Phillips. Totally unaware of my research, she refers to the line as 'beginning on the Isle of Wight, passing through Winchester (seat of the ancient Kings of England including Aelfred), travelling upwards, through the west of Oxfordshire, gathering intensity at the Rollright Stones before whizzing up to Trinity Church at Stratford-upon-Avon. Further north the line is marked by Long Meg in Cumbria'.

Interestingly, Phillips omits to mention both Stratford-upon-Avon and the Rollright complex because neither one falls on his projected line through the south of England. So I became intrigued with Cortens' claim that the line connects with Trinity Church, which stands 2.9 km (1.8 mile) east of the alignment. In fact, I believe she was actually referring to the serpent energies when she says 'it gathers intensity at the Rollright Stones before whizzing up to Trinity Church'.

I rushed to find my dowsing notes made on the last visit through Warwickshire and found that I had written 'Holy Trinity Church'. Even though this building is on the outskirts of the town, it is the main parish church of Stratford and the final resting place of Shakespeare. In naming this church, Cortens had not only intuitively discovered a serpent path of energy but also pointed to a significant place of power along the terrestrial spine of Britain.

Stratford and the Bard

If Stratford-upon-Avon is at the heart of Warwickshire and the county of Warwickshire is the heart of England, then one could safely say that this town must be at the very heart of the heart of England. Stratford-upon-Avon is famous all over the world as the birthplace and final resting place of William Shakespeare, the celebrated and enigmatic Elizabethan playwright who in the words of Arthur Mee (1937) became 'better known than Caesar'. However, Stratford's natural surroundings are important too, set in beautiful countryside along a widening stretch of the River Avon, full of wildfowl and lined with willow trees. The picturesque town has some of the oldest surviving Tudor and Elizabethan half-timbered cottages in the country with delightful narrow streets making it the quintessential old English town.

The name of the town derives from *Strat* or 'street' and *forde* refers to the ford that once crossed the Avon at a junction of several important roads, including a trade route from London to Wales. Bronze Age artefacts were found near the ford as well as evidence of a minor Roman settlement. Saxon settlers, part of the kingdom of the Hwicce, utilised this important crossing of the Avon, where the Clopton Bridge stands today, and built a monastery nearby in AD 691.

The monastery raised its status to a minster upon a charter awarded by Beorthwulf, King of Mercia, in AD 845. In 1192, Richard the Lionheart granted Stratford the privilege of holding a market, established further along the river from the religious settlement next to the ford. By the 14th century, the town had become an important centre for trade, bringing with it much prosperity and a thriving wool industry between the 15th and 17th centuries. During the Elizabethan period, John Shakespeare, William Shakespeare's father, moved to Stratford to become a wool trader at a time when the industry was at its peak. Today, as a world-renowned cultural centre, the place thrives from the millions of visitors it receives every year, visiting its historic buildings and packing out the theatres to watch the famous Royal Shakespeare Company perform Shakespeare's plays.

Holy Trinity Church, Stratford-upon-Avon

In 2004, I returned to Stratford with Caroline to spend a few days researching the course of the currents and the crossing place. After a hearty breakfast at the suitably named Templar House guesthouse just north of the town, we parked the car by Holy Trinity Church. I began dowsing where I last encountered Belinus some years ago at the bend in the road heading towards the west door of the church. In 1331, a stone-built college for a community of chantry priests stood somewhere in this area. This school of priests who chanted continually for their benefactors reminded me of Marwell Manor and the medieval college built by Henry of Blois on the alignment in Hampshire. Nigel Pennick mentions that chantries were 'geomantically sited chapels' built by medieval geomancers who were initiated into the secret knowledge of the dragon force. The word geomantic derives from geomancy, the ancient art of divining centres of energy on the Earth's surface and the artificial modification of the terrain to express their geometric relationships with other centres.

Locals still refer to this built-up area to the west of the church as the 'old town', even though much of the thriving medieval trading industry took place nearer the ford. Perhaps the Saxon stonemasons were geomancers and built the monastery over an energy point. The exact site of this religious house is unknown, although historians and traditions say that it stood on or near the site of the present church, along a stretch of the Avon where swans have nested for over 2000 years. Swans were sacred within royal circles and protected by law, their meat reserved purely for kings and monks.

Sections of Holy Trinity Church date back to 1210, and shortly after in 1269 its welfare became the sole responsibility of the Guild of the Holy Cross, which developed most of the town in medieval times.

The path from the road to the main visitor's entrance has an avenue of lime trees that, like a Druid grove, seems to initiate visitors as they enter this sacred sanctuary. According to local tradition, the twelve trees either side of the path represent both the Apostles and the Tribes of Israel. We decided to first explore the exterior of the church before attempting to mingle with the numerous visitors inside. Belinus enters through the west door of the nave, his flow now 4.5 m (14 ft 6 in) wide. Elen, meanwhile, approaches from the River Avon to enter through the south transept. Her width was equally as wide, marked by a piece of masonry lying on the ground carved with the threefold trinity. Belinus leaves the church through the northeast corner of the chancel and Elen partially through the north transept and nave, establishing a Node beneath the tall spire.

With great reverence and anticipation, we stepped across the threshold of the porch only to be confronted by the most peculiar bronze doorknocker, modelled as the face of a wizened monk. According to the guide, this ancient piece of ironwork is 700 years old and was the original sanctuary knocker. By grasping the handle, a fugitive from the law could find safe sanctuary here for 37 days before facing trial. This tradition reminded me of the Molmutine Laws, which decreed that temples along the sacred highways, including those built by King Belinus, act as safe sanctuaries for all citizens.

Inside the church, we found the male serpent travelling between the pillars along the axis of the nave, the earliest contribution of the ancient Guild of the Holy Cross, to meet with Elen beneath the tower. Wooden screens partitioning the transepts and the chancel enclose this hallowed crossing point of the serpents. Directly above are two roof bosses of St Catherine holding a wheel and a Green Man. On the pulpit nearby, a carved relief of St Helen, Elen's Christian counterpart, holds the cross and faces towards the Node as if indicating this special place of power. A guide informed us that the ceiling boss of St Catherine recalls an early chapel dedicated to the saint that still houses her altar in the north transept. This seemed a fitting location for St Catherine's Chapel, as her wheel symbolises the cosmic axis.

Elen passes through this former chapel, now a vestry, and partly through the Clopton Chapel alongside it, which before the Reformation was the Lady Chapel. Her flow incorporates the monuments of the protestant Carew family and the previous site of a Catholic High Altar that once stood by the north wall.

The Cloptons from Clopton House were a prominent family in Stratford. Hugh Clopton was Mayor of London in 1492 and a member of the Guild of the Holy Cross, the mysterious fraternity that built the chapel at Alderminster. The male current also passes through the Clopton family tombs in St Swithun's Church at Lower Quinton.

Curiously, the church has a 'weeping' chancel and transepts, which are offset by just over a metre, 4 degrees from the axis of the nave. This rather unusual misalignment is said by church historians to be a symbolic allusion deliberately mimicking the position of Christ's head on the cross. However, it is likely that a magnetic compass, introduced to stonemasons in Britain in the 13th century, was used to reset the new chancel and transepts to a more accurate east–west alignment.

John of Stratford, another successful Stratford resident, built a chantry in the south aisle in 1331, having achieved the position of Bishop of Winchester. In the chancel on the path of Belinus is the tomb of William Shakespeare, possibly the most visited spot in England. He died in Stratford aged 52 on St George's Day, 23 April 1616, and is buried alongside his wife and daughter. The rather strange inscription on the plain slab of stone set into the floor beneath his memorial, allegedly composed by him, reads:

'Good friend for Jesus sake forebear,
To dig the dust enclosed here,
Blest be the man that spares these stones.
And curst be he that moves my bones.'

This crude epitaph is hardly the poetry of Shakespeare and most unfitting for this great figure of English literature. I was also curious as to why such a curse would appear on his tomb. Perhaps his grave conceals a vital secret relating to some of the many mysteries that surround this famous playwright.

More importantly for us, what was Shakespeare's connection to the Spine of Albion? At Place House in Hampshire, once the Abbey of Titchfield where both currents Node, he composed and performed some of his plays, he spent time at Ettington Hall and at Luddington, just to the southwest of Stratford, where he married Ann Hathaway at the old chapel on the path of the Belinus current.

Just above his tomb, the Shakespeare memorial is partially obscuring a stained-glass window depicting the biblical Elijah confronting the priests of Baal and Asherah as they stand over a sacrificial bull on the High Altar. It glorifies an event from the Old Testament where God sent down bolts of lightning to destroy the sacrificial altar and kill the pagan priests. Baal, the sun god, and his consort Asherah, the mother goddess, were ancient Semitic pagan deities worshipped by many Middle Eastern cultures. It seemed symbolic to us that we find the pagan spirits of Belinus and Elen crossing so close to an image of the old pagan idols of Baal and Asherah behind the memorial of Shakespeare. Incidentally, a public outcry followed the installation of this fascinating window, many demanding its removal, distraught at finding their favourite bard overlooked by such a wantonly pagan scene.

Many writers claim that Shakespeare had a clandestine side to him, working as a spy for the statesman and politician Lord Francis Walsingham, spymaster for Elizabeth I. Other sources say he was associated with a syndicate of prominent men who used him to front their own plays, revealing forbidden subjects such as Hermetic thought and other teachings from the ancient Mystery Schools of the East. Perhaps this window was placed here as a clue to the many sides of this man of mystery.

The splendidly carved figures on the 16th century misericords, a small wooden shelf on the underside of a folding seat in the choir stalls, include dragons, demons and St George killing the dragon. Marking the point where the male current exits by the east window is a statue of St George subduing the dragon at his feet. St George, the earthly aspect of the 'Heavenly Twins', has become for me the guardian of the Belinus Line and it intrigued me that this saint is specifically positioned to overlook Shakespeare's grave. Ignored by many researchers is the coincidental fact that this great playwright was born and died on 23 April, St George's Day. The town of Stratford celebrates this day with great pomp and ceremony during which a large street procession journeys from Shakespeare's birthplace on Henley Street to Holy Trinity Church. This annual pageant existed long before Shakespeare's time, however, when it celebrated St George and the Dragon until it was suppressed in 1545. Whether it is by chance or not, the great playwright is associated with a saint who symbolically represents the English nation and a cosmic axis of Britain.

The Guild and the Mulberry Tree

Outside the church, we follow Elen through the graveyard and a group of old yews to a low wall where we discovered a walled-up feature, possibly the site of a well. She continues through Avonbank Gardens into buildings situated between Halls Croft and Other Place Theatre.

A chapel built 700 years ago by the Guild of the Holy Cross is one of Stratford's most historic buildings, now part of the King Edward VI Grammar School. Researchers say that although the Guild's true origins have now been lost, they were known to have been an influential and devout brotherhood existing before 1269, owning objects that were primarily religious. This medieval fraternity was so renowned that people from all parts of the country were eager to join. Their membership included not just local merchants, but priests, bishops, nobles and even kings. Through generous donations, the Guild was able to supply the town with a grammar school, a guildhall, almshouses and a new bridge. It also contributed to the development of Birmingham, which at the time was a minor town. However, it later became the second largest city in Britain and a world centre of manufacturing during the 19th and 20th centuries.

Elen passes through the chancel of the Guild Chapel close to the altar, above which is an old stained-glass window depicting Shakespeare's father John. He was one of the Guild's former masters and achieved this status as a prosperous glover and wool trader in the town. More windows depict other former masters including Sir Hugh Clopton, who in 1401 became Lord Mayor of London. The Stratford Guild of the Holy Cross fascinated me, for many of its members became prominent bishops and key players in the development of the town. Robert de Stratford who built the chapel in 1269 became Bishop of Chichester and John de Stratford became Bishop of Winchester in 1323 and Archbishop of Canterbury (1333-1348). Interestingly a guide informed us that Prince Charles often attends a private carol service here at Christmas.

Chapel of the Guild of the Holy Cross, Stratford-upon-Avon

Sir Hugh Clopton, buried on the female current in the Holy Trinity Church, may have been responsible for the paintings that once decorated the walls of this chapel in the 15th century, covered by whitewash in 1559 following a royal injunction declaring that all superstition and idolatry to be removed from churches in England. Some of the themes included the death of Thomas à Becket, the legend of the Holy Cross, St George and the dragon and an allegorical painting of the 'Whore of Babylon'. The St George painting, although now impossible to discern, once depicted an enormous dragon made to look twice the size of the saint and his white horse.

Elen enters the chapel after visiting the King Edward VI Grammar School, on the site of the early Elizabethan school where according to local tradition Shakespeare composed his first poems. Opposite the chapel, she passes through an open garden, once the site of Shakespeare's home called New Place House, funded by the Underhills of Ettington Hall. New Place was the first brick-built house in Stratford erected by Sir Hugh Clopton. Shakespeare purchased the house from the Cloptons for his retirement and died there in 1616. A contemporary of Shakespeare, John Ward, one time vicar of Stratford, explained his death by stating: 'Shakespeare, Drayton and Ben Johnson had a merry meeting and it seems drank too hard for Shakespeare died of a fever there contracted'.

His daughter Susanna Hall inherited New Place and intriguingly in 1643 the Queen of England, Henrietta Maria, wife of Charles I, stayed here as her guest for three days. In 1702, the house was once again in the ownership of the Clopton family who undertook a major refurbishment. A mulberry tree planted in the garden by the Bard was a major attraction in the town and survived until the 18th century, when the house was under the ownership of Parson Gastrell. Irritated by the numerous tourists leaning over his wall to view the tree, he took an axe to it, selling the wood to subsequent visitors. His unpopularity increased further when out of sheer spite for the local population he demolished the house, although some say it was to avoid paying taxes.

Archaeologists have recently excavated the garden at New Place and surprisingly they found evidence of an Iron Age settlement and grain storage pits dating 400BC–43AD. The prehistoric pits are unique in the area of Stratford making this an important site close to the ford and far enough away from flooding of the Avon.

Elen passes through the well in the garden close to the grain pits before entering Nash's House Museum. She then disappears through houses on Chapel Street crossing Ely Street to Bell Court, once the town square and now a shopping centre. She emerges on Henley Street heading straight for the preserved half-timbered house said to be Shakespeare's birthplace.

As the evening light faded, we continued north through the outskirts of the town towards Clopton House, a Carolean mansion built in the 17th century and former home of the prominent local family of that name, now converted into private apartments. Hugh Clopton enlarged the house in the 15th century and received a royal visit from King Henry VII. A large double bed said to be the one slept in by the king was sold in Victorian times for 170 guineas. Ambrose Rookwood, one of the key conspirators of the Gunpowder Plot, resided at Clopton House with Lord Carew and held meetings with his fellow plotters until their riotous plans were discovered.

Behind Clopton House, I dowsed Elen through an old brick vaulted spring known as Margaret's Well. As we stood overlooking the shrine in the shadows of the setting sun, I immediately felt that the energy was out of balance and malignant. We performed a healing ceremony in an attempt to cleanse the site. Within minutes I soon started to feel weak and dizzy and this worsened, making it difficult to walk. After resting for a while, I was able to return to the car, although it took two weeks for my health to recover fully.

That evening we discussed the results of our dowsing and the remarkable coincidence that Elen visits significant places associated with Shakespeare's life. Moreover, her connection with the powerful Clopton family and the Guild of the Holy Cross also seemed important.

Most people are familiar with the official story of Shakespeare's life written by countless authors over many centuries. Yet recent researchers such as Michael Wood (2003), Graham Phillips and Martin Keatman have concluded that his dramatic career is shrouded in mystery with little documented evidence even of his existence. In 1994, Phillips and Keatman published *The Shakespeare Conspiracy* in which they analysed the numerous written accounts concerning Shakespeare and found that many failed to provide any conclusive evidence about his playwriting years; in fact much of his life was based on romantic opinion and guesswork.

There are, however, records proving that his wealth came from successful property deals and trading in grain. He was paid 20 pounds for his part in producing some 'comedies' and he did have a minor share in the Globe and Blackfriars Theatres in London. However, unlike Christopher Marlowe, Ben Johnson and countless other poets and dramatists, Shakespeare was barely recognised in his day and there were certainly no heart-warming obituaries directly after his death. In the Stratford burial register, he is described as 'gent' whereas his son-in-law is described as a skilful physician. Actually, there is no mention at all of him being a successful playwright in the annals of Stratford.

Phillips and Keatman felt that a group known as the 'School of Night', made up of mostly playwrights and poets under the tutelage of Sir Walter Raleigh, used Shakespeare's plays as a way of disseminating to the masses important knowledge about the universe, esoteric views, magic, astronomy and anything else that was considered subversive at that time. Interestingly, this group regularly met at the home of the Third Earl of Southampton at Place House in Titchfield. It could be that this School left us a legacy of lost knowledge from the early Mystery Schools through the plays of Shakespeare, which has remained in the psyche of the people and inspired so many future generations of his followers. It is remarkable that people have loved, revered and honoured him so intensely and for so long. Perhaps the continual celebration of this man on St George's Day perpetuates his memory. Such strong associations with our mythological hero, perhaps endows Shakespeare with a similar status in the minds of ordinary people.

However, let us assume that, like Mozart, Shakespeare was purely and simply a genius admired and patronised in his time by the elite members of the School of Night. Perhaps this genius took inspiration and nourishment from his very exposure to the Belinus Line and its currents.

Margaret's Well, Clopton House

The next morning we visited the local library and discovered a tragic story associated with Margaret's Well behind Clopton House, where we had detected the female current the previous day. During the time of Shakespeare, Margaret Clopton committed suicide by drowning herself in this sacred spring after being spurned by a lover. This terrible event apparently inspired Shakespeare to create the character of Ophelia who drowned in the play *Hamlet*. However, this was not the only sad tale associated with this house to inspire Stratford's Bard.

During the plague of 1564, the year of Shakespeare's birth, it was assumed by the family of Charlotte Clopton that, after many days of suffering, she had died from the disease. Due to the nature of her death, her interment in the Clopton vault in Holy Trinity Church was swift. However, in their haste, the family failed to realise that she had only fallen into a deep state of unconsciousness. Her lifeless body was found on the steps of the vault when it was opened for another family burial a few weeks later. One of the symptoms of the plague was the lapsing into a sleep so deep that the victim appeared to be dead. Shakespeare must have known this popular local tale and some say it was the inspiration for the manner of Juliet's death in his most famous play *Romeo and Juliet*.

It was reported that when Elizabeth Gaskell, the famous Victorian novelist visited Clopton House, the story unnerved her, especially when she was informed that Charlotte's ghost still haunts one of the bedrooms and is often seen walking to the chapel on the upper floors. Gaskell often gazed up at Charlotte's portrait showing her dazzling beauty with her piercing blue eyes and golden locks. Clopton House was also the scene of a murder committed long ago in the chapel and an old bloodstain still marks the dreadful crime.

Gaskell describes another gruesome feature of the house: 'There was a curious carved old chest in one of these passages, and with girlish curiosity I tried to open it; but the lid was too heavy, till I persuaded one of my companions to help me, and when it was opened, what do you think we saw? Bones! But whether human, or the remains of the lost bride, we did not stay to see, but ran off in partly feigned, and partly real terror.' (Howitt 1840).

Gaskell's story and that of Charlotte Clopton, reminded me of the tragic tale of the Mistletoe Bride at Marwell Hall, close to the alignment in Hampshire, and Minster Lovell Hall in Oxfordshire on the Belinus current. Perhaps we have an allegorical tale here too, for there is no documented evidence of a Charlotte interred at the church, neither is there any genuine proof of Margaret Clopton's suicide. Collectively these accounts have given the place a reputation as one of the most haunted houses in England. Another strange coincidence is that both females from the ancient Clopton family died on the path of the female current. I was beginning to sense that long ago occult practices were at work here, no doubt utilising the feminine energy that resides at the church and the well – no wonder I received a psychic backlash at the well!

Returning to the Holy Trinity Church, we began following the path of the male serpent. An ordnance insignia on the northeast corner of the church marks the flow of Belinus as he exits towards the opposite banks of the river. Taking the little passenger ferry across the Avon, we located him up at a bowling green but, to our surprise, he curved back in a gentle arc to cross the river heading for the theatre buildings. Back on the other side, I dowsed Belinus passing through the rotunda of the Swan Theatre built on the side of the larger Royal Shakespeare Theatre.

This bizarre and deliberate behaviour of the current here seems to indicate that human consciousness certainly has an influence. Both currents appear to be drawn by large gatherings of people, such as at theatres and churches, where excited or heartfelt fervour is transmitted. In fact, the currents seem to enjoy the energy of such focused emotion, whether it is through prayer, pagan ceremony or creativity.

We were surprised to find ourselves back at New Place Garden, once part of Shakespeare's former home. Here we dowsed the male current very close to Elen passing through a large tree, seeded from a cutting of the original Mulberry tree planted by Shakespeare and later felled by Parson Gastrell. Within its twisted and gnarled branches, I noticed, through natural formation, the shape of a winged dragon; perhaps this was nature's way of immortalising the presence of the male serpent at this site.

The mulberry tree became a sacred symbol for

The 'dragon' within the mulberry tree in New Place Garden

both Eastern and Western cultures. In the West, the plant was sacred to the goddess Minerva and Athena and the three colours of its fruit during its life cycle, white, red and black, were seen to represent the triple aspect of the goddess. In Eastern mythology, the mulberry was a symbol of the 'tree of life' due to the fruit's nutritional value. When fermented into wine the shaman drank it for its intoxicating effects during fertility rituals. Shakespeare features the sacred tree in his play *A Midsummer Night's Dream*, where the forbidden lovers, Pyramus and Thisbe, meet secretly under a mulberry tree. Tragically, they were soon discovered and slain beneath the tree, their blood staining the white berries dark red. The tree planted at New Place by Shakespeare supposedly came from the garden of James I. After its unfortunate end, many cuttings were transplanted to various places around England. Interestingly the juice of the leaves is a remedy for serpent bites.

Walking along Sheep Street, we dowsed Belinus entering the cobbled courtyard of the 16th century Shrieve's House between two stone dragons. Here you can take part in the Falstaff Experience, a popular tourist attraction that includes a waxworks museum. During Shakespeare's lifetime, a tavern stood here and the Bard had close connections with the tavern keeper and his family. Some say that the travelling players who frequently performed in the courtyard may have inspired the young playwright. Local history states that there has been a dwelling on this site for at least a thousand years and the name Shrieve derives from its earliest known resident, William Shrieve or Shreyve, an archer of King Henry VIII. Its reputation continued as the dwelling place of three of Stratford's Lord Mayors. For tourists today it has the distinction of being the oldest house of continuous occupation in Stratford and one of the most haunted in England, having over thirty recognised ghosts.

In order to satisfy our curiosity and track the male current through the building, we decided to take part in one of the regular organised late night ghost hunting events. Although we had watched programmes of this nature on TV, we were slightly apprehensive, this being a new experience for us. The doors opened promptly at 10 pm and a character dressed for the occasion, but with a slightly sinister air, ushered us in. As we expected, the whole experience was a bit corny and of course, no ghost in their right mind would want to be party to such a charade, particularly when noise from a neighbouring wine bar intruded upon the rather bizarre proceedings.

However, we did learn something of its history as it was also the meeting place of a witches' coven. At one particular spot where mediums have sensed the residual energy of their old practices, I felt the presence of the Belinus current. As soon as the opportunity presented itself, we dropped behind the group to see if we could dowse his current. As we fumbled our way through the house with only the light of the torch to guide us, we traced its flow, jumping at the sight of the waxwork figures that loomed out at us from every dark corner. We followed the direction of our rods towards one of the rooms where most of the ghostly activity supposedly occurs and through the site of the witches' coven. Perhaps these spirits are feeding off the electromagnetic energy emanating from the Belinus current in order to keep them in the physical realm, where they were evidently causing frequent commotion!

Belinus next appears in Guild Street at a curious half-timbered building and then through the Baptist Church on Payton Street. He continues across fields towards the old Clopton estate to Clopton Tower, an unusual octagonal three-storey building, complete with battlements, before entering the Welcombe Hills Country Park.

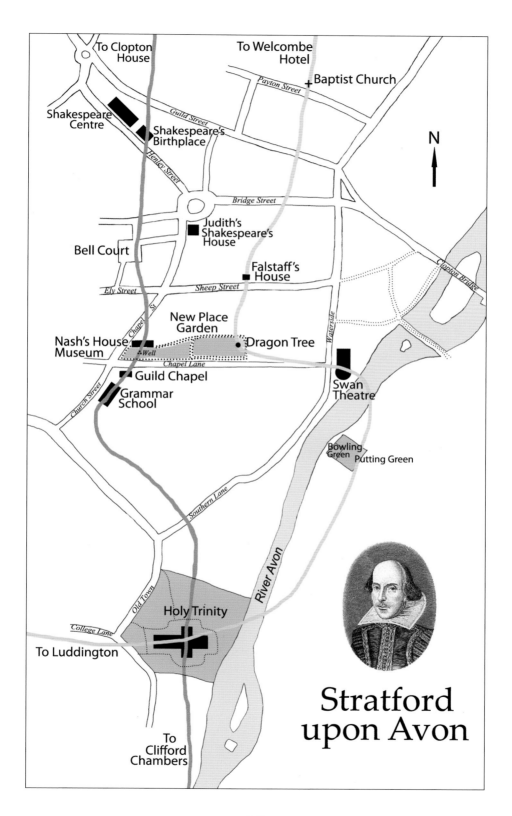

To Clopton House
To Welcombe Hotel
Payton Street
Baptist Church
Guild Street
Shakespeare Centre
Shakespeare's Birthplace
Henley Street
N
Bridge Street
Judith's Shakespeare's House
Bell Court
Falstaff's House
Ely Street
Sheep Street
Clopton Bridge
Chapel St
New Place Garden
Nash's House Museum
Well
Dragon Tree
Chapel Lane
Waterside
Guild Chapel
Grammar School
Church Street
Swan Theatre
Bowling Green
Putting Green
Southern Lane
River Avon
Old Town
Holy Trinity
College Lane
To Luddington
To Clifford Chambers

Stratford upon Avon

The Welcombe Hills

The Welcombe Hills, a short distance northeast of Stratford, are those viewed on the horizon from the King Stone at the Rollright complex. It is over these hills that Deneb hovered when Vega aligned with Draco over Brailes Hill around 1500 BC. With this knowledge, we were curious to know if we would uncover anything obvious about the hills that marked them as sacred to these early cultures.

Belinus first takes us to a Jacobean-styled mansion, now the Menzies Welcombe Hotel. As we approached the hotel by its main driveway, Caroline focused her dowsing rods to detect the male current and they swung to the right just as we passed a curious tall mound, located on the edge of a golf course. After leaving the car in the hotel parking area, we walked across to the cone-shaped earthwork and followed a spiral path leading to the top. At first glance, it appeared to resemble a grand garden feature with water cascading down from its summit. We asked the hotel receptionists if she knew anything of its history, but she could only tell us that the house dates from 1866 and the mound is called Temple Hill. The name fascinated us, but I reasoned that it might have derived from a temple-like folly that once stood on the mound.

Later, I came across a reference to this place in a gazetteer of medieval castles on the *Gatehouse* website, which states that the mound at Welcombe was originally a Norman motte and its earlier name was Castle Hill. Although the Victorians destroyed evidence of an earlier fortification during re-landscaping of the grounds, excavations in and around the mound revealed a human burial and an ancient weapon resembling a pike.

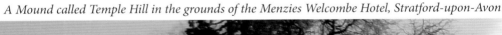

A Mound called Temple Hill in the grounds of the Menzies Welcombe Hotel, Stratford-upon-Avon

Perhaps the Clopton family knew that these hills were sacred when they purchased the land.

On a recent visit, we found that the hotel had published a new history of the estate, which supplied more information on this curious site. The name 'Welcombe' derives from *combe* or 'valley' of the sacred well located at the base of the mound. The revised history mentions that another tumulus once existed on the site of the garden wing where Saxon weapons were uncovered. Also along the main drive, excavations revealed a series of deep Y-shaped trenches or ditches in some places 12 m (40 ft) deep. However, historians believe these trenches were formed by water erosion seeping from a geological fault. The drive also marks the route of an old Roman salt trail where carts would ford the river from a small garrison at Tiddington.

During the reign of Elizabeth I, the land became the property of John Combe, a friend of William Shakespeare; coincidentally the Bard also purchased this estate in 1602. Robert Needham Phillips built the present house in 1876 for his brother Mark, having purchased Welcombe Manor in 1845 after both brothers had become wealthy merchants and politicians. Through marriage, Sir George Otto Trevelyan (1838–1928) inherited the estate after the death of his father-in-law Robert Needham Phillips. He and his wife used the house as a winter resort for many years and their third son, historian George Macaulay Trevelyan, was born in the house. One of their grandchildren, also called George, was a renowned visionary and pioneer of the New Age Movement. The house became the property of the London, Midland and Scottish Railway Company, until 1931 when it was converted into a hotel.

We dowsed Belinus passing north–south through the mound to the right of the hotel flowing through the landscaped garden before ascending to an obelisk. The male current is invariably drawn to obelisks, many standing proud and mighty on hilltops. This particular needle of stone has commanding views over the Stratford landscape, with Brailes Hill and Meon Hill visible in the distance. We later discovered it is a beacon hill, another link in the chain of such hills along the Spine of Albion. I believe our early ancestors regarded the Welcombe Hills as the embodiment of earth, water and celestial energy, but now it is just a pleasure ground for golfers.

In the village of Snitterfield, we encountered Belinus passing through a superb 14th century octagonal stone font with carved heads at the church of St James the Great. Shakespeare's father John and his uncle were baptised here and like at the Guild Chapel in Stratford we find former Bishops of Winchester, depicted here in the east window.

To the west of Stratford, the alignment passes through Wilmcote, a focal point for tourists visiting the cottage of Mary Arden, Shakespeare's mother. There was a chapel here, first mentioned in 1228 and given to the Guild of the Holy Cross in 1481, but its whereabouts is unknown. Elen, from the well at Clopton House, and Belinus, from Snitterfield, are now both heading towards the oldest church in Warwickshire at Wootton Wawen, a few miles north of Stratford.

The Saxon Sanctuary

I had a feeling that the little village of Wootton Wawen, on the Stratford-upon-Avon canal, had an underlying history of some importance, for the alignment and both its currents converge here. The Celts settled the area next to the meeting of ancient tracks, to guard the strategic fording of the River Alwen, or Alne, meaning 'shining', profiting from the trade carried along its waters. The Romans adapted this old track through 'Wooton', which they named 'Raven's Street', linking Stratford and Birmingham, possibly one of the Iron Age roads built by King Belinus. In AD 700, the Benedictine monks, those guardians of the dragon paths, chose this site to build a monastic settlement. Our first visit here coincided with the summer solstice, a timely day to visit the ancient sacred sanctuary now St Peter's Parish Church.

While exploring around the outside of the church, I was amazed to find a prominent mound in the upper graveyard where someone had conveniently

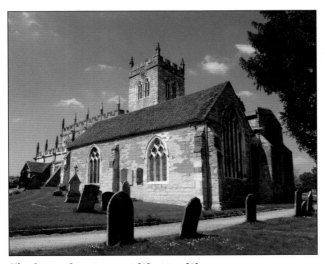

The Saxon Sanctuary at Wootton Wawen

placed a wooden seat. While Caroline investigated the church interior, I sat on the tumulus and marvelled at the lovely view across the valley. Bathing in the hazy heat of the midday sun, I had a sense of timelessness, until one of those unusual synchronistic events took place. An old man walking his dog in the churchyard felt the urge to approach me, remarking, 'You know it is the summer solstice today', and with that the church bell started to sound the noon chime. I suddenly realised the importance of the moment, for it was midday on the summer solstice, when the sun god Belinus is at the height of his power. I knew this was the perfect time to dowse and tune into the dragon energies here.

I soon found the Elen current passing through the tumulus entering the church through a walled-up Saxon doorway under the tower. Sir George Gilbert Scott, the architect of many buildings on the Belinus Line, restored this church in the 1880s and described it as 'an epitome in history of the church of England and nation'.

Inside, my instincts guided me to the ancient masonry supporting the tower, enclosed by four arches. The guidebook calls his section of the church the Saxon Sanctuary, believing it to be older than AD 900. Standing on this hallowed ground, I started to sway due to the intense energies emanating from this spot. After dowsing around the arched walls of the enclosure, I found Belinus flowing along the axis of the church, crossing with Elen at a Node in the middle of the Sanctuary and leaving through the west window. I felt sure that this was a sacred place long before both the Saxons and later Normans laid foundation stones here.

Back in the churchyard, we both dowsed Elen at the south transept window and continued following her south, across the busy road and along an old track that took us to some earthworks and a mound in a field next to a dried-up section of the River Alne. According to a local guide, this was the site of a Saxon moated manor house, later adapted by the Normans as a motte and bailey. North of the church, she passes through a row of modern houses, built over the site of monastic buildings from the Benedictine settlement. The Normans abandoned these buildings and built a new priory in front of the present church. This too disappeared over time to become the grassy earthworks you can see today in the field between the road and the church. The presence of these sacred buildings was a clear indication to us that the Saxons and Normans understood the power of this place.

Belinus approaches this site from the east through Austy Wood, bordered by an ancient track called Monarch's Way. He too focuses on the field where we found Elen at the motte and bailey site, to connect with separate earthworks of an early settlement to the northeast. We then followed him through the grounds of Wootton Hall before entering the church through its east window to meet with Elen in the Saxon Sanctuary. The alignment passes through the village to the west of the currents through the Catholic Church of Our Lady and St Benedict, built over an earlier chapel.

Henley and the Beautiful Wilderness

Continuing north, we drove through the picturesque town of Henley-in-Arden, with its charming black and white half-timbered Tudor houses. The dowsing rods suddenly moved as we passed the remains of an old market cross in the High Street. Here we find Belinus at a place once used for proclamations for at least 500 years, the last occasion was during the Jubilee celebrations of Queen Elizabeth II in 1977. The current continues through the rear of the half-timbered Guild Hall and enters the church of St John the Baptist on the High Street. The old stonemasons who built the church left a clue for those seeking the serpent lines, for exquisitely carved dragons adorn the main entrance. Inside, several more stone creatures stared down at us from the ceiling and pillars, as we dowsed the current across the centre of the church through a north window, the only one carved with dragons.

Dragon carvings on the exterior of St John the Baptist Church, Henley-in-Arden

Less than a kilometre to the east of the church is Henley-in-Arden's twin village of Beaudesert, its name derived from Norman French meaning 'a beautiful wilderness'. A hill overlooking the village known as 'The Mount' is the site of Beaudesert Castle, once an imposing Norman motte and bailey located on a natural conical-shaped ridge, its banks and ditches very similar to the feminine contours of Glastonbury Tor. Thurston de Montfort built the castle in the early 12th century, possibly over an ancient British fort. The construction consisted of an oval enclosure with two outer baileys and a stone keep, which by the end of the 16th century had all but disappeared.

Elen visits the church of St Nicholas at the foot of this hill built by Thurston in the hope of it becoming an abbey. Having supported Queen Matilda during the civil war against King Stephen, he was awarded a grant to hold a market nearby, its success eventually creating the town of Henley-in-Arden. Elen passes through the east side of the church to the High Altar and leaves in a northerly direction after making a dramatic right-angled turn underneath the finely carved Norman chancel arch. Her focus is the Mount, its spectacular views were a refreshing change to all the dank and musty churches we had visited that day. Even Elen seemed to widen her flow as she crossed the hill free from the confines of old buildings.

Situated on a hill surrounded by a yew hedge, Lapworth's church dedicated to St Mary the Virgin is another ancient monument on the Elen current. The church,

Site of Beaudesert Castle at the Mount, Henley-in-Arden

thought to be the site of a Saxon chapel, has a separate tower reflecting a peculiar tradition of that era. The Normans also built a wattle church here. The expressions of the carved heads and grimaces of the dragons that surrounded us would certainly appeal to the lovers of the grotesque.

Elen, however, prefers the company of a beautifully carved modern stone statue of the Madonna and Child by John Poole, inspired by the works of the famous modern sculptor Eric Gill. Gill's work is also included here, having sculptured an exquisite memorial plaque also on Elen's flow at the east end of the church. The south aisle, once the site of a chapel built around 1200 and dedicated to St James, was incorporated into the church in the 15th century. Elen leaves through the unusual west porch added around 1250, housing a room above originally built to store holy relics. A tomb in the churchyard belongs to the family of Robert Catesby, one of the main conspirators of the Gunpowder Plot of 1605. He was born in the village and christened in the church.

Elen journeys through the small village of Nuthurst, to an obelisk opposite an abandoned chapel next to Obelisk Farm. The present chapel, constructed in 1834, replaced one built in the 12th century abandoned 500 years later due to disrepair and neglect. Thomas Archer of Umberslade Hall celebrated his peerage by erecting the obelisk in the field opposite in 1747, crowning it with a copper globe and gilt cross. Archer's family came to Britain with William the Conqueror and settled at Umberslade in the 12th century during the reign of Henry II. Many locals believed there was a secret tunnel built under the base of the obelisk to the Hall.

Tolkien's Lost Paradise

Ahead of us lay the southern suburbs of Birmingham, its land once covered by the great Forest of Arden. The housing estates and industrial parks that inhabit this area today presented us with a difficult set of challenges, the busy traffic and one-way systems being the least of our problems.

Elen flows through the marshy area south of Cheswick Green, once littered with ancient earthworks before crop fields and housing developments took over. One of these was 'The Mount', a circular fortification consisting of a platform surrounded by 3 m (10 ft) banks and a 1.8 m (6 ft) deep moat. Some authorities believe it to be either a Celtic settlement or British encampment while others date the complex as medieval.

Elen stays with the watercourses of the Blythe and Cole Rivers just west of the alignment near Sarehole Mill. A mill has stood on this site since 1542, one of two surviving examples of around seventy mills that once operated within Birmingham. The great 18th century industrialist Matthew Boulton leased the mill from 1756–61, converting it to roll metal and grind blades. This sheet metal production continued until his Soho manufacturing plant was built at Handsworth in the 1760s. We dowsed Elen close to the alignment crossing the main road towards a bridge by the entrance to the mill, heading northwest across a park to woodland known locally as Moseley Bog.

Sarehole was the childhood haunt of author J.R.R. Tolkien, who moved to Birmingham with his mother and brother from South Africa in 1895. He lived very close to Sarehole Mill for four years while living in a house in Wake Green Road. His father sent his family on ahead while settling affairs in South Africa, but died before he could return to his hometown. The young Tolkien spent much of his time playing around Moseley Bog which inspired the setting for 'The Shires' in his book *The Hobbit*, written in 1937, and *The Lord of the Rings* published in 1954 and now an award-winning film. In a *Guardian* newspaper interview in 1966, he mentioned Sarehole as 'a kind of lost paradise ... I loved it with intense love ... I took the idea of the hobbits from the village people and children'.

The idea for the two towers featured in *The Lord of the Rings* came from the nearby Perrot's Folly and the Edgbaston Reservoir Tower. Before attending Oxford University, he lived in rooms in Edgbaston shared with his brother, having lost their mother a few years before. It was at Oxford that he became interested in 'Old and Middle English' and other ancient languages such as Old Norse and Welsh.

Moseley Bog, which inspired Tolkien's fictional characters the Hobbits

The bog once contained two pools (now drained) which acted as secondary reservoirs to feed the millpond for Sarehole Mill. The woodland is full of old oak, beech, sycamore and hazel trees, and although surrounded by residential Birmingham, this little oasis is now a nature conservation area and haven for wildlife. We continued walking until the woodland opened up to grassland and a playing field, where a geophysics team found a Bronze Age settlement. The famous reggae band UB40 while producing some of their earliest recordings occupied a house adjacent to the reserve (since demolished).

Elen then visits St Agnes Church at Wake Green built in 1881, set within a circular graveyard where the road splits to encircle the site. As we walked along Oxford Road towards Moseley with Elen to our right, our great friend Darrell, who was born and brought up in the area, pointed out the site of his old primary school, now replaced by a modern block of flats in School Road. Here we dowsed Elen and were astounded to hear that Darrell and his fellow pupils were encouraged by their teachers to dream, which led to some interesting and magical experiences.

The 14th century church of St Mary at Moseley was once described as 'the Church on the hill which tells a city's history'. Although much of what you see today is Victorian, it is the site of one of the oldest churches in Birmingham and Norman masonry is still evident in the church tower. However, standing at the heart of the town, this religious site was once part of a Saxon settlement in the kingdom of the Hwicce. Today, Moseley is an affluent suburb of Birmingham clearly cared for by the community, at one time winning the Britain in Bloom competition. More intriguingly, over the years, strange phenomena have been recorded in the area such as balls of light, cyclones, frogs and fish falling from the sky and UFO sightings.

As well as numerous dragon gargoyles, we spotted two stone carvings of a Green Man on the exterior of St Mary's that mark Elen's flow as she enters the church. Her route then passes through the back of the Zen Bookshop and a pub called the

Fighting Cock, where many famous bands made their debut.

Returning to the path of the male current from Henley-in-Arden, we dowse him passing through two interesting hilltop sanctuaries unusually dedicated to female saints, including the old chapel of St Mary at Chapel Gate near Ullenhall. Standing some distance from the village, the hill is a likely site of pre-Christian worship. Most churches built on hilltop beacon sites are St Michael sanctuaries, so the female dedication here is unusual. The second site is at Tanworth-in-Arden, just 2 km from the alignment, once a circular hilltop settlement of the Saxons, highlighted today by the semicircular wall that surrounds it. The church dedicated to St Mary Magdalene was first recorded here in the 12th century and possesses two windows commemorating the saints Chad and Columba, both of whom feature strongly during our forthcoming adventures along this alignment. Today, the churchyard is a place of pilgrimage for fans of Nick Drake, a 1970s cult singer-songwriter.

Just to the southwest of the suburb of Shirley is Berry Mound, a large prehistoric fortification surrounded by watercourses and marshes; Bury or Berry refers to a defensive position. It was the perfect haven to provide safe sanctuary to the local Iron Age and later Saxon tribes, also known as 'Danes Camp Field' or 'Danes Bury Field'. This once-mighty bank and ditch defensive earthwork covered 11 acres but only the southern section remains today. A local tradition mentions that the Danes at Berry Mound were under siege by an army led by King Alfred the Great for many months and recent excavations uncovering 9th century refortifications may provide evidence for this.

The alignment passes through a place called Three Maypoles just north of Nuthurst. Maypoles are yet another concept of the 'world tree' or 'axis mundi' often placed at the omphalos of a village or town on the green.

Interestingly, as the Belinus current edges closer to Birmingham city centre, he seems to avoid the metropolis of housing estates and shopping centres, preferring the natural surroundings of Billesley Common, Highbury Park, Cannon Hill Leisure Gardens and Edgbaston Park.

On the fringe of Edgbaston Park, where Tolkien spent his teenage years, is Edgbaston Old Church dedicated to St Bartholomew. Approaching the church from the south, we noticed that the town sign of Edgbaston displays a dragon; perhaps a clue to what lies hidden here. This large imposing church, with its numerous dragon gargoyles, is a perfect haven for the male current in this hectic but extremely affluent part of the city. It is set high on a hill and dedicated to a male saint whose name translates from Old English to 'town of the bold sword'. It was first chosen as a place of worship in the 13th century when Henry de Edgbaston built a small chapel of ease adjacent to his manor house around 1270.

The church's exceptionally tall tower draws Belinus to this high place where numerous wealthy individuals associated with the Industrial Revolution are buried, many choosing plots directly on the Belinus current. Since then it has been restored and rebuilt many times and, like so many churches in Birmingham, is largely Victorian.

The dowsing of Elen and Belinus through the centre of the second largest city centre in Britain awaited us. This would be a first-time experience for us, so we prepared ourselves for what was to be a fascinating albeit daunting adventure.

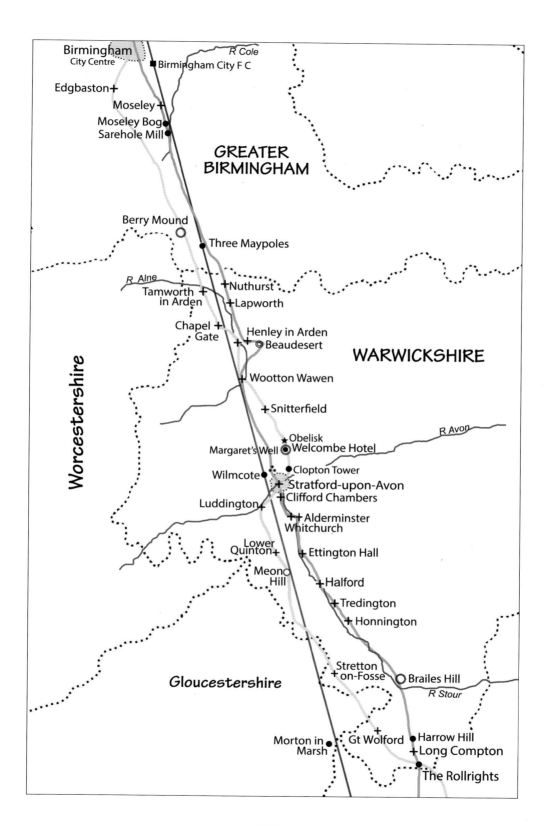

Birmingham
City Centre
■ Birmingham City F C
R Cole

Edgbaston+

Moseley+
Moseley Bog●
Sarehole Mill●

**GREATER
BIRMINGHAM**

Berry Mound
○
● Three Maypoles

R Alne
+Nuthurst
Tamworth +
in Arden
+Lapworth

Chapel +
Gate
Henley in Arden
+●
○ Beaudesert
WARWICKSHIRE

+ Wootton Wawen

+ Snitterfield

R Avon

★ Obelisk
Margaret's Well ○ Welcombe Hotel

Wilmcote ●
● Clopton Tower
+ Stratford-upon-Avon
+ Clifford Chambers

Luddington+
+ Alderminster
Whitchurch

Lower
Quinton+
+ Ettington Hall

Meon ○
Hill
+ Halford

+Tredington

+ Honnington

Stretton
+ on-Fosse
○ Brailes Hill

Gloucestershire
R Stour

+
Morton in ● Gt Wolford ● Harrow Hill
Marsh
+Long Compton

The Rollrights

Worcestershire

185

Chapter 7

Through Birmingham and Staffordshire
Masons, Saints and the Christian Omphalos

A Masonic City of Craftsmen

According to the latest archaeological evidence, Birmingham has a history dating back long before the Norman Conquest. The Romans built a fort a little west of the city centre and occupied land for farming around the present Bull Ring and Moor Street railway station. The Hwiccas had occupied most of the Midlands, but also at that time another body of Saxon invaders known as the *Ingas* or Family of Berm established a ham or home on the banks of the River Rea. This was at a location not far from the Roman Ryknild Street or Icknield Street that ran through the centre of Birmingham from the Metcheley Fort all the way to Wall near Lichfield. The Domesday survey mentions, 'Richard holds of William four hides in Bermingham and it is worth twenty shillings'. It also states that Ulwine held the lands of Bermingham during the reign of Edward the Confessor. Like so many of the Saxon Barons, Ulwine had to relinquish his estates to the Norman nobility, and William Fitz-Ansculf of Dudley Castle became the recipient of the surrounding manors of Edgbaston and Aston.

In the 12th century, the manor of Birmingham was awarded to Peter de Bermingham who brought prosperity to the town, having acquired a charter in 1166 from Henry II to hold a market every Thursday outside his castle. As a result, the town began to thrive, being the sole place of trade in the whole region. In 1250, Henry III granted a William de Bermingham the right to hold a fair on St John the Baptist day in the market area north of the castle called the Bull Ring, which continued into Victorian times.

Throughout the medieval period, the Norman castle or fortified manor house surrounded by a moat became the hub of Birmingham along with the moated parsonage to the west near Lady Well. However, recent excavations of these enclosures suggest they originate from the time of the Saxons. The medieval St Martin's Church, situated near the site of the old castle may also be a place of prehistoric significance, as early maps show it within a sizable semicircular-shaped graveyard.

The Bull Ring was the city's meat and cattle market in medieval times and possibly where bulls were baited before being slaughtered, an ancient custom to tenderise the meat which continued until the 16th century. However, there is no evidence of an actual bull ring existing here and it is not referred to by name on any maps older than 1750. In the early Norman period, the area of the Bull Ring was a public square at the centre of the town, surrounded by shops with a *high cross*, a freestanding Christian stone cross which symbolically and geomantically marked its centre.

To the north was a priory or hospital dedicated to St Thomas, founded soon after St Martin's Church. According to Michael Hodder in *Birmingham: The Hidden History*, which details much of the excavation work carried out in the city centre, the buildings stood at what is now the Priory Square Shopping Centre at the intersection of Bull Street and Dale Street.

In the 14th century, members of the Guild of the Holy Cross, encountered previously at Stratford-upon-Avon, were invited to build a chapel in New Street. They also erected a guildhall in the town and founded a chantry within the church of St Martin. Across the River Rea to the southeast, the Guild of St John the Baptist built a chapel at Deritend in the parish of Aston. The lack of historical accounts makes it almost impossible to ascertain how prominent these Guilds were at the time, but we do know that they had the support of high-ranking political and religious leaders. Their knowledge of the hidden secrets of stone masonry and architecture also wielded great influence in the town; they probably preceded the powerful Freemasonic fraternity that grew to prominence in the 17th century.

The de Berminghams remained in control of the town until 1536 when Edward de Bermingham was mysteriously imprisoned and his lands dispossessed by John Dudley, Duke of Northumberland. In Tudor times, the town continued to flourish and by the 17th century its population had increased to around five thousand, every one of them contributing to its thriving industries.

During the Civil War, the Birmingham blade-makers manufactured 15,000 swords for Cromwell's armies. Whilst Charles I was staying at nearby Aston Hall, Parliamentarian forces from Birmingham cut off his baggage train and captured his 'plate and furniture'. However, their antics were soon thwarted by Prince Rupert, the nephew of Charles I, who captured the town and burnt it to the ground.

A map in Hodder's book shows a fault line running southwest–northeast through the centre of Birmingham, just to the east of St Martin's Church and the Bull Ring, with the River Rea running parallel to it. The fault line is a meeting of two different geological landscapes, sandstone to the west and mudstone to the east. Most of the city lies on the sandstone plateau, rising in places to 200 m (656 ft) above sea level. The telluric energy released from this fault is almost certainly attracting the earth serpents that utilise it to restore and empower their life-giving force. As discussed in previous chapters, the effects of living on or near fault lines can be dramatic and may explain the mysterious phenomena experienced at Moseley.

Having decided to take the train into the heart of the city, we soon found ourselves immersed in the throng of a bustling metropolis. Birmingham is renowned for its cultural diversity, evident by its inhabitants, who happily intermingle as they go about their daily activities. In comparison to other cities, Birmingham grew to be an internationally celebrated centre of craft-making, industry and trade, drawing together silversmiths, jewellers, cutlers, watchmakers, gunsmiths and later engineers, from all walks of life and cultures. Although the streets are brimming with shops and warehouses there are few signs of the manufacturing companies that made Birmingham famous. In fact, at one time almost every household in Europe owned an item made in Birmingham.

St Martin's, the Centre for Healing

We began our quest at Birmingham's oldest surviving building, St Martin's Church. Its tall spire is conspicuous despite its position in the lowest part of the city centre, hidden amongst a mass of modern buildings. Like many ancient churches visited by Elen, it once stood next to a tributary of the River Rea, which also fed the moats surrounding the manor and parsonage. First constructed in 1166 by the de Berminghams, it was replaced by another of red sandstone in 1290. The structure was further adapted and enlarged in 1690 to meet the needs of the growing congregation. Unfortunately, severe erosion of the red sandstone resulted in the Victorians enclosing the building with brick to preserve the fabric, although the edition of a splendid Burne-Jones window may have softened the congregation to this rather severe restoration.

Today, the church is a 'Centre for Healing' where volunteers counsel and support the city's homeless and needy, following in the spirit of its patron Saint Martin and his renowned service to the poor. As we wandered around the church, we detected Elen's path travelling north–south from a side chapel in the chancel, across the High Altar and choir stalls and through two old tombs displaying effigies of knights, members of the de Bermingham family.

Elen visits the chantry of the Guild of the Holy Cross established in 1383. Their members, which included both men and women, paid great sums of money to belong to this powerful order; they even had great influence over local government and royalty. The church guide mentions that stones from the earlier medieval church make up the wall of this chapel. The old stonemasons also left us with a clue to Elen's exact path here in the form of a female head above a dragon carved into each of the two arches either side of the choir stalls. There is an abundance of superb carvings on the exterior of the church, including griffins, dragons and a Green Man.

Dragons biting the ears of a Green Man, St Martin's Church, Birmingham

As we looked south towards the busy metropolis of market buildings and shops bustling with people, we thought it would be easier to first dowse a street plan to determine her flow. To the west of the church, we noticed a multi-storey car park on Elen's path next to the curiously named Moat Lane. When we later compared this map with an old map of Birmingham, we realised that the car park exactly marks the site of the de Bermingham castle that later became the moated manor house. The map dated 1731 shows the manor house with its moat and two entrance towers still in existence (Masterman 1920).

Returning to St Martin's, we followed Elen north through the Bull Ring shopping centre, crossing Corporation Street to the impressive Georgian edifice of St Philip's Cathedral, said to be the smallest cathedral in the world.

St Philip's Cathedral

In Georgian times, a patch of ground called Barley Close, on the highest point of the crystalline sandstone hill, was the site chosen for a new place of worship. St Martin's Church had now become insufficient to house the growing population and money supplied by the many wealthy inhabitants of the town contributed to the building of one of the grandest edifices in Birmingham. The Georgian-styled church, built in 1708 and consecrated in 1715, stands on a hill 111 m (365 ft) above sea level, the exact height of the cross on top of St Paul's Cathedral in London. Incidentally, the height in feet also corresponds with the number of days in a year. St Philip's eventually took the status of a cathedral in 1905 when Birmingham became a city. The original builder and designer Thomas Archer was a close friend of Queen Anne and knew the Italian architect Francesco Borromini well, resulting in a design more elaborate and Italianate than anything produced by Sir Christopher Wren.

Crossing the street called Temple Row, we entered the grounds of St Philip's, following Elen along a path to its southeast corner. Temple Row, which runs along the southern border of the cathedral grounds, represents the financial and political sector of the city. A little to the west I dowsed Belinus entering the cathedral through a large obelisk on its south side. The extremely elaborate interior, with its gilt-painted ornamentation, reminded me of a miniature version of St Paul's Cathedral, yet the strange mix of the highly romantic style of the Edward Burne-Jones and William Morris windows and Georgian extravagance somehow added life and vibrancy to the atmosphere here. We dowsed Elen and Belinus crossing at the High Altar, after which they behave in an unexpected way. First, the female current diverts off at an acute angle to the southwest and Belinus heads to the northeast, his interest taken by a small obelisk in the churchyard made of Shap granite. Elen's propensity to this southerly direction was a mystery but we felt sure the reason would reveal itself shortly.

After studying old maps of Birmingham and researching its history further, we could find no references to anything earlier on this site before the cathedral. Such a high position in the centre of the city, however, may indicate the site of a mound or temple lost to the realms of history long ago. This new Georgian building set at the highest point in the town became the new spiritual focus and reflected the growing success of the city, almost rivalling London. Signs of Masonic influence are obvious in its design such as the five-sided pentagonal shape of its grounds, a potent sacred symbol used by the Freemasons in their rituals and architecture. The number five represents Venus, the morning star, bringing light and knowledge. It also represents the marriage of the male and female. This landscaped pentagram with well-kept lawns and colourful flowerbeds is certainly a lively gathering place for the people of Birmingham, particularly during the summer months. Joining them, we basked in the warm sunshine and ate our sandwiches before undertaking another few hours of dowsing around this fascinating city centre.

We continued to weave in and out of the shoppers as we followed the female current across the street called Bennett's Hill. Here at No. 11, close to the Elen current, the brilliant artist Edward Burne-Jones was born, a leading member of the Pre-Raphaelite Brotherhood. In 1848, a group of art students from the British Royal Academy of Arts, unhappy with the direction the Academy was taking, formed a Brotherhood. This would include William Holman Hunt (1827–1910), John Everett Millais (1829–92) and Dante Gabriel Rossetti (1828–82). They painted in a realistic style, emphasising the aesthetic value of nature and the traditions and techniques of the old masters prior to the early 16th century Italian artist Raphael, hence the name Pre-Raphaelite.

A second generation of artists to join this movement were Edward Burne-Jones (1833–98), William Morris, whose home we visited at Kelmscott by the Thames, and John William Waterhouse (1849–1917). The group strongly influenced Morris and inspired him to create the Arts and Crafts movement. The Pre-Raphaelites also laid seeds for a style of design called Art Nouveau and Art Deco. Medieval culture and more especially the Arthurian romances were prominent subjects for many of their works. They believed the latter to possess a spiritual and creative integrity that had been lost in the midst of the soul-destroying Industrial Revolution, which in their mind had devastated so much of the natural world.

'The floozie in the jacuzzi' in Victoria Square

In Victoria Square, we dowsed Elen at a magnificent fountain surmounted by a huge bronze figure of a reclining female nude called 'The River'. This surely had to be the greatest statement of the divine feminine within a city centre. This marvellous sculpture is one of the largest fountains in Europe and would be at home in the city centres of Rome or Paris. The locals, however, have nicknamed the sculpture 'the floozie in the jacuzzi'. The 'goddess' fountain is certainly in keeping with the female current and has been possibly placed here to provide a modern focal point at the centre of the city. Princess Diana, the immortal goddess of Britain, officially opened it in 1994.

Elen then passes through the northern edge of the Town Hall, modelled on the Temple of Castor and Pollux in Rome. Several months later, I was looking through some old photographs of Birmingham and noticed one showing a church with a tall spire and a façade designed as a classical temple called Christchurch. This magnificent church once stood in Victoria Square exactly on the path of Elen. Built between 1805 and 1813, it soon became redundant and was demolished around 1899, its site used to construct offices just before the new millennium. Many regard Victoria Square as the new heart of Birmingham, due to the changing size of the city during the Industrial Revolution. Christchurch became a symbol of the new omphalos, marking the point from where local road sign distances were measured. Around 1864, the church housed the offices of John Henry Chamberlain and William Martin, the leading Gothic architects in Birmingham. It seemed strange to me why this church at the omphalos of

Sketch of Victoria and Chamberlain Squares, Birmingham, dated 1886 showing Christchurch in the centre, the Town Hall bottom right, St Philip's Cathedral top left and St Martin's Church top right

the city became redundant only 86 years after its construction.

Just beyond the Town Hall, Elen visits a small memorial in Chamberlain Square surrounded by water, dedicated to Joseph Chamberlain who was Birmingham's MP in Victorian times. We noticed that a number of people were sitting in deck chairs around the monument. We were impressed that the council had created a sandy beach here complete with a paddling pool and ice cream vendor for the public to enjoy.

The Lunar Society Trail

Also in Chamberlain Square, Elen passes through the city's museum and art gallery housing the world-renowned collection of works by Burne-Jones and other members of the Pre-Raphaelites. Some claim that these artists inspired the young J.R.R. Tolkien, his stories featuring many of the mythological scenes portrayed in their paintings. Passing to the west of the Telecom Tower, the current continues to the Georgian church of St Paul, set within a geometrically landscaped square. Built in 1774 by Roger Eykyn of Wolverhampton, with Samuel Wyatt of London as consultant, the church has a similar design to St Martin-in-the-Fields in London with an almost identical tower, under which Elen passes.

Brass plaques inside commemorate the two great industrial pioneers Matthew Boulton and James Watt, both members of the Lunar Society who regularly worshipped here. The church has an interesting orientation as its axis follows the summer solstice sunrise alignment rather than the usual east–west course adopted by most Christian churches. I mentioned this to the guide but he had no explanation and seemed rather puzzled by my observation. He mentioned that the plot chosen to build the church was a spare piece of land donated in 1779 when all the cemeteries had become full. For such a significant church of this size and the considerable cost of construction there would have been no room for error and certainly not one of this magnitude, which suggests its orientation was a deliberate choice by its founders.

The fabulous southwest window above the High Altar depicts the Conversion of St Paul painted by Sir Benjamin West, copied and then mechanically applied to glass by Francis Eginton, who installed it in 1791. Eginton, another member of the Lunar Society, also applied this technique to the paintings of Angelica Kauffman, which hung on the walls of almost every Regency drawing room of society's elite at the time. Elen passes through the High Altar and another exquisite stained-glass window showing a young woman wearing a flowing white gown carried by angels. The scene commemorates the death of the wife of another member of the Lunar Society, architect and sculptor William Hollins (1763–1843), who also lies buried here. He was Birmingham's first true architect and responsible for many of the town's buildings. Elen's flow also incorporates the spot where Matthew Boulton's pew once stood. Interestingly, as a founder member of the Lunar Society, he was born very close to the male current in the once affluent and grand Colmore Square. He also met with his fellow members at his home on the Elen current a little further north of here.

Just beyond the Jewellery Quarter, we arrived at Soho House, once surrounded by vast landscaped gardens complete with a lake and waterfall, now swallowed up by the suburban sprawl of Handsworth. Matthew Boulton built the house for his mother and sister and later lived there himself from 1766–1809. In 1796, he employed the top architect of the day James Wyatt to redesign the house; its name Soho is adopted from the nearby wayside inn. We dowsed Elen passing through the Visitor's Centre and diagonally through the house.

Matthew Boulton, Birmingham's most successful industrialist, was born on September 1728 into a family of button and belt buckle manufacturers. After attending a local school, Boulton joined his father's business in the early 1740s. In 1761, he acquired land at Handsworth, about 3 km from Birmingham town centre, and began building the great Soho Manufactory. After introducing modern production methods and a pioneering workers' insurance scheme, he set about becoming what Josiah Wedgwood called 'The Most Complete Manufacturer in Metals in England'. Jewellery, toys, Sheffield plate and sterling silver tableware, ormolu (gilded ornamental wares), coins, medals and tokens poured out of his workshops and were exported all over the world.

His factory just south of Soho House attracted around a thousand skilled workers from all over Europe and soon gained a considerable reputation for the excellent craftsmanship of its products, becoming a school of design. However, he soon required a greater form of power to carry the ever-expanding production line, which he achieved when he met James Watt, the inventor of the steam engine. So began the making of the first steam engines at the Soho factory and this new source of power was made available to mines and factories throughout Britain which did more to shape the Industrial Revolution than any other invention. A famous line by Matthew Boulton to James Boswell in 1776 reads, 'I sell here, Sir, what all the world desires to have – POWER!'

Another man attracted to Boulton's enterprise was the young William Murdoch who arrived on his doorstep wearing a wooden hat produced on the first ever lathe which he had made himself. He later designed the first prototype for the steam locomotive and, during a test run on the roads of Cornwall, he terrified the local vicar who believed it to be the devil (Masterman 1920). Murdoch went on to invent coal-gas apparatus for lighting homes, the equipment manufactured at the Soho factory.

The house is open to the public, which gave us the opportunity to explore its interior. We first found the female current flowing through the fireplace in the dining room. Its design is reminiscent of a Greek temple with Doric pillars standing either side of the fireplace and its carved gilt mantle decorated with lions' heads. Interestingly, Boulton's bedroom was directly above this room. We wondered whether the serpent energy affected his dream state or perhaps inspired him to create a society of inventors and craftsmen. According to the information leaflet, Lunar Society members such as Erasmus Darwin, James Watt and Joseph Priestley regularly met in this room to discuss various topics, from the advancement of science to the abolition of the slave trade. These discussions and exchanges of ideas inspired many new discoveries and inventions that placed Birmingham at the heart of the Industrial Revolution.

Perhaps it was here in this dining room that these great innovators were somehow inspired to turn their ideas into reality. It is particularly fascinating that these extremely ingenious men not only sought each other out to share their ideas, but also actively participated in realising their dreams, founding one of the greatest manufacturing movements in the world.

Handsworth

The northern suburb of Handsworth was once a Saxon settlement centred on the River Tame and through here the Romans later constructed a road between Birmingham and Wall called Ryknild Street. Amongst one of the busiest multicultural communities in Birmingham, we find the ancient site of St Mary's Church on the edge of Handsworth Park. In 1160, the first church was built next to the Roman road, remains of which can be seen within the lower stages of the tower. St Mary's is described as 'the cathedral of the Industrial Revolution' for it houses the memorials of James Watt, Matthew Boulton and William Murdoch.

Elen visits the chancel highlighted by medieval carvings and continues through the graveyard, where many other notable industrialists lie buried. Amongst the many famous locals who rest under the hallowed turf is William McGregor, the founder of the football league, and George Ramsay, a key figure in the early history of Aston Villa football club. This seemed poignant to me as my grandfather Fred Biddlestone was an Aston Villa goalkeeper from 1930–39.

The church is now lost in a modern busy urban landscape, with few people attending services and many failing to preserve the graveyard. However, what saddens me most is that the church is continually locked and the tombs of the greatest British inventers that ever lived, men who made this country great, gather dust in the darkness.

Perry Hall Park, also next to the River Tame, seemed like a desert oasis after the many hours spent walking the hectic streets of this urban metropolis. Elen passes through a rectangular moat, all that remains of Perry Hall today. This once magnificent Elizabethan manor house, with its enormous moat fed by the nearby river, was destroyed in 1929 by the city council. Natural springs once surrounded this area and during medieval times, numerous mills existed here powered by the Tame. In its heyday, the three-storey stately home was one of the grandest in the area along with Aston Hall. For financial reasons Birmingham Corporation chose to pull it down to save Aston Hall, but allowed the moat to survive though its history is now long forgotten. Nevertheless, the parkland remains for public recreation and as a habitat for wildlife.

Elen also visits the lakes of Great Barr Park and the ruined 17th century Great Barr Hall, yet another former meeting place of the Lunar Society. It seems we have been following the trail of this powerful society all the way from the centre of

Birmingham, described by one notable historian as 'the most remarkable group of thinkers and inventors in the eighteenth century, which had a more potent effect upon civilisation than that of any other society in history. Members were unusually distinguished and a few of them became members of the elite Royal Society in London'. Their interests covered an astonishing range of subjects including geometry, geology, engineering, medicine, instrument making, chemical manufacturing, assaying, electricity, canals, roads and education. Their meetings were generally informal discussions amongst friends concerning new ideas and theories. Many of them were in contact with famous scientists and thinkers from around the world and often these great men would travel to the Midlands to attend as guests at Lunar Society gatherings. One such man was Benjamin Franklin, founding father of the United States of America.

Just to the south of Great Barr Hall, in the grounds of the Queslett supermarket, are eight commemorative standing stones to the Lunar Society. Each stone displays a member corresponding to a different phase of the moon. According to some authorities, they met at the full moon, specifically to aid their journey home after their late night discussions. Perhaps a more likely explanation is that the energy produced by the full moon gave them greater insight and revelation.

Sir Francis Scott of Great Barr Hall invited Sir George Gilbert Scott, the great Victorian architect of many Belinus Line churches, to design numerous ornamental buildings in the grounds, including a chapel, and created parkland of national renown. I was intrigued to know whether any of these buildings contained occult symbolism similar to others designed by this architect on the alignment. Today, this privately owned Gothic-styled mansion, hidden amongst trees and out of bounds to the public, has been left to crumble. Locals are incensed that the present owner has allowed it to remain in such a poor state of repair and live in hope that English Heritage will restore this once great landmark.

Also visited by Elen is the nearby St Margaret's Church with a handsome spire and, although mainly Victorian, parts of the building date to the 13th century. Interestingly it represents a significant part of my mother's life, as she worshipped here while growing up in the area. It seemed fitting that the female current connects with a church my mother described as 'her special place'. According to its early history, there has been a site of worship here for 700 years and a preaching cross once stood here prior to the 13th century, possibly Saxon, erected by one of the missionaries of St Chad from Lichfield.

As well as depicting various historical characters, the northwest window shows St Margaret kneeling at the foot of the throne of Christ piercing the dragon with a cross. The window commemorates Lady Bateman-Scott, widow of Sir Francis of Great Barr Hall.

Lunar Society members used the old road next to the church, now a track, which leads to Great Barr Hall. Elen's flow seemed to be meandering towards the great eminence of Barr Beacon, which we could see in the distance, and soon we would be walking up its slopes to discover another Node. In the meantime, we return to the city centre to follow the trail of Belinus from the cathedral.

The Guild Chapel and St Chad's Cathedral

To the west of St Martin's Church, we located the male current crossing St Martin's Queensway, travelling close to the unusual cylindrical-shaped building called the Rotunda and through the Odeon Cinema. I later discovered that the cinema is on the site of the old Grammar School built over the chapel of the Guild of the Holy Cross. This great Guild seemed to have knowledge of the serpent energies, as many of their constructions, such as Alderminster Church, the Holy Cross Church and Guild Chapel at Stratford-upon-Avon and their chapel in St Martin's Church, all fall on the flow of either Elen or Belinus. Despite its various uses over the years, the male current has remained loyal to the site, perhaps fixed there by the medieval pre-Masonic builders.

Often stonemasons incorporated special stones in the foundations of their new churches, particularly those from an earlier church or prehistoric monuments, to draw and fix the serpent energy to the new site. My friend and author Peter Knight mentioned the presence of an ancient stone in the walls of the restaurant below the Odeon Cinema. Perhaps it is a remnant of the Guild Chapel or an even earlier sacred temple that continues to hold the serpent to this modern centre of leisure.

Before it was demolished, Belinus would have visited the site of King Edward VI Grammar School on New Street, built in 1553 and later redesigned by Thomas Barry in 1835, architect of Highclere Castle and the Houses of Parliament. It was here that Edward Burne-Jones first encountered the classical myths of ancient Greece and Rome. During his later school years, he discovered the legends of an ancient culture called *Elder Edda*, the *Prose Edda* of Norse mythology and the Irish and Welsh myth cycles.

Tolkien also attended this school and, inspired by William Morris and Burne-Jones, he began to introduce fantasy to modern literature. Burne-Jones regarded the past as a largely imaginary one where Arthurian courts and the Middle Ages were for them full of beauty and chivalry rather than the brutal reality of endless wars and cruel persecution. Perhaps it was a way of escaping from the dark clouds of coal smoke that rolled from the Birmingham factory stacks. Like Tolkien, Morris was enchanted by the Norse myths, writing such poems as *The Wood Beyond the World*, *The Well at the World's End* and *The Hollow Land*. *The Earthly Paradise* also written by Morris tells of Norse seafarers who find the descendants of a band of Greek wanderers living on a remote island in the West, which inspired Tolkien's *The Silmarillion*.

It seemed to me that the Guild of the Holy Cross and the Lunar Society, whose sacred places lie on the path of the currents, were directly responsible for the development, growth and prosperity of the city of Birmingham and British industry as a whole.

North of St Philip's, the male current enters the rather plain and austere St Chad's Cathedral, standing aloof on a traffic island surrounded by major commuter routes to and from the city. Although originally built as a Georgian classical chapel in 1808, a new larger church took its place designed by Augustus Pugin (1812–52) in the German style of the 13th century.

Apparently, this church was the first Catholic shrine erected in England since the Reformation and later proclaimed as a minor basilica by Pope Pius XII in 1941. Even though the red brick exterior of St Chad's is rather uninspiring, the interior is much more splendid with its towering ceiling. Outside I dowsed the male current entering its southwest corner through a chapel that has the illusion of being a later extension, as it seems out of place with the overall design of the church. As we entered, the building appeared empty but, to our surprise, we discovered a crowd of worshippers lost in prayer in the side chapel where we dowsed Belinus.

Built in 1933 and dedicated to Edward the Confessor, this popular chapel displays magnificent windows illustrating the story of the relics of St Chad, the 7th century Bishop of Lichfield. Tradition says that during the Reformation, Arthur Dudley rescued the relics from Lichfield Cathedral and handed them to his nieces for safekeeping. Some of the saint's bones ended up under the altar of a private chapel at Aston Hall near Stone. After their rediscovery in 1840, they were delivered ceremoniously to St Chad's Cathedral and now reside in a gilded casket above the altar. Little did we know that it was from this point onwards that we were about to embark on a sacred trail of St Chad through the Midlands.

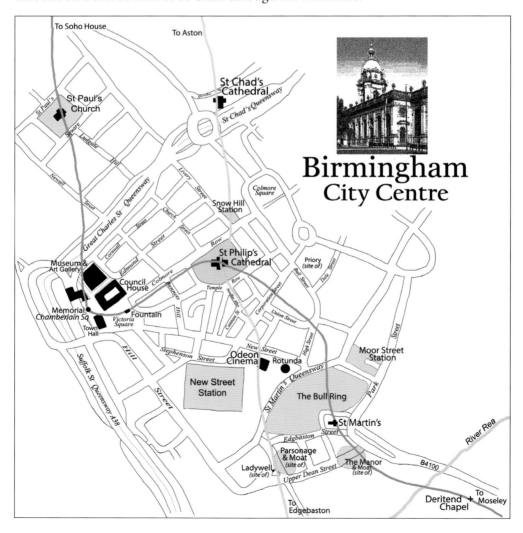

The Alignment at Aston

A few kilometres northeast of the Catholic cathedral, within the once grand Aston Park, stands Aston Hall, designed by the renowned architect Inigo Jones and said to be one of England's greatest Jacobean country houses. The site, however, has a history of settlement dating back to the Norman Conquest. In 1618, building work began on this splendid house funded by Sir Thomas Holte and completed in 1635 just in time for the family to provide refuge for Charles I during the Civil War. The house remained in the family right up until 1817 and today Birmingham City Council has preserved it as a museum. Together with Perry Hall on the path of Elen, it was considered in its day to be one of the most impressive and ornate historic houses in the Midlands.

Just metres away, the alignment passes through the parkland between the Hall and Aston's parish church, clipping the Villa Park football ground, one of the oldest and most famous stadiums in Europe where my grandfather played in the 1930s as Aston Villa's goalkeeper. Curiously, it also passes through the Birmingham City football ground in the southeast of the city.

Opposite the entrance to the hall, the male current visits Aston's church of St Peter and St Paul with its medieval tower. The Domesday Book records a church within a manor valued at a hundred shillings whilst Birmingham was in comparison only worth twenty shillings. Aston was an important religious and economic centre over a thousand years ago, at a time when Birmingham was a minor settlement. The church stands on the site of a Saxon minster and has many fine memorials including one to Ralph Arden dated around 1360. Shakespeare is a direct descendant of Arden through his mother Mary Arden, whose family home also stands close to the alignment at Wilmcote near Stratford-upon-Avon.

The Creation window at Aston Church depicting a swan at its centre

There are many tombs inside the church of the Holte family of Aston Hall, and gravestones in the churchyard of those killed in the siege during the Civil War. Hidden behind a display screen, we uncovered the remains of a very early preaching cross, carved with the Crucifixion and the figures of St Peter and St Paul that once stood in the graveyard. Belinus enters the church from the southeast through the tower and then changes course to continue his journey north.

One of the stained-glass windows called 'the Creation Window' intrigued me for it depicts heavenly angels creating man and animals and at its centre is a swan. I believe the swan represents the constellation of Cygnus and its creative power, drawn through the Spine of Albion by its very orientation to its setting stars and the Great Rift in the Milky Way.

Having passed through one of the largest cemeteries in Birmingham at Witton, we find the male current at an unusual place of power in the middle of a housing estate on a prominent hill in the northern suburb of Kingstanding. Here stands the only prehistoric monument to survive in Birmingham, a Neolithic or late Bronze Age mound next to an old Roman road measuring approximately 20 m (65 ft) in diameter and 1 m (3 ft) high, showing faint traces of a ditch around its base. On the 19 October 1642, King Charles I chose this mound to address local recruits and gentry during the English Civil War. Curiously, the name Kingstanding is older than this event and dates back to at least medieval times, when the mound was used as a platform by the king during the hunting season to observe game within the heathland of Sutton Chase. According to G.B. Benton writing in 1906, the mound was destroyed in the 19th century when the ground around was cleared for agriculture and subsequently reconstructed (Hodder 2004).

Soon we were back on the alignment at another beacon site called Barr Beacon where Belinus also meets with Elen. With all three present, this had to be an important place, although frustratingly its history seems to have been lost to the ravages of time.

Barr Beacon: Sanctuary of the Archdruid

Standing at 199 m (653 ft) above sea level, Barr Beacon is one of the highest points in the West Midlands, its extensive views making it a natural local beauty spot. Barr is an ancient British word for 'hilltop' and the name Beacon suggests it to be another fire sanctuary along the Spine of Albion. Some authorities believe that during the Iron Age a hillfort existed on the summit, although no evidence of it survives today.

Seen from above, the hill resembles a long mound or a giant finger, pointing exactly NNW along the axis of the Belinus Line towards the northern horizon where the stars of Cygnus set during the Iron Age. At precisely 340 degrees, I could just make out a cleft between two hills, which I later discovered to be the Hednesford Hills on the southern edge of Cannock Chase, a notorious UFO hotspot close to the alignment. It also points towards Castle Ring 16 km (10 miles) to the north, the largest hillfort in the Midlands. The summit of Barr Beacon is crowned by a clump of trees called the Scott Plantation, and a little to the north is an unusual circular pillared Grecian-style temple, built as a folly to commemorate those who had fallen in World War I.

Over the years, archaeologists have unearthed finds from the Stone Age, Bronze Age and Iron Age and surveyed the possible location of Neolithic standing stones, a medieval ridge and furrow plough marks. Unfortunately, Barr Beacon's northern summit has suffered through the construction of a vast reservoir, destroying much of its underlying history and archaeology.

Elen approaches from the west to form a Node with Belinus inside the Scott Plantation on the summit, now surrounded by metal railings. The Scott family of Great Barr Hall planted Scots pine and beech trees around the year 1700, complete with a flagpole, which has since disappeared. No archaeological excavation has taken place in the plantation, so evidence of any prehistoric importance beneath the surface remains unclaimed. From here, the male current continues to the folly before proceeding north.

Folly on Barr Beacon

According to legend, Barr Beacon was a place of Druidical sacrifice and the summer and winter seat of the Archdruid himself. Along with the Isle of Wight and the Rollright Stones, this is the third site where we have encountered the most powerful religious leader of the Druids. On more than one occasion, locals have seen ghostly processions of Druids slowly traversing the hill in single file. Some recall the waters from a pool, on or near the hill called Druid Mere, as possessing a supernatural quality whenever it unexpectedly overflowed.

Similar to other significant sacred places on the Belinus alignment, we discovered that the geology is an important factor here. The formation of the hill is the result of a north–south folding of Triassic sandstone over carboniferous rocks. In addition, an east–west crack called the Barr Beacon Fault cuts straight through the hill. Other sites on the Belinus Line with Nodes on or near geological cracks are the Rollrights, Uffington and the Isle of Wight.

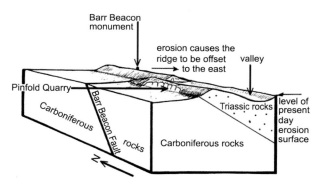

Diagram showing the geological strata of Barr Beacon

Where there are fault lines in strata containing silica such as sandstone or granite, you will often find sightings of plasma or strange lights, which is conducive to what is termed as a 'thin veil' area, where people experience ghosts, time-slips and UFOs. This usually occurs under specific conditions, particularly when the faults are under stress either by the passage of the full moon, slight earth movements or after a period of heavy rain. The crossing of two faults here may also be a key to the Beacon's unexplained paranormal activities; in fact, I discovered there have been numerous sightings of ghostly activity relatively recently.

Below Barr Beacon, on the female current is Great Barr Hall, home of Sir Joseph Scott who invited the Lunar Society to meet regularly there. Exactly when the hill came into his possession is still in dispute amongst local historians but it remained in the family until 1909. We could imagine members of this exclusive society climbing to the summit during one of their 'full moon evenings', connecting with the Node point and tuning into its celestial influences. Perhaps the site's orientation towards the Great Rift in the Milky Way and the stars of Cygnus as they set into the horizon enables people to absorb their celestial influence at this powerful spot, possibly inspiring the Lunar Society to change the face of history.

Standing on the hill looking north across the Midlands towards Cannock Chase, I sensed that Barr Beacon was a very important site during the time of the hillfort builders. The presence of two fault lines, telluric energies, a Node and a north–south corridor of power leads me to believe that this might be another chakra site along the Spine of Albion.

From the hidden Node within the woods, Elen heads north to the church of St Mary at Aldridge, one of the oldest churches in Staffordshire dating from the 13th century and containing several monuments of the Scott family. On Grove Hill near Stonnall Church, Elen connects with the site of a tumulus that once stood on its summit and regarded as a sacred sanctuary of the Druids, now marked by a solitary tree. Here her course starts to move away from the alignment to the northeast, meandering towards the little Staffordshire village of Wall, another hidden gem and secret place of ancient sanctity.

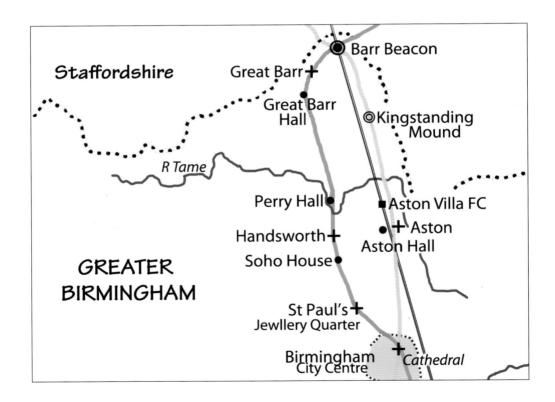

Letocetum: The Navel of England

Two thousand years ago, the Romans built a city at Wall called Letocetum, a name derived from its earlier Celtic name of *Caer Llwyd Coad* or *Caer Luitcoyt* meaning 'camp in the grey woods', grey possibly referring to the colour of the lichens that once covered this area. The two major routes of Watling Street and Icknield Street converged here, which during pre-Roman times created a significant centre of trade. However, as with many ancient tracks, the Romans rebuilt them, in particular Watling Street, an important route between London and Wales. Icknield or Ryknild Street was also an old road that ran from the Fosse Way near Stow-on-the-Wold in the Cotswolds. Its journey passes close to many of the Belinus Line sites through Birmingham as it continues to Templeborough in Yorkshire.

We pulled off the busy A5 into the small car park in the quiet rural village of Wall and walked along the marked tourist path to the church. At first there appeared to be no visible traces of its ancient past until we spotted in the field to the right of the path the footings of several Roman buildings. On a high ridge overlooking these old foundations is a small Victorian church dedicated to St John. Here the female current sweeps through the building at a slight angle through the only stained-glass window depicting a female saint. The church stands on a pagan site once occupied by a pre-Roman temple dedicated to the god Cernunnos, often depicted cross-legged with an antler headdress equivalent to the Roman god Pan. Cernunnos is the horned god of nature, invoked by the Druids to integrate man with his natural environment. As a shrine to the goddess, a Roman temple to Minerva also stood on the site, later transformed into a Christian monastic centre. Architect George Gilbert Scott, a character we see repeatedly on this journey, designed the church, which the local authority plans to convert into a Visitor Centre to serve this historic site.

After spending time exploring the church and the Roman ruins, I started to get a strong sense that this site was more than just a British settlement but an important sanctuary used for sacred ceremony by the Iron Age priesthood. Later research revealed that a clue to its lost history might lie in the place name of a 2-acre field near the museum called Castle Croft. No stone-built castle ever existed here, but I believe

Roman ruins at Wall with St John's Church in the background

the name refers to an earthen bank and ditch fortification, typical of those built by the Iron Age peoples, such as the nearby Castle Ring hillfort on Cannock Chase.

When Stukeley examined the remains of Wall in 1690, he recorded between the village and Pipe Hill to the north the blackened half-rotted remnants of an immense wooden barricade. The ancient wall was made of huge oak trees laid side-by-side and stretching for over a quarter of a mile, which he believed was part of a Roman military works. However, a century later Revd Stebbing Shaw, author of the *History and Antiquities of the County of Stafford* (1801), declared them to be much older. He noticed that 'they were strutted with balks of oak about a foot in diameter and twelve long', similar to the foundations he had seen uncovered during the excavations of prehistoric lake villages around the country. Letocetum was located next to a thoroughfare of ancient roads leaving its people vulnerable to attack during troubled times. In other parts of the country, many settlements moved to swampy ground, creating 'lake villages' or settlements surrounded by a protective moat.

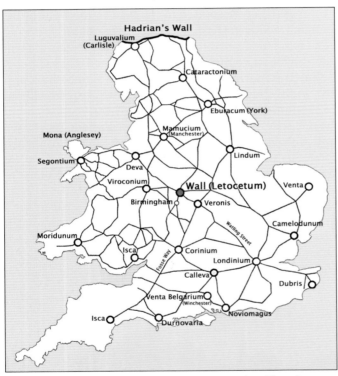

Roman map of England showing at its centre the old settlement of Letocetum, now called Wall

Wall continued as a site of importance even after the Romans departed, being the focus of many recorded raids by the Saxons and Danes. A Welsh poem called *The Lament of Cynddlan* tells that in AD 665, a local chieftain called Moriael joined the Welsh Prince Cynddlan in a victorious but devastating battle against the invading Angles at *Caer Luitcoyt* (Wall). Just a stone's throw from Wall, archaeologists uncovered the great Staffordshire Hoard consisting of Anglo-Saxon gold and silver metalwork dating from the 7th century, possibly hidden from the Angles during the battle.

Baram Blackett and Alan Wilson, researchers of Welsh history, were examining the king lists of Owain, son of Hywell Dda, and found an inventory of West Midland kings, the first of which was Mormyl. He was said to derive from a place called *Glastunun*, whose people came originally from a place called Loytcoyt (Gilbert *et al.* 1998). Nennius, the 9th century monk, also mentions Caer Loytcoyt as one of the 28 major cities of the Britons.

In the *Harleian MS 3859*, a warrior called Glast (*c.* AD 485) is referred to as 'one who came to Glastening [Glastonbury] from a place called Loyt Coyt'. Glast defends Loyt Coyt against the Angles with the aid of the warrior Arthur, successfully driving them back. If Letocetum was a great spiritual centre during the Dark Ages linked to Glastonbury, as the manuscript suggests, then, like Glastonbury, it was almost certainly an important Culdee or early Christian site.

Although the local tribes were victorious against the Saxons in the great battle of AD 665, according to historical and archaeological data the town suffered severe destruction and a new town was developed shortly afterwards just a few kilometres away at Lichfield. As the present cathedral city of Salisbury replaced the ancient centre of Old Sarum, so the city of Lichfield replaced the old centre of Letocetum. Even in the 7th century, during the time of the Venerable Bede, this area was regarded as an omphalos and Lichfield was said to mark the centre of England (Pennick 1979).

According to the *Victoria County History of Staffordshire*, the nearby city of Lichfield stands on the site where a thousand Christian holy men were massacred by the Romans, upon the orders of Emperor Diocletian in AD 286. However, excavation beneath the city reveals no evidence of a settlement dating back to this time, which leaves me to believe that this genocide took place at the early Celtic Christian centre at Letocetum rather than Lichfield, which only became an important religious settlement after the 7th century. Further evidence of this comes from the discovery of a bronze bowl at Wall bearing the early Celtic Christian symbol of *Chi-Rho*, one of the earliest monograms of Christ combining the Greek letters *chi* with *rho*, the first two letters of Christ's name, and various carved stones said to be 4th century.

Furthermore, the pre-Roman Watling Street that passes through Wall links London to Anglesey in northwest Wales, the holiest island of the Druid priesthood. It is therefore highly likely that before the Romans invaded Britain, Wall was a very important centre of the Druids, located where ancient tracks meet at the centre or omphalos of the combined nation of England and Wales. I also believe that these early Christians were in fact either Celtic or Culdee whose teachings of Jesus came with Eastern traders to Britain in the 1st century AD.

Of course, many historians still hold the view that the Druids were unholy pagans, superior magicians and sorcerers lusting for sacrifice and blood. This originates from the Roman biographers who recorded their own version of British history and the events that followed their invasion, being no more than political propaganda to justify their assault on Britain and the subsequent massacre of the Druids on Anglesey and in other areas of Britain.

In fact, Druidism was the centre and source from which radiated the whole system of organised civil and ecclesiastical knowledge and practice throughout Britain. Members of its order acted as diplomats, legislators, priests, physicians, lawyers, teachers and poets. Moreover, before their invasion of Britain the Romans sent their brightest students to be educated at Druidic schools (Elder 1962).

I believe that the desecration of the old sanctuary at Letocetum scarred and wounded the land for future sacred usage, and necessitated the building of a new religious centre at Lichfield nearby. Despite the long history of conflict and massacre that has left its stain within the land here, the Elen current still chooses to remain loyal to the old site. By bringing attention to this now forgotten sanctuary of the goddess, we hope this place will once again be revered and acknowledged as the former sacred omphalos of England and Wales.

Taking into consideration the sites we have already visited along the Belinus alignment, the serpents appear to transfer easily from the old centres of worship to the new, as if the stonemasons of the new churches deliberately manipulated them.

Lichfield and St Chad

Before arriving in Lichfield, we found Elen at Aldershawe Hall, once a moated manor house with a spring within its grounds that feeds Lichfield's water supply. As we approached the city, we could see in the distance the 'Three Ladies of the Vale', the name given to the three mighty spires rising out of Lichfield Cathedral dedicated to both St Mary and St Chad. Built in the 12th century, it stands on high ground above two great ponds giving one the impression from the south that its stands on an island. Adorned with intricate medieval carvings of England's past monarchs, this red sandstone building is beyond doubt one of the finest places of worship in the Midlands, rivalling the cathedrals of Salisbury and Wells. We were therefore thrilled that Elen had guided us to this architectural masterpiece.

However, before the cathedral ever existed, this area was a swamp fed by the numerous springs that surround it, providing natural defences against any invading forces. The Christians, after abandoning Letocetum, built a wooden church around AD 700 as a shrine to St Chad, the former Bishop of Mercia, which according to historians stood on the site of the present cathedral. St Chad's Church next to a lake a little further east at Stowe was possibly where St Chad retired and died in AD 672.

Map of Saxon England showing the Kingdom of Mercia

The Saxon Kingdom of Mercia covered most of the Midland counties that stretched from Wales to the realms of the Eastern Angles of East Anglia and from the Humber River at the southern border of Northumbria to the edge of the Kingdom of Wessex in the south.

Chad spent his early years as a pupil of St Aiden at Lindisfarne who sent him to Ireland for his education. The Archbishop of Canterbury, recognising his great devotion and character, later chose him for the position of Bishop of Mercia. He was successful in Christianising the local pagan kings and brought peace to Mercia by uniting the Britons and the Angles.

Chad first built his Christian cell by a well on the low-lying swampy area at the centre of Mercia here at

Lichfield. Pilgrims flocked to his shrine dedicated to St Mary after his death and when miraculous cures started to occur, many more started to arrive. As a result, Bishop Hedda built a new larger church in AD 700 dedicated to St Peter to house Chad's relics and later those of Hedda and St Cedd. Soon the power of Lichfield grew, becoming not just the ecclesiastical centre of Mercia but also of the Kingdom of Wessex, now the holiest place in Saxon England.

Lichfield began to thrive when in 1153 a charter granted by King Stephen allowed the town to hold a market. A Norman cathedral replaced the Saxon church of St Peter, later transformed by skilled stonemasons using a magnificent English Gothic design. During the 19th century, considerable restoration was carried out, undertaken by our old friend Sir George Gilbert Scott.

In the city centre, we dowsed Elen passing through the Guildhall that stands on the site of the old Guild House built around 1380. It is interesting to note that the male and female currents along the Belinus alignment pass through many Guildhalls, which were largely places of ceremony for members of the medieval Guilds, the forerunners of the Freemasons.

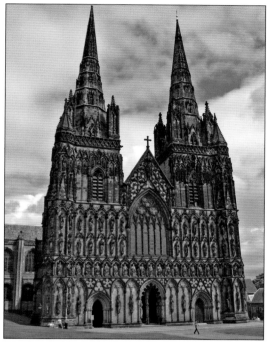

Lichfield Cathedral

The current continues to St Mary's Church in the market square, which doubles as a Heritage Centre, displaying the history of Lichfield spanning 2000 years. A succession of churches have resided here since 1150, but now the present Victorian Gothic building only provides a small chapel at its northern end for public worship.

A preacher called George Fox, who would later establish the Quaker movement, had a vision when he arrived here in 1612 that the streets would run with blood, with a 'pool of gore' forming in the marketplace. He stood without shoes outside St Mary's Church and denounced the people of Lichfield. Perhaps he had foreseen the devastation the city was to suffer later at the hands of the Parliamentarians who also desecrated the cathedral.

From St Mary's Church Elen crosses the pond, abundant with wild fowl, and enters the cathedral through a side door of the nave. We were greeted by the harmonious sound of organ music, transforming the vast interior into an angelic realm. We dowsed Elen crossing with a male current (not Belinus) by the Nave Altar, although were surprised that she avoided St Chad's shrine. However, a chance encounter with a cathedral guide brought our attention to the true significance of this spot. She informed us that recent excavations beneath the Nave Altar had uncovered foundations of the earliest church that originally housed the shrine of St Chad. Amongst the finds were the remains of a carved angel that may have been a part of his shrine, now displayed in the cathedral. Bede in the 7th century refers to the relics of Chad as being housed in:

> 'a wooden monument, made like a little house, covered, having a hole in the wall, through which those that go thither for devotion usually put their hand and take out some of the dust, which they put into water and give to the sick cattle or men to drink upon which they are presently eased of their infirmity and restored to health.' (Dumville 2003)

There is an ancient well underneath the cathedral similar to those beneath Winchester Cathedral. The early stonemasons understood that underground water amplifies the energy of the structure, for liquids are good conductors of electromagnetism, an important factor in the building of cathedrals.

To the north of the cathedral, Elen passes through a large mound at the rear of a row of houses, believed to be a Saxon burial place but more likely to be prehistoric. After leaving the city, she curves to the northwest following Cross in Hand Lane to visit the tiny village and church at Farewell. The name derives from the Saxon word for 'clear spring' that rises close to the church dedicated to St Bartholomew. The church guidebook informed us that a priory administered by Benedictine nuns once stood on this site founded by a Bishop of Lichfield in 1140. Cross in Hand Lane was so-called when pilgrims or travellers walked its path to the sanctuary of the church.

The Mysterious Chase

The elderly people of Staffordshire refer to their environs as 'the Hidden County' because within the rolling hills, now covered by factories, potteries and farms, many secrets lay hidden, waiting for those who seek them. In this great central plain of England nestling to the south of the Pennine Hills, ancient settlers cleared vast areas of forest to create villages and land for farming. When food was no longer the imperative, hunting became less popular and mining took over as the new source of trade. The underground veins of Staffordshire are rich in iron, coal and clay, their prolonged extraction having shaped the landscape we see today.

North of Barr Beacon the alignment strikes through the very heart of Cannock Chase, an area of wild heathland once part of the ancient forest that consisted of lakes and dense woodland. According to local lore, the Hednesford Hills, close to the line, were a religious centre of the Druids.

However, the Chase's modern-day mysteries are just as intriguing, for strange balls of light are commonly seen floating above the wild landscape. Was this another 'window' or 'thin veil' area, like the Isle of Wight and Barr Beacon, where our three-dimensional world interacts with higher dimensions? People witness all sorts of unexplained events at such places and indeed Cannock Chase has had its fair share over the years, including sightings of strange Yeti-like creatures and UFOs and bizarre tales of people experiencing loss of time. Many researchers believe that these types of phenomena relate to anomalies in the local magnetic field of the Earth, causing a rip in time, which can allow such strange incidents to occur. The rich deposits of iron under Cannock Chase could partially be the cause, for iron-bearing rocks emit a weak magnetic field.

Eager to uncover some of the mysteries of this hidden county, we started to explore this strange landscape following the male current from Barr Beacon to the medieval church of St Michael on the outskirts of Rushall. However, Belinus just misses the church to visit a large mound behind a fence in a private garden almost hidden amongst foliage. This Bronze Age tumulus is oval and measures about 2.1 m (7 ft) high and 11.9 m (39 ft) in diameter. Excavations here uncovered Saxon and medieval burials and the mound is now a scheduled, although somewhat neglected, ancient monument. Belinus then continues north through Pelsall Common, once part of the Arden Forest, across the large Chasewater Lake to Red Moor to connect with the site of a Cistercian abbey.

Turning off the old straight road between Barr Beacon and Castle Ring hillfort, we took a footpath between residential houses that led us through fields into a picturesque wooded valley. Here we came across the scant remains of a medieval manor house in an area known then as 'Radmore' (now Red Moor). King Stephen gave this land to hermits, who with others founded the abbey in 1141. However, by June 1155, the monks preferred another site at Stoneleigh in Warwickshire, after which the land fell back into the possession of the king. Two years later, a manor house with a surrounding moat was built over the site by Henry II, later becoming the private hunting lodge for the Bishops of Coventry and Lichfield until its dissolution.

Unfortunately, the dense woodland and barbed wire fencing hampered any extensive dowsing of the site. Most ramblers taking the footpath through here would never suspect that they were walking on former hallowed ground. The map indicates the site of 'Nun's Well' just a little further north along the edge of the wood, which at first remained elusive, until we heard the faint sound of a bubbling spring hidden by dense foliage. As we gingerly made our way through bramble and tall grass, we came to a large pool stained red by the iron-rich soil. Half-buried old stone slabs indicate the possible site of the old Nun's Well, but barbed-wire fencing made it impossible to inspect it thoroughly. We were further hindered by a large sign next to it placed there by the farmer stating 'End of path, please retrace your steps'. The spring would have supplied the monks and nuns with fresh drinking water and filled the moat around the manor house. Despite the numerous obstacles, we successfully dowsed Belinus through the supposed site of the old hermitage and hunting lodge, although the site's inaccessibility prevented us from enjoying this enchanting spot.

Castle Ring and the Hidden Node

Just over a mile east of the alignment is one of the largest Iron Age hillforts in Britain, standing on the highest point of Cannock Chase at 244 m (800 ft) above sea level. Castle Ring, constructed around the same period as Uffington Castle in Berkshire and St Catherine's Hill near Winchester, has massive double ramparts protecting an interior of 8.5 acres, and five impressive banks still survive on its southeast side.

In Britain there are few hillforts of this magnitude other than Maiden Castle in Dorset, indicating the former significance of this site. When it was first constructed, its position would have ensured commanding views in all directions; today, however, only the north and west horizons are visible due to the modern pine plantations. This fortified hill was also a safe haven for the British from the invading forces of the Angles

Castle Ring hillfort, Cannock Chase

and Saxons. In *The Holy Kingdom: The Quest for the Real King Arthur*, the co-authors Blackett and Wilson found a reference in the Welsh chronicle *Hanes of Gruffyd ap Cynan* that says Arthur fortified the Lichfield area against the Saxons. Perhaps he instructed the locals to refortify the walls of Castle Ring.

Before the Romans invaded our shores, the Druidic priests, who calculated so precisely the movements of the heavenly bodies, would have perceived this hill as the perfect location to observe the risings and settings of both the sun and moon, surrounded by sacred oaks within the ancient forest.

After dowsing around the ramparts, we detected several lines of energy intersecting at different points within the fort. However, two well-defined paths of energy corresponding to Elen and Belinus cross near the centre. The unusually broad width of our serpents often distinguishes them when faced with numerous other lines of energy at such a large site as this.

Elen enters the fort from the southeast and leaves by the northwest entrance through a tree below the ramparts decorated with clootie. This is an old pagan custom of hanging strips of cloth or 'cloot' on branches of sacred trees. Each ribbon or cloth represents the sick or dying, placed there by a friend or relative in the hope that as it rots the illness will disappear. In recent times, people hang clootie in the tree as an offering, honouring the sacred place, particularly at the Celtic festival of Beltane.

Belinus meanwhile enters not far from the main entrance in the south and heads for the centre, crossing with Elen close to a junction of well-trodden paths. The number of lines that intersect here reminded me of the hillfort on St Catherine's Hill. In fact, both places have radiating energy lines like that of a Catherine wheel. Symbolically, Castle Ring and St Catherine's Hill act like great junction boxes of earth energy, similar to St Michael's Mount and Glastonbury Tor on the St Michael Line.

This area has a wealth of ancient hidden history that can be determined through the study of 'geomythics'. By understanding the symbolic meaning of the many folktales and local traditions, and how they relate to the natural landscape of this area, we are able to get a better sense of the way our ancestors understood and utilised the earth energies along the Spine of Albion. Here we have a local oral tradition retold by 19th century Staffordshire antiquarians that Castle Ring and Barr Beacon were the headquarters of the Archdruid of Britain. Interestingly, both places are Node points along the Spine of Albion and beacon hills. Moreover, the final resting place of an

Archdruid is by a Node at the Rollright Stones. Another resides at the Needles on the tail of the Isle of Wight serpent ridge. Either there were an inordinate number of Archdruids around the country or these eminent leaders of the Druidic priesthood resided at important sacred sites to their religion.

Inside the ramparts are footings of a 12th century stone building, probably a hunting lodge for the Bishops of Coventry and Lichfield, once part of their estate of Beaudesert. Beaudesert translates as 'beautiful wildernesses', which perfectly describes this site. However, when Henry VIII came to the throne he was solely interested in the carboniferous coal seams beneath the forest floor. He confiscated the estate and hunting lodge from the Bishops after the Dissolution of the Monasteries and placed them in the hands of his Secretary of State, Sir William Paget, who took control of the mining operations that have long since scarred the landscape. His ancestors took the title of Marquis of Anglesey in 1815, the Sixth Marquis having sold Castle Ring to Cannock Urban District Council in 1933, who scheduled it as an ancient monument.

We decided to avoid the great expanse of forest that lay ahead of us and travelled instead to its northern outskirts to investigate the next significant place on the alignment at the Shugborough Hall estate, home of the Earls of Lichfield. Both currents enter the estate from the southeast, Elen slightly further north than Belinus. However, it occurred to us that the currents were the wrong way around, so somewhere between here and Castle Ring they must have crossed. Rechecking our dowsing once more, we resigned ourselves to the fact that somewhere within the impenetrable Cannock Chase forest, with its vast network of footpaths, both serpents seek another site of power.

Sometimes when we find ourselves in this predicament, we meditate at the previous Node and ask the spirits of the line to show us a mental picture of the next important crossing site. Quite by surprise, we independently received the same image of a distinctive hill with great rocks on its summit half hidden within the forest. Looking at the map there seemed to be no such place, so we geared ourselves for the challenging journey ahead following the serpents with our dowsing rods from Castle Ring.

North of Castle Ring, we eventually found Belinus crossing over two ancient tracks at a high point called Wandon Hill, an area rich in archaeology and the site of an ancient settlement. He then leads us to the historic town of Rugeley, which dates back to the late Saxon period. Rugeley's earliest known church, built in 1150 and dedicated to St Augustine, is now a ruin, but judging from what remains it must have been an impressive building before it was replaced by a new church immediately across the road in 1823. Belinus passes through the new church before entering the ruins of the medieval chancel, which still has its 13th century tower. The old church stands on raised ground, indicating that the site might have an earlier history. We spotted some interesting graves in the old churchyard such as a stone slab carved with the Rosicrucian cross and a tomb showing a couple in a death shroud, complete with the Masonic skull and bones motif.

From the church, he curiously turns towards the housing estates on the western suburbs of the town, which made us query what might be drawing him so dramatically from his usual northerly route. Meanwhile, Elen journeys through miles of forest crossing the A460 at Moors Gate through Lady Hill Coppice to the northwest edge of Rugeley, now very close to Belinus. It was then we realised that both currents were heading for a place called Etching Hill. As we approached the promontory along one of the many footpaths around its base, we immediately recognised it as the high rocky mound we had visualised in our meditation at Castle Ring. The 137 m (450 ft) high steep-sided hill displays a magnificent crown of Triassic sandstone impossible to see from the road below.

On the very summit of the hill, Elen and Belinus cross over a hole, once a Bronze Age burial cist. Those hoping to find a valuable artefact here in Victorian times destroyed the mound of earth or stone, exposing a 0.6 m (2 ft) deep burial cist, now lined with concrete, having once been the base for a flagpole. The site, with fine views over the Chase, recently showed signs of neglect and vandalism but thankfully the local community has come together to improve it, clearing away litter and broken glass from the slopes and maintaining the footpaths.

Etching Hill, Cannock Chase

The burial cist on the summit of Etching Hill marking the Node

After visiting Chapel Hill, the site of a medieval chapel, we located Elen flowing over a lake in the grounds of a garden centre, once part of the Wolseley Hall estate. The Wolseleys have owned the land since Saxon times, and it was only in the 1980s that the family sold the estate and demolished Wolseley Hall. We follow the current to a domed temple, which the family apparently used for meditation. The lake is all that remains of a moat that surrounded a Norman manor house, built over Saxon foundations.

Belinus passes through a tower within the forested Wolseley Park, along a valley called 'Hell Hole' to Beggars Hill before crossing the River Trent to the Shugborough estate.

Colwich and Great Haywood

Elen continues to the ancient church of St Michael and All Angels at Colwich in the Trent Valley, where members of the Wolseley family lie buried. The earliest church here dates from 1086, and fragments of gravestones from that period, possibly Knights Templar, are set into the wall and a carved female head sits above a medieval stoup. The church guidebook informed us that the foundations of a 7th century Saxon chapel lie beneath the north aisle, where we found the female current crossing with two other male energy lines. According to a local tradition, St Chad was a frequent visitor to this area, and probably visited the chapel on many occasions while travelling through the Saxon Kingdom of Mercia. Again, we have the curious case of a St Michael church set low in a valley next to a river rather than the hilltop shrine we normally associate with this saint. As observed in *The Sun and the Serpent*, St Michael represents the slaying of old pagan practices, which may indicate that the site of the church at Colwich replaced an earlier shrine of a pre-Christian culture.

Elen's flow includes the choir stalls and pillars surmounted by corbels carved with cherubs peering through oak leaves, a younger version of a Green Man perhaps. The church also houses the tomb of the First Lord of the Admiralty, George Anson of Shugborough Hall, and the plaque reads that he was born on 23 April 1697 and died on 6 June 1762. This great man had something in common with Shakespeare, for they both shared the same birthday on St George's Day as well as an interest in the sacred knowledge of the occult.

From the church we followed Elen a short distance to a large brick-built Victorian house surrounded by a high wall called St Mary's Abbey, now a private residence. We decided to visit the local shop to see if anyone there knew of its history. Luckily, the shopkeeper was a mine of information and informed us that the Abbey was built initially as a private residence until French nuns of the Benedictine order acquired the land and house in 1836.

At the village of Great Haywood, we find both the alignment and the female serpent. The Catholic Church of St John the Baptist marks the Spine of Albion, and the church was curiously moved here from the nearby village of Tixall, then a private chapel of the Aston family of Tixall Hall. Later, when Earl Talbot purchased the estate, builders dismantled and rebuilt it on the alignment at Great Haywood, whether deliberately or by divine intervention. Its tall narrow eight-sided tower adorned with fabulous carved beasts stands like a long pole daring you to discover its hidden meaning. Here we find yet another connection with the famous author J.R.R. Tolkien. Great Haywood was the home of his wife and it is here that he wrote *The Silmarillion* while recovering from trench fever.

However, Elen avoids the Victorian St Stephen's Church to cross the River Trent a few metres away where it meets the Sow River, just to the west of the old Essex Bridge on the eastern edge of the Shugborough Hall estate.

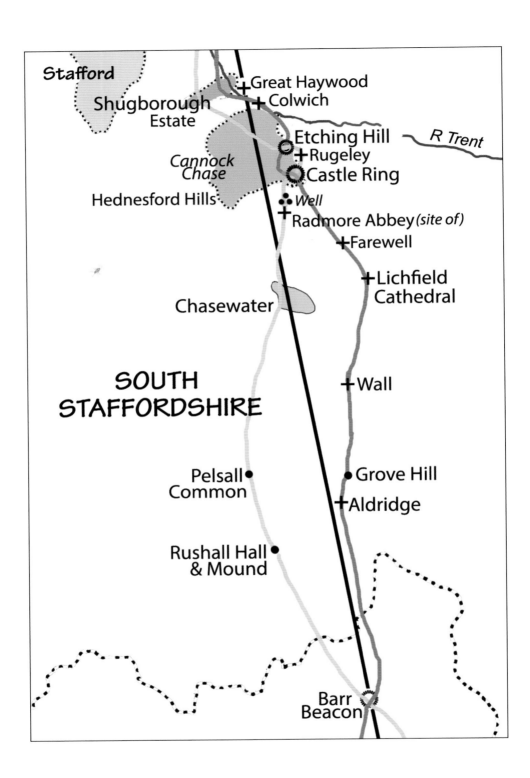

The Great Mystery at Shugborough

Shugborough Hall nestles on the edge of Cannock Chase where the Trent meets the Sow. Our ancient ancestors venerated the area around the meeting of two rivers as hallowed ground, building their temples and places of worship in close proximity to them. The powerful force generated by the collision of two bodies of running water creates subtle energies the Chinese call *chi*, a hidden energy linking all things in the Universe, finer than the electromagnetic force of the Earth and beneficial to the well-being of nature; indeed the most powerful Saxon Bishops in the country built a palace here.

The Bishops of Lichfield once wielded great influence over most of Saxon England and chose to build a moated manor house at Shugborough, which King John later used as a hunting lodge. The estate remained the property of these powerful religious men until the Dissolution of the Monasteries, changing hands several times until William Anson purchased the whole estate in 1695. He demolished a village that stood 0.8 km from the manor house in order to extend the grounds for his new three-storey brick mansion. The grand house we see today, however, was the work of his great grandsons George and Thomas. George Anson (1697–1762) became Admiral of the Fleet, making his fortune through the successful capture of a Spanish galleon laden with treasure during one of his sea voyages. This was the largest prize ever seized at sea by an English captain amounting to £400,000 at the time, which his brother Thomas inherited together with the estate after his death. This vast fortune allowed Thomas Anson to extend and improve Shugborough in a way that would fully realise his passion for classical and sacred architecture. The National Trust took over the running of the house in 1960 as part payment for death duties. Staffordshire County Council also contributed towards the cost of its upkeep and after acquiring the lease took over the administration of the estate.

Having discovered that the alignment is less than 0.4 km away at Great Haywood and both currents enter the grounds from the east, we prepared ourselves for an interesting afternoon. We first walked across the grounds to where we had last located Elen at the meeting of the Trent and Sow. She appeared to be heading to an island formed from an 18th century channelling of the Sow. There seemed to be no way across until we noticed a tiny bridge to the island next to the ornamental Chinese House.

Almost obscured by trees we came upon the peculiar Cat Monument with a carved stone figure of a crouching cat peering down from the top of a classical stone urn supported by the heads of four horned goats. This stands upon a square stone column carved with a relief panel depicting two winged griffins either side

The Cat Monument by Daniel Pincot carved in 1767

213

of a Rococo-styled Grail cup. Symbolically, griffins are the guardians of treasure and ancient knowledge, so we were curious as to what these creatures represented. Perhaps they provide an allegory or code to alert us to the presence of the female serpent energy, as the Grail cup is symbolic of the divine feminine. The monument is made of a type of concrete called Coadestone, completed in 1767 by Daniel Pincot, a close associate of the Coade family, who invented this artificial stone, found elsewhere on the estate.

The cat carving itself has an almost comic expression and stares at the enigmatic Shepherd's Monument which stands directly across the river from there. This we felt was significant as Elen also connects with this infamous elaborate stone feature. It was carved by the Dutch artist Scheemakers in 1640 and includes a marble relief depicting a mirror image of a painting by Nicholas Poussin entitled *Et in Arcadia Ego* and a Doric-style portico. Poussin's painting shows two lovers listening to an elderly shepherd who is reading aloud an inscription on a tomb – *Et in Arcadia Ego* (And I in Arcadia) – which means even in the heavenly lands of the gods, which the Ancient Greeks called Arcadia, there is still no escape from death. An inscription or code on the monument reads:

O U O S V A V V.
D. M.

According to a *Sunday Times* article dated 29 November 2004, Bletchley Park, the centre that made its name cracking Hitler's Enigma Code, has itself put forward its own theory regarding this inscription made by one of its professional code breakers who remains anonymous. The code breaker refers to the code as representing the

The Shepherd's Monument by Scheemakers carved in 1640

hiding place of a stone tablet handed down from Jacob, the Old Testament prophet, and used as a talisman by a secret society known as the Priory of Sion, a group explored by Baigent, Leigh and Lincoln in *The Holy Blood and the Holy Grail*. Admiral Lord George Anson, who organised the building of the Shepherd's Monument at Shugborough, is said to have captured the tablet from a French ship somewhere along the American coast and then buried it on an island off the shores of Nova Scotia, Canada. Anson was possibly a member of the Priory of Sion himself, as was the artist Poussin (Baigent *et al.* 1982).

Allegedly, this stone tablet, carved in an ancient script, belonged to the lost tribe of Benjamin, having eventually found its way into the hands of the Knights Templar and eventually the Priory of Sion. Apparently, even the Jacobites acquired it, some sources suggesting that the mysterious code denotes the Jacobite struggle to restore a Catholic monarch to the throne. Was Admiral Anson, who lived during the time of the Jacobite Rebellions, somehow part of this conspiracy and does the monument describe the final resting place of this ancient stone?

In a recent competition to decipher the code, one researcher substituted each letter for another and came up with 'Jesus H defy', believing it could be an exhortation to the reader to deny the divine nature of Jesus. *Et in Arcadia Ego* has also been translated as 'In Arcadia I go'. Arcadia was also the early French name for Nova Scotia and New Brunswick in Canada, territories seized by the British and visited by Admiral Anson; the famous 'Money Pit' associated with the Templars was also discovered in this area.

One of the architects closely associated with the installation of both the Shepherd and Cat Monuments was Thomas Wright (1711–86), who was also an astronomer and mathematician. Andrew Collins revealed that Wright had written a book called *Theory of the Universe* which demonstrated a true insight into mystical cosmology based on medieval concepts of heaven and hell, including fallen angels and Satan. Many writers believe that his inspiration came from Robert Fludd (1574–1637), the infamous Rosicrucian and leader of the Priory of Sion. He was also an alchemist and a mystic with a great interest in Druidism (Baigent *et al.* 1982).

There is some suggestion that originally the Shepherd's Monument, which also features the deities of Isis and Serapis, was to be set above the fire surround in the dining room at Shugborough Hall. Thomas Anson's deep interest in the mystical clearly included Ancient Egypt as his tomb at Colwich Church is in the style of an ancient Egyptian catacomb. Investigating Anson further, we found that he was a member of the Royal Society, although according to an article by Andrew Baker called *Shugborough and Rennes le Chateau*, he was not a Freemason and there is no evidence to suggest his involvement with the occult. However, he was closely embroiled with the famous Sir Francis Dashwood of the Hellfire Club, which had a reputation for 'devil worship' (Mannix 1961). Although there is no record of his association with this notorious Club, he did know many of its key members. More importantly, he was acquainted with many members of the Lunar Society and patron to Wedgewood and Boulton, two of its founders.

To the east of the Shepherd's Monument is possibly one of the oldest and definitely one of the largest yew trees in England, its canopy measuring over 152 m (500 ft); large yews such as this are often said to ward off evil spirits.

To the west of the monument, Elen passes through a tall sweet-chestnut tree with a twisted trunk before continuing along the front of the house beside the Sow to another unusual monument called 'The Ruin'. It once extended further to the west and incorporated a Gothic dovecote. On the rubble crag is the seated figure of a Druid made out of Coadestone. Apparently, there is a duplicate monument at Croome Park, home of the Earls of Coventry. Coadestone is a type of concrete specifically mixed and used to face much of the exterior of the house here. Its secret ingredients were handed down over generations of the Anson family, which according to the guidebook was lost when one of the family members died. Although it has been recently analysed, its ingredients continue to baffle experts. The figure of the Druid may be significant to the history of the site, as this ancient order often had their ritual sites close to the confluence of two rivers. After connecting with this strange monument, the female current crosses the river to an island where a classical colonnade once stood, said to be a copy of the Temple of Saturn in the Roman Forum.

Having previously located Belinus entering the estate from the southeast, we made our way along a path signposted to the tearooms just south of the main house to yet another monument called 'the Tower of the Winds'. The white octagonal building completed in 1765 is a copy of a famous classical Greek temple called 'The Horlogium of Andronikos Cyrrhestes' in Athens. Its two entrances are accessible by a small bridge over the surrounding moat and once featured a frieze of sculptured reliefs showing the nature of the wind and its effects on the human body. In the past, the lower floor of the tower was used as a dairy and the upper floor as a gambling den. Boards covering the windows now prevent us from observing the delights of its interior. However, peeping through a slit in one of the boards of the ground floor we could just make out the furnishings of a chapel, now used for wedding ceremonies. An image of the serpent-footed God Boreas once adorned this temple, which in Greek mythology has two faces, similar to the Celtic Janus head, each looking in the opposite direction. We wondered if Thomas Anson, with his knowledge of the occult, used this temple originally as a place for ceremonies of a more mystical nature, no doubt harnessing the solar serpent energy of Belinus, protected and enhanced by the surrounding water.

Belinus then targets two further monuments in the grounds modelled by James Stuart. The 'Triumphal Arch', next to the exit road, is the supposed copy of the Arch of Hadrian erected by the Athenians in honour of the Roman emperor. Thomas would later adopt it as the memorial to his brother George. Another to the northwest is the elaborately carved 'Lanthorn of Demosthenes' or Dark Lantern, copied from a 4th century BC monument in Athens.

It seemed to us that this unique collection of monuments situated around Shugborough Park were featuring very strongly on the path of the currents, almost as if they were themselves charged with some magic power that lures the dragon force. The official guide describes them as a 'haphazard medley of whimsical ideas' conceived in 1748 by Thomas Anson based on designs by the architects Thomas Wright of Derby and James Stuart. Influenced by the Classical Greek style, their purpose was to fuse the principles of harmony, symmetry and proportion with the laws of nature to create the ideal landscape.

We left Belinus and Elen heading northwest crossing the Sow. As we made our way back to the car, we stopped to chat to a guide who by chance was walking through the grounds. He was happy to answer our questions, but our jaws well and truly fell open when he announced that the word Shugborough actually means 'territory of the dragon' – *Shug* being an ancient word for dragon; interestingly, other historians believe that Shug means 'demon'.

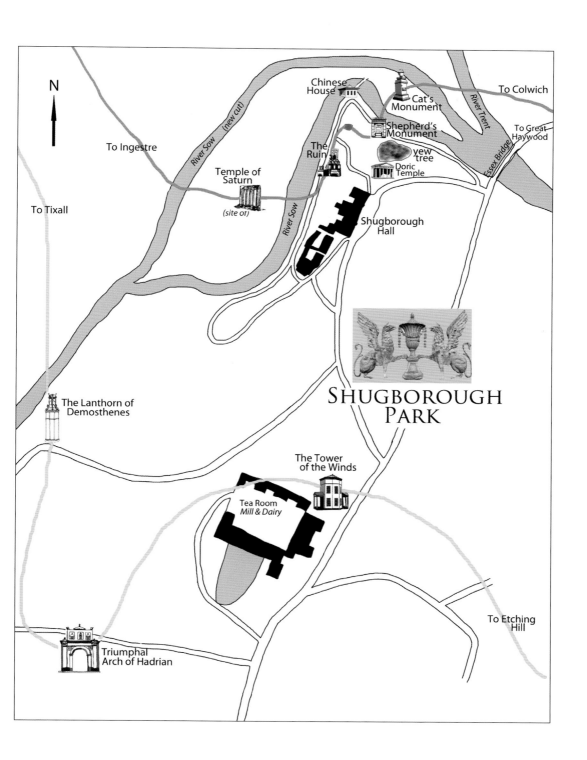

N

To Colwich

To Ingestre

Chinese House

Cat's Monument

River Sow (new cut)

Shepherd's Monument

To Great Haywood

The Ruin

yew tree

Temple of Saturn

Doric Temple

River Sow

(site of)

Shugborough Hall

To Tixall

Essex Bridge

River Trent

SHUGBOROUGH PARK

The Lanthorn of Demosthenes

The Tower of the Winds

Tea Room
Mill & Dairy

To Etching Hill

Triumphal Arch of Hadrian

217

Chapter 8

The Chase to the Edge
The Trail of St Chad Through
Staffordshire and Cheshire

Tixall and Chartley

After crossing the Sow from Shugborough, both currents flow north through a sacred peninsular formed by the Trent and Sow valleys. Belinus heads for the village of Tixall and Elen towards Ingestre. This area has many prehistoric tumuli or burial mounds (called Lows in Staffordshire) including Kings Low and Queens Low, possibly the burial of ancient British or Saxon Mercian royalty.

Edward Aston (1494–1568), a prominent Staffordshire Protestant, built an Elizabethan hall at Tixall in 1555. Around 1580, his son Sir Walter Aston constructed a grand gatehouse, through which Belinus flows, and this was described in 1598 as 'one of the fairest pieces of work made of late times in all these counties'. This accolade, however, was not to last for it later became a shelter for cattle.

Mary Queen of Scots was incarcerated at nearby Chartley Hall, built in the 15th century, having arrived on Christmas Eve 1585 as its prisoner. A chair cover and set of bed curtains embroidered by her are still preserved in the house. While there, she

The remains of a long barrow called the Bridestones in the saddle of the Cloud

became involved with Sir Anthony Babington, who plotted to assassinate Elizabeth I and crown Mary as Queen of England and Scotland. Having intercepted letters incriminating Mary in this plot, Walsingham, Elizabeth's Spymaster, removed her to Tixall Hall while his men searched her rooms at Chartley.

Whilst at Tixall, she was completely oblivious to what was about to befall her. On 11 August 1586, she accompanied her captor, Sir Amyas Paulet, on a hunting expedition and saw a group of riders galloping towards her. Believing them to be Babington's men, she hurriedly rode to meet them only to find that they were English soldiers sent to arrest her. Realising the severity of her situation she dismounted and sat on the ground refusing to move, requesting the armed guard to kill her there and then. Her close aid eventually persuaded her to return to Tixall Hall quietly, but before doing so she knelt against a tree and prayed loudly. After a further two-week stay under guard at Tixall she returned to Chartley Manor. As she rode through Tixall Gatehouse she cried out to the beggars who were amongst the assembled crowd, 'Alas, I have nothing for you, I am a beggar too; all is taken from me'.

Today the Gatehouse is a holiday let, but whoever stays there will have to share it with a few ghosts. Nearby is the 12th century church of St John the Baptist, rebuilt in 1772, where we dowsed the male current passing through the High Altar. We follow him through the grounds of Tixall Hall estate where he visits a healing pool before heading for Queen's Low tumulus, curiously avoiding King's Low to the west. Instead, he prefers the lofty heights of Beacon Hill to the northeast of the county town of Stafford. Looking across the Staffordshire countryside from its summit, I again had a sense that the Spine of Albion route may have been laid out by ancient surveyors using beacon hills.

Meanwhile Elen crosses the road a little east of here drawn to a golf course at Ingestre Hall. This grand Jacobean mansion is one of the finest in England built in 1613 by Sir

Tixall Gatehouse, north of Shugborough estate

Walter Chetwynd on the site of an earlier manor house. Today it is a residential art centre, so we were able to visit the magnificent church of St Mary the Virgin situated in its grounds near the old stable block.

Elen flows through the High Altar overseen by magnificent stained-glass windows of numerous female saints and various depictions of Mary the Virgin. Sir Walter Chetwynd was a most interesting character, being a renowned antiquarian, patron of architecture, mathematician and Fellow of the Royal Society. Walter commissioned the building of Ingestre Church in 1673 with designs from his friend and fellow society member Sir Christopher Wren.

St Mary's Church replaced an earlier chapel that stood in Church Field a short distance away, now the private Ingestre Park golf course. I later discovered that a great healing shrine once stood on these green fairways. According to local history, St Erasmus' Well was a sulphurous spring said to be famous for the cure of the 'king's evil', a skin disease called scrofula. Its popularity grew, necessitating the building of a chapel next to the healing waters during the reign of Henry VII.

According to the Chetwynd Manuscripts in the Salt Library at Stafford: 'the adjoining wells were much frequented by lame and diseased people, many whereof found there a cure for their infirmity, inasmuch that at the dissolution thereof, the walls [of the chapel] were hung about with crutches, the relics of those who had benefited thereby. Nor was the advantage small to the priest, the oblations of the chapel being valued in the king's books at £6 13s. 4d'.

Many of these healing pools have disappeared, except for Tixall Park Pool visited by Belinus to the east and another on the golf course visited by Elen. The geology may explain this healing phenomenon as the minerals from the iron-rich soil would have enhanced the many springs scattered around this sacred peninsular. Alternatively, the curative powers may be due to the presence of Belinus and Elen; in mythology, pools and lakes are the abode of dragons and serpents.

Elen veers towards the east from Ingestre Church to Stowe-by-Chartley and the Norman church of St John the Baptist. Here she connects with an ancient preaching cross in the churchyard and a stained-glass window of the Virgin and Child. Ranulph Gervons, Earl of Chester and Lord of Chartley, founded the first church on the site in 1150. Even though the name Stowe is an Old English word for 'holy place', little remains from the time of the early Christians apart from the base of the old cross which may date to the Saxon period.

Nearby stands the imposing ruin of Chartley Castle, built upon a prehistoric camp

Ruins of Chartley Castle

and an artificial hill. One of the first wooden castles in Britain stood on this site followed by a Norman motte and bailey castle within a single bank and ditch enclosure. All that remains of the royal castle today are two round towers and a portion of the walls of a structure originally built in 1220 by Ranulph Blundeville, Earl of Chester, who also founded the church nearby.

A strong atmosphere shrouds the area around Chartley, pervading it with an air of sanctity that reaches far back into history to a period when the mysterious Bronze Age peoples settled on the hill. The appearance of a crop formation in a field below the castle in the summer of 2006 drew many New Age enthusiasts to the area. It was during that same year that other formations had appeared at key places along the Belinus alignment in Hampshire, Oxfordshire and Berkshire, as if the circlemakers were deliberately marking the alignment.

We located the Elen current crossing over the artificial mound or motte within the ramparts of the Norman castle where other energy lines meet with her on its summit. We now had a sense as to why Elen veered so sharply to the east from Ingestre; she was clearly attracted to this ancient mound, yet another dragon's lair of telluric power like the many other mounds we have encountered along the Spine of Albion.

Unfortunately, there was a tense atmosphere pervading this hill and as we walked around, I could feel psychic disturbance. Soon after our visit, I discovered that a very strange event had occurred near the castle in 1986. One day, while driving along the road by the ruin, a couple suddenly encountered a large stag galloping across the road in front of the car, forcing them to brake sharply. Before they had time to gather their thoughts, another creature, which they described as monkey-like, came bounding after the stag and charged their vehicle. This strange creature seems to be unique to Cannock Chase and has been witnessed on many occasions, including running across the grounds of Shugborough Park in 1987. There have been many reports of occult practices and strange phenomena taking place all around the Chase. I believe at certain times when the highly magnetic subterranean ironstone rocks under Cannock Chase are stressed, a high magnetic field creates an opening or 'rip in time', through which such creatures and events from the past or the future enter this time and space.

Moreover, exposure to high magnetic fields and plasma (balls of light) can cause hallucinations.

This I believe has occurred at many pagan places of power along the Belinus Line, particularly on the Isle of Wight, Meon Hill, at the Rollright Stones, Uffington and St Catherine's Hill in Winchester.

After the rather unsettling sensations of Chartley, Elen guided us to the tranquil setting of St Mary's Church in the pretty village of Gratwich. The brick-built church looks recent but the list of its rectors dates back to 1230.

North of here we arrived at St Mary's at Checkley, which the English poet and writer Sir John Betjeman describes as one of the finest medieval churches in North Staffordshire. It has three ancient carved Saxon crosses in the graveyard standing by the south entrance of the church, a very rare sight indeed. According to legend, they commemorate three Saxon bishops slain by the Danes in a nearby battle.

Remains of Saxon crosses at St Mary's Church, Checkley

Elen enters the church through one of the most ancient fonts in Staffordshire dating from the Saxon period. St George and St Margaret pinning the dragon at their feet feature in the stained-glass windows. Elen meets this female dragon slayer again at the village of Draycott-in-the-Moors just north of here on a high mound that typifies a 'dragon hill'. Here St Margaret's Church looks down upon an old straight track, now the A50, between Derby and Stoke, standing close to a Roman settlement. Although it dates from Norman times, recorded evidence of a Saxon cross in the churchyard indicates a much earlier Christian site. Other features of interest are the numerous gargoyles and a Green Man who stares down from the ceiling near the entrance.

King Arthur and Caverswall Castle

Along the eastern outskirts of Blythe Bridge, Elen returns to the alignment at the Tudor-styled village of Caverswall. Here stands a fairytale castle set within an idyllic landscape designed with high parapet walls, turreted towers and a deep moat with a long and fascinating history dating back to Saxon times.

Ernulphus de Hesding built a manor house on this site within an ancient oak forest by the source of the River Blythe. After the Norman invasion, William the Conqueror gifted the estate to Robert de Stafford, his friend and kinsman. Near the end of the 12th century, Thomas de Caverswall acquired the house and King John visited the 'Mansion of Caverswall' whilst hunting in the area; a carving over the mantel in the present dining room commemorates his visit. In 1275, Sir William de Caverswall, a knight serving Edward I, was given a licence to fortify the Saxon manor house. The house stands in close proximity to the two ancient roads mentioned above said to be Roman, one of which passes by St Margaret's Church at Draycott-in-the-Moors.

The medieval castle, built of sparkling red sandstone, became the home of the Earls of Huntingdon by descent, but they were forced out after the Reformation due to their Catholic persuasions, leaving the building to fall into decay. However, a wealthy merchant from Wolverhampton called George Craddock rescued the building during the reign of James I, having made his money from the lucrative wool trade during the Elizabethan era. His son, Matthew, a staunch Puritan and Parliamentarian and later Mayor of Stafford, restored the ruined site, incorporating much of the medieval walls and Norman tower into a new castle in the typical Jacobean fashion.

During the Civil War, Caverswall became a garrison for Parliamentarian troops who burned down most of the surrounding forest, including ancient oaks and elms. The estate then passed through many hands, including the Wedgwood family who sold it to a community of Benedictine nuns in 1811. They converted it into a girl's boarding school, which became a convent in 1931. Once again, this medieval religious order seeks out a place of power inhabited by the female serpent.

Caverswall Castle on the alignment

As we approached the castle along a majestic tree-lined avenue set in glorious parkland, we sensed an atmosphere of enchantment, a truly inspiring place for those who enjoy connecting with the spirit of the land. This was such a contrast to the grey and cheerless suburbs of Stoke-on-Trent we had just passed through. I first visited Caverswall Castle when it was still a hotel in 1995 and was fortunate to meet the owners who informed me of its history. I had to stifle my excitement when they told me that according to local tradition it was one of the fabled courts of King Arthur.

There are in fact several myths and legends associated with this castle, but to find an Arthurian tale was remarkable. To think, I would never have visited this hidden place were it not for the fact that it marked the alignment. In the medieval romances, King Arthur and his Knights ardently pursue the Grail and encounter many obstacles during their quests. One was to seek out Christ, but in the acceptance of this task, they were required to battle against evil forces. In the Caverswall legend, Arthur rescues the 'Lady of the Castle' from impending danger; some stories say the lady in question was actually his future wife Guinevere. The owner gifted to me a little guidebook on the history of the castle, which states:

> 'King Arthur kept his court at Caverswall on occasions. It was, perhaps, at one of these festivities that the "fair Lady of Caverswall" distinguished herself. One of the features of such gatherings seems to have been a competition to see who was the most virtuous of the ladies present. During the dancing, each lady in turn donned a garland of fresh leaves on the occasion of Arthur's visit, the honour was won by the "fair Lady of Caverswall", upon whose shoulders the magic kirtle of chastity did not wither, but retained its pristine freshness.'

Such intriguing associations made us wonder if long ago Caverswall was a place of fertility rituals where young women of noble birth were groomed to become royal brides. Remarkably, King Alfred of Wessex is also said to have married a Lady of Caverswall. If this is true then, perhaps, the beauty and chastity of these highborn 'ladies of Caverswall' gained such a reputation that kings and princes came here from all over England to choose a wife or mistress. However, these stories may hide a factual truth in allegory, for both King Arthur and King Alfred seem to feature in the folklore of many places along this north–south Spine of Albion. Perhaps one of the roles of the Celtic King Arthur is to protect the mystical pathways associated with the northern stars, or keep 'watch' over the celestial pole, as his name, according to some, derives from Arcturus meaning 'Bear Guard' or *Arth Fawr*, the Welsh term for the Great Bear constellation.

The blood of the 'once and future king' runs through the veins of George Craddock who rebuilt the house. His descendants stem from a long line of Welsh nobles including Arthur, which ironically seems fitting, for he returned to restore one of the courts of his legendary ancestor.

Some historian's question why this elaborate and well-engineered castle was constructed in such an exceptionally boggy and inaccessible terrain, particularly in the 13th century, a time of considerable strife and poverty. However, I believe that the architects understood the significance of this site as a sacred abode of divine feminine power on the Belinus alignment, enhanced by the presence of natural springs in an old oak forest bordered by ancient roads.

I dowsed Elen through the morning room of the castle, possibly connecting with some of the underground springs. She crosses with an unidentified male current in the terrace garden on the west side of the castle and then heads to the 13th century St Peter's church in the village built by Sir William Caverswall, her flow marked there by a corner-stone inscribed with an ordnance insignia.

On the outskirts of Stoke-on-Trent, the alignment passes through a church situated on a prominent hill just north of Caverswall in the village of Bagnall. The site of the church has a history dating back to Saxon times and is dedicated to St Chad. Inside we find a beautiful stained-glass window of the saint between Jesus and Mary. In the churchyard, a very early altar stone, used now as a base for a sundial, indicates an early Christian site possibly founded by St Chad. So far, this now very familiar saint has visited several churches on both the male and female currents as well as the alignment; perhaps he too was following the dragon currents 1500 years before us!

To the northwest of Caverswall in the Trent Valley is Park Hall Country Park, one of Stoke-on-Trent's most important natural sites. Its sandstone canyons are fascinating to geologists and for dragon followers too, as Elen flows through here on her way to the mystical waters of the Trent.

Close to the edge of Stoke is the site of a once significant Cistercian abbey dedicated to St Mary, known as Hulton Abbey. All that remains today is a few foundation stones amongst a large council estate on the eastern outskirts of the city. The surrounding road names such as Abbey Road, Cloister Way, Chantry Way and Abbey Way clearly indicate the true extent of the grounds long ago. From as early as 1219, the Abbey thrived as an important centre for spiritual devotion and economic activity right up to the Reformation. The layout followed a standard Cistercian plan of building based on the Christian cross, but after its dissolution the great edifice became a quarry for material used in the construction of newer buildings. Here we dowsed Elen still holding to the memory of this site as she connects with the tracings of the west transepts and the High Altar. Sadly, these few remnants fail to provide much of a picture of this once magnificent abbey.

Knypersley and the Druid Grove

Crossing the Trent, Elen visits the church of St Bartholomew at Norton-in-the-Moors, which has a history of a Saxon church on the site. Unfortunately, locked doors forced us to continue to Greenway Bank Country Park, formerly the old Knypersley estate near Biddulph. This local beauty spot frequented by picnickers and walkers is located next to Knypersley Reservoir set within extensive woodland.

In 1808, John Bateman, an industrialist from Salford, purchased the estates of Biddulph and Knypersley from Sir Nigel Gresley. Bateman's son James, moved to Knypersley Hall in 1838, an Evangelical preacher and industrialist obsessed with pagan rites and creation myths. He landscaped the park and re-erected a 2000-year-old Etruscan tomb in the grounds, aided by the Victorian marine painter and landscape architect Edward William Cooke.

Two of the estate's most sacred features are Gawton's Well and the Gawton Stones, comprising a great boulder balanced on three stones, located in the woods to the east of the reservoir. The Victorians believed that the Stones were a Druidic cromlech and the name stems from a hermit who resided there in the 1600s. Bateman was convinced that the whole area was once a Druidic sanctuary rededicated and Christianised by the presence of the hermit.

Doug Pickford, a local author with a fascination for folklore and Earth Mysteries, mentions in his book *Staffordshire, Its Magic and Mystery* that the Gawton Stones was a traditional place of healing for those who crawled beneath them. He also states that the remains of a Druid grove surround the well, one of the finest still surviving in Britain. More significant is the fact that many believe this well to be the spiritual source of the Trent and a place of pilgrimage to partake of its healing water and to honour the spirits. The actual source of the Trent is to the east of here in a field on the edge of the

A stone marking the source of the River Trent on the edge of the village of Biddulph Moor

village of Biddulph Moor through which the alignment passes, marked by a stone inscribed 1935. The Trent is the third largest river in England, which historically and culturally divides England in two. Its surging waters are obviously a natural focus for the currents and the alignment.

When I first visited Gawton's Well, I was amazed to find a strong flow of water still swelling out from the ground over a cascade formed by ancient stones and a protective dry-stone perimeter wall. Despite Victorian restoration and considerable alteration since then, a strong 'spirit of place' still resides here.

The Elen current passes through this idyllic spot surrounded by old yew trees and crosses a footpath to an old stone stump set in the ground, possibly a broken cross shaft, said to mark Gawton's hermitage. Perhaps Gawton chose this site due to its proximity to the beneficial curative powers of the natural spring water rising here. Elen avoids the cromlech, meandering instead towards a cliff-face

Gawton's Well, Knypersley

with a cave or crevice above, which I believe to be the true site of the hermitage. This reminded me of a similar natural feature I visited in Arizona in the US and at Ayers Rock in Australia. Indigenous tribes around the world revere naturally formed caves or fissures. I believe the old hermits knew the secret power inherent in caves, for the entrances lure the beneficial qualities of orgone energy or chi. Inside,

Gawton's Cave, the possible site of Gawton's hermitage

cosmic forces filter through the rock and combine with the therapeutic earth energies to create an environment conducive to connecting with one's higher consciousness through meditation.

At the entrance to the woods by the edge of the lake, Elen passes through the Wardens Tower, built by the father of James Bateman in 1828. Perhaps he took inspiration from the current to build this structure here for meditation. The chi radiating from the source of the Trent imbues the surrounding area with healing energy, even the beautiful flora and fauna clearly benefiting from its vital force – a truly magical place.

Walking north along a footpath, we continued to follow the dragon path to Biddulph Brook and the parish church of St Lawrence on the edge of the town of Biddulph. This grand church, with its massive spire, stands on sacred ground once occupied by a small oak-built chantry, possibly destroyed by the Danes in AD 850–900. The Saxons rebuilt it in stone, as evidenced in the arch to the belfry, becoming a larger church under the Normans. On the exterior of the church by the south wall, stone slabs now arranged as seating are thought to be Knights Templar graves, possibly transferred from Hulton Abbey that administered the parish. Although Hulton Abbey had no known associations with the Knights Templar, its Cistercian order was closely linked with its military arm. It is also possible that there was a Templar site not far from St Lawrence's Church near Biddulph Grange, also owned at one time by the Cistercian monks of Hulton Abbey.

The Meonia at Biddulph Grange

John Bateman purchased Biddulph Grange as part of the Biddulph estate and with his son James Bateman moved there from Knypersley Hall in 1840, transforming it into a grand mansion and created one of the finest Victorian gardens in England. With the help of artist and landscape architect Edward William Cooke, they created an antiquarian theme park, which included an Egyptian temple with four stone sphinxes, a statue of the 'Ape of Thoth' and an Egyptian Apis Bull with a sun disc between its horns. A Chinese temple with a pagoda stands next to a miniature lake and the finished plan is fashioned as the perfect outline of Britain's coastline. Curiously, according to this garden plan of Britain, the Egyptian temple falls exactly on the area of Biddulph in North Staffordshire.

Perhaps Bateman and Cooke followed the principles of the old Chinese geomancers who were renowned for transforming the full range of nature into microcosm, where mountains, green hillocks, rivers, streams and pools are reduced to the scale of a garden. In this way, the fast-flowing course of the dragon lines as they run across the land become modified and refined to a slow meander by the creation of a series of gentle curves, diverting them like a river to fertilise the land more effectively. From this secluded landscape the serpent can be modified by the angles and shapes of trickling waterfalls, abundant foliage, rocky caverns and well-proportioned features, all laid down in harmony to enchant the senses of the observer, and in this case to nourish and harmonise the female serpent.

In 1872, Robert Heath purchased the Grange and in 1923 it became an orthopaedic hospital. When the hospital closed in 1991, the National Trust acquired the house and

Egyptian temple in the gardens of Biddulph Grange

gardens to ensure its survival.

Elen enjoys the extravagant melding of fauna and form as she snakes her way through the grounds, first visiting a stone tunnel, a glen and the lake by the Chinese temple. Here she highlights for us a group of mock standing stones reminiscent of the Bridestones, a prehistoric monument a few kilometres northeast of here. She passes through the Apis Bull and enters the doorway of the Egyptian temple through a side room, just avoiding the statue of Thoth.

Andrew Collins included some fascinating and controversial information on Biddulph Grange in his book *The Seventh Sword* (1991). Using a combination of traditional and psychic research, he discovered that in the 19th century the Grange was a ritualistic and mystical centre for the Rosicrucian Meonia Group. They specifically chose this site because of its ancient association with nearby sacred sites such as the enigmatic hill called the Bosley Cloud just east of Congleton. The contours of this hill are shaped in such a way that the sun gives the appearance of setting twice at the summer solstice when viewed from the churchyard at Leek.

I wondered if the Meonia Group were aware of the female dragon force at Biddulph Grange. Perhaps they drew inspiration from its wisdom in the course of their rituals. Certainly, the water features, exotic flowers, shrubs and trees in the Biddulph gardens would have heightened the divine powers of the female serpent as she flows through the grounds. Although there is no documented proof that such a group ever existed, the psychics working with Collins say that their leader was a young woman called Mary Heath who posed as a housekeeper or nanny to Robert Heath, owner of Biddulph Grange. Curiously, although not related, they shared the same surname. Her family supposedly had bloodline links to the House of Guise in France, one of whom was Mary of Guise, the mother of Mary Queen of Scots.

The name Meonia is similar to Meon, the Old English word for 'middle', a name that features at key places along the Spine of Albion. The Belinus Line enters the country at the Meon Estuary and connects with Meon Hill near the centre of England. In the Bible we have 'Baal-meon', meaning the 'Lord's (Baal) dwelling' or 'house' (*meon*). Collins believes Meonia is an anagram of 'I am one', the name given to the Supreme Being.

Although Collins' work is controversial, his practice of using psychic questing has led to the retrieval of many physical objects under mysterious circumstances, including a short sword with an inscription on the blade that reads 'Meonia for Marye'. Also on the weapon is a monogram that resembled the personal insignia of Mary Queen of Scots. The term 'psychic questing', first introduced by Collins, means the use of inspired thoughts and visionary information to seek new insights into hidden history and to locate concealed artefacts. In some ways, both Caroline and I apply a form of psychic questing as well as dowsing through meditation and visualisation to seek the hidden pathways of the dragon force along the Spine of Albion.

Close by is Biddulph Old Hall, once the home of the de Biddulph family whose descendants were of the royal house of Mercia. Their original settlement, dating around AD 900, is now an earthwork in Bailey's Wood almost opposite the Grange. The descendants of Bertram de Verdon, first overlord of Biddulph who fought in the third Crusade, built the present hall during the reign of Elizabeth I. As staunch supporters of Charles I, they left the Hall to fall into ruin after fleeing Cromwell's troops during the Civil War.

Elen passes through the old tower of the house, which at the time was undergoing restoration by its new owners. She then travels to an unusual stone feature by the road on the edge of the grounds called Shepherd's Cross, possibly carved from an old standing stone showing large veins of iron. On the opposite side of the road are the remains of a holy well surrounded by old oak trees. James Bateman restored both these monuments, creating steps and a courtyard around the cross and enclosing the well with elaborate stonework, including a small offering shelf incorporated into the masonry. It is possible that early Christians shaped the pagan standing stone into a cross to Christianise the site. Unfortunately, these two monuments are not ideal to explore as they stand either side of a sharp bend of a busy country road. Despite this, the site still holds a spiritual significance thanks to the restorations of Bateman.

Shepherd's Cross near Biddulph Old Hall

The Bridestones

Elen continues north across Biddulph Common crossing the main road between Congleton and Leek to visit the Bridestones, a group of standing megaliths placed in the saddle of the hill called Bosley Cloud or the Cloud. According to excavations carried out in 1936 by Professor Fleur of Manchester University, the Bridestones were once part of a late Neolithic long barrow dating from 2300 BC, with a paved court in front of the burial chamber, a feature rarely seen in Europe. Incredibly, the barrow once measured 10 m (33 ft) across and over 91 m (300 ft) long, with an internal chamber 9 m (30 ft) by 12 m (40 ft), making it larger than the famous West Kennet Long Barrow at Avebury and therefore the greatest chambered long barrow in Britain.

The barrow would have been orientated east–west in honour of the equinox sunrises. A box structure existed near the entrance to the chamber consisting of two compartments separated by a holed stone through which the spirits of the dead are supposed to pass. In many cultures around the world they are called 'spirit-holes' through which spirits from other dimensions can cross into our world. Fleur also reported: 'There is an old resident of the district who recounts that many years ago an engineer engaged in the cutting of the Manchester Ship Canal, visiting the spot, actually used one of the biggest monoliths for the purpose of carrying out a demonstration with a detonator. As a result of this the great stone was broken off close to the ground'. This demonstrates the complete lack of respect people felt towards these monuments at that time. Thanks to Fleur's excavations, the remaining monoliths were uncovered, having been buried deep underground, piecing one together that had split apart and returning it to its original position.

According to a drawing by Mr Simms in 1766, the long barrow consisted of twelve standing stones in an ovoid shape that surrounded two further stones. The lidded two-compartment chamber was at the west end of this group of twelve stones with four taller standing stones leading away from here aligned to the west. The remains you see today formed part of the chamber; the rest of the stones were broken up to make roads, field walls and landscape gardens, including a rockery and water feature at nearby Tunstall Park.

Sketch by Mr Simms dated 1766 of the Bridestones long barrow

The name of the monument derives from Bride, Bridie or Brigit, the ancient goddess of the Brigantes tribe, who represented the fertility of the land, invoked using fire ceremonies.

Despite the wanton destruction of the Bridestones, Elen still chooses to honour this ancient site, perhaps attracted by an essence of the old pagan worship of the goddess and the old shaman practice of communing with the ancestors that took place here. Her north–south flow through the monument connects precisely with the prior location of an inner chamber, an artificial cave or symbolic womb of birth and death.

Dial Road passes the entrance to the old long barrow, which according to some historians derives from 'deiseal', *deas* being the Celtic word for right hand and *sul* meaning 'sun'. This refers to a very ancient ceremony of walking three times around a stone circle east–west, depending on the course of the sun, their right hand pointing towards the centre as the ancient priests circled the stones; walking in the opposite direction is termed 'widdershins'.

Doug Pickford in his book *The Bridestones* mentions a poem by The Revd J.E. Gordon who wrote:

'he could never approach the Cloud and the Bridestones without becoming conscious that his presence there constituted a challenge to the genius of the place to disclose the secrets of the ages. Nor could he divest himself of the consciousness of a strange atmosphere of mystery and awe, of a sense of being watched by an indefinable presence, not unkindly, but vastly aged, pathetically wistful and jealous of departed glories who replied to his challenge.'

Pickford also recalls a story told to him by a man who experienced a strange event near the Bridestones. Whilst driving home late one night, he stopped the car opposite the long barrow to relieve himself in the hedge. Suddenly, he saw a golden light shining over the stones and sparks flying from the megaliths. In his panic to get away, the car failed to start. With his head under the bonnet, he turned around to find the ball of light hovering over his head. With that, he blacked out and woke up to find himself in a copse about 200 m (656 ft) away from his car wearing only his trousers, which were full of static electricity. Looking at his watch he also found that he had lost time. Could this be one of those classic UFO abductions, or was his experience the result of exposure to a plasma light form. As mentioned previously, those who come into close contact with these earthlights often experience loss of time due to the strong magnetic field affecting time and space.

Locals tell how they often break into a run when they pass the stones to avoid their powerful influence. Psychics have sensed a woman lying buried by the stones, sacrificed there during a ceremony. Arthur Mee in *The King's England, Staffordshire* mentions a legend associated with the Bridestones where a Viking, having married a Saxon woman in the village, was slain along with his wife and buried there. Others have seen a ghostly white lady wandering around the stones; light-ball phenomena may explain such apparitions.

The Cloud

The Cloud stands on the border of Cheshire and Staffordshire just east of the Derbyshire Peak District. Its highest point, called Cloud End, faces towards the northern horizon overlooking the River Dane. As we were soon to discover, this entire region is part of a forgotten sacred landscape full of mystery.

The Cloud can tell us much about our Earth's history through its geological layers. At the base of the hill are mudstones with layers of millstone grit and sandstone above. The passage of ice around the hill's flanks during successive ice ages has fashioned these layers into the shape of a gigantic long barrow, reminiscent of Barr Beacon near the southern border of Staffordshire.

View of the Cloud marking the alignment and a Node on the borders of Staffordshire and Cheshire

As mentioned at the beginning of the book, John Michell noticed how the shape of the Mump and Glastonbury Tor point in the direction of Avebury, leading to the discovery of the St Michael Line. The Cloud and Barr Beacon point NNW and mark not only the Belinus alignment but also the northern and southern boundaries of Staffordshire.

The shape of Cloud End allows for a unique solar phenomenon to occur when viewed from the Leek area during sunset at the summer solstice. The sun appears to set into the summit of the Cloud, and then reappears a few minutes later in a hollow of the hill's vertical northern slope. However, because of the obliquity of the ecliptic, the double sunset is no longer visible from the traditional site of Edward the

Looking north towards Alderley Edge from the summit of the Cloud called Cloud End

Confessor Church at Leek. This is due to the Earth being slightly pear-shaped and the variance of its axial tilt. The gravitational pull of the sun and moon causes uneven pressure on the Earth's northern and southern hemispheres, which results in a slow wobble of the rotation axis that takes a cycle of 41,000 years to complete. Thanks to the research by Jeff Kent in his book *The Mysterious Double Sunset*, you can still view the double sunset at the summer solstice from a new location, southeast of the churchyard.

We decided to join a group of local people in 2011, who gather every year to witness this unique event on a hill just on the outskirts of Leek. With excited anticipation, we waited in the hope of witnessing this double sun phenomenon for the first time. However, just as the sun was about to set, a bank of cloud suddenly appeared and ruined the spectacle. Although hugely disappointed, I realised that it was not the viewing place that was significant but the sacred hill itself and its unusual and unique shape that allows for this rare phenomenon to occur.

There are remnants of a prehistoric settlement on Cloud End consisting of a single ditch carved into solid rock and beehive huts. J.E. Gordon believed it to be a Bronze Age encampment settled by Iberians. Some historians suggest a Celtic tribe resided here around 1100 BC, having taken over the abandoned site of the previous occupants.

Flowing at the foot of the hill is the River Dane, which some say is a reference to the Danes who invaded these shores over a thousand years ago. Alternatively, the name may derive from the race of Dan or Don, known as the Tuatha De Danann who settled in Ireland around 1800–1200 BC. They worshipped the goddess Cattha or Cat Anna derived from Danu, Anu and then Ana. According to Pickford in *Earth Mysteries of the Three Shires*, this tribe used the Catstones for their sacrifices located on the western edge of the Cloud. Interestingly, the local Iron Age tribe known as the *Cornovii* was also referred to as the 'Cat people'.

Andrew Collins in *The Seventh Sword* refers to psychic information that suggests the Cloud was a significant place to the Neolithic and Bronze Age races. They perceived this area as the heart of Britain's energy matrix and communed with this vital force in caves or chasms such as Lud's Church and the Dove Holes at Dovedale in Derbyshire, where visitors still witness the light-ball phenomenon. In the absence of caves, these tribes would build artificial cavities such as long barrows like the Bridestones and Wayland Smithy at Uffington.

Research by Graham Phillips, using psychic information, revealed that around 1320 BC, a group of Egyptians fleeing persecution from the Amun priests after Akhenaten's downfall carried with them precious relics including a Greenstone gem. When they first arrived in southern England, the Egyptians visited many prehistoric sites, conducting ceremonies along the way. Some of these sites were Node points of the St Michael Line and the Belinus Line. They were to meet with the later descendants of the megalithic builders who were responsible for taking care of the energy matrix of Britain, including the area around the Cloud where they eventually settled (Phillips & Keatman 1984). Interestingly, Phillips received this information long before Miller and Broadhurst discovered the Nodes on the St Michael Line. Doug Pickford also mentions a tradition that gypsies with red hair, who were also stonemasons, settled in the area and bred with the native people; the locals even referred to them as Egyptians.

We chose a bright sunny day for our exploration of the Cloud and were soon ascending the steep stony path through woodland, gorse and heather to the summit. We stood for a while to tune into the site and admire the stunning views over the plains of Cheshire and the Derbyshire hills. Elen approaches along the spine of the hill from the direction of the Bridestones, passing through a solitary megalith in a field. Near the trig point on the highest part of the hill, we found her crossing with Belinus.

Later research revealed that before the quarrying of the summit there were four rock features here. One of them called Bully Thrumble stood over 18.3 m (60 ft) high and had the appearance of a giant corkscrew. Such rock formations seem to attract telluric dragon energies like the famous Cheesewring on Bodmin Moor in Cornwall visited by the Mary current of the St Michael Line. Moreover, Stowe Hill, on which the Cheesewring stands, is reputedly the sacred ritual centre of Cornwall. Perhaps the prehistoric tribes once revered the Cloud as the sacred centre of their region, incorporating what is now North Staffordshire and South Cheshire.

The male current approaches the summit from the west near the small village of Timbersbrook through a 15.2 m (50 ft) high rock face, a sheer cliff with a plateau at the top called the Catstones in the private garden of Catstones House. Pickford cites a local story that worshippers of the goddess Cattha threw sacrificial victims from the plateau to die on the altar at the base of the cliff. It is also the legendary place of a Celtic burial or battle. Up until recently, thousands of people from Congleton and Macclesfield would ascend the Cloud every Good Friday, a possible throwback to the days of sacrificing to the goddess.

Belinus crosses Gooseberryhole Lane above Catstones House through two stones either side of a gateway, that were possibly remnants of megaliths. He then continues through woodland across a prehistoric settlement with hut circles towards the summit.

Having discovered the Cygnus connection, we calculated that the point where Deneb sets into the horizon in 500 BC is a high eminence called Alderley Edge where legend says King Arthur and his Knights lie sleeping.

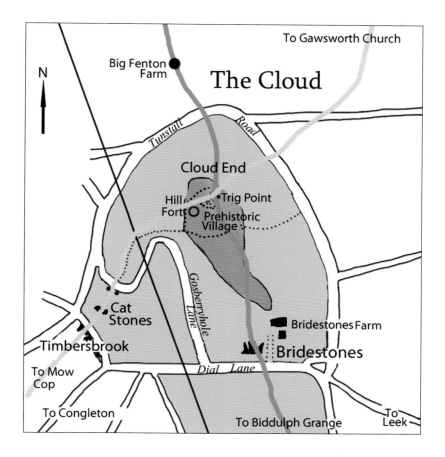

To Gawsworth Church

Big Fenton Farm

The Cloud

N

Tunstall Road

Cloud End

Hill Fort · Trig Point
Prehistoric Village

Cat Stones

Gosberryhole Lane

Timbersbrook

Bridestones Farm

Bridestones

To Mow Cop

Dial Lane

To Congleton

To Biddulph Grange

To Leek

The King of Mercia and St Chad

From Beacon Hill near Stafford, the Belinus trail to the Cloud swings towards the east to the villages of Salt and Burston just south of the town of Stone. In the tiny hamlet of Aston-by-Stone, I located him near St Saviour's Church passing through a chapel of the moated Aston Hall where the relics of St Chad were stored before their interment at St Chad's Cathedral in Birmingham. It seems that St Chad was bound to the male serpent in life and in death. As we soon discovered, his spirit continues to haunt the male current through the old middle kingdom of Mercia.

Arriving in the ancient town of Stone, we decided to rest by the Trent and Mersey canal to read a book I had just purchased about the town's local history. Stone possibly takes its name from the Saxon *stanas*, meaning 'a pile of stones' or cairn, which local tradition says marked the graves of two Saxon princes murdered by their father King Wulfere of Mercia in AD 665. Wulfere was a staunch pagan who only converted to Christianity to win the hand of the beautiful Princess Ermenilda from the Royal House of Kent. Once married, he reverted to his old pagan ways and refused to allow his sons Wulfad and Rufin to be raised as Christians, only his daughter Werburgh was permitted to practice the new faith.

According to a local Staffordshire legend, his son Wulfad met a hermit in a cave while hunting in the forest near Stone. So inspired by his Christian teachings, he spent the night with the hermit, inviting his brother to join them. The hermit was St Chad, who converted the two princes to Christianity. Their conversion remained a secret until Werebode, a pagan and unsuccessful suitor of their sister Werburgh, exposed them to their father. Wulfere swore to kill his sons and promptly pursued them across the region, killing Rufin at Burston and Wulfad at Stone. Later, filled with remorse and relenting to the new religion, Wulfere allowed their mother Queen Ermenilda to build a priory over the site of their graves, which became a Christian sanctuary in AD 670, possibly consecrated by St Chad.

We had already dowsed the male current at Burston but found little to inspire us. However, armed with the knowledge that Rufin was martyred here and that St Chad's cave was situated nearby, we returned in the hope of finding a hidden shrine.

The picturesque village of Burston surrounds a millpond by the River Trent. Having parked our car, we spotted an elderly man on his way to feed the ducks. I asked him if he knew about the history of the village and although he had some knowledge, he was the caretaker of the church and offered to unlock it in case there was anything there that might help us. The tiny unassuming chapel is dedicated to St Rufin and one of the stones on the gable reads: 'The stone beneath is supposed to have been part of the ancient chapel that stood near this place'. Another is inscribed 'WTAI IB 678' , 678 possibly referring to the date of its original foundation, eight years after Queen Ermenilda built a priory at Stone in memory of her sons.

Having found no sign of the male current there, we headed back to the pond to return the key. It was then that we were approached by the author of *A Short History of Burston*, having heard of our interest in the history of the area. He informed us of a newly discovered well, recently restored, in a field just to the northwest of the village dedicated to St Chad, where an ancient chapel once stood. He gave us directions to a footpath leading to the entrance of the field, where we found a sunken depression next to the canal containing the well.

Local history says the ruins of the chapel of St Rufin, founded by his grieving mother, remained until the end of the 16th century and were 'much frequented by the pious'. Interestingly, the well is known by three different names: St Chad's Well, St Rufin's Well and Druid's Well. Perhaps it was originally a sacred place of the Druids before St Chad arrived to Christianise the pagan site. To our surprise, we dowsed Belinus just to the east of the sunken well with its new blue brick surround. Perhaps he was showing us the site of the old chapel that once stood next to the well. Thrilled by our discovery we set off back to the car, but before we departed the area, we were informed of another important piece of local history relating to our quest.

The Burston historian informed us that a cave near the village of Salt is supposed to be the one where the sons of Wulfere met with St Chad, although he was unsure of its exact location. We decided to stop at the local pub in Salt to ask whether anyone there might know of the cave's whereabouts and, luckily, a young man who worked there was a local and knew the area well. He told us that there are several caves on the escarpment above the village, having played there as a child, but he was not aware of one called St Chad's Cave.

Having supplied us with directions, we set off in the hope of finding this elusive cave. Taking a permissible footpath across fields, we soon found Belinus passing through dense woodland ahead of us. Using the current as our guide, we followed him up a steep slope through bracken to a path just below a cave with an entrance carved as an inverted 'V'. Inside, two long seats or ledges carved out of the solid rock provided us with a place to rest. Could this be where the two Saxon princes had sat and listened to the preaching of St Chad? If so, they would have bathed in the flow of the male dragon.

St Chad's Cave near the village of Salt

The cave entrance faces north towards the sacred River Trent, unlike the other caves in the wood that face to the east. Having visited many Christian hermitages that seem to face either a river or the sea, I felt sure this was the hermitage of the legendary St Chad. Later research confirmed pilgrims once visited this particular cave over many centuries. Several folk tales around the world tell us that certain caves were the lair of dragons and St Chad's Cave certainly lives up to this tradition. Interestingly, its high position on the escarpment would at one time have given its resident a good view of the northern skies, and more particularly the rising and setting stars of the northern constellations.

Stone and the Palace of the Mercian Kings

Returning to Stone, we stood before the church of St Michael and St Wulfad, the burial place of the Mercian princes. A succession of religious buildings stood over the foundations of Ermenilda's original priory, including one established by an Augustine order of monks in 1135 dedicated to St Mary and St Wulfad. During the 13th century, the priory prospered to become the largest in Staffordshire. After its dissolution, it was downgraded to a parish church, later replaced by the present church in 1749. All the old gravestones were re-laid to form a footpath through the churchyard, leaving only a memorial cross, various stone pillars and a few Elizabethan tombs to mark its former sanctity.

The church, next to a busy road and surrounded by housing estates, emanates an atmosphere of neglect and irreverence, the modern world no longer recognising the spirit of this place. We found it difficult to believe that this was once a thriving religious centre of the Mercian Kingdom, which at the time was the most powerful in England, even above that of Wessex. Thankfully, Belinus still resides here to remind us of its former status, connecting with the tower at a 45-degree angle. He also sweeps across the open ground to the south of the church where the cloisters of the priory once stood.

Stone is a pleasant town made famous for the brewing of ale and shoemaking, where barges daily negotiate several locks on the Trent and Mersey canal. As the warm sun beat down, we lingered for a while enjoying the tranquil setting and watched canal boats queue at the locks. Belinus also visits St John's Church on a high piece of ground on the northern edge of the town before making his way to a prominent hill overlooking a busy roundabout.

The great hill called Bury Bank is now inaccessible to those wishing to explore its summit, for it lies between two busy trunk roads, the A51 and A34. Dense woodland also shrouds the site of the former royal palace of the Mercian kings, complete with a mound and ramparts. Early maps refer to Bury Bank as Wulferecester or 'Wulfere's Town' where St Chad attempted to convert the pagan King Wulfere. The mound inside the fort is one of the possible sites of Wulfere's grave, but this is unlikely as burials were usually sited outside the walls of a settlement or on a prominent ridge or hilltop. Although Wulfere used the mound as a motte or watchtower, excavations date the mound from the Bronze Age period. The ramparts may date from before Wulfere's time, possibly during the Iron Age, as this high hill provides commanding views over the Trent and the major trading routes along the valley. This royal palace of Mercia was without doubt a significant place of sacred ceremony positioned at the centre of what was for a time the largest Anglo-Saxon kingdom in England.

The male current passes through the mound and ramparts on Bury Bank towards the northwest, connecting with two more 'lows' or tumuli as it flows parallel with the A34 towards Stoke-on-Trent. One of them called 'Saxons Low' is another reputed grave of Wulfere; its size and position seem more fitting for a king who once ruled over much of England during Saxon times.

Trentham Priory

On the outskirts of Stoke-on-Trent is Trentham House estate, the former home of the Dukes of Sutherland with one of the finest gardens in England nurtured by the River Trent that feeds the lake as it flows through the grounds. Belinus visits the church of St Mary, which stands directly behind the now derelict house. The gardens are the only reminder of the former splendour of this Victorian stately home still filled with beautiful blooms, shrubs and trees. The Trent is the third longest river after the Severn and the Thames, journeying 274 km (170 miles) from its source at Biddulph Moor to join the Humber near Kingston-upon-Hull in Lincolnshire. Its river valley has become one of the prominent features on our journey through the Midlands and the male and female serpents follow its course as far south as Cannock Chase, visiting such sacred places as Etching Hill and Rugeley, Colwich, Shugborough, Tixall, Salt, Burston, Stone, Bury Bank, Trentham Gardens and Hulton Abbey.

As we wandered around the outer buildings of Trentham House, we realised the true extent of the decay that has reduced this particular site to a complete eyesore. Trentham was one of many fine houses in Staffordshire to suffer during the agricultural depression of 1873. During this time, the power of the landed gentry declined and many of the families disappeared completely, their heirs killed during the Great War of 1914–18. Later, crippling inheritance taxes would also lead to the abandonment of these great mansions, many of them soon falling into ruin.

St Mary's Church still draws Belinus through the area, having been a site of continuous religious worship since at least the 7th century. Trentham was a royal Saxon Manor and there is some evidence that Werburgh, sister to Rufin and Wulfad and daughter of King Wulfere, created a small Saxon nunnery here in AD 680 and became its abbess. She lived as a nun for most of her life, tutored by St Chad and her great aunt Etheldreda, abbess of Ely in Cambridgeshire. Local legend says that she possessed the gift of prophecy and could psychically read 'the secrets of hearts'. One miracle associated with her is the banishment of a flock of wild geese causing havoc in the cornfields of Weedon, and since that time these birds have never returned to the area.

In AD 907, Ethelfleda, daughter of King Alfred the Great, established a priory here; one of her titles was the 'Lady of the Mercians', having wed Ethelred, the Earl of Mercia. An ancient stone cross in the churchyard marks the male current, reputed to be where Ethelfleda's saintly remains rested during her burial procession to Chester. The heavily worn steps at its base indicate centuries of pilgrims kneeling before this sacred rood. Records refer to a fortification known as the Castellum de Trentham existing near the church in 1168, although nothing remains of it today.

The once great industrial metropolis of Stoke-on-Trent lay before us as we continued north, but we were somewhat relieved when Belinus suddenly veered to the northwest avoiding the city completely. He crosses the road from Keele University to a church on a hill dedicated to St John the Baptist. The present 17th century building is believed to have been proceeded by one built by the Knights Templar in 1168, although nothing survives today. Henry II gave the lands of Keele to this mystical order in 1162. Here they built a preceptory that included farm buildings, living quarters, kitchen, stables, a watermill and windmill, said to have stood on the grounds of the university and partly on the site of the old vicarage.

The alignment is to the east of Stafford and Stoke, passing through yet another airfield at Weston and through the villages of Gayton and the Wheatsheaf pub at Coton, burned down after a lightning strike in 2011. Saverley Green also marks the alignment before Blythe Bridge and Caverswall Castle.

The Audley and Church Lawton Mounds

North of Keele, we found the male current flowing through the medieval church of St James standing on a high ridge in the old mining village of Audley. The church was first documented in the foundation charter of Hulton Abbey in 1223, possibly built over an earlier Saxon religious site. Audley or *Aldidelege* was held by first a Saxon noblewoman and later by two Saxon Thanes called Uluric and Godric. A tomb lid in the graveyard against the south wall may belong to a knight of the Audley family; the Twenty-Third Baron of Audley became Sir Winston Churchill's son-in-law. The male current also passes through an earthwork or mound just north of the church on Castle Hill, thought to be the site of a 13th century motte and bailey castle. Unfortunately a busy road now separates the church from the castle making the motte difficult to access.

At the village of Church Lawton just a few kilometres north, we find Belinus passing through another church on a raised earthwork. In *A History of All Saints' Church, Church Lawton*, Revd Ron Sutton suggests that the church, built in 1180, has an ancient origin. The Saxon meaning of *Hlaw-tun* (Lawton) is 'settlement by a mound', and it is assumed that the mound in question is the one on which the present church stands. Local historian Robert New believes it to be an Iron Age burial mound within what was once a circular churchyard. However, it is more likely to date from the Bronze Age, part of a complex of sites excavated a short distance away near Alsager, a highly significant religious centre in prehistoric times consisting of two stone circles and several barrows.

William the Conqueror's Chief Counsellor Hugh d'Avranches, First Earl of Chester, was a character notorious for his riotous living, but on his deathbed he vowed to establish a church at Lawton, 'If the Lord would only spare him'. Church Lawton also boasts the legend that the bodily remains of St Werburgh, daughter of Wulfere, rested here while being taken to Chester to avoid the marauding Danes. These legends attached to sites on the path of the Belinus and Elen currents through Staffordshire may be an allegory representing the spiritual hold that the Saxon kings had over the land. It seems more than a coincidence that the powerful King Wulfere constructed his fort at Bury Bank and martyred his sons at Stone and Burston, all on the male current. Was this a memory of a ritual practice of harnessing the male serpent to enforce the king's masculine sovereignty over the land?

In the summer of 1652, whilst a service was in progress, lightning struck the church during a terrible thunderstorm. An entry in the church register reads, 'A great black cloud poured down hail over an area 60 miles by 2 miles. It killed small animals by hundreds and beat down men and horses'. Despite the commotion, the minister continued his sermon and it was not until afterwards that eleven men were discovered lying dead in the bell house, having been killed by the lightning strike. Lightning often seeks underground water to ground it to earth and the mound under the church may have precipitated this tragic event. Many dowsers have found prehistoric mounds positioned over the crossing of underground streams, the friction of which creates telluric energy. Oak trees too are often struck because their root system penetrates much deeper than most other trees to connect with underground water streams metres under the ground, making them good lightning conductors.

The Old Man of Mow

Ahead in the distance, we could see a huge outcrop of rock topped by a ruined castle. The prominent hill above the village of Mow Cop has dramatic views over Cheshire and accommodates a folly on its summit in the form of a two-storey tower with a cone-shaped roof. Built in 1754 by local stonemasons, it was utilised as a summerhouse by its owner Randle Wilbraham of Rode Hall.

According to local history, it was built over the site of a Roman watchtower next to an Iron Age quarry that extracted crystalline rock known as millstone grit. The hill itself is formed from a geological fault, sandwiched by limestone with deposits of coal and millstone grit. Mow Cop also witnessed a grand meeting of the Methodists in 1807, to instigate the return of a simpler form of worship by removing the 'Ranters' from the movement, later known as Primitive Methodism; a small standing stone commemorates the event near the path to the folly.

To the north of the folly in an old quarry stands a 19.8 m (65 ft) high rock pinnacle known as the Old Man of Mow. Locals believed this was an idol used for worship, similar to an altar. Historians suggest, however, that it marks the site of a cairn that would have stood on top of the hill, originally a large Neolithic burial chamber, possibly resembling the Bridestones in the saddle of the Cloud. After quarrying removed large quantities of stone from the top of Mow Cop Hill, some of the workers left this rock stack to mark the old site. The loss of the cairn

The Old Man of Mow, Mow Cop

that once defined this dramatic hill as sacred to the ancient cultures is typical of the destruction of monuments in the area, many lost due to the burgeoning Industrial Revolution.

Interestingly, standing at the remains of the Bridestones at dusk on the midwinter solstice, you can see the sun set into Mow Cop Hill. In the opposite direction, the sun rises out of the Bridestones from Mow Cop at the summer solstice. Kevin Kilburn who discovered this solar alignment in 2002 states, 'the Bridestones monument was not a prehistoric observatory but simply a ritualistic burial site incorporating astronomical alignments' (www.megalithic.co.uk).

Belinus passes alongside the folly and straight through the Old Man of Mow, alerting us to this sacred sanctuary of the ancestors lost to the ravages of the modern age. In the distance, we could see the familiar shape of the Cloud as we followed Belinus along the Gritstone Trail back to Catstones House at the foot of Cloud End.

North of here, amongst the fertile plains of Cheshire, we enter the realm of dragons, giants and sleeping knights.

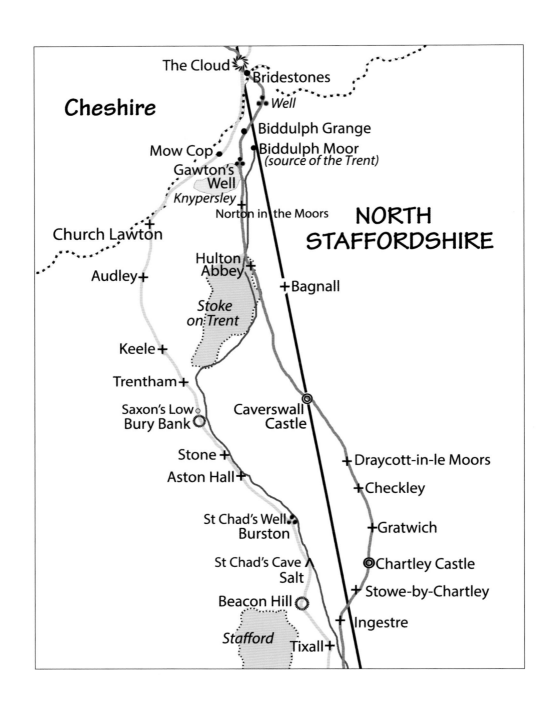

Gawsworth and the Dragon Church

From Cloud End, Belinus crosses the River Dane to Gawsworth and the old parish church of St James the Great. This architectural gem, situated next to a charming little lake filled with ducks and swans surrounded by ancient yews and conifers, is festooned with carved winged dragons and images of St George. Nearby is Gawsworth Hall, home of the Fytton family from 1316–1633. According to the church guide, the ghost of Mary Fytton haunts the churchyard, the grounds of the hall and the old rectory. She was an attendant at the court of Queen Elizabeth I and caught the attention of Shakespeare, inspiring the character *The Dark Lady* in his famous sonnets. Some writers believe she was the Bard's mistress, which provides us with an intriguing link with the towns of Stratford-on-Avon and Titchfield, also associated with Shakespeare, and where we have two important Node points on the Belinus Line. Interestingly, another Elizabethan spirit who worked at the Queen's Court also haunts the area, that of a jester known as Maggoty Johnson.

The hamlet of Gawsworth dates back to Norman times with the building of a chapel of ease. By the 13th century, a tower was added adorned with a carving of a winged dragon holding a stone, possibly representing the foundation stone of the church. The fabric of the chancel and tower is pink sandstone while the remainder is limestone. Sandstone is highly paramagnetic containing large amounts of silica acting as a powerful conductor for orgone energy. The porch has a Sheela-na-gig in the form of a rather gruesome looking balding creature with its legs straddled to expose its vulva, reminding me of similar carvings we encountered at Binstead Church on the Isle of Wight and Burford Church in Oxfordshire. Again, the position of this effigy at the entrance of the church is symbolic of the gateway to rebirth through the *Yoni* of the goddess, the womb of regeneration.

Near the south porch, we dowsed the current through an ancient preaching cross with unusual carvings placed at all four corners of its base, two of which depict a dragon and a serpent. The gaze of the many ominous dragons seem to mark the direction of the male current as it passes through the tower and a window just to the left of the south porch incorporating the Sheela-na-gig carving as well as a serpent's head and a mermaid. Inside, a coloured sketch shows St George rescuing a princess by slaying a dragon, a replica of an old mural now destroyed. St George seems to be strongly associated with many places on both the male and female dragon currents, representing Christian control over old pagan sanctuaries. Two carvings of a bear mark the current as it passes through the north wall, possibly symbolising the northern constellation of Ursula Major and Ursula Minor, the Great Bear and Little Bear. We sensed an eerie atmosphere around the church despite its beautiful setting and fascinating features, perhaps due to the restless spirits that haunt this area.

The male current leaves through one of the gateposts of the church, carved with a skull and bones,

Sheela-na-gig, St James the Great Church, Gawsworth

before taking a sharp turn across the lake to Gawsworth Hall and the site of a medieval 'tilting ground' where, according to Cheshire historian George Ormerod, writing in 1819, knights would joust and practise their skills in preparation for battle. The guidebook suggests that it was created in the hope that Queen Elizabeth I would visit the hall during her royal tour.

Before the Fytton's, the house belonged to the de Orreby family from 1130–1316. The present building is Tudor, incorporating a chapel erected in 1364. The chapel replaced one built by the Knights Templar, bringing with them foreign stonemasons whose descendants built Gawsworth Church. We dowsed Belinus passing through this tiny chapel now incorporating fabulous stained-glass windows designed by the Pre-Raphaelites Edward Burne-Jones and William Morris, depicting St George and the dragon, St Agnes, St Alban and St Stephen. Belinus flows east–west, crossing with a mysterious female energy line at the altar, which we followed to a well in the garden.

North of here, Belinus wanders through the villages of Warren and Henbury, avoiding the church to pass through fields near New Farm where a stone circle once stood. A single megalith from this circle stands in a hedge adjoining the field. The alignment is marked to the west of here by the 18th century Henbury Hall. The house was demolished by Sir Vincent de Ferranti in 1957 and replaced by a new mansion based on the famous 16th century Villa Rotunda near Vicenza in northeast Italy, very similar in design to the Temple of the Four Winds at Castle Howard in North Yorkshire. The site goes back to the 11th century owned by the Mainwaring family and then the Davenport family, until it passed through marriage in 1657 to Sir Fulk Lucy of Charlecote Manor near Stratford-upon-Avon.

According to *The History of a Village* published by the Henbury Society in 2003, Henbury was laid waste by William the Conqueror in 1069 as punishment for a serious rebellion organised by the landowner Earl Edwin of Mercia.

Looking at the map, I could see that the path of Belinus was on a direct course to the popular beauty spot of Alderley Edge, also known as 'The Edge', situated on a high wooded escarpment next to the B5087 to Macclesfield.

Caught between the Moon and Big Fenton

Back in the shadow of Cloud End, a timber-framed black and white building marks the path of Elen next to a small lake called Big Fenton Farm. In the old Cornish language *Fenton* means 'holy well', and perhaps alludes to a spring that feeds the lake. The house has some fascinating but strange tales attached to it. One in particular, mentioned by Pickford, says it was carried through the air by angels in search of a suitable location, but on passing Bosley Cloud they became frightened by its jagged edges and dropped it on the crest of a small hill in the valley. It hit the ground with such force that it split the ground open. The angels decided to fill this hole with water so that the house could see its reflection in its shimmering surface.

The present house has existed since at least the 17th century, and became the setting for Beatrice Tunstall's novel *The Dark Lady*, based on the story of Mary Fytton at Gawsworth. In the novel, Big Fenton Farm was given the name 'Silverpit' (Pickford 1996).

After seeking permission from the farmer, we dowsed the Elen current passing straight through the house along a corridor that long ago was a strange public right of way, allowing access through the farmhouse. The passer-by could dismount outside the front door and then lead his horse through the corridor that separated the kitchen from the living room, then remount again at the back door to continue his journey. It was believed that a house built

Big Fenton Farmhouse

on a fairy path or ley line would suffer supernatural events unless the building was demolished or a passage or corridor was built linking the front door to the back door to let the fairies through at night (Pennick 1996).

In one of the wings of the house was a small chapel with ancient Latin inscriptions on its walls. Outside was a wooden structure heavily stained with blood, said to have been there for centuries. This tale is reminiscent of the bloodstain that is said to still exist in the chapel at Clopton House near Stratford-upon-Avon, also on the Elen current. Elen also crosses the large pond at the back of the house, which is called 'silver mirror' in one of the tales. In Tunstall's novel, the name of the house was Silverpit, which I believe refers to the pond capturing the silvery light of the moon. In folklore, certain ponds were used for scrying to obtain spiritual visions or divination, a practice associated with witches and the Druids. The tales may be an allegory that Fenton was a site for honouring the lunar goddess, with Cloud End as the place of solar worship, later used for sacrifice by the Iron Age followers of Cattha.

Yet another strange tale refers to a mound at the back of the farmhouse, which according to Tunstall's novel is haunted by a Grey Lady. Perhaps this is a manifestation of the feminine energy here, which flows through the corridor of the house, once a right of way, and across the pond.

Marton and the Solar Mound

Elen continues to an unusual and rare half-timbered black and white church in the pretty village of Marton, said to be the oldest of its type in Europe. The autumn sunshine greeted us as we arrived to find a wedding party posing by the entrance for photographs. It is of no surprise that this charming little church set in such an exquisite landscape is widely sought after for such ceremonies. However, for us the sight of a church on a large mound meant something quite different.

Dedicated to St James and St Paul, it was founded and endowed in 1343 by Sir John de Davenport who once owned nearby Henbury Hall on the alignment. Looking southeast from the churchyard by the old cross, I could clearly see the prominent outline of the Cloud with a notch or saddle on its back cradling the Bridestones. It then occurred to me that I might be standing on a prehistoric mound used for observation. My compass confirmed that from here one would have a marvellous view of the sun rising from behind the saddle in the Cloud at the midwinter solstice. I was later to discover that Kilburn, who discovered the Bridestones/Mow Cop alignment, was the first to photograph this event in 2002.

St James and St Paul's Church on the sighting mound at Marton

I am certain that the prehistoric priests utilised this mound under Marton Church as a viewing platform to observe the most sacred time of the year, when the sun stands still for three days until its rebirth on the 25 December.

Kilburn also notes that in the Bronze Age, the midsummer sun set into this notch when viewed from a prehistoric mound that existed in the playground in Spring Gardens in Leek called Cock Low, now flattened by urban development. He realised that an alignment from here extends through the Bridestones to the mound at Marton Church.

Southeast of Congleton is Astbury Church with its 1200-year-old yew tree. This medieval building, with its Green Man and wall painting of St George, may also stand on a prehistoric site that long ago observed the sun rising out of the Cloud at the spring or autumn equinox. I also noted that a true north line extends from the Node point on top of the Cloud to St Michael's Church on a hilltop in Macclesfield. This would suggest that the Cloud is at the centre of a prehistoric astronomical clock used to observe and plot the time of the seasons accurately. This enigmatic hill and its surrounding monuments reveal a

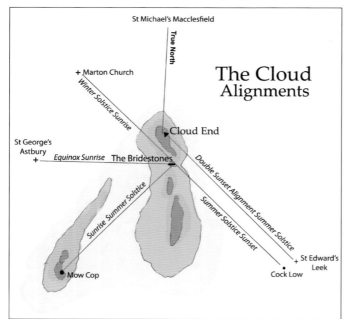

Plan of the Cloud's solar alignments

significant sacred landscape that could easily rival Avebury in Wiltshire.

I dowsed the female current from the car park in front of Marton Church passing first through a rowan tree, planted by the Marton Women's Institute to commemorate their 60th anniversary, before continuing to the remains of an ancient cross and the tower and nave of the church. Behind the building, the current travels along some stone steps to a courtyard with a wishing well created as a feature during the last hundred years by the occupants of nearby Church Farm. Examining the old stone steps, I observed cuts in the slabs, identical to those I had seen on ancient stone blocks in Greece and Egypt, which allows them to be jointed together by metal strips for added strength. I then discovered more old stones displayed in the little garden next to the well, one appearing to have the faint markings of a cross, reminiscent of the old Greek cross.

Centuries ago, the little village of Marton would have been at the centre of an ancient oak forest, the mound possibly standing on high ground within a clearing. Perhaps these stones came from a sun temple built on the mound by the prehistoric priests and reused by the Druids. The early Christian cross is also an indication of the sacred importance of this mound.

The Marton Oak and the Alderley Yew

Elen then weaves around the back of a café, part of the Marton Craft Centre, across fields in a northeasterly direction. Walking along Oak Lane in search of the current, we arrived at the entrance of Marton Oak House where a notice invites you to visit the Marton Oak. Intrigued, we followed the driveway towards the house where we found a magnificent oak tree, reportedly the oldest in Britain. The girth of the tree is enormous and its interior lovingly preserved with African Violets. After seeking permission from the owner of the house, we stood inside the tree and gazed up through its majestic boughs, feeling instantly nurtured by its ancient wisdom.

According to experts, it is at least 1200 years old and the oldest native species of its kind, known as Sessile oak. The life of the tree probably began during the Anglo-Saxon period but it may be much older. Its circumference measures a staggering 17.7 m (58 ft), much wider than any known oak in Britain. Ancient oaks are revered all over Britain, including the Major Oak in Nottinghamshire and the Gog and Magog trees at Glastonbury. However, the solitary Marton Oak, standing within the shadow of Cloud End, is less well known. Close to the tree is a spring bubbling out of the ground, adding to the enchanted atmosphere here.

Elen continues along a footpath to visit All Saints' Church at Siddington, a restored black and white

The Marton Oak

timbered church on raised ground set apart from the village. In the churchyard the current passes through the very early stone stump and base of a preaching cross. The earliest mention of a church here is in 1337. The interior has some of the finest stained-glass windows in Cheshire, showing such mystical characters as King Alfred, St George and St Mary Magdalene. The church also contains the tombs of the Bromley-Davenports of nearby Capesthorne Hall, their family seat since the Norman Conquest.

We follow Elen into the grounds of this fine Cheshire mansion, where she connects with a mound or tumulus near the entrance, listed as a 'round barrow on the summit of a knoll', now crowned by a pedestal.

Due north of here is another St Mary sanctuary at Nether Alderley, where Elen targets an ancient yew tree and the stump of a Saxon cross in the churchyard, signifying an early site of Christian worship. Like the oak, the yew is a sacred tree once venerated by the Druids and early Christians who for centuries carried their branches on Palm Sunday and during funerals. The church dates from around 1300, built over an earlier Norman chapel. A crypt under the church and a mausoleum in the churchyard contain the tombs of the powerful Stanley family of Alderley Hall. They were responsible for making several improvements to the church over the centuries when they acquired the manor in 1450. Inside, we noticed the carving of a Green Man on one of the pews. Elen flows through the tower and the 14th century font. Curiously, its upper portion was found hidden under the yew tree in 1821 and its base used to support a seat in the porch. Elen heads across the road through the grounds of Alderley Hall and on to Brynlow Farm near Alderley Edge. The name is interesting for *Bryn* is a Welsh/British name for hill and *Lowe* is a Staffordshire name for burial place.

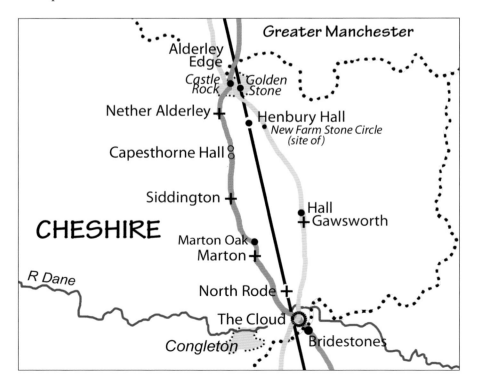

Alderley Edge and the Sleeping Warriors

Alderley Edge is set within a strip of woodland on an east–west prominent red sandstone ridge rising 183 m (600 ft) above the Cheshire plain. There are spectacular views northwards towards the River Mersey, the ancient boundary of Mercia, now shrouded by the southern suburbs of the city of Manchester. To the south, we have fine views of Mow Cop and the Cloud and, on a clear day, the Welsh mountains to the west. According to archaeological finds, many cultures native to the area have utilised this strategic ridge from the earliest times. A bronze shovel found in one of the numerous mines in the area dates to 1750 BC. Many prehistoric mounds also survive along the Edge including one on the highest point called the Beacon. This impressive Bronze Age mound once had a beacon on top, first referenced on Sexton's map of 1578, which records it as having a 'hollow square room with a door and an iron pot kept in it for the purpose of holding pitch and tar', later destroyed in a storm in 1931. When the Edge was devoid of trees this stone structure would have been seen for miles around and another link in the chain of beacon hills along the Spine of Albion.

The name Alderley refers to the Alder or Eller tree that grew on the ridge and was sacred to the early cultures of northern England. An ancient game called the 'eller tree' invites children to dance around the tallest of their group whilst trying to jump on each other's toes. This is probably a remnant of the practice of dancing 'sunwise' or clockwise in a circle around a sacred object such as a standing stone or stone circle. The Cistercian monks of Dieulacres Abbey near Leek once owned the Edge but it is now in the hands of the National Trust.

Alderley Edge is another significant site on the Belinus Line for both currents and the alignment pass through its great ridge. There are a number of magical features contained within its wooded interior including the Wizard's Well and Castle Rock. A whole day is required to fully appreciate this enigmatic place and explore the meandering paths of the serpents through its undulating terrain. However, despite having a detailed map, I soon started to feel disorientated, similar to my experience at the Rollright Stones. I realised much later that the cause was the highly geomagnetic fields radiating from the special rock and minerals under the Edge, which contain rich copper seams within high crystalline sandstone; the Edge would not give up its secrets easily.

However, Caroline seemed relatively immune to the effects of this magnetism and was able to continue the dowsing. Taking a footpath from the carpark by The Wizard pub, we soon came to the tall artificial hill called the Beacon, where we found numerous energy lines intersecting with Elen. Therefore, it was imperative that we remained totally focused on her frequency as we walked through the labyrinthine paths of this woodland.

Elen then disappears down a steep bank, but luckily narrow steps provided a means of descending to the foot of what turned out to be a rock escarpment just northwest of the Beacon. After clambering over boggy ground, we arrived at one of those hidden places that seem timeless. The rods guided us to a holy well and a little cave, not unlike one of those hermitages frequented by early Christians and hermits. She passes through the side of the cave, emerging further along the path at another well, which appeared just as ancient and with a stone trough to collect the water just like its neighbour. After some research, we found that the well by the cave has the reputation of being a wishing well and the other a holy well. Nine separate wells are said to exist along the Edge but the waters of these and another called the Wizard's Well near Castle Rock are the most renowned for their healing properties.

From the wells, Elen continues across a ravine to the east of a viewpoint on the Edge called Stormy Point. Here she reappears through the mouth of a small cave before descending to the flat plains

One of the wells at Alderley Edge on the path of the female current

of Greater Manchester. Elen approaches the Beacon from the west along a footpath that eventually took us to Castle Rock where she forms a Node with Belinus. The rock is a huge outcrop, part of the fault that runs right through the Edge. It has acquired its name from a story about the many unsuccessful attempts made by the Earl of Chester's stonemasons to build a castle on this spot. Hollows in the rock still survive to indicate where the stonemasons attempted to build this stone fortification.

It was here within these footings that we found Elen and Belinus crossing. It seemed a mystery why the stonemasons had such difficulty building their foundations, many of them no doubt being highly skilled. Perhaps after cutting the foundations the stonemasons decided this site was unsuitable for a castle, or given the supernatural quality of the Edge some unseen force may have hindered its construction. Quarrying and mining for copper has taken place around Alderley Edge since the Bronze Age and lead during medieval times. Such activities are known to disrupt earth energies, which geomancers refer to as geopathic stress; perhaps this was the real reason the masons abandoned their project at Castle Rock.

Castle Rock at Alderley Edge looking north towards Greater Manchester and the hills of Turton Moor where the stars of Cygnus set in prehistoric times

Looking north from the Edge over Greater Manchester and its southern suburbs, I had the feeling that this ridge marks a border that divides the rolling hills of the Midlands and the flat industrial plains of the North of England. Castle Rock also provides a perfect platform to view the northern constellations and the stars of Cygnus setting into the horizon, similar to Dragon Hill at Uffington and the ridge at the Rollright Stones. My sighting compass showed that the hills of Turton Moor in the distance once marked the setting of these stars. However, around 2500 BC Deneb had become circumpolar in this region of the country, actually setting into the horizon at the true north position. In 1500 BC, it remained circumpolar, skimming above true north by 2.5 degrees.

After crossing with the Elen current, Belinus visits a well at the base of Castle Rock called the Wizard's Well. The water runs into a stone trough, above which an inscription carved into the cliff face reads 'Drink of this and take thy fill for the water falls by the Wizard's will'. This is the supposed site of a cave where the legendary Arthur and his Knights sleep waiting for a call to rescue Britain during her hour of need.

Doug Pickford gives the best rendition of the tales of this area in *Myths and Legends of East Cheshire and the Moorlands*. One particular story associated with Alderley Edge tells of the day a farmer from Mobberley, crossing the Edge with his pure white horse on his way to Macclesfield market, was approached by an old man dressed in a dark flowing gown. Having the appearance of a wizard, the old man offered a price for the horse, but when the farmer refused, the wizard gave a warning that no one would purchase the horse at Macclesfield market. He further declared that he would remain at that spot until the farmer returned with his horse. Just as the old man had predicted, the farmer failed to sell his horse and so agreed to take up his offer. The farmer was ordered to follow the old man until they came to a rock, which opened when struck to reveal a massive pair of iron gates at the entrance to a deep cavern. The gates then flew open with a terrible noise that made the farmer fall to his knees begging the old man to spare him. After entering the cavern, he found many men and their white steeds fast asleep. After paying for the horse, the wizard told the farmer that these men and horses would awaken and come forth to decide the fate of a great battle and save the country but, until that time, no one should ever know of their existence behind the iron gates.

This legend, first published in the *Manchester Mail* in 1805, was 'collected from the tradition of the neighbourhood and some slight written documents and chiefly from the report by a very old man, Thomas Broadhurst'. In the same year the story was published, the Coach and Horses pub at Monks Heath changed its name to the Iron Gates, and the Miners Arms at the Edge later became The Wizard.

Another rendition recited by Parson Shrigley, Curate of Alderley Edge in 1753, reads, 'Following the old man, the farmer went past Seven Firs, past Stormy Point and Saddle Boll finally stopping against a blank rock face. He struck with his staff and a vast door appeared. The two entered and the farmer was told to take what payment he wanted from the gold lying in piles about the cave. Before he left, he had the chance to see the bodies of King Arthur and his Knights as they lay in suspended animation; after this the door in the rock and the old man disappeared never to be seen again'.

The entrance to the cave has been sought by many people over the years but to no avail, but according to Pickford, the real Wizard's Well is actually one of the wells just below the site of the Beacon where we found the female current earlier. He felt the promotion of the Wizard's Well near Castle Rock was a way of diverting visitors away from the real source of healing power within this wooded ridge.

The familiar story of sleeping warriors, encountered at other Node points along the Spine of Albion, may be an allegory for the dormant telluric power that lies hidden within the Edge. Finn Low is another burial mound situated just across the road from Alderley Edge. Finn (or Fin) MacCool was a hero warrior associated with the Irish Celts and the stories of valour surrounding him are very similar to those of King Arthur. He too slept in a cave with his elite band of nine warriors called the Fianna, who were made to carry out many initiations before given the right to join the circle.

Pickford also refers to the white horse being a Celtic symbol for underground earth energies and local people believe that the Edge is one of Britain's major chakra points. Could this place be yet another chakra point along the Spine of Albion, like the Uffington White Horse in Berkshire?

The Golden Stone marking the alignment at Alderley Edge

Other chakra points on the Belinus Line, such as the Isle of White and the Rollright Stones, like the Edge, are also associated with witchcraft and the occult. A witches' coven practised at Stormy Point on Alderley Edge within a fissure called the Devil's Grave. However, after a newspaper took a photograph of them in the 1960s, clad in white robes walking sunwise around a large fire, they abandoned the site. Yet people still gather here at the Edge on Halloween, some aware of its power whilst others just assemble for the fun of dressing up. A group of Manchester University students during WWII visited the Edge in an attempt to awaken the sleeping warriors through a powerful invocation in the hope that they would defeat Hitler's army; perhaps it worked!

Further to the east at the edge of a field, we came upon a large glacial boulder by the side of a track that marks the alignment. The pebbly sandstone rock called the Golden Stone is unique to the area. Locals say it is a boundary stone or a megalith fallen on its side, its name deriving from the colour of the aura it gives off. Both Alfred Watkins and Nigel Pennick discovered that these types of stones are often geomantically placed to mark ley lines on hilltops and ridges. Interestingly, a worn spot on the stone may be due to pilgrims placing their feet or hands there as a form of worship or veneration. Perhaps it was an inauguration stone for a local king or a 'golden milestone' placed at the omphalos of Roman cities and towns or at the meeting of several tracks. Regardless, this 'golden' stone marks the Spine of Albion.

As we sat on the stone contemplating our fascinating day of dowsing, we surveyed the beautiful landscape that stretched out before us and felt a tremendous sense of well-being, a truly 'golden' moment.

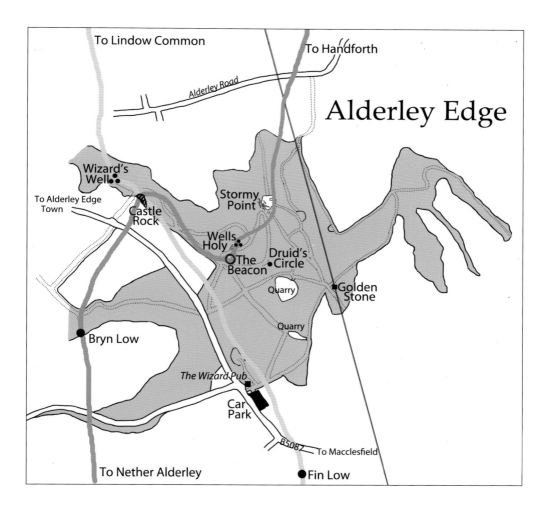

Chapter 9

Brigantia, the Middle Kingdom
Between the Mersey and the Ribble

The Mighty Brigantians

Leaving behind the enchanted woodland of Alderley Edge and its strange disorientating energies, our journey continues northwards into the once powerful Celtic state of Brigantia. This influential province stretched from Chester across to the Wash and as far north as the borders of Scotland and the Solway Firth.

Looking north from the Edge, I had a sense of homecoming for I was born in Brigantia, on the west coast of Lancashire. I decided to take a trip to the Fylde coast to visit Poulton-le-Fylde and the ancient church where I was christened. Not having returned to this church since childhood, I was surprised to find it dedicated to the Mercian St Chad, whose trail we had just followed through Staffordshire. As a native of Lancashire up until my early thirties, I was familiar with many historical sites in the

*View of Clitheroe by
Mathias Read c. 1715*

county, so was excited at the prospect of where Belinus and Elen might lead us.

With the serpents as our guide and the alignment providing the direction, Caroline and I set out across the marshes of Cheshire towards the industrial heart of Manchester. Our journey would take us through the rugged north–south spine of hills called the Pennines, with their 'dark satanic mills', to the gentler moorland of the once great Bowland Forest and the dramatic fairytale mountainous landscape of the Lake District in Cumbria. Brigantia is also the 'middle' territory of Britain and we were soon to discover some of its hidden mysteries.

The Iron Age tribe that inhabited this vast region were the *Brigantes*, a distinct race of people with their own elite aristocracy who ruled over middle Britain. Ralph Ellis, author of *Scota, Egyptian Queen of the Scots* (2006), states that the race originated from a city called Brigantia in northern Spain, which from early geographical descriptions is the modern city of Betanzos in Galicia. According to old maps and literary accounts, this town up until the 17th century was referred to as 'the former city of Brigancia'. The name Betanzos is also phonetically derived from Brigantium.

In 1435, Walter Bower, Abbot of Inchcolm Abbey in Scotland, compiled a history of Scotland called the *Scotichronicon*. In this remarkable but controversial book, Bower states that the Irish and Scots were descended from Scota, daughter of an Egyptian Pharaoh. Ellis identifies her as the fourth daughter of the Pharaoh Akhenaten also known as Ankhesenpaaten. Her husband Gaythelos was an Amarna royal prince who Ellis believes was Aye, vizier to Akhenaten, and later called Milesius. The *Scotichronicon*

mentions that Scota and Gaythelos left Egypt during a great exodus in 1300 BC with the help of Phoenicians and settled with their many followers in southern Spain by the River Ebro. Later they moved into Portugal and built a fortified town called Brigantia, their descendants eventually settling in Ireland and Scotland.

Around AD 145, a Greek geographer working in Alexandria published a map of the world based upon information gathered by early Greek/Phoenician traders and the Roman expeditionary forces. His map of Britain was remarkably accurate except for Scotland north of the Tay, which stretched eastwards rather than northwards. He named the southeast region of Ireland Brigantes after the tribe who settled there.

These Irish colonists adopted the name *Scotii* after their Queen Scota, many of them eventually migrating to Western Scotland. The Brigantes of northern Britain were another group of these colonists making their capital at York. This popular tourist city formerly known as Eboracum took its name from the River Ebor, which is uncannily similar to Ebro, the name of the river where Scota first settled in Spain.

The Venerable Bede described the Brigantes along with the Scottish tribes of the *Novantae* and *Selgovae* as the southern Picts. Other sources say they came originally from Germany or northeastern Gaul, whilst others suggest they travelled from the Braganca region of Portugal or Bregenz in Austria, both places renowned for the worship of the goddess Brigantia, a name that literally means 'the highest'.

During the time of the Roman invasion, the Brigantes held the largest territory in Britain ruled over by Queen Cartimandua from another of their main centres at Stanwick in Yorkshire. Many historians regard her as a traitor, having handed over the great British war leader Carodoc or Caractacus in chains to the Romans, although many sources say she did so to protect her people.

The Romans recorded the Brigantes as a proud and war-like nation with a tradition of imperial conquest. Despite her pro-Roman stance, Cartimandua's tribe rebelled several times under the leadership of her husband Venutius, until General Ostorious finally suppressed them in AD 79. However, according to the Roman poet Juvenal, the Brigantians continued their bid for independence in the second century AD, as Roman soldiers were encouraged by their families to win glory for their country by 'destroying the forts of the Brigantes'.

Some historians now believe that the intention of Hadrian's Wall, built after AD 122, was to prevent the Brigantes and the lowland Pictish tribes from joining forces, as the strength of their combined armies would have almost certainly outnumbered the Roman legions.

After the Romans departed Britain, the northwest region of Brigantia became the Kingdom of Rheged, one of the most powerful kingdoms of the post-Roman Britons, ruled over by a legendary warrior called King Urien. Its territory stretched as far south as Manchester and the western Pennines to Galloway in the north, but its heartland was the Eden Valley and Carlisle. They successfully defended their realm against the Saxon tribes and stayed independent until the 7th century when, through a royal marriage alliance, they peacefully joined with the Angles to become part of the Kingdom of Northumbria. Celtic Christian missionaries from Ireland also roamed the Kingdom of Rheged during the Roman occupation, converting many pagans to the early teachings of Christ.

The Great Estates of Manchester

After a few kilometres following the path of the Belinus current from the Wizard's Well at Alderley Edge, we arrived at an area of heathland called Lindow Common near Wilmslow. Just to the east of the common is Lindow Moss, an area of peat bog where archaeologists discovered the preserved body of an Iron Age man together with other human remains. Affectionately known as Pete Marsh, his three-fold ritual death from a blow to the head, strangulation and throat cutting suggests it was at the hands of the Druids. However, based on his manicured nails, neatly trimmed beard and grave goods, the Lindow Man may himself have been a Druid priest.

The Common is now a conservation area, proud of its increasing population of water voles. It has a history dating back to prehistoric times and remains relatively undisturbed by building. Locals used to graze their cattle here for hundreds of years until the 1890s when it became a place of recreation.

Heading northwest through the Common, the male current flows through the southern end of Black Lake, a murky expanse of water that dominates this natural environment; Lindow comes from the welsh *llyn ddu* meaning 'dark lake'. The pool remained stagnant for years through neglect and the dumping of rubbish from fly tippers. Although the council stepped in and restored it to its natural state, we felt the place still needed to undergo a healing ceremony to release some remaining negative energy. According to the principles of Chinese Feng Shui, if an area suffers from neglect or is cluttered with unwanted items, the energy will stagnate and become detrimental to the environment. Next to the Common is a pub, now a Thai restaurant, appropriately named the 'Boddington and Dragon'.

Just to the west of the alignment, the male current dips into the flowing waters of the River Bollin in the picturesque Styal Country Park. As we sat by the fast-flowing river near a waterfall in the gorge, the scene reminded me of the famous British legend of *Sir Gawain and the Green Knight*, whose adventures according to some historians were set in the Cheshire countryside. According to an Arthurian poem written in the 14th century, Gawain journeys to seek the Green Knight at the Green Chapel for a return contest of strength and courage. One of the places mentioned on his journey from Wales was the Wirral Forest, the peninsular bordered by the Mersey. Some folklorists believe the Green Chapel was actually Lud Church, mentioned earlier as the natural ravine just east of the Bridestones. Another location described in the poem was a cascading waterfall, which seems to match the environs of Styal.

In 1784, Samuel Greg moved his mill to Styal to provide a better environment for his workers, relying on the fast-flowing River Bollin to power the huge mill wheels. We traced Belinus following a footpath over Oxbow Bridge, mapped out by the National Trust as the Northern Wood Walk. He crosses a large bend in the river to connect with a sandstone escarpment curiously called Giant's Castle, very similar to Castle Rock on Alderley Edge. As we climbed to the top via a well-marked path, a large country house standing on a high plateau came into view called Norcliffe Hall, which the current just clips. A large clump of Scots pines just to its left gave me the impression that this was once an important prehistoric site, possibly an Iron Age hillfort, perfectly placed above the powerfully paramagnetic sandstone escarpment. Perhaps this was the site of the legendary castle belonging to Bertilak de Hautdesert mentioned in the poem as visited by Gawain.

This tranquil setting now borders the busy Manchester International Airport over which Belinus crosses on his way to the suburban metropolis of Greater Manchester. Here we find a hidden gem in Baguley Hall. The *Pevsner Guide to Fine Buildings* describes it as 'one of the oldest and finest surviving medieval timber-framed halls in the northwest'. This privately owned hall has a fascinating history for a building has stood on this site for over a thousand years owned by the noble Baguley family and sections of the present house date between 1320 and 1650.

A little further north, we enter another country house with extensive grounds called Wythenshawe Hall, now administered by Manchester Art Gallery. The present black and white half-timbered construction dates from 1540, built by Robert Tatton over the site of an earlier medieval building. His successors continued to add to the house until Manchester City Council took possession in 1926.

The male current passes through the now dilapidated hall that combines antiquated Tudor architecture with grotesque modernist design at its worse. In the grounds, opposite the front entrance is a huge statue of Oliver Cromwell, moved here from Deansgate in the city of Manchester. This addition to the grounds is rather ironic for the Tatton family successfully fought off Cromwell and his troops on two occasions. When the Parliamentarians finally managed to seize it, they only held the estate for two years, receiving payment from the family for its return.

Crossing the River Mersey, the male current continues through Longford Park, built in 1857 in the Italianate style by Lancashire's self-made millionaire John Rylands, also known as the 'Cotton King'. The once magnificent grounds and gardens, similar in design to those of Chatsworth House in Derbyshire, eventually became a municipal park with only the front façade of the house remaining.

The male dragon appears to be avoiding the more densely populated areas of Manchester preferring instead to travel between public parks including Gorse Hill Park in the Stretford area, where we stumble upon one of the city's hidden historical landmarks.

The Arthurian Stone

Standing by the old entrance to the Trafford Park estate, next to the busy A56, is a sacred stone known as 'the Great Stone'. This rectangular hewn grit-stone boulder probably originates from one of the numerous quarries between Mow Cop and the Cloud.

According to local tales, the two deep holes cut into the top of the stone were filled with vinegar or holy water at the time of the Great Plague of 1665 as a cure for the sickness. Coins were also dipped into this solution as a form of sterilisation, to help prevent any further spread of the disease. Stretford meaning 'straight-ford', similar to Stratford-upon-Avon, was an important crossing place of the River Mersey in Celtic and Roman times. The stone possibly served as a boundary marker and its deep holes may have previously supported a cross shaft for religious worship.

According to an ancient legend, this stone landed at Stretford thrown by a giant called Tarquin. He was a foreigner who became a local overlord residing at Knott Mill close to the River Medlock, now called Castlefield, south of Manchester city centre. Tarquin was a bad-tempered individual and after an argument with another giant at Stretford, he lifted this rock from the Medlock and threw it at his rival. However, he missed his target, the stone landing instead on the western side of Chester Road. The two depressions you see on the stone are the supposed marks of the giant's thumb and forefinger. Tales of stone-throwing giants or devils always missing their targets are familiar to the folklore of many counties in England.

The Great Stone at Gorse Hill, standing by the old entrance to the Trafford Park estate

Another version of the story places the Arthurian knight Sir Lancelot as Tarquin's rival. The inclusion of this Arthurian hero as the vanquisher of Tarquin perhaps indicates a dim memory of a struggle between the British and invading foreign forces during early Saxon times.

The name Tarquin is also intriguing as it refers to an Etruscan title equivalent to a prince. An Etruscan prince called Lucius Tarquinius Priscus, from the royal city of Tarquinia in Italy, was the founder of Rome in *c.* 575 BC (Keller 1975). Perhaps Tarquin was an Etruscan warrior of royal birth who came to Britain with the Romans and settled to protect the remaining Romano-Britons from foreign invaders.

The inherent healing power that the Great Stone emanates still attracts the male current despite its removal from its original site across the road, where a war memorial now stands. Perhaps the stone was a geodic marker or omphalos that once stood at the centre of a tribal region.

Nearby, the alignment passes 0.6 km east of Old Trafford, the Manchester United football stadium, one of the most famous amphitheatres of football in the world. Birmingham City and Aston Villa football stadiums also mark the line

Ordsall Hall and the Radcliffes

A little further north, only 274 m from the alignment, is the ancient Ordsall Hall, a recently restored Tudor house that originally stood on the bend of the Irwell before the river became part of Salford Docks and the Manchester Shipping Canal.

The first mention of the Hall was in 1177 and from 1232–1335 it was owned by the Earl of Derby and the de Hulton family who bequeathed it to the Radclyffe (Radcliffe) family of Radcliffe Tower. This important Catholic family, descended from the Angevin dynasty of France, was known to have substantial influence over kings and queens, governments and religion until Protestantism ruled over England in 1662.

Sir John Radcliffe developed the moated manor house to include a grand hall, five chambers, a kitchen and a chapel. This place of worship, designed for the family's private use, was the first to be built in Salford, although its whereabouts is presently unknown, having been demolished long ago. Before the Industrial Revolution, the alignment passed through the grounds of the Hall, which then included a farm, dovecot, watermill, sawmill and a brick kiln.

John Radcliffe was also said to be responsible for the thriving textile industry at Salford through the introduction of Flemish weavers from Belgium. Their skills, having been passed on to the locals, continued through subsequent generations in both Salford and Manchester contributing to the creation of the most important textile manufacturing centre in the world. Sir John distinguished himself in battle alongside Edward III, who granted the family the right to use one of the oldest mottoes for service: *Caen, Crecy, Calais*. Many heads of this wealthy and illustrious family fought in important English campaigns such as the War of the Roses and the Civil War against Cromwell. The Radcliffes continued to stay loyal to the Catholic faith, so much so that Sir John was deemed a 'dangerous temporiser' and considered a potential threat to the government of the day. His defiance led to the demise and bankruptcy of the family in the 1650s, having been forced to pay a fine to practise their religion.

Ordsall Hall, Manchester

Much of the 14th century building was demolished, but an unusual room called the Star Chamber still survives, its ceiling covered in gilt-painted lead stars, thought to be the earliest domestic apartment to still exist in England. The restorers believe that this is where the Radcliffes would have conducted most of their business affairs, held meetings and heard small court petitions.

Curiously, Ordsall Hall featured in a Victorian novel written by Harrison Ainsworth about the Gunpowder Plot in 1899, where Guy Fawkes and Robert Catesby fell in love with a fictional character called Vivien Radcliffe. The novel also includes fleeing Catholic priests, perhaps reflecting the continued support of the Catholic Church by the Radcliffes after the creation of the Church of England. This story links with other places along the Belinus Line such as Chipping Norton on the male current, where Catesby was said to have hatched the plot to blow up the Houses of Parliament in 1605 in the Crown and Cushion Hotel, and Lapworth where he was born and christened, on the Elen current.

Also of interest is an acacia tree that once existed at the front of the Hall said to have been brought back from the Holy Land during one of the Crusades. As to be expected with such an historic house on the alignment, it has many ghost stories associated with it. From the end of the 17th century, various families owned this moated stately home including Sir Humphrey Chetham and Earl Egerton of Tatton. The Pre-Raphaelite artist Frederick Shields also rented it for a time until 1875, when it became a Working Men's Club before being used as a Clergy's Training College in 1908. Today the Hall is open to the public and includes a local history museum.

Again, the Belinus Line passes through an important centre that once had great influence over its surroundings and was a base for the powerful Angevin bloodline in the North of England. We later encountered another of their houses also on the alignment situated on the northern outskirts of Greater Manchester at the small town of Radcliffe.

The alignment continues through the city of Salford, where various cultures have settled since Neolithic times. The Saxons called it Salfordshire, an ancient division of the county of Lancashire held by Edward the Confessor. In *Salford, a City and its Past* by Bergin and Shaw (1975), Salford is said to derive from 'willow by the ford', *sal* or *sahl* meaning 'sallow' or 'willow'. Alternatively, it could refer to a salt route that crossed the ford of the River Irwell.

A considerable network of trade routes called 'salt ways' once existed around Britain and Europe dating back to prehistoric times. I believe the Romans reused some of these ancient tracks to build their system of roads, including the Manchester to Bury road that passed through the centre of Salford. The town grew in size due to the thriving textile industry but eventually, like many other northern towns, suffered a massive decline after the closure of the mills. It eventually received city status in 1926. Salford Quays enjoyed extensive renovation in the 1990s and now boasts elegant housing, hotels and restaurants.

As we followed the Belinus current through this old district, now part of Greater Manchester, we arrived at St Luke's Church known locally as 'the church on the hill' built in 1865. This is yet another church designed by the prolific Sir George Gilbert Scott, which stands on a small green mound next to Liverpool Street. The path of the male current avoids Manchester city centre preferring instead a straight route to the once medieval town of Radcliffe.

Farewell to St Chad

Returning to Alderley Edge to follow the route of Elen through Greater Manchester, we eventually arrive at Handforth. Here she visits the Victorian church of St Chad and the fine 16th century half-timbered manor house of Handforth Hall close to the alignment. Still in private hands, the owners have created a medieval-style garden complete with a labyrinth.

Cheadle was once a sacred place in prehistoric times as many burial mounds were reportedly destroyed during the building of the town. Its name derives from Cedd or Chad, who according to local history preached on the hill above the Mersey. Elen visits St Mary's Church in the centre of the town, which stands on 'Chad's Hill'. The present building mostly dates from Tudor times although a church was recorded here as far back as 1200.

Inside the church is an ancient Anglican cross, dedicated to St Chad and described as 11th century despite some authorities believing it to be much older. The cross, found in 1873, once stood 3 km (1.8 miles) northwest of the church where the Micker Brook meets the River Mersey. A local tradition states that St Chad baptised many pagans at this spot by the river and built a church on the hill nearby. Although it might seem that

Chad was a long way from his home in Lichfield in Staffordshire, this was the most northern boundary of the Kingdom of Mercia marked by the Mersey. As we stood looking down upon the river, we realised we had reached the end of St Chad's trail. We said our farewells and thanked his spirit for guiding us through the hidden sacred places between the two great cities of Birmingham and Manchester.

Just to the northwest of here is the exclusive town of Didsbury, which dates back to Norman times, although the site of its parish church goes back as far as the 7th century. Here we meet St Oswald for the first time who built on this site 'the most ancient of all the chapels in the parish of Manchester'. St Oswald (AD 604–642) was a Northumbrian king and the most powerful ruler in Britain north of the Humber and the Mersey and, like St Chad, promoted Christianity throughout his realm.

In 1235, the Saxon chapel became a private chantry, limited to the use of the Lord of the Manor. The church stands on high ground by a bend of the Mersey close to the ford where Bonnie Prince Charlie crossed when marching south during the Jacobite Rebellion. Elen still connects with the church, rededicated to St James in 1855, and an old yew in the churchyard.

Castlefield and the Captive Knights of the Round Table

The female current than takes a direct route to the heart of the city of Manchester through Withington and the university district, crossing the River Medlock at Castlefield. Manchester was the first purpose-built industrial city in the world, growing to become the third largest city in Britain and presently regarded as the UK's second city of cultural and historical importance. Yet, very few people know of the city's hidden history that stretches back to pre-Roman times when the Britons called it *Caer Maunguid*. Nennius, the Welsh monk, author of *Historia Brittonum* in AD 828 refers to it as one of the principal cities of Britain. From remote times, Maunguid became an important and thriving centre of trade, strategically placed next to the busy River Irwell by the junction of two important track-ways, one linking the south to the northwest of the country and the other running from the port of Chester to York.

In prehistoric times, there were two prominent hills in Manchester utilised for settlement and defence. One of them, near the Granada Studios, is a sandstone outcrop between the rivers Irwell and Medlock, now covered by buildings at the bottom of Deansgate; the other is above the meeting of the rivers Irk and Irwell now occupied by the cathedral and Chetham's Library. Early remains found on and around these hills indicate important settlements of the Brigantes. When the Roman General Agricola (AD 40–93) passed through here on his way to Chester, he obviously recognised the strategic importance of these hills, for he later built wooden stockades on both sites, perhaps as a way of deterring the troublesome Celts. A local tradition says the Roman General called the site by the Medlock and the Irwell *Mamuciam* or *Mamucium*, meaning 'a breast-shaped hill', from which Manchester takes its name.

Later Agricola constructed a stone fort in a wooded area a little further downstream from the hill that covered some 5 acres in the region known today as Castlefield.

However, this site was already settled by the *Setantii* or *Sistuntii* tribe, who introduced wool making to the area from Gaul. An extract from Dr Hibbert's pamphlet recorded in *The Traditions of Lancashire* by J. Roby (1879) states:

'Upon the site of Castlefield near Manchester, was originally [before the Romans] erected a British fortress by the Sistuntii, the earliest possessors of Lancashire, comprising an area of twelve acres. It would possess on the south, south-east, and south-west, every advantage, from the winding of the River Medlock, and on its west, from the lofty banks which overlooked an impenetrable morass. By the artificial aid, therefore, of a ditch and a rampart on its east and north sides, this place was rendered a fortress of no inconsiderable importance. This fell afterwards into the hands of the Brigantes, the ancient inhabitants of Durham, York, and Westmorland. Upon the invasion of the Romans, Cereales, their general, attacked the proper Brigantes of Yorkshire and Durham, and freed the Sistuntii of Lancashire from their dominion, but reserved the former to incur the Roman yoke.'

After Queen Cartimandua made her truce with the Romans, the Brigantes eventually settled alongside them, even occupying their forts.

This highly populated settlement at Castlefield had five great roads branching off in all directions possibly built by the earlier Sistuntii tribe and later paved by the Romans. After the Romans withdrew from Britain in AD 411, their fort gradually fell into disuse, its stones carted away to construct new buildings or roads. Once the Saxons arrived, they soon occupied the site, which by the 10th century was part of the Kingdom of Northumbria. The *Anglo-Saxon Chronicle* mentions 'Mamecestre in Northumbria' in AD 923, when Edward the Elder sent a force from Mercia to repair it.

The fort stood close to the district of Knott Mill, next to the River Medlock, now Deansgate railway station, where the giant Tarquin hurled a stone at his rival on Gorse Hill, on the Belinus current. Legend describes Tarquin's castle as surrounded by vast ramparts and flanked at the corners with high and stately towers. Roby (1879) refers to another legend, which states that Tarquin gained the fortress through treachery, imprisoning the former keeper, a British knight, and some of the fabled Knights of the Round Table.

'Within this ancient British land,
In Lancashire I understand,
Near Manchester there lived a Knight of Fame,
Of a prodigious strength and might,
Who vanquished many a worthy knight,
A giant great, and Tarquin was his name.' (Ballad of Sir Tarquin)

Sir Lancelot, upon hearing of Tarquin's evil deeds, arrived at Knott Mill where he encountered a maiden who warned him that Tarquin would slay him if he knew of his presence there. Seeing this as a challenge Lancelot asked to be shown the castle. The young woman took him along a path that crossed the ford over the Medlock towards the great castle. Near the entrance by a large ditch or rampart was a tree with an array of weapons and shields hanging from its branches, spoils of war taken from the defeated knights. On the lower branches hung a copper basin with an inscription that read, 'Who valueth not his life a whit, let him this magic basin hit'. After hitting the basin and circling the fortress several times, Lancelot finally met with Tarquin, promptly defeating him and freeing King Arthur's knights.

If Sir Tarquin was an Etruscan who came to Britain with the Romans, then he may have remained after the Romans departed to defend the area. He may even have led a retinue of Roman soldiers left behind, perhaps becoming a chief of the local Romano-British people while aiding them in their struggle against the invading Picts and Scots. Later these foreign war leaders would befriend the incoming Saxons, allowing them to settle in areas around northern Britain. It was during this tumultuous period that a legendary noble brotherhood surfaced, led by a British warrior called Arthur. Having sworn to avenge the wrongs of their country, they began to harass these Saxon intruders and the leaders who invited them in, driving them out and returning their ill-gotten gains to the native British.

The Tarquin story may be a geomythic rendition of actual events or perhaps alludes to an historical connection between the Medlock and Stretford. Alternatively, it may refer to an energetic relationship between the two sites, for the giant lifted a stone from the Medlock where we dowsed the female current and threw it at the Stretford giant where we found the male current at Gorse Hill.

The newly renovated Castlefield is now full of trendy cafes and tasteful apartments all placed next to the canal, very different from the dreary and neglected place I knew 20 years ago. In Victorian times, this area was full of warehouses, later abandoned and left to decay when the mills closed down. Today, it is bustling with activity of a different kind, with many people coming here to sip cappuccinos and stroll around the delightful waterways now frequented by Canada Geese rather than the old barges packed with wool and cotton.

Next to a bridge, Elen passes through an old well opposite Barca Bar. The well may have supplied fresh drinking water for the Iron Age settlement and Roman fort and continued in use for centuries afterwards. We follow her northeast weaving through cobbled streets surrounded by ugly cast-iron and red-brick pillars that support the complex system of railway lines and roadways above.

We soon arrive at the newly reconstructed Roman North Gate at the bottom of Deansgate, which until recently was an eyesore with just a small section of Roman stones on a much-neglected site. A diagram on the information board shows the ancient fort once hugged the banks of the Medlock River, now covered by raised roadways and viaducts. Elen passes through the west side of the North Gate entrance across the reconstructed ditch defences.

Deansgate is a long and straight north–south road that linked the sites of the two hillforts between Knott Mill and the site of the cathedral, a possible meridian or polar axis in earlier times. Elen flows to the west of this now famous shopping street, crossing Camp Street, where we stopped to survey the location of Mamucium, the breast-shaped hill that gave Manchester its name and where Lancelot rescued the knights of King Arthur. Elen clips St John's Gardens nearby, once the site of a medieval chapel, a good place for us to rest and connect with the goddess energy of the hill.

Soon we found ourselves staring up at the Opera House in Quay Street where the current passes through its classical façade, elaborately adorned with Greek columns and a depiction of Apollo on his chariot driven by three horses. Behind Quay Street, Elen enters through the modern entrance of the John Rylands Library. The main body of the building is a magnificent example of Victorian Gothic architecture created to emulate an Oxford college library but on a much grander scale. This 'cathedral of learning' made of Penrith red sandstone certainly exudes within its design the ancient art of sacred proportion. Enriqueta Rylands commissioned the building, fronted on Deansgate, in 1889 for her late husband who lived at nearby Longford Park on the Belinus current. Many criticised her decision to build on a piece of land already very crowded with tall buildings, derelict cottages and narrow streets, fearful that valuable manuscripts would be housed in 'that dirty, uncomfortable city ... [with] not enough light to read by'. However, the resulting structure must have enhanced this area no end through its harmonious and elegant proportions.

We dowsed Elen inside the café in the modern glazed extension at the west end of the original building, before entering the library. As we wandered around the outside of the Gothic building, we were astounded at the sheer number of elaborately carved winged dragons and serpents that festoon not only the exterior but also every single room and corridor inside. We spotted a Green Man on a ceiling boss just as you walk into the men's toilets and another just to the left of the entrance to the historic Reading Room. As we strolled around the atmospheric corridors and rooms of the library, we sensed the divine qualities of sacred measure incorporated into the building's design that bestows upon its interior the appearance of a cathedral. It came as no surprise to read that ghosts have been witnessed drifting through the library including a White Lady. Elen

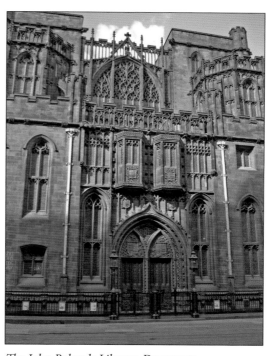

The John Rylands Library, Deansgate

led us to a quiet corridor on the ground floor at the northwest corner of the building, to show us a row of ceiling bosses displaying a rose, a Green Man and a dragon.

Parsonage Gardens was another interesting site on her route, where St Mary's Church once stood. Erected in 1756 in Parsonage Fields, it was to accommodate the upper classes and more affluent residents of that area in competition with the nearby St Anne's parish church. The church, elegantly designed in the Greek style with columns and architraves, had an exceptionally high spire. However, by the 1850s it found itself in one the poorest districts of the city and was eventually abandoned, creating 'sepulchral gloom'. Now a delightful garden displaying colourful flora and fauna, it is the perfect place to take time out from the hustle and bustle of this fast-moving yet exciting city.

Before entering the cathedral precinct, Elen afforded us one more revelation, a fine carving above a doorway in Parsonage Lane off Blackfriars Street depicting a 'green lion', once part of the old Hayward & Co. glass and china factory.

The Cathedral on the Hill

Elen crosses the Hanging Bridge, one of the city's oldest serving structures dating from the 14th century, to enter the cathedral, which has an unusual dedication to three saints: St Mary, St Denis and St George. The bridge once spanned a ravine or great ditch over the mythical River Dean from which the name Deansgate derives. The Hanging Bridge was recently discovered during construction of the cathedral's new visitor centre, which now stands above it.

The cathedral stands on the site of Manchester's second sacred hill, which long ago was a sandstone outcrop by the confluence of the rivers Irwell and Irk. A Norman manor house and castle were built on the site in 1184, held by the Greley family. Excavations in the area have revealed three rings of ditches surrounding the supposed site of the castle; two of them ran together under Long Millgate and Hanging Ditch in Exchange Square, and another through the yard of Chetham's Library nearby. After many centuries, the importance of the old fort site at Castlefield by the Medlock was long forgotten, the Norman planners of the new city preferring instead the hill by the Irwell and Irk. This became the new spiritual omphalos of Manchester represented by the building of a grand cathedral.

The Saxon carving of an angel, found embedded in the wall of the south doorway and now displayed by the entrance to the choir, is evidence of early Christianity in Manchester. Experts believe it came from the old St Mary Chapel that once stood on this site and mentioned in the Domesday Book.

In 1441, during the reign of Henry V, an important Collegiate Church dedicated to St Mary replaced the earlier church, but today most of the building is Victorian Gothic. We were surprised to learn that in 1596 its ninth warden was Dr John Dee, the famous astrologer to Mary Tudor and her sister Queen Elizabeth I. He was also a theologian, mathematician, astronomer, politician, architect and medical scholar and possessed the largest library in England at the time. However, according to some sources, he was also a renowned alchemist and occultist and 'communicated with angels'. Many even suspected him of practising black magic, making his time in Manchester less than convivial. Perhaps he was also aware of the hidden path of the Elen current, having once written:

> 'For the true mathematical science is that which measureth the invisible lines and immortal beams which can pass through clod and turf; hill and dale. It was for this reason, it was accounted by all ancient priests the chiefest science; for it gave them power both in their words and in their works.' (Dr John Dee in *Mathematical Preface*)

As with most cathedrals at the time of Oliver Cromwell, the building suffered the ransacking of Parliamentarian troops, who used it as a stronghold with snipers stationed on the roof. From 1715–45, it became the region's centre of operations for Bonnie Prince Charlie and his army during the Jacobite Rebellion.

The female current enters through the south doorway and crosses the widest nave in the country through the beautifully carved 16th century choir stalls embellished with mystical beasts, serpents and dragons. They were commissioned by Lady Margaret Beaufort, grandmother of Henry VIII and wife of Thomas Stanley First Earl of Derby who owned many large estates in Lancashire. Elen then enters the impressive chantry chapel dedicated to St John the Baptist, also built by the Stanley family. In 1936, it was rededicated to commemorate those who died during WWI from the Manchester Regiment.

As we stood admiring this small but impressive building, it was hard to believe that two bombs almost destroyed it during the 20th century; one delivered by a German bomber during WWII and the other planted opposite by the IRA in 1996 in the Arndale shopping centre. Although not on Elen's flow, we came across a very early defaced and worn wooden carving of St George slaying the dragon set into a medieval screen at the entrance to the Lady Chapel. Rector Walter de Langton, later Bishop of Lichfield, originally built the chapel dedicated to Our Lady Mother of Jesus in 1299; the screen is now all that survives from the WWII bombing. As we were leaving, we noticed two dragons and guardian winged lions staring down at us from the vaulted ceiling.

Chetham's Library

Behind the cathedral and standing on the highest part of the hill is Chetham's Hospital and Library, the only group of medieval buildings to survive in Manchester and Elen's final destination in the heart of the city. Although some of the buildings date from Elizabethan times, the original edifice was a moated manor house first recorded in 1184, similar to the structure that once stood at the centre of Birmingham. The manor house eventually became Manchester Castle held by the Greley family in the 12th and 13th centuries.

After 1421, it became one of the collegiate church buildings, and a grammar school was added in 1515, which survived up until the 1930s. Under the will of Sir Humphrey Chetham (1580–1653), any buildings that remained after his death were to be purchased for the development of a Free Library and Blue Coat Charity School. Blue Coat Schools began in London to provide clothing and education for children of little means. Despite the damage caused by the WWII bomb, much of the old building survives, including the old Elizabethan library, Baronial Hall and Audit Room.

Chetham's Library is now part of the International School of Music so an appointment was required prior to our visit. At the gate, the guard told us to cross the courtyard to an entrance that would take us to a small door where we had to ring a bell. The grey-haired librarian kindly beckoned us in and we mounted the rickety old stairs to a 15th century library filled with the aroma of old leather-bound books. The dark rooms had finely carved oak bookcases, some filled with ancient manuscripts, a scene straight out of a Dickensian novel.

Although distracted by the fascinating old books, the purpose of our quest was an unusual carving in the Audit Room on the ground floor lined with aged oak panelling and reputed to be haunted. It was hard to believe that just over 500 years before, when these buildings were part of Christ's College, Dr John Dee worked from the Audit Room and met here with Sir Walter Raleigh during his time as warden of the cathedral. They say a scorch mark on a table in the room is reputedly the result of a visit by the devil, but presumably it was the product of one of Dee's alchemical experiments.

Looking up at the ceiling we spotted the carving depicting the grotesque face of the legendary Manchester giant Tarquin feasting on a small child, who according to legend

Carving of the head of the giant Tarquin on the ceiling of the Audit Room in Chetham's Library.

devoured one a day for breakfast. I was intrigued to know why the only depiction of Tarquin, who seems so integral to the foundation myths of this area, was in this building. Unfortunately, records no longer survive as to who commissioned it. Curiously, our photograph of this carving captured numerous orbs, a clear indication of elemental or paranormal activity in this room.

Curiously, we found no hint of the current in either the Old Library or the Audit Room, and it was not until we walked back through the courtyard that we detected Elen's flow through the ancient Hyde Cross, which stands within a landscaped garden. Donated to the school in 1913, the old cross was erected here after its removal from a position at the junction of Fennel Street, Hanging Bridge, Withy Grove and Todd Street, when the road was widened to create the main thoroughfare to the North. Some historians believe it was a sanctuary cross, for it predates the establishment of the medieval marketplace. However, the cross, which once stood at a major junction of roads, may have marked a centre or omphalos of the city. Whether Elen connected with the cross at its original location we cannot be certain, but moving a monument imbued with such sanctity to this site may have deliberately fixed the female serpent to flow through these buildings.

Although intrigued by our findings in this cosmopolitan city, I also wondered why Belinus avoided the centre, for these two historic hills from which Manchester had grown would normally be a focus for him. Instead, they are dominated by the female serpent along with many of the city's important and historical buildings past and present. Perhaps the Celts who settled on the 'breast-shaped hill' and

Hyde Cross at Chetham's Library marking the female current

the hill on which the cathedral stands worshipped the goddess, later usurped by the Christians who revered the divine feminine as St Mary, for many of the churches in the city centre were dedicated to female saints including St Anne.

Elen leaves the city centre for Kersal Dale, to bathe in the healing chi created by a sharp U-bend in the Irwell River, one of the loveliest green areas amongst the industrial suburban sprawl. The alignment also passes through the district of Kersal to the west of here close to the Agecroft Cemetery.

Kersal stands out as a sacred place in times gone by; Arthur Mee describes it as 'a green hill on top of which is a prehistoric earthwork below a bend in the River Irwell' (Mee 1937). According to local folklore, the elementals of the area took revenge when a Saxon knight murdered Richard Peveril at nearby Kersal Hall (now demolished) and took possession of his house. The lifeless corpse of the knight was later found on the threshold of the hall with a notice written in his own blood across his temple warning that any other trespassers would be prosecuted according to fairy law.

The female current continues to one of the oldest parish churches in Lancashire at Prestwich built by the old Roman road between Manchester and Ribchester, where it passes north–south through the nave. St Mary's Church is one of the finest medieval Gothic churches in Greater Manchester, built on an Anglo-Saxon place of worship evident by the discovery of a wheel cross head fragment nearby. Before arriving at the town of Radcliffe, Elen visits the second largest Jewish community in Britain at Whitehead.

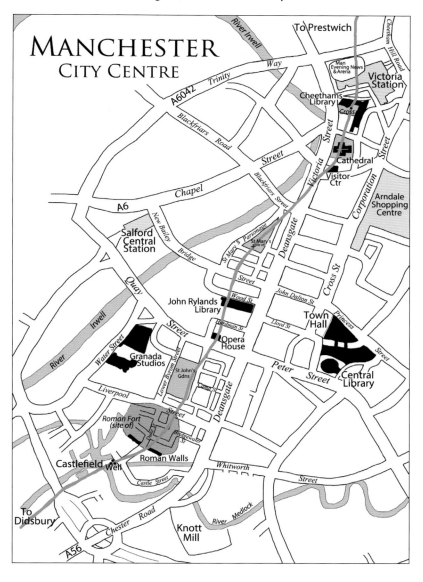

Fair Ellen of Radcliffe Tower

The alignment passes through Radcliffe just over half a kilometre away from its parish church dedicated to St Mary, and both currents appear to focus here as they enter this southern district of Bury. The town sits in a favourable geomantic position by a bend of the Irwell River where it meets with the River Roch; the name Roch derives from the red iron-rich sandstone escarpment next to the Irwell. The origins of this place go back to Edward the Confessor (1042–66) who once held the manor known then as Radeclive, part of the 'hundred of Salford' mentioned in the Domesday Book. After the Norman invasion, William de Radeclive (Radcliffe) settled the land, taking his name from the town while holding the office of High Sheriff in the 11th century. During Norman times, Radcliffe was under the diocese of Lichfield, which continued up until 1540.

Radcliffe Tower started life as a simple manor house possibly with a fortified keep called a Pele tower, later renovated by James de Radcliffe in 1403, enlarging it to include two towers. The family also owned Ordsall Hall previously visited, also on the alignment within the city of Salford. A description of Radcliffe Tower at the time says it was one of the 'noblest manor houses in the county'. However, by 1781 the house was reduced to a two-storey timber house with a ruinous tower. It was finally dismantled in the 19th century, leaving only the remains of the tower overlooking Close Park and the River Irwell.

We parked the car by St Mary's Church, which at the time was partially concealed by scaffolding due to crumbling masonry. According to local information, William de Radcliffe, a descendant of William de Radeclive, replaced a Saxon church here in 1202, having already built himself a chantry chapel in the grounds of the manor house. The church, formerly dedicated to St Bartholomew and St Mary, is perched on the edge of the town looking rather dejected.

Ruins of Radcliffe Tower where the male and female serpents form a Node

Added to which, we have the forlorn remains of Radcliffe Tower, now standing on a piece of privately owned ground at the edge of a housing estate. A sign greets you at the entrance to the field with a firm message that any trespassers are most unwelcome. During our first visit to this site, we immediately sensed a dark and lingering presence reinforced by three pit bull terriers charging around the tower stopping now and again to manically shred any sticks their owner happened to throw at them.

Waiting until the dogs and their owner had disappeared we wandered over to the neglected ruin. An information board informed us that after the demolition of the manor house, the tower became a stable for cattle and sheep. To our surprise, we found the crossing point of Elen and Belinus inside the tower rather than the church. However, their flow was weak and difficult to detect, seeming faint and fragile, preventing us from confidently determining which one was which. This was an unfamiliar experience for us and we concluded that there was something more to this ruin than just another case of neglect. After spending time tuning into the site, we both had a sense that something was causing a drain on the Node, hence the foreboding atmosphere.

We then stood at a specific spot, determined by dowsing, to carry out a healing ceremony to cleanse and rebalance the currents. However, later research of the local folklore revealed a geomythic clue that may explain the disrupted energy here.

A gruesome tale, recounted in the aptly named ballad *Fair Ellen of Radcliffe*, seemed to resonate with us. According to the story, Ellen, the daughter of the Lord of Radcliffe Manor, was murdered and cooked in a pie upon the orders of her wicked stepmother, the Lady Isabella. The brave scullion boy tried to save her and cried 'O save her life, good master cook and make your pies of me'. Unsuccessful, the frantic young man was, however, able to stop the Lord from eating her! Justice was eventually served with the execution of both the cook and Lady Isabella, the distraught Lord leaving his estates to the scullion boy. According to local folklore, after this dreadful event pilgrimages were made to Radcliffe Church to honour the effigies of Ellen and her father. Pieces of their tombs were broken off to make amulets or charms in the belief that they would cure sickness.

Although there is a lack of historical proof to support this story, it may be yet another allegorical clue relating to some sort of desecration that took place here specifically affecting the feminine energy. We have come across similar stories before along the Belinus Line such as the tragic tale of the Mistletoe Bride at Marwell Manor in Hampshire and Minster Lovell Hall in Oxfordshire.

The ghostly presence of a black dog at Radcliffe witnessed by many locals over the years may also be a clue to the state of the currents here. The black dog is a manifestation seen all over the country over many centuries at places associated with ley lines or places of power. But more often than not they represent unbalanced earth energies; the menacing pit bull terriers we encountered when first arriving at the tower were perhaps symbolic of this too.

Another local folk tale set in the neighbouring town of Unsworth may be related to our findings at Radcliffe. In medieval times, the townspeople were terrorised by a dragon that had a particular liking for women and children. Thomas Unsworth tried in vain to shoot the dragon with his musket but the scales deflected the shot. For his next attempt, he loaded his gun with a dagger. As he approached the carnivorous beast, the dragon rushed at him and, as it reared, he fired the knife into the dragon's throat, killing it instantly. We concluded that this was another allegory attempting to explain that the out of control serpent energy was not just affecting the land but also its people. Unsworth Hall, now Bury Golf Club, once housed a carved oak table that illustrated the legend, later purchased by an American. However, it ended up at the bottom of the ocean with the ill-fated *RMS Lusitania*, torpedoed by a German U-Boat.

The healing ceremony at the tower seemed to have improved the energy of both currents for during our next visit we had better luck with our dowsing. Circling the tower, we both detected the Belinus current arriving from the south passing through the southern doorway of the tower and exiting the northern entrance. Elen meanwhile enters St Mary's Church and flows through the tower's east and west doorways, crossing with Belinus inside.

It began to dawn on us that the feminine current along the Belinus alignment has suffered more manipulation than the male. I have discovered over the years that occasionally some groups of occultists seek empowerment over the land and the psyche of its people by abusing the earth energies in their rituals at specific sites of telluric power. More often than not, they target the feminine force, leaving nothing to nourish the land, as Miller and Broadhurst found along the St Michael alignment. This is not a new phenomenon, for throughout history many cultures in Britain and Europe have misused the Earth's vital veins of life force either for self-aggrandisement or to control and influence its people, through their environment.

All serpent lines consist of the dual qualities of light and dark, positive and negative, which can be manipulated either way, depending on the intention of those who wish to control them. Adolf Hitler knew this very well, building many of his regional headquarters on sacred sites. One of these was the strongly fortified encampment known as Fort Wolf, placed at the heart of a configuration of earth energy lines in the East Prussian Woods, now part of Poland. One of these lines linked the site with Moscow, which Hitler's team of occultists used to direct psychic attack upon its inhabitants (MacLellan 1999).

Elen follows the old Roman road between Manchester and Ribchester towards the northwest through the remains of an old stone cross in the tiny village of Affetside, where Juluis, Tenth Legion Commander of the Romans, set up a camp. The name Affetside is an Old English word for 'half each side', in the belief that it was the halfway point between the capitals of London and Edinburgh.

The cross, only 1.5 km east of the alignment, is actually a pillar with a rounded top, which suggests that the site was an omphalos or centre. Pillars of this design represent a world pillar or axis mundi, and many of them still mark the centres of the old Celtic regions throughout Europe. On the Spine of Albion, we have seen other representations of sacred centres in many forms: Meon Hill, St Catherine's Hill, the Marton Oak, the Golden Stone at Alderley

The world pillar at Affetside

Edge and the King Stone at the Rollrights. All of these objects and places express a symbolic point of connection between the heavens and earth where the four compass directions meet.

The Affetside pillar is now part of a landscaped garden including a lily pond created to celebrate the millennium. Apart from the female current, this place has another significant link to the alignment through its choir. Before leaving St Mary's Church at Radcliffe earlier that day, I noticed on the information board that the Affetside Choir was performing there the following evening. We had the strong feeling that this synchronistic and joyful event would somehow reinforce the positive effects of our healing of Elen and Belinus at the tower.

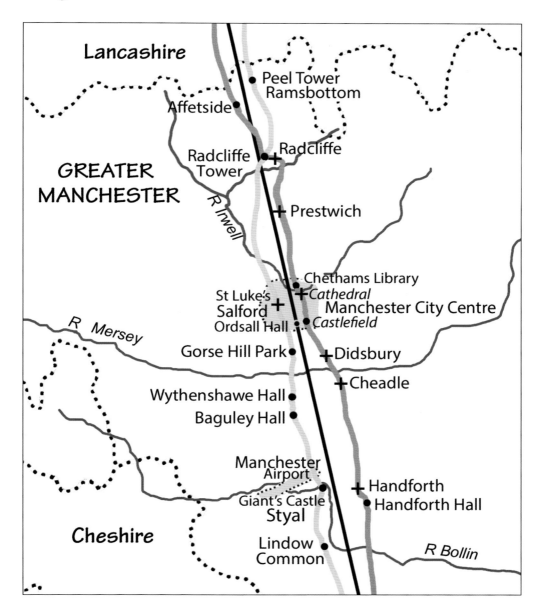

Turton to Great Harwood

Just to the north Elen visits the Victorian church of St Anne at Turton, called the 'church on the hill'. A chapel has been on this site for hundreds of years, the first built in 1111 by Roger de Poictou, a cousin of William the Conqueror, who acquired lands between the rivers Mersey and Ribble.

Humphrey Chetham, founder of Chetham Hospital Library in Manchester also on Elen's flow, rebuilt the church in 1630. He donated 'goodly books' to the local parishioners, which are now displayed in nearby Turton Tower. The church, rebuilt in 1779 and again in 1840, has a richly decorated interior with a grand marble reredos, font and pulpit. Like so many churches on this journey, a window of St George marks the path of the current, but in this instance Richard the Lionheart joins him. Another window on her path depicts the three Mary's entitled Faith, Hope and Charity.

Due to its position high on a hill, the church has fine views over the surrounding landscape. Behind it to the west is a row of hills known as Chetham Close, comprising the remains of an Iron Age enclosure and a stone circle called the Druidical Circle that dates from the Bronze Age. More importantly, it is these particular hills that can be seen from Castle Rock on Alderley Edge mentioned earlier, where the star Deneb made its lowest transit to the northern horizon as far back as 1500 BC.

The female current surprisingly bypasses this sacred enclosure, preferring to seek the open moorland towards Oswaldtwistle, named after the Northumbrian St Oswald who visited this area. Elen also misses St Immanuel Parish Church close to the alignment and visits the now abandoned church of St James in the village of Church Kirk.

Somewhere close to this church, but now lost, was a holy well dedicated to St Oswald. The tower, built in 1284, is all that reminds us of the medieval church recorded as All Saints' Church in the 16th century. A river once flowed close to its walls before authorities diverted its course to make the Leeds and Liverpool Canal. In 1837, the building was abandoned in favour of the larger St Immanuel Church in Oswaldtwistle, due to the flood of new workers arriving to take advantage of its thriving industries. Curiously, the 16th century Thorn Inn opposite may recall another object of devotion at this forgotten sacred place, as an old thorn tree once stood nearby, possibly next to the old spring or Oswald's Well. Intriguingly, the Thorn Tree pub sign portrays a young fair-haired maiden crossing a wooden stile.

Elen visits the little church of St Bartholomew at Great Harwood, once the site of the early 'Chapel of Harwode', recorded in 1315 as dedicated to St Lawrence standing next to the Hyndburn Brook. The church you see today dates from the 16th century. Early maps show a holy well nearby but there is no sign of it today. From here, she continues over a hill called Whalley Nab to an ancient abbey.

Whalley Abbey

The little town of Whalley still attracts visitors to its ruined Cistercian abbey, but very few know of its relatively new status as the most central town in the British Isles excluding her outer islands, as determined by Ordnance Survey. The charming town sited deep within the valley of the Calder River consists of attractive stone houses, a coaching inn, antique shops, tearooms and an ancient church.

There has been a long history of Christian worship at Whalley dating back to the early Celtic missionaries, who came to our shores from Whithorn in Scotland and Ireland and left here three finely carved but worn Celtic crosses in the parish churchyard. The Domesday Book records that 'the church of Saint Mary and All Saints had in Whalley two carucates of land free of all custom'. This is indicative of its important status before the Norman Conquest, and like Glastonbury Abbey, it was exempt from paying taxes and tithes.

Elen crosses the Calder from Whalley Nab into the grounds of the abbey. Here we stopped in our tracks, rather puzzled, for instead of making for the main abbey church, Elen turns to pass through a flower garden. This curious avoidance of the main sanctuary and the High Altar seemed strange; nevertheless, we continued to follow her through what would have been the monk's day room and the abbot's kitchen to the tiny ruin of Peter de Cestria's Chapel, now attached to the main building used as a conference venue. We cross the courtyard to find her curiously disappearing through the toilet block next to the little museum. Luckily, the museum provided us with some of the Abbey's history, which may explain the behaviour of the female current here.

The origins of the abbey begin with the Cistercian monks seeking a new site after Stanlaw Abbey, on the banks of the Mersey, suffered from constant flooding. Henry de Lacy granted them the lands of Whalley in 1283, which consisted of a rectory and chapel belonging to the parish church built by Dean Peter de Cestria. The Cistercians arrived and built their great abbey, converting the old buildings into the abbot's house and lodgings. After the Dissolution of the Monasteries in 1537, Ralph Assheton acquired the abbey and adapted the lodgings into an Elizabethan manor house. It remained as a private residence until the Church of England took it over in 1923.

Despite the many changes to the site, the original chapel built by Peter de Cestria has survived, albeit restored many times and is now roofless. We assumed that something or someone had fixed her current here, as she makes no attempt to connect with the main abbey building. Although there is little evidence of anything earlier on this site, we wondered whether the tiny chapel was originally built over a pagan temple connected with the worship of the river goddess. Next door to Whalley Abbey in the grounds of the Presbytery by the Roman Catholic Church is a former monastic building called the Lay Brothers Dormitory. At the northeast corner of the building is an unusual carved stone of uncertain origin used as a gatepost and known locally as the Sun Stone. Upon this mysterious pillar is carved the face of the sun, a human head and a spiral insignia, having possibly been dug up or moved from the parish church or the Abbey.

Carved pillar known as the 'Sun Stone' in the grounds of the Presbytery, Whalley

The Church at the Centre of the Kingdom

From the abbey, Elen visits the parish church of St Mary, said to be the oldest in Lancashire. The name Whalley comes from the Saxon word *Walabaeg* meaning 'field of the wells'. Dr Whitaker refers to this name in *History of the Parish of Whalley* (1872):

> 'No term more strikingly descriptive could have been chosen, for, situated as it is upon a skirt of Pendle, and upon the face of those vast inverted mineral beds, popularly denominated the 'Rearing Mine', the Earth, if drained, bleeds almost at every pore, and there are no less than six considerable springs within the immediate precincts of the village.'

Whitaker refers to Whalley as an extension of Pendle Hill, which is an ancient place of assembly and one of the most renowned occult sites in Brigantia.

Bede and the *Anglo-Saxon Chronicle* both record in the year AD 664 that Bishop Tuda visited the area west of the Pennines to oversee the submission of the Celtic church to Roman Catholic rites. Bede states that there was a monastery at Whalley then called Paegnalaech where Bishop Tuda died of bubonic plague. In *Journeys Through Brigantia, Volume Nine* by John Dixon and Phillip Dixon, the authors refer to archaeological excavations at Whalley between 1985 and 1988 which uncovered earthwork boundaries of a large monastic settlement.

The first recorded church at Whalley dates from AD 628 during the time of St Paulinus, who according to local tradition preached here. The monks of Whalley Abbey also record a tradition that St Augustine founded a shrine here in the 7th century dedicated to All Saints. Pope Gregory sent Augustine on a mission to Britain and ordered him to build churches over the sites of pagan shrines, particularly those held by the Celtic church. These 'centres of light' often stood over old Druid sanctuaries long before the Saxons and Romans came to Britain. The Saxons dedicated the first wooden church at Whalley to St Mary, known as the 'White Church under the Hill'.

The oldest of the three ancient stone crosses in the churchyard dates from the 7th century; the others were erected in the 11th century. At some stage in the past, they were broken up and used for gateposts but later restored to their original sockets in the churchyard. In both Britain and Ireland, the early Roman missionaries often planted crosses inside stone circles or henges as if staking their authority upon the powerful terrestrial energies at these places. This suggests that the site of Whalley Church may have once been a prehistoric or Druidic sanctuary, or an earthwork similar to the Welsh 'Cors' or the 'Rounds' of Cornwall.

The largest of the crosses is 3 m (10 ft) tall and has an interesting piece of folklore attached to it. According to an inscription on its shaft, any person who can decipher and transcribe its hieroglyphs 'will be awarded the power to become invisible'. This story has its roots in pagan times, before Roman Christianity arrived with Augustine. In one of the carved panels of the cross are two open-mouthed serpents either side of a haloed saint with his arms held aloft, a stance similar to that of an Indian snake charmer. On the badly worn cross nearest the church, you can just make out two haloed figures linked by the Celtic knot patterning. On both the east and west faces of the third cross is the carving of a central rounded shaft or pole rising from the apex of a gable. Some believe this represents the Celtic 'Tree of Life', others say it is the Christian

'Tree of Calvary'. I suggest, like the Affetside Pillar, it represents the axis mundi or world pillar, which seems a most fitting symbol for a town at the centre of Britain on a central north–south axis we call the Spine of Albion.

By the time the Normans arrived in 1080, the church at Whalley was the largest in Lancashire, later replaced in 1200 in stone, remnants of which are visible in the south entrance. For 500 years, the priests held their office through hereditary title here, known as Deans, holding sway over a wide area. The Bishop rarely visited the region due to its inaccessibility and 'the wild animals that roamed the road' between Whalley and his home in Lichfield, awarding greater power to the Dean.

The first rector was Peter de Cestria (1235–95), who built the old chapel next to the river on the female current, a man of great 'ecclesiastical and political influence'. He was buried in the churchyard but his tomb was removed to its present position by the font in 1950 (www.ian-opc.org.uk).

Access to the parish church is

The Saxon cross showing the axis mundi in the churchyard of Whalley Church

limited to certain days and times, so it took a couple of visits before we managed to unlock some of the wonderful secrets it holds. We dowsed Elen passing through the cross nearest to the church next to a Laburnum tree, grafted onto the base of its ancestor. She then enters the church through a 13th century priest's door with its original sanctuary knocker. The priest's door is a feature often found in early churches at a time when they were able to give fugitives safe sanctuary during periods of turbulence.

The current enters the oldest part of the church through the sanctuary and the choir, with its finely carved wood misericords originally made for the abbey in 1430. Amongst them is St George slaying the dragon and a unique triple-faced Green Man. Others include the comical depiction of a warrior with discarded sword being beaten by his wife with a frying pan and a scene from 'the flight of Alexandra'.

Another striking feature is the oak roof, also transferred from the abbey, with beautifully carved bosses. A 1920s stained-glass window just on the edge of the Elen flow was installed to commemorate those lost in WWI and shows King Arthur with the Grail cup, St George slaying the dragon and St Nicholas. The church also has a window by Edward Burne-Jones and William Morris portraying the Good Shepherd between two angels.

I was delighted to see King Arthur represented at the omphalos, for although it is a relatively modern window, symbolically, like St George, this great warrior acts as a guardian and protector of Britain, particularly along the Spine of Albion.

In the north aisle, a remnant of a Roman altar stone shows what many believe to be the horned god Mars but it also has the likeness of a local Brigantian god called Lugh. There is also a fragment in the arch over the inside of the north door inscribed with the name 'Flavius', which some believe came with the altar stone from a Roman structure at Ribchester. However, excavations revealed a drainage system beneath the Abbey made up of well-cut arched stonework, indicating a Roman origin. John Dixon, who took part in the excavations at Whalley, believes that because there is good stone available nearby at Whalley Nab, it is unlikely that they came from Ribchester and that there is evidence that Whalley was 'a very large Roman civil settlement' (Dixon and Dixon 1993).

Stained-glass window of the legendary King Arthur, Whalley Church

Roman altar stone of the horned god Mars

This church is full of mysterious stones, the greatest of which is in the churchyard at the foot of the south side of the tower. According to my dowsing, this intriguingly

Mysterious stone discovered in the foundations of the old tower of Whalley Church

large square block of black stone was emanating a strong energy field. The guidebook says it was found in the foundations of the tower close to where it now rests and exhibits Roman tooling, although this may be later. We felt impelled to say a few words of healing over this stone to help restore and rebalance the energies at this sacred site. This ancient stone with its mysterious radiating energy is certainly symbolic of an omphalos stone perfectly placed at the modern centre of the British landmass.

Without doubt, this fascinating church has a remarkable history and an interesting collection of ancient stones and crosses, possibly the best so far on this trail. Although Whalley is designated the most central place in Britain without her islands, the precise spot according to Ordnance Survey is on the northwest outskirts of the town just under a kilometre from the church. This is just south of the intriguingly named Calderstones Hospital.

After leaving the church, Elen crosses Church Lane to pass through Abbey House opposite, the first chapel of the Methodist Society. She then enters a field just north of the church called 'Imps' or 'Little Imps', where tradition says stood a stone circle in a grove of oaks (http://northernantiquarian.forumotion.net). Just north of here the alignment crosses a ford of the River Calder on the old Roman road from Ribchester to York, very close to one of the finest medieval churches in the north of England at Great Mitton. The village and the alignment are very close to the confluence of three rivers: the Ribble, Hodder and Calder. The ancient British and the Druids regarded such a meeting of major rivers as sacred and in the vicinity are the remains of prehistoric barrows and tumuli.

Also close to the alignment to the west of Great Mitton is Stonyhurst College, built as a Catholic Boarding school in 1794 over the site of a medieval Oratory founded by John de Bayley. It was here that J.R.R. Tolkien wrote much of his epic novel *Lord of the Rings*, being a frequent visitor to the college from 1942–47. Before continuing Elen's trail into the town of Clitheroe on the Ribble, we return to the Belinus current at Radcliffe.

The Devil's Trail

From Radcliffe Tower, the male current took us to the suburbs of Bury through the beautiful Kirklees Valley. Here he climbs the blustery slopes of Harcles Hill where the colossal Peel Tower dominates the skyline from its position on a high ridge overlooking the town of Ramsbottom. The 39 m (128 ft) high tower is a spectacular landmark as you drive along the A676, erected in 1852 as a memorial to the former Prime Minister Sir Robert Peel by the people of Ramsbottom.

To the north, a modern memorial stone marking a junction of tracks indicates the serpent flow as it cuts across Holcombe Moor. It replaced a much older cross, confirmed by an inscription on one of its faces: 'On this site stood the ancient pilgrims cross. It was standing AD 1176 and probably much earlier. Pilgrims to Whalley Abbey prayed and rested here'. Unfortunately vandals in 1901 destroyed the original socket of the cross necessitating some form of replacement in commemoration of this geomantic marker.

Across the curiously named Tor Hill, Belinus travels past Holden Wood Reservoir near Haslingden, and then to Thirteen Stones Hill where we find a hidden historical gem. On the south side of this hill on the path of the current are the scant remains of a stone circle.

Such monuments are rare in Lancashire and few have survived, suffering destruction from either farmers or urban expansion during the Industrial Revolution. Judging by the sheer number of stones scattered here, this megalithic ring must have been sizeable, possibly the largest in Lancashire. Sadly, it is not marked on the map and has only one upright stone remaining, with the faint traces of a few more. Avoiding the town of Accrington, Belinus then heads northeast to a prominent hill called Great Hameldon.

The village of Sabden, beneath the great eminence of Pendle Hill, has many folktales, mostly fictitious, that relate to the ancient Sabden treacle mines and wells. Sabden's treacle is probably bitumen seeping from many of the mines on the slopes of Pendle Hill often into local wells or springs renowned to 'treat all complaints'.

The church of St Nicholas at Sabden in a valley to the south of Pendle Hill has an exceptionally tall spire that lures the male current. This stone antennae acts to amplify the solar aspect of his energy, widening his flow. Founded in 1841, the church was originally a chapelry of Whalley Abbey, dedicated to St Simon and St Jude in the former parish of Heyhouses, the district only taking the name Sabden in 1904. In 1342, Richard de Radcliffe held land here when it was part of the Forest of Pendle. As we followed Belinus to the spire, we noticed what appeared to be a huge megalithic stone next to an old village well.

The current follows the old prehistoric route to Clitheroe Castle visiting a famous viewpoint at the foot of Pendle Hill called the Nick o' Pendle. The name Nick refers to 'the devil' or 'giant'; the Saxon term *Nick*, or *Niki* in Scandinavian, means 'demon'. The lower slopes of Pendle Hill are scattered with stones that according to legend were dropped by a giant or devil on his way from Hameldon Hill also on the path of Belinus. From here he threw a stone at Clitheroe Castle, perhaps an allegorical clue relating to the energetic relationship between these two sites.

Nick o' Pendle is a flat-topped hill with what appears to be the remains of a defensive bank and ditch. As we stood admiring the magnificent views, we realised we could clearly see four great eminences: Ingleborough standing due north, Clitheroe Castle to the northwest, Hameldon Hill in the south, and Pendle Hill just to the east.

Pendle Hill

Pendle Hill stands brooding over the Lancashire landscape from a height of 557 m (1827 ft), just short of 2000 ft, the official height to designate it as a mountain. The terrain consists of rough moorland grass with patches of peat exposed through weathering over the top of several geological layers of millstone grit and limestone. Although Pendle Hill was renowned for the mining of gold, rubies and lead, it was mostly significant as a place where cultures gathered over thousands of years for ceremonial worship; even the Romans came to honour their own gods here.

View of Pendle Hill from St Mary Magdalene Church, Clitheroe

A tradition recorded by H.V. Morton in his popular book *In Search of England* describes an ancient celebration of Beltane on Pendle Hill, the origins of which may go back to ancient times. In the early 1900s, 'Springers' would arrive at the hill on May Day and travel from village to village singing until midnight, having climbed to the top of Pendle Hill. After reaching the summit, they would light a fire and face the east to await the rising sun. During Easter, the hill once attracted huge crowds of festival-goers and even today many climb the hill on Good Friday and at Halloween. I remember visiting Pendle Hill on a couple of occasions in my youth, organised by local pubs specifically to climb its slopes at midnight on Halloween. The sight of hundreds of drunken revellers trying to climb the hill at night in pitch darkness was quite a spectacle, but for some it was an attempt to continue an age-old tradition.

In 1612, the famous Pendle Witches, who lived in the forests around Pendle Hill, were involved in one of the most famous and very public witch trials in English history, charged with the murder of ten people by the use of witchcraft. Up until then, they made their living from healing, begging from neighbours and extracting doles, a charitable gift of the church, with the threat of some terrifying spell if they refused to pay up. However, it was the great rivalry between two witch clans that forced their eventual demise. After their incarceration in Lancaster Castle dungeons, the town witnessed the hanging of ten of the Pendle witches.

Of interest are the paranormal events experienced by many on the hill, with several people witnessing balls of light and another rare but natural phenomenon. Occasionally the pressure of water builds up inside the hill under the limestone core and, when the millstone grit above fails to contain it, water bursts through to the surface at a weak point and cascades down the hillside. Near the summit or 'Big End', as it is locally known, is a spring called Robin Hood's Well, formerly Robin Goodfellow's Well. Seventeenth century literature describes this character as a popular trickster fairy and Shakespeare mentions him as Puck or the devil. Perhaps a ball of light was witnessed hovering over the well and became mistaken for a mischievous fairy. A round-headed cross once stood next to the well, marking it as a place of pilgrimage. Perhaps the pillar marks a geomantic centre as the hill was reputed to be the cosmic axis of the Northern Celts, the sacred hill of the Brigantes.

Clitheroe and the Lion

Clitheroe lies in the heart of the Ribble Valley, nestling between the two hills of Longridge Fell and Pendle Hill, all three places associated with tales of ghosts, witchcraft and folklore of the devil. The devil was said to stalk the streets of Clitheroe offering any locals he encountered three wishes in exchange for their souls. However, when several stood up to him he disappeared at Hell Hole Bridge, which spans the Ribble River.

Clitheroe Castle dominates the skyline from all directions standing on a reef knoll made of limestone. It is one of two hills in the town, the other bearing the parish church of St Mary Magdalene. Although most of the town's recorded history only goes back to Norman times, there is evidence of Roman occupation. The Saxon King Edward the Confessor held Clitheroe until the Norman Conquest, when William the Conqueror granted it to Roger de Poictou, who also held the lands at Ordsall for a time. Langshaw writing in 1947 proposed that a wooden Saxon structure existed on the site before the Normans built their fortification, as a castle at Clitheroe was mentioned in the Domesday Book, but without proper archaeological analysis this is only supposition. William Rufus, who built many such strongholds in the region, probably constructed the Norman fortification. Alternatively, it was his brother Henry I, for there was a mention of a castle here in the 1120s.

During the reign of Henry II, Robert de Lacy, a descendant of one of the many nobles who came to England with William the Conqueror, built a motte and bailey castle at Clitheroe. This included a chapel within the inner bailey dedicated to the Archangel Michael for the benefit of his household servants, shepherds and foresters. The chapel was eventually annexed to the parish church of Whalley. After dowsing around the outside of the castle, we discovered that both currents were crossing in the keep, said to be the smallest in England with an interior measuring around 40 m². We noticed a large hole in the south wall of the keep known as the Devil's Hole, which according to folklore was made from a stone thrown by the devil standing on the Nick o' Pendle. In the guide to Clitheroe Castle, the author David Best mentions that 'whilst the subsequent history of the castle can be mapped out reasonably well, the origins of the keep and the precise nature of the overall site are still obscure'.

Best also noted that 'The castle was a religious centre, it had a gaol, an administrative centre, stables and the other important buildings in order that the de Lacy family could control their land from one regional centre'.

Standing in the keep looking at the Node in the middle, we were accompanied by the most disharmonious sound recording of several people humming out of tune. The composer believed it emulated the feelings of the Pendle witches during their final months of captivity whilst awaiting trial. However, to our annoyance, somebody has failed to do some historical research because the witches never set foot in the castle. We then had the complicated task of plotting the path of two currents around the castle.

Elen approaches the town from the direction of Whalley through the park below the castle and passes straight through a seven-fold classical labyrinth near the bandstand. It was designed with two entrance paths and we dowsed Elen passing through its right side. Land artist Jim Buchanan and Willem Kuipers created it for the Ribble Valley Borough Council on the site of an old bowling green. I wondered whether it was intuition that guided them to build it here or was it somehow divine coincidence. We were excited at the fact that Clitheroe has the only labyrinth in the county of Lancashire along with the only Node point, and the female current links both places. The labyrinth is a great tool for guidance and healing and we sensed that the area certainly needed it due to the many battles fought in the area over the centuries.

Clitheroe Labyrinth

Elen passes through the southwest corner of the keep crossing with Belinus and leaves through the opposite corner towards the High Street in the town. Belinus enters the keep from the direction of Nick o' Pendle through the paved courtyard and a part ruined building that we later discovered was St Michael's Chapel. After crossing with Elen, he leaves through its northwest corner towards the village of Bashall Eaves.

Looking down at the town from the outer walls, I noticed a housing estate where I had worked as a painter and decorator in the early 1980s. I remember even then sensing the powerful energies emanating from this castle, visiting it on many occasions during my lunch break. In the lower terrace of the keep, I noticed benches with iron serpents at each end as if indicating that earth serpents are present.

In the town we dowsed Elen passing through the Swan and Royal Hotel in Castle Street where Sir Winston Churchill stayed between 1940 and 1941 to observe Sir Frank Whittle's jet engine factory, which was moved to Clitheroe after Coventry was bombed. Whittle spent much time at the hotel where he held many important meetings, namely one where he signed a deal with Rolls-Royce in December 1942. Gandhi also stayed here in 1933 when he visited Mrs Garnett's cotton mill nearby. Gandhi was so impressed with the mill that he took the idea back to India, where they manufactured their own cotton.

Elen then continues down the hill to the public library on the corner of Church Street and York Street, which stands in front of the old Market Square. The Library was refurbished in 1990 incorporating the 1905 Andrew Carnegie Library, the old

Town Hall, and the Victorian Police station and prison cells. Interestingly, Elen flows through the site of the Old Town Hall that replaced the Moot Hall around 1610, its exterior carved with the heraldry of the House of Lancaster and the de Lacys.

Elen then visits the church of St Mary Magdalene perched on Clitheroe's other hill to the north of the town centre. An ash tree, another reminder of the axis mundi, marks her current as she enters the church, first established in 1122, becoming a chapel of Whalley Abbey in 1283. Inside we noticed a 15th century tomb belonging to Sir Richard Radcliffe of Radcliffe Tower along with other family members by the High Altar. A curious feature here is a brass plaque engraved with the horoscope of Dr John Webster, the infamous organiser of many witch-hunts in the area. From a spot in the churchyard, there is a view of Pendle Hill, which to some resembles a lion in a sphinx-like pose.

Clitheroe and Pendle Hill also feature in a landscape zodiac contained within an elongated irregular eclipse 51 km (32 miles) across, discovered by Robert Lord in the 1970s. There are many examples found around the country, including the famous Glastonbury Zodiac where, within a circle or ellipse in the surrounding landscape, are twelve astrological signs, each outlined by rivers, roads and footpaths. The lion figure, representing Leo, is the guardian of the Zodiac and the Belinus alignment travels through its heart. The front paw of the sovereign lion figure rests upon the ancient religious centre and omphalos at Whalley.

The Romans called the River Ribble that flows through Clitheroe by the name Belisama, a goddess associated with lakes and rivers, fire, crafts and light. The Britons and the Gauls of France worshipped Belisama and statues of this deity show her bearing serpents; she also equates to Minerva or Athena and Bride or Brigit. Interestingly, many sources mention her as the consort of Belenus. Our journey through southern Brigantia, between the rivers of the Mersey and the Ribble, has taken us to several lost religious and historical places of ancient significance on both the currents and alignment, their mystery enhanced with thrilling legends and folklore. According to an ancient Lancastrian rhyme:

'When all England is aloste
Where so safe as in Chrystes croft
Where do you think Chrystes croft be
But between the Ribble and the Mersey.'

Perhaps 'Christ's Croft' is the hallowed ground of Whalley near the confluence of three rivers, the new navel of Britain.

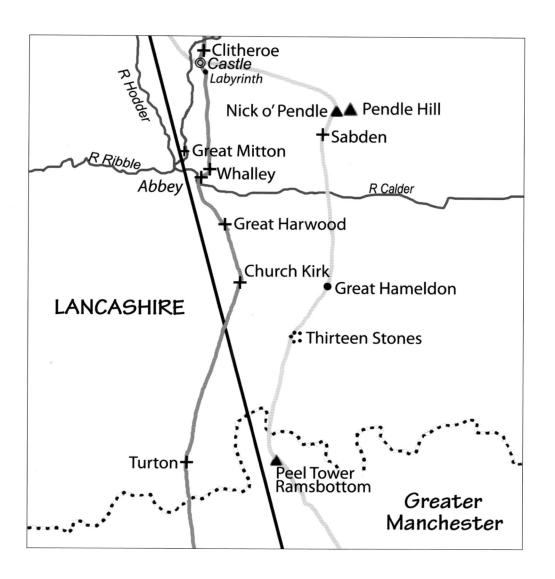

Chapter 10

Brigantia and the Heart of the Rose
Between the Ribble and the Eamont

The Sarmatian Knights of Arthur

After crossing the River Ribble, the currents take us through a landscape of gentle heathland and pleasant wooded valleys. The verdant countryside of the Forest of Bowland with its rolling green hills, fast-flowing rivers and ancient forests have now replaced the peaty dark moorlands of Lancashire.

Just west of Clitheroe, at the southern edge of the old forest, the male current enters the private grounds of Bashall Hall, originally the 16th century home of the Talbot family, lying close to Bashall Brook as it flows into the Ribble. He then crosses the alignment meandering northwest through the village of Bashall Eaves to Browsholme Hall.

Browsholme Hall, pronounced 'Brewsom', is one of the oldest surviving family homes in Lancashire. The Parker family were originally 'bow bearers' from the Forest of Bowland and in the 13th century they became 'park-keepers' to John of Gaunt. Successive members of the family have lived at Browsholme Hall since 1507 and it is now open for weddings, conferences, craft fairs and music events.

The 'screaming scull' of Browsholme Hall is a popular local tale that tells of the strange and alarming events that affect the house and its occupants on every occasion the skull is removed from its rightful position. The last time this occurred, a spontaneous fire broke out in the house and members of the family suddenly died. There are many bizarre legends of screaming skulls attached to large stately homes in Brigantia, as we were about to discover!

Shap Abbey

According to Guy Ragland Phillips, the house is a star feature on his Belinus Line; however, our more accurately aligned axis of sites through the country is about 0.8 km (0.5 mile) to the east. The male current visits rooms at the back of Browsholme Hall on its way across Birkett Fell to Knowlmere Manor, another stately home in the area where the alignment passes through the grounds, 290 m east of the house.

That night we stayed in bed and breakfast accommodation in the village of Bashall Eaves. After chatting to the proprietor and telling him about the places we had visited that day, he recalled a fascinating legend that appears to link all these sites together. On the eve of a great battle, the spectral cavalry of King Arthur and his Knights ride out from the grounds of Knowlmere across Birkett Fell, passing through Bashall Eaves on their way to Bashall Brook.

The 9th century British historian Nennius, who wrote *Historia Brittonum*, records that Arthur fought his sixth battle on a river called Bassas. This location is a mystery, but locals here believe it to be Bashall Brook. John Dixon (2003) also refers to this ancient tale in his informative walking guide of Bowland Forest, which we purchased at the little shop at Dunsop Bridge. His rendition says that every year on the eve of the battle, Arthur's Knights rise from the grounds of Knowlmere Manor, mount their horses and with standards streaming in the wind, charge up the side of Birkett Fell through the grounds of Browsholme Hall to meet their foes at Bashall Brook near Bashall Hall.

According to Alice Peel in *The Manor of Knowlmere*, written around 1913, a later Victorian Gothic mansion was built by the descendants of Sir Robert Peel over the site of a lost village that lay within the earthworks of a Roman cavalry station manned by Sarmatians. These great nomadic warriors from the Russian Steppes arrived in this country under the banner of the Romans to garrison the region of the Brigantes at Ribchester. After the Romans left in the early 5th century, many thousands of Sarmatians remained in the area and used Whalley and the Forest of Bowland as a base to breed horses. They eventually created a territorial cavalry to protect the locals against the Saxon incursions. Their greatest leader known as 'The Bear', with his standard depicting the dragon, was said to have fought a great battle at Bashall Brook.

Knowlmere Manor

Some stories equate this Sarmatian leader with the legendary King Arthur, as in the old Welsh language Arthur means 'bear'. The Sarmatian warriors were known as 'Dracomen' or 'Dragonmen' because their standard was designed as a silken windsock with a dragon's head, made of small copper plates. As the bearer's horse charged into battle, the windsock made a frightening hissing noise, terrifying the enemy into believing it to be a real dragon. More intriguingly, these ghostly warriors were following the path of the male serpent between Clitheroe and Knowlmere.

Locals suppose that three ancient battles were fought in the area of Bashall. One took place in the 6th century between the Britons under Arthur and the Saxons under Tarquin. Another was was at Brunanburgh, where a key battle was fought for the supremacy of Britain fought between a Norse–British confederacy led by Constantine, King of the Scots, Anlaf of Dublin and Athelstan, King of England in 937. Although there is little archaeological evidence of these two battles, skeletons and weapons at nearby Backridge were unearthed dating from the Iron Age, which Dr Whitaker in *History of the Parish of Whalley* (1872)

Artist's rendition of a Sarmatian cavalryman with a 'dragon' wind-sock standard, taken from an image engraved on a stone found at Ribchester

referred to as 'some place of a great engagement between the Romans and the British Celts'. Perhaps a Celtic Arthur defeated the Romans here.

Just north of Knowlmere, Belinus clips the remains of an unusual knoll called 'The Knot' or 'Sugar Loaf', its southern slopes now defaced by lime quarrying. A gibbet once stood on the hill where local offenders hung from a noose for months as a deterrent; gibbets are often located on important energy points such as on the Neolithic long barrow at Walbury Hill on the female current.

The name Sugar Loaf derives from a local myth recounting the antics of the Old Man of Bolland, a local name for a rounded hill called Mellor Knoll, which from a distance looks like a sleeping man with a big belly. He is said to awaken on moonlit nights in order to feast on the Sugar Loaf, but each time he tries to take a bite a black boggart (a mischievous pixie) frightens him back to his bed. As we have already found with the legend of the Sarmatian warriors, these tales are an allegorical reference to the local earth energies and may refer to an energetic relationship between these two sites.

Sugar Loaf Knoll near Dunsop Bridge

Perhaps they are leaving us a clue to a possible solar alignment here, for the winter solstice sun can be viewed setting into the belly of the Old Man of Bolland from the Knoll or Sugar Loaf. Moreover, on this winter solstice alignment is the village of Dunsop Bridge. According to Ordnance Survey, it is the most central village in Britain when calculated with the country's outer islands. Interestingly the dedication of its little church is to St George the dragon slayer.

Middle Britain and the Sacred Ash

The male current enters the Forest of Bowland across Beatrix Fell and along the southern slopes of the curiously named Middle Knoll. Just to the north of here on bleak moorland are the Whitendale Hanging Stones, the nearest natural feature to mark the exact geographical centre of the British Isles and her outer islands.

The dome-shaped Middle Knoll is the most central hill of this omphalos and has the remains of a Romano-British camp or fort near the summit. How it received its name is a mystery, but its association with the centre of Britain goes back before the calculations of Ordnance Survey. Indigenous peoples in many different parts of the world regard such dome-shaped hills as sacred. This hill, however, once rich in seams of silver, seems to stand out from the others. Residing at the fort, the Brigantians were the first to extract the silver from here until the Romans arrived and took over the mining.

For the long trek to Middle Knoll we chose a fine day and set off from the car park at Dunsop Bridge. Following the River

Middle Knoll

289

Dunsop along the designated footpath, we eventually dowsed Belinus at the foot of Middle Knoll passing through Brennand Farm, which has the distinction of being the most central dwelling in Britain.

According to Dixon's walking guidebook, Brennand is a Viking word meaning 'the burning one' and in the days when Bowland Forest was a hunting ground for local kings, the farm was a lodge where they could rest after a day's chase. A chapel once stood on the site of the barn and a portable altar stone, inscribed with 'IHS' and surrounded by five crosses, was uncovered near here and later transferred to Whalley Abbey. It can now be found set into the base of a table in the garden courtyard beside the abbey café.

Altar stone found at Brennand Farm

According to local tradition a bottomless pool, called Brennand Tarn to the east of the farm, is the hiding place of precious gold and silver plate belonging to Whalley Abbey. This valuable hoard was secreted at the bottom of the pool by the monks for fear it would fall into the hands of Henry VIII's men during the Dissolution of the Monasteries. Many have tried in vain to recover the treasure over the years, but only Abbot Paslew, whose ghost haunts Whalley Abbey, knows the secret of how to recover it. The powerful monks of Whalley must have known the significance of this area, as Brennand and Middle Knoll including the silver mines were part of their manor.

Dixon also mentioned a curious event called by the locals 'the Middle Knoll Phenomenon'. Apparently during late May and early June when the sun sets over Morecambe Bay, a minute after total sunset in the Hodder Valley a shaft of the sun's final rays strikes through one of the many ravines which bisect the Bowland Fells. The light appears to run up Middle Knoll like a forest fire until the whole west side is illuminated (Dixon and Dixon 1993). The Brigantes must have seen this natural phenomenon as remarkable as the Cloud's double sunset.

The shrill song of a pair of lapwings hovering nearby greeted us as we entered through Brennand Farm's main gates. We dowsed the male current visiting the site of the old chapel, now a shearing shed, and the farmhouse, once the old lodging house for the kings. From here Belinus heads north for the inaccessible moorland of the Forest of Bowland. We then decided to follow a footpath around the base of Middle Knoll to the east where we located the green oasis of Whitendale, the remotest farmstead in the county.

In its grounds stands a large ash tree, which Dixon refers to as '*the greatest ash in Bowland Forest*'. In Norse mythology, the 'World Tree' or *Yggdrasil* was an immense ash tree where Odin, the pagan God of the Scandinavians, found enlightenment and received knowledge of the Runes. It is also home to the serpent or dragon *Nidhogg*, which lurks at its base. The Norse believed that the great ash tree nourished gods, humans and animals, connecting all living things and all phases of existence.

Important meetings of the Norse clans were often held under the sacred boughs of the ash and the name 'Whitendale' is derived from the Old English word 'Witan' or 'moot', where kings would gather as a form of council in a valley or dale during Saxon times. At these gatherings both kings and bishops discussed royal grants of land, church benefices, charters, aspects of taxation, defence, foreign policy, customary law and the prosecution of traitors; the Witan even acknowledged the succession of kings. As we stood beneath the ash tree, with Belinus to the east and the alignment less than a kilometre to the west, we marvelled at the thought that we were standing beneath the symbolic central axis mundi of Britain.

Lonsdale and the Dragon Mounds

For about 20 km (12 miles) the Forest of Bowland and its bleak, boggy and inaccessible terrain conceals the path of the Belinus current until it surfaces near the village of Wray, northeast of the city of Lancaster. The village is famous for its rather creepy scarecrow festival held in May, a popular modern event rather than an ancient tradition. The George and Dragon pub in the village seemed an appropriate detour for a well-earned drink.

However, the current's focus is not the church but an oval enclosure on a small hill next to the meeting of the rivers Hindburn and Roeburn, said to be the site of an ancient village. We then continued to the church of St James the Less at Lower Tatham, a tiny hamlet near the River Wenning, where a place of worship has existed since Saxon times. The church is set high on a mound, comprising a fine Norman arch, with little remaining from Saxon times except for the remnants of an early stone altar lying beneath the present one.

A little further north we were in the valley of Lonsdale through which flows the River Lune, a name that may derive from 'Lunar' (moon) or the Celtic word for 'pure'. At the pretty village of Melling we were surprised to discover Belinus visiting a large overgrown mound behind St Wilfred's Church in the middle of the Vicarage garden. The church guidebook describes it as the remains of a Norman motte and bailey castle built by the de Montbegon family in the 11th century. The earthen mound is just one of many clustered along the Lune Valley between Lancaster and Kendal, the largest concentration of mottes in Britain.

We dowsed Belinus through the mound and along the east–west axis of the church, his flow almost enveloping the entire width of the central aisle. The church of St Wilfred has the historical distinction of being the old mother church of the region and early manuscripts mention that a Saxon cross once stood in the churchyard. Interestingly, a massive grave slab in the porch, said to be 14th century, has what appears to be Celtic inscriptions. An ancient wooden church may have once stood within the earthworks of the bailey here, but nothing remains of it today.

Melling received its name from the followers of the family of Mellor, a tribe of Angles who settled and worshipped on this site by the banks of the River Lune in AD 570. The Normans built a church on top of the old settlement, which the Scots led by Robert the Bruce and the Earl of Moray destroyed in 1322. The present building dates back to one rebuilt shortly afterwards.

The supposed Norman motte seemed to emanate a powerful energy, which we dowsed as a series of lines radiating out like the spokes of a wheel. Moreover, the close proximity of an ancient church and the presence of the Belinus current indicate that this may have been a sacred place of worship to the Druids. The great evangeliser St Wilfred was known to Christianise Celtic pagan sites this far north, possibly converting this ancient sanctuary at Melling just as he had on the Isle of Wight and at Titchfield in Hampshire.

We continued along the Lune Valley to Thurland Castle, just south of the village of Tunstall where the River Greta meets the Lune. It once comprised a circuit of walls and towers surrounded by a moat constructed in 1402 by Sir Thomas Tunstall, knighted by Henry V at Agincourt. After its partial destruction by Cromwell's troops during the Civil War, it remained as a ruin until its transformation as a Gothic mansion in the late 19th century by the North family, now turned into luxury apartments.

Around AD 650, the St John the Baptist Church at Tunstall stood within a large manor owned by St Wilfred when he was Bishop of Ripon. It was one of the many Saxon churches in Lonsdale destroyed during Viking raids. In Norman times, the manor became the property of the de Tunstall family who restored the church around 1415.

Charlotte Bronte based one of her characters in *Jane Eyre* on the Revd Carus Wilson (1791–1859) who was a vicar here. He became Mr Brocklehurst, the much-feared benefactor of Lowood School. Wilson founded a school in Tunstall for clergymen's daughters in 1824, which Charlotte attended for a time with her sisters.

Inside the church, we found the male current flowing through a Roman votive stone embedded into the north window jointly dedicated to *Aesculapius*, the Roman god of medicine, and *Hygeia*, goddess of healing. Discovered buried in the churchyard, this sacred altar may be linked to the Roman fort which marks the alignment just north of here at Burrow.

The ancient High Altar stone is also considered significant, dating from the 7th or 8th century when St Wilfred was in the area converting the Celtic population to Roman Christianity. Close to the church is the major crossing point of two Roman roads, one running from the fort at Burrow to Ribchester and the other from Burton-in-Lonsdale to the Lune Estuary at Lancaster. Local field names such as Tunstall Barrows and Cantsfield Barrows could suggest that this entire area next to the alignment was once an important Bronze Age burial ground.

The current then crosses the Lune to the village of Whittington and the church of St Michael the Archangel on a raised knoll, recorded as a Christian place of worship since 1200. Next to the church is yet another dragon mound, where at one time a sundial was set upon a square base with five worn steps, probably once supporting an early cross. The mound may have been another Norse Moot Hill or meeting place that later became a motte and bailey fortification to guard the Lune Valley. Belinus passes through both the mound and the church including its two fonts.

Inside is a magnificent stained-glass window depicting St George taming a green dragon with a lance, St Michael spearing a red dragon and St Oswald holding a green cross. St Oswald, who we encountered on the southern border of Brigantia, converted local pagans and Druids to Celtic Christianity in the 7th century over a hundred years before St Wilfred arrived from Rome to preach his Catholic teachings. The early Christians often depicted serpents and dragons on their crosses as if to alert the world that they were now the new keepers of the power of the serpent force within the landscape. The image of Oswald, holding a green cross next to the two great dragon slayers, symbolically represents his control over the male and female serpents that twist around the green pole or axis mundi like a caduceus; the Belinus alignment lies about a kilometre east of this church. Nearby is the appropriately named pub the Dragon's Head.

This symbolic window seemed to be an omen for what we were about to discover next, for just a short distance away at Kirkby Lonsdale both Elen and Belinus serpents meet with the alignment. Before we begin our investigations into the mystery of this lesser known South Cumbrian town, we return to the path of Elen where she crosses the Ribble just north of Clitheroe.

The Devil's Stones

From Clitheroe Elen guided us to the picturesque village of Waddington and its church dedicated to her Christian counterpart St Helen. Two magnificent beech trees in the churchyard stand as guardians of her flow before she enters the nave of this heavily restored church. Only the tower remains of the medieval building and some fine monuments of the Parker family from Browsholme Hall visited by Belinus. The name Waddington derives from an Anglo Saxon chieftain named Wada who had his *tun* (settlement) on the site; he features in a stained-glass window in the church along with Henry VI, who was held captive nearby.

As we strolled around this delightful village, we admired the colourful blooms that seemed to cover every verge and adorn every garden and hanging basket. The locals are obviously very proud of their village, perhaps inspired by the essence of the female current, becoming one of Britain's winners of the 'best kept village' competition.

We followed the spectacular Fell Road north to a spring emptying into a tough by the side of the road called the Walloper Well before heading towards Easington Fell and the little church of St Andrew at Slaidburn. This picturesque town with stone-built cottages is set in an Area of Outstanding Natural Beauty at the centre of the Forest of Bowland, but its looks are deceiving as in medieval times it was once an important administrative centre complete with its own court.

The original Norman church was built over Saxon foundations in 1450 and the Victorian restoration retains the magnificent wooden pews dating from the 17th century. Elen connects with several graves in the churchyard of various members of the Peel family of Knowlmere Manor, a crusader grave slab, an early Celtic stone and a Norman font. Set into the fabric of the north interior wall is a Celtic stone head, a remnant perhaps of ancient worship at this site. Also discovered near the church in a wall to the east of the rectory was a stone, probably Saxon, carved with an angel, now in the local Heritage Centre. We follow her through the village to the well and a very old pub called the 'Hark to Bounty', where my friends and I spent many enjoyable evenings in the 1980s.

Following the road to High Bentham past Tatham Fells, we came to a high point where the current is marked by the remains of a cross, known as 'Cross of Greet' or 'Top of t' Cross'. This large boulder once held a wooden cross and the carved-out depression that remained was later used to hold holy water during times of plague, similar to the 'Great Stone' at Gorse Hill in Manchester. The cross also once marked the county boundary with Yorkshire's West Riding until 1974, when the Slaidburn area became part of Lancashire. From here you have a clear view of Pendle Hill in the south and the great prominence of Ingleborough to the north. The remoteness of this area is evident by the existence of just three villages encountered since Clitheroe, over 40 km away.

Continuing through this beautiful moorland wilderness we crossed Tatham Fells before descending to the River Wenning in the valley below. In the shadow of Burn Moor within open moorland, Elen takes us to a large natural glacial erratic boulder called 'The Great Stone of Fourstones'. As we approached the enormous rock along a footpath, we noticed steps carved into its side allowing access to a level platform on its summit.

Folklore suggests that Finn McCool, a hunter-warrior of Irish mythology akin to the Arthur of the Celtic myths, hurled the stone across the Irish Sea in a fit of anger. Another legend says that it was one of a group of four stones 'from the beginning of time', until the devil took three away, dropping two on Casterton Fell and the other in the River Lune near Kirkby Lonsdale to build a bridge, known today as Devil's Bridge. More significantly, the stone 4 m (13 ft) high with a circumference of 27 m (88 ft) apparently marked an important boundary where local Celtic tribes gathered to hold council.

The Great Stone of Fourstones above the village of High Bentham

The platform that forms the top of this huge stone provides a perfect viewing place to monitor the rising and setting of the sun, moon and stars. From here you can see the three counties of North Yorkshire, Lancashire and Cumbria across Wenningdale. Ingleborough, once known as the 'fiery beacon' mountain, dominates the surrounding countryside to the east and marks the rising of the sun at the summer solstice. The star Deneb rises out of Whernside to the NNW, one of the famous 'three Yorkshire peaks' 736 m (2400 ft) above sea level. In *The Lost World of Agharti* the author A. MacLellan tells a fascinating story of a local man who discovered that one of the caves on the western slopes of Whernside led him deep into the bowels of the Earth where he met with a race of inner Earth people (MacLellan 1983).

From the Great Stone of Fourstones, true north is marked by a dimple at the eastern edge of another hill called the Howgills, with the village of High Bentham at its base. It is here we find Elen at a church on a mound dedicated to St Margaret of Antioch, nestling by the banks of the Wenning River on the northern edge of the Forest of Bowland. The present edifice is Victorian Gothic with a stained-glass window showing St Margaret subduing a dragon. High Bentham grew to become a market town in the 14th century and later a centre for weaving.

St Margaret according to one legend was the daughter of Aedesius, a pagan priest from Antioch, now the modern city of Antakya in Turkey. Margaret's father was so horrified by her Christian tendencies he arranged to marry her off to Olybrius, the Governor of the Roman Diocese who would only form this alliance if she renounced her faith. When she refused, she was cruelly tortured, during which various miraculous incidents occurred including her disappearance within the jaws of a dragon. However, irritated by the cross she carried, it soon regurgitated her back into the land of the living. During the time of the Crusades, the Knights Templar in Britain revived her status as a saint. Another common depiction of St Margaret is one where she is riding on the back of a dragon.

The quaint village of Burton-in-Lonsdale by the River Greta became famous for its potteries, producing stoneware and earthenware from 1650–1944. The elaborate Victorian Church of All Saints stands on an impressive knoll but Elen misses the building by a metre, entering a field just to the west. Within this field the current focuses on a large mound at the centre of an extensive group of earthworks.

Little is known concerning the history of this area but a 'castro de Burtona de Lanesdala' existed here in the 13th century. The large circular bank and ditch dates from the 12th century and was modified a hundred years later as a classic motte and bailey. This historical site has the rare privilege of having two baileys, one in the south and the other on the west side of the site.

Large mound behind All Saints' Church, Burton-in-Lonsdale

We continued to the small church of St Peter's in the village of Leck on the outskirts of Kirkby Lonsdale. In 1066, Leck was part of the manor of the Saxon Earl Tostig but, like so many Saxon manors after the Norman Conquest, it was awarded to a French Baron, who also acquired the manor of Tunstall. The present church built in 1879 stood on the site of a medieval chapel.

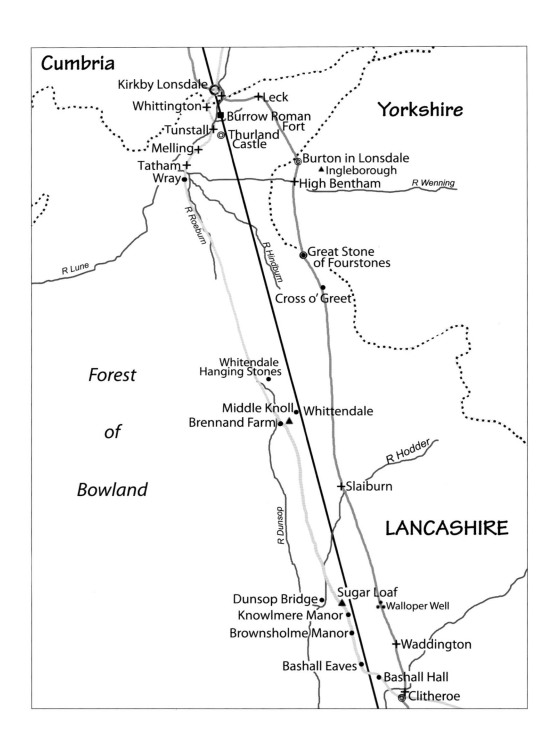

Cumbria

Kirkby Lonsdale

Whittington +

+Leck

Burrow Roman
Fort

Tunstall +

Thurland
Castle

Yorkshire

Melling +

Tatham +

Burton in Lonsdale

Wray •

▲Ingleborough

+High Bentham

R Wenning

R Roeburn

R Lune

R Hindburn

Great Stone
of Fourstones

Cross o' Greet •

Forest

of

Bowland

Whitendale
Hanging Stones

Middle Knoll ▲
Brennand Farm • ▲ Whittendale

R Hodder

+Slaiburn

R Dunsop

LANCASHIRE

Dunsop Bridge •

Knowlmere Manor •

Brownsholme Manor •

Bashall Eaves •

Sugar Loaf
▲

• Walloper Well

+ Waddington

• Bashall Hall

Clitheroe

Kirkby Lonsdale and the Belinus Sanctuary

Having crossed over the county boundary into Cumbria, we arrive at Devil's Bridge, a famous landmark just to the southeast of Kirkby Lonsdale. As a youth, I visited this place many times with my motorcyclist friends at the weekends. Little did I know that many years later I would return here to dowse its earth energies and discover one of the most enigmatic sites on the Spine of Albion.

The old market town, settled since Neolithic times, stands above a bend of the Lune River just within the border of Cumbria, tucked between the fells of the Lake District and the Yorkshire Dales. The Celtic tribes of the Brigantes and *Segantii* settled in the area, on nearby Casterton Fell and at the neighbouring villages of Leck, Barbon and Middleton. The Romans also came to the town, constructing a road just to the east and a fort to the south at Burrow.

Kirkby Lonsdale developed as a major fording place over the Lune for drovers and packhorses and a place for trade for the many early farmers who cultivated the highly fertile land in the surrounding area. The Domesday Book records the town as *Cherchibi*, meaning 'a village with a church', which, according to the *Annals of Kirkby Lonsdale* (Pearson 1930), the Saxon Earl Tostig owned at the time. However, William the Conqueror took the entire estate for himself, later inherited by his son King William Rufus who fortified a mound next to the old church. A wooden tower was erected on the top of the mound used as a stronghold to 'administer power and control' over the surrounding area, overseen by a knight of William the Conqueror called Ivo de Taillebois (1036–94), who became Baron of Kendal.

After the Dissolution of the Monasteries, many of the Catholic families were persuaded to relinquish their lands to the Crown, which Henry VIII sold off to his loyal servants. Thomas Carus, the new owner of the manor of Kirkby Lonsdale, was one such benefactor who later became a justice of the Bench during Elizabethan times. Around 1678, Sir Thomas Lowther of Lowther Park purchased the estates, a wealthy and powerful politician who, as we were about to discover, also owned much of the land north of here including many important sacred sites on the Spine of Albion. However, by the 18th century it was in the possession of Sir Thomas Tunstall of nearby Thurland Castle.

The town has attracted many interesting characters throughout history, such as Bonnie Prince Charlie when he held the place for a short time during the Jacobite Rebellion in 1745. The natural beauty of the Lune that flows below the town brought many famous artists to its banks including J.M.W. Turner (1775–1851) who in 1818 painted one of its finest views just below the churchyard. The picture inspired the famous writer, poet and artist John Ruskin (1819–1900) who wrote, 'I do not know in all my country, still less in France or Italy, a place more naturally divine'. This wonderful scene became the renowned 'Ruskin's View'.

The twisting serpent-like valley of the Lune naturally attracts the female current and we dowsed Elen crossing the river to the east of Devil's Bridge by the old fording place. Here an enlightened soul had left a bunch of wild flowers next to the water possibly as an offering to the goddess of the river, precisely where the current crosses the Lune. The narrow bridge is an ancient structure with unusually tall

Devil's Bridge over the River Lune, Kirkby Lonsdale

arches that rises at its highest point to 11 m (36 ft), reminding me of an Etruscan bridge visited some years ago near the ancient city of Vulci in Lazio, Italy. As we stood mesmerised by the fast-flowing river rippling over the rocks, I wondered why this beautiful place had such a sinister name attached to it.

In *The Folklore of the Lake District*, the local author Marjorie Rowling tells the story of an old woman who, while crossing the Lune River, became separated from her cow. The devil appeared and offered to build a bridge in return for the soul of the first living thing that crossed over. With that, the woman tricked her dog to cross before her and the devil had to be satisfied with the soul of an animal. This legend reoccurs in many places around Britain albeit in a slightly different form. This particular legend relates in many ways to the folk memory of a foundation sacrifice, such as the black dog. In the remote past, the superstitious locals would sacrifice an animal before laying the first stone when constructing a new bridge to guard against the spirits of the river. Another legend says that the bridge was created by the devil using one of the four stones from Tatham Fells, visited earlier on the path of Elen.

From the river, Elen crosses a field into the town of Kirkby Lonsdale to a preaching cross in an old square called Swine Market. It was here that Bonnie Prince Charlie stood in 1745 to marshal local men to join him in the Jacobite Rebellion against the Duke of Cumberland's English Army. As we were to discover later, this is one of many places on the female current where we encounter this Scottish hero. The cross dates from medieval times and was moved to this spot from Market Street, site of the original medieval market.

She slips through an alleyway into the churchyard of the ancient parish church of St Mary, entering through the southeast corner, where we find the Underley Chapel. Long ago, pews in this particular chapel were for the exclusive use of the Earls of Bective and their families from Underley Hall and often the chapel 'was full of Dukes'. The Domesday Book mentions that a Saxon chapel stood on this site, its lands later given by Ivo de Taillebois in 1093 to St Mary's Abbey at York, which retained it until the Dissolution of the Monasteries. The northeast section of the present church stands over the site of this early chapel, chosen because of its commanding position high above the old river crossing at the bottom of Mill Brow. St Mary's still contains some of the finely sculptured masonry from the original Norman church including three pillars, two carved with diamond patterns very similar to those found in Durham Cathedral and in the crypt at York Minster dating from 1096–1115. Many believe that the same stonemasons worked at all three places.

One of these pillars marks the Elen flow, made obvious by the carvings of a Green Man, a dragon and the familiar centaur that represents Sagittarius, encountered at many churches on the currents in Hampshire and Oxfordshire. The dragon represents the female serpent and the Green Man symbolises the silent intelligent power within the land. The centaur poised as if about to fire an arrow alerts us to the presence of the north–south axis of the Belinus Line, which passes just a few metres from the church. Moreover, as Sagittarius he also represents the direction of

Norman pillar carved with a Green Man inside St Mary's Church, Kirkby Lonsdale

the line, as the stars of Sagittarius are in the region of the heavens closest to the centre of our galaxy. In the Glastonbury landscape zodiac, the outstretched arm of the figure of Sagittarius points to the omphalos of the zodiac at Park Wood near Butleigh in Somerset.

A Templar grave slab lies on the edge of her flow by the tower and a corbel carved with a rose marks her exit in the northwest corner. There are several remnants of 12th and 13th century masonry including the magnificent Norman doorway on the west side of the tower. The 14th century font was rescued from a disused chapel at Killington, where it was used as a drinking trough for the neighbouring farmer's cows and sheep.

From here, Elen makes a sudden swing to the north to enter the private grounds of the Vicarage, once called Glebe Field. As we dowsed around the large churchyard, I found the Belinus current approaching from the southwest having passed through the town's war memorial. Now travelling parallel with Elen, he too disappears into the grounds of the Vicarage, behind a high wall. Finding a suitable place to peer over, we soon realised the object of their focus, an enormous 'dragon' mound right at the end of the garden, now completely overgrown. This we realised must have been where William Rufus built his wooden tower on a motte to 'administer power and control'. Dowsing around the perimeter of the vicarage wall, Caroline picked up Elen entering the mound from the southeast and I dowsed Belinus joining her from the southwest to form a Node on its summit. It was at this point that we

Kirkby Lonsdale Mound in the Vicarage garden by Ruskin's View

decided to visit the local library to find out more about its history.

We discovered through the *Annals of Kirkby Lonsdale* (Pearson 1930) that it was indeed the remains of the Norman motte built by William Rufus. I believe the deliberate positioning of the tower over the mound was to focus and amplify the telluric energy created by the meeting of two great earth serpents, ritually manipulated to affect the psyche of the local population by those who held the power. As always, the underlying geology is also a factor here, for the town lies on an arc of highly paramagnetic carboniferous limestone that is almost crystalline in substance, which includes the rim of Morecambe Bay. The Node point was further desecrated in the 18th and 19th centuries when the mound was adapted for cock fighting, known then as Cockpit Hill. During WWII, this important power centre became a weapons dump.

During prehistoric times, the mound was constructed on the ridge overlooking the sharp bend of the sacred Lune to harness *chi* which naturally occurs here, to create balance and fertility within the surrounding area. The old tribes possibly viewed the male serpent as symbolic of their solar god and Elen as representative of the divine feminine within the land who brings healing and wisdom. To our amazement, we discovered that the town is associated with the Iron Age god Belinus or *Belenus* (also Belenos). According to one source, his shrines were found all over Europe from Aquileia on the Adriatic and significantly at the British town of Kirkby Lonsdale in England.

Such a bold claim can be verified by the discovery of an altar stone unearthed in the northeast end of the churchyard near the Node in 1684, being the only one of its kind ever found in Britain. The Latin inscription on the altar, NVMINIB AVG N ET GENIO COLGF APOLLINIS BELLINVS VSLMI, roughly translates as 'a dedication to the guiding spirits of the twin brotherhood of Apollo and Belinus fulfilling the vow'. Although described as Roman, its discovery here implies that a temple to Belinus must have existed at Kirkby Lonsdale almost at the heart of the Brigantian nation, perhaps on the very site of the Node that lies within metres of the Belinus alignment. Looking due east from below the mound near Ruskin's View, we could

see in a dip between two hills the flattened summit of Ingleborough, perhaps a marker for the equinox sunrise.

From the mound, the male current follows a high ridge called Fisherty Brow to a field, where we find a large deep bowl-shaped depression in the ground known locally as the Devil's Punchbowl. Rowling mentions it as the place where the devil buried an early church so deep that it now lies beneath the crater. As a child, she was told that if she placed her ear to the ground at the bottom of the bowl she might hear the chiming of bells from the buried church. This story may be another allegory indicating a hidden pagan place of worship that existed here long before Christianity came to the area.

A similar crater, also called the Devil's Punch Bowl, can be found at Hindhead in Surrey, now owned and maintained by the National Trust. This natural phenomenon is believed to be the result of erosion caused by natural spring water beneath the sandstone, gradually collapsing the upper level.

We continued along a footpath to a quaint stone bridge crossing a stream where Belinus disappears over a ridge of earthworks into private grounds of Underley Hall, once home of the Earls of Bective who founded the Underley Chapel at St Mary's Church. The design of the house is Jacobean in style built over the footprint of a former mansion within an estate established since the 16th century. Today Underley Hall is a specialist residential and day school that caters for both boys and girls aged 8–17 years with behavioural, emotional and social difficulties.

We were in no doubt as to the enormity of such an important find as the Belinus altar, placing Kirkby Lonsdale as a highly significant sacred sanctuary of this ancient solar deity on the Spine of Albion. It may have originally stood on the mound where we found a powerful Node point of the male and female serpents, which makes this find even more astonishing. Sadly, for those visiting Kirkby Lonsdale today its sacred history still lies well-hidden with only the folklore to tantalise us.

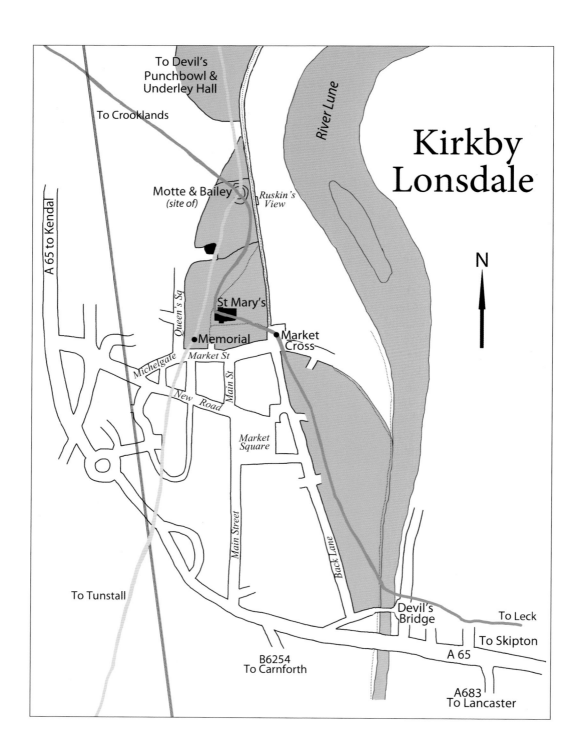

Kirkby
Lonsdale

To Devil's
Punchbowl &
Underley Hall

To Crooklands

River Lune

A 65 to Kendal

Motte & Bailey
(site of)

Ruskin's
View

N

Queen's Sq

St Mary's

Michelgate

•Memorial

Market St

Main St

•Market
Cross

New Road

Market
Square

Main Street

Back Lane

Devil's
Bridge

To Leck

To Tunstall

To Skipton

A 65

B6254
To Carnforth

A683
To Lancaster

The Last Frontier of the Celts

In *People Called Cumbri*, F.J. Carruthers describes Cumbria as a lost and forgotten 'region of greatness' ruled over by illustrious kings that remained independent of England until long after the Norman Conquest. Cumbria, previously known as Cumberland, was the northern realm of the Brigantes and the *Carvetii*, a place rich in traditions and history, much of which was set into verse by the ancient Welsh bards. This mystical land was also the centre of the cult of *Brighida* or *Brigga*, a goddess later Christianised as St Bride, Bega or St Bridget. It has stories of King Arthur and Sir Lancelot and early Christian missionaries such as St Ninian, who established religious communities before the time of St Augustine.

This ancient county also has a wealth of prehistoric monuments scattered around its glorious fells, silent remnants of the mysterious Neolithic and Bronze Age cultures, its archaeological finds showing them as intelligent, enterprising and prosperous. Neolithic polished stone axes from one particular mountain in the Langdale area of Cumbria have been uncovered in many places around Britain and Europe. Later tribes utilised many of the rich seams of minerals such as iron and lead, found beneath this dramatic mountainous terrain.

Cumbria was particularly important to the Neolithic and Bronze Age peoples who built over a hundred stone circles in the region, of which sixty-five still survive, amounting to almost a fifth of the megalithic circles in the country. Some of the more impressive monuments include Castlerigg, Long Meg and Her Daughters and Swinside. Shap once had two stone circles and two stone avenues, a complex similar in design to Avebury, before its destruction. The prehistoric henges of Mayburgh and Arthur's Round Table, just south of Penrith, are also impressive monuments still preserved and accessible to visitors today.

It always amazes me how little emphasis is placed on the great monuments of Cumbria in comparison to their southern counterparts, overshadowed perhaps by Hadrian's Wall and the overemphasis on the Roman occupation here. Throughout Cumbria, we find remains of cairns and long barrows, many dug into and destroyed during the end of the 19th century by the Cumberland County Council, the locals taking away cartloads of material for road building. By the time the antiquarians arrived, most of the precious artefacts had disappeared. However, they did manage to rescue a number of intricately carved gold torques, now on display in the British Museum. The famous Embleton Sword, uncovered at Maryport on the west coast of Cumbria, dates to around 50 BC. This veritable 'Excalibur' is decorated with silver, bronze, jewels and enamel, obviously forged for a great warrior of considerable wealth and prestige by skilled and accomplished craftsmen, designed to be strong, long and light.

When the Romans arrived in the north of England, they encountered a people with an already strong and well-established culture. According to archaeology, the local tribes changed very little throughout the Roman occupation and continued their religious and administrative practices, with the tribal hierarchy maintaining their civil authority. As the Cumbrian Celts belonged to the same branch of those on the Isle of Man and Ireland, much of their folklore survives intact.

Early victors of many a conquered country were renowned for rewriting their history and after the Brigantes fell to the Romans and the later Angles and Danes, many of their early churches and written records were destroyed. The importance of Cumbria's ancient kingdoms and their great and noble deeds eventually became the source of myth and legend. Although very few archaeologists are willing to consider folklore and legend as a means of uncovering lost history, I believe they help us to re-remember our ancient past. With the loss of our oral tradition as an accurate way of retelling historical events, local folklore and legends surely have a place in explaining our history, if examined in context. Certainly, some of the old traditions that still survive in Northern England and Scotland have helped us to piece together some of its fascinating past.

George Fox and the Quaker Vision

The Barbon Cross

To the northeast of the Punchbowl, Belinus follows the general direction of the old north–south Roman road along the Lune Valley, stopping briefly to visit a few places along the way including a megalith carved as a cross, situated on a high ridge in a field south of the village of Barbon. The quality of the cross carving is superior to similar crosses we have encountered so far. Apparently, it was re-erected at this spot in the 19th century after the stone was found buried nearby.

In the shadow of the old settlements of both the Brigantes and Segantii tribes, Belinus visits the church towers of St Bartholomew at Barbon and the nearby Holy Ghost at Middleton, both once part of the manor owned by the Saxon Earl Tostig, but little remains of any antiquity today. The Holy Ghost is an interesting dedication, which I believe relates to the spirit force, the intelligent nature of the earth energies that reside within the land sensed by the old priests at these sites long ago. Belinus also visits the castellated Middleton Hall, once owned by the powerful Middleton family of Westmorland from the reign of Edward III until the time of Charles I.

Travelling north along the Lune Valley by the Rawthey River near Sedbergh, Belinus took us to a renowned place of worship at Brigflatts. Here we dowsed him at the Friend's Meeting House, where the Quakers have worshipped uninterrupted since the 17th century and considered to be their oldest meeting house in the north. The present building was constructed in 1675 over the site of a simple single-roomed farmhouse with a dirt floor.

The gentle power of prayer over hundreds of years is an obvious draw for the male current – the serpent energy subtly radiates their religious message and influences the psyche of the people as it travels along the Belinus alignment. Moreover, the male current may have inspired the founding of the Quaker Movement when its instigator, George Fox, experienced a vision while connecting with its flow during a visit to Pendle Hill. In the vision, Fox saw a place by a river where people in white would come forth to meet with him:

'A mighty meeting there was and is to this day, near Sedbergh,
which I gathered in the name of Jesus
And the Lord opened to me at that place: and let me see a great
People in white raiment by a rivers side coming to the Lord;
and the place was near.' (Fox 1694)

Fox believed that his vision referred to the community of white linen workers who lived by the Rawthey at Brigflatts. During his stay there in 1652, the workers invited him to their little chapel on top of Firbank Fell to hear him preach, but instead he chose a rocky crag nearby to spread his message. Today this crag is known as 'Fox's Pulpit', situated 3.2 km (2 miles) northwest of Brigflatts, and a plaque there reads:

'Let your lives speak. Here or near this rock George Fox preached to about one thousand seekers for three hours on Sunday June 13, 1652. Great power inspired his message and the meeting proved of first importance in gathering the Society of Friends known as Quakers. Many men and women convinced of the truth on this fell and in other parts of the northern counties went forth through the land and over the seas with the living word of the Lord enduring great hardships and winning multitudes to Christ.'

The chapel at Firbank was destroyed in the 19th century but the enclosure of the churchyard remains along with a few stunted trees and a solitary gravestone.

We followed Belinus to Fox's rocky podium and assumed that his unusual choice of venue was inspired by his wish to connect directly with the power of the male serpent energy that resides there, having previously experienced his flow at Pendle Hill and Brigflatts. As we sat on the rock in the company of skylarks, buzzards and moorland sheep, it certainly felt very peaceful and tranquil.

Across the sparsely inhabited moors of the Cumbrian hills, Belinus ascends the high fells near Tebay to Shap, a village on the A6, which for thousands of years has stood next to a busy thoroughfare frequented by travellers to Scotland.

The Auld Grey Town

We next located the female current at the church of St Patrick's at Crooklands, northwest of Kirkby Lonsdale near the small village of Preston and close to where the Peasey Beck crosses the Lancaster Canal and the M6 motorway. The church stands on an ancient place of worship first established by Thomas de Wyrkington for the Premonstratensian Canons in 1190, the same order that founded Titchfield Abbey in Hampshire. She then changes her course to journey north to a prominent hill called

'The Helm', south of the town of Kendal. Here Elen passes through a small hillfort at its southern tip called Castlesteads.

Soon we were entering the bustling town of Kendal, also known as the gateway to the Lake District. This chartered market town has ancient origins mainly due to its topography. The earliest settlers here recognised the strategic importance of its hills and constructed their fortifications on them, located either side of the River Kent just below where it converges with the River Mint. On the summit of the western hill are the impressive ruins of Kendal Castle, where according to Arthur Mee the Romans built a camp. Gilbert Fitz Reinfred erected the first castle there in the 12th century as an earth ring-work and bailey fortress, later reconstructed in stone by William de Lancaster in the 13th century. Sir William Parr acquired it in 1383, the rumoured birthplace of Katherine Parr, one of his descendants and the sixth wife of Henry VIII.

We had attempted to explore Kendal during a three-day weekend break in the Lake District, but after experiencing disturbing nightmares relating to the town on two consecutive nights before our planned visit, we left it until the last day. Over the years, my dreams have been a great source of insight but sometimes they present me with a warning and, in this instance, I was shown a dark presence disrupting the energy matrix of Kendal and particularly the feminine energy. Caroline also had dreams of demonic beings flying over its streets, confirming that there was a definite distortion within the energy field, which was probably allowing a 'diabolical' entity to pervade the town. I also believe there are times when the earth energies wax and wane, corresponding with the phases of the sun and moon, the period around the solstices and the equinoxes is particularly strong. Being naturally sensitive to such effects upon the Earth, I often intuitively feel when it is appropriate or not to visit a sacred place. As I awoke on this cold but sunny Sunday morning, I had a strong sense that all would be well for our trip to Kendal.

Walking towards the entrance of Kendal's parish church, the sound of choral music wafted over the car park, which somehow reassured us as we opened ourselves up to the energies of Kendal. Strolling around the outside of the 13th century building dedicated to the Holy Trinity, we could strongly sense the spiritual act of worship emanating from its ancient walls. Its five aisles make it the widest church in the country, enabling it to house a congregation of twelve hundred people.

The Domesday Book provides evidence of a much older site of worship and the shaft of an Anglican cross now housed in the Parr Chapel dates back to AD 850. The tower and central section dates from 1201, made from sandstone blocks taken from the ruins of the Roman fort to the south of the town. The 15th century Flemish aisle acquired its name from an influx of Flemish weavers during that time, which boosted Kendal's woollen trade.

The area around the parish church was originally within the separate township of Kirkland, next to an important crossing point of the Kent River. It became a monastic estate with its own court and customs. Today Kirkland contains an art gallery, museum and the Abbots Hall.

We spotted numerous carved dragons on the exterior of Holy Trinity, especially above the east window where we dowsed the female serpent. On its west side, it passes through a sundial set on a much older stone base, possibly the socket to the old Celtic cross that once stood here, its replica standing nearby.

Once the service had ended, we entered the church to a warm welcome and the sound of beautiful and uplifting organ music. After the congregation had dispersed, we started to dowse Elen's path from the east window and through the part of the church called the Old Sanctuary. She leaves through the 'Resurrection' window at the west end of the church, her flow also incorporating the organ, which stands close by.

From there, we walked towards the town centre and noticed that this once ancient and potentially attractive place appeared dowdy and sombre. Curiously, the width of Elen responded to this atmosphere as she suddenly began to shrink and weaken as we followed her up the steep Captain Frenches Lane before veering along a footpath into a park overlooking Kendal. Standing on a mound here is the ancient motte and bailey earthworks of Castle Howe, earlier known as Castle Law Hill. Catching our breath after the steep climb to the base of the mound, we stood for a while to admire the panoramic view that stretched out before us. Across the River Kent we could clearly see the ruins of Kendal Castle standing on the opposite hill, and to the south the huge spur of land called the Helm.

Ivo de Taillebois, of the Angevin Dynasty, who also owned the castle at Kirkby Lonsdale, built Castle Howe in the 11th century as a wooden motte and bailey fortress. It was abandoned by the 13th century after its total destruction during a Scottish raid. The earthworks of Kendal's earliest castle consist of a circular mound surrounded by a ditch and rampart at its base and a secondary ditch encircling the plateau at the top, now occupied by an obelisk commemorating the Revolution of 1688. The original name Castle Law Hill may give us a clue to its earlier purpose, as 'law hills' were moot places where local tribal chiefs would gather to discuss the region's affairs.

On the level area just to the east of the mound was the site of the bailey, deliberately carved out of the steep incline. However, such an impressive feat of engineering was well beyond the capabilities of the Normans, being more on a par with the Iron Age hillfort builders of Maiden Castle in Dorset and Old Sarum near Salisbury. I could imagine sacred ceremonies taking place here as early as the Bronze Age, where the British tribes would have practised their pagan rituals, honouring such festivals as Beltane and the summer solstice sunrise.

Castle Howe, Kendal

We followed the footpath that spirals clockwise up and around the mound and just as we reached the top, where the obelisk stands, we heard the bells tolling from the parish church below. We dowsed the path of Elen approaching the mound from the southeast and, after uniting with the obelisk, she changed course to head northeast towards the centre of Kendal.

After spending time tuning into the site we sensed that the disruptive energy of the town, first alerted to us in our dreams, was affecting the quality of the serpent flow here, so before continuing to the town centre we performed our usual healing ceremony. The previous day we had collected several special rose-coloured granite stones from the River Lowther near Shap Abbey and I could feel strong healing energy emanating from one of them. I placed this particular stone on the mound to help recharge and realign the current. During the visualisation, I sensed that the real source of this energetic disturbance was somewhere in the town centre. We passed the Town Hall, once the old Exchange Hall for the wool trade known as the White Hall, and found ourselves outside the tourist office. Here we noticed an ancient stone at the base of the building laid there in 1893, believed to have been the foundation stone of the old market cross that stood by Strickland Gate. Its local name is the *Ca Steean* or 'Cauld Stone', used for proclamations for at least three centuries. The Quaker George Fox also preached there in the same year he founded the Meeting House at nearby Brigflatts. In 1745, Bonnie Prince Charlie used it to proclaim his father, son of the deposed James II, the true King of England. Before its removal to the tourist office, this omphalos stone once marked the true geomantic centre of the town from which all measurements were taken.

Now dominated by a large war memorial, the old Market Square still has remnants of an old cobbled street and Tudor houses, although much reduced in size due to the building of new shops and houses. We found an information board in Strickland Gate that informed us that a chapel dedicated to St George also once existed in the marketplace within a building constructed in 1754, close to the present war memorial. Its design was unusual in that it consisted of three floors; the chapel of St George occupying the upper floor, the ground floor used as the butter market, and beneath was the notorious town jail, encapsulating the typical Victorian ideal of heaven, earth and hell. A notice board in Strickland Gate reads:

> 'The dungeon was nicknamed the black hole, and an old rhyme associated with it reads: "there is a spirit above and a spirit below, a spirit of love and a spirit of woe, the spirit above is the spirit divine and the spirit below is the spirit of wine".'

I believe it was geomantically placed here over the site of the stone cross, which formed the original omphalos. In fact, this strange building represented the perfect ideology of the World Tree. In the old cosmology of the bards, the World Tree has three planes of existence viewed as concentric circles. The plane at the base of the tree represents the underworld, the *Annwn* or 'Abyss'. The middle plane is the earthly realm in which we live and strive through good and evil. The upper level equates to the heavenly realm of enlightened beings, having transcended the cycle of earthly lives (Pennick 1996).

A dungeon or 'black hole' placed at the omphalos of the town would certainly contribute to the disrupted energies, but we both sensed that something else was also causing this phenomenon. Having found Elen passing through the eastern part of the marketplace, we felt sure we would find a clue here as to what else was troubling her current. At the information centre, we found our answer. A small pamphlet entitled *A Quaker Guide to Kendal* by Donald A. Rooksby informs us that the marketplace once included three of the town's ten slaughterhouses. In my experience, the presence of one slaughterhouse in a town, let alone ten, can have a detrimental effect upon the local earth energies and the psyche of the people living around them, negatively influencing their general well-being. The work of the Fountain Group founded by Colin Bloy can also attest to this.

In the marketplace, the female current visits the Unitarian Chapel built in 1767 next to the George and Dragon pub at the top of Braithwaite Brow. Unitarianism grew out of the Protestant movement in the 16th century when the people of Kendal were seeking a simpler and purer form of worship.

As we stood and tuned silently into the marketplace and the old omphalos site, now a war memorial, we dowsed her flow as stagnant and weak which seemed to reflect the general decline and neglect we were observing in the town. As we stood amongst the shoppers, we discreetly directed healing towards the old chapel and dungeon with the intention of releasing Elen from the shackles of the dark and menacing residual energy. We felt that this energy had accumulated here over centuries through the activities at the slaughterhouses and the events experienced by both men and woman incarcerated in the grim underworld of the 'Black Hole'.

Despite our initial experience of Kendal, it is a fascinating place and was once an important commercial centre for the South Lakes. It is particularly famous for its mint cake, renowned for its high energy-giving qualities, and the medieval woollen mills that once produced 'Kendal Green', a hard-wearing cloth worn by the Kendal Bowman at the Battle of Crecy in 1346. In the 19th century, 'K Shoes' were made here and became one the biggest brands of footwear in Britain until they were taken over by Clarks. Tiny alleyways leading off the main streets, known as 'Yards', are full of quaint little shops and restaurants similar to the 'shuts' of Shrewsbury, and once filled with the workshops of stonemasons and craftsmen.

We continued to follow Elen across the River Kent to the main Museum and College of Creative Arts; perhaps her presence there helps to inspire the young students. Elen then runs northeast along the River Mint towards the alignment to cross Shap Fells, reputedly haunted by the spirit of King Arthur's father, Uther Pendragon.

The Shap Serpent Temple

'a great temple of the old Britons, such as that at Abury [Avebury],
which it resembles very much' (Stukeley 1776)

Before its destruction in the 16th and 17th centuries, Shap was one of the most important prehistoric centres in Britain, having the largest serpent stone temple outside of Avebury. The name Shap is said to derive from either *Heape*, meaning 'pile of stones', or *Hep, Heppe, Heps, Hips*, the fruit of the dog-rose. The rosehip may refer to the distinctive colour of the unique pink or rose-coloured granite that only exists in this region of Britain.

Shap lies at the southern end of the Lower Eden Valley, a geographical meeting place where for thousands of years various cultures have settled and built their ceremonial temples. While living in Lancashire during the 1970s and 1980s, I spent much of my time exploring Cumbria's fascinating prehistoric sites, often witnessing strange natural phenomena, which I realise now was initiating me into the pathway of the earth serpents. One of the remotest and windiest places I visited was Shap, its atmosphere always leaving me with a sense of sadness and loss, probably due to the massive level of wanton destruction and disrespect levelled at one of our ancestors' most powerful and sacred sites.

Just south of the village by the A6, in the shadow of the ugly lime works near the River Lowther, are the remains of a stone circle called Kemp Howe. The construction of a railway line destroyed most of it, cutting right through its centre in 1845 leaving us with an arc of six stones to the west of the embankment, the largest being 3 m (10 ft) long. These large stones are Shap granite boulders, which display a radiant rose pink colouring said to be biotitic granite with large crystals of pink plagioclase feldspar.

The remaining stones of Kemp Howe stone circle, Shap

Many years ago, I discovered from observing a large map of northern England that Kemp Howe lies on an equinoctial east–west axis from St Bees Head lighthouse in Cumbria to Whitby Abbey on the coast of Yorkshire, which appears to divide Britain at its halfway point. I wondered if Alfred Wainwright, the famous author of many Lakeland walking guides, knew of this line, for his popular coast-to-coast route starts at St Bees Head and passes through the village of Shap. St Bees Head is another omphalos of Britain if you include the whole of Ireland, calculated by the author Andrew Collins and outlined in Alex Langstone's book *Bega and the Sacred Ring*.

According to John Waterhouse in *The Stone Circles of Cumbria*, Kemp Howe circle was part of a Neolithic complex that included a stone row known as the Shap Stone Avenue. Descriptions from antiquarians who visited this site over a hundred years ago suggest that the Kemp Howe circle was approximately 30 m (98 ft) across and stood at the southern terminus of a great avenue of parallel megaliths heading north for over a mile, very similar to the West Kennet avenue of megaliths at Avebury.

William Camden (1551–1623) was a leading member of the Society of Antiquaries, established around 1588, and one of the very first antiquarians to explore Britain's stone monuments. He noted that the northern and southern avenue at Shap consisted of large stones 'in the form of pyramids set almost in a direct line and at equal distances, for a mile together'. When Stukeley visited the site in 1725, he observed that the avenue resembled a 'megalithic serpent', and produced accurate surveyed plans, which have sadly disappeared.

The width of the avenue, according to Thomas Pennant writing in 1769, was 27 m (88 ft) in the south, gradually reducing to 18 m (59 ft) as it passed through the village. The avenue then turned towards Skellaw Hill in the northwest, on top of which was a large barrow. All that remains of the avenue today is the Goggleby Stone and one other, a massive tilted megalith called the Aspers Field Stone.

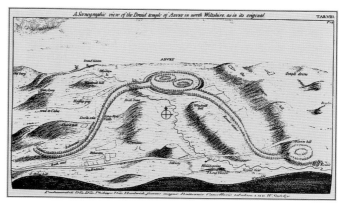

William Stukeley's drawing of the Avebury serpent temple

According to a local antiquarian, who was also the vicar of Shap during the mid-1800s, called the Revd J. Simpson, cup and ring marks could also be observed on these stones. Another stone in the wall below Skellaw Hill is in line with these megaliths and some researchers believe they indicate the point where the avenue reached its northern terminus.

In 1777, Joseph Nicolson and Richard Burn in *The History and Antiquities of the Counties of Westmorland and Cumberland* refer to another large stone circle existing at Shap, previously known as Karl Lofts. Revd Simpson also confirmed that it stood halfway between Kemp Howe and Skellaw Hill:

'The largest stone circle near the English border – the Stonehenge or Avebury of the north of England – formerly stood near Shap. The stone avenues leading to it are said to have been nearly two miles in length.' (www.themodernantiquarian.com)

The Karl Lofts circle lay north of the old Greyhound Inn now a Hotel, thought to measure 121 m (400 ft) in diameter with a large stone at its centre. Revd Simpson also mentions that the huge centre stone was eventually cut up into seven pairs of 'yat stoops' or gateposts. Some of the circle's smaller stones are still visible in the wall alongside the pavement of a row of terraced houses called Carl Lofts. If we are to assume that all these early accounts are true, then the village of Shap lies on the site of the second largest stone circle in England after Avebury.

Yet this rich variety of sources and descriptions fails to indicate the exact layout of the Shap complex. However, a painting shown in Burl's *From Carnac to Callanish* (1993) entitled *The Shap Avenue sketch by Lady Mary Stuart, wife of the first Earl of Lowther in 1775*, clearly shows

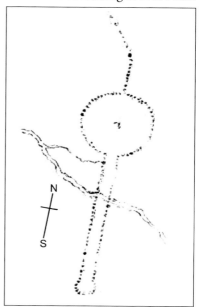

Sketch by Revd Simpson of Shap's stone circles and avenues

Kemp Howe stone circle standing at the southern terminus of the avenue.

In the 1970s, archaeologist Tom Clare noted that the northern and southern avenues were separate monuments, the northern stones being tubular in form whilst the southern stones were more diverse in shape. The type of stone used also highlights the difference between these avenues; the southern avenue consisted of granite stones and the northern avenue was mostly of limestone (Clare 2007).

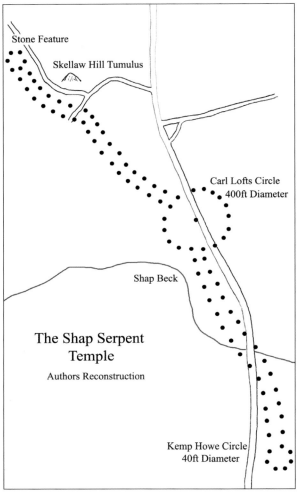

Author's plan of Shap's serpent temple

I have spent many years researching this site in an effort to piece together how this great megalithic ceremonial landscape was constructed. I believe an avenue of granite boulders ran from Kemp Howe to the larger stone circle called Karl Lofts, with a separate avenue continuing northwest curving to the left of Skellaw Hill and terminating at 'a four stone feature'. From the air, the whole complex would have resembled a giant serpent temple similar to Avebury.

It is interesting to note some comparisons here between Shap and the serpent temple at Avebury envisioned by Stukeley. Like Kemp Howe, the Sanctuary on Overton Hill at Avebury was a stone circle at the southern terminus of a great stone avenue. Another stone avenue called the Beckhampton Avenue, now destroyed, began at the western entrance of the Avebury circle and snaked its way to the Longstones. In a similar manner, Shap had a separate avenue from the main circle running to a stone feature further north. I am convinced the monument at Shap was potentially a serpent temple and a prototype for Avebury.

Many antiquarians describe how the gradual destruction of the temple began in the 16th century. William Camden in his book *Britannia* (1586) describes the monuments of Shap as 'a remarkable Druidical monument but upon the enclosure of the parish of Shap the stones were blown up by gunpowder, and were converted into rude fences'. Around 1640, members of the Puritan movement also destroyed many of the stones with dynamite. Lady Lowther captured these shattered remains in her sketch of 1755.

I also felt sure that the presence of the earth serpents of Elen and Belinus here would unlock some of its secrets. On many occasions, I have dowsed the male serpent passing through Kemp Howe and from there he follows the course of the original avenue parallel to the railway line, crossing the little bridge over Shap Beck to the Greyhound Hotel.

As Caroline and I followed the male current north through fields next to the railway line and parallel to the A6, the old main road to Scotland, we spotted several megaliths broken up and lying in the hedgerows or carved into gateposts. Just after the little bridge over Shap Beck, the current crosses the road to the west side of the village. Looking down from the bridge, we noticed a massive megalith in the stream, possibly a stone from the avenue. Early accounts state that Shap Beck once ran across the avenue between Karl Lofts circle and Kemp Howe as shown in the sketch by Revd Simpson.

Just north of the Greyhound Hotel, at the centre of the village, the road rises to an elevated platform of land on which I believe the large central circle stood, now marked by a row of houses similarly called Carl Lofts. Remnants of the stones belonging to this circle are in the foundations of the walls alongside these houses.

We continued following Belinus through a field to the west of the village where we encountered several megalithic stones marking his flow, including a large one on its side known as the Giant's Foot.

Megaliths in the wall in front of a row of houses called Carl Lofts, possibly from the Karl Lofts stone circle

The Giant's Foot marking the Belinus current at Shap

Belinus then aims for Skellaw Hill but no longer follows the avenue, which is to the west of him, its original course now marked by a copse of trees where we find a large megalith in the wall, and further along the great Goggleby and Aspers Field Stones. According to Robert Farrah in *A Guide to the Stone Circles of Cumbria*, these two stones and Skellaw Hill align with a stone circle on Knipescar Common to the northwest of Shap. The male current surprisingly avoids these major stones as it targets the tumulus on Skellaw Hill, passing

Goggleby Stone, once part of the Shap Avenue

through a fallen megalith by a wall and another in front of Skellaw Hill in the wall opposite. Here on the mound, we find a powerful Node, where Belinus meets with Elen arriving from the west.

All that remains of the large mound or tumulus on Skellaw Hill is a slight rise, its size reduced during the enclosure of the common land in 1815. Some sources suggest that the mound was in fact a stone cairn. This may be the origin of the name Shap, a possible rendering of the Old English word *Heape* meaning 'heap of stones'. According to local legend, Skellaw means 'hill of skulls', perhaps derived from the many skulls discovered during excavation or the destruction of the cairn.

The hill was obviously an important feature of the Shap temple, as from its summit looking south you can view the whole complex, including Kemp Howe, just under 3.2 km (2 miles) away. Similar to Silbury Hill at Avebury, this hill may have been also significant as a sighting place for the priests to coordinate processions from Kemp Howe. As well as the alignment found by Robert Farrah, it also falls on a possible summer solstice sunrise alignment with a stone circle on Iron Hill above the hamlet of Hardendale, just over 3 km away. However, there is little evidence to suggest this hill has any astronomical significance. Like the Bridestones, I believe the purpose of Skellaw Hill was to specifically honour and harness the dragon force in the land, channelled through these great avenues of stones.

We dowsed the signature of the Node point to be the usual six-pointed star with a spiral uncoiling from the centre. However, also residing here is another line of energy of equal width to that of Elen and Belinus, heading south from the Node. We followed this to both the Aspers Field Stone and the Goggleby Stone as if it was seeking out the old avenue. We dowsed the colour of this mysterious line to be orange or gold in contrast to the violet of Elen and the pale yellow of Belinus. At the Avebury circle, Hamish Miller and Paul Broadhurst found the 'birthing' of a new line from a Node of the Michael and Mary currents, which followed the lost Beckhampton Avenue.

I sensed that this new line, birthed from the Skellaw Hill Node, was nourishing the serpents and the surrounding landscape. Perhaps many energy lines once radiated out from this hill, as we see at many places of telluric power such as St Catherine's Hill and the Beacon at Alderley Edge. It seemed incredible to us that this bleak and remote landscape desecrated by large mines and quarries, its ancient monuments destroyed by dynamite, still has something positive to offer us. Perhaps this is why so many people, like me, have been drawn over the years to connect with

Skellaw Hill marking the Node at Shap

this tumulus and the great megaliths such as the Goggleby Stone, and still do so in their hundreds.

Interestingly, the Shap serpent temple lies at the heart of the Belinus Line, almost exactly halfway between Sandown on the Isle of Wight and Durness in Scotland. Likewise, the Avebury megalithic serpent temple lies at the heart of the St Michael Line, roughly halfway between Land's End and the Norfolk coast. The great circle of Avebury is located at the most convenient place for tribal gatherings, at the omphalos of the southern counties and close to where major ancient trackways converge from different parts of the south. Likewise, Shap lies within a natural level plain between the Cumbrian Fells and the Pennine Hills next to the main thoroughfare to and from Scotland, a route that has existed since the Ice Age.

Today its altitude at 304 m (1000 ft) makes it a cold and harsh environment to live, but in Neolithic times when the climate was equal to that of the South of France it would have been a pleasant place for tribal festivals and ceremonial practices. In the Neolithic and Early Bronze Age period, there were no boundaries dividing Britain and it is possible that this geographically suited meeting place was chosen as the ideal place to create a magnificent ritual temple. The fact that this area has the largest concentration of prehistoric stone circles and monuments than anywhere else in Britain is indicative of its former importance.

Another definition of the word Shap may refer to it as an ancient centre, for *Heppe*, its name in early Victorian times, is an Old English word for *hip* meaning the 'fruit of the rose', or symbolically the 'heart of the rose'. Interestingly the geology around Shap has seams of unique rose-coloured granite very similar to that of Aswan granite in Egypt, the most precious of the highly paramagnetic stones used in the building of the monuments of Ancient Egyptians. Collins in *The Seventh Sword* refers to 'the heart of the rose' as a place of great power in the English landscape known only to the mystical Rosicrucians. The builders of the Shap complex may have chosen this site because of its proximity to geological faults. Kemp Howe's position is very close to the meeting of four types of geology: slate, carboniferous limestone, a crystalline rock called Hornfels and blue and pink granite. Was the function of the Kemp Howe circle and the Shap Avenue to draw the telluric power from the faults and channel it towards the great circle called Karl Lofts.

From the Node, the male current continues northwest towards the Thunder Stone, a massive glacial erratic boulder almost the size of a car. One local tradition says that the northern avenue extended to this stone and continued for over 8 km (5 miles) northwest to the Cop Stone on Moor Divock.

Interestingly, the female current avoids the stone circles and avenues completely, approaching Skellaw Hill from a narrow lane signposted to Shap Abbey.

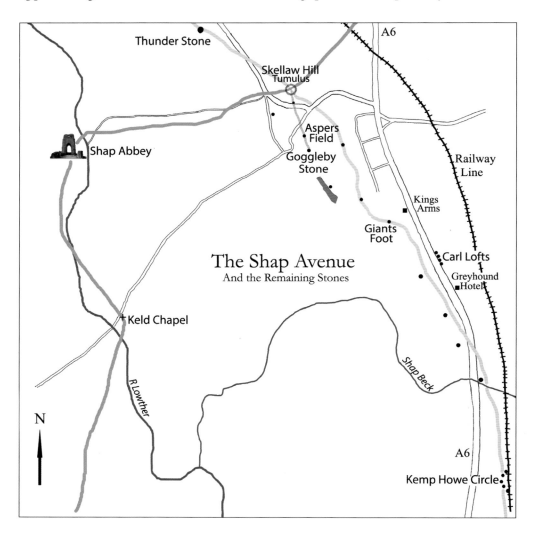

The Shap Avenue
And the Remaining Stones

Shap Abbey

This imposing ruin of Shap Abbey, dedicated to St Mary Magdalene, stands deep in a luscious valley by a bend of the Lowther River, veiled by trees and surrounded by green fields in stark contrast to the bleak uncultivated moors of Shap Fell. The Premonstratensian Order or White Canons founded the abbey in 1199, having moved here from their abbey at Preston Patrick, now the site of St Patrick's at Crooklands also on the Elen current. This was one of the most northerly establishments of the White Canons from their mother church at Titchfield Abbey in Hampshire.

The abbey was one of the last to surrender to King Henry VIII during the Reformation, afterwards granted to Thomas, Lord Wharton in 1544. By 1729, it was the property of Robert Lowther of Maulds Meaburn Hall, eventually becoming part of a vast estate owned by the Earls of Lonsdale. In 1896, the Fifth Earl of Lonsdale retrieved some of the finest pieces of carved stone from the abbey ruins to adorn his new gardens at Lowther Castle in readiness for a visit by the Kaiser of Germany. In 1948, the family gave the abbey to the Ministry of Works following public concern over its dilapidated condition.

Today the abbey ruins mostly date from the 13th century consisting of the church, cloisters, chapter house and warming room. The female current flows along its east–west axis intersecting with various other feminine energy lines before connecting with the High Altar, a medieval sunken stone coffin and the 16th century tower.

She then swings to the south to follow the Lowther River to a little 14th century chapel in the tiny village of Keld. This former chantry chapel, now preserved by the National Trust, was under the auspices of Shap Abbey and stands close to an important fording of the Lowther just to the west of Shap. According to a local legend, an underground tunnel once linked the chapel to the nearby abbey. However, this is almost certainly allegorical and refers to an energetic link between the two sites, as the extreme hardness of the rock terrain would make the cutting of a tunnel almost impossible.

Shap Abbey

At Avebury, the Michael and Mary currents form a Node at a site called the Sanctuary, once a stone circle that symbolically forms the head of the serpent complex. Perhaps before its severe destruction Belinus and Elen formed a second Node at Kemp Howe stone circle, the head of the Shap serpent complex. The desecration may have caused Elen to seek another place of power to the west, perhaps attracted to the congregation at Keld Chapel and Shap Abbey. Alternatively, the Premonstratensian monks, whose mother church was on a Node point at Titchfield Abbey, may have deliberately manipulated the currents to their present form, bringing Elen's flow through their chapel and abbey.

Moor Divock and the Earls of Lonsdale

From Skellaw Hill, Elen travels northeast towards the A6 where she passes through Brinns Well in a field just below Brinns Farm before visiting the tiny chapelry of Little Strickland dedicated to St Mary. This medieval church was transported here in 1814 by William Lowther, First Earl of Lonsdale, from its original site on the opposite banks of the River Leith at Thrimby, claiming the land was needed for agriculture.

Elen passes through a cairn circle at the Leacet Plantation about 6 km (3.7 miles) southeast of Penrith. Although only five of the original nine upright stones remain, it would have measured 11 m (36 ft) in diameter with its tallest stone 1.75 m (5½ ft) high. The majority of ring cairns in this country have much smaller stones around their base often surrounding a mound or burial cist, so this one is unusual, reminding me of a Dorset stone circle called The Nine Stones.

Looking at the map, I felt sure Elen would lead us to Penrith and the enigmatic prehistoric monuments of Arthur's Round Table and Mayburgh Henge, but again she surprises us by taking a northerly route towards the Whinfell Holiday Park. Here she crosses the old Roman road now the A66 into the great valley of the Eamont River, once an ancient boundary.

Returning to the male current at Shap and the Thunder Stone, Belinus took us to a church on a mound at Bampton Grange by the meeting of the rivers Lowther and Haweswater Beck. Before restoration, the church of St Patrick was another chapelry of Shap Abbey built by the White Canons in 1199, much earlier than the chapel at Keld. They must have known the importance of this prehistoric mound by the meeting of two ancient rivers.

Following the current through the narrow lanes towards Moor Divock and its necropolis of burial mounds and stone circles was a challenge but a red squirrel conveniently stopped us dead in our tracks to show us the correct turn-off. As we approached open moorland, my dowsing rod pointed to a lonely standing stone in the distance. Known as the Cop Stone, this megalith is set on a high point on the moor with marvellous views over the Lakeland Fells. I noticed some smaller stones nearby forming a ring around a central mound, hollowed out long ago by treasure seekers. This seemed to infer that the Cop Stone is part of a cairn circle and a legend refers to the northern avenue from Shap continuing to this very stone, a distance of over 8 km (5 miles). However, there is no evidence to support this, with most antiquarians believing it only travelled as far north as the Thunder Stone.

However, Moor Divock has a strange atmosphere where in the past balls of light and

Cop Stone, Moor Divock

other strange phenomena have occurred. The male current approaches the stone from the southeast but upon contact with it curiously diverts off its course to the northeast. Observing the Cop Stone more closely we could almost make out the shape of a male head.

Moor Divock marks the exact centre of the alignment travelling 0.5 km (0.3 miles) east of the Cop Stone, just clipping the edge of the sacred plateau. Not far away is the pretty village of Askham with its whitewashed cottages lying deep in the lush valley of the River Lowther. Here Belinus visits another church on a raised mound, which sits close to the banks of the river. Dedicated to St Peter, it was restored in 1832 by Sir Robert Smirke, an architect renowned for designing the façade of the British Museum and nearby Lowther Castle for the Earls of Lonsdale. However, this has been a site of worship since the time of St Kentigern, who came to this area in the 6th century before becoming the Bishop of Glasgow. We dowsed the male current passing through a part of the church built over the site of St Kentigern's Chapel. The south transept was rebuilt over the ground plan of a 13th century church and incorporates the Sandford family burial chapel.

The Sandfords originally came from Sandford in Westmorland, having been lords of the manor there since 1174. Through marriage, they acquired the manor of Askham and lived at Askham Hall from the time of Edward III until 1724. The Earls of Lonsdale made it their new home after abandoning Lowther Castle in 1936.

Leaving our car at Askham, we crossed the river over the old bridge into Lowther Park, where in the distance we could just make out the shell of the once grand home of the Earls of Lonsdale, dismantled in 1957. The estate of this once rich and powerful family included the area of Shap and it was the Second Earl who ordered the final destruction of the great Shap Avenue in 1845, to make way for the railway. By the 1930s, however, their wealth and influence had diminished substantially, mainly through mismanagement of the estate and the extravagant lifestyle of the Fifth Earl. Eventually most of their land and property were sold and the grand castle abandoned. Recently, the castle and gardens have been part of a massive restoration project and are now open to the public with a splendid restaurant and tearoom. The grounds provide a fine view overlooking the enchanting valley of the River Lowther along which the male current flows between Moor Divock and Askham church.

The current heads north to the isolated church of St Michael in the grounds of the Lowther estate, standing high on a plateau overlooking the River Lowther with stunning views across the valley. Remnants of the Norman church, built in 1165, are still visible in the northern section of the present building.

Belinus passes through a line of graves and memorials of the Earls of Lonsdale and their family in the churchyard including the impressive tomb of Lancelot Edward Lowther, Sixth Earl of Lonsdale, built in 1857 and adorned with stone dragons and the family coat of arms. The Lowthers were first recorded living in this area during the reign of Henry II, when they part-owned the surrounding lands with four other families. By 1422, they were the sole landowner 'partly by purchase and partly by other means and being always lucky'. Sir Hugh de Lowther was attorney-general to King Edward I, his descendants remaining trusted officers of the law and knights of the shire of Westmorland and Cumberland, Sir Richard Lowther having conveyed Mary Queen of Scots to her prison at Carlisle Castle. In 1696, Sir John Lowther was created Baron Lowther and Viscount Lonsdale for services to William III, and by 1807 the family was known as the Earls of Lonsdale.

Belinus also visits the stump of an early stone cross in the churchyard now supporting a sundial and passes through the tower. Displayed in the porch are two hogback tombs dating from the 9th century and remnants of three Celtic stone crosses. Inside under the tower is a marble monument to the Tenth Earl and Countess of Lonsdale and a statue of a dragon holding the church standard. On the north side of the nave are three Norman pillars with corbels individually carved with various figures including a Green Man, a green lion and a menacing bat.

We also found Knights Templar grave slabs, one engraved with the St Clair Cross, underneath the tombs of more members of the Lonsdale family. One of the marble monuments is to John, Viscount Lonsdale, Baron Lowther inscribed: 'most eminent amongst his ancestral knights in the reign of the undefeated William III of Great Britain … secret advisor and most experienced of the English counsellors to the Hanoverian kings, keeper of the Privy Seal who was guardian of the far flung areas while the king's away …. He died when destiny came too soon July 6th 1700 having lived forty-five years'. A memorial window to the Fifth Earl of Lonsdale depicts St Cuthbert and St Michael slaying the dragon.

Key members of the Lowther family have played a major role in British politics for centuries, their power and wealth influencing the decisions of kings and their parliaments. Many of them were great sportsmen and patrons of art and music. However, they also wielded their power to cause the destruction of many prehistoric monuments such as the serpent temple at Shap, which stood in the way of progress during the Industrial Revolution.

A pair of standing stones in a field next to the River Lowther marks the path of Belinus as he snakes his way to the little village of Clifton. Close to the appropriately named George and Dragon pub is St Cuthbert's Church, built on a prehistoric mound, possibly the site of an early Christian sanctuary when the remains of St Cuthbert rested here after his death in AD 687. In order to escape desecration by Viking raids, monks carried his bones from Lindisfarne in Northumberland, stopping at different locations until they arrived at Durham where they built his shrine.

Cumbria only became a county of England during the time of the Norman kings, as before then the region was part of the old Kingdoms of Strathclyde and Rheged. Henry II named it the Barony of Westmorland, awarding the manor of Clifton to Gilbert Engayne. Later Thomas Wybergh inherited it through marriage and mortgaged the land to Sir John Lowther for £100. However, he failed to redeem it after losing the land to the Parliamentarians during the Civil War, and it remains to this day the property of the Lowthers.

The name Clifton actually derives from two 'very remarkable stone cliffs' which stand on the eastern banks of the Lowther, one of white hard stone like marble, the other of a softer fine-quality stone, both heavily quarried. Two burial mounds and two Roman altars were found nearby, one dedicated to Jove, now in private hands, and the other incorporated into the wall of Clifton Hall Farmhouse.

A tombstone in the churchyard marks the burial of those who died at the infamous Battle at Clifton Moor on 18 December 1745, between the Jacobite Army led by Bonnie Prince Charlie and the Duke of Cumberland's English forces. After the battle the Jacobite Army retreated to Penrith, almost exactly a month after Bonnie Prince Charlie was proclaimed King of Scotland and England in Carlisle, in honour of his grandfather the deposed James II.

Belinus avoids the Pele tower at nearby Clifton Hall, to arrive at the southern fringes of the ancient town of Penrith, where next to the River Eamont we discover some of the most fascinating sites found so far in the North of England.

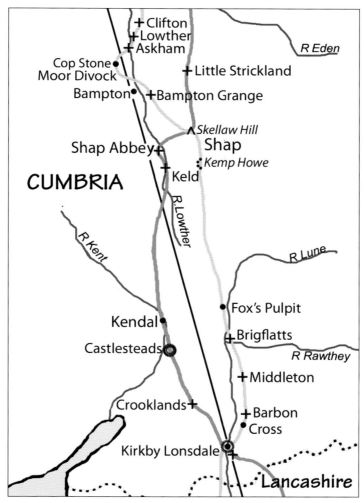

Chapter 11

The Grail and the Knights of the Round Table
Between the Eamont and the Eden

The Curse of Brougham Hall

Across the fields from Clifton, Belinus enters the grounds of Brougham Park to visit the enchanting ruins of Brougham Hall, once a grand Victorian mansion known as 'the Windsor of the North'. The castellated building stands on a raised plateau of land above a bend of the Lowther River near its confluence with the Eamont, once an important fording place. This strategic site overlooks the crossroads of two Roman roads, one that linked the old Roman port of Ravenglass on the west coast of Cumbria to the city of York, now the A66, and the other from Manchester to Carlisle, now the A6. Ravenglass served around 45,000 troops stationed at Hadrian's Wall and the city of York was the capital of the kingdom of the Brigantes.

A fort built about a kilometre west of the hall, near the ruins of Brougham Castle, had a substantial *vicus* or settlement that Stukeley suggests stretched all the way to Brougham Hall. The Romans built a tower on the hill as a lookout to spy on the ford next to the crossroads and as a signal station during times of impending danger. Its later history is uncertain, but given the strategic importance of the location, there must have been a post-Roman presence here. The earliest local written records state that a licence was given to the de Burghams, the local lords of the manor, to build a tower here in 1307.

Looking east from its high castellated walls, I noticed that the nearby prehistoric henges of Arthur's Round Table and Mayburgh seem to be in alignment with the ruin and a detailed OS map shows they are almost equidistant from each other. Furthermore, aerial photographs reveal that the shape of the hill and defences around Brougham Hall resemble a henge. Striking a line through all three sites using Google Earth, I

Mayburgh Henge near Penrith

found that it extends west to the saddle of Blencathra and the summit of Skiddaw Mountain. The geographical relationship of all three sites aligned with these sacred mountains towards the equinox sunset suggests that Brougham Hall lies within a ritual landscape of some importance.

In 1480, a Tudor mansion of white stone was constructed over the site of the tower and chapel 'of very ancient

Aerial view of Brougham Hall

erection' dedicated to St Wilfred, which later became Brougham Hall's private place of worship. Around 1690, Lady Anne Clifford of Brougham Castle pulled it down and replaced it with a more substantial building. The church housed a font, continuously supplied by a natural spring until a new road diverted its flow in the 19th century.

The name Brougham derives from the nearby Roman fort called *Brocavum* Latinised from the original Celtic name 'home of the badgers'. Alternatively, it refers to a 'homestead near a fortification', *burh* meaning 'fort' and *ham* a Saxon word for 'homestead'. When the Romans left around AD 410, the Angles moved in and established their 'ham' on the site of the 'vicus'.

The de Burghams, later known as the Broughams, were 'an ancient and warlike family', taking their name from the area. They held lands here long before the Norman Conquest, possibly from the time of the Angles. The place also had more than its fair share of misfortune that, according to Benjamin Furnival in *Windsor of the North*, started with the later Broughams' inability to produce a male heir, resulting in their holding only partial ownership of the estate for centuries.

By 1830, the family held the title of Baron, during which time their fortunes thrived. William, the Second Baron, restored the chapel and rebuilt Brougham Hall, incorporating an earlier mansion but adding a heavy Norman-styled tower to emulate a medieval castle, perhaps in the hope of recapturing his noble ancestral roots. It was during this time that it became known as the 'Windsor of the North',

renowned for its grand exterior and luxurious internal furnishings. In 1846, William discovered the tombs of two Crusader knights at nearby Ninekirks Church, found to be his ancestors Odard and Gilbert de Burgham, and displayed their relics in the great hall.

It was also around this time that a skull was unearthed and taken to Brougham, thought to be that of Edwardus de Burgham, who also fought in the Crusades. There are many tales concerning this skull and, like the 'screaming skull' of Browsholme Hall in Lancashire, its aversion to any form of removal from the house has caused endless trauma for the family. Once, when it was tossed onto a dung heap, the hall suffered the 'most awful torment, disturbances and hauntings'. When thrown into a lake 'screams … and terror resumed' until returned. During restoration work in the 1980s, the skull was finally uncovered and only the present owner knows of its current resting place (Furnival 1999).

Sadly, many of William's descendants failed to share his love of Brougham Hall, preferring to live elsewhere, and eventually the house became neglected and forgotten. However, Brougham Hall's problems were not to end there. In 1927, Victor Brougham, having inherited the estate from his father, squandered his fortune on an extravagant lifestyle and gambling which led to the hall being sold for a pittance at a time of deep recession. According to Furnival, the new owner, resenting old money and privilege and having a particular aversion to the Brougham family, ordered the demolition of much of the hall soon after the sale in 1934, despite local opposition. After purchasing the site in 1978, a local builder proceeded to demolish the castle still further. The present owner Christopher Terry has restored much of the remaining fabric of the hall, converting some of the buildings into small business units, creating an aesthetic blend of enterprise and historical conservation. However, for a while his plans were thwarted by a group of dishonest businessmen who offered to finance the building work. After a successful court case against them, Terry commenced with the conservation of the hall, albeit at a much slower pace than originally envisioned. Artists, crafts people and small local businesses have now moved in together with a lovely café that serves coffee and lunch to visitors, right at the heart of the complex.

We entered the hall through its huge Elizabethan oak doors into a delightful open courtyard, with well-kept lawns and craft shops. As we walked around the interior, we could see that the outer castellated walls have remained almost intact. We dowsed the male current passing through a small outer doorway on the southeast side of the complex and heading west to connect with the remains of a tower built over earlier Roman foundations. Apparently, it has the same dimensions as 'turret no. 41' from a Roman wall at Bank in London, constructed around AD 120 from standard military manuals.

We believe the ill luck of Brougham Hall was caused by the desecration of this ancient sacred site during the time of the Romans, when they built their tower, disrupting the energy of the inner sanctum of the original henge. At Old Sarum, a prehistoric enclosure near Salisbury, medieval masons were subjected to strange and terrifying events during the construction of the cathedral and even when they finally succeeded, the structure was often plagued with bad luck and was part destroyed by a lightning strike.

Arthur's Round Table

A little west of the hall, at the village of Eamont Bridge on the south bank of the Eamont River, is a circular henge 90 m (295 ft) in diameter called King Arthur's Round Table. Dating from 2000 BC, it has a deep circular ditch and a 1.5 m (5 ft) high external bank surrounding a raised level platform at its centre. The general design of the earthwork is flat and round, and according to 17th century diagrams included two stones standing at its northern entrance; this quadrant is now lying beneath the road and the adjacent public house. Another henge called the 'Little Round Table' stood 75 m (246 ft) south of here, although nothing remains of it today.

Folklore refers to Arthur's Round Table as the place where a giant 'six yards tall' dined with another even taller giant, which he later killed. He is said to rest in the 'Giant's Grave' at Penrith Church. The Round Table was also a fabled venue of many tournaments between chivalrous knights, where the legendary King Arthur instituted the order of Knights of the Round Table for the encouragement of young warriors in the use of the lance. Local legends place his 'Camelot of the North' and one of his great battles in this region of the country. *Sylva Caledonis*, the supposed site of his seventh battle against the Saxons, was said to have been fought in the Forest of Inglewood between Penrith and Carlisle. Here Arthur gained a most significant victory, forcing the entire Anglo-Saxon army into submission. It is possible that the henge, recognised as an important sacred site of the ancestors, witnessed festivities that took place directly after the battle, strategically placed near an ancient boundary and fording place.

Local folklore also describes the gathering of fifty champions of the realm at the Round Table to take part in a contest to win the hand of King Arthur's daughter Gyneth. In fact, the outer banks of the henge with its inner platform forms a sacred enclosure, perfect for tribal gatherings and festivities, no doubt serving many cultures throughout the ages, including the post-Roman Kingdom of Rheged.

Some historians believe the henge received its name from the Clifford family, owners of nearby Brougham Castle since 1268. They considered themselves descendants of Welsh kings of the bloodline of Arthur. Their fortification on the Mallerstang estate near the source of the River Eden was renamed Pendragon Castle. Leland, writing in 1538, mentions the henge as 'Arthur's Castle'. Its present name has been in existence since at least the time of William Stukeley who visited the site in 1725. It has a long history of being a place of country sports and military exercises, and Hutchinson (1794) recounts a local tale that the site was a 'tilting ground' during medieval times, where jousting and wrestling matches were held 'within living memory'.

As we have observed so far along this Spine of Albion journey, many key sacred ceremonial sites are aligned to the north and some are associated with King Arthur. Here at Arthur's Round Table we find that the original entrance is marked by two stones facing north. Standing in the centre of the henge, looking through where the entrance once stood, I noticed the outline of Beacon Hill on the northern outskirts of Penrith. The ancients believed that the Pole Star not only marked north but also was a portal for souls to the afterlife, protected by the constellation of Ursula Major or the Great Bear. Perhaps the name of this henge has a celestial significance, for the name Arthur derives from *Arcturus* meaning 'Bear Guard', possibly symbolising his role

A circular henge called Arthur's Round Table at Eamont Bridge

as 'watcher' over the celestial pole. Observers at the southern entrance of the henge around 1500 BC would have seen Ursula Major, also known as King Arthur's Chariot, skimming the summit of Beacon Hill.

Mayburgh and the Solar Alignment

The Belinus current crosses the northern section of the Round Table and then heads across to the entrance of Mayburgh Henge, located 155 m (508 ft) to the west. This huge complex, considered one of the greatest prehistoric structures in England, measures 110 m (360 ft) in diameter and lies on a tongue of land between the rivers Eamont and Lowther. Long ago it enclosed a four-stone feature, of which only one huge, 2.8 m (9 ft) high megalith remains, the rest, including four entrance stones, having been dynamited in the 19th century. The lone standing stone sits at the centre of the monument, surrounded by a steep oval bank over 6.5 m (21 ft) high, made from literally millions of small cobblestones collected from the rivers nearby, an extraordinary feat of engineering. Considering the amount taken away over the centuries for use as building material, the bank is still an impressive sight. Sir Walter Scott, a friend of the Brougham family, once wrote, 'Mayburgh's mound and stones of power, by Druids raised in magic hour'.

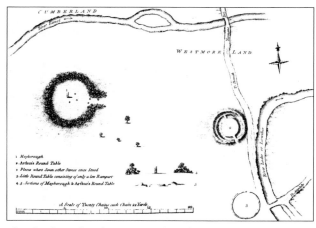

Sketch of Maybergh Henge and Arthur's Round Table by Thomas Pennant dated 1769

The east–west alignment formed by Mayburgh Henge, the Round Table and the former circular enclosure of Brougham Hall suggests an important equinoctial ritual landscape. Here people would have gathered twice a year to honour the sun between 21/22 March and 22/23 September, when the hours of daylight and darkness are equal, a time when nature is reborn and the fruits of the harvest were celebrated. An observer standing within the Mayburgh Henge at dawn on the equinox facing the eastern entrance will see the sun rising over Brougham Hall in alignment with the northern entrance of the Round Table. Farrah observed that when facing west on a clear day from the location of the Round Table's northern entrance, the saddle of Blencathra is visible spanning the bowl of Mayburgh's entrance. Blencathra, also called Saddleback, is one of those sacred mountains aligned with many megalithic sites in Cumbria. We have also noted that 'devil' sites are places of power and the name *Blencathra* in old Cumbrian means 'Devil's Peak'.

According to Marjorie Rowling, this mountain is another resting place of King Arthur; even its earlier name the *Roakes of Blenkarthure* means 'mountain of Arthur'. Perhaps the naming of Arthur's Round Table was an allegorical indicator to the ritual function of this site, where the prehistoric cultures observed the equinox sun through Mayburgh's megalithic entrance setting into Blencathra, where King Arthur sleeps; a later metaphor for their Celtic solar god.

The male current enters the eastern entrance of Mayburgh towards the standing stone at its centre. As Belinus passes through the large megalith, he surprisingly changes direction and heads northwest towards Penrith, the old capital of Rheged. We also picked up a female energy line emerging from the megalith proceeding to flow westwards towards Yanwath Hall and the Belinus alignment, 2.4 km (1½ miles) away at Stainton.

The megalith is the only surviving stone from a group of four that, together with the other four entrance stones, may have formed a 'solar' avenue. This would have served as a way of focusing both the powerful energies of the equinoctial sunrise and the terrestrial solar power of the male earth serpent into the monument. The collective energies would be stored by the huge circular bank of pebbles, ready for dispersal at the appropriate time into the local energy grid, to revitalise and fertilise the surrounding landscape.

Long ago, all three henges must have formed a trinity of immense power and are without doubt one of the most impressive megalithic complexes in Britain.

The Treaty of Eamont

During late Saxon times, the monuments at Eamont Bridge may have witnessed one of the most significant political events in British history that changed the shape of English monarchy forever. Many historians believe that one of the most important treaties ever signed in Britain took place at Eamont Bridge near the monuments.

After the Anglo-Saxon King Athelstan defeated the Danes at York in AD 927, he forced the submission of all the kings of northern England, Wales and Scotland. According to the *Anglo-Saxon Chronicle*:

'King Athelstan took to the Kingdom of Northumbria, and governed all the kings that were in this island: first, Hywel Da, King of West-Wales; and Constantine, King of the Scots; and Owain, King of Gwent; and Ealdred, the son of Ealdulf [Eadwulf], of Bamburgh. And with covenants and oaths they ratified their agreement in the place called Eamotum on the fourth day before the ides of July [12 July]; and renounced all idolatry, and afterwards returned in peace.' (Ingram 1912)

Although William of Malmesbury, the 12th century English historian, surmised that 'Eamotum' was further west along the River Eamont at Dacre, most sources agree that it was Eamont Bridge at the ancient boundary with the Kingdom of Northumbria and close to an important junction of major roads mentioned earlier.

After the signing of the treaty, Athelstan became the first supreme sovereign of pre-Norman Britain, dashing any hopes of a Celtic resurgence by the Welsh and Scottish. Athelstan reigned until AD 940, during which time coins were minted with the abbreviated inscription *Rex Totius Britanniae*, 'King of the whole of Britain'. However, the *Anglo-Saxon Chronicle* written by Roman Catholic monks recorded little during his reign, preferring to emphasise the achievements of his grandfather King Alfred and father Edward the Elder.

This prestigious gathering of so many noble warrior kings must have been an intriguing sight for the locals of Eamont Bridge. The exact location is still a mystery, but it is possible that Athelstan chose Arthur's Round Table because of its reputation as a place of ritual and sacred ceremony in earlier times and its association with King Arthur. Athelstan may have used this mystical place to unite the fractured tribes of Britain under one ruler, just as Arthur had accomplished centuries before. During his reign, Athelstan was a great collector of powerful Christian relics including the Holy Lance of Charlemagne and the Sword of Constantine, said by some authorities to be the real Excalibur of King Arthur.

At one time or another, these relics had all belonged to various Emperors of Rome, and historian and broadcaster Michael Wood speculated that they represented a *translatio imperii*, a symbolic transfer of imperial power from the rulers of the Carolingians to the West Saxons (Wood 1983). Athelstan, through receiving these iconic relics linked with these powerful and successful rulers, would aspire to become a great king, perhaps explaining why he self-styled himself 'Emperor of all Britain'.

There seems to be no explanation as to why Athelstan, whose royal seat was Winchester, chose 'Eamotum' for the most important council of kings ever held. The obvious choice would surely have been only a few kilometres north at Carlisle, which at the time was the regional capital of northern England. I believe these locally renowned monuments of solar ritual and celestial sovereign power here at Eamont Bridge, next to an ancient boundary and only a short distance away from the middle of the alignment, may have served as a national omphalos at the time.

Stainton and the Lost Abbey

Just west of Eamont Bridge is the small village of Stainton, marking the Spine of Albion. However, behind the façade of modern affluence, a much deeper mystery unfolds, for a local legend states that, during Saxon times, this was the site of an important religious centre. According to Dugdale in *Walks in Mysterious North Lakeland* (1998), the legend also refers to the complete destruction of a large abbey here during the Reformation at the hands of a local baron, who hired men to strip it to its foundations in preparation for the building of his new grand mansion. Nevertheless, karma prevailed, as during one of his many visits to monitor its destruction from a nearby hill, his horse suddenly reared, causing him to fall and break his neck. The spectral figure of a galloping rider is still seen today on a spot called Baron's Hill.

One of the stone figures of a bear hugging a pole at Dacre Church near Penrith

About a kilometre to the west of here is the church of St Andrew at Dacre where four mysterious ancient stone figures stand in the churchyard, locally known as the 'Dacre Bears'. Each bear appears to be either clinging or chained to a pillar, which I believe has a celestial connotation. The bear represents the constellation of Ursula Major, which protects the polar north, shown in the stone figures as a pillar. The image of a bear chained to a pole is a common depiction in paintings and carvings from ancient civilisations around Europe and the Middle East, representing a symbol of the celestial gateway to the afterlife protected by the stars of the Great Bear. Perhaps a star cult of the bear existed here in Celtic times, later personified as Arthur, the sovereign protector of the sacred north.

Some historians believe they survive from an earlier monastery that once stood on this site, although there is little archaeological evidence to suggest this. It is more likely they originated from the supposed abbey at Stainton that once stood on the Belinus alignment.

Penrith, Capital of Rheged

Penrith, once the capital of Cumbria, is located less than 3.2 km (2 miles) east of the alignment, just outside the boundary of the Lake District National Park. During the Iron Age, the Carvetii, a sub tribe of the Brigantes, settled in the region, possibly establishing two important north–south and east–west roads to York and Carlisle, later built over by the Romans.

Between the 6th and 10th centuries, Penrith was the capital of the British Kingdom of Rheged, an area that stretched from Galloway in southern Scotland all the way down to the western ridge of the Pennines in Lancashire. In AD 573, a famous battle was fought between two rival Rheged kings at Arthuret on the borders of Scotland. One of them, named Gwenddollau, was a descendant of Hen Coel, later portrayed as Old King Coel in nursery rhymes.

In medieval times, this once-fortified capital grew as a marketplace for traders and travellers resting at the ford and crossroads by Eamont Bridge and perhaps taking a moment to honour their ancient ancestors at its sacred monuments. In legend, Penrith may have been a seat or court of the warrior Arthur or King Arthur of the romances referred to as *Penrynydd* in the 14th century *Welsh Triads* (Bromwich 1961). It mentions Mynyw (St David's) in Wales, *Celliwig* (Callington) in Cornwall and *Pen-Rhionydd* or *Penrynydd* in the North of England as the 'Three Tribal Thrones of the Island of Britain'. The latter, said to be the northern seat of Arthur as Chief Prince, has yet to be identified. Some scholars are certain that this northern throne of Arthur lies somewhere in the borders, either in southern Scotland or around Carlisle in Rheged, but, of all the major towns in this region, Penrith is the most likely to derive from Penrynydd. The closest derivation of Penrith is from the Welsh *Penrhudd* meaning 'red hill', referring to the nearby Beacon Hill. The legendary Penrhyndd (*Pen* meaning 'promontory' or 'cape' and *Rhionydd* meaning 'royal') could be a phonetic version of Penrith, for in the Welsh language *ydd* is pronounced *ith*, thus Pen-Rhion-ith.

At the time of Arthur, a great legendary king called Urien ruled this kingdom and reunited the lands of Rheged after the Romans withdrew from Britain. The great bard Taliesin recalls this mighty warrior, whose name means 'city born', in a poem describing him as 'Sovereign supreme ruler all highest' who courageously defended his kingdom against the invading Angles. Like King Arthur, he was known as the Raven King, because of a talisman or good luck charm depicting a raven that he carried constantly. His son Owain succeeded him, inflicting further defeats upon the Angles, but after his demise in AD 593 the Kingdom of Rheged fades from the pages of the Bardic poems.

Urien is also reputed to be buried in the 'Giant's Grave' in St Andrew's churchyard in Penrith, where his bones rest alongside his son Owain, also known as Hugh Caesario. The four hogback stones surrounding the grave are said in legend to represent the numerous wild boar he killed in nearby Inglewood Forest; the wild boar is also the emblem of the Picts of Scotland. However, hogback tombs appear all over the north of England and Scotland, many associated with burials of Norse warriors.

In 1070, the town became the territory of William the Conqueror, transferring to Scotland in 1242 when the manor of Penrith was handed over to King Alexander in exchange for Cumberland, Westmorland and Northumberland. This tussle for Penrith between the English and Scottish crowns continued, when Edward I seized it from John Balliol of Scotland, promptly awarding it to the Bishop of Durham.

We detected the male current crossing the Eamont River to a housing estate before entering the ruins of Penrith Castle. The constant Scottish raids demanded the building of a great wall around the town, and in 1397 William Strickland, later Bishop of Carlisle, received a licence to fortify the castle. At the time it consisted of a single Pele tower, built over the site of a Roman fort. In 1419, Ralph Neville, First Earl of Westmorland, added the Red Tower. Judging from the ancient earthworks that surround it, the Roman fort may have stood over a prehistoric settlement.

It was described as 'the Castle of the Kings' even though historians record no reigning monarch having actually lived there. Could this be the site of Arthur's illusive royal seat of the north or the later Rheged kings? Prior to becoming king, Richard, Duke of Gloucester, resided here, the Crown remaining as the chief landowner of the area until the reign of William and Mary (1689–1702). It eventually passed to the Earls of Portland and later to the Dukes of Devonshire, who sold it to the Lancaster and Carlisle Railway Company. Its transformation into a public park came when the Penrith Urban District Council acquired it in the 1920s.

The Belinus current enters the castle ruins over a bridge, passing through Ralph Neville's great Red Tower to a well, now grated over and filled with rubble. It then continues through a war memorial by the castle exit. As we made our way towards the town centre through the old narrow streets, we detected Belinus disappearing into the theatre of the Penrith Players built in 1922, and through White Hart Yard, once the site of the Griffin pub. Soon we found ourselves in the delightful ancient precinct of St Andrew's Parish Church. A church has stood on this site since 1133 but the present building dates from 1720, constructed from a design by Nicholas Hawksmoor, a pupil of Sir Christopher Wren.

A sundial in the churchyard marks the path of the current to the Giant's Grave next to the north wall of the church. It is formed by two 9th century Anglian crosses, standing over 3 m (10 ft) high either end of four hogback tombstones, collectively making this one of the most remarkable monuments in the north of England. Carved with spirals and serpents, the hogback stones are the finest examples of the many found in Cumbria and Lancashire.

Giant's Grave, St Andrew's Church, Penrith

Another local legend places this monument as the supposed resting place of the giant Tarquin, otherwise known as Owain Caesario. The name is very similar to Hugh Caesario, better known as Owain of Rheged. According to Lancashire folklore, Tarquin was also the so-called giant who resided at his fort at Knott Mill in Manchester; could this giant also be the former King of Rheged?

Curiously, while staying at the Crown Inn in Penrith in 1599, a local schoolmaster and historian called Mr Page showed antiquarian William Camden a document that stated Sir Hugh or Owain Caesario, 'a knight killing monster of man and beast', lived in the caves near Ninekirks Church by the Eamont River and was buried at the parish church in Penrith. Mr Page then took Camden to the church to see the grave for himself and remarked that when he was a child the opened tomb revealed the shank bones of a very tall man, together with bones of another holding a broad sword.

However, this part-circular churchyard suggests a site of greater antiquity, perhaps a prehistoric burial ground later used by the many early kings of this region. When examining the upright crosses or pillars in more detail, they seemed reminiscent of early megaliths but with later carvings, perhaps taken from a circle of stones that once surrounded one of the early cairns or burial mounds here.

The Roman Trail of Belinus

From the town centre, Belinus takes us north to another important beacon hill on the Spine of Albion, where the locals once lit the Beacon Pike to warn of the approaching Scots. Beacon Hill is the 'Red Hill', in old Welsh *Penrhudd*, from which Penrith possibly takes its name. Today a hideous red sandstone monument stands on its summit called Penrith Beacon, erected in 1719. It takes the form of a 285 m (937ft) high square tower with a pyramid-shaped roof. The hill has witnessed many executions over the centuries, including that of the notorious murderer Thomas Nicholson in 1767; many believe his unhappy spirit still haunts the hill.

Belinus continues north along the old Roman road, now the A6, to Carlisle, to the Church of St John the Evangelist in the tiny village of Plumpton, with an unusual tower. According to local history, it was part of 'the manor more anciently called Plumpton Park and was a demesne of the crown' held by the Earl of Annandale. It was sold in 1653 to Mrs Eleanor Lowther, passing eventually to the descendants of the Earls of Lonsdale. The present church, built in 1907 by Sir Robert Lorimer, includes a castellated Pele tower that unusually tapers up from the base and contains a William Morris window. Intriguingly, Plumpton also features in one of the Arthurian romances. In a poem called *Adventures of Arthur at Tarn Wadling*, a jousting contest took place on the levels at Plumpton, where, as a reward for beating Sir Galeron, King Arthur grants Sir Gawain lands in Wales and Brittany.

However, the actual site was possibly just a little further north on the A6, which today is the extensive earthwork remains of a Roman fort next to Castlesteads Farm, known as 'Old Penrith'. Originally, the Roman fort of *Voreda* served as a station for a task force of legionaries from the 20th Legion during the entire period of their occupation of the north of England. Based on inscriptions on some of the stones found at the site, it was renovated and enlarged by a unit of Gauls in AD 178, formed from various Gallic tribes of central and northern France, and further extended by German mercenaries in the 3rd century. Finds from this site include altars honouring the Roman gods Silvanus and Mars and the Germanic gods of Belatucador and Mogons.

Looking over the hedge, we could see some large finely cut blocks still in position marking the old east entrance. The grass banks that make up the huge walls are still visible, indicating the grandeur and size of the structure.

The Castle of the Green Knight

A couple of kilometres to the west of Old Penrith we find the alignment passing through the grounds of Hutton-in-the-Forest, a beautiful historic house, owned by the First Lord Inglewood. It stands over the site of another Pele tower where one of Edward I's Foresters, Thomas de Hoton, stood guard over the whole area. The house stands within Inglewood Forest, once the second largest hunting ground of the English kings and an ancient site of a battle.

From Roman to Norman times, Kings of Carlisle and Penrith held this once vast forest, serving as a buffer zone between the Scottish Borders and England. The

Hutton-in-the-Forest, marking the alignment

ancient woodland was also the mystical realm of questing knights, inspiring many local ballads and legends including *Sir Gawain and the Green Knight*, one of the most famous of the Arthurian romances. According to one medieval story, written in the 14th century, Hutton-in-the-Forest is the legendary castle of the Green Knight

sought by Sir Gawain who 'rode into a deep forest that was wonderfully wild'. After encountering the Green Knight, he rode with him to his *'Castle of Hutton'*. This particular story may possibly derive from post-Roman times known as the Dark Ages. Some sources say the character of Sir Gawain was based on Owain, King of Rheged. Perhaps Hutton was Owain's favourite hunting ground, and he built a lodge there on the site of the present house.

In a courtyard above an ancient well set into the wall of the house is the unique stone carving depicting a figure emerging from a bough of a tree, possibly symbolising the Green Man or his other guise, the Green Knight. Another on the terrace is carved on two sides with a serpent coiled around a pole, representative of the polar axis around which the constellation of 'Serpentanus' rotates. Alternatively, the pole may indicate the presence of the Belinus alignment.

In the grounds of the house is the 13th century parish church of St James. The interior houses an 11th century Viking cross and a medieval tombstone carved with a chalice, or Grail. We were about to discover this potent symbol featuring in many places between Penrith and Carlisle.

Stone carving of a snake entwined around a pole on the terrace of Hutton-in-the-Forest

The Sacred Lake

From the site of Old Penrith, the male current passes east of the village of High Hesket over a low-level plain, once covered by a sacred lake called Tarn Wadling. Its waters spread over a hundred acres, and the Gough map of Great Britain dated 1360 shows it as the size of Lake Windermere. During the 19th century, the lake bred some of the finest carp in the country until farmers required the land for agriculture. They reduced it to half its size and it continued to exist up until WWII, when Italian prisoners of war drained it again. It has now disappeared completely.

The lake nestled beneath a high ridge that separates the valleys of the rivers Petteril and Eden on property owned by the Nunnery at nearby Armathwaite. According to Stephen Matthews in *King Arthur Lives in Merrie Carlisle*, *Tarn* is a Norse word but *Wadling* has its roots in the Celtic language. On a hill overlooking the lake, a ruined fortress existed up until the 18th century. Many authors have speculated it to be the remains of Castle Hewen, the legendary base of King Owain Caesario of Rheged. However, the site of this 6th century royal castle is more likely to be at the old Roman fort now called Old Penrith, strategically built next to the busy north–south thoroughfare between Manchester and Carlisle. It was common for British nobles, after reclaiming their land from the Romans, to build their fortifications within the abandoned Roman forts.

Tarn Wadling also appears in an old local ballad called *Awntyres off Arthure at the Terne Wathelyne* (Adventures of Arthur at the Tarn Wadling) set in the Inglewood Forest featuring once again the hero Sir Gawain. After a long day hunting with King Arthur, he volunteers to stand watch during the night at the 'Tarn' to guard against an attack by a great wild boar.

Interestingly, balls of light have been witnessed rising out of Tarn Wadling, a phenomenon seen at many lakes all over the world. Such an event was even included in one of the Arthurian poems, when Guinevere and Arthur's Knights witness a mysterious light over the lake, which glides towards Sir Gawain 'All glowed as a glebe the ghost there she glides, unbeclipped in a cloud of clothing unclear, circles with serpents all about the sides'. He comforts the frightened queen exclaiming that it must be an eclipse of the sun while the other knights believe it to be a ghost (Matthews 2009).

A little further north between High and Low Hesket, Belinus passes close to a thorn tree growing through a hole in a squared slab on a verge next to the A6 called the Court Thorn. Many believe tenants assembled here to pay their feudal services to the Lord of the Manor on 11 June, the feast day of the apostle St Barnabas. The stone marks the location of the original tree. According to Marjorie Rowling in *Folklore of the Lake District*, in the region of the Lakeland the White Thorn, May Tree or Hawthorn was traditionally associated with the holding of courts of justice and trials.

Soon we reached the outskirts of the ancient city of Carlisle, where we discovered another Node, the last before the Scottish border. However, before exploring this historic 'Capital of the North' and the last city to mark the alignment in England, we return to the River Eamont to trace the path of Elen.

Ninekirks and the Giant's Caves

As we began the research of the female current through Penrith's ancient landscape we both felt something special was about to unfold. We last dowsed Elen crossing the A66 from Whinfell Park just south of the town, heading for a loop of the serpent-like Eamont River. Here she visits the site of a solitary church dedicated to St Ninian, standing in a field by the banks of the river, locally known as Ninekirks. Many historians believe it to be on the site of the oldest Christian settlement in Cumbria.

The church of Ninekirks next to the River Eamont

However, this area may have been a sacred place of worship long before Christianity for a large megalith covered with cup and ring marks, now in Carlisle Museum, stood on a sandstone escarpment above the church on the lands of Honeypot Farm. We travelled to the Tullie House Museum in Carlisle to see this remarkable stone and wondered if the markings, enclosed within an incised border, actually represent a map of the energy vortices around Ninekirks; the shape of the border even appears to mimic the great loop of the Eamont River.

Large boulder with cup and ring marks in Carlisle Museum that once stood above Ninekirks at Honeypot Farm

St Ninian was an Apostle of the Picts and the mainspring of the northern Celtic church before St Patrick. He was born by the Solway Firth in Cumbria and tutored in Rome, returning to Cumbria in AD 397 just before the departure of the Romans from Britain. In *The History of Penrith* published in 1894, William Furness wrote of St Ninian:

'after visiting Rome he became the Apostle of Cumbria. … That he built a church at Withern, in Wigtownshire, is certain. That was in 397, and it is a probability almost amounting to certainly, that he erected a church at, or near to Brovacum [Roman fort], as early, if not at an earlier date, and that, whilst ministering to the garrison and people at Brovacum, at the church we now call Nine Churches, he dwelt in the caves close by.'

The caves in question, carved out of the red sandstone cliffs, lie on the opposite banks of the Eamont River to Ninekirks. They have the curious name of *Isis Parlis*, and legend says that it was the abode of the giant Hugh or Owain Caesario.

An early monastic settlement founded by a group of Culdee monks is said to have stood to the east of the present church, similar to those found in Scotland. Many of the Culdees adhered to the teachings of St Ninian so it is quite likely that their settlement absorbed the church and caves associated with this saint. Long ago, when this area was covered in thick forest, refugees would have seen the Culdee monastery as a safe sanctuary during turbulent times. A hoard of Roman coins dating from the 3rd century AD was found close to the little church along with an altar and tombstone from the same period.

As previously discovered, the so-called giant Hugh or Owain Caesario who dwelt in the caves here also lived at Castle Hewen at Tarn Wadling on the male current. Owain was King of Rheged and possibly fought alongside King Arthur against the Picts and the Angles. In the poem *Dream of Rhonabwy* from the 12th century Welsh *Mabinogion*, Arthur allies himself with the 'Ravens of Owain ab Urien' during the Battle of Badon Hill around AD 516; Owain's father Urien was also known as the Raven King. According to many Arthurian romances, knights would often retire to caves after particularly bloody battles to become hermits. Therefore, the legend associated with Sir Hugh or Owain Caesario at these caves at Ninekirks may be a distant memory of this.

Marjorie Rowling points out that the giant that frequented the caves at Ninekirks is variously called Owain, Sir Ewen, Hugh Caesario, or Tarquin. She believes that *The Mabinogion* story, written during medieval times, may have confused Owain of Rheged with a later hero from the 10th century called King Eugenius or Owain of the Kingdom of Strathclyde, which included Cumbria at that time. According to various antiquarians, King Owain lost a major battle against the Saxon King Athelstan on the Solway Firth and retreated to the cave at Ninekirks to become a hermit where he ended his days. The main royal court of this 10th century King Owain was Penrith and his burial may have usurped that of the earlier Owain of Rheged – the Giant's Grave at St Andrew's Church. His son was Duvenald or Dunmail, the last king of Cumbria, a great hero who in *c.* AD 945 resisted the Angles and the Scots. He is immortalised at Dunmail Raise, north of Grasmere, where a cairn or tumulus marks his grave.

William Furness refers to an Arthurian ballad in which Sir Tarquin held 'three-score and four' Knights of the Round Table as prisoners in a cave. The challenger in the form of Sir Lancelot, the famous Knight of Arthur's court, succeeded in slaying Tarquin and released the knights (Rowling 1976). The story is very similar to one recounted in Malory's *Morte d'Arthur*; Malory may have been familiar with the local legend of Tarquin at Ninekirks as his family lived in a manor house close by.

The reputation of this mighty Tarquin travelled as far south as Manchester where legend says he resided at his fort at Knott Mill by the River Medlock, close to the female current at Castlefield. Sir Owain, Ewen or Hugh Caesario and Tarquin may in fact be the same person. Tarquin is a title for an Etruscan prince and Caesario may have been the Italian family name of this legendary warrior. After the Romans conquered the Etruscan empire in Italy in around 396 BC, many of the Etruscan aristocracy were seconded into the Roman legions and Tarquin Caesario may have been a descendant of one of these families, remaining in northern Britain after the Roman withdrawal, to fight the invading forces of the Scots and the Picts.

While we were researching these legends, I came across a story that places the tomb of Sir Lancelot at St Lawrence's Church in the village of Crosby Ravensworth. Ironically, this church is located just 5 km (3 miles) east of the Shap prehistoric complex. Many prominent families of the area later adopted his name, including Sir Lancelot Threlkeld, also buried at the same church, and Lancelot Edward Lowther, the Sixth Earl of Lonsdale from nearby Lowther Castle. There must have been a church here contemporary with Lancelot, for it has a Saxon cross shaft in the churchyard.

William Furness recalls another local story associated with the caves at Ninekirks written in 1860 by Revd B. Porteous, vicar of nearby Edenhall. An annual assembly of over a thousand people would gather on the third Sunday of May called the 'Giant's Cave Sunday', when mysterious ceremonies took place. Below the caves was St Ninian's Well, now lost in the undergrowth, where young men and woman would collect water to mix with liquorice in bottles which they would then shake vigorously to create froth. Honeypot, the name of the nearby farm, may be another clue to this ceremony, as honey mixed with well water was an earlier alternative to liquorice (Rowling 1976).

We gained access to Ninekirks along a footpath leading from a parking area next to the A66 opposite the entrance to Winfell Park. The day was gloriously sunny as we set off along a ridge above the Eamont River lined with old oak trees and surrounded by freshly cut wheat fields. We soon descended to the solitary church next to a loop in the river and as we entered through the old wooden gate, it felt as if we had stepped into the past, as little has changed since Victorian times.

To extend his hunting grounds, de Veteripont of Brougham Castle demolished the Saxon village surrounding Ninekirks in 1284. A hundred years later, a new chapel dedicated to St Wildred was built at nearby Brougham Hall to serve the surrounding population and in 1659 Lady Anne Clifford, having inherited the castle in the 17th century, completely rebuilt the original Norman church of Ninekirks. As we entered the church through the south entrance, the carved terracotta head of St Ninian looked down upon us, a possible relic of the old church now incorporated into the Victorian masonry.

It was hard to believe that this picturesque and tranquil setting of Ninekirks opposite the mystical caves was once a thriving religious centre. However, the female current avoids the church, passing instead through a roofless stone building in the southeast corner of the churchyard, perhaps used to stable horses during services. Immediately we entered this shed, we noticed amongst the undergrowth two huge white quartz crystal stones marking her flow, which we sensed were pinning her current to this abandoned shed and draining her energy.

We quickly removed the stones and cleared the ground of other debris. After carrying out a healing ritual to cleanse the space and to release and rebalance Elen's flow, she instantly moved away from the shed to flow east of the church through a rough strip of ground, which we believe was the site of the early Christian Culdee monastery.

We followed her to the river where she disappeared through the mouth of a cave, which we could just make out on the opposite banks of the Eamont. Was this the cave inhabited by Owain Caesario or Tarquin?

Isis Parlis or Giant's Cave by the River Eamont opposite Ninekirks

Interior of Isis Parlis cave

The Revd C.E. Golland proposed that its local name Isis Parlis or *Isey Perlis* derives from the Celtic *Aesidhe* (*Eashea*) meaning 'fairies', while *Parlis* originates from the Scottish *parrlie* meaning 'small barrel' or 'container', which he interpreted as 'Jar of the Fairies'. It may also refer to the cave as a place of worship of the Roman and Egyptian goddess Isis, *perlis* or *parlis* meaning 'parlour' (Rowling 1976).

The caves are difficult to visit as they are now on private land, the farmer having made public access impossible. However, by chance we met a local Earth Mysteries researcher who knew the farmer and helped us obtain permission to visit the caves. Taking out our dowsing rods, we proceeded to walk along a path next to the river and soon found Elen entering one of the caves. Here she passes through a carved recess or altar, perhaps used long ago to place offerings in honour of the goddess Isis.

Our dowsing also indicated a spiral emanating from the ground just before the altar denoting a blind spring or crossing of underground water streams under the cave. Dowsers have often found rising vortexes of energy such as this before the High Altar in many churches and cathedrals.

Carving of a running maiden at the entrance of Isis Parlis cave

On a crevice of rock next to the mouth of the cave, we noticed the faint image of a running maiden sculptured into the sandstone rock. Despite its badly damaged head, the billowing skirt and part of the torso and arms are still visible. This carving may have prompted Furness to recall a story about a damsel who ventures down to the river next to the cave unaware of the gruesome giant that resides there. Luckily she spots him just as he is about to grab her and leaps to safety across a cleft in the rock face. Missing his step, the pursuing giant falls into the river and drowns. The locals still call this part of the River Eamont 'The Maiden's Step'.

Elen continues across fields through a curious mound overgrown with trees by the road to Udford before visiting the village of Edenhall and its parish church dedicated to St Cuthbert.

The Luck of Edenhall

The village of Edenhall takes its name from a grand mansion owned by the Musgrave family complete with palatial landscaped gardens. Its architect was Sir Robert Smirke, who also designed Askham Church and nearby Lowther Castle, building the house in an Italianate style over an earlier structure in 1824. A few years later, Edenhall passed through marriage to Lord Henry Charles Brougham when he married Zoe Musgrave. Nothing remains after its demolition in 1934, except for the gate pillars, the lodge and stables, which are now private dwellings.

In Norman times, William the Conqueror awarded the manor of Edenhall to Henry Fitz-Swein, passing to Robert Turp during the reign of Henry III. Eventually through the female line of descent it passed down to the Stapletons and then to the Musgraves, a family who also came to Britain during the Norman invasion.

According to Rowling, an event of a more mysterious nature may explain the fate of the Musgrave family and their home Edenhall. It involves a Venetian glass beaker dating from the 13th century called 'The Luck of Edenhall' owned by the Musgrave family and now in the care of the Victoria and Albert Museum in London. Experts have examined the relic and determined it as originating from Aleppo in Syria, possibly brought to England by a Crusader knight. The letters *HIS* inscribed on the glass are the Greek initials of Jesus, which suggests a religious purpose similar to a chalice.

Several folk tales surround the origin of the Luck, including its discovery by a butler while fetching water from the nearby well. As he stumbles down to the well, he spots a group of dancing fairies encircling a glass cup and decides to snatch it for himself. Angry at the butler's actions, the elementals announce, 'If ere this cup shall break or fall, farewell the luck of Edenhall'. Some stories differ in their telling of this event; in one, the butler encounters the fairies dancing outside the nearby St Cuthbert's Church.

Another tale pertains to a Duke who often visited Edenhall and when drunk would throw the Luck into the air to prove he could catch it. However, one day he nearly dropped it, saved only by a quick-handed servant catching it in his napkin. Despite the servant's dexterity, the Luck received a crack to its rim and from that day 'bad luck befell Edenhall'. Many old villagers also believed the story that its removal from Edenhall would seal the fate of the house and its family.

Sir William Musgrave published the first account of the Luck and its folklore in *The Gentleman's Magazine* in 1791. According to Rowling, there were at least six old families of Cumberland who until recently owned relics similar to the Luck, on the presumption that its safe preservation controlled their fortunes. Dr Hartland, who wrote *The Science of Fairy Tales* in 1925, suggested that the Luck of Edenhall was in reality a goblet dedicated to the pagan worship of a female guardian spirit particular to Cumbria. This form of honouring came with early Norse settlers, who believed that this guardian bestowed 'peace and plenty' upon the family and house if the goblet was in safe-keeping and handed down to subsequent generations of the family (Rowling 1976).

Folk tales of cups stolen from fairies and preserved by the families originate from Scandinavia, and in Sweden such goblets were said to be gifts from the *berg* or mountain women.

A local tradition says that the Musgrave family used the Edenhall Luck during certain ceremonies held in the caves at Ninekirks. It seems that a number of Lucks associated with some of these old Cumbrian families were in fact sacred relics honoured in a

The Luck of Edenhall. (Taken from an engraving from Robert Chamber's Book of Days published in 1864)

way that seemed reminiscent of Grail worship. One of the canons issued during the reign of King Athelstan (AD 925–940) reads 'Sacer Calis fusilis sit, non ligneous', translated as 'Let the sacred chalice be fusile [glass] not wooden'. Even Golland referred to the Edenhall Luck as 'Jar of the Fairies', another possible memory of Grail worship in the area.

In 1937, Arthur Mee wrote that the area of Edenhall was once a Saxon settlement and remnants of that time are still visible in the foundations of the Norman St Cuthbert's Church nearby. The house of the Musgraves also stood on the route taken by monks as they carried the body of St Cuthbert to safety. Most of what is left of the estate is privately owned so we decided to wander along a charming country lane to the local church dedicated to St Cuthbert to see if we could find any further clues about the history of the village.

The isolated church nestles in an idyllic spot next to the River Eden, with a backdrop of the majestic Pennines in the distance. This 12th century church once stood within Edenhall's deer park, said to be built over a holy spring called St Cuthbert's Well, where folklore says the Luck was taken from the fairies.

The shields carved into the western face of the tower are those of the Musgrave, Stapleton, Veteripont and Hilton families, past owners of many of the estates in the region. We found several members of the

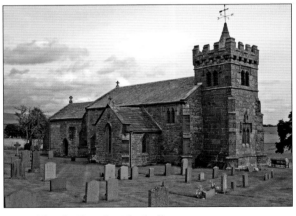

St Cuthbert's Church, Edenhall

Musgrave family buried here, their coat of arms showing a circle of six gold rings with a red hand at the centre, reminding me of Tolkien's epic tale The Lord of the Rings. We found Elen passing through a Saxon window, now bricked up, below which we find a white crystal stone set into the exterior of the wall.

Before returning to the centre of the village, Elen connects with St Cuthbert's Cross next to the road where a Victorian replica stands on what appeared to be the original 8th century base. The cross, erected on top of a plague stone, is renowned for its healing powers, which I sensed still linger here. She also visits a huge old oak tree in a field, the remains of the old forest of Ingleborough that once covered this area. After dowsing her from the Vicarage, she took us to the Edenhall Hotel, passing through part of the restaurant.

We decided to have our evening meal there and detected a table on Elen's flow. Our conversation soon turned to the enigmatic 'Lucks' of Cumbria and I remembered that Guy Ragland Phillips in his book *Brigantia* mentions one at Burrell Green, a farm in the Eden Valley, and at Muncaster Castle near Ravenglass. I could not help but wonder whether these important families including the Musgraves, whose crest depicts the six gold rings, were somehow associated with a corrupted form of ancient Grail worship. Perhaps, like the Norse people who settled here, they might have been hereditary guardians of an artefact that embodied their local goddess, some authors referring to them as 'Grail Families'. Their role was one that ensured the powerful telluric energy remained balanced and nourished to promote well-being in the land, a duty once performed by the Druids and Culdee monks. Most likely, these families were groomed for this task over generations, fulfilling their role through ritual and ceremony using the Grail cup at sacred places where the presence of the divine goddess is at her most potent.

The story of the giant Sir Hugh or Owain Caesario is an intriguing one. Was he a great warrior of Rheged, who fought valiantly beside the legendary King Arthur at the battle of Badon Hill and lived in the caves opposite Ninekirks? Perhaps he too was a Grail keeper. I also believe the early Culdees specifically chose their site by a bend of the River Eamont at Ninekirks because of its proximity to the sacred caves and the holy well, where the goddess of the land also resides.

Such ceremonies in the cave at Ninekirks have now faded from memory, abandoned after ill luck befell the Musgrave family.

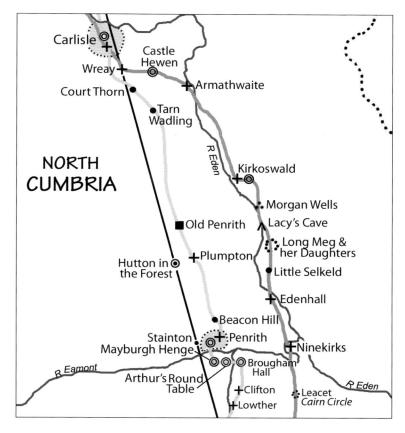

Chapter 12

Camelot and Avalon of the North
Along the Eden to the Borders

Long Meg and the Sacred River

We now enter the Eden Valley with its enchanting landscape, steeped in magic and mystery, once part of the northern lands of the Brigantes. The vale of the River Eden begins its journey on Wild Boar Fell just north of the Yorkshire Dales, a sacred hill that from a distance resembles a face looking up towards the heavens. From this great terrestrial guardian, the trickling waters gather momentum to become a spectacularly wide river that flows all the way to Carlisle, eventually entering the sea further west at the Solway Estuary near the Scottish border. The Eden is one of the very few rivers in the world that is orientated north–south, with its waters flowing north. The ancient and aboriginal cultures around the world believe that such rivers are sacred and reflect the Milky Way, the 'road to the stars', because the north-flowing waters take the departed souls towards the realm of the 'great spirit', the abode of our ancestors. Another north-flowing river is the Nile, where the Ancient Egyptians sailed their dead upon its waters in 'boats to the afterlife'.

After crossing the Eden from Edenhall, Elen visits the village of Little Salkeld where a medieval church once existed dedicated to St Mary. Perhaps a dwelling close to the current called Church House may be a clue to its original location. Elen passes alongside a working watermill as she makes her way north towards the nearby stone circle called Long Meg and Her Daughters.

A farm track leads you into an open field where sixty-nine colossal megalithic stones still survive dating to the late Neolithic and early Bronze Age. The stone circle is actually a great oval or ellipse measuring approximately 94 m (308 ft) north–south and 109 m (357 ft) east–west. The monument is certainly the largest and finest stone circle in the north of England, having some of the biggest individual megaliths seen outside

Long Meg and Her Daughters stone circle

of Stonehenge and Avebury. All the stones, of which only 27 remain upright, are made up of unhewn greenstone, limestone and granite glacial erratics, some standing over 2 m (6 ft 6 in) high and one measuring 3.3 m (11 ft) wide and weighing over 28 tons. When the early British archaeologist John Aubrey investigated the site in 1650, locals informed him that giant bones had been uncovered within the circle, a story familiar with other megalithic sites around the world (Waterhouse 1985).

Just a short distance from the main circle on the highest point of the complex is a tall tapering outlier called Long Meg standing to the southwest. Its curious name derives from an old nickname for anything of great size dating back to its association with an extremely tall woman called Meg, buried at Westminster Abbey during the reign of Henry VIII. Others say that the name refers to a local witch known as Meg of Meldon who lived in the 17th century. Local folklore refers to Long Meg and Her Daughters as a group of witches turned to stone by a Scottish wizard named Michael Scott (1175–1234), because they danced there on the Sabbath. He apparently endowed the stones of the circle with magical powers, 'making it so that no one could ever count the stones twice alike'. According to British archaeologist Aubrey Burl (1976), this huge piece of Triassic sandstone, measuring 3.8 m (12 ft 6 in) high, is older than the stone circle because the flat face of the stone points NNW. Farrah also suggests that Long Meg predates the circle, stating that 'from the centre of the circle the stone is not central to the portal stones that define the entrance'. He also cites recent research indicating that the shadow cast by Long Meg at sunset on the winter solstice strikes the stone in the circle to the north and east of the farm track, 'suggesting the shadow path helped determine the circle'. Moreover, at Samhain and Imbolc its shadow crosses the two southeast portal stones before reaching the largest stone in the circle to the east. Therefore, the height and position of Long Meg on a higher platform of land suggests that this pre-existing standing stone was used as a *gnomon* (like an arm of a sundial) to determine the proportions of the circle during its construction.

The standing stone has numerous carvings on one of its deliberately flattened surfaces, including spirals, cup and ring marks, grooves and concentric circles. These are similar to those found on many other megaliths around Britain and Ireland, including New Grange in Ireland, which dates to 3800 BC. Researchers of such phenomena have begun to realise that these enigmatic markings may have been created through shamanistic inspiration, the drawings communicating to us the unique nature of the energies emitted at these sacred places of power. Many dowsers have found spirals of energy

Long Meg standing stone, casting a shadow towards the circle at winter solstice sunset

emanating from individual stones at many circles and at isolated cup and ring marked rocks. The aboriginals painted certain sacred rocks with their strange designs and symbols, believing that such images stimulated the life essence within them, providing a source of energy capable of producing rain and fertilising the crops. The geology of the stone was also an important factor to the Neolithic and Bronze Age races, the minerals within its strata crucial to creating the desired effect upon the land.

William Camden described the circle based on a description given to him in a letter around 1600 from a Cumbrian antiquarian and schoolmaster Reg Bainbrigg:

'Besides Little Salkeld ... Where the Romaines have fought some great battle, there standes certain ... pyramides of stone, placed there in the manner of a crown. They are commonlie called Meg and hir daughters ....' (Rowling 1976)

Over seventy stones were said to have formed this circle before Lieutenant Colonel Samuel Lacy dynamited some of them in 1725. However, work was suddenly halted when:

'the slumbering powers of druidism rose in arms against the violation of their sanctuary; and such heavy rain and hail ensued as the Fell-side never before witnessed. The labourers fled for their lives, vowing never more to meddle with Long Meg.' (Burl 1976)

This apparent act of god saved the remaining stones, for a short time later Lacy began to preserve the megaliths by restoring the site and protecting it from any future damage or desecration. According to Farrah (2008), Lacy commissioned a painting of the monument called *The Druids cutting Mistletoe* by Jacob Thompson, dated 1832 and exhibited at the Royal Academy.

We dowsed Elen entering the site through the south-facing edge of Long Meg, then diverting to a new course towards the northeast, passing through the circle between the portal stones at the southwest entrance to the centre, following the shadow of the mid-winter solstice. Here she crosses with two other energy currents – one male, the other female. The male travels through the circle on an east–west equinoctial course and the female flows from southeast to northwest. As Elen crosses a large stone lying on its side at the northeast quadrant, she abruptly changes her path to the north, passing into an area which aerial photography shows as the site of a large ditched enclosure or henge.

It is almost certain that the circle was part of a much bigger prehistoric complex as a mound and another smaller stone circle existed southwest of Long Meg on higher ground, recorded in a drawing by Stukeley in 1725.

It was at this stage that I noticed that Long Meg leans not towards the circle but to the NNW towards the setting stars of Cygnus and the Dark Rift in the Milky Way. Furthermore, using a compass along its flattened eastern face, its precise orientation is 335 degrees. If Burl is correct, and the placing of the standing stone was earlier than the stone circle, then it may have been located there for an entirely different reason than its suggested purpose as an indicator for the sun setting at the midwinter solstice.

I realised that by taking the elevation and the height of the hills on the horizon into consideration, and using Skyglobe, the early priests standing at Long Meg would have viewed Deneb setting at 335 degrees between 3500 and 2500 BC. I believe that the standing stone was deliberately orientated and shaped to emphasise this point on the northern horizon where Deneb or the Dark Rift sets. A ridge near the village of Kirkoswald marks the actual setting point and its place of rising would have been at a hill known as Cross Fell, now shielded by a group of trees. This name is interesting as Cygnus is often referred to as the Northern Cross.

During this same period, the long barrow at Uffington called Wayland Smithy, constructed in 3500 BC, was exactly orientated to the setting of Deneb, and Collins found the axis of the stone circle at Avebury also aligned perfectly to the setting of Deneb around 2600 BC. Therefore, the dating of the outlier Long Meg to 1500 BC may be incorrect, for it aligns with the setting of Deneb between 3500 and 2500 BC. The circle's close proximity to the sacred north-flowing Eden also reflects an ancient belief in a cosmological river as a bearer to the afterlife, the point in the sky where we find the Dark Rift and the constellation of Cygnus.

Lacy's Caves

From Little Salkeld we followed a footpath along the banks of the Eden bordered by wild flowers and woodland. In the distance we could see the goddess hills of Blencathra, Skiddaw and Carrock Fell, a spectacular backdrop to this enchanting walk. As we followed the path of a former tramway, which connected the Long Meg Mine with the nearby Settle to Carlisle railway, we noticed ahead of us what appeared to be a red sandstone structure on a ledge jutting out over the river.

This grotto, known as Lacy's Cave, was carved out in the 18th century by Colonel Lacy, owner of the Salkeld Hall estate. He was also responsible for the near-destruction of Long Meg and Her Daughters. The caves, of bright red sandstone rock streaked with quartz seams, consist of a series of five chambers all hand carved with pillars and arches, very similar to ancient oracle sites such as Cumae in Southern Italy. It was fashionable at the time to build romantic follies and the Colonel planted the outside of these caves with an ornamental garden where laburnums and rhododendrons still

Entrance to Lacy's Cave by the River Eden

flower today. He also enjoyed entertaining his guests here, going so far as to employ a man to sit in the caves as a hermit to add authenticity and 'make his friends envious'! He may have been attempting to emulate Constantine's Cells situated further up river near the village of Wetheral, gouged out of solid rock centuries ago.

The atmosphere here was heavy with psychic energy captured by our photographs in the form of numerous orbs. We dowsed the female current passing through its chambers, one having four vertical recesses carved into the walls tall enough to stand in. There were other smaller alcoves clearly carved as shelves for either candles or sacred objects. Caroline and I both had the impression that Lacy hollowed out these caves for some ritual purpose, perhaps honouring the feminine serpent energy. Certainly, after his extraordinary experiences at Long Meg whilst attempting to blow up the stones, he acquired a new-found respect for the hidden power within the land.

Elen's serpent energy felt very powerful in these caves, her flow amplified by the high levels of silica-quartz embedded in the walls.

Further along the east bank of the river, before the footpath meets the road at Daleraven Bridge, is Kirkbank. Before several devastating floods in the 12th century, an early chapel stood here attached to the ancient village of Addingham situated on the opposite bank. All that remains today is St Michael's Well, standing alone in the middle of a field. The village and church were rebuilt in the 13th century further east of here, using stones from the old chapel. Just a short walk north of Long Meg, the present St Michael's Church at the new village of Addingham contains several artefacts retrieved from the ancient chapel, including part of a hogback tomb and pieces of an early cross shaft and its base.

Elen connects with some sadly neglected springs emerging from the banks of the Eden north of the bridge known as the Morgan Wells. It is interesting that in this Cumbrian landscape steeped in Arthurian myths we have the name Morgan, reminiscent of Morgan le Fay or perhaps the Welsh goddess Morrigan. We were surprised at the lack of a Christian dedication here, perhaps a site overlooked by the missionaries from Rome.

The Castle of the Stars and St Oswald

A little further north, we arrived at the picturesque red sandstone village of Kirkoswald, where we discovered several fascinating historical features. Its ancient church lies to the east of the village below a prominent mound crowned by a bell tower. On another hill close by is a large double-ditched earthwork of a ruined castle with the remains of a moat.

Elen arrives first at the castle visiting the remains of its northwest turret, now standing precariously amongst dense trees and foliage. This once grand building, built by the new lord of the manor John de Castre in the early 1300s, stands on the site of a Norman motte and bailey castle. However, it only lasted a hundred years before its destruction at the hands of the Scots under Robert the Bruce. Lord Ranulph Dacre later restored the castle and his son Sir Thomas added a moat in 1485. It was described as 'one of the fairest fabrics that eyes looked upon, having a great hall, one hundred yards long, ornamented with pictures of all the kings of England'. Amongst these rare portraits of ancient kings was the legendary King Brutus of Troy, Molmutius of Winchester and King Belinus. The entire collection was lost in a fire after their removal to Naworth Castle around 1601.

Like many other places on the male and female currents, the Norman motte and bailey may have occupied the site of a prehistoric mound, perhaps originally constructed as a celestial marker as Deneb set into this mound when viewed from Long Meg between 3500 and 2500 BC.

Remains of Kirkoswald Castle

From the castle, Elen skirts the slopes of the large mound with the bell tower erected in 1893 over the foundations of one built in the 18th century. The hill resembles a miniature Glastonbury Tor and at its base is St Oswald's Church, set on the banks of the Raven Beck that feeds into the Eden. Oswald was a Saxon king and a local tradition says that when he visited the area in the 7th century he found the local people worshipping the deity of a spring that issued from the hill. With the help of St Aidan, he converted the villagers to Christianity and built a wooden Christian church over the stream.

Elen flows down the axis of the church and out through a lovingly restored holy well, which still gushes forth at the west end of the church, its source, according to Colonel Fetherstonhaugh in *Our Cumberland Village* (1925), now under the church nave.

We first encountered St Oswald at Didsbury on the ancient southern boundary of Northumbria below Manchester. He was the son of Ethelfrid and nephew of Edwin, both Kings of Northumbria, and succeeded to the throne in AD 634, later converting to Christianity during his 17-year exile on the island of Iona in Western Scotland.

Around the walls of the church are several grave slabs of Crusader knights and one much older with Saxon markings. Inside are tombs of the Musgraves from Edenhall, having intermarried with many of the important families of the area including the Grahams, the Earls of Lonsdales and the Broughams.

Perhaps the real site of ancient goddess worship here is the bell tower mound, out of which gush the sacred waters revered by the early Britons. Like the gardens at Chalice Well, where waters flow out of the base of the Tor in Glastonbury, this hill is a possible site of pagan worship dating back to the time of the Druids and beyond. Many local sources believe that Cumbrian place names that include the word 'Kirk' are more likely to be associated with prehistoric ceremonial sites than the later Christian churches. Kirkandrews, Kirkby Stephen, Kirkby Lonsdale and Kirklinton all have churches with very early Christian foundations built over ancient pagan sites of worship.

Holy well at St Oswald's Church, Kirkoswald

Throughout our journey in Cumbria, we have discovered many ancient sites renowned for their goddess worship, such as those next to rivers and holy wells or in caves, in fact more so than in any other county in England. Holy wells in Cumbria were visited during Beltane to celebrate the fertility of Spring. Perhaps the well at Kirkoswald was also renowned for its Beltane festivals as the church is orientated to the Beltane sunrise rather than aligned on the usual east–west axis. Oswald would have intentionally built his church over this sacred well to stamp out this ancient practice, forcing people to worship a Christian god. The sacred waters were channelled to flow under the nave to serve a new Christian holy well created at the west entrance of the church.

From here, Elen passes through the curious square outline of a double-ditched enclosure that appears to resemble a Roman fort. The large moated site may have been the motte and bailey castle recorded in the early 12th century as a wooden structure with a tower built by Ranulph d'Engayne, Lord of Cumberland, later destroyed by fire in 1314. The earthwork was possibly the bailey, while the motte stood on the large mound under the Bell Tower. However, square double-ditched baileys are generally unheard of, which suggests it was originally constructed as a ceremonial henge, part of a much larger sanctuary, its sacred significance inspiring King Oswald to journey all the way from Northumbria to build a church here.

Meandering north, Elen follows the course of the Eden River towards Nunnery House to connect with its waters once more at Croglin Beck just south of the village of Armathwaite. A Benedictine convent was established here in 1018, the order of nuns having been awarded the lands by King William Rufus. They originally came from a nunnery in Carlisle founded by St Cuthbert, with Ermenburga, Queen Dowager of Northumbria, as its Abbess. The convent was dedicated to Our Saviour and the Blessed Virgin Mary, holding lands as far west as Tarn Wadling. Nunnery House took over the site in the 18th century, its estates including the scenic Nunnery Walks. Sadly, they are no longer accessible to the public due to high maintenance costs. Just to the west of the house, Elen passes through the scant remains of a chapel next to a sacred spring called Chapel Well.

Why Rufus granted land at such a remote site is curious; perhaps it was due to its proximity to the well. However, like the Benedictine order established by Henry of Blois at Winchester, these nuns may have been initiated into the ancient knowledge which included an understanding of the dragon energies of the Earth, perhaps establishing themselves here as guardians of the Grail.

As we continued through the Eden Valley, the spirit of this large but gentle river enchanted us. We began to linger for a while to admire its picturesque views. The stretch of river between Kirkoswald and Armathwaite is without doubt the most stunning and further enhanced by the presence of Elen as she weaves her way through woodland and meadows above its banks. At the point where she crosses the river to the village of Armathwaite, we found several sculptured heads carved in relief on the sandstone bluff next to its eastern banks. The position here is a precarious one for walkers, the narrow footpath requiring nimble footwork as the fast-flowing

waters bubble beneath. The faces have a magical presence about them, perhaps portraying elemental guardians as they watch over the sacred river. As we sat amongst the glowing red rocks at sunset, we sensed the strong energy of the female current nourished by the chi of the churning waters of the nearby weir, the same invisible force that must have inspired the carvers to capture the spirits at this place.

On the opposite bank, Elen connects with the site of a Pele tower, now Armathwaite Castle, built by the Skelton family. She then enters the village through the old forge, now a cottage and part of the Duke's Head pub where we enjoyed

Sculptured heads on a sandstone buff next to the River Eden near Armathwaite

several evenings during our stay in the area. Elen's connection with the forge came as no surprise, attracted once upon a time by the alchemical processes used during the forging of metal. Carruthers writes that the smiths in Celtic traditions used a magical formula to smelt iron ore and forge metal into swords, spears and arrowheads, symbolised in the story of Merlin and the sword in the stone. The blacksmiths would use water during the quenching process to harden the metal and temper the sword to produce a fine edge, a magical alchemical procedure that gave the British Celts a technical advantage over the Romans and Saxons.

The magnificent Burne-Jones stained-glass windows depicting Christ and St Mary is a wonderful feature reflecting the dedication of Armathwaite's 15th century church, set high up on the slopes of a hill overlooking the Eden. At one time it became a cattle shed, until its restoration in 1660.

Castle Hewen

Driving along the narrow country lanes towards Carlisle, the rods picked up Elen crossing a hill above a group of farm buildings called Aiketgate. Walking up the bridleway next to the farm, we arrived on a high ridge where we noticed large cut stones in the undergrowth either side of the track. As we stopped to admire the views, we could see the site of the legendary lake at Tarn Wadling below, visited by the male current. The blocks of stone may have been remnants of the legendary Castle Hewen, royal residence of the 5th century King of Rheged, Owain or Hugh (Hewen) Caesario. Leland in 1553 refers to these ruins, overlooking the sacred lake of Tarn Wadling, as a possible medieval stronghold.

Moreover, in the 18th century an antiquarian recorded ruins of a very strong and ancient building with 2.4 m (8 ft) thick walls and outer defences standing on the top of a ridge adjoining Aiketgate to the northeast of Tarn Wadling. By the 19th century, the only visible remains were the foundations of a huge round tower.

Was this the castle of the legendary Tarquin, also known as Owain or Hugh (Hewen) Caesario, a warrior buried in the Giant's Grave in the churchyard of St Andrew's Parish Church in Penrith? During the 14th century, this area was romanticised in many ballads, including one entitled *The Marriage of Sir Gawain*, which describes King Arthur living at his court in 'Merrie Carlisle' with his wife 'Genever'. According to the story, one day at Christmastide Arthur meets with the giant Baron of Castle Hewen. The Baron carried an enormous club upon his back, demanding that Arthur either fight him or return on New Year's Day with the answer to 'what thing it is that a woman will most desire'.

While returning to Castle Hewen on the appointed day but still with no answer to the riddle, Arthur comes across a hideous old woman in the forest. The hag promises to give him the answer if Arthur provides her with a 'fair and courtly knight to marry her'. Arthur agrees and the hag tells him 'that all women will have their wille, and this is their chief desyre'. Having duly satisfied the Baron with this answer, Arthur returns to court with the dilemma of how to persuade one of his knights to marry the hag. He explains his predicament to Gawain who gallantly agrees to wed the old woman. His reward was swift, however, when, after the marriage vows were exchanged, the hag transformed into a beautiful princess, having been placed under an evil spell by her wicked stepmother.

The county archaeologist Tom Clare excavated the site of Castle Hewen in 1978 and his discoveries, recorded in an interim report now in Carlisle Library, suggest that it was a Romano-British fortification, possibly a Roman signal station, and one of a line that runs south from Carlisle. Although there are indications of occupation during the 5th and 6th centuries, at the time King Owain allegedly resided here, there is no substantial evidence that this was the site of the castle of the King of Rheged. However, Hutchinson, who visited the remains of a castle in 1773, was certain it was Castle Hewen and came across a tradition that neighbouring tenants would pay the Lord of the Manor the 'Castle Hewen rent' (Hutchinson 1794).

The Sacred Basilica

Elen follows the River Petteril to another site of a Roman signal station before entering the pretty village of Wreay. Here, on the alignment, we find a most remarkable building resembling a Roman basilica. St Mary's Church is a highly original work of architecture built under the direction of Miss Sarah Losh between 1840 and 1842, as a memorial to her beloved sister Catherine. She was described by Simon Jenkins, in *England's Thousand British Churches,* as 'an individual genius, a Charlotte Bronte of wood and stone'. The church stands on ancient hallowed ground; the earlier building here dates to 1319 recorded as a chapelry belonging to St Mary's Priory in Carlisle.

The inspired design of the rectangular nave and semicircular apse we see today was an ancient style of building observed by Miss Losh during her 'grand tour' of the Continent. Her local workforce included the stonemason William Hindson and his sons, sent to Italy to learn its building techniques. This included the practice of incorporating sacred measure within the proportions of the building, a method that surely promotes an exquisite atmosphere of harmony and balance. The church is full of symbolic ornamental carvings, some created by Miss Losh herself.

According to a local guidebook, this accomplished young woman was born in 1785 to a prominent Cumberland family who mixed with such literary greats as William Wordsworth. She was educated 'far beyond the reach of her own sex and indeed of most men', her particular interests being science and art, with many of her ideas and designs reproduced in this magical church.

St Mary's Church, Wreay

By the entrance is a holy well, restored by Miss Losh and still flowing freely. The main door of the church displays exquisite carvings of lilies, birds, beetles, butterflies, caterpillars and fossils. To the right of the entrance is an enormous head of a serpent just under the eaves of the roof, with other stone carvings of serpents, tortoises and alligators also adorning the exterior.

Upon opening the door, the church gradually lights up to reveal the semicircular apse with its fabulous symbolic paintings of Jesus and the twelve apostles. The pulpit is fashioned out of a trunk of a bog oak, rescued from a submerged forest and in such fine condition that the carvers were able to retain its shape, sculpting it as a palm tree and fossils.

Marking the Elen current is a fabulous alabaster font decorated with butterflies, bees, grapes and figs, its lid carved as water lilies floating on a pool. Before leaving this remarkable church, we took one last look at the exquisite carvings and paintings all contained within an ancient style of building enhanced by sacred proportion. We felt that the expression of nature here at its most abundant was the perfect environment to honour and nourish the female current.

The village of Brisco on the outskirts of Carlisle was our next destination where Elen passes through a well dedicated to St Ninian, also restored in the 19th century by Miss Losh. According to a local tradition, the 4th century saint utilised the well for baptisms during his travels to Carlisle. The name Brisco may be associated with the long-forgotten Celtic goddess of the Brigantes, known as Brighida or Brigantia, Christianised to St Bridget. We found this remote well, once an ancient sanctuary of the goddess, now cared for by locals and its clear water still flowing from the well-head.

As we headed towards the town centre of Carlisle, we followed Elen through St John the Baptist Church at Upperby, off St Ninians Road. We also noticed a St Ninians Avenue nearby, possibly an indication that a church founded by this northern saint once stood in the vicinity.

Carlisle, 'the Camelot of the North'

'In Carlisle dwelt King Arthur,
A prince of passing might,
And there maintained his Table,
Beset with many a knight.' (Child 1882–98)

Carlisle is a key historical city on the Spine of Albion with many similarities to the old southern capital of Winchester. It was the capital of the north of England during Saxon and Norman times and is the only city in England that bears a purely British name, referred to as *Caer-Luel*. Like Winchester, it has mythological origins, founded by a legendary king of the bloodline of King Brutus. Geoffrey of Monmouth, who wrote *History of the Kings of Britain* in the 12th century, stated that King Leil (1001–976 BC), son of Brutus Greenshield, ruled Britain for 25 years and founded the city of *Kaerleil*; *Caer* being Welsh for 'fortress' or 'castle'. Leil built his palace on the highest and most northerly area of the city where Carlisle Castle stands today. In addition, according to 12th and 13th century ballads and romances, Carlisle and Winchester were both courts of King Arthur and the Round Table.

Geographically, the city, which lies close to the main ancient route between England and Scotland, has the natural protection of three rivers: the Eden flowing in the north, the Caldew on its western side and the Petteril to the east. The Carvetii settled on the site of the British camp and remained there during the early stages of the Roman occupation. Carlisle grew to become a major Roman centre, which they called *Luguvallium*, meaning 'as strong as Lugus', a Celtic God also known as Lugh or Lot from which the name Lancelot derives. The Latin invaders may have named the town after this Celtic god to appease the Carvetii. The Romans transformed the settlement into a place of civic splendour, strengthening the outer walls, paving the streets and building drainage systems. A forum, marketplace, baths and tiled-roofed houses were also added. The area of the Roman city stretched from the southern part of the castle to an area now partially covered by Tullie House Museum and Gardens. On the opposite side of the River Eden, in the suburb of Stanwix, the Romans built one of the largest forts in Europe. It housed a regiment of cavalry at least a thousand strong to garrison Hadrian's Wall, which once crossed the Eden close to the site of the present castle.

Many legends as well as several British and French medieval poems and ballads maintain that the legendary King Arthur held court in Carlisle and some even refer to the city as Arthur's 'chief town'. A 12th century poet known as Marie de France, thought to be a member of the court of Henry II and his wife Eleanor of Aquitaine, mentions Carlisle as Arthur's Court in her *Lais de Lanval*, one of a collection of short poems written between 1160 and 1215. Marie de Champagne (1145–98), daughter of Eleanor of Aquitaine by her first husband Louis VII, was patron to Chrétien De Troyes, the most famous writer of Arthurian romances. Chrétien too mentions Carlisle or Carduel as Arthur's Court, and credits Marie de Champagne for supplying material for his poem *Lancelot the Knight of the Carl*, *Carl* referring to Carlisle.

Henry II, already associated with numerous places on the Belinus alignment, was ceremoniously knighted in Carlisle by his great uncle King David I of Scotland, before becoming King of England. Henry usurped the city from the Scots in 1157, making it an English stronghold once more by replacing the wooden city with stone buildings. Through his marriage to Eleanor of Aquitaine, he became well acquainted with the Arthurian romances and built his castle and Great Hall at Winchester on a site known for its association with King Arthur. Did he also build his stone castle and court at Carlisle because of its many legends relating to Arthur?

During the historical period of Arthur around the 5th and early 6th centuries, Carlisle was part of the Kingdom of Rheged ruled over by the Welsh-speaking Britons. Arthur could have utilised this stronghold as a base to defend his northern territories from the constant invasions of the Picts, Scots and Angles. According to the written romances, Sir Percival, one of the most famous of the Knights of the Round Table, set out on a quest for the Holy Grail from Arthur's Court in Carlisle. Gawain also began his quest to seek the Green Knight from the city.

Several other stories associate Arthur with Carlisle. Sir Thomas Malory mentions it as a place of Arthur's Court, where the great warrior met with a Roman delegation. Arthur imprisoned his wife Guinevere at Carlisle after her adulterous affair with Lancelot, who later rescues her and carries her off to his castle known as 'Joyous Gard', thought to be Bamburgh Castle in Northumbria. In the 14th century ballad *Sir Gawain and the Carl of Carlisle*, Arthur and his Knights set out on an adventure into the wilderness around Carlisle. Steve Matthews in *King Arthur Lives in Merrie Carlisle*, cites several 14th and 15th century poems that mention Arthur's Court in Carlisle, four of which have him hunting wild boar in the nearby Inglewood Forest.

Evidence of a real-life historical Arthur is stronger in Carlisle than at any other place in England; even the highly respected modern historian Michael Wood (2010) suggests that Carlisle was the most likely base for this legendary king. Excavations in the grounds of the castle revealed a wooden stronghold dating from the 5th century and timber structures were uncovered near the cathedral and under Blackfriars Street.

Rowling mentions that a charter from the time of Henry I (1100–35) gives documented proof that Carlisle was a military stronghold of Arthur. This document records a transfer of land stated to lie near 'Arthur's Burgh' in Carlisle; *burgh* meaning 'fortified dwelling'. This suggests that a fortification associated with Arthur existed long before 1100, which Henry II must have known of through his grandfather Henry I and from the poems of Marie de France, who attended his court on many occasions.

The same charter further mentions Arthur's Burgh in connection with a nobleman called Randulf, son of Walter, who was granted 'land which was around Arthur's Burgh in Carlisle, next to the house of the Canons'. 'The Canons' probably refers to the Augustinian monks who founded the priory church of St Mary in the city in 1122, later established as a cathedral by Henry I in 1133. Local historian John Denton of Cardew wrote in 1610 of the tradition:

> 'Waldeive, son of Gospatrick, Earl of Dunbar gave to the priory (of Carlisle) some saintly relics together with a mansion near St Cuthbert's Church where at that time stood an ancient building called Arthur's Chamber taken to be part of the mansion house of King Arthur, son of Uther Pendragon ….' (Rowling 1976)

It is also interesting to note here that Waldeive gifted to the priory an ancient building called 'Lyons Garde', also mentioned in Arthurian romances. This was possibly a Roman building at Ravenglass, a port on the west coast of Cumbria known to have existed during the time of Arthur.

With such a wealth of prose and documents associated with this legendary king, there is much confusion between a real-life historical figure and the fictional character of the medieval romances. Nevertheless, one cannot help but be persuaded that a local king named Arthur actually lived here in Carlisle during the Dark Ages. However, many have argued that Arthur was purely a title, awarded to great British warriors stretching back through the mists of time. Perhaps the people of Cumbria awarded this title to King Owain (Hewen) of Rheged, who successfully fought off the Angles and the Picts.

From written documents we can safely assume that Arthur's Burgh or mansion house stood somewhere near the 'house of the Canons' and St Cuthbert's Church, built 200 years after the supposed time of Arthur. However, Christianity sprung from roots established in the fells and estuaries of this northern region long before Arthur and the coming of St Patrick to Ireland. St Ninian, an apostle of the Picts and the mainspring of the northern Celtic church, was born by the Solway Firth in Cumbria and studied in Rome before being ordained a bishop. He returned to Cumbria in AD 397, founding a church in Carlisle. A photograph on display at Carlisle Museum shows a stone found in the area carved with a Chi-Rho. Unfortunately, like so many controversial relics, it has since disappeared.

Later, St Cuthbert visited Carlisle as Bishop of Lindisfarne, establishing one of his many monastic centres here when it was still part of the Kingdom of Northumbria. During a tour of the 'town's old walls' accompanied by Waga, the Saxon Reeve, he was shown a fountain 'wondrously constructed by the Romans and still in order'. St Cuthbert was gifted 15 acres of land by King Ecgfrith of Northumbria in AD 685 to build a religious centre here and Bede records that this was to include an abbey. It was King Ecgfrith's intention to make Carlisle his northern capital and the ecclesiastical equivalent of York, but before this could be realised he died in battle against the Picts at Nechtansmere. Legend says St Cuthbert foresaw the death of the king as he stood waiting at Carlisle for news of the battle with Ecgfrith's queen, Eormenburg.

By the mid-9th century the Danes had desecrated much of Cumbria, reducing the highly populated and prosperous Carlisle to ruins. According to early historians, the destruction was so great that it remained uninhabited for 200 years except for some 'Irish who lodged themselves among the ruins' (Carruthers 1979). Carlisle remained at the heart of numerous conflicts between England and Scotland, finally established as an Earldom of England in 1092 by William Rufus.

Our dowsing investigations began at the two great round towers called the Citadel at the old southern entrance to the city, built as part of a secondary fortress by Henry VIII. The male current passes through the western tower and a building on the corner of Blackfriars Street and Victoria Viaduct, where the Blackfriars Convent stood in 1233. He then disappears through buildings to the west of Blackfriars Street, where archaeologists discovered wooden structures dating to the time of Arthur. He then enters the precincts of the cathedral opposite St Cuthbert's Church.

A local tradition says that when William Rufus came to Carlisle in 1092, he saw the ruins of Cuthbert's Church as a heap of stones with great oaks growing out of them, which his brother Henry I completely rebuilt. During major reconstruction work in 1778, the remains of a Saxon building were uncovered amongst the footings of the Norman church. However, a local tradition says that the church's foundation may be more ancient, for the chancel possibly stands over the site of a Roman temple. Curiously, this part of the church is still the responsibility of the cathedral rather than the wardens of St Cuthbert's. I also noticed that its main body points to the northwest, a pagan orientation found in many pre-Christian temples. A holy well dedicated to St Cuthbert once existed by the main entrance but is now lost to the rigours of modern development.

Inside we find splendid stained-glass windows depicting the story of St Cuthbert, including one that shows Queen Ethelreda offering him an embroidered stole and mantle. We dowsed Belinus flowing northeast through the chancel and High Altar over the site of the supposed Roman temple.

The Great Cathedral of St Mary's

Having created a parliament in Carlisle in 1307, it was at the entrance of this once great cathedral that Edward I mounted his white horse before riding to Scotland to face Robert the Bruce in battle.

The building of the cathedral began when Walter the Norman requested permission from William Rufus to construct a church dedicated to the Blessed Virgin Mary. In 1123, when Augustinian Canons took charge of the building it was known as St Mary's Priory. Below here, excavations have produced evidence of Roman buildings and roads and an 8th century burial ground with carved Saxon crosses. Many historians believe the crosses may be remnants of a very early church dedicated to St Mary, possibly the Royal Nunnery established in the vicinity as the abode of King Ecgfrith's queen and her sister during the time of St Cuthbert. Panels unearthed during excavations show artefacts honouring both St Kentigern and St Cuthbert.

When Henry I established Carlisle as a diocese in 1133, the priory became a cathedral and Prior Athelwold became its Bishop. His actions enforced his authority over the border regions and ended the 'spiritual' control over Cumberland by the Bishop of Glasgow. During the mid-14th and 15th centuries, an extensive rebuilding

Carlisle Cathedral with its once extensive buildings from an engraving by Sir Charles Nicholson dated 1906

programme was undertaken. During the time of the Dissolution of the Monasteries, St Mary's closed and the Augustinian monks were secularised, the cathedral was then refounded and rededicated as the Holy and Undivided Trinity in 1541.

The next hundred years saw the decay of this once grand building, causing great concern to Charles I in 1639. Part of the nave had to be demolished along with several other monastic buildings close by. During the Civil War in 1652, it suffered damage to its newly constructed west end and further destruction arose when it became a prison for the Jacobites during the 1745–46 rebellion between the Highlanders led by Bonnie Prince Charlie and the English under the Duke of Cumberland.

Carlisle Cathedral

Restoration to what remained of the cathedral began in 1764 and again in 1853, but many of the original medieval features were lost. The cathedral is now only a fraction of its original size with the additional loss over time of its priory buildings including the cloisters, friary, stables and chapter house. The great walls consisting of very soft sandstone failed to stand up to the harsh northern weather and consequently much of the exterior stonework you see today is considerably later.

The Belinus current enters the cathedral from the south through the cathedral shop by the main entrance, formerly St Catherine's Chapel. Just by the entrance to this chapel, recent excavations revealed a stairwell that leads down to a well. It was still in use in 1830 when it provided water to wash the cathedral floors. Under the tower we discovered the male current forming a Node with the female current; Elen having journeyed to this spot along the east–west axis of the cathedral from the great east window. The letter 'W' in the stone floor curiously marks the crossing point. According to a knowledgeable cathedral guide, this marks a subterranean well under the floor, now dried up and filled with rubble. Similar to the well in the crypt, under the Node in Winchester cathedral, this subterranean well would have once enhanced the telluric power of the crossing point. Now defunct, it no longer provides nourishment for the serpents at the Node.

Near the spot where Elen and Belinus Node, I noticed an exquisite medieval carving on the uppermost member or capital of a pillar depicting a male and female dragon kissing. The spirits were certainly with us that day as my camera captured a large orb hovering just below these enamoured dragons.

The male current continues to the western edge of the St Wilfred Chapel and leaves the building through the Song Room in the north transept. Originally, it was the

Carving of a pair of kissing male and female dragons on a capital of a pillar in the choir of Carlisle Cathedral

Bishops' Consistory Court, which housed an altar dedicated to St Michael. Rebuilt in 1979, it became St Wilfred's Chapel named after the church at Brougham Hall, and a triptych found at Brougham is on display here.

Elen's journey begins in the city through a little park in Portland Square, St George's Reform Church in Warwick Road and a 17th century cross in Green Market, said to mark the centre of the city. Interestingly this geomantic omphalos stands on the supposed site of the legendary Roman fountain shown to St Cuthbert during his tour of the city in the 7th century. The female current then passes through the 14th century Guildhall before diverting towards the east window of the cathedral.

Inside, Elen connects with the site of another well to the northeast of the High Altar, pointed out to us by the same helpful guide. She then stays parallel with the north aisle through the choir stalls to the tower where she meets with Belinus. She exits through the nave at the western end, once the site of the old parish church of St Mary incorporated as part of the Norman priory built in 1122.

Amongst the carvings on the capitals is a wonderful example of a Green Man and the misericords in the choir show many examples of dragons and griffins, perhaps reflecting the presence of the powerful dragon energies crossing within the precinct of one of the finest Norman cathedrals ever built in England.

We follow Elen along Abbey Street north of the cathedral, crossing over the busy bypass to the western end of the castle grounds at a modern ironwork pedestrian bridge. Part of its design incorporates a bow and arrow rising high into the sky, much to the distaste of many of the locals who felt it out of keeping with its historic surroundings. However, the design symbolically reflects the archer who fires an arrow at the omphalos or the centre of our galaxy, similar to Sagittarius and the centaur, an image adorning many of the churches on our journey through the country.

Locals are still annoyed with the decision to build the busy A595 bypass called Castleway, which has decapitated the castle from the main body of the town. This careless piece of planning by the local council serves to disconnect the spiritual energy that exists between the two most historic and sacred hills in Carlisle.

Tullie House

North of the cathedral, Belinus enters the charming garden and Jacobean-styled mansion of Tullie House Museum, built in 1689 by a German family who came to England to work the gold and silver mines in Keswick. Their descendants, called the Waughs, continued to live there until 150 years ago when it became a cloth warehouse. In 1893, the house was converted into a cultural centre, having been purchased by public subscription after its threatened demolition. Much of the original building remains and it is now the city museum and art gallery. The garden provides outdoor seating for the museum café, where we relaxed with some refreshments surrounded by ancient carved stones.

The museum is a treasure house of Cumbrian history from the dawn of civilisation. The bronze and iron weapons uncovered in the area were precisely tooled and shaped using highly sophisticated methods, including sandstone moulds to produce spearheads. As we strolled around the museum, we noticed a carved sandstone figure of a king dressed in a tunic and holding a horn of plenty in one hand and a club in the other, possibly a depiction of Owain Caesario.

The most controversial stone, however, resides outside the Millennium Gallery, near the northern entrance to the museum by the underpass. Known as the 'Cursing Stone', it is a large piece of granite inscribed with a 16th century curse, said to have caused much of the city's misfortunes since its installation in 2001. Situated close to the Belinus current on its way to the castle, the stone depicts a 1,069 word-long curse against the 'reivers' or raiders, men from the Border regions of Scotland who terrorised the area 500 years ago. Surrounding it on the tiled floor are lists of surnames of the families involved in these crimes. Although it has historical context, this surely perpetuates the curse aimed at those families and the negative energy suffered in the city all those years ago.

Carlisle Castle

When William the Conqueror's son William Rufus recovered Carlisle from the Scots in 1092, he built a wooden castle over the remains of an earlier stockade and re-established the town as an important economic and religious centre, one of the greatest achievements of his 13-year reign. However, by 1135 Carlisle was back in the hands of the Scots, David I of Scotland later adding a keep in 1150. The might of the Norman forces was no match for the Scots and soon it became the northern royal court of Henry II and his Queen Eleanor of Aquitaine. Henry improved the defences and added a grand palace, gatehouse and chapel. When Edward I came to Carlisle in 1307, he installed a bath for his second wife Queen Margaret.

John of Gaunt, son of Edward III, stayed at the palace as its governor and later it was procured by Richard Duke of Gloucester, who became the notorious Richard III. In 1567, the Warden's Tower was utilised as one of the many prisons of Mary Queen of Scots, after her arrest for treason upon the orders of her cousin Elizabeth I. She came with several attendants and 'an enormous quantity of belongings'. All that remains of this tower today is a panelled stairway still with its 14th century mouldings.

The old wooden drawbridge became a stone bridge, which crosses the moat to the 12th century gatehouse with its old portcullis, now serving as the ticket office. As we walked from the gatehouse to the inner courtyard, we imagined it as the fabled 'Camelot of the North' with its giant ramparts surrounding the motte and bailey. After climbing to the top of the keep, we looked down at the grassy area known as Lady's Walk, once frequented by Mary Queen of Scots as part of her daily exercise. During that time, Mary drank from a Roman well now incorporated into the north wall of the keep.

Carlisle Castle

The castle has seen much excitement over the centuries. In 1745, the townspeople watched as Bonnie Prince Charlie marched on foot across the drawbridge ahead of 4,000 men to the sound of bagpipes to garrison the castle. They were on their way south to meet the English army of the Duke of Cumberland, only to return defeated and demoralised months later; the chair Bonnie Prince Charlie rested on is in the nearby museum. Unfortunately, the Duke of Cumberland was hot on his trail and a battle ensued in the city, leaving 300 of Bonnie Prince Charlie's men imprisoned and left to die in the cathedral.

Belinus passes through the castle keep through a room known as MacIvor's Cell, carved with intriguing Christian and pagan images, including a Sheela-na-gig. He then leaves through a well built into the north wall. Curiously, Elen visits a series of old barracks, some still in use by local regiments and others rented out to local enterprises. However, this particular area of the castle may have been a crucial sacred place of the early British tribes who settled on this site long before the Romans built their town.

The guide told us that when the new by-pass was laid between the castle and the museum, remains were found of the old Roman fort mainly around the area of the barracks and the museum.

The alignment just over 1 km east of the castle and is marked by an octagonal folly in Rickerby Park built by the 19th century banker George Head Head.

Although now a minor city, Carlisle retains an air of its former grandeur and religious importance. However, due to the various changes made by the city council, the energy matrix of the town has become disrupted, its spiritual heart severed from the castle, now the Military Museum of Cumbria. The much reduced energy of the Node of Elen and Belinus earth serpents at the blocked-up well in the cathedral also fails to provide nourishment for the area. Perhaps through bringing awareness and healing to this historic city, Carlisle will once again experience greatness and see the return of the legendary Arthur, 'the once and future king'.

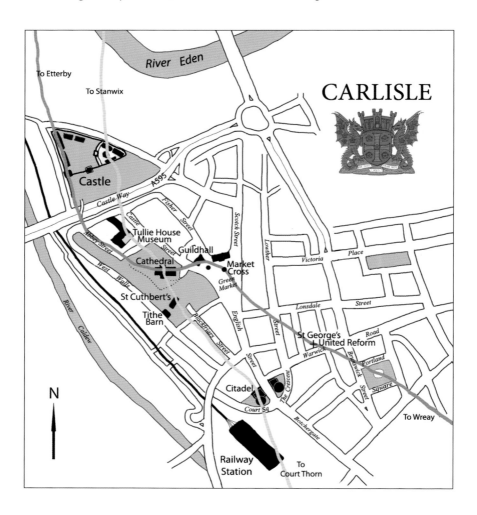

St Kentigern and the Avalon of the North

Set high on a hill across the River Eden is St Michael's Church at Stanwix, built over the site of one of the largest Roman forts in Britain called *Uxellodunum* or *Petriana*. Hadrian's Wall also passed through the town, although nothing remains of this section today. An ancient stone unearthed here in 1787, now in Carlisle Museum, dates from the time of the Roman occupation and is carved with a Roman cavalryman riding over the body of a native Briton portrayed as a naked barbarian.

According to archaeological evidence, the present Victorian church is just one of many to stand on this hill, the first built at the time of the Roman occupation. Fragments of early masonry from the various churches that once existed at this site lie scattered around the churchyard including a reproduction of a hogback tomb, similar to one found here dating back to the 11th century, carved with angels and a figure grappling with a serpent. Perhaps Norse or Danish masons, who carved this design on their tombs, drew their inspiration from the Belinus serpent, which passes through the church.

The church of St Michael and All Angels at Arthuret just south of Longtown lies 0.7 km west of the alignment near the border of Scotland. This has been a site of Christian worship since the Dark Ages on an eminence once partly surrounded by shallow water and marshland. The churchyard may have been an ancient burial ground for it has the remains of a tumulus in the southeast section.

St Michael and All Angels' Church, Arthuret

Historian Michael Wood, in his TV documentary *In Search of Arthur*, states that the legendary battle at Camlann was in fact Camboglana, the name given by the Romans to the fort known as Birdoswald just a short distance to the east of Carlisle next to Hadrian's Wall. Wood believes if Birdoswald was Arthur's last stand against rival factions of the North, then Arthuret was his final resting place. Hutchinson's *History of the County of Cumberland* claims that the name Arthuret may be a corruption of 'Arthur's Head', the name given to the land around the church, leading many to believe that Arthur's head is actually buried here. Writing in 1688, Dr Hugh Todd, the rector of Arthuret, also believed that the name Arthuret or 'Arthuridd' derives from the famous warrior. Moreover, just north of Longtown on high moorland is a place called Arthur's Seat.

Such place names, along with centuries of deeply entrenched local folklore, suggest that this hallowed ground is an 'Avalon of the North' and like Glastonbury lies on an elevated ridge above low-lying flood plains. However, Arthuret was not an island but a peninsular, flooded by the River Esk to the west and the River Lyne to the south and east.

Norma Goodrich, author of *King Arthur* (1989), also researched traditions and poems of the legendary king in the Carlisle area. Goodrich, an American scholar and etymologist, believes 'the name implies that the land at Arthuret was an important part of Arthur's own tribal territory'.

Welsh traditions and ballads refer to Ardderydd as the site of a great battle in AD 573, where Rhydderch, the Christian King of Cumbri, defeated Gwenddollau, the pagan King of the Scots. According to some authorities, the Battle of Arthuret marked the beginnings of the Kingdom of Strathclyde. In *The three frivolous causes of battle in the Isle of Britain*, Ardderydd is named as the second battle where '80,000 men were slain of the nation of Cymry' (Probert 1823). According to local legend, the mounds in Arthuret churchyard are the graves of the warriors killed in this decisive battle.

Alistair Moffat in *Arthur and the Lost Kingdoms* also refers to this great battle and mentions that Gwenddollau had a fine lineage, being a descendant of Old King Cole of the line of Brutus. Myrdin or Merlin was Gwenddollau's chief Druid and Bard, but having been driven insane by the resulting slaughter of the battle he exiled himself in the woods of Celidon, surviving on the fruits of the forest and offerings given by the locals. Merlin also feared Rhydderch, the King of Strathclyde, who 'is a lover of monks and a hater of bards'. Celidon Woods, now Ettrick Forest, was once the territory of the Selgovae, the last of the southern tribes to convert to Christianity.

However, the chosen site of the battle may be due to its more sacred associations as mentioned in the Welsh poem *Triad of the Three Horses*. Each horse carries a valuable cargo of the Isle of Britain; the second horse carries two Welsh princes 'to see the sacred fire of Gwenddollau at Ardderydd'. Welsh bards once told stories of princes travelling far to attend the 'balefire of Gwenddollau', also referred to as the 'Bull Protectors of Britain'. The prominent hill that overlooks the church called Arthuret Knowes was possibly a beacon site or a pagan sanctuary of the Druids, where the sacred fire would blaze to reanimate the land.

The first recorded church at Arthuret dates from the 6th century established by St Kentigern while on route to Glasgow where he became Bishop. A church was also on this site in 1150, when Turgis Brundis, Lord Liddle, granted Arthuret to the Northumbrian Abbot of Jedburgh Abbey. Due to its situation close to the border, the church suffered from numerous border raids by Scottish reivers and had to be rebuilt twice in the 14th century. During the installation of the organ, a vault was disturbed revealing a 14th century heart brass of a Crusader knight.

The remains of a very weathered Celtic cross lies in the churchyard dating from the 12th century, apparently placed there by the Angles who installed many throughout Cumbria. A native of the parish was a court jester from the court of King James I, buried in the churchyard on All Fools Day 1672. He was reputedly banned from the court for being disrespectful to the Bishop of Canterbury.

When King James I of England unified Scotland and England, peace finally descended upon the region. During his reign he organised a collection from 'all the churches in the realm' to pay for the cost of building a new church at Arthuret in 1609.

Belinus approaches the church from the southeast across Arthuret Knowes, which the locals say is the site of the great battle of Arthuret where the British Christians defeated the British pagans and changed the shape of a nation. From the tumulus in the southeast corner of the churchyard, Belinus enters the tower of the church. Here the current is curiously marked in the wall by a stone-carved chalice a couple of metres from the ground, as if old stonemasons were leaving us a clue to its flow and reminding us of the Grail worship here in Brigantia.

We then followed him through the graveyard along the edge of a ridge to an enclosed holy well dedicated to St Michael. This sacred place stands below the church facing the flat marshy plains of the River Esk, the scene of many battles between the English and Scots. The well dates from the 7th century and its source is thought to originate under the church. It was here that St Kentigern allegedly baptised the Christian princes after they defeated the pagan Gwenddollau. In 1609, during the building of James I's new church, stone slabs were placed here to enclose the well.

Carving of a Grail cup in the tower marking the Belinus current at St Michael and All Angels' Church, Arthuret

St Michael's Well, Arthuret Church

The monk Jocelyn of Furness Abbey wrote *The Life of St Kentigern* around 1180, taking as his source an ancient book in Ireland. He wrote that Kentigern was the son of 'the daughter of a certain king most pagan in his creed who ruled the northern parts of Britannia'. Some believe he was a Cumbrian king called Chenderin or Cynderyn, son of Owain of Rheged. Legend says that Kentigern's mother was Thenew who became pregnant by a young nobleman disapproved of by her father, which was punishable by death. She managed to escape and sailed to Culross where she gave birth. Her young son was taken in and educated by a community of monks run by St Serf. There he was nicknamed Mungo meaning 'the beloved one'.

As a young man, Kentigern left Culross and settled on the banks of the Clyde where he discovered an old cemetery dedicated to St Ninian. As a missionary, he founded many churches on the sites of earlier Christian places of worship, which had existed since the Roman occupation. In Strathclyde he built a church beside the Molendinar

Burn from which the city of Glasgow grew. Today St Kentigern is still the city's patron saint and his bones are entombed in its cathedral.

Impressed by his 'good works and the miracles attributed to him', the King of Strathclyde consecrated him as the Bishop of 'Glasghu', soon becoming Bishop of Strathclyde and Cumbria. Kentigern was expelled from Glasgow around AD 553, having fallen out with a later king who ridiculed him for his magical powers.

According to Jocelyn, he found sanctuary at Karleolum (Carlisle) where he 'converted to the Christian religion many from a strange belief, and others who were erroneous in the faith'. His dedication to the teachings of the early Celtic church ensured their survival long after the Synod at Whitby in AD 664, which decreed that all of England should conform to the Roman Catholic Christianity as preached by Augustine.

He spent several years in Wales meeting St David, its patron saint, before returning to Scotland where he later befriended St Columba. He performed many miracles throughout his life and had an encounter with Merlin, the magician from the Court of King Arthur. He has left a strong and lasting mark on Cumbria with many churches dedicated to him and we continued to connect with his sacred places through the Border regions of Scotland.

Longtown is the last town in England on both the Belinus alignment and male current. In ancient times, the town developed as a trading place close to a major ford of the River Esk. It was rebuilt in a grand style in the 18th century by Dr Robert Graham of Netherby Hall, replacing the old hovels by the river with a wide tree-lined street fronted with fine Georgian buildings. In the 1750s he drained 1000 acres of his estate to create more villages and roads in the region. However, Graham's ancestors were not so respectable, becoming one of the many notorious Scottish border-raiding families known as reivers. In 1745, Bonnie Prince Charlie and his retreating army waded across the Esk to Longtown, dancing to the sound of bagpipes as they dried themselves in the sun (Mee 1937).

This part of the alignment has absorbed much conflict over the centuries including Anglo-Saxon disputes and the repeated border raids carried out by the reivers, who stole cattle and crops from innocent farmers. It was also the site of the Battle of Solway Moss in 1542, which the Scottish King James V lost against the English. His young daughter and sole heir Mary inherited the throne when she was only six days old, becoming Mary Queen of Scots.

Beyond Longtown, the male current passes through Dr Robert Graham's old home Netherby Park to visit the earthworks of Liddel Strength. This was the stronghold of the pagan King Gwenddollau, who lost the battle of Ardderydd to Rhydderch, the Christian King of Cumbri. The current passes through the mound, another possible moot or hill of Druidic sun worship. The bailey may have been the site of the palace where Merlin attended as chief bard.

Elen's journey from Carlisle to the border of Scotland passes to the west of Stanwix, through Austin Friars St Monica's School in Etterby, a private Roman Catholic school founded by members of the Order of St Augustine in 1951. The ancient name for Etterby was *Arthuri-burqum*, or Arthur's town, and a local tradition states that King Arthur stayed here in the year AD 550 while pursuing the Danes. At one time, the Earls of Lonsdale of Lowther Castle also owned the manor of Etterby.

Further to the northwest, we arrived at the church of St Mary the Virgin on a high spur above the Eden River at the picturesque village of Rockcliffe. The village was once a thriving port next to the Solway Firth and an important centre for shipbuilding. During September, thousands of geese rest on the marshes before flying off to their winter destinations. We found Elen connecting with an ancient stone cross in the churchyard, a clear indication of the sanctity of this site. Lord Dacre, owner of Kirkoswald Castle on the Elen current, built another castle here in the 16th century, now called Old Hall. At the edge of Rockcliffe Marsh there once existed three turf-cut labyrinths all known as the 'Walls of Troy', one recorded as cut in 1815. Soon both currents cross the border into Scotland, continuing the trail of Merlin and Arthur.

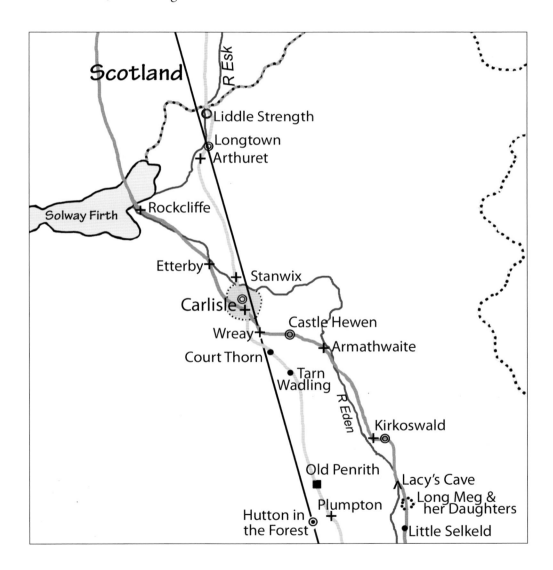

Chapter 13

The Border Lands
On the Trail of Merlin to the Firth of Forth

'The march of the intellect is gradually trampling underfoot the legends, omens and superstitions which formerly flourished in their strength amid the wild fastnesses of the land; and they are seldom talked of now but as things that have been, but never will be again.'

(John Mackay Wilson in *Tales of the Borders*)

Land of the Brave

The wild and rugged country of Scotland has an ancient past dating back thousands of years to a period when the earliest megalithic tombs and stone circles dotted the landscape. Some of the most impressive monuments include Maeshowe and the

St Mary's Loch

Stenness circles on the Orkney Islands, Callanish stone circle on the Isle of Lewis, the megalithic stone complexes at Kilmartin in Argyll, and Machrie Moor on the Isle of Arran. These early settlers were an advanced and sophisticated society derived from Indo-European stock arriving in around 8000 BC.

Much of Scotland's ancient history and oral traditions have been lost due to centuries of conflict and religious control. Yet, there was a time when the early cultures of Scotland lovingly honoured and nurtured the land, which continued despite the constant threat of invasion. In time, they would be forced to continually battle with their enemies to retain their independence and freedom from foreign invaders such as the Romans, Angles and Vikings.

Nennius, the 9th century Bishop of Bangor, wrote that when Brutus and other survivors of Troy arrived in Britain in around 1103 BC, known then as Alban or Albion, he occupied the country as far north as the River Tweed and began the task of uniting the various tribes of the Picts under his rule. According to the *Welsh Brut*, 'Ynys Pridein' (the Isle of Prydain or Britain) had three realms, Cymri, Alban and Lloegyr. Geoffrey of Monmouth in *History of the Kings of Britain* (1136) wrote that these realms were divided between the three sons of Brutus. Locrinus was given land that covered the area we know today as England, called Loegria, Albanactus ruled over Alba or Alban, now Scotland, and Kamber was given Wales, which he called Cambria. This legend was also included in the *Chronicle of the Alban Duan*, believed to have been written around 1070 to commemorate the crowning of King Malcolm

Roman historians were the first to produce a written history of Scotland, which they called Caledonia, describing it as 'wild, waterless mountains and desolate swampy plains, and possess neither walls, cities, nor tilled field, but live on their flocks, wild game and certain fruits'. Tacitus wrote that its people were 'aggressive, awkward, and difficult to subdue, many of them with red hair and large limbs', reminding him of the barbarians they fought against in the Rhine. Dio Cassius, writing in Rome without ever setting foot in Scotland, described the tribes as constantly forcing the Romans back behind Hadrian's Wall. In fact, the Romans were continually plagued by the clever guerrilla tactics of the Picts throughout their occupation of Britain, resulting in the construction of the Antonine Wall across from the Firth of Forth to the Clyde on the west coast and when that fell they built Hadrian's Wall above Carlisle.

However, far from the 'noble savages' described by the Romans, the Picts were in fact a highly civilised, cultured and literate race, their kinsmen residing in Germania and Gaul. From the moment the Romans set foot on Scottish soil, its precious land became stained with the slaughter and carnage of constant conflict.

The Romans described these tribes as variously fair-haired and tall and short and swarthy like the Iberians of southern Spain. Whatever their origins, these people, who had inhabited Scotland for centuries before the Romans invaded Britain, formed a confederation of tribes which successfully stopped any Roman attempts to completely conquer their sacred realm.

Most scholars agree that the Picts were an amalgamation of different tribes that included the indigenous peoples of Scotland. Although many of the early sources are unreliable, it seems that the descendants of the Picts occupied the northern regions, then known as Alba, long before the Celtic tribes arrived in Britain in 700 BC. Scottish historian Michael Lynch states that 'Whatever the Picts were, they are likely, as were other peoples either in post-Roman Western Europe or in contemporary Ireland, to have been an amalgam of tribes, headed by a warrior aristocracy which was by nature mobile. Their culture was the culture of the warrior' (Lynch 1992).

Pictii, the name given by the Romans to the various tribes living in Scotland, has been widely translated as 'the painted ones'. Yet McHardy, in *A New History of the Picts*, believed that the Romans used an accepted literal form of the term *Pecht* translated as 'the ancestor peoples', which was then replaced by the name *Picts* by the later Latin writers having misheard the name rather than mistranslating it. The word *Pecht* also survived in place names from earliest of times and it is very possible that the descendants of the Neolithic and Bronze Age megalithic builders in Scotland were the Pechts. Anthony Roberts in *Atlantean Traditions in Ancient Britain* (1975) believed the Picts had '*many* fairylike, magical connotations, and were long credited with strange, prophetic powers' and worshipped the alchemical 'serpent power' within the land. He stated that Pechts or Pechs in Scottish fairy lore are variously described as small beings with long red hair, long arms and large feet. He believes that the stone monuments were built by this ancient race of people using magical powers.

The Picts also had to forge an alliance with new settlers from western Scotland – the Gaelic-speaking *Scotii* of the Dal Riada kingdom having migrated from Ulster around AD 500. According to Moffat, the Western Isles were at the time already inhabited by a tribe called the *Atecottii* meaning 'the old people', who spoke a language unrecognisable to the Picts and the Gaelic-speaking immigrants from Ireland later known as the Scots.

'A true picture of one Pict' and a female Pict by John White. Illustrated in Thomas Heriot's
A Brief and True Report of the New Found Land of Virginia, dated 1588. (© Wilson Special
Collections Library, University of North Carolina Chapel Hill)

According to historian Ralph Ellis in *Scota, Egyptian Queen of the Scots* (2006) the Scots were descendants of the Egyptian Princess called Scota. Although inter-tribal raids were common between these various tribes they stood side by side to fight the Angles of Northumbria, and later the Vikings and Danes.

After several intermarriages between the Picts and their Gaelic confederates, historians tell us that they were easily absorbed into the Dal Riada kingdom by the 11th century. Cináed mac Alpín or Kenneth MacAlpin, the son of a Dal Riada king and a Pictish princess from the royal house of Fortrenn, created the first single kingdom of the Scots having proved himself against the Vikings. Considered by many as the founding father of Scotland, he compares to Alfred the Great of England. MacAlpin would later move the Celtic church from Iona to Scone, bringing St Columba's remains to the Pictish church at Dunkeld in AD 849.

MacAlpin's descendants became the Kings of Alba and by the 11th century ruled over all of Scotland. They spawned the longest living royal family in Britain which included Malcolm III of the House of Canmore, whose daughter Matilda married Henry I of England, and the Houses of Bruce and Stewart. It is uncertain when the Pictish elite converted to Christianity but there are traditions that place both St Palladius and St Ninian in Pictland before the Roman Catholic missionaries. It seems that their efforts hardly created a dent in the way the Pictish tribes lived their lives, the task falling to St Columba in the 6th century to further the Christian cause.

There is much debate about the fate of the Picts. Having written much of their history, the later Latin scholars and Gaelic Scots allowed them to fade from our memory, renaming their lands as the Kingdom of Alba. Many ignore their oral traditions, relegating them to myth and legend. However, much of their ancient heritage was lost; the Vikings reportedly throwing large quantities of manuscripts plundered from abbeys into the sea from their long ships. Hundreds more were looted by King Edward I of England in the 13th century who sought to rob Scotland of its identity. He was known as the 'Hammer of the Scots' who, according to a contemporary writer, was 'like a common thief'. Sixty-five boxes of Scottish documents were taken from Scone Abbey and Edinburgh Castle alone. Yet more was lost during the Reformation and during the later religious wars of the 17th century (Henderson 2008).

McHardy believes that such a noble warrior society as the Picts, who over the centuries successfully fought off the Romans, Angles, Vikings and Danes to retain their freedom and independence, would never have allowed their race to be completely eradicated by one single tribe. Perhaps a remnant of these people and their way of life carried on within the clansmen of the Highlands, their descendants still walking the streets of Scotland today. Until the Scottish archaeologists start concentrating their efforts on excavating more sites in the old Pictish territories rather than those of the Romans, we only have their stone monuments to rely on.

Arthurian Scotland

As we began to explore the trail of Belinus and Elen through southern Scotland we encountered more legends of King Arthur and Merlin. The very first mention of Arthur in Scotland is in the *Y Gododdin*, written as an epitaph to the tribe of the *Gododdin* who ruled the Lothians as they prepared for battle against the Angles at Catterick in AD 600. Part of it mentions their great cavalry warrior Gwawrddur, who was killed during the battle, 'though he was not Arthur ... [he was] Among the strong ones in battle'. In another poem, Gwawrddur's mount was compared to 'Arthur's horse'. Why should these warriors of southeastern Scotland mention Arthur?

Geoffrey of Monmouth sets him firmly in Wales but curiously states he was born in Caerlaverock in Scotland. Arthur was king and war leader fighting for the survival of Britain long before the country became divided into England, Scotland and Wales, so it is quite possible that Arthur travelled this far north to protect Britain from the invading Angles and Saxons from his 'Camelot in the North' in Carlisle. He is often described like Gwawrddur in the *Y Gododdin* as riding a huge war horse, courageous and formidable.

Moffat (1999) believes that Arthur's seventh battle, fought at Celidon Woods, was in the area now called Ettrick Forest to the west of Selkirk, part of the territory of the Selgovae tribe. It is possible that he fought the Picts there, the old enemy of the Gododdin. According to Philip Coppins in *Land of the Gods* (2007), Arthur married the sister of King Lot or Loth of Lodonasia, which is Latin for Lothian, at the heart of the Kingdom of the Gododdin. He argues that the twelfth battle at Badon Hill, where Arthur killed 960 men in one single charge, securing his military reputation and peace over the land, may have been at Dowden hillfort on the border of the territory of the Gododdin, the lands of his brother-in-law.

Following the male and female serpents across the borderlands of Scotland, we prepared ourselves for the vast wildness of craggy, boggy and forested terrain that awaited us. The Romans called this area the 'wild lands', where bears roamed the forests that once covered this region. A famous story tells of a bear from 'far Caledonia' captured by the Roman Governor of Britain, Agricola, and sent to Rome to appear in the Colosseum.

North of Liddel Strength motte and bailey, Belinus journeys to Halgreen across a mound between the River Esk and the Liddel Water, once the site of Canonbie Priory and home to a community of Augustinian canons from 1170 until its destruction after the Battle of Solway Moss in 1542. The mound could be the site of St Martin's Church, which once stood near the priory during the 12th century called the 'Church of Liddel'. Just over a kilometre to the northwest is the town of Canonbie named after the canons. Here Belinus passes just to the west of the United Saints Church built in 1822, preferring the older churchyard by the banks of the River Esk. North of here on the way to Langholm, his path is marked by an earthwork on a high promontory above the Esk called Gilnockie Castle. Although it is reputed to be medieval, it has the feel of a much earlier fortification with ramparts and a causewayed entrance.

Langholm

Ancient tracks dating from the time of the Neolithic and Bronze Age often follow the river valleys and where a number of them converge, the ancient tribes established a settlement for trade. Langholm, a small market town next to the alignment is one such place lying at the confluence of the River Esk, Ewes Water and Wauchope Water. From a geologist's point of view, the area is of great interest as a fault of volcanic strata and oceanic bedrock runs straight through the town, which marks the point where two great continents collided millions of years ago.

Other than its proximity to the Belinus alignment, Langholm has something in common with Birmingham and Manchester, as during medieval times it was a manufacturing town, particularly renowned for the making of tweed. We located the male current passing through the old market cross behind the Town Hall, known as the Mercat Cross. However, it is actually a sandstone pillar holding aloft a flattened spherical stone with a carved equal-armed cross on its upper surface. It once stood by the old crossroads in the middle of the town on a square stone plinth, later used as a platform for important proclamations.

This is a perfect representation of an omphalos stone formerly marking the geomantic centre of the town. For the early tribes, the pillar represented a world axis, a link between heaven and Earth. These

Mercat Cross, Langholm

pillars were the forerunners of the Christian cross, erected in towns and villages across Europe, taking the form of a pillar topped by a stone ball representing the sun and a square base fixing it to Earth.

Belinus continues through the Town Hall before crossing the road to the scant remains of a castle. Its strategic location on a flat plain next to the confluence of three river valleys was an ideal position to guard a very important fording place that linked the north of England with Scotland. Christopher Armstrong built the castle as a small garrison to police the fording place in 1526. His brother, the infamous reiver Johnny Armstrong, had leased the lands from the Maxwell family. The Earls of Buccleugh procured the castle in 1643 and it remained occupied until about 1726.

The confluence of the River Esk, Ewes Water and Wauchope Water, once the site of a castle

Although this site has no recorded history before medieval times, it may have been an important sanctuary for the ancient priests such as the Druids, possibly a ceremonial mound that drew upon the energy of the three rivers.

In 1455, the town was the site of the Battle of Arkinholm. According to W. S. Young in *A Spot Supremely Blessed: The History, Lore and Legends of Langholm*, the battle was fought between the great grandsons of Archibald Douglas, the most powerful man in Scotland save for the king. Their brothers were the exiled James, Earl of Douglas, known as 'Black Douglas', and George Douglas, Earl of Angus, also called 'Red Douglas'. The conflict broke the power of the great Douglas clan of Eskdale after which the River Esk ran red with the blood of those who fell on the 'Lang holm'. This is just one of many key battles fought along or close to the alignment throughout Britain, its telluric power amplifying the negative effects of war, remaining in the psyche of the people for years to come.

The witches of Eskdale also terrorised the region. A local clergyman was so 'forsaken of God and wretched under their evil influence' that he committed suicide. Several reputed witches burned at the stake in the 18th century near the old castle, which according to a local myth prevented Ewes Water from ever freezing over in winter because of the heat still emanating from their burned corpses. The number of men and woman burnt at the stake in Scotland accused of practising witchcraft amounted to 4500, compared to only 500 executed in England during the same period. The frenzy surrounding witchcraft was at its height during the reign of James VI (James I of England), who particularly sought those still practising the pagan arts of healing and herbal medicine. Over the centuries, ecclesiastical authorities have endeavoured to rid Scotland of its pagan Druidic practices and even as late as the 11th century, remnants of the old Pictish tribes were still worshipping the sun, moon, rocks and rivers at wooded shrines and on hilltops.

The many ghost sightings in the town are probably due to the great fault and the powerful convergence of three rivers. This potent force of chi and telluric energies allows all manner of supernatural phenomena.

The Esk Valley

Belinus guided us along the old prehistoric route through the Esk Valley to the ruined church at the remote hamlet of Staplegordon situated on the banks of the Esk River. It was described by the Hawick Archaeological Society in 1904 as 'perhaps the most historical spot in the valley of the Esk'. Like Canonbie, its history stretches back to the reign of David I (1124–40) when William de Cunigburg, Baron of Staplegordon, granted the church and lands to the monks at Kelso in 1127.

The male current still connects with the main body of the old chapel, its outline indicated by a raised area of ground and a few exposed foundation stones, continuing to a nearby motte and bailey, once the Castle of Barntalloch and feudal residence of the Barons of Staplegordon. The church and castle were eventually destroyed in a raid led by Lord Dacre, who reported to Henry VIII that he had 'burned and destroyed

Remains of Staplegordon Kirk with the motte and bailey earthworks behind

… the whole water of the Esk from Staplegordon to Canonbie'. He also stated that he had left 'no man dwelling in any of them in his daye, save only to the towers of Stepel and Walghapp [Staplegordon and Wauchope]'. In 1637, King Charles I annexed the Kirk of Staplegordon and the lands to the Bishopric of Galloway.

Belinus also connects with what appears to be a pagan cross-stone set into a wall, a remnant perhaps of an early Celtic Christian sanctuary. According to Young, St Patrick's Fountain once existed in the vicinity. Like St Patrick in Ireland, many saints Christianised pagan sites in Scotland, regarding them as 'heathen' places.

Hugging the alignment, the male current weaves its way north through Eskdalemuir Forest to the tiny hamlet of Ettrickhill, visiting the tower of its tiny church. Its history spans 800 years, the present Victorian church being the third built on this site. Standing at this beautiful hallowed spot, we looked south to admire the picturesque valley of Ettrick Water with its dense plantations of pine trees, which cover vast areas of this region.

Belinus leaves us for the more rugged terrain of Ettrick Forest, once part of the ancient Caledonian Forest. The area is largely open moorland, the forest now severely depleted due to the advent of sheep farming and industrialised forestry. Ettrick Forest was also the hunting ground of the medieval Kings of Scotland, but according to Moffat, in *Arthur and the Lost Kingdoms*, its earlier name was Celidon Woods. This ancient realm was Merlin's place of exile after the battle at Arthuret, once a stronghold of the ancient tribe of the Selgovae. Moffat believes King Arthur fought his seventh battle here, defending the later tribe of the Gododdin against their old enemy, the southern Picts. The Scottish hero Sir William Wallace set up his base in the forest, from where he led a revolt against the oppressive rule of Edward I of England in 1296.

Vivien and Merlin Repose. Illustration by Gustav Dore for Tennyson's Idylls of the King (1868)

So far it appears that the trail of the male current was following the route taken by the Arthurian wizard Merlin from Carlisle to this forest in the southern lowlands of Scotland.

After negotiating the roads across bleak moorland, we arrived at the largest natural body of water in the Borders. The picturesque St Mary's Loch is the only notable feature to mark the alignment in this vast wilderness. After refreshments at the Glen Cafe, we headed further north along its shores until our dowsing rods abruptly pointed east at a junction about a kilometre up the road.

We followed a narrow lane beside Megget Water until we spotted a mysterious mound, which according to the map was the site of a ruin called Chapel Knowe. The information board states that a chapel once stood on this tranquil knoll, which by 1603 was described as 'altogether down and equal with the Earth'.

This strange description may refer to a chapel constructed over a sunken depression on top of the mound, perhaps to immerse the congregation with its telluric force. There is no sign of a depression or a chapel today, only a grave slab within metal railings, later erected on the Knowe in 1841. I dowsed the male current flowing through the mound, but as we continued to explore the site further, we sensed the energy of Belinus was out of balance, the atmosphere feeling strange and unsettling. To clear the negative energy, we carried out a brief meditation visualising the mound and the male serpent bathed in light. Instantly, the site felt clearer and healthier, the dragon energy of Belinus radiating his true power once more and in response widening his flow. He then led us to the remains of a castle behind Chapel Knowe variously called Henderland or Cockburn's Castle.

Further along the road skirting St Mary's Loch we noticed a graveyard on the side of a hill and after consulting our map we realised the alignment passes very close to it. A chapel stood here long ago dedicated to St Mary, mentioned in many legends and ballads and from which the loch takes its name. All you see today is a pile of rubble, but open-air or 'blanket' preaching still goes on in the graveyard during the summer months.

Leaving Belinus to wander north over the hills and glens towards the historic town of Peebles, we returned south to the River Esk to trace the flow of Elen as she crosses into the borders of Scotland from Rockcliffe.

The first Scottish site of interest visited by the female current is a tiny church at Cadgill near Chapelknowe. A few miles further north she ascends St Bride's Hill where once stood St Bride's Chapel, considered the most ancient in the whole of Eskdale. Bride is the Celtic British mother goddess identical with Brigantia of the northern Britons. Her origins date back to the end of the Bronze Age and possibly earlier. Hundreds of 'Bride' place names exist throughout northern Britain that date back to unknown periods in history. The Bridestones monument, visited earlier on the borders of Staffordshire and Cheshire, is one such example. In Ireland, she became St Bridget and early Irish missionaries visiting Britain named churches after her. St Bride is also associated with the worship of the northern constellation of Cygnus and the swan goddess. Although lost to us today, a large stone on top of the hill, known as the 'church stone', is a remnant of this early chapel. Despite its desolate position, Elen still breathes life into this once sacred sanctuary of the British goddess.

As the current meanders northward through the border areas of Scotland, we encounter a wondrous landscape of dense forest and high crags. She soon descends to the River Esk and the village of Bentpath, which in ancient times was highly populated. On the river's northern bank, we find Elen at Westerkirk Parish Church, built in 1880 over an earlier chapel, now by the entrance of a private house.

Here we had another chance to marvel over the magical and tranquil landscape of Eskdale, leaving us with a sense that little has changed here for many centuries. Like Belinus, much of Elen's flow through these parts crosses wild and inaccessible terrain. From Bentpath she follows the Esk northwest, before negotiating the pine plantations of Castle O'er Forest. We took the road to Eskdalemuir, known as the most ancient route along the river valley of the White Esk surrounded by hillforts.

Lulled by the stunning scenery, the sudden movement of our dowsing rods diverted our attention towards a field on the right, indicating that Elen had crossed the road. Stopping the car and peering over the hedge, we could see a megalithic stone circle nestling beside the river called the Girdle Stanes. It once consisted of about forty stones but only half of the circle remains, washed away over the centuries by the expanding riverbed. In the *Stone Circles of the British Isles*, the author Aubrey Burl describes the Girdle Stanes as being 'tree ringed and standing in an inconspicuous hollow, its grassy outer bank showing clearly in the north. Some of the stones can still be seen in the river. Opposite there seems to be an eastern entrance of double portal stones'. He suggested that rather than being a site for astronomical purposes, as some surveys have claimed, this stone circle served to worship the spirits of the river.

The Girdle Stanes, Esk Valley

Just over a hundred yards further along the banks of the White Esk, I dowsed Elen visiting another larger stone circle called the Loupin Stanes, with two great entrance stones. This circle of twelve megaliths, shaped as an oval, is set on an artificial platform rising towards the southwest, where we find remains of yet another circle.

The Loupin Stanes, Esk Valley

Elen connects with both the Girdle and Loupin Stanes circles, passing through what I believe was the course of a stone avenue that linked them. As Elen approaches the larger circle, her width narrows as she slips through two portal stones that form the entrance, crossing with another line of energy at its centre. As we left this hallowed place, we gazed at the feminine-shaped hills either side of the fast-flowing river, the perfect realm for the female dragon.

Just a little north of here, we arrive at the Kagyu Samye Ling Tibetan Monastery. This Eastern temple streaming with multicoloured flags seems out of place in this wild landscape. However, Elen was attracted to its delightful gardens, artificial lake and a stone feature, and no doubt lured by the highly spiritual Buddhist form of worship encouraged and taught here. Founded in 1967, this was the first Tibetan Buddhist centre established in the West. It is a centre for wisdom and learning within the Karma Kagyu tradition of Tibetan Buddhism and is open to people of all religions and creeds. The temple, built in classic Tibetan style welcomes people to attend for just a day or to join their longer retreats available throughout the year.

Kagyu Samye Ling Tibetan Buddhist Centre, Eskdale

Further north Elen passes through the remains of a circular earthwork in an area called Fingland. The name derives from the Nordic *Fing*, an indication of Viking occupation of these lands in the 9th century and a possible tribal meeting place similar to the moot hills of the Celts and Druids.

At Tailburn Bridge, on the A701 between Moffat and Selkirk, Elen leads us to a well-known tourist beauty spot called the Grey Mare's Tail. The 'Tail' refers to the 60 m (200 ft) waterfall, one of the highest cascades in Britain flowing into Tail Burn and Moffat Water from nearby

Grey Mare's Tail waterfall, Tailburn Bridge

Loch Skeen. A mound above the car park is an ancient earthwork called the Giant's Grave, said to be the remains of a defensive hillfort built about 2000 years ago, before centuries of flash floods eroded its banks. Excavations in 1792 and 1987 have shown that it consisted of an outer north ditch 5 m (16 ft) wide and 2 m (6 ft 5 in) deep.

We certainly felt the powerful chi of this beautiful place as we followed Elen along the rim of the Giant's Grave to the waterfall, enjoying the spectacular southern views of Bell Craig and Bodesbeck Law. Elen too appears to enjoy this stunning landscape, her width expanding to over 3 m as she heads up to Loch Skeen and Hogg's Well. To the north is the towering hill of Bran's Law, the name Bran being a possible reference to the last Archdruid in Britain. Many early Welsh kings were called Bran to emulate their solar god.

Merlindale

As Elen crosses rugged moorland and bog, she looks down upon the fast-flowing Tweed River before descending the steep slopes of Drumelzier Law to arrive at the village of Drumelzier. This remote area, with place names more akin to the Welsh Cymric language, is locally known as the 'The Old North'. Dr Gunn in *The Book of Stobo* believed a Welsh tribe called the *Cadeni* inhabited this particular area, part of the territory of an Iron Age British tribe known as the *Damnonii* and the Gododdin during the time of the Romans. From AD 800–1100 it remained in British hands as a region of the Kingdom of Strathclyde.

Local legends here recall the tale of Merlin, the last of the royal Druidic bards, who fled into these parts after the Battle of Arthuret. We found the female current flowing along the east–west axis of Drumelzier Kirk, supposedly founded by St Cuthbert or one of his disciples. Its origins are a mystery but parts of the present building seem centuries older than its Post-Reformation structure.

According to the church guide, Drumelzier is a Cymric name, meaning 'the dun of Myrddin' or 'Merlin's fort'. Deike Rich and Ean Begg, who wrote *On the Trail of Merlin*, suggest *Dunmeller* as one of its earlier names, meaning 'hill of Merlin'. Of interest is a house in the village aptly named Merlindale. To the east of here are the remains of the 16th century Tinnis Castle, a crumbling ruin built within an Iron Age fortress, perhaps the site of the *Dun of Myrddin*.

Just below the Kirk by the river, marked on the map as Burnfoot Pool, is the spot where in 1807 the famous poet Sir Walter Scott recalled the 12th century rhyme by Thomas the Rhymer:

'When Tweed and Pausyl meet at Merlin's grave
Scotland and England shall one monarch have.'(Moffat 1999)

The prophesy seems to have come true, for on the 25 July 1603, the day James VI of Scotland was crowned James I of England, a terrible flood changed the course of the Powsail Burn causing it to join the Tweed at the supposed spot of Merlin's grave. Moffat reminds us that during the last century, the Powsail diverted into the Tweed 500 yards further southeast of its original position.

The River Powsail or Pausel is the old name for Drumelzier Burn and where it now meets the Tweed there is said to be an old thorn tree that locals point out as Merlin's grave. According to legend, as Merlin lay entranced under the thorn tree the spiders gathered from all sides and bound him in their threads, making him only visible to the fairy realm. The tree became famous as 'Merlin's Thorn', an oracle place where his spirit could be invoked to receive his wisdom and prophesies; the present thorn may even be a descendant of this original tree.

Jocelyn, a 13th century monk who wrote *The Life of St Kentigern*, likens Merlin to the Scottish prophet *Lailoken* and recalls his place of passing near the River Tweed. After killing many men in battle, a voice from Heaven condemned Lailoken to wander the woods until his death. He also prophesied his own demise, stating where it would occur and how his three-fold death would befall him. The very same day, he was caught and stoned by local shepherds before being impaled upside down on stakes left by fishermen, having fallen over a ridge into a river, and eventually drowned when the tide unexpectedly rose.

Further north along the banks of the Tweed there is a standing stone on the edge of fields. The 2 m (6 ft) tall megalith stands near the original meeting place of the Rivers Powsail and Tweed before flooding changed its course. Was this standing stone the real grave of Lailoken or Merlin? Having found no trace of Elen at either the standing stone or the supposed site of Merlin's grave, perhaps her flow through the kirk is indicating the real site of Merlin's grave. Drumelzier Kirk, perched on a high plateau, is safe from the sudden floodings of the Tweed, unlike the banks immediately below the church, which have endured centuries of erosion. Therefore, the only suitable site for a grave, which befits such an important figure as a prophet of the Strathclyde Britons, would have been the site of the church.

Drumelzier Kirk, the possible site of Merlin's grave

At the side of the road, a little further along the valley near Altarstone Farm, the current passes through a large boulder with a flattened top half hidden in the undergrowth. A local poem quoted by Dr Gunn (1907) refers to this peculiar stone:

'Hard by this monolithic altar stone
Merlin the sage met saintly Kentigern,
And communed. 'neath the Druid oaks of Caledon,
The mysteries of the New Faith come to learn,
Bard of the golden torques of Vortigern,
From the tangled scrub emerged Lailoken,
Burst through the golden gorse and russet fern,
Stretched forth to take the Holy Symbol broken,
Paused at the Apostles warning spoken,
"If thou the Christian Creed can full believe,
Who then am I to keep the Holy Token?
From off this altar thou thyself receive,"
Twas thus the old faith's heathen bard, from Cymric lands,
With Kentigern, who met Columba, here joined hands.'

The story describes the day when St Kentigern was surprised in his solitude by an apparition of a wild and naked savage, who commanded to speak to him. He said that his name was Lailoken, a bard also known as Merlin in the British court of King Vortigern who had converted to Christianity after a great battle. Now a homeless wanderer 'living amongst the beast of the fields', he believed himself a grievous sinner seeking repentance after causing the terrible slaughter of so many men at the Battle of Arthuret. After hearing his confession, St Kentigern received from him the Holy

Sacrament and baptised the bard on the altarstone. Later that same day Merlin suffered his deadly fate.

To the northwest of Drumelzier is the church of Stobo dedicated to St Mungo, also known as St Kentigern, which Dr Gunn believes was founded over a hermit's cell built during the time of this saint. It was here that Merlin was allegedly baptised, as depicted in the stained-glass window in the north aisle.

Elen passes through this part of the church, reconstructed in 1928

Piece of the altarstone, near Altarstone Farm. (Taken from The Book of Stobo Church by Dr Gunn dated 1907)

from the body of the earlier 15th century mortuary chapel, thought to be the original site of St Mungo's or St Kentigern's Cell. Stobo is derived from an Anglian word meaning 'a holy place', which according to Moffat suggests that the story of Merlin and St Kentigern was very much alive during the Angles' occupation of this area in the 8th century.

Interior of the north aisle, Stobo Kirk.

The reconstruction of St Mungo's Cell is identical to others found in Scotland built by the mystical sect of the early Celtic Christians. Here, Elen also connects with a fragment of the original altarstone found at the side of the road near Altarstone Farm visited earlier. Set into the exterior wall of the reconstructed cell is a megalithic standing stone, perhaps part of a pagan sanctuary that once existed here and preserved by the early Christians.

In the aisle are stone slabs, one carved with an effigy of a knight and another with Celtic writing.

The churchyard contains early stonemasons' graves, one carved with a rather curious figure of a man wearing a strange headdress holding what appears to be a rifle. Unusually this church is orientated north–south which suggests that Kentigern's Cell, like St Chad's Cave near Salt in Staffordshire, was facing towards the northern horizon.

Similar to Ninekirks in Cumbria, the Culdees established their religious settlements on or near places where the feminine serpent power is at its most potent, further enhanced by their proximity to rivers. Stobo next to the Tweed is no exception, where in the absence of a cave, the monks built beehive-like structures in order to directly commune with the Earth.

Window showing Merlin with St Kentigern, Stobo Kirk

The Culdees in Britain

Many early writers held the notion that a form of pure Christianity free from Roman corruptions survived in isolation in the western confines of Britain. Scottish poet Thomas Campbell enshrined this view in *Reullura* (1824):

'Peace to their Shades. The pure Culdees
Were Albyn's earliest priests of God.
Ere yet an island of her seas
By foot of Saxon monk was trod.'

Isabel Hill Elder, having endeavoured to unravel legend, tradition and early writings, has revealed that churches flourished in Scotland as early as the 3rd century. They were established by a religious order known as the Culdees, their name derived from the original word *Culdich* meaning 'distant strangers'. Old church records describe them as *Cele Dei* or *Keledei*, meaning 'children of God'. During the Roman persecution of the Christians, they were forced to flee the Holy Land by sea, taking the old established trade routes to Europe and Britain.

Often referred to as the *Pythagorean Essenes*, the Culdees were inspired by Gnosticism, a form of Christianity linked with the Petrine Church of Rome known as Coptic. The Druids, having foreseen the coming of a future saviour called *Hesus*, instantly embraced the Gnostic faith brought by the Culdees. This priestly order successfully merged these teachings with Druid lore, corresponding to the original structure of the Celtic Church, Glastonbury having become its most important centre.

By AD 156, the Culdees established themselves as the natural successors to Druidism, and many of the peace loving Druids, already highly educated in the ancient classics, soon became Culdee priests. Similar to the Celts, the Culdees believed in the divinity of nature, often dedicating their church to the Trinity, their prayers offered to the third element, the dove or Holy Spirit. They honoured the existence of the Supreme Being, the creator of all things, and believed in the evolution of the soul and life after death.

Monastic communities adopted the special places of the Druids to 'ground' the new Christian message of love and compassion. They built circular huts and temples to imitate stone circles and Druid groves, paying heed to the wider cosmic significance of the number twelve, their settlements consisting of twelve monks modelled on the twelve original disciples. The planting of herb gardens next to healing springs provided remedies to heal the sick. Marriage and private ownership of land were part of their equalitarian doctrine in direct opposition to the later 6th century religious settlements founded by the Roman missionaries who preferred communal ownership of land, celibacy and larger monastic buildings.

Sharing the same beliefs and way of life of the Celtic tribes, they were able to settle amongst them peaceably. Many towards the end of their lives lived in caves or beehive cells of stone, surviving on meagre rations to help induce visions and maintain balance and harmony in their lives.

According to Barry Dunford in *Vision of Albion, the Key to the Holy Grail* (2008), descendants of these Judean apostles, called by the 9th century monk Alcuin as 'the Children of Egypt', intermarried with the royal families of Scotland. Their offspring eventually became the so-called Grail Line, including the Stewarts and Sinclairs (St

Clair), whose bloodline is rumoured to be directly related to that of Jesus. Jackie Queally, who wrote *The Culdees, An Ancient Religious Enigma in Scotland*, also states that the Stewarts considered themselves 'custodians of the land' and often built their chapels or strongholds on energetic places held originally by the Culdee church. One such site is St Mary's Church at Grandtully, built next to ancient stones.

The Order of the Knights Templar, to which the St Clair family belonged, continued the work of the Culdees after both the Danes and the Normans destroyed their churches. The Scottish Templars had their headquarters at Balantrodoch, known today as Temple, not far from Rosslyn Chapel.

After fleeing from France in the 14th century, the Templars came to Scotland bringing with them the Cistercian order of monks. They acquired lands to build their churches and monasteries over old Culdee sites, adopting their way of life. In Scotland they were free from persecution by the papal church and continued to exist in one form or another up until the Reformation of the Scottish Church in the mid-16th century.

Cademuir Hill and Arthur's Battle

Just to the southwest of the town of Peebles, the alignment passes through the tiny hamlet of Cademuir, at the foot of Cademuir Hill. Nearby, Elen led us to the 17th century Kirkton Manor Church. This hidden sanctuary stands amongst old Scots pine trees at the head of the beautiful river valley known as Manor Water. An earlier church, recorded here before 1656, was dedicated to Gordianus or Gordian, an obscure Roman saint of the 2nd or 3rd century AD.

About a kilometre northwest of the church, Elen visits a large standing stone set into the dry-stone wall next to a field near Bellanrigg Farm. Its size is impressive and faint traces of cup marks are just visible on its surface. Later research informed us that the 2 m (6 ft 6 in) high megalith known as the Dwarf's Stone was moved here from a position near the meeting of the Tweed and Manor Water, by a wood called *Arter Brae*. A local tale of a Black Dwarf living near Kirkton Manor recalls him carrying the standing stone from Peebles for a wager, but, having grown tired, he dropped it halfway to his home. Other legends say it was the stone taken out of the boot of a giant passing through the area or an old woman turned to stone by the devil. The sheer number of legends associated with this solitary stone may indicate that its presence marks an earlier pagan sanctuary. Likewise, Bellanrigg, the name of the nearby farm right at the foot of Cademuir

The Dwarf's Stone near Bellanrigg Farm

Hill, possibly alludes to its summit being the site of solar worship to the ancient sun god Bel.

We were delighted to find bed and breakfast accommodation next to the alignment at nearby Lyne Farm, where it passes just 30 m east of the house through a curious cross-shaped plantation above the site of a Roman encampment. The camp stands high above Meldon Bridge, built over an ancient fording place. About a kilometre north of here the alignment caresses the western slopes of Black Meldon, supplanted by a cairn and an Iron Age hillfort.

The view from our bedroom window looked across to Kirkton Manor Church and Cademuir Hill, a prominent dome-shaped eminence, comparable to Middle Knoll, which stands high above soft rolling hills and fertile plains. As we both stared across the fields of the river valley, we sensed a magical landscape awaiting our discovery and that Cademuir had a secret to share. Indigenous peoples all over the world consider rounded feminine-shaped hills such as Cademuir as sacred, perhaps because their shape attracts orgone or cosmic energy from the upper atmosphere.

Perhaps this hill on the Spine of Albion represented to the ancient inhabitants of this region a 'middle hill', or axis mundi. The remains of four pre-Roman camps on its summit highlight its sacred importance, one with a dry-stone wall 'five yards' deep. Cademuir, anciently called *Cadhmore*, signifies in Gaelic 'the great fight'. According to local history, long ago a battle took place here so significant that nearly 200 monumental stones stood on the hill to commemorate the historic event. Over the centuries, due to the removal of the stones for building material, the memory of this great battle has faded from the nation's memory.

A Neolithic dolman called 'Arthur's Oven' also located on the hill suffered the same fate, its stones removed by the father of the Scottish poet Sir Walter Scott. The name Arthur's Oven may relate to local folklore, which we found in several fascinating books in Peebles Library, stating that Cademuir Hill was the location of King Arthur's seventh battle. Nennius, the 9th century Welsh chronicler of British history, mentions this battle as taking place at *Coit Celidon* or Celidon Forest, which modern researchers believe to be Ettrick Forest, just south of Peebles.

I suggest that the exact location of the battle was at the tiny hamlet of Cademuir,

Cademuir Hill, near Peebles

from which the hill takes its name, located at the foot of the hill to the southwest on the alignment. Not far from here is the wood named Artur Brae or Arthur's Brow, *Brae* being a lowland word for 'brow' or 'slope of a hill'. Perhaps the Dwarf's Stone that once stood near the woods commemorated Arthur's victory.

We were surprised at just how many places Arthur is immortalised around the border area of Scotland and Cumbria, including 'Arthur's Mansion' in Carlisle and 'Arthur's Seat' in Edinburgh. Moreover, this was a region known as 'The Old North', held in Celtic times by the Welsh-speaking Britons; therefore are we encountering in the North a merging of the three Arthurs – the warrior, the Grail seeker and the hero of the Celts? In 1120, the French Chronicler Lambert de St Omer refers to 'a palace of Arthur the soldier, in Britain, in the land of the Picts, built with various and wondrous art, in which the deeds of all his acts and wars are seen to be sculpted' (Moffat 1999). We can only guess where this palace may have stood, having been lost to myth and legend long ago.

Neidpath Castle, Peebles and the Sacred Cross

The following day, as we drove along the idyllic Tweed Valley towards Peebles, we noticed the tall and ancient walls of Neidpath Castle and decided to pay it a visit, having the sense that Elen might be nearby. Although there was no sign of her current inside the castle, she appeared to be immortalised in a poem called 'The Maid of Neidpath' which we spotted framed on the wall. The poem refers to a legend of a young woman called Elen, left bereft after her father sent her lover away to war, believing him unsuitable for his daughter. Seeing his precious Elen dying of grief, the father recalled the suitor in the hope of saving her. Sadly, when he encountered her deteriorating state of health he realised that she was no longer the girl he knew and loved.

Neidpath Castle, near Peebles

The castle is set high on a bank overlooking the Tweed, which up until 1810 was renowned for its exquisitely terraced gardens. Below, we dowsed Elen meandering along the banks of the river attracted no doubt by the romantic grounds of the castle. Perhaps the legend is an allegory for a bygone age when the Celtic peoples of this area worshipped the goddess of the land here.

Both currents cross the Tweed to enter the town of Peebles, Belinus from the eastern slopes of Cademuir Hill and Elen from the west. Before exploring the historic town of Peebles, we decided to wander down to the river below the castle to find a quiet spot to meditate and connect with the spirit guardian of the area. Immediately I could see in my mind's eye a ruined church with a surrounding wall and railings set amongst modern houses, which I felt was highly significant to our quest.

At the western outskirts of the town, Elen passes through a large cemetery with a church tower and ruined nave dedicated to St Andrew. Here she takes an east–west course mimicking the axis of the old nave. Local history informed us that this 12th century church stands over the site of an earlier religious shrine built by St Kentigern or St Mungo. A well in the town is also dedicated to him.

Although Robert the Bruce granted Peebles the right to hold a market in the early 14th century, it was already a royal burgh at the time of David I (1124–53), one of the oldest in Scotland. Some believe its name derives from the Cumbrian or early Welsh word *Pebyl* meaning 'a place where tents were pitched'. The old market town today has great character with a pleasing high street of traditional buildings filled with delightful craft shops, restaurants and cafes.

After following Elen through a maze of residential streets, we suddenly came to a ruined church on a high point north of the high street, surrounded by a wall with metal railings, exactly as I had envisioned in the meditation by the river in the grounds of Neidpath Castle.

Cross Kirk was once a Trinitarian priory built in the late 1100s. The Trinitarians, also called the Redfriars, were an order founded towards the end of the 12th century at Cerfroy in France. Their original aim was to obtain the release of Christians captured by the Saracens during the Crusades and provide sanctuary for them, but they continued to exist long after this need had passed. There were once seven Trinitarian houses in Scotland but only the remains of this church and another at Dunbar exist today. The information board provided us with an illustration of the monks dressed very similar to the Knights Templar and carrying a banner of a Maltese cross.

However, further investigation provided us with another more fascinating version of the church's origins. According to local sources, King Alexander III (1249–1286) founded a priory here in 1261 after witnessing the discovery of an ancient holy rood or cross and an engraved stone. At the same time, a stone urn was uncovered a few metres away containing the ashes and bones of a human body. John of Fordun, a 14th century historian who wrote *Chronicles of the Scottish Nation*, stated that the cross, which became associated with miracles, was hidden by 'the faithful' about the year AD 296. The urn was thought to contain relics of St Nicholas, Bishop of Myrna, for engraved on the stone were the words 'The place of St Nicholas, the bishop'. St Nicholas lived around the early 300s in Turkey and was revered in Europe as a patron saint of sailors as well as connected with the myth of Santa Claus. Britain became a beacon for Christian missionaries from Eastern Europe during the Roman occupation so this story may well be true.

In 1474, the priory's status grew to that of a monastery with the building of a bell tower. After the Reformation of 1560, it became Peeble's parish church, replacing St Andrews, destroyed by the English in 1548. Cross Kirk became a ruin after its abandonment in 1784, itself replaced by a new church constructed on the High Street, now called the Old Parish Church. The old priory has some unusual features, the masons having defied convention by constructing domestic buildings to the north in the shadow of the church. Unusually, the simple rectangular building also lacks a division between the nave and choir.

Elen presented herself strongly, weaving her way through the ruins in an east–west direction, connecting with a large uncut megalith set into the ground at the threshold of the northwest entrance. Having entered the site from the southeast, the energy of Belinus, however, seemed surprisingly faint and out of balance. He forms a Node with Elen inside a small sealed chapel attached to the north wall of the ruin, similar in style to the Culdee shrine at Stobo.

Dowsing the signature of the Node on the grass beside the chapel, a distorted and irregular six-pointed star presented itself, which I felt reflected the out of balance nature of Belinus. The region has been subject to many battles and inter-tribal conflicts between power-mongering lairds over the centuries. Such activities are commonplace on the Spine of Albion, especially where there is an important Node of the male and female serpents. Their magnetic field is able to retain the memory of an emotional or violent event creating a negative charge within their flow, which can if left unchecked affect everything on their path over considerable distances for generations.

For some reason, Belinus has recovered less well from these dramatic events than Elen, no doubt her flow benefiting from the nourishing chi of the Tweed River, which she stays close to all the way from Drumelzier. However, as we discovered earlier, certain sites on the Belinus current succumbed to wanton destruction and desecration, such as at the mound at Chapel Knowe just south of here, causing his flow to become almost untraceable.

Ruins of Cross Kirk, Peebles

My dowsing also indicated that a large stone circle once stood on this site, perhaps destroyed by the Christian missionaries during their conversion of the area in the 7th century. The holy rood discovered by Alexander III was possibly an attempt to Christianise the pagan site, to diminish its power and exorcise the old cult of the goddess. I further dowsed that the existing boundary walls of the church mark the edge of the circle and the threshold stone over which Elen flows was an outlier, with many of the megaliths possibly broken up to build the priory. I also noticed that before the construction of the surrounding houses a clear view of the setting sun at the summer solstice would have been seen rising over a hill called White Meldon, which has a cairn and the remains of a hillfort on its summit.

A pagan ceremony survived in Peebles until medieval times to celebrate the Celtic festival of Beltane called 'Peebles to the Play'. Although a Christian festival of 'Finding the Cross' superseded this ancient practice, it continued to be held on the same day, the first Monday of May, which culminated in the crowning of the Beltane Queen. There was also a festival in August called 'The Elevation of the Cross' or *Rood-mass*. On these occasions, miracles were common, attracting pilgrims from all parts of Scotland and northern England.

From the south, Belinus enters Peebles from the eastern slopes of Cademuir Hill through Gallow Hill, now a housing estate, the name referring to a gibbet site, a place of execution. He then crosses the Tweed to the present 18th century parish church at the eastern end of the High Street, built with an extremely tall tower, before ascending Castle Hill to the ruins of Cross Kirk.

The parish church resides over the site of a medieval royal castle, possibly destroyed during the 13th century Wars of Independence. It stood on a motte or mound, which once sat on the neck of a promontory overlooking the confluence of Eddleston Water and the Tweed; perhaps the desecration of the mound during the building of the motte also affected the flow of Belinus. From Cross Kirk, the male serpent continues northwest to the remains of the fort on White Meldon. Elen meanwhile heads northeast to another hillfort on Milkieston Hill.

Before we left this ancient sacred shrine, we visualised pure light flooding through the energy currents and the Node to help this site realign and restore it to its natural balance.

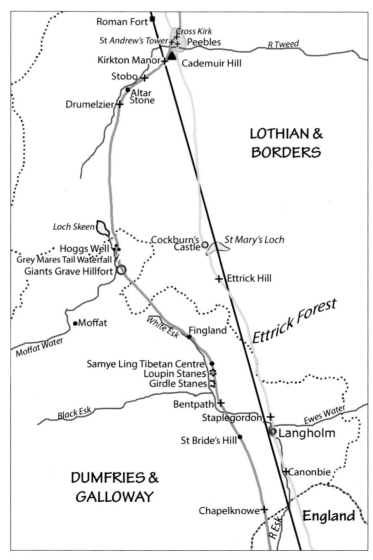

The Pentland Hills

Southwest of Penicuik overlooking the North Esk River is the 'Gowk' Stone, also known as the Auchencorth Stone just east of Auchencorth Farm, a large sandstone monolith over 2 m (6 ft 6 in) high. The name has been applied to many other standing stones and glacial erratic boulders in Scotland and means 'place of the fold', perhaps referring to a lost stone circle. The stone has distinct vertical fluting due to weathering, with some fragmentary lettering in Latin still visible.

Just to the north of there, situated on the edge of a deep ravine, are the ruins of Brunstane Castle built in 1568, the old seat of the Crichtons. Around the beginning of the last century, a deep *fosse* or ditch surrounded it creating a very effective place of defence.

The stone and castle mark the path of Elen to Glencorse Reservoir, the site of the medieval religious and administrative centre of the Pentlands. It included a chapel dedicated to St Catherine in the Hope, located just where the Kirk Burn flows into the reservoir, now a pile of stones lying on the bottom. The original name for this area was Glencross, said to derive from an ancient cross standing within the burial grounds of the old church.

Sir Henry de Brade first bestowed a chapel there upon the monks of Holyrood Abbey in 1230. In 1314, Sir William St Clair evidently acquired the land having won a wager with Robert the Bruce. The wager required two hounds to bring down a renowned white deer before it got to a particular burn or stream. At a critical moment in the chase, Sir William invoked the spirit of St Catherine, which ensured the dogs succeeded in their mission. In gratitude, he built a chapel at the very spot of invocation. Although there is no truth to the tale, it may be associated with a geomythic memory alluding to the sovereign taking charge over the land through the subjugation of the feminine serpent, represented by the white deer. Just to the north is an area called Knightfield and to the east is the hillfort known as Castle Law with a souterrain or underground chamber.

The Pentland Hills are at the heart of the territory once ruled by the Celtic tribe of the Selgovae, who built their hillfort next to an already existing souterrain from a much earlier culture. About 9 km (6 miles) to the east of here is Rosslyn Chapel built by Sir William St Clair in 1446, made famous by Dan Brown's novel *The Da Vinci Code*.

Meanwhile, we find the male current further to the southwest at an old stone bridge in the small hamlet of Romanobridge before heading to St Andrew's Church in the ancient village of West Linton. A charter mentions a church on this site in 1160, under the auspices of the Abbot of Kelso Abbey, a date also confirmed by an inscription on the gate. The early name for this parish was Linton Roderick, the latter part of the name deriving from Rhydderch Hael, the Christian King of Strathclyde who defeated Gwenddollau in the 6th century and who was the patron of St Mungo. It is possible that Mungo arrived here at the invitation of the king to set up a religious community. Several roads radiate out from the village and a Roman road passes just to the west, implying that this ancient fording place of Lyne Water was seen as strategic by the early cultures.

Inside the church we found an early stone font, which predates the church's medieval foundations; its shattered remains were pieced together after its recovery from the riverbed in 1929. We also trace him at Cross Well in the main street, later restored and surmounted by a clock tower. Also incorporated into it is a replica of a sculpture of Lady Gifford by her husband James, the local laird.

The current continues north over the Pentland Hills visiting Bavelaw Castle on its northern slopes, once a 13th century hunting lodge held by Henry de Brade, Knight and Sheriff of Edinburgh. Among its noble guests were Mary Queen of Scots and her son James VI. Just to the north, another church associated with St Kentigern or Mungo marks his flow at Balerno. Kentigern, reputedly the son of the infamous Owain of Rheged, is another saintly companion to escort us along the dragon paths of the Spine of Albion, this time through the border regions and along Merlin's trail to Stobo, continuing all the way to the great northern boundary of the Firth of Forth.

Driving along the road towards Ratho we crossed the alignment just west of the little chapel at Entry Head known as St Mary's of Dalmahoy, which we felt was worth a look. In the churchyard we spotted a megalithic stone carved with a crude cross which, according to the church guide, once stood in a field on a ridge above the old eastern avenue of Hatton Hall, burnt down in 1955. This megalith may have once marked the alignment, as according to our OS map it crosses the remains of this avenue just to the northwest of the church. Built in the 17th century, Hatton Hall replaced a site once occupied by the 'Tower of Haltoun'.

Further north is another St Mary's Church at Ratho, set within a circular churchyard, which stands next to a spring known as the Ladywell, now lost to the ravages of time. In 1436, it came under the auspices of the Collegiate Kirk of Corstorphine in the western suburbs of Edinburgh. Remnants of a Norman arch still survive incorporated into the west wall of the church. The Victorian entrance protects an ancient Celtic cross, found during refurbishment, which stands next to an old stone bearing the sword and cross emblem of the Knights Templar. As we traced the male current's flow north through the main body of the church, we spotted megalithic stones built into the foundations, the possible remains of a sacred sanctuary of the early Pictish tribes.

Huly Hill, a Lost Prehistoric Sanctuary

Belinus then brings us to the alignment at the busy Lochend Industrial Estate at Newbridge, about 11 km (7 miles) west of Edinburgh set between the River Almond and the western tip of the Edinburgh Airport runway. Here we find one of Scotland's most important prehistoric sites in a rather frenzied position next to a major junction of the M9 motorway, a burger restaurant and a busy petrol station.

Known as Huly Hill, it consists of a large circular cairn surrounded by three standing stones made of greenstone, one marking its east side and the others located to the southwest and northwest. This early Bronze Age ceremonial complex also has another megalith belonging to it nearby called the Gauger Stone on the premises of a company called Bodycote Materials Testings separated from the Huly Hill tumulus by the M9 motorway and Newbridge roundabout.

Although the council has made a great effort to restore this once neglected and forgotten site, they have failed to provide road signs, so we had to rely on our dowsing

Huly Hill tumulus and one of its three standing stones, Loch End Industrial Estate, Newbridge

rods to show us the way. We found the male serpent entering the tumulus from the south and connecting with the northwest standing stone at 310 degrees, deviating to 320 degrees as he leaves towards the small town of Kirkliston.

The tumulus or burial cairn measures 30 m (98 ft) wide and 3 m (9ft 7 in) high and dates from 2500 BC. A stone circle once surrounded the mound, which one antiquarian stated consisted of twelve standing stones, which survived up until the 18th century. Other sources suggest it was the possible burial place of a great Bronze Age chieftain, his cairn placed inside what may have been a pre-existing stone circle. In 1903, historians proposed that the three standing stones formed part of two separate concentric stone circles. The website *Undiscovered Scotland* states that it is possible that the tumulus and standing stones were constructed at different times, the cairn in relation to the stones being significantly offset to the northwest. With the discovery of both Bronze Age and Iron Age burials nearby, it is almost certain that this site has been used by consecutive races since the Neolithic age, perhaps believing it to be an important sacred place of their ancient ancestors.

Excavation of the tumulus in 1830 revealed a bronze spearhead, a heap of animal charcoal and small fragments of bone, although they found no trace of burial cists, urns or any human remains. In 1878, Joseph Anderson argued that the spearhead was in fact a dagger with rivets as 'no authenticated instance of bronze spear-heads had been found with an interment in Scotland' (www.cyberscotia.com).

During the building of the industrial estate in 2001, a complete Celtic chariot was uncovered to the south of the tumulus, believed to be part of a burial dating to around 250 BC. Although little survives of the organic remains, it is of a type previously unknown in Scotland, being more akin to those found on the mainland of Europe. Similar chariots have been found in East Yorkshire where the Gaulish *Parisi* settled but, unlike the one at Newbridge, they had been dismantled before burial (Coppins 2007).

On the north side of Edinburgh Airport runway is the Cat Stane, with an inscription translated by Sir James Young Simpson in 1861 as 'On this Mound lies Vetta son of Victi'. Also in the vicinity, Robert Hutchison in 1864 uncovered nine rows of 51 burial cists of varying types, further substantiating that up to the Roman period this site was in constant use as a burial ground by different races over several centuries. A tribe known as the *Vecturians* settled this area around AD 364, as well as peoples of the *Meatea* and *Damnonii* tribes. Further excavations in the 1970s, led by Trevor Cowie, uncovered several more prehistoric graves. Numerous tumuli existed around the Cat Stane towards the Huly Hill tumulus, which suggests that before extensive farming and the building of the airport runway this was a massive and extremely important complex of prehistoric monuments (www.canmore.rcahms.gov.uk).

When viewed from the top of the mound, the streamlined shape of the eastern outlier aligns with Arthur's Seat in the centre of Edinburgh. Grahame Gardner, Chairman of the British Society of Dowsers who accompanied us on one of our visits to the site, also pointed out an alignment found by Harry Bell that links the Huly Hill tumulus and the Gauger Stone with Edinburgh Castle to the east and the Cairnpapple tumulus near Bathgate to the west.

However, we also discovered an equinoctial line that connects the Huly Hill tumulus with the old parish church at Corstorphine and Arthur's Seat. The church at Corstorphine stands within a circular graveyard, the possible site of a prehistoric henge similar to Arthur's Round Table at Penrith. We felt sure that the ancients built the Huly Hill tumulus as a platform to observe the rising sun through the entrance of the henge at Corstorphine as it rose behind Arthur's Seat during the equinox.

Without doubt, Huly Hill is one of Scotland's most important prehistoric monuments, and like many other important sacred sites on the alignment, there are numerous stories of witchcraft and dark occult practices occurring here.

Kirkliston and the Templars

North of Huly Hill, the alignment is marked by the ancient town of Kirkliston, once part of the monastery of Abercorn. Built around 1200, Kirkliston Parish Church stands on a grassy knoll next to one of the most important royal routes in Scotland, linking the castles of Edinburgh, Linlithgow, Falkirk and Stirling. According to the parish history written by Donald Whyte, very little remains of the medieval structure after several 19th century restorations, except for the finely carved Norman arch over the entrance, likened to the western doorway of Holyrood Abbey in Edinburgh. The original dedication of this church is unknown but two ancient annual fairs dedicated to St Jude and St Symon were held here long ago.

The earlier name of the town was Temple Liston, a name referring to the Knights Templar who acquired the land from Robert the Bruce as they fled from France during their persecution by the Pope in the early 1300s. They purchased several plots of land in the area, including Temple near Rosslyn Chapel. The Knights were keepers of esoteric and Masonic knowledge, which went underground after the royal line of the Stuart kings became extinct. However, a few records tell us the true history of the Knights Templar in Scotland and the exact nature of these sites whilst in their hands.

In the graveyard of Kirkliston Church the great number of Masonic headstones with distinctive carvings and symbols signify the reverence given to this sacred site by the later Freemasons and the Knights Templar order that still exists in Scotland today. However, the interior of the church displays nothing to indicate this ageless

Norman doorway, Kirkliston Church

site of sacred worship. We dowsed Belinus ascending the hill from the south through the impressive Norman doorway to visit the High Altar; the Presbyterians always placed their altars in the south of the church.

Also situated on the alignment is Dundas Castle, first built as a keep by James Dundas in 1416. Oliver Cromwell stayed here and a statue of him stands in the grounds. In 1818, Henry Dundas tore down a 17th century building in the hope of reconstructing a grander home, but the resulting costs forced him to sell the estate in 1846. The Stewart-Clark family took possession in 1899 and after extensive restoration in 1995 the castle became an exclusive wedding venue and the keep is used for marriage ceremonies.

Abercorn

During our first visit to the area, major road works forced us to make several detours to trace the male current as he makes his way to the Firth of Forth. We soon lost our way amongst a maze of narrow country lanes, not helped by a severe shortage of signposts. After tuning into Belinus, our dowsing guided us along a lane following a tall dry-stone wall that marked the western boundary of Hopetoun House estate. We eventually arrived at the tiny hamlet and church of Abercorn, the memory of the frustrating journey soon fading as we stood within its tranquil churchyard next to a river called Midhope Burn. The site is located on a promontory overlooking the banks of the Forth opposite Forsyth Naval Base. *Abercurnig* was the original name for Abercorn, a Proto-Celtic word meaning 'a horned confluence' or 'mouth of the Cornie Burn'.

We were delighted to see a small museum there housing a unique collection of 8th century stone crosses, hogback tombs and Pictish stone slabs, many of them finely carved with mysterious but exquisite designs, including Celtic knots, scrolls, stylised animals and the Tree of Life.

The Romans built a small fort here and after they departed the Christian missionaries arrived. The Venerable Bede wrote that St Serf, a student of St Ninian, founded a church here in the late 400s, having journeying to these parts to Christianise the Picts. Many historians believe St Wilfred and the Celtic monks of Lindisfarne also founded a monastery here around AD 635–663.

At one time Abercorn nestled between the tribal territories of the Britons of Lothian and the Picts in the North. When the Northumbrian Angles successfully invaded the region, they established a monastery at Abercorn under Bishop Trumwine to serve as a frontier against the invading Picts and Scots.

The architecture of the church is mainly 11th century Romanesque, except for the south transept, which has larger stone blocks and roof tiles, similar in style to the sanctuary of St Mungo at Stobo, even having an identical circular window. The earthworks of several raised mounds survive in the churchyard, possible remains of the earlier monastery.

We dowsed Belinus passing through the south transept and the 'Laird's

South aisle of Abercorn Kirk, possibly a Culdee cell

Loft', built in 1637 at the back of the altar as a private place of worship for the Earls of Abercorn and Hopetoun. Perhaps they believed the solar power of the male serpent would imbue them as they contemplated God.

Corstorphine and Cramond, a Roman Port

After Glencorse Resevoir, Elen meanders across the eastern slopes of the Pentland Hills to the suburbs of Edinburgh, where she heads northwest through a curious old dovecot between residential houses at Corstorphine. Just to the north is the old collegiate church of St John the Baptist with a circular churchyard and Corstorphine Hill, one of Edinburgh's seven ancient hills.

The name Corstorphine refers to an ancient cross, found buried on the site of St John's, now the suburb's main parish church. Its earliest known dedication, however, was to St Mary which, according to Cowper in *Historic Corstorphine and Round About*, may have been one of the many small rectangular churches that started to spring up in Scotland during the 7th century. During the reign of King David I (*c.* 1084–1153), the Sheriff of Berwick built a new chapel here, bestowing it upon the abbey of Holyrood.

After buying the land and church around 1400, Sir Adam Forrester built a chantry chapel next to St Mary's, dedicated to St John the Baptist. The chapel became a Collegiate Church under Sir John Forrester, St Mary's ceasing to exist as the parish church by 1593. Its ruins were finally demolished in 1646, making way for a further extension to St John's, now the new parish church.

The Forresters, encountered before at the sacred church at Kirkton Manor near Peebles, were an important clan family believed to be of Celtic origin. During the Wars of Scottish Independence, the Forresters supported Robert the Bruce and fought against the English at the Battle of Halidon Hill in 1333. Sir Adam's son, Sir John Forrester, became Keeper of the Great Seal of Scotland, Chamberlain of Scotland and Keeper of the Household to King James I of Scotland. The tenth chief, Sir George Forrester, became a Baronet of Nova Scotia and Lord Forrester of Corstorphine in 1633. Upon his death, the title became dormant and even today awaits a claimant.

The Forresters built a castle over earlier foundations, just to the south of the church, now Castle Avenue, with a moat supplied by water from two lochs that stood either side of it. All that remains today of their estate is the dovecot, located next to the aptly named Dovecot Lane between the old castle site and the church, all on the Elen flow.

An avenue of trees once passed close to the dovecot that led to the castle, and until 1998 a single sycamore tree remained at the corner of Dovecot Road and Saughton Road. The ghost of Lady Christian Nimmo is said to haunt this area, having been executed for the murder of her uncle and lover Lord James Forrester in 1679. She still holds the sword in her spectral hand, dripping with his blood. Curiously, some refer to her as the 'White Lady'.

As we discovered earlier, the circular site of the church stands on an equinoctial alignment with the Huly Hull tumulus and Arthur's Seat. We felt sure that it was originally the site of a henge constructed in prehistoric times to capture the sun's power during the equinox. The 7th century missionaries from Rome may have Christianised the site by the supplanting of the cross, from which Corstorphine gets its name. Sadly, the church stays locked and barred, the people who visit the site today no longer respect it as a sacred sanctuary but only use it as a place to walk their dogs.

The old coastal village of Cramond is located in a picturesque spot on the south shore of the Forth River. A distinct feeling of antiquity greeted us as we strolled along the cobbled streets passing old whitewashed cottages to the quaint little harbour and sandy beach. This important port used by the Romans long ago is the oldest known site of human habitation in Scotland.

Ice Age hunter-gatherers frequented the raised beach where much of their waste from flint workings has been uncovered at a place where the River Almond meets the Forth. The port was already a strategic landing site during the time of the Celts and possibly before. In AD 142, the Romans erected their own fort here called *Caer Amon*, meaning 'fort on the Almond River', to defend the southern shore of the Forth from the invading Picts. They occupied areas of Scotland right up to the Forth and the Clyde Rivers, building the Antonine Wall using wood and turf. The Welsh-speaking tribe of the Gododdin, whom the Romans called the *Votadini*, originally named this area *Din Eidyn*. When the Northumbrian Angles captured the fortress in AD 638 it was renamed Edinburgh.

Cramond Kirk, showing a possible Culdee cell

Cramond Kirk stands over the site of Roman baths within the precincts of a large fort. A chapel was founded here by King David I and gifted to the Bishops of Dunkeld in 1160. The present church boasts two altars, dedicated to the Virgin Mary and St Columba.

Elen flows through an eastern protruding chapel of the church, which is architecturally identical to those at Stobo and Abercorn, perhaps another Culdee cell. She then crosses over the Roman foundations said to be the barracks and bakery towards Cramond Tower on the edge of the church grounds, built in 1580. This unusual four-storey freestanding structure, now a private house, appears to have earlier foundations.

After enjoying a fascinating afternoon exploring the area, it was time to cross the Firth of Forth, the largest body of water encountered so far along the Belinus Line and once an important boundary between the ancient realm of the Picts and the British.

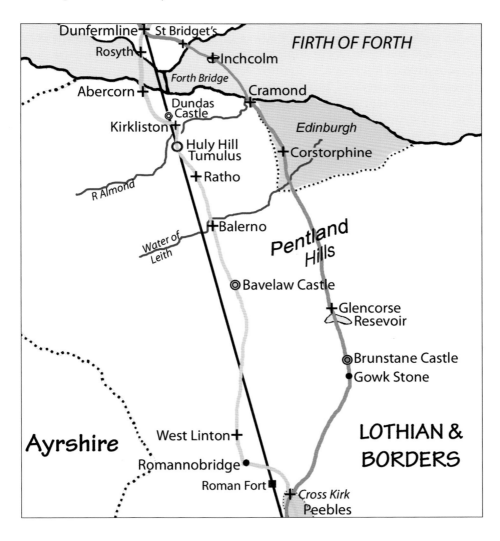

Chapter 14

The Forth to the Tay
From the Iona of the East to the Royal Burgh

The Belinus alignment crosses the Firth of Forth, the ancient southern border of Pictland, close to the famous Forth Railway Bridge built between the towns of South and North Queensferry. Opened in 1890, the great steel cantilever construction was the first of its kind in Europe, becoming an internationally recognised symbol of late 19th century engineering. This highly significant through-route along the north–south axis of the Spine of Albion marks the shortest crossing of the Forth aided by a protruding finger of land from the north shore and Inchgarvie Island. From the 12th century, a regular ferry service existed here and both landing places became the towns of North and South Queensferry, perhaps marking a renowned fording place of the prehistoric cultures when sea levels were lower.

Inchcolm Abbey, Isle of Inchcolm

Inchcolm

The beach below Cramond Kirk on the south shore of the Forth marks the northern edge of the old kingdom of the British. From here we could just make out the distant outline of our next destination, the Isle of Inchcolm 5 km (3 miles) east of the Forth Railway Bridge. Our only opportunity to visit this small island, referred to by some writers as the Iona of Eastern Scotland, arrived on a grey and damp morning in July. We were soon bouncing our way across the choppy waters through the fog aboard the small ferryboat that regularly takes visitors to the tiny island from Queensferry. From a distance, the skies over Inchcolm appeared to be dark and foreboding, but as we docked the weather started to improve and the sun burst through to reveal the ancient ruined abbey in all its glory. As we stepped down onto the little stone pier, nesting gulls cried incessantly as if annoyed by our presence. The ferry boatman warned us that they were prone to dive-bomb the odd visitor if we got too close to their nesting young on the craggy rocks that surround the abbey. However, we were too enthralled with the majestic ruins of the abbey to mind the gulls circling overhead and soon found ourselves wandering through its delightful gardens.

The ancient Gododdin tribe, who inhabited lands south of the Forth, regarded Inchcolm, anciently known as *Emona*, as their Avalon, the sacred abode of the dead placed at the extreme north of their territory. The island has also been an important Christian sanctuary from the earliest beginnings of the Culdees in Scotland. According to local legend, it was to this holy island in the Forth that the wounded Celtic King Arthur went to receive healing after his final battle. Its reputation as a sacred burial ground continued in the 11th century, when the Danes paid a large sum of gold to have their dead buried here after their defeat by Macbeth at the Battle of Kinghorn.

The Scottish King Alexander I was given shelter on the island during a storm around AD 1123 and in grateful thanks he built a monastery completed by his brother and successor David I. The Augustinian monks settled on Inchcolm soon after under the supervision of the Bishop of Dunkeld, who held the diocese. It was raised to full abbey status in 1235.

Walter Bower, Abbot of Inchcolm (1417–49) wrote the ten-volume *Scotichronicon* during his time there, one of the most infamous books of Scottish history. Like Geoffrey of Monmouth, he collected annals from earlier writers and chronicled a history of the Scots, who he believed descended from the mythical daughter of an Egyptian Pharaoh called Scota. Bower, as an acclaimed scholar and an ordained priest, quickly climbed the monastic ladder and left the monastery at St Andrews to become Abbot of Inchcolm. He frequently travelled to the royal court of James I in Edinburgh and it was during this time that he was commissioned by the Scottish Laird David Stewart of Forsyth to chronicle the origins of the ancient Scots.

My instincts guided me past the ruined abbey dedicated to St Columba to a small rectangular building on the far side of the exquisitely kept garden with a stone-vaulted roof, identical to those found at the ancient Culdee sanctuaries at Abercorn and Stobo. We realised after reading the official guide that we had found the hermit's cell or oratory, which judging from the old stones in its walls was much older than the abbey. I later discovered that the oratory is in fact one of the oldest relics of Scottish Christianity, a memorial to the visit of the apostle St Columba and his disciples. In the ancient *Book of Cupar*, a manuscript in Bower's Scotichronicon, it is said that St Columba occupied the Isle of Emonia (Emona), and it was here that the light of the Gospel was first kindled in the east of Scotland. The modern Gaelic name Inchcolm is derived from *Inch* meaning an island and *Colm*, St Colm, perhaps another title for St Columba.

Columba was the son of Prince Fedilmith of the Ur-Neill kings of Tara and the decision to allow him to enter the church of Ireland was due to St Patrick who foretold his birth. He attended one of Ireland's many Druidic colleges where he pleaded the case for the teachings of Jesus Christ to replace Druidism, and declared 'Christ is my Druid; he is my true miracle worker'. At 25, he became a chief advocate for the Celtic Church and soon climbed the ecclesiastical ladder.

According to Adamnan who wrote the *Life of Columba* in the late 7th century, the saint arrived with a group of monks in Argyll on the west coast of Scotland in AD 563 as a Christian missionary from Ireland, having had a vision of crowning a great king. His main purpose was to reinstate the exiled King Aidan who was seen as an ambitious and ruthless warrior. However, another legend states that he was exiled there for provoking a battle between the northern and southern Irish tribes where thousands died. Aidan presented Iona to Columba where he established a monastery to spread his brand of Christianity across the whole of the kingdom. Iona was previously known as *Innis-nam Druidbneach* or Isle of the Druids, a sanctuary for meditation and ritual and therefore perfect as a place of learning and writing for Columba and his monks. Columba was an advisor to the king and eventually became ambassador to Pictland and Ireland. King Bridei of Fortriu invited him to his royal 'house' or hall within a fortified hillfort, but knowing of his reputation as a powerful wizard, Bridei requested that St Columba meet him and his chief druid Broichán outside rather than in the hall, believing his magic would not be as effective in open sunlight (Oram 2006).

Elen passes in an east–west direction through the dark and damp interior where our dowsing detected a blind spring, a crossing of underground streams beneath. We dowsed one of the streams to a stone-lined well just to the south of the cell.

The intense magnetism created by this underground crossing combined with the presence of the powerful female serpent promotes a potent and heady atmosphere inside the cell, encouraging one to have strong visionary experiences. I decided to settle down on a ledge inside and as the sun illuminated the ancient walls through a tiny east window, I drifted into a meditative state. Images came to mind of the early Culdees sitting on these seats honouring this telluric place of power. I had a sense they recognised the strong vital force of Elen flowing through this site as they communed with god or the spirit of the place. They also projected their pious thoughts from here, to heal the land and its people, a practice learned from their predecessors the Druids.

Hermit's cell, Isle of Inchcolm

Interior of the hermit's cell

Elen also visits the nave of the abbey, the oldest part of the building dating from the mid-12th century, passing through the old bell tower and across to the magnificent chapter house, an octagonal building erected using sacred proportion. This type of centralised polygonal structure is architecturally rare, other examples in Scotland being at Holyrood Abbey and Elgin Cathedral. The information board informs us that the chapter house was the main meeting room of the Augustinian canons in the early 13th century, where their chants must have resounded like a hundred voices due to the remarkable acoustics here. At the centre of the building Elen intercepts with an anonymous male current. No doubt the old stonemasons understood the powerful effects of resonance enhanced by the use of sacred geometry within its design. The sound vibration created by the monks chanting would also help to harmonise the life essence of the feminine force.

The mist that surrounded the island upon our arrival had now completely cleared, leaving us with fabulous views of the northern coastline of the Forth. My dowsing indicated that Elen targeted a ruined building on the opposite shore in Dalgety Bay.

St Bridget's Church

After the ferry returned us to Queensferry, we drove across the Forth Road Bridge and navigated our way along the north coastline of the Firth of Forth and parked close to the church. After a pleasant walk through arable fields, we arrived at an idyllic spot by the beach surrounded by trees at Dalgety Bay. Looking east from the church, we had a perfect view of Edinburgh Castle and the hill called Arthur's Seat.

We found Elen passing through the roofless remains of what appeared to be a grand structure with superior architecture, built by skilled stonemasons. Its design appeared similar to the Knights Templar churches we had previously visited at Kirkliston and Ratho, and the information supplied on the site supported this.

King William I (1165–1214), who founded the first church on this site, was a great supporter of the Knights Templar, having given them several hundred acres of his lands. Alexander Seton, First Earl of Dunfermline and Lord Chancellor of Scotland, added an aisle in the 17th century but was taken to task for placing 'superstitious images in the windows of the church', which sounded most intriguing. Perhaps he adorned the church with too many fertility symbols or dragons! The graveyard is full of elaborately carved gravestones and tombs showing the Masonic mortality emblem of the skull and crossbones.

The dedication to St Bridget is an early one, supposedly named after a 5th century nun from Kildare. Myth and legend bind Bridget with the ancient goddess of the Irish and the Brigantes of northern England called Bride. Both Bridget and Bride share the same Celtic feast day of Imbolc held on 1 February. We also noticed the carving of a five-pointed star or pentagram over the main doorway, a pagan symbol rarely

seen in churches, perhaps one of the 'superstitious images' placed there by the Earl. The pentagram is also symbolic of Venus, possibly showing us that the spirit of the ancient goddess Bride still resides here, honoured by the Picts on the ancient border of their lands.

Just northwest of Dalgety Bay, the current visits Fordell, an estate once belonging to a Flemish family called de Camera. They acquired the land as a gift for their support of the

St Bridget's Kirk, Dalgety Bay

king during the fourth Crusade. A keep and chapel were constructed in 1210 next to a holy well dedicated to St Theriot. In 1511, King James IV handed the estate to James Henderson who extended the keep and rebuilt the chapel.

This beautiful rural estate with its forest walks and waterfalls is an obvious draw for Elen who passes through the well and chapel dedicated to the obscure 8th century evangelist. The renowned healing quality of the water from the well was perhaps the focus for these medieval settlers. Amongst the many royal visitors to the house was Mary Queen of Scots, when one of her ladies-in-waiting married George Henderson. In the 20th century, the lawyer and Conservative politician Sir Nicholas Fairbairn (1933–95) purchased the ruins of Fordell Castle and restored it for his private residence. Today it is still in private hands, the owners no longer providing access for visitors to this historic area.

As Elen heads towards the city of Dunfermline, she passes close to a megalithic standing stone amongst the suburban sprawl of Pitcorthie, a place visited by the Saxon princess Margaret before she met her new bridegroom, King Malcolm III.

We found Belinus further west near the coastal village of Limekilns passing through the old burial ground and ruined church at Rosyth dedicated to St John. Marking the alignment south of Dunfermline is the site of Hill House and its windmill, built in 1623 for William Monteith of Randford, now part of a housing estate.

The Royal City of Dunfermline

Dunfermline, like Winchester and Carlisle, was once a royal city on the Spine of Albion and another of those key places where the alignment and both currents converge. Dunfermline was the Scottish capital long before Edinburgh and one of the oldest settlements in Scotland, just as Winchester was the former capital of England and a prehistoric sanctuary. Malcolm III of the House of Canmore made this ancient town the new seat of royal power, having transferred the centre of government from the old Pictish centre at Forteviot in the mid-11th century. Edinburgh became the new capital after the assassination of James I of Scotland in 1437.

Historical records refer to Dunfermline as a monastic centre of the Scottish Culdees, having established a Celtic church here around AD 800, which still existed in the late 12th century. The church became the venue for the marriage of King Malcolm and his second wife Margaret, their union producing eight children and a remarkable royal dynasty. Three of their sons, Edgar, Alexander and David, became future kings of Scotland.

Queen Margaret invited Benedictine monks from Canterbury to establish a priory and religious centre here on the site of the Culdee sanctuary. Her influence also established a new royal burial site for Scottish kings at Dunfermline, breaking with the age-old tradition of interment on the sacred Isle of Iona. The new royal seat also saw the building of a palace next to the priory. King Malcolm's son David I later transformed the abbey in the early Norman Romanesque style.

Why Malcolm Canmore made this small town his new royal centre is a mystery. Did he know of its geomantic placement on an alignment that connected it with other cities in Britain? Perhaps a good deal of research and dowsing of the city might provide us with some answers.

Dunfermline Abbey

As we began to explore the area around the cathedral and ruined palace, we noticed that despite their magnificent presence, Dunfermline no longer displays the grandeur of former times. The pervading atmosphere of dreariness that we could see all around us reflects the lack of respect held for this former sacred capital of the kings of Scotland. Even though Winchester has lost its title as the old royal capital of England, its history and medieval buildings are still the focus of great reverence and enjoyment by its inhabitants and frequent visitors. Nevertheless, the environs of Dunfermline Abbey appear to hold a glimmer of light, with its well-kept lawns and stunning interior.

More significantly, enhancing its sanctity is the presence of the alignment, passing through the eastern edge of the abbey, and the male and female serpents, which form a Node near the tomb of Robert the Bruce. Outside, we dowsed the Elen current entering the abbey diagonally through the north corner of the impressive east window, whilst Belinus enters through its southern corner, both clipping the edges of a black marble tomb just below the east window encased by a now roofless chapel. A plaque on the railings informed us that it is the Catholic shrine of St Margaret, which for hundreds of years was one of the most famous places of pilgrimage in Europe for those of all religious persuasions.

Margaret was of royal Saxon blood, having been born in Hungary during the exile of her father, Edward Atheling or 'Edward the Exile'. King Canute had banished him, along with his father King Edmund Ironside, after the Danish conquest of England. When the throne was restored to the Saxons under King Edward the Confessor, he recalled Edward to England in 1056, making him his heir with the intention of thwarting any attempt by the House of Godwin to take the throne. When King Harold II fell at the Battle of Hastings, the English elected Edgar Atheling as their king. However, after only three months on the throne he had to concede the crown to William the Conqueror and flee the country with his mother and sisters, Margaret and Christine.

Marriage to Margaret gave Malcolm the perfect opportunity to gain a foothold in the south by creating a new dynasty allied with the English Royal House. Finding the Scottish church rather backward, Margaret influenced religious practices by promoting the more progressive ways of Europe and at court she introduced Saxon ceremony, European fashion and refined tableware.

Margaret died shortly after hearing of the death of her husband and son, killed fighting William the Conqueror's army in 1093 near Alnwick. She was canonised in 1250 by Pope Innocent IV, and nine years later her relics were transferred from their position before the High Altar of the cathedral to a new shrine by the east wall of the abbey. At the Reformation, Margaret's remains were moved around to preserve them from desecration and her skull came into the possession of Mary Queen of Scots who venerated the relic during her pregnancy. It later perished in France during the Revolution while in the guardianship of the Jesuits at Douai. The remainder of Margaret's relics and those of her husband Malcolm III went to Spain where Philip II (1527–98) placed them in the church of St Lawrence at El Escorial near Madrid, but they have since disappeared.

This remarkable Saxon–Scottish alliance spread into the Norman dynasty with their one daughter, Matilda, who married King Henry I. They too had a daughter called Matilda who became the wife of Geoffrey of Anjou and for a short time Queen of England. Their son Henry, however, became one of the most powerful kings of England as Henry II. It interested me that this dynasty spawned by Malcolm and Margaret created royal courts on the Belinus Line, with Henry II at both Winchester and Carlisle and his great grandparents at Dunfermline. King Malcolm gained more power and prestige during his reign than any Scottish king in history, his legendary status remaining in the hearts and minds of the Scottish people even today. According to the testimony of St Berchan he was:

'A king, the best who possessed Alban;
He was a king of kings fortunate.
He was the vigilant crusher of enemies.
No woman bore or will bring forth in the East
A king whose rule will be greater over Alban;
And there shall not be born for ever
One who had more fortune and greatness.' (Skene 1867)

Many miracles and legends are associated with St Margaret's shrine, including the story of a crippled knight called Sir John Wemyss. On 3 October 1263, the knight had a vision in which he saw a great portal swing open in Dunfermline Abbey to reveal St Margaret mounted on a horse accompanied by her husband King Malcolm and their noble sons and knights, riding out to fight for Scotland in her hour of need. On the same day, King Alexander III routed Hakon IV, King of Norway, at the Battle of Largs, saving Scotland from Viking rule. Enlightened by this vision, Sir John immediately visited St Margaret's shrine where his infirmity was cured. Many sites on the male and female serpents and the Belinus Line in England have similar tales associated with them, but it is often King Arthur and his Knights who reside in their subterranean slumber in readiness to defend their country.

As we entered the abbey, we soon realised that Elen and Belinus were approaching each other to

St Margaret's shrine, Dunfermline Abbey

Node near the pulpit where the High Altar of the old abbey was situated. Beneath the pulpit is a commemorative plaque that indicates the tomb of the infamous and revered Robert the Bruce who lies beneath. His most glorious achievement was the defeat of King Edward II's English army at the Battle of Bannockburn. When restoration work in the 19th century revealed his grave, the church authorities relocated his relics to this spot. Not all of his remains are here, however, for James, Earl of Douglas, took his heart with him on the Crusades to the Holy Land inside a silver casket. After Douglas' death in Spain fighting the Moors, the embalmed heart returned with a knight for burial in Melrose Abbey.

The Elen current passes through the south wall of the old nave with its carved Norman pillars to the ruins of the nearby royal palace, residence to many Scottish kings and where Charles I of England and his sister Princess Elizabeth, the Winter Queen, were born. This piece of history fascinated us, having already acquainted ourselves with Princess Elizabeth at Ashdown House in Oxfordshire and Hamstead Marshall in Berkshire. Like her brother who became Charles I, King of Scotland, Ireland and England, she was destined for great things, although this was never fulfilled.

In 1651, in an attempt to regain the British throne after his father's execution, Charles II met Cromwell and his Parliamentarian forces in a field below Pitreavie Castle at Inverkeithing, southeast of Dunfermline. This site, marked by the Belinus alignment, was to prove disastrous for Charles, losing nearly 2000 of his men, and a tragedy for Scottish independence, forcing the end of 600 years of royal residency in Dunfermline Palace. In the words of Sir Walter Scott (1808):

'Tradition, Legend, Tune, and Song,
Shall many an age the wail prolong;
Still, from the sire the son shall hear
Of the stern strife, and carnage drear,
Of Inverkeithing's field,
Where shiver'd was fair Scotland's spear,
And broken was her shield.'

The ruined remains of St Catherine's Chapel in Pittencrieff Park

From the abbey, the male current enters Pittencrieff Park through an ivy-covered buttressed wall, supposedly the site of a chapel dedicated to St Catherine and an almshouse destroyed in 1420. Its date of construction is unknown, but a charter mentions the chapel in 1327. It is interesting that St Catherine surfaces here at the former royal and Christian omphalos of Scotland, for in cosmology her wheel and spindle represents the rotating wheel of the axis mundi.

A stone's throw from here and next to the alignment are the City Chambers, a French-styled building adorned with numerous carvings of winged dragons and other Masonic symbols, built by French stonemasons. Our attention focused on one particular carving showing two 'green serpents' either side of a central pole with another serpent entwined around it. This seemed to mimic the Belinus Line and its currents, which also reminds us that the alignment itself holds its own serpent power.

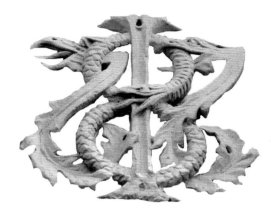

Carving of two 'green serpents' with another entwined around a central pole on the exterior of the City Chambers next to the Belinus alignment

Malcolm's Tower

'The King sits in Dunfermline tower
Drinking the blood red wine.' (*Ballad of Sir Patrick Spens* (Child 1882–98))

Dunfermline means 'fortress by the crooked stream', referring to an early fortification in the form of a tower on the rocky outcrop built by Malcolm Canmore in 1057, the foundations of which are still visible west of the abbey in Pittencrieff Park. Standing on a flattened prominence above a deep gorge, this extraordinary building would have once dominated the skyline for many kilometres around. It consisted of two storeys and an attic, the design emulating a typical Pictish Broch.

It was here that King Malcolm and the Saxon princess Margaret consummated their marriage on the day after Easter 1068. According to one local legend, immediately after introduction they proceeded to the tower for nuptials. This may have been a sacred fertility ceremony formerly practised by the Pictish kings at key sites of serpent power. Sometimes this would include 'sex magic' ritually performed between

Malcolm Canmore's Tower, Dunfermline. (Reproduced from a sketch in the Annals of Dunfermline 1089–1878 by Dr Ebenezer Henderson)

the king and a priestess. Known as the 'Great Rite', this ancient tradition originally took the form of the king 'marrying the land' to exercise his sovereignty over the nation. In some cases it involved the symbolic act of plunging a sacred knife, representing the male, into a cup or chalice filled with wine held by the high priestess, signifying the female. This powerful act would also have the potent effect of harmonising the serpent currents at key nodal points to ensure fertility in the land.

Belinus arrives at the ruined tower through the old western entrance and crosses with Elen at its centre, having appeared through another opening from the south. We detected four further energy lines radiating from this crossing point, two of which were serpents, one male and one female, almost the width of Elen and Belinus. When we meditated upon these newly discovered serpents, we discovered they connect with the ancient sanctuary of St Andrew's Cathedral, the headquarters of the medieval Scottish Church on the east coast of Fife.

The tower, made from highly paramagnetic sandstone blocks and built on a high mound on a sharp bend of the river, is a very powerful conduit or antennae for the enhancement of earth energies. It also represents the axis mundi of Malcolm and Margaret's new kingdom. Cosmology was the secret knowledge of the medieval elite who embodied its principles to create a sacred centre, using mountains, mounds or a manmade building, such as a tower, to empower their territory. They believed the energies of the cosmos would enter the world at this point and flow across the landscape towards the cardinal points. Malcolm Canmore's Tower, with walls also facing towards the cardinal points, would be the perfect place to act out a ceremony of marrying the land.

The six-pointed star signature dowsed at this Node was warped similar to Cross Kirk at Peebles, indicating the out of balance nature of the earth energies here, perhaps brought about by its desecration at the hands of Edward I when his English forces burnt much of Dunfermline in 1304. The image of the great towering seat of the powerful Scottish Royal House of Canmore standing on a rocky outcrop in flames reminded me of the Tower in the pack of Tarot cards, representing false structures.

At the museum, I noticed a seal depicting Malcolm and Margaret's son David as King of Scotland with his grandson Malcolm IV, between them two coiled serpents. I wondered whether this signified the integration of sovereign power with the male and female earth serpents inherent in the land here. Vestiges of the tower and the gorge

became part of Pittencrieff Park when a local aristocrat landscaped the area to enhance the flow of the river in the early part of the 20th century. Here, amongst the maze of footpaths, bridges and exotic trees, we find the Elen current flowing along the edge of the stream to Wallace's Well, having come from the ruined palace. Local tradition states that in 1303 Sir William Wallace took refuge here and drank from the well while being pursued by the soldiers of King Edward I after visiting the shrine of St Margaret.

A seal depicting King David I and Malcolm IV with two coiled serpents

St Margaret's Cave

From the tower, Elen veers off to the northeast outskirts of the park across the road to a car park, where we find the entrance to St Margaret's Cave, one of the most unique pilgrimage sites in Britain. This now subterranean chamber was uncovered during excavations in the 1970s. In medieval times the mouth of the cave looked down upon a ravine and pilgrims climbed up to the cave from the stream below. This was possibly a hermitage site later used by the Culdee monks and St Margaret. Today, a modern concrete entrance gives access down 87 steps to the hidden shrine. After paying the entrance fee, we descended into a softly lit cave reputed to be where St Margaret prayed and found refuge.

I noticed the sandstone walls are highly paramagnetic due to their high iron content. The trickling of spring water from a holy well further enhances the potent atmosphere here. Testing the magnetism in the cave with a compass, I found anomalies above the head of the fibreglass statue of St Margaret, kneeling and praying before the altar. The needle began to waver from side to side, suggesting a very strong magnetic wave. We placed the palms of our hands over the

Interior of St Margaret's Cave

head of the model and could feel a tingling sensation, which I believe is a manifestation of healing energy. We dowsed the female current passing straight through the kneeling figure.

Perhaps the focus of prayers from thousands of pilgrims over 900 years has imbued the crystals and minerals of this cave, further enhanced by the power of natural spring water, to make a healing shrine that is still powerful today.

Elen connects with many of the sites associated with St Margaret, such as the standing stone in the suburbs of Dunfermline, her shrine at the cathedral and this cave. Was Queen Margaret drawn intuitively to the path of the female dragon at these sacred places?

Andrew Carnegie

The male current continues north to the Andrew Carnegie statue, having already visited his birthplace in Moodie Street to the south of the city. Elen too passes through Carnegie Hall as she enters the city from the east. As previously experienced, the currents seem to connect with certain key individuals at major centres of power. In the 19th century, Andrew Carnegie left a great artistic, musical and literacy legacy to his beloved birthplace here in Dunfermline, as well as creating community welfare and bathing facilities.

Despite his humble beginnings, Carnegie became the second-richest man in history after John D. Rockefeller, making his fortune from the steel industry. As the son of a handloom weaver, he was born in the living-room attic of a cottage at the corner of Moodie Street and Priory Lane on 25 November 1835, and died in America in 1919. He expounded a new philosophy of wealth and wrote, 'Fortunate in my ancestors, I was supremely so in my birthplace'.

Having invested his earnings well during his time as a superintendent of the Pittsburg Railway, he soon found himself a wealthy man. By 1889, he owned the Carnegie Steel Corporation, cementing his name as one of the 'Captains of Industry' after revolutionising steel production in the United States. However, some believe that his success came at the expense of his workers and when he tried to lower wages in one of his plants, his workforce went on strike, the first in American history.

In 1901, at the age of 66, he sold his business for $200 million and dedicated his time to expanding his philanthropic work, setting up a trust fund 'for the improvement of mankind'. He built libraries, contributed to charities and established various institutions, including the Carnegie-Mellon University in Pittsburg. He also created the Endowment for International Peace in an effort to prevent future wars, and set up large pension funds in 1901 for his former employees. By the time of Carnegie's death in 1919, he had given away $350,000,000.

He wrote a series of books including *Triumphant Democracy* (1886), in which he compared the egalitarianism of America with the class-based inequalities of Britain and other European countries. In June 1889, he wrote an article called the *Gospel of Wealth* arguing that it was the duty of rich men and women to use their wealth to improve the welfare of the community. He wrote that a 'man who dies rich dies disgraced'.

He always maintained an interest in his hometown and in Scotland in general; even as a small boy, the writings of Robert Burns and such historical Scottish heroes as Robert the Bruce, Sir William Wallace and Rob Roy fascinated him.

Carnegie was also a prominent Freemason, attending many Lodge meetings at his own Carnegie Hall in New York. Many believe he was obsessed with becoming rich and destroyed the lives of many people in the process, turning to charitable endeavours in compensation for his ruthless deeds of the past. Whatever his motives, he was truly a remarkable man, born and possibly conceived on the male serpent.

We took refreshments in the Abbots House Heritage Centre, a grand old building with red-painted exterior walls that marks the alignment, formerly on the site of the old abbey burial ground. We mulled over the day's findings and realised that during Norman times it was clear that the Spine of Albion was utilised to heighten the power of the kings in England and Scotland. Dunfermline was the royal and religious capital of Scotland in 1068, at the same time that Winchester was the royal and religious centre of England under William the Conqueror. His son William Rufus completely rebuilt and restored Carlisle, constructing a castle and religious houses in order to make this town a powerful city in the north.

Was this a deliberate act by the Normans to reanimate the serpent power of Albion, after the tumultuous period of the Romans, Saxons, Angles and Danes, and to reverse the wilting fortunes of the country? Alternatively, was it to influence the psyche of the people to accept their rule? Even though Winchester and Carlisle are the mythological courts of King Arthur, it seems that Dunfermline has created its own legends around Malcolm and Margaret, who held court in the city just as King Arthur and Guinevere had at Camelot. Legend tells us that they even lie sleeping under the abbey ready to awake and ride out like Arthur's Knights to rescue Scotland in her hour of need.

The city also gave birth to one of the most powerful men in the Western world in the 19th century, Andrew Carnegie. His birth on the Belinus current may have had a profound effect on his character and created a genius who, like Matthew Boulton in Birmingham, became one of the greatest pioneers of industry.

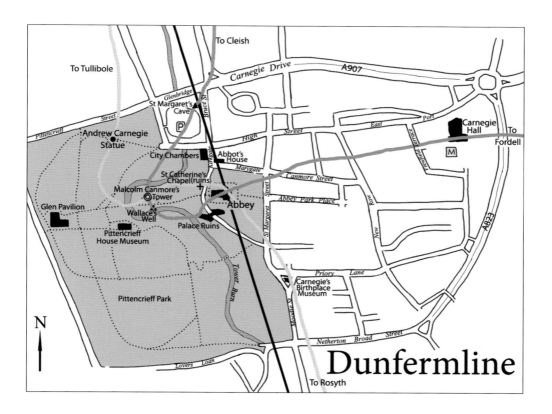

The Mound of the White Church

After leaving the suburbs of the old royal city Belinus stays close to the alignment, visiting an Iron Age hillfort at Dumglow, the highest of the Cleish Hills, and a ruined church just north of Tullibole Castle.

The parish of Tullibole is reputed to be the oldest in Scotland. Its ancient burial ground just above Tullibole Castle occupies a slight elevation or mound next to the remains of a church, a site used by the indigenous peoples since the Bronze Age. This enchanting place now lies forgotten amongst a wilderness of vegetation with just the foundations and a handful of gravestones to stir the imagination. A cist grave was discovered buried in the graveyard together with a 9th century Norse hogback tombstone, considered rare in this region of Scotland.

Remains of Tullibole Church

Tulybothwyn, the ancient name for Tullibole, means 'mound of the white church' and a local legend suggests that St Serf, whose mother *Ingen ri-g Cruithnech* was a Pictish princess, founded an early Christian sanctuary here over a Pictish sacred site, confirmed by the discovery of a Pictish stone in the churchyard. Now displayed in the National Museum of Scotland in Edinburgh, it shows two horned serpents coiled together standing on their tails. Such symbols have become synonymous with the Belinus and Elen current as they follow the Spine of Albion through Britain.

We dowsed the male serpent flowing just west of the mound through the foundations of the church. The presence of the circular mound, surrounded by four yew trees within the oval churchyard, is an indication of its great antiquity. The obelisk erected on its summit stands on an earlier stone base, possibly that of a Celtic cross. The boundary wall around the church, particularly near the east entrance, contains large blocks of stone similar to those used to build the early Celtic shrines in Ireland dating from the 6th century. Geophysics resistivity surveys carried out at this site show signs of several grave features and a possible manse or mort house. In 1217, Malcolm, Earl of Fife, granted land for the building of a church to the Cistercian Abbey at Culross. A succession of churches has stood on this site but the remains you see today are Victorian.

To the east of the churchyard, there is access via a footpath to a hedge maze built within the grounds of Tullibole Castle by the Moncreiffe family. According to the information board, its creation was to commemorate the lives of eleven innocent men and women executed for witchcraft in 1662 at the nearby Crook of Devon. The trial, claimed as the worst persecution for witchcraft Scotland has ever seen, was presided over by William Halliday, laird of Tullibole, together with his son and three others. The eleven were burned at the stake on a mound near the current village hall. Clearly, the Moncreiffe family still holds to the memory of this heinous act that occurred over 350 years ago.

The Dunning Dragon and the Royal Centre of the Picts

Having crossed over the beautiful Ochil Hills, the male current arrives at Dunning, a village steeped in history from prehistoric times. Six roads meet at its centre, an indication that it was once a thriving town. Several megalithic monuments and earthworks still survive in the area, including burial mounds surrounded by three ring ditches, perhaps part of an important prehistoric ritual landscape. An Iron Age hillfort called Dun Knock once existed here, from which the town takes its name. Although nothing of it remains today, lines or crop marks of the ditches are still apparent from the air, as they radiate out from woodland to the southeast of the church.

We soon detected the Belinus current entering the village from the site of Dun Knock heading towards a thorn tree protected by a circular wall in Thorn Tree Square. Here a thorn once stood planted in Jacobite times, revered for its magical powers by the locals and used as a protective talisman. The tree you see today is a descendant of the original. The current continues through the fountain to the medieval tower of the parish church dedicated to St Serf, who reputedly died at Dunning.

Born in AD 470, St Serf, also known as St Servanus, having studied in Alexandria, embraced the Gnostic teachings banned by the Roman Catholic Church. An angel then guided him to Adamnan, Abbot of Iona, in the Western Isles of Scotland, and soon after he established a Culdee monastery at Loch Lomond. As the supposed son of Eluid, King of Canaan, many historians believe he was one of the many Judean apostles who fled from persecution in the Holy Land. According to local legend, the saint built a Culdee cell here and rescued the locals from a terrifying dragon, which he killed with his staff. Mentioned in an old manuscript, he had a vision while in his cell that 'a dragon great and terrible, and very loathsome was coming into his township whose aspect no mortal could suffer'. Andrew de Wyntoun (1350–1420) also describes this event in *The Orygynale Cronykil of Scotland*:

'In Donnyng, of his devotion
And prayer, he slew a fell dragowne;
Where he was slain, the place was ay
The Dragownes Den called to this day.'

The 16th century *Breviary of Aberdeen* states, 'In a place called Dunnyne the inhabitants were harassed by a dreadful dragon, which devoured both men and cattle, and kept the district in continual terror. Saint Serf, armed with the breastplate of faith, attacked the monster in his lair, and slew him with a blow of his pastoral staff. The place where he fought and killed the dragon was renamed the "Valley of the Dragon", later known as the "Dragon's Den"'. Interestingly Newton of Pitcairns just to the southeast of Dunning village is known today as 'The Dragon'.

411

According to various sources, its actual lair, however, was in the wooded valley of the Dunning Burn, marked by the alignment. This energetic association allows the legend to remain fixed in local memory as on the eve of the last new millennium, a 'dragon' procession took place in the village; a witness describes the event: 'almost a thousand torches shone like a river of fire that night, mimicking the serpentine body of the mythical beast with the effigy of a green dragon leading the way'.

The 12th century tower is the oldest part of the church but masonry in the north wall is of Saxon workmanship, possibly a doorway of St Serf's cell or church. A friendly guide pointed out to us some of the more curious aspects of the building, particularly the stained-glass windows, one showing the curious image of Christ wearing only one sandal and another of St Michael protecting the 'righteous in the world', portrayed as a woman. Above him is St Mary Magdalene with the tower of Dunning Church behind her. These allegorical windows seem to denote the male protecting the divine feminine; they also recall certain Scottish legends that refer to Mary Magdalene visiting Scotland after the crucifixion of Jesus (Dunford 2008).

Within the tower, Belinus passes through one of Scotland's finest ancient monuments, a Pictish stone known as the Dupplin Cross. It once stood in a field on the northern banks of the River Earn overlooking the old site of the Pictish palace at Forteviot,

Dupplin Cross inside St Serf's Church, Dunning

just to the northeast of Dunning. The carving is exquisite, detailing a warrior king on horseback accompanied by foot soldiers carrying shields and spears. Anna Ritchie, an authority on Pictish art, believes that much of the imagery on the stone relates to righteous and powerful kingship, organised for war and governance (Ritchie 1989). Based on Latin writing found on the cross, the mounted warrior was thought to be the Scottish King Constantine (AD 789–820).

A standing stone in a field behind the church marks the male current as it continues northeast. The stone is said by locals to commemorate the death of Doncha, Abbot of Dunkeld, slain during the Battle of Duncrub in AD 965. The Norman Baron Eric Rollo owned the Duncrub estate, a Dane descended from a long line of nobles including William the Conqueror.

The alignment is further marked in the vicinity by the vitrified Iron Age sanctuary of Dun Knock, where we dowsed Belinus on the eastern suburbs of the town, and the site of a very large Roman marching camp to the northeast. In the fields surrounding Dunning, some authorities on Scottish history believe the legendary Roman General, Agricola, fought an epic battle against the Picts. In 2009, the *Roman Scotland* website identifies it as the site of the Mons Graupius battle that took place around AD 83–84, the scene of ferocious fighting and slaughter.

Interestingly, both the male serpent and the alignment pass through the site of the Roman camp said to be large enough to house 25,000 men, the actual size of the Roman army who fought at Mons Graupius. Likewise, the line held by the northern tribes during the battle was at the multi-ditched hillfort of Dun Knock. Tacitus records the speech made by the great 'fair-haired' warrior Calgacus, meaning 'swordsman', to his warriors as they prepared to do battle with the Romans:

'Shielded by nature, we are the men off the edge of the world, the last of the free. Britons are being sold in Roman slavery everyday .... When that happens there will be nothing left that we can call our own: neither farmland, nor mines, nor ports. Even our bravery will count against us, the imperialists dislike that sort of spirit in a subject people. Therefore as we cannot hope for mercy, we must take up arms for what we cherish most. We will be fighting for our freedom.' (Handford 1971)

Although many sources say the northern tribes lost the battle, it was not decisive. What became of the famous Ninth Legion has been the subject of a book and several movies, but many Scottish historians believe the Picts defeated them. After the recall of Agricola to Rome, the Roman army never again entered the ancient realms of these great warriors, regarding them as too hostile and their terrain too difficult to control. When you consider the original purpose of the alignment, laid down by the British Iron Age geomancers to harmonise and enchant the land, such a ferocious conflict at the hands of the Romans, particularly at the sacred stronghold of Dun Knock, would almost certainly pervade the region with a sense of chaos and fear for centuries to come.

A little northeast of Dunning, Belinus flows through the fertile fields of the Earn Valley just to the west of the village of Forteviot, in an area where once existed one of the most extensive concentrations of early prehistoric ritual monuments and Iron Age tombs in mainland Scotland. This forgotten sacred landscape has recently been revealed as one of the most important royal centres of the Picts and the later Kings of Alba.

Forteviot or *Fothuir-Tabaicht* is located above a flood-plain of the River Earn occupying a slight eminence on the east bank of the Water of May close to where it merges with the Earn. It encompassed an area where one of the most sacred enclosures in Scotland once stood, including a mound known as Haly Hill (or Holy Hill) to the northeast of where Forteviot's parish church stands today. Over the years, devastating floods have dramatically changed the landscape around Forteviot, but aerial photography has revealed a complex of prehistoric monuments, seen as faint outlines of rectangular and sub-circular enclosures, linear ditches, henges, round barrows and long graves, possibly long barrows. Many of them date from 2600 BC, all destroyed by river flooding or ploughed out over the centuries.

In 2009, an archaeological dig carried out by the University of Glasgow near Forteviot unearthed a burial chamber of great significance. The tomb dating from 1950–2100 BC was covered by a 4-ton capstone carved on one side with a spiral and an axe, similar to those found on stones at Kilmartin Glen in Argyll. Inside they found a body lying within an interwoven lattice of birch bark on a bed of quartz pebble surrounded by possessions including a bronze dagger with a tabbed gold hilt, indicating an individual of some importance in Bronze Age Scotland, perhaps a local king.

Archaeologists call this ritual complex the 'Scottish Valley of the Kings' which they believe would have dwarfed the Stonehenge area of monuments. According to Nick Aitchison in *Forteviot, A Pictish and Scottish Royal Centre*, it was situated within the Kingdom of Fortriu which the *Irish Annals* mention as *Fortrenn*, a region known today as Strathearn and Menteith. This northern tribe of the Picts built their royal palace between Dunning and Forteviot, overlooking the plains at the core of a ritual landscape of their prehistoric ancestors. However, much of Forteviot's early history as a royal centre is still open to debate, as most of the Pictish records were destroyed before the 9th century; anything earlier is considered myth and legend.

Fortriu was the most powerful of the seven kingdoms of the legendary Alba, its earliest recorded King being Bridei, son of Bile (AD 671–692). The royal centre would have consisted of a palace, church, cemetery, assembly place, a possible focus for ritual ceremony, and an area for agricultural production. Some historians believe that the warrior King Constantine (AD 789–820) resided at Forteviot, hence the inscription on the Dupplin Cross. Kenneth MacAlpin, king of the Dal Riada Scots (AD 842–858), would later usurp the Pictish palace at Forteviot for his own royal residence after winning a decisive battle against King Bruidi; according to folklore, signs and portents were seen in the skies before this battle, foretelling Bruidi's downfall.

Although many believe Forteviot was once the greatest Pictish capital of Scotland, MacAlpin and the earlier Pictish kings had no permanent place of residence. Instead, they would travel to different royal centres within their kingdom including Dunfermline, Scone and Dunkeld: 'Together with their entourage, the kings would engage in such pursuits as hunting expeditions, feasting and ceremonial festivals. This form of royal progress would enable them to exercise royal governance maintaining the king's authority over the land and its inhabitants making laws and dispensing justice' (Stewart 1926).

Aitchison believes Forteviot became a theatre for rituals of royalty for these kings by reusing the ancient monuments of their ancestors. The henges became places of gathering, and by connecting with this ceremonial landscape, the king reinforced the legitimacy of his sovereignty, made all the more powerful by the terrestrial energy inherent within the land and its situation next to the confluence of the Earn and the Water of May. The Druids would have understood the importance of this site close to the Spine of Albion and perhaps honoured and utilised the vital force of the Belinus current to reanimate the land and empower their kings.

The Pictish kings were considered 'heads of the kindred' where 'kinship' was more important than 'kingship'. The warrior chief would engage in fighting for the prestige of himself and his clan rather than for any territorial or material gain. It has been suggested that sometimes the boldest, most courageous and noblest of warriors was chosen as their chief rather than for his aristocratic bloodline. He would have been surrounded by an elite band of warriors who themselves earned this status through valour on the battlefield (McHardy 2010). Perhaps such 'righteous and powerful kingship' is depicted in the carvings on the Dupplin Cross at Dunning, which shows a mounted warrior king with a line of soldiers beneath the horse's hooves. Aitchison also suggests that Pictish kings were inaugurated here, before their ritual centre was transferred to Scone. The Stone of Scone, originally brought over to Scotland from Tara in Ireland, resided here for a time when Kenneth MacAlpin was king.

Forteviot was also the court of Malcolm Canmore before he moved his centre of power to Dunfermline, and his palace was said to have stood on Haly Hill. Nothing remains of this ancient fortress but a memory. A plaque above the entrance archway to a group of houses in the village of Forteviot reads:

'This village was rebuilt by John Alexander first Baron Forteviot of Dupplin in the years 1825–26 and occupies part of the site of the Pictish Capital Fothuir–Tabaicht a royal residence from the VII to the XII centuries. Here Kenneth I (MacAlpin) died AD 860.'

The Culdees also established themselves at Forteviot, building a place of worship within the site of the palace, and Aitchison (2006) quoting MacGibbon and Ross writing in 1897 mentions an ancient church that occupied the site within the *rath* or stronghold at Haly Hill. In 1241, the Bishop of St Andrews consecrated a church where the present parish church now stands; the focus of worship having moved from the banks of the Water of May when flooding destroyed the original church. Various worn fragments of finely carved masonry including a 9th century arch were discovered in the 1820s in the riverbed of the Water of May after severe flooding had eroded its banks. The carvings show an influence from the Carolingian palaces at Aachen and Maastricht. The arch, thought to have adorned a royal stone chapel, is now on display at the National Museum of Scotland in Edinburgh, and shows a reclining Pictish king holding a sword, two clerics holding staffs, and a bull. This collection of intricate carved stones is only a fragment of the incredible work by the early stonemasons that once adorned this Pictish capital.

Aitchison refers to the *Liber Floridus* or 'book of flowers' compiled from 1090–1120 by Lambert of St Omer which mentions 'a palace of the soldier Arthur in Britain, in the country of the Picts, constructed with marvellous art and variety in which may

The Forteviot Arch. (© National Museums Scotland)

be seen sculptured all his deeds and wars'. Only Forteviot's ancient palace and chapel seem to match the marvellous art described, although there is no evidence that this legendary British warrior king ever visited this area.

Surprisingly, the male current avoids both St Andrew's Church and the proposed site of Haly Hill mound where the Picts built their palace. Instead, we dowsed him passing through a farm a little further north called Milton of Forteviot. Aitchison states that Milton of Forteviot may have been the site of a mill where remnants of a cross slab carved with Pictish designs were uncovered in the walls of the farm buildings. Other fragments found nearby include one carved with intricate knotwork and the other of a beast holding a serpent in its mouth.

John of Wyntoun states in the *Orygynale Cronykil of Scotland*, written in the 15th century, that the mill is significant to the birth of King Malcolm III. According to the story, Malcolm's father King Duncan I (1034–40) was out hunting one day and took refuge at the mill after being separated from his companions. There Duncan met the miller's daughter who became pregnant by him, eventually giving birth to the future King of Scotland. Perhaps the mill stood over a much older site, its true significance now relegated to myth and legend. Did Malcolm's conception on the male current somehow influence his future as a great leader and inspire him to build Scotland's new capital on the Spine of Albion at Dunfermline where both currents Node not once but twice?

After a fascinating afternoon, we decided to enjoy the delights of the local hostelry at Dunning to reflect on the story of the dragon slaying St Serf and the incredible history of this area, including Mons Graupius, the biggest battle ever fought in Scotland.

Just north of Dunning, the alignment runs close to a battle site near the town of Methven. Here the English, led by Edward I, fought a fierce skirmish against the Scots, defeating the great Robert the Bruce in 1307. Fortunately, for the Scots, Bruce survived and went on to defeat the English at the Battle of Bannockburn in 1314. The sacred significance of this tribal centre around Forteviot and Dunning reminded me of the Uffington complex, another region of legendary battles.

Not far from where the Dupplin Cross once stood on the north bank of the Earn are the ruins of Dupplin Church, where we find the male current before he passes through the grounds of nearby Dupplin Castle, now a hotel. The church stands over medieval foundations, becoming the burial site of the Earls of Kinnoull.

Huntingtower Castle and the Green Man

On the western precincts of the city of Perth, we found a rare kindred spirit in the little ticket office at Huntingtower Castle. After handing over the information leaflet, the attendant announced that many ley lines converge at the castle and inside we would find a painted Green Man and winged dragons in one of the interior rooms. After this intriguing interlude, we were keen to find out for ourselves what secrets lay in store for us in a place visited by Belinus and clearly teeming with esoteric symbolism.

As we explored the grounds, we spotted the remnants of a wall on the north side with a very steep drop. The natural escarpment here was obviously utilised over the centuries as a form of protection; the Romans built a tower here as one of their northern outposts.

The powerful Ruthven family built the present structure in the 15th century to replace a wooden fortress. In 1297, Walter Ruthven played a major role alongside Sir William Wallace during his defence of Scotland against the invading forces of Edward I. The Third Lord Ruthven entertained Mary Queen of Scots here with her second husband Lord Darnley during their honeymoon excursion in March 1566. Interestingly, the Fourth Lord Ruthven assisted in Queen Mary's incarceration at Loch Leven Castle.

The east tower boasts a magnificent tempera-painted ceiling dating from 1540, said to be the earliest in Scotland, uncovered with the removal of a pine ceiling in 1913. Belinus passes through the main hall in the oldest part of the castle marked by the esoteric images of the Green Man and a dragon mentioned by the female attendant, but accompanied also by a male angel. Other painted images in the room depict the biblical Adam, a rabbit, a galloping horse, flowers, and a male figure with a lion's head, all centred around the serpent flow here at Huntingtower.

Loch Leven and Moncreiffe Hill

From Dunfermline, Elen skirts the eastern slopes of the Cleish Hills to visit the tiny Victorian church in the village of Cleish. Here we find clear indications of an early Christian site, for the church perches on a raised mound near a holy well, situated across the road from the church, and the remains of a 9th century cross slab, both on the flow of Elen. By the entrance we noticed a little circular stone font, perhaps another early remnant of this now forgotten ancient sanctuary.

As we entered the town of Kinross, the gloomy weather seemed to reflect the rather austere and neglected state of the main street. However, a veil of otherworldliness shrouds the town, for it has the reputation for being the abode of witchcraft where the 'old religion' was once openly practised.

The sight of Loch Leven from the town's main street with its tiny islands more than compensated for our disappointing first impressions. The magical shores of Loch Leven lie in a wide basin bounded in the north by the Ochil Hills, with the Lomonds and Bishop Hill to the east and Benarty and the Cleish Hills to the south. Dowsing confirmed that Elen heads straight for the loch and one of its islands. A ferryboat carried us to Loch Leven Island, once the domain of the Picts ruled by King Dongart around AD 490. Today, the ruins of a castle dominate the island, made famous as the prison of Mary Queen of Scots in 1567. The first castle to be built over the Pictish fort was one ordered by Alexander III in 1257. It was the focus of many conflicts between the English and Scots, and at one time was captured from Edward I by Sir William Wallace during the first war of Scottish Independence in the latter part of the 13th century.

The castle became a state prison in 1390 and the present 14th century tower that forms its nucleus is one of the earliest and best preserved in Scotland. Under the ownership of the noble Douglas clan, the tower confined Mary Queen of Scots, after being escorted there by Scottish nobles convinced of her role in the murder of her second husband, Lord Darnley. A letter written by the Queen's secretary described the harshness she endured during this ghastly period:

'At the Edge of the lake she was met by the Laird and his brothers, who conducted her into a room on the ground floor, furnished only with the Laird's furniture. The Queen's bed was not there, nor was there any article proper for one of her rank. In this prison, and in the midst of such desolation, her Majesty remained for fifteen days and more without eating or drinking or conversing with the inmates of the house, so that many thought she would have died.' (Watkins 2009)

During her imprisonment here, she miscarried twins by her third husband Lord Bothwell, who had since fled to the Isle of Orkney, and soon lapsed into a weak and distressed state. Taking advantage of her illness, the nobles forced her to abdicate the

Loch Leven Island

throne of Scotland in favour of her 13-month-old son Prince Charles James. He later became James VI of Scotland and James I of England.

Fortunately for Mary, Sir William Douglas' dashing 16-year-old brother George had fallen hopelessly in love with her and plotted her escape nine months after she first set foot on Loch Leven Island. In the dead of night, Mary was secreted back to the mainland by rowboat, meeting young George in Kinross. They fled by horse to North Queensferry where they crossed the Forth River to safety. After a failed attempt to reinstate herself as queen, she fled to England, only to be immediately arrested and imprisoned at Carlisle Castle under orders from Elizabeth I.

Despite its history, the island exudes an atmosphere of enchantment, no doubt nourished by the passage of Elen. Perhaps it was a sacred sanctuary of the Neolithic or Bronze Age peoples, later used by the Picts. As we strolled across the beautifully kept lawns in front of the castle, we marvelled at the beautiful surroundings. Elen enters the tower from the south, having passed over a ridge of low hills, called Benarty Hill, said to resemble a sleeping giant if viewed from the east. The great number of standing stones and mounds in this area would also indicate that the early cultures that once lived here revered this region as a sacred landscape.

On the Loch's northern shores is the ruined chapel at Orwell, gifted to Dunfermline Abbey by Robert the Bruce in 1315; it was later abandoned in 1729, when a new parish kirk was established at Milnathort. Orwell derives from a Gaelic descriptive word meaning a 'green or fertile retreat'. Parking our car just beyond the entrance to Orwell Farm, we could see two large standing stones on a long ridge that mark Elen's current. One stands 3 m (9.8 ft) tall, said to be part of a Druidical circle, although cremation deposits found at the site date to the Bronze Age.

The megaliths at Orwell are the first to mark the path of Elen since the Loupin Stanes in Eskdale, northwest of Langholm. These mighty stones give the impression that this was the site of a very large circle, which would have dominated this area for miles around.

We next visit the romantic ruins of a church at the little hamlet of Arngask next to the village of Glenfarg. This overgrown site, now completely abandoned and forgotten, stands high on a ridge. Its foundations go back to 1281, the church later becoming a mortuary chapel of the Barclays of Balvaird which continued to be used until 1951.

Red sandstone effigy of Virgin and Child at the ruins of Arngask Kirk

Beside the roofless mort-house Elen passes through a red-sandstone effigy of the Virgin and Child. Although now completely masked by vegetation, a cup and ringed marked stone built into the eastern wall of the churchyard suggests the site's origins are more ancient.

Before entering the medieval burgh of Perth, we dowsed the female current on a peninsula called Moncreiffe Hill situated between the rivers Earn and Tay. This area was once part of the Forest of Black Earnside, formerly extending along the banks of the Earn, celebrated for the adventures of Sir William Wallace. Moredun hillfort stands on its summit associated with the lighting of fires at Beltane. The name Moncreiffe derives from the Gaelic *monadh croibhe* or *Monid Croib* meaning 'hill of the sacred bough'. Moncreiffe was at the centre of a great battle in the 8th century fought between rival contenders for Pictish dynastic control. It is also another contender for the site of Mons Graupius, the great battle between the Picts and the Romans.

When the Moncreiffe family held the lands, they built a chapel in 1208, now in ruins. They were descended from Ramerus de Moncreiffe, keeper of the wardrobe in the court of Alexander I (1107–24); a branch of this family also own Tullibole Castle. A stone circle stands in the grounds of Moncreiffe House on the southern base of the hill, moved there along with a cup-marked boulder during the construction of the M90 motorway. However, Elen chooses to flow between the remains of a former seat of the Moncreiffes at Moredun Hall at the base of the hill, to visit the Butter Well.

The Dragon of Kinnoull

Across the great Tay River lies Kinnoull Hill, an extinct volcano with a castle-like folly on its summit, situated just to the southeast of Perth city centre. Fascinating folklore associated with the hill refers to St Serf slaying a dragon that frequented a cave overlooking the river. The local legend takes us back to the 6th century when the dragon was busy terrorising the area, slaughtering cattle and abducting local women. The large fearsome creature was no match for the locals so they sought help from St Serf, a holy Christian monk living in a stone cell at Dunning. Agreeing to help he picked up his staff and headed for Kinnoull Hill. At the mouth of the cave he called forth the creature and as soon as it appeared the monk summoned the power of God and slew the beast with his staff.

This particular dragon had an enormous diamond at the centre of its forehead, said to be the source of its power. Over the centuries locals have searched for this treasure with the knowledge that its magical powers would render them invisible. Dragon slaying or taming was a popular pastime for the early saints, the best known being St George and St Michael. In *The New View Over Atlantis*, John Michell reminds us of the many stories of dragon killing found throughout most cultures around the world. Its true origins, however, lie within the principles of fertility. As an annual process, the Chinese believe the dragon is created from a seed born from the Earth, fertilised by the union of yin and yang within the elements of sky, wind and water. The dragon, nourished by the celestial influences, reanimates the landscape until its life force wanes at the end of the cycle. As the dragon grows stronger, it devours the land, until it dies at the hands of one that is initiated into the ways of the Earth (Michell 1983), such as the Druids and the later Christian priests like St Serf and St Patrick. The role of the saints was replaced in medieval times by local noble families, continued over the coming centuries by their descendants, which may explain some of the myths surrounding the so-called Grail families such as the Musgraves at Edenhall in Cumbria.

The memory of this ancient pagan fertility ritual is translated into annual festivals such as those continued by the locals of Kinnoull Hill in honour of St Serf on 1 May. Perhaps the hill was a sacred site of the Druids who held their festivals here, lighting fires on its summit before the advent of Christianity. The steep-sided hill with its ruined tower is situated in a commanding position overlooking the Firth of Tay. This volcanic plug, once the lair of a dragon is also visited by the female current as she heads across the hill towards the city of Perth.

Perth, a Royal Burgh

Perth, once an important Pictish centre, is centrally located in the old territory of the Scottish Celts called the *Venicones*. A Perthshire legend says that Regan, the second daughter of King Lear (909–849 BC) had a son called Cynedda or Cunidad (d. 772 BC) who ruled over Britain. He built three temples, one to Apollo in Cornwall, another to Mercury in Bangor, and the third to Mars, the god of war, in Perth. The Romans, seeing one of their own gods already in place, built a grid of streets around this sacred temple, which they named Bertha. The old foundation myths of Perth are believed to be fictional, its actual name deriving from the Pictish word *pert* meaning 'wood' or 'copse', a settlement at the heart of the territory of the Pictish tribe. However, some argue that the name Perth came originally from Bertha, the nearby Roman fort; the p and b were interchangeable in the old languages and often had the same sound. From the evidence of Roman remains found beneath the streets, it is likely that modern Perth was built over the Roman town. Over the centuries, its strategic position on the west bank of the Tay at the conjunction of two fertile plains next to a major fording point has enabled Perth to grow into a thriving city.

In medieval times, Perth was considered the capital of Scotland because of its proximity to the royal palace at Scone, having been fortified and made a royal burgh by David I (1124–53), the youngest son of King Malcolm III and Queen Margaret. It remained the fourth leading burgh in Scotland until the 17th century. In 1126, King David granted the Benedictine monks of Dunfermline Abbey a piece of land there to construct a church, which they dedicated to St John the Baptist, later built over by the present 13th century St John's Kirk. Excavations have revealed the site was more extensive than previously thought, archaeologists having uncovered a ditched enclosure around the holy precinct dating to the 10th or 11th century, suggesting that the medieval church lay within a sacred sanctuary of the Picts.

Perth was also endowed with four friaries; the oldest and most prestigious was Dominican, founded by Alexander II in 1231 and run by the Black Friars, which also served as the parliament house and lodgings for the king. In *Dunkeld, An Ancient City*, Elizabeth Stewart writes that the Bishop of Dunkeld had a palace off St John's Street erected before 1461 within its own garden, later demolished in 1821. A medieval castle stood to the north of the town, built by Malcolm IV between 1157 and 1160, now the site of the Concert Hall.

Perth today is a vibrant lively city with street cafés, smart restaurants and grand architectural buildings. We found the streets and gardens full of colour as we followed Elen from Kinnoull Hill crossing the Tay through the old Water Works building. Its design is reminiscent of the temples to Venus in Rome, built as a rotunda in 1832 and crowned by a classical urn. It served

The Fergusson Gallery, formerly the old Water Works building

as a huge reservoir holding around 146,000 gallons of water, but ceased to supply the city after 1862 when it became a pumping station. It is now the Fergusson Gallery and a sculpture of the torso of a female nude marks Elen's flow by the entrance.

A short distance away, we are in the grounds and cemetery of the old Franciscan monastery of the Greyfriars, founded in 1496. This walled enclosure contains several elaborately carved grave slabs belonging to the early masons, some with Pictish symbols as if honouring their ancient ancestors. Here, Elen melds with two sycamore trees before disappearing across Canal Street to the Salutation Inn in South Street, once part of the grounds of the Grey Friars. In the early 1600s, the building was the private residence of the Murray family of Arngask and Balvaird, eventually becoming a coaching inn. In 1745, Bonnie Prince Charlie used Room 20 to discuss his plans for the Jacobite Rebellion.

Almost opposite, Elen marks the location of a medieval chapel dedicated to St Anne, confirmed by a plaque in the narrow St Anne's Lane. We soon arrive at the focal point of the city, St John's Kirk, where Elen enters through the south transept. An old map shows that canals once surrounded the church on three sides with the wide River Tay to the east. A mason's mark on one of the pillars marks her flow, as does the modern pulpit, which replaced the original used by John Knox to preach the new Scottish religion in 1559. His passionate sermon against idolatry encouraged the congregation to riot, stripping the church and the city's friaries of all their ornaments and furniture. Unlike the Reformation in England, where the wealth of the monasteries ended up in the coffers of King Henry VIII, the church and friary endowments were gifted to the King James VI Hospital for the sick and destitute.

Elen crosses the High Street just to the west of a building said to be the site of Cynedda's temple of Mars. Historians have claimed that it stood on the site of a house belonging to Colonel Mercer of Aldie called the 'Kirk or House on the Green' on the corner of High Street and Watergate, an ancient north–south thoroughfare. Stonemasons working on the construction of a new building in 1788 uncovered a rectangular subterranean chamber orientated north–south measuring 8 m (26 ft) by 4.3 m (14 ft) with walls built of large stones 1.1 m (3 ft 6 in) thick, with a door in the north and one in the south. A plaque above a restaurant is all that reminds us of this historic, perhaps mythical, site, bearing the coat of arms of Colonel Aldie and an inscription stating 'The Green House'.

Plaque marking the possible site of Cynedda's temple to Mars

A short distance from here is a grand domed structure that houses the city's museum and art gallery. With no religious site left to draw her current north of St John's, Elen has instead found the creative and inspiring atmosphere of this fine building.

After a busy day tramping the streets of Perth, we sat reading up on the history of the city in the warm afternoon sun, opposite St John's Kirk in one of Perth's outdoor cafes. I came across a curious Scottish legend in *The Guide to Mysterious Perth* by Geoff Holder that refers to Guinevere, wife of King Arthur, as originating from Perth. An old children's rhyme also tells us that, 'Frae Perth came Guinevere, to make the king revere. He saw her face in the Loch of the north, and never went more forth'. Holder also mentions the 16th century writings of Hector Boece who states that Guinevere was imprisoned at a castle on 'Barry Hill' where she was violated by Mordred and then killed by wild animals. As far as the Scots are concerned, Mordred was the son of Loftus, king of the Picts who usurped King Arthur's kingdom and kidnapped his wife while Arthur was away on a pilgrimage to Rome.

Today Barry Hill is the site of an Iron Age hillfort to the northeast of Perth at Alyth. Some say that Stone No. 2 at the Meigle Museum depicts Guinevere's demise, while others interpret it as the biblical David in the Lion's Den. This elaborately carved stone once stood on a grassy mound north of Meigle Church, known then as Vanora's Grave, another name for Guinevere.

Elen leaves the city through North Inch Park by the Tay towards the ancient inauguration place of Scottish kings.

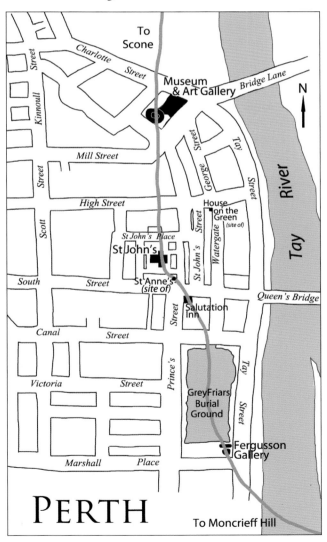

Scone, the Axis Mundi of the Scots

'If destiny deceives not, the Scots will reign 'tis said
in that place where the stone has been laid.'
(John of Fordun; Skene 1871–72)

Located north of Perth on the eastern banks of the River Tay is Scone Palace with a sacred mound called the Moot Hill. Shakespeare mentions it as the place where MacDuff slew King Macbeth, a man who 'was not of woman born', and Malcolm, his successor, 'invited all his adherents to see us crowned at Scone'. The *Scottish Chronicles* referred to it as a place of inauguration for the 'high kings' of the Picts, and a Pictish cross slab from here is displayed in the Perth Museum.

According to an article in *The Scotsman* by Frank Urquhart, published in September 2010, archaeologists from Glasgow University confirmed the date of the Moot Hill as between the late 9th century and early 11th century based on analysis of a massive ditch that once surrounded it. Significantly, the new dating evidence also matches the earliest historical accounts of royal ceremonies held at Scone from the time of Kenneth MacAlpin.

The mound, now topped by the Victorian neo-Gothic Stormont mausoleum, is reminiscent of one of the many motte hills we have previously encountered in England frequented by the male and female currents. Many are prehistoric, built next to fast-flowing rivers to enhance the dragon power within the land.

In 1114, Alexander I invited Augustinian canons to Scone to build a priory on land to the south of the Moot Hill. In 1163, King Malcolm III raised its status to an Abbey,

The Moot Hill, Scone Palace

which after the Reformation in 1580 was dismantled by Lord Ruthven of Huntingtower Castle, its stone used to transform the Abbots Palace into a grand residence.

The Moot Hill is particularly famous for the fabled Coronation Stone or 'Stone of Scone' on which the early kings were inaugurated. Abbot Bower from Inchcolm explains in the *Scotichronicon* that, before the kings were crowned in front of the High Altar in the abbey, they would be inaugurated sitting on the stone on the mound, which allowed them to receive the authority to rule over the land and its people. Scone witnessed the crowning of Kenneth MacAlpin, the first King of Alba, in the 9th century and Robert the Bruce in 1306. The very last king inaugurated on the Moot Hill was Charles II in 1651.

However, several legends refer to this stone as the *Lia Fail* or 'Stone of Destiny', a sacred stone of the Irish Kings of Tara, brought over from Ireland with the migration of the Scots in the 6th century. When we arrived at Scone Palace, I discussed the various myths and legends surrounding the Stone of Destiny with the steward at the admission gate. There are many versions of the story, but my favourite is the story of Scota mentioned earlier.

After Scota's descendants defeated the local inhabitants called the Tuatha De Danaan, they placed their marble stone on a sacred hill at Tara, the royal centre in the county of West Meath, where they inaugurated their future kings. One of them was Fergus MacEre from County Antrim, who with his followers settled in Argyll in the Western Isles of Scotland around AD 500 and set up his kingdom of Dal Riada. MacEre took the precious stone of Tara with him to be inaugurated as the first Dal Riada king. In AD 873, Kenneth MacAlpin, of the bloodline of King Aidan of Dal Riada and the son of a Pictish princess, formed a new dynasty of kings after defeating King Bridei of Fortriu and King Drust IX near Scone.

Many historical writers, including Giraldus Cambresis in *De Instructione Principus*, state that MacAlpin acquired the crown through treachery, killing the Pictish King Drust IX and the remaining nobles at a conference. Thereafter the seat of the Dal Riada kings or Scots along with the Stone of Destiny moves to Scone, where MacAlpin officially accepts the crown as overall ruler over the lands of the Picts. However, many writers believe the later Scottish churchmen and church historians created this story, eager to provide a church-approved version of how the Gaelic line of kings came to conquer the Picts, ending their culture and destroying their history along with the Celtic Church. However, many early sources, such as the *Irish Chronicles*, portray MacAlpin and his immediate successors as Picts and founders of a new dynasty rather than a new kingdom.

Moreover, McHardy suggests that such a great warrior society as the Picts, who over the centuries successfully fought off the Romans, Angles, Vikings and Danes to retain their freedom and independence, would never have allowed their culture to be so brutally eradicated. In fact, MacAlpin was often recorded as the 'King of the Picts of Fortriu' and not of the Scots, and it was only after AD 904 that his descendants become known as the Kings of Alba.

Many claimed that the Stone of Scone was the biblical pillow of Jacob. In 1526, Hector Boece called it the 'Stone of Fate', invested with a *mana* or magical power. Others have described it as imbued with the spirit of the ancestors, the newly appointed king receiving the *luck* or mana from his predecessors through having direct contact with it (Westwood 1986). When Edward I of England (1272–1307)

Coronation chair, Westminster Abbey

fought the Scots, he knew the stone at Scone was a powerful talisman of the Scottish nation and after defeating the Scottish army at Dunbar, he stripped John Balliol of his crown and took the stone to Westminster Abbey.

A local story informs us that the protectors of the Stone of Destiny, realising that the English troops had no idea of its appearance, gave them a fake, hiding the true stone in the Tay River. This is highly probable, their spies no doubt informing the Scots of the intentions of Edward I after the massacre of Berwick.

Recent analysis of the stone by geologists confirmed that its geology matched that of the local Perthshire sandstone rather than Egyptian marble, which is intriguing as early descriptions of the stone, by those who witnessed inaugurations at Scone, described it as shiny and smooth. A former schoolteacher, who has lived in the area for 50 years, informed us that the real stone was black in colour and carved with hieroglyphs. Many locals believe the actual stone given to Edward's troops was a cesspit cover, taken at the time from Scone Abbey. The rusted iron handles still attached to the stone were probably a means of lifting the stone off the foul pit.

There is of course another famous story associated with this stone, its abduction from Westminster Abbey by four Scottish University students on Christmas Day 1950. Having successfully removed it from the abbey without detection, they unfortunately damaged it as they dragged it to their car. Once repaired, they left the stone outside Arbroath Abbey. After members of the British government retrieved it, rumours of its authenticity soon started to circulate and many believe that, yet again, the British were given a duplicate.

In 1996, John Major of the Conservative Government finally agreed to return it to the Scots and a ceremonial exchange took place on the borders of Scotland between the Home Office and the Scottish government. The stone, now safely ensconced at Edinburgh Castle and displayed for all to see, receives thousands of visitors every year. But as to the whereabouts of the original polished black 'Stone of Destiny' brought to Ireland by Scota over 3000 years ago remains unanswered.

Elen enters the grounds from the southeast, crossing the river called Catmoor Burn near the main gate. Here she visits a star-shaped modern hedge maze and an old graveyard, where we found her crossing at a Node with an unknown male current near an obelisk memorial stone.

Following her to the enigmatic Moot Hill, she passes through the Stormont mausoleum on top of the mound. This impressive building replaced an earlier chapel, and observing its architecture and symmetry, it seems apparent that the old masons used sacred proportion within its design. An octagonal tower, capped by a pyramidal roof, stands at each corner of the chapel with windows designed as an eight-petalled rose.

As we continued dowsing the exterior of the chapel, we detected Belinus entering from the southwest forming a Node with Elen inside the mausoleum, 11.3 km (7 miles) away from the alignment, the furthest so far. The building's ornate interior with its elaborate tombs is out of bounds to the public, so we could only guess at the exact location of the crossing. On its north side are a set of steps leading down to the locked doors of what appears to be an underground crypt. Although we were unable to connect directly with the Node point, we sensed that this was where the stone of Scone originally sat, moved to its present position after the building of the chapel.

Before Belinus arrives at the Moot Hill, he passes through the southeast corner of Scone Palace and clips the replica coronation stone standing in front of the mausoleum. Elen then proceeds to the northwest through Scone Racecourse while Belinus heads northeast.

As we overlooked the immediate area from the Moot Hill, we noticed archaeologists surveying the lawns below with what looked like a device for geophysical analysis. We soon got chatting to one young archaeologist, who informed us that the Earl of Mansfield, Scone's present owner, had requested the University of Glasgow to find the foundations of the lost abbey. The use of magnetic resonance imaging had given them a clear indication of the footings of a large building on the lawns just in front of the palace incorporating the old graveyard. I mentioned we were dowsing earth energies here and one student immediately took an interest. I indicated where the current passes through the graveyard and he announced to our surprise that it was the location of the High Altar of the abbey. Perhaps the Node we found there between Elen and an unknown male current was the site of the old High Altar where the Scottish kings knelt before they were crowned after inauguration had taken place at the Node of the Moot Hill.

During a tour of the palace, we noticed a painting of a king on the Moot Hill striking the mound with his sword. The ancient act of placing the sword in the mound perhaps refers to the old alchemical practice of symbolically marrying the king to the land, called the 'Great Rite'. This potent act particularly on the nodal point of two powerful male and female serpents of the Spine of Albion would ensure the king's sovereignty over the land and its people. It reminded me of St Catherine's Hill in Winchester, also considered a sacred omphalos and kingship site of the Saxon and Norman kings of England.

As we sat on the slopes of the mound in the warm afternoon sun recording our findings in our notebook, we observed the archaeologists as they continued to map their newly discovered plan of the old abbey. We were delighted that their discoveries had confirmed our dowsing of the old Abbey's High Altar – a perfect juxtaposition between science and Earth Mysteries.

Belinus follows Stormontfield Road from Scone, lined with magnificent copper beech trees. He crosses the River Tay just below the town of Luncarty to a standing stone on a mount near Over Benchil Farm, just west of the village of Stanley. Made of local quartzose schist, it stands over 2.1 m (7 ft) tall with a sandstone sundial now adorning its flattened top.

North of here, the tall tower of the ruined Auchtergaven Parish Church at Bankfoot

Standing stone near Over Benchil Farm

draws his flow. It was destroyed by fire on 25 February 2004 while builders were demolishing a house next door on a particularly windy day. It is the third church to be built on this high prominence, the first recorded here in the 10th century.

Another standing stone, once known as the Saddle Stone within a clearing of Gelly Woods, marks the path of the male current as he heads in the direction of the popular tourist town of Dunkeld. He crosses the Tay once more through a small island next to Craig Tronach to connect with two large monoliths on the north bank, at the disused quarry at Newtyle by the A984. They are referred to by locals as 'the Druid stones near Doo's Nest', part of a stone circle destroyed during the construction of the road. Like the stone at Over Benchil Farm they are of quartzose schist and when Alexander Thom visited the site he wrote in 1990 that they aligned with the setting sun at summer solstice (www.megalthix.wordpress.com). Another unlikely tradition is that they mark the graves of two Danish warriors who died during a battle at Dunkeld in the 10th century (Stewart 1926).

After Scone racecourse, the female serpent visits Pitmurthly Old Manse, next to a graveyard. She travels along the Tay Valley following the A9 to the impressive Court Hill tumulus, next to a farm called East Mains just south of Bankfoot.

Interestingly, the landscape here is covered with the remains of prehistoric

Court Hill tumulus, south of Bankfoot

monuments, perhaps an ancient burial ground or ritual site. Although now lost, the old location of St Bride's Well is still a draw for Elen as she targets the Witch's Stone further north. The 2.2 m (7 ft) high megalith made of glistening schist stands at the side of the lane leading to Meikle Obney Farm. Elizabeth Stewart in *Dunkeld, An Ancient City* recalls a legend associated with the stone that tells of a witch, willed by Satan, accidentally dropping it at this spot while flying through the air. Such folk tales, encountered throughout our journey along the Spine of Albion, still fix the serpent trail in the memory of the locals. This fertile area of land between Scone and Dunkeld has an abundance of megalithic stones and mounds, perhaps built to honour the goddess energy in the land – Bride's Well just a couple of kilometres south of here may be a remnant of those times.

As we approached the picturesque town of Dunkeld with its historic part-ruined cathedral, we had an overwhelming sense that we were entering a hallowed realm. Its illustrious past also reveals it to be another important sacred centre, but as we were about to discover there were a few more magical secrets waiting to unfold.

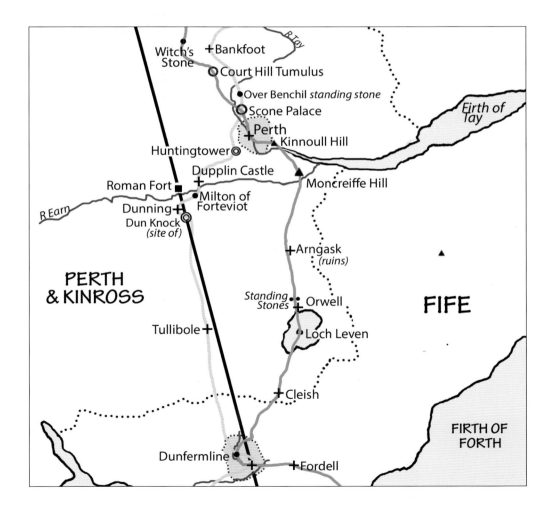

Chapter 15

Through the Sacred Centre of Scotland
From Dunkeld to Faraid Head

Dunkeld, Capital of an Ancient Kingdom

'Ye ancient hills, and thou, Duncaledon
Could ye but speak, and tell of friend or foe
Then would we hear of deeds both strange and great
Deeds that were old, a thousand years ago!' (Stewart 1926)

Early historians describe Dunkeld as the gateway to the Highlands, a frontier town with only mountains and wilderness beyond. The Pictish Kings of Fortriu built a royal centre here to guard the ancient route through this border where the River Braan meets the powerful Tay. It was also an important stronghold of a Celtic tribe the Romans described as red haired and longed limbed called the *Caledonii*, meaning 'cunning people'. Dunkeld derives its name from two ancient British words: *Dun kaled* meaning 'the stronghold of the rough, mountainous country called Caledonia'. Another source derives it from *Dun Chuildich* or 'the stronghold of the Culdees'.

In AD 84, the Romans penetrated the Tay Valley and built a camp next to the river, 9.7 km (6 miles) south of there at Inchtuthill, under the command of Agricola. This proved to be their last outpost in Britain, as they never successfully captured this strategic Caledonii stronghold.

Dunkeld Cathedral

During the 9th century, Dunkeld was the scene of many attempted takeovers by the Scots, finally achieved by Kenneth MacAlpin in AD 834. When this new king of the Picts came to power, he established his political centre at Forteviot and his ecclesiastical capital at Dunkeld, realising that this small Pictish settlement lay at the heart of his newly combined Pictish and Scottish state. Finding the omphalos or the geographical centre of a kingdom was important to the early Celts when establishing their territory, for the navel is the source of connection between the upper and lower worlds and nourishment, just like the umbilical cord that connects us to the womb of the mother.

MacAlpin enlarged the Culdee church to become a monastery to house the relics of St Columba and the Stone of Destiny after the Vikings sacked the Isle of Iona. St Columba was considered 'an indispensable talisman of Gaelic success' and twenty-four of the saint's miracles were said to have been later painted over the High Altar of the cathedral. It soon became the main church of southern Scotland, due to its status as one of the most important places of pilgrimage in northern Britain.

Dunkeld continued as a significant religious centre for hundreds of years, attracting constant strife particularly from the Danes, who raided the area in the 10th and 11th centuries, plundering the cathedral of all it precious relics.

Elen approaches Dunkeld over Birnam Hill noted for its cup-marked stones. The Southern Highland Boundary Fault, one of the biggest in Britain, runs through this hill, which splits the Highlands from the Lowlands all the way from the Isle of Arran on the west coast to Stonehaven, just south of Aberdeen.

The current then descends to Birnam, just south of Dunkeld on the west bank of the Tay. Birnam developed as a town during the advent of the railway within the ancient realms of the great Birnam Wood. This enchanting forest was once a royal hunting ground transferred to the Bishop of Dunkeld during the reign of James IV in the early 16th century. In the High Street, Elen visits the Scottish Episcopal Church of St Mary which stands on the site of an ancient preaching cross where pilgrims knelt in prayer long ago.

The Birnam Oak

She then enters woodland at the back of houses by the river to the mighty Birnam Oak next to a giant sycamore tree called the 'Young Pretender'. According to the information board, the magnificent oak, 7 m (24 ft) high, dates from the 11th century and may have been the inspiration for one of Shakespeare's plays when he visited the area in 1589; 'Macbeth shall never vanquished be, until great Birnam Wood to High Dunsinane Hill shall come against him' (*Macbeth*, Act 4, Scene 1).

This was a prophesy told to Macbeth by three witches, which led him to believe he was impermeable to defeat, encouraging him to murder his way to the throne of Scotland. According to the play, the prediction comes true, when Malcolm III's forces attacked Macbeth and his army at Dunsinane Hill using branches from the trees of Birnam Wood as camouflage; in reality, Malcolm Canmore killed Macbeth in 1058, during the Battle of Lumphanan in Aberdeenshire. Shakespeare portrays him as a mad yet tragic ruler, but history disputes this myth. Although dogged by many uprisings during his 17-year reign, he still found time to visit Rome, where he 'scattered money like seed corn to the poor'.

We continue along Elen's path by the Tay, to the 18th century church at Little Dunkeld. This tiny church was for centuries a place of worship, which held the status of mother church of the parish until the early 16th century. Many believe it stands on the site of a Culdee settlement and in fact the present church still houses a Celtic bell, and linear mounds found nearby may be the remains of the ancient outer walls of the earlier building.

Dunkeld Cathedral and the King's Seat

On the bridge over the Tay heading towards the centre of Dunkeld, I dowsed Elen crossing the river targeting the cathedral. Continuing into the town along the north–south Atholl Street, Caroline detected Belinus passing through the haunted Royal Dunkeld Hotel, a former coaching inn with its famous Gargoyle Lounge Bar. Behind, he passes through a long north–south orientated mound called Stanley Hill; its three terraces having been created around 1730 by James Murray, the Second Duke of Atholl.

This unusual tree-covered sculptured eminence was earlier known as Shiochies' Hill and, according to some authorities, was the original sacred seat of Pictish royalty up until AD 843. The hill or elongated mound may be the Dun or stronghold of the Caledonians from which Dunkeld receives its name. Without any archaeological evidence as to its origins there is little to suggest that this mound was anything more than a natural geological feature. However, the presence of the male serpent may suggest otherwise, perhaps serving as a place of kingship for the early Picts. Curiously, Stanley Hill is orientated to 330 degrees, pointing directly towards the stars of Cygnus on their lowest transit.

Stanley Hill, Dunkeld

The current then changes course to enter St Ninian's Garden before heading through the Duchess Anne Hall in the little square in Cathedral Street. Here we also find the Victorian fountain richly embellished with Masonic symbols and dragons, which replaced the old market cross. In 1745 at the old navel of the town, Bonnie Prince Charlie proclaimed his father king while mustering more troops for the march south to Preston to meet the English.

Arriving at the precincts of the cathedral next to the roaring waters of the magnificent River Tay, we witnessed one of the most magical and harmonious settings on our quest so far. The rose-coloured walls of the cathedral glistening in the sunlight blended perfectly with its idyllic surroundings, nestling in a pine-wooded valley with the Caledonian Mountains as its backdrop. The early morning mist hanging over the river added to the already heady atmosphere, luring us into this enchanted landscape, until the sudden interruption of the church bells jolted us back to reality. The ruined walls of the nave and the restored chancel, now the parish church, display both Norman and Gothic styles of architecture, reflecting the long and chequered history of this cathedral.

Legend tells us that St Columba resided at Dunkeld for some time, teaching and preaching to the people of the district who came in great numbers to hear his 'godlie instructions'. Some sources believe the earliest missionaries to the Tay Valley were St Ninian and a contemporary of St Columba called St Colm, as a chapel dedicated to Ninian existed here centuries before. Perhaps St Ninian's Garden, behind the Royal Dunkeld Hotel, is a reminder of his visit. St Colm, whose name derives from 'dove', also resided on the island of Inchcolm on the Firth of Forth. However, there is some confusion as to whether this saint is actually St Columba, their names becoming interchangeable at several sites around Scotland. Judging from the sheer number of churches and wells dedicated to them, this is certainly possible.

Having defeated Cinaed, the Pictish King of Fortriu, Castantin or Constantine mac Uurguist came to Dunkeld and built its first stone church in AD 810 over the site of a wooden structure constructed by the Culdees, possibly St Ninian's Chapel. Forty years later, his kinsman, Kenneth MacAlpin, transformed it into the ecclesiastical capital of Scotland.

In 1127, the church was given the status of a cathedral by David I, occupied by Augustinian canons from Rome. The construction of a grander cathedral dedicated to St Columba was begun in 1260 by Bishop William Sinclair, brother of Henry 'the navigator' Sinclair, and later extended in 1406. Nothing remains of the Bishop's Palace, however, once standing to the southwest of the cathedral. Like Winchester, the Bishops and Abbots of Dunkeld held considerable power in Scotland, influencing numerous kings and their courts. Many of them were members of noble families, including Bishop Athelred, third son of Malcolm III.

Accompanied by the sweet sound of the choristers as they sung the morning prayers, we dowsed around the outside of the cathedral. From the east, Belinus travels along its axis strong and wide to the tower within the romantic ruins at the western end of the building, its Gothic arches now open to the elements. I noticed that his flow incorporates a carved stone set into the base of the tower depicting a Pictish warrior on horseback holding a spear and blowing a horn. It was previously in the grounds of nearby Dunkeld House, built on an earlier Pictish site and now an exclusive country house hotel.

From the river, Elen appears through the nave, crossing with Belinus within the ruins. However, her flow seemed weak and her width narrow as she crossed Belinus without forming a Node or developing a signature. For this to occur, we instantly knew that their energies had suffered through some form of negative interference. Furthermore, we were surprised to find the crossing point at such an unacknowledged spot so far from the High Altar, so something was definitely amiss here. Up until now, we have always dowsed Node points inside cathedrals, such as at Winchester, Birmingham and Dunfermline Abbey, either under the main crossing of the transepts or at the High Altar.

Feeling unsure as to what action we should take to help the flow of Elen, we decided to stroll around the grounds in the warm sunshine to gain a better perspective of our findings. As we took the woodland trail by the river in the direction of the Hilton Dunkeld House Hotel, once the summer residence of the Dukes of Atholl, I wondered about the location of the Culdee Collegiate College, said to have existed in the vicinity around AD 570.

St Adamnan of Iona records that St Fintan, a disciple of St Columba, built a *Muintir Kailli-an-Find* at Dunkeld meaning 'a monastery of St Fintan among the Caledonians'. A *Muintir* is a family of twelve monks who created a college of education, which produced and copied ancient manuscripts. Each monk was assigned their own circular beehive dwelling constructed of wattle, twigs and mud-plastered walls, very similar to the Culdee community at Glastonbury in Somerset. One possible site is Little Dunkeld Church previously visited by Elen. Upon our return to the cathedral, we were able to gain access to the church, but as soon as I stepped through the entrance, I started to feel uneasy, sensing immediately that the energy was out of balance; after reading the guidebook, purchased on the way in, I began to realise why.

In 1689, the cathedral witnessed the horrific clash between government troops, loyal to the new English King William III, and the Catholic Jacobite army mainly consisting of Highland clans. The Highlanders fresh from their victory at Killiecrankie, massacred a group of enemy soldiers barricaded in the church; the musket shot are still visible in the masonry today. Having garrisoned themselves in Dunkeld, a 700-strong regiment known as the Cameronians were unaware that the Jacobites had hidden themselves in houses around the town ready to ambush them. Short of bullets, the government soldiers stripped the lead off the cathedral roof and set fire to the town to root out the Highlanders. After several skirmishes, the Cameronians sheltered in the church, only to find themselves trapped. The Highlanders forced their way in and massacred them; a mass grave found when new drains were laid shows remains with wounds to the sculls.

In 1560, the Privy Council of Scotland ordered the cathedral's dismantlement and any remaining Catholic idols and relics destroyed. However, the two local lairds appointed to this task merely sat back and observed their men wantonly and illegally vandalising the site. In 1691, John Murray, the Marquis of Atholl, commenced repairs on this eastern limb and restoration continued into the 19th and early 20th century to form the parish church we see today.

Such traumatic events in the cathedral's history have left their mark within the magnetic field of the local energy matrix, forcing the feminine serpent away from her true path. However, the geology of the area also plays its part, its highly paramagnetic minerals and the seismic activity of the Southern Highland Boundary fault line amplifies the wavelengths of electromagnetic energy which holds on to the negative charge in the land created by these horrific acts of desecration.

Sitting under a tree next to the river, we visualised a shaft of pure light radiating through the building and releasing the dark emotions that had manifested from this terrible massacre. We then projected our healing thoughts through the flow of Elen and Belinus, to restore their ability to bring harmony and balance to the land.

We returned to the cathedral and dowsed that Elen had immediately shifted from the ruined nave to the church to form a Node with Belinus at the High Altar. This spot is also the exact site of the old Culdee church. At last, she had found her way back to her rightful place with Belinus, at a sacred place chosen by the Culdee monks long ago. From the crossing point, Elen now enters the Chapter House Museum, once the mausoleum of the Dukes of Atholl. Here she connects with the tomb of John, Marquis of Atholl, and the remains of an 8th or 9th century Pictish cross-slab known as the Apostle's Stone. It shows twelve standing figures, said to represent the apostles.

St Colm's Well

However, it may also depict the twelve Culdee monks who founded their college here.

The following day we continued dowsing Elen through Dunkeld Park to a megalithic standing stone in a field to the south of General Wade's military road. She disappears into woodland to an enchanting holy well, located at the foot of an eminence called the King's Seat. Luckily, our dowsing rods were able to guide us along a myriad of tracks in this dense woodland, now part of the grounds of the Hilton Dunkeld House Hotel. Secreted away by nature, the well is set into a moss-covered rocky escarpment, the mid-morning sun illuminating the water as it gushes out of the womb-like opening of a dry-stone well house. Its dedication to St Colm provides us with the only vestige of his presence in Dunkeld, the possible founder of one of the most important early Christian centres in Scotland. For thousands of years this spring would have served the local inhabitants and been revered by the local Druids as a place of the goddess. The well house is similar to the covered holy wells found in Cornwall and faces east to receive the potent rays of the early morning sun.

We ascend the steep banks of the King's Seat, to a commanding spot set high above the Tay, just northeast of Dunkeld. According to Stewart, this was the other contender for the great stronghold of the Caledonii from which Dunkeld derives its name. Here Pictish royalty up until AD 843 controlled the passes leading to the north. To reach the summit of King's Seat is a challenge, for we had to clamber up an extremely steep slope through overgrown vegetation and fallen trees with no path to guide us. However, both the male and female currents led us to a grass-covered clearing strewn with wild flowers, positioned on a level shelf facing the Tay River where we find yet another Node.

Long ago when King William I, also known as 'the Lion', stationed himself here during a deer hunt, the hill was devoid of trees, revealing spectacular views along the Tay Valley. The hillfort on the summit above us has natural rock-faces, precipices and four ramparts to defend it with, which according to some sources has traces of an inner walled enclosure, now overrun with rhododendrons.

As we walked back to our car, we turned to take a last look at the King's Seat, quite convinced that we had discovered a long lost site on the Spine of Albion. Dunkeld held a significant position in the early history of Scotland, as a vital stronghold of the Iron Age tribes and an important religious centre for the Kings of Alba. Perhaps early warrior kings chose this area as a place to heighten their power over the land, where

two great earth serpents Node not once but twice in close proximity to the great boundary fault line. As we have discovered already, the currents seem drawn to these major geological places of telluric power. Tectonic movements within these faults cause paranormal activity such as balls of light (plasma) and Dunkeld has certainly seen its fair share over the years.

Pictish Stone at Logierait Parish Church showing a mounted warrior riding over a serpent coiled around a pole or staff

The Stones of the Picts

North of the King's Seat next to the confluence of the rivers Tay and Tummel, Belinus visits the parish church at Logierait. Here in the churchyard is a rather unique Pictish stone intricately carved showing a mounted warrior carrying a spear riding over a writhing serpent coiled around a staff, similar to a caduceus. Perhaps this is another depiction of the dragon-slaying practices epitomised by St George and St Michael. Stewart suggests, 'such sensitive and imaginative images we see on the Pictish stones around Scotland were carved by artists cleverly depicting a stylised form of nature interwoven with Christian symbols'.

A church was founded here as early as AD 650 by St Cedd who was passing through the area from Iona with his brother St Chad, a saint who founded many churches on the male and female currents in Staffordshire. St Cedd's Well once flowed near Logierait House high above the church but dried up when, according to a local tradition, St Cedd's market ceased to be held in the village. Until, that is, a strange event occurred in June 1968 after the Atholl Association revived a very successful market. Within one week, the back premises of the house were entirely flooded with water pouring down the embankment after a thunderstorm; an event that had never occurred before even during far worse storms.

In the churchyard, a stone wall encloses the burial ground of the Stewarts of Ballechin, lineal descendants of Robert II and known as a race of big-boned, strong and brave swordsmen. One of the most curious features of the churchyard is the iron mort safes, heavy cast-iron coffin covers used in 1828 to protect the newly buried from body snatchers.

Closer to the Tay, Belinus visits yet another hillfort of the Picts from which Logierait derives its name, *laggan* meaning 'hollow' and *rath* meaning 'fortress'. King Robert III (1390–1406) used the fort as a hunting-seat and built a castle nearby. When the Dukes of Atholl set up a court at Logierait, they erected a gibbet within the fort, now marked by a Celtic cross. Little remains of this glacial knoll, although a defensive ditch is still evident on its west and north side.

A Pictish cross slab known as the Dunfallandy Stone, just south of Pitlochry, is the next site visited by the male current. Colin Liddell in *Pitlochry, a History* mentions that it is made of sandstone not native to the area, some believing it was transported here just before 1900 from the old chapel at Killiecrankie. It is also likely, however, that the mound on which it stands has always been the site of this stone, situated next to an early chapel now incorporated into the nearby farmhouse.

The Dunfallandy Stone

437

As we surveyed the two flattened sides of the cross slab, known locally as the 'Priest's Stone', we were impressed with the fine carvings of serpents, angels and shamanistic animal designs. A crescent moon, a mounted warrior and two seated figures also adorn the cross, as does a pair of smelting tongs and bucket, implying perhaps their ability to cast hot metals. I sensed that this site had been an important ceremonial centre of the highly cultured and skilled Caledonii. Curiously, a local minister writing in 1845 notes that the cross slab was 'long the object of much superstitious attention from the natives'.

That evening we decided to visit the famous Moulin Inn just north of Pitlochry, lured by its reputation as one of the best hostelries in Scotland. As we entered, we could see the main bar area was crowded and the only seats available were two rather small chairs around an even smaller table positioned by the aisle to the busy bar. As we settled down with our drinks with one eye on another table becoming available, we both sensed that the male current was around us. However, believing the drink might be affecting our judgement, we decided to discount the feeling.

Moulin, the Ancient Navel of Scotland

Described as the geographical centre of Scotland, Pitlochry is located 13 km (8 miles) north of Dunkeld and just over 1.5 km (0.93 miles) to the east of the alignment. It first grew as a settlement when General Wade built one of his military routes through Moulin in 1728 called the Great North Road, part of the English government's attempt to make this area of Scotland more penetrable. However, its name alludes to a much earlier settlement derived from the curious name *Pit-clochaire* meaning 'place by the sentinel stone'. This busy tourist resort by the Tummel River soon thrived after the building of the railway in 1863, bringing visitors from all over England and mainland Europe.

Liddell (2008) mentions the numerous megalithic standing stones in the area, many found in groups of four known as 'Four Posters'. Probably the most impressive were the *Clachan an diridh* or 'stones of the ascent' that once stood as a prominent feature on open moorland south of Pitlochry. Long ago, locals would annually process to the site at Beltane on 1 May to walk sunwise or clockwise around the stones.

After breakfast we dowsed the male current in the town at the Holy Trinity Church next to the railway bridge, opposite the Pitlochry Dundarach Hotel. The Episcopalians had been in the area since 1725 and first worshipped in a carpenter's shop until they built the church in 1858. Perhaps the 24-year-old designer Charles Buckeridge was inspired to locate his church here on the male dragon.

Belinus avoids the rest of the town as he turns northwest towards the little hamlet of Moulin, an ancient town on the old route to the Highlands, long before Pitlochry existed. This now quiet picturesque village made up of old stone-built cottages is on the site of a former Pictish royal fort, thought to be the capital of Atholl or *Fodla*, the central province of Scotland. Its great defences consisting of a double circle of outlying hillforts indicate the importance of this settlement, perhaps built to guard the sacred omphalos of the Pictish nation. Many believe Moulin is the ancient settlement of 'Lindum' shown on the north bank of the Tay on Ptolemy's Map of the

World of AD 145. It is the Latin name for 'fort by the pool', which is similar to Moulin translated as 'place by the pool'.

According to local legend, a Pictish chief invited St Colm to establish a church within his fort, although other sources argue it to be another name for St Colman of Kilroot, who came to Moulin in AD 490. However, a market once held here on 18 February commemorated St Colm's feast day, called locally *Feill-ma-Chalmaig* meaning 'the market of the Blessed Colm'. Several churches were built on this site, two having been destroyed by fire, and the present building, constructed in 1875, is now a heritage centre.

Moulin or 'place of the pool' refers to a lake that once protected and surrounded the peninsular. Although it was drained around 1720, the land still consists of boggy marshland. According to Liddell, St Colm's Church was originally sited on the northern edge of the pool or *lochan* not far from a *crannog*. Crannogs were artificial islands surrounded by water, usually circular or oval in form and built as defensive homesteads during the Iron Age possibly as protection from raiding parties and wild animals.

The Earls of Atholl held the Moulin estate from Norman times, and in 1180 the lands and the church were granted to Dunfermline Abbey. During the time of Robert the Bruce, it was handed to his faithful brother-in-law Sir Neil Campbell of Lochee. His son John succeeded to the Earldom of Atholl and built a castle called *Caisteal Dubh* or 'Black Castle' on the site of the crannog in the pool around 1326. When its inhabitants became stricken with the plaque in 1500, the locals fearing contamination destroyed the castle with cannon fire, burying its victims under the rubble.

Belinus visits the old ruins of this castle before passing through the Moulin Heritage Centre, formerly the church of St Colm. His flow incorporates two crusader grave slabs in the churchyard, said to be Knights of St John, and an ash tree, or 'world tree' in Scandinavian lore, revered by the locals as an ancient place of meeting, similar to the symbolic centre at Whitendale near Dunsop Bridge, another important geographical navel.

We then followed him to the Moulin Inn and to the very table where we were sitting the previous evening. To the northwest he glances a solitary megalith in a field called the Dane Stane, which some believe was part of a stone circle. According to folklore, this was the site of St Colm's market, encircled by a moat. Each time two farmers struck a deal, they clasped hands over the stone. The Northern Antiquarian website refers to a story regarding the present farmer. Apparently, in his grandfather's day, several more stones stood in this field and those saved from demolition are still lying half-buried in the field.

After climbing Craigower Hill, Belinus drops down towards Glen Garry Bridge passing close to a 19th century house called *Tigh-na-Geat*. We later discovered that this house has a curious legend. Its former name was *Tigh-na-Teud* meaning 'house of the harp string'. Historians presume that this unusual name evolved from a local story concerning Mary Queen of Scots who, while passing through here on her way to Blair Castle, stopped to replace a damaged string of her harp. The owner, who was also a ferryman, just happened to be a harp player and offered to repair her instrument. Although Mary did indeed have a harp with her at the time called the Lude Harp, many doubt this story.

There may be more to this tale than first meets the eye, however, as the house has the reputation locally of being a 'navel' of Scotland. Meon, meaning 'middle', is also the name for the middle string of Apollo's harp or lyre; it is also an allegorical name for the Belinus Line, which is just 0.8 km to the west of here, and the Meon sites associated with the alignment reinforce its role as a central cosmic axis.

The Grail Chapel of St Chad

From the Node at the King's Seat, Elen heads northeast across the Tay and through the great expanse of Tay Forest Park. In order to locate her flow further north we turned off the A9 at Ballinluig and headed west along the A827 towards Aberfeldy. After a few kilometres, the dowsing rods indicated Elen crossing the road just after the gates to Grandtully Castle, the seat of the Stuart-Fothringham's since the late 14th century.

We noticed on the map that almost opposite the castle to the south stands a small church. We turned left up a narrow track leading to a farm where we found it standing on a rocky hilltop having the unusual appearance of an old barn. Beautifully restored, St Mary's Church at Grandtully is a rare treat, boasting a well-preserved hand-painted barrelled roof commissioned by Sir William Stewart in 1636.

Of main interest to us is the original founding of this church. According to Liddell, St Chad of Mercia built a church at Grandtully while his brother St Cedd founded another at nearby Logierait in AD 650. They visited this area after returning from the Isle of Iona where they took instruction from St Oswald. Ancient stones litter the fields around St Mary's Chapel, indicating that this may have been the former site of a stone circle or Druidic temple. In *The Holy Land of Scotland*, Barry Dunford outlines the various claims by many of the noble Scottish families, including the Stewarts and Sinclairs, that they were descended from the Royal Davidic line of Jesus. According to Queally, descendants of these noble families became members of the Knights Templar who built their churches over the remains of Culdee religious

Painted ceiling inside St Mary's Church, Grandtully.

Detail of the painted ceiling at St Mary's Church, Grandtully, showing an angel and two dragons

sanctuaries after their destruction by both the Danes and the Normans. The royal dynasties of Scotland intermarried with some of the high priests of the Culdees, who themselves were apparently descended from the royal line of David and that of Jesus. Queally also states that the Stewarts considered themselves 'custodians of the land', so perhaps they realised the significance of this site as possessing feminine dragon energy.

Interestingly, one of the paintings on the ceiling in St Mary's Church depicts a Grail knight, said to be Percival or Galahad, holding a chalice while a stone appears suspended in mid air between his hands. The main mural shows the Judgement (Resurrection) Tarot symbol, but the most intriguing is an image of two female angels clearly heavy with child. If the Stewarts who commissioned this work were keepers of the Grail, was St Mary's their symbolic Grail chapel?

Under the canopy of these allegorical paintings, Elen seeks out the High Altar, having first visited two cup and ring-marked stones to the south of the church.

Across the Tay to the north are the remains of a megalithic tomb called the Giant's Grave, which marks Elen's path as she continues north through rugged and wild terrain once covered by the ancient Caledonian Forest. Only one per cent of the original forest survives today mainly in the area of the Cairngorms.

Belinus too experiences its rough crags further to the east before arriving at the ruins of an old chapel in the grounds of Old Faskally House next to the village of Killiecrankie. Orientated to the solstice, the old church was erected on an ancient barrow or burial mound just below a place called Druid. A stone socket, part of the base of a stone cross, once existed close to the church.

Another monument called the Claverhouse Stone marks his flow as he approaches the famous Killiecrankie battlefield. A recent legend states that it also marks the scene of the death of General John Graham Claverhouse, Viscount Dundee, the famous Jacobite leader, a character surrounded with several myths and legends. Many say he was invincible, protected by superhuman powers by the devil himself. While resting against the megalith, he died after receiving an assassin's silver bullet under the arm, fired through a gap in his armour.

The Battle of Killiecrankie

The first Jacobite Rebellion took place during the reign of James VII of Scotland, also James II of England. His autocratic style of governing and his Roman Catholic beliefs made him unpopular in certain circles of government. After his son was born in 1688, many feared the beginning of a new Catholic line of monarchs, which spurred a powerful group of Protestant nobles and landowners to invite the King's nephew, Prince William of Orange, to usurp the throne of Scotland and England. William was already married to James' daughter Mary, both staunch Protestants. While James was in France seeking support to reinstate his throne, the Highlanders rebelled against the new Protestant royals, forming a division in Scotland between the Catholics and the Presbyterians who supported the new Protestant monarchs. James' supporters became known as the Jacobites derived from *Jacobus*, the Latin for James.

The famous Battle of Killiecrankie in 1689 was the first major clash between the Gaelic-speaking Scottish army under General Claverhouse, also known as Bonnie Dundee, and the Government troops led by General Hugh MacKay. General Claverhouse's plan was to fight for both his deposed king and his lost heritage.

The Government troops stayed at Dunkeld the night before the battle, marching through Moulin the following day to meet the Jacobites at the Pass of Killiecrankie. Related by marriage, John Murray, the First Duke of Atholl, pledged his allegiance to King William, leaving his family seat at Blair Castle, just a few kilometres from the battle site, exposed to attack by the Jacobites.

During the battle, the Highlanders charged down from the ridge above Killiecrankie Pass with such speed and fury that the opposing army had no time to fix bayonets. The battle became a rout for Dundee whose forces chased their enemy across the fields killing over 2000 of them. Yet, for General Claverhouse it was not so victorious, as at the very moment of glory he was shot and killed by one of his own men. Despite their victory, the loss of their great leader was a psychological blow for the Jacobites and paved the way for their eventual defeat at Dunkeld.

Legends sprang up after this great battle including several involving General Claverhouse. According to one story, the night before the battle, the spirit of a ghoulish spectre visited him three times. On the first occasion it appeared dripping with blood from a head wound demanding before vanishing that he wake from his slumber. The second time it pointed to its head and said 'Remember Brown of Priesthill', a reference to Claverhouse's killing of the Covenanter John Brown. During the final visitation, the ghost pointed to the plain of Killiecrankie below and said 'I'll meet thee yonder'. Dundee immediately called in a Highland chief and told him what had happened, but made him swear to say nothing if the Highlanders won the battle.

The Killiecrankie Visitors Centre next to the River Garry displays a full account of the battle and from there you can walk to the famous 'Soldier's Leap' where some of the government troops leapt to safety over the river.

The male current passes through the battle site, where the English troops lined up awaiting the charge of the Highlanders. However, this area was once an important burial ground of an earlier culture and their mounds are still evident on the ridge above. The alignment too is only metres away and, as a result, the memory of the battle endures, particularly as it is so close to Tigh-na-Geat, a national omphalos just over 3 km away. As mentioned before, in areas of high electromagnetic energy these terrible events can continue to haunt an area, and the numerous incidences of locals as well as visitors witnessing ghostly re-enactments of this battle prove that Killiecrankie is no exception.

Aldclune, the King's Palace

Further south opposite the 'house of the harp string', the alignment passes through the remains of a stone cottage called Coillebhrochain next to the confluence of the Garry and Tummel rivers. Here Robert the Bruce rested before the Battle of Innerhadden against the English. On the western edge of the Killiecrankie battlefield, the alignment is marked by a set of Iron Age earthworks at Aldclune, also visited by the male serpent, lying in a strategic position next to the Garry between two passes.

Aldclune's history is intriguing, as archaeologists have uncovered the remains of two ring forts described in the 18th century as castles. According to Liddell it is known locally as the 'King's Palace' and in the centre of the site, occupying the highest crest, was a plateau encircled with a triple ditch or moat. Here, according to a statistical account dated 1793, several obelisks stood positioned in a zigzag formation. Liddell includes a photograph in his book *Pitlochry, a History* taken in 1925 in which the three circular banks and ditches could be clearly seen. Excavations here produced many finds including an ornate cast silver brooch and pin dated to the 9th century now on display at the National Museum of Scotland in Edinburgh.

The ancient earthwork is hidden amongst woodland next to the A9 near Snow Gate and almost impenetrable by foot. We found ourselves once again stumbling through dense vegetation, fallen trees and bramble in the hope of investigating this curious historical complex. The building of the A9 has destroyed its northern section but you can just make out one of the banks on the southern side. The male current flows over a high point within this early hillfort that may have been one of its southern ramparts. Also from this site, two ancient roads emerge, possibly old chariot tracks, known today as the 'Queen's Drives'.

The male serpent continues along the banks of the Garry to an area of land called King's Island, which until the 20th century lay midstream. The name refers to Robert the Bruce who rested there after escaping the Battle of Methven in 1306.

Just to the northwest, Belinus flows along the old military road built by General Wade to a little church situated at the edge of a field dedicated to St Adamnan (AD 628–704), Ninth Abbot of Iona and chronicler of the life of St Columba. The Victorian church is all that remains of the old hamlet of Kilmaveoniag, meaning 'the chapel dedicated to the blessed Eonan', Gaelic for Adamnan. The Irish saint reputedly founded a church here around AD 665.

Belinus continues along Wade's road to a hamlet called Old Bridge of Tilt, where he visits an early stone bridge known as the Black Bridge and then climbs a hill to an obelisk called Balvenie Pillar, erected to commemorate the last public hanging in Scotland in 1630.

Blair Castle and the Sanctuary of St Bride

At the southern frontier of the Highlands near the town of Blair Atholl is Blair Castle, situated at a strategic position in the valley of the Garry where it meets the River Tilt. Now one of Scotland's grandest stately homes, this seat of the Earls and Dukes of Atholl once controlled the main route through the Highlands from medieval times. The Norman Earls of Atholl died out in the early 1300s but King James II of Scotland reinstated the title in 1457 when he granted the earldom, the castle and estates to his half-brother Sir John Stewart of Balvenie. After the Fifth Earl died in 1595 without an heir, his grandson John Murray inherited the title, his descendants became the Dukes of Atholl in 1703. Lord George Murray, sixth son of the First Duke of Atholl, born in Huntingtower Castle on the male current, commanded Bonnie Prince Charlie's army during the Jacobite Rebellion, taking part in the famous Battle of Culloden in 1746. The name Atholl may derive from *Ath-fhodla* meaning 'new Ireland', a name perhaps given to this province by Kenneth MacAlpin when he became king of all Scotland. MacAlpin is a direct descendant of the Celtic kings of Ireland whose tradition was to determine the centre or omphalos of their country. Once achieved, they divided their territory into four provinces radiating out from that centre. The central province of Meath in Ireland, meaning 'middle', is a reminder of this tradition and had at its centre the royal palace at Tara.

The Irish Celts or Scots predominantly settled in the Western Isles of Scotland around AD 500, their noble families intermarrying with those of the Picts. With this tradition in mind, MacAlpin may have sought to find the omphalos of his newly acquired territory to build a new royal palace. Several other contenders for Scotland's geographical centre include the 'house of the harp string' north of Pitlochry, already visited, a stone at Abernethy near Grandtully, and Mount Schiehallion, the 'fairy hill of the Caledonians', just to the southeast of Blair Atholl.

Having ventured across a wild and rugged landscape from Grandtully, Elen visits the grounds of Blair Castle and a little mound or tumulus with a tree on its summit, close to the ornamental pond in Hercules Garden. Ignoring the grand castle, she instead continues north through the grounds to a ruined church on a raised mound dedicated to St Bride.

The earliest mention of a church on this site is in 1275 when it contributed taxes to help fund the Crusades. According to a legend, the angered spirits of this hallowed site nearly caused the death of Angus Og, son of John McDonald II, Lord of Islay, after he attacked and damaged the church in 1475. Having experienced the near loss of his ship during a freak storm on his trip home to Islay, he immediately returned to St Bride's to compensate for the damage, seeing the storm as some divine retribution.

Ruins of St Bride's Church, Blair Castle

Although much of what you see today dates from the 16th century, its dedication to the Celtic goddess St Bride suggests the site's antiquity. Revered by the early Celts and Picts, this may have been one of her shrines, one of many Bride sanctuaries visited by Elen in Scotland.

We came to believe that the early tribes associated with the Picts were connected with the spirit of the land and knew how to benefit from its healing and rejuvenating energy and in particular the feminine serpent energy. Their Druids understood how to maintain the balance and harmony of this terrestrial power through positively working with the energy matrix of Scotland. Despite their war-like reputation, the Picts had a sacred relationship with all elements including plants, animals and stones. They felt part of nature and not separate from it, regarding everything as an extension of the Universe. According to the folklorist Stuart McHardy, 'Their rituals were a celebration of the unfolding of creation itself and the extraordinary spiritual vitality and sacredness of life. They had the freedom of spiritual expression honouring and revering nature spirits rather than worshipping divinity'.

St Bride's Kirk may also have been a sacred burial ground, reused by the Dukes of Atholl. Amongst the tombs are the Sixth Duke and his wife and John Graham Claverhouse, buried here after his death at the Battle of Killiecrankie. We dowsed the female current through the side chapel housing the Atholl tombs to a cup-marked stone and part of a larger megalith placed in the footings of the north wall. She also visits the more recent private burial site of the Dukes of Atholl and their family before entering woodland connecting with a giant redwood tree sited on a small mound called Mount Strange. The mound was shaped by the Second Duke of Atholl in celebration of taking his seat in parliament; he had also just inherited the title of Baronry of Strange from his grandmother. Other redwoods were later planted throughout the grounds in 1853, from seeds taken from Yosemite National Park in California.

Statue of the goddess Diana within a grove in the grounds of Blair Castle

We then encounter the most unusual sight, the statue of the goddess Diana within a grove of these giant trees. The statue, which stands on the flow of Elen, was originally designed by John Cheere and erected by the Second Duke of Atholl in 1737 after planting the grove. It was replaced when damaged after the great storm of 1893 and further restored in 1997. Diana is the goddess of the hunt, associated with animals and woodland, often worshipped in oak groves. She is also a moon goddess representing the preservation of man through childbirth and often seen as active in securing the succession of kings. Perhaps the builders of this exquisite recreation of a pagan shrine had placed the statue here to attract the feminine serpent.

During a tour of the interior of the Castle, the portraits of the various members of this family allude to an illustrious bloodline, many of them demonstrating huge influence in both England and Scotland over the centuries. Did the situation of their castle help their extraordinary rise to power, being located close to the omphalos of Scotland, the Spine of Albion and the ancient Celtic sanctuary of the prehistoric goddess Bride?

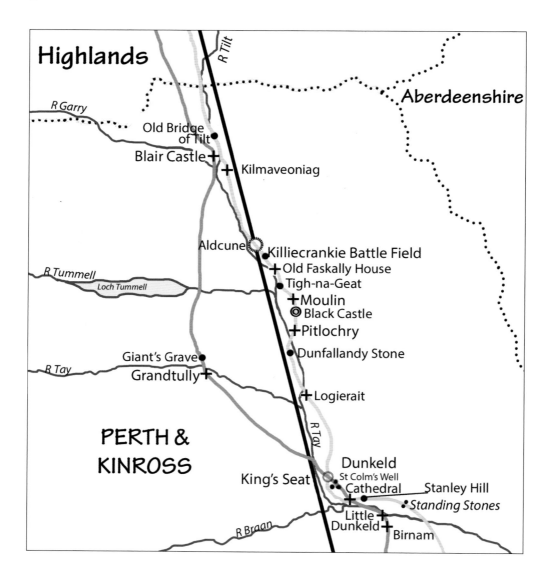

Loch Insh

Leaving behind the beautiful landscape of North Perthshire, with its spectacular river valleys and historic towns, the male and female serpents disappear into the inaccessible regions of the Highlands, passing through the Cairngorms National Park and the Grampian Mountains. In a bid to locate them further north, we enter the area of Badenoch deep in Glen Truim, which includes the towns of Newtonmore, Kincraig and the ski resort of Aviemore.

The alignment crosses the River Spey through the Insh Marshes National Nature Reserve near Loch Insh, an area once occupied by the Caledonii and the site of another key battle for the freedom of Scotland fought between the Vikings and the Picts. The grave of the defeated leader of the Vikings King Harold lies on the side of a nearby hill called *Creag Righ Tharailt* in the shape of an upturned boat through which the alignment also travels. He apparently viewed the battle on a hill called *An Suidhe*, meaning 'fairy hill', to the east behind Kincraig House. The nearby Dunachtonmore Farm may refer to the Dun or settlement of Nechtan, a great Pictish king.

Dowsing around the ancient battleground there was no indication of the currents; instead we found Elen just over a kilometre away flowing through the beautiful Loch Insh, next to the town of Kincraig. As we stood on the shore, its ethereal setting surrounded by Scots pine trees with an old white church overlooking the scene on a tall mound instantly captivated us. As the sun broke through the clouds bathing the magical landscape in a shimmering glow, we watched swans and ducks gliding upon the tranquil waters.

After climbing the many steps to the church, we discovered it has a remarkable history. Local legend says that this site was sacred to the Druids, later built over by Culdees as a place of worship. The guidebook informed us of its dedication to St Adamnan and, judging from its northeast–southwest orientation, this mound may have been a platform for the Druids to honour the summer solstice. St Adamnan, St Columba's biographer, would have preached here in an attempt to convert the pagan tribes.

St Adamnan's Church at Loch Insh

The marshy terrain of the surrounding landscape may indicate that the church once stood on an island. The only surviving remnant of its antiquity is an ancient granite bowl possibly used for baptism and a damaged bronze bell displayed in the church. The bell has wrought iron supports in the form of doves, symbolic of the Holy Spirit and the totem bird of St Columba or possibly St Colm. This ancient relic is reputed to have healing properties and according to local legend must never leave the church. On one occasion, when taken to Perth for safekeeping, the bell rang without aid perpetually producing a sound that seemed to call the words 'Tom Eunan, Tom Eunan', the name of the sacred hill on which the church stands, so it was duly returned. This legend may be an allegorical clue to the magical ways of the old Druids who revered this place.

Furthermore, the source of the bell's healing power may possibly originate from the sacred mound by the lake, probably cast within the energy of this ancient earthwork. According to some sources, such practices facilitated the alchemical processes involved with the craft of bell foundry, using specific metals to aid the resonance of the bell as it was rung.

Behind Kincraig House, the female flow ascends the hill of An Suidhe or 'fairy hill', where the Viking King Harold viewed the defeat of his army. The Monadhliath Mountains prevented any further investigation of her path for several kilometres. We relocated her much further north crossing the River Nairn to a church in the small village of Daviot south of Inverness, having passed through a ring cairn between the Nairn and the River Farnack. Here a vitrified citadel called Dun Davie hillfort sits next to the alignment high above the church.

Further east of Kincraig, Belinus visits the Duke of Gordon Monument, set high on the summit of Torr Alvie within the Cairngorms. Below he visits the ruined castle on Loch of Eilein just south of Aviemore, once the stronghold of Alexander Stuart, Earl of Buchan (1343–1405), and connected to the shore by a causeway. He was the third son of King Robert II, earning the nickname 'Wolf of Badenoch' due to his notorious cruelty and greed – his tomb resides at Dunkeld Cathedral.

At Rothiemurchus near Aviemore, Belinus passes through a church next to the River Druie built in 1886, now used as the Cairngorm Mountain Rescue Centre, formerly dedicated to St Columba. Belinus continues to the old Duthill Parish Church, now the centre for the Grant Clan where a place of worship has stood since medieval times. Once dedicated to St Peter, it stands on a raised mound surrounded by marshland, perhaps an ancient burial ground of the early Picts, as traces of their early settlements are extensive in this area. Records show that its original name was *Glenchearnich* meaning 'glen of heroes'. Opposite, the male current visits the grand mausoleum of the Grant Clan enclosed by Scots pines. They became the Earls of Seafield and this has been their chosen site of burial since 1585.

The Clava Cairns

The alignment crosses the Findhorn Valley west of Findhorn Bridge before eventually passing through the eastern suburbs of Inverness at Inshes, once a site of a Neolithic settlement and the royal seat of the old Pictish King Brude. We had a pleasant stroll through the city along the riverside walk but both currents avoid this most northerly capital of the Highlands on the Spine of Albion, preferring one of Scotland's best preserved prehistoric sites further to the east known as the Clava Cairns.

From Daviot, Elen weaves her way northeast along the valley of the Nairn River strewn with countless signs of prehistoric settlements, including cup-marked stones. At a bend in the river, Elen crosses a field to a ruined cairn and standing stone, one of a group of seven along a ridge that includes a group of Bronze Age burial tombs called the Clava Cairns. There are over 50 in the area, but this group, known also as the Burial Cairns of Balnuaran, are the most impressive. They are in fact smaller versions of the passage tombs that make up the Newgrange complex in Ireland.

The Clava Cairns

This unusually large number of cairns overlooks the Moray Firth situated on an area of land formed by the Great Glen Fault. Balls of light or plasma are often witnessed emerging from such faults, which early tribes may have revered as the manifestation of the Earth Spirit, marking the site where they appeared with stone monuments. The Great Glen Fault is the result of a massive collision during a tremendous cataclysm between two landmasses millions of years ago. It runs southwest–northeast almost exactly in line with the winter solstice sunset and the summer solstice sunrise. The enigmatic Loch Ness is part of this fault, famous for not only its monster but also the many paranormal events that occur there including floating balls of light.

Our journey along the Spine of Albion has revealed several Node points over geological faults, drawing upon the fountain of telluric energy produced during periods of movements and stress in the Earth's crust. The Clava Cairns actually stand upon a ridge formed by a secondary fault of the Great Glen Fault. Often these minor faults produce more plasma, because the larger faults release the built-up energy more efficiently. For example, minor faults in Arizona in North America produce more light-ball activity than the great San Andreas Fault in California.

Before entering the sacred enclosure of the Clava Cairns, Elen visits the stone foundations of a chapel at Milton of Clava, next to an ancient route that leads to the Black Isle and Northern Highlands. The information board could tell us little about the chapel's history except its possible mode of construction using the stones of a large cairn. Its northeast–southwest orientation, similar to the church at Loch Insh, perhaps indicates a place of worship of the early Culdees. A standing stone still

Remains of St Bridget's Church, Milton of Clava

survives next to the foundations of the chapel, perhaps part of a stone circle that once surrounded the former cairn. The Culdees built many of their churches over former ceremonial temples of the Druids, who themselves continued honouring the sites sacred to the Bronze Age dwellers. While researching the chapel in Inverness library, I discovered its former dedication was to St Bridget, the Christian aspect of Bride, the goddess of the Celts.

Having travelled along the axis of the chapel, Elen crosses with Belinus at its east end. If a burial cairn did indeed exist here, its construction over the Node where both yin and yang forces were present would have been seen as favourable by the early priests. The ancient Chinese geomancers would have viewed such positioning as auspicious to future generations, safeguarding dynastic success. For those disputing dynastic control, many of the tombs placed over these Nodes were destroyed, to sever their enemies' control over the land (Michell 1983).

Both currents now direct us to the nearby Clava Cairns, enclosed within a beautiful wooded glade next to the Nairn River, imbuing the site with nourishing chi. All three cairns have central circular chambers, but only two have passages leading to them. They are unique in that each includes an outer circle of standing stones, originally consisting of twelve in all. Unfortunately, because the site was once utilised as a quarry by the locals, the central chambers of the cairns are now open to the elements.

Our dowsing indicated that Belinus enters from the southwest, from a cairn near the chapel at Milton of Clava, passing through all three monuments. Elen enters from the southeast, forming a second Node with Belinus inside the most northerly cairn.

The chambered cairn where the currents form a Node at the Clava Cairns

Recent research by Douglas Scott has revealed that the cairns, along with their cup-marked kerbstones and outer standing stones, form a prehistoric calendar charting the passage of the sun and moon throughout the year. The passages in both the outer cairns align to the winter solstice sunset, the day the sun dies before the rebirth of a new solar cycle. As the early morning sun casts its golden rays into the chamber to illuminate the back stone, the Bronze Age priests would already be inside communing with their ancestors whose bones were stored in the chamber (Scott 2006). The cairns were once covered in red and white stones, possibly a combination of sandstone and quartz, high in silica, to store the energy from the sunlight and enhance the telluric power built up inside.

Culloden and the Highland Conspiracy

We soon realised our next destination was Drumossie Moor near the village of Culloden, the scene of perhaps one of the most karmic events in Scotland's history, just under a kilometre away from the cairns. The outcome of the Battle of Culloden in 1746 shook the nation and its effects still reverberate amongst its people today. Culloden was an important victory for the English, decimating the Highland forces almost completely and ending the Jacobite Rebellion for good.

Although the alignment is over 4 km (2.5 miles) away to the west, we had a horrible feeling that both the male and female serpents had entered the old battleground. A guided tour seemed the best way of confirming this and understanding exactly what went on that day and how it might have affected the currents. As we wandered through the site, we had to navigate our way across difficult and boggy terrain just as the Highlanders had experienced over 260 years ago.

A local wizard, known as the Brahan Seer, uttered the following prediction:

'Oh! Drumossie, thy bleak moor shall, ere many generations have passed away, be stained with the blood of the Highlands. Glad am I that I will not see the day, for it will be a fearful period; heads will be lopped off by the score, and no mercy will be shown or quarter given on either side.' (Mackenzie 1909)

The Battle of Culloden was the final showdown between the English troops under the direct command of the Duke of Cumberland and the Jacobite army led by the Young Pretender, Charles Edward Stewart, also known as Bonnie Prince Charlie, grandson of the deposed James II. The first attempt to restore the Stewart line of kings began in 1689 with the Jacobite uprising under General John Graham Claverhouse at Killiecrankie, also on the alignment and visited by the male current. In 1745, Bonnie Prince Charlie managed to rally the Highland clans once more, hailing his father James III as the rightful king.

The site of the battle in 1746 was at Drumossie Moor near the village of Culloden, chosen by Bonnie Prince Charlie's quartermaster, the Irishman John William O'Sullivan. Why this occurred was a mystery because Lord George Murray, the Jacobite leader's long-time army commander who had always served him well up until then, would usually have made such decisions. To the dismay of Murray, O'Sullivan for the first time ever was placed in charge of the battle. He first ordered the ill-equipped Highlanders to stand downhill from a 5000-strong English army, located just out of sight below the brow of the hill. Their drastically depleted numbers were partly due to many of their comrades having failed to return from home leave just before the battle.

Although unaccustomed to such a disadvantaged position, the Highlanders felt reassured by the presence of the French and Irish armies standing in the wings ready to support them. As the Duke of Cumberland ordered his men to charge, O'Sullivan held the Highlanders back. However, realising their disadvantage, they ignored his command and surged forward, only to be bogged down by the treacherous terrain. The Scots, already weary from previous campaigns, were easy targets for the lethal 'grape shot' fired at them by the English, cutting swathes through their ranks. For Bonnie Prince Charlie, the final straw came when, due to a mistake by O'Sullivan, the Scottish artillery found their cannon balls too large for their field guns. The young Prince fled the scene, abandoning his army to their fate. The Irish and French stood back as the slaughter went on around them, later reports suggesting they saw no action that day.

Only an hour after the first charge, the battle was over and more than a thousand Highlanders lay dead on a blood-soaked moor. Any wounded survivors were finished off where they lay and those who deserted the field were hunted down and killed along with their families. Curiously, the only punishment endured by the French and Irish armies was a brief imprisonment.

The Disarming Act of 1746 that followed was a direct attack on the culture of the Highlanders as it forbade them to carry arms, to wear their tartan and to play the bagpipes. Many of those shipped abroad ended up in 'His Majesty's Plantations overseas' or the colonies. 'The Highland Clearances', as it became known, was devastating for the region, and the lairds according to John Knox 'began the devilish custom of ejecting fifty or a hundred families at a time to make room for a flock of sheep'. Those who escaped the colonies were herded into cities such as Edinburgh and Glasgow. Although many flouted the law, the Highland traditions began to die as the pipers, fiddlers, poets and sennachies (Gaelic for bards who recite family history and Gaelic heroic tales) disappeared. Those who remained lived in poverty while the wealthy landowners enjoyed the fruits of sheep farming on land once owned by the Highlanders.

As our guide described the battle, it became evident that a conspiracy had taken place, to rid the lands of the Highlanders in readiness for the great Protestant takeover. Their fierce independence was their downfall, many clan chiefs having refused to trade with the lowlanders. The English army, made up of many of the lowland clans, were loyal to the new Protestant regime in England, seeing the modernisation of farming as an opportunity for huge prosperity. If the Jacobite cause had prevailed, the Highlanders planned to derail the planned union between Scotland and England.

Bonnie Prince Charlie escaped to France disguised as a woman's maid and died some years later in exile as a poor and embittered man. Why the Prince trusted his incompetent Irish friend O'Sullivan over his loyal and successful general Lord Murray remains a mystery. Perhaps he was duped, for, according to our guide, O'Sullivan was later rewarded by King George II for his mistakes to the tune of £12,000 and a title.

Many visitors speak of 'an atmosphere of spiritual desolation' that shrouds the site even on a bright summer's day and ghostly Highlanders are often seen wandering the old battleground. Many locals in the 19th century witnessed the phantom re-enactment of the battle, while others have seen ghostly soldiers lying dead on top of grave mounds.

To our dismay, we dowsed the Elen current snaking her way through a line of gravestones and mounds representing the various clans that died here. Her real focus, however, is a sacred spring at the heart of the battlefield known as the 'Well of the Dead', where it is said Alexander MacGillivray of Dunmaglass was killed. Caroline sensed that such an act left the female serpent violated, injured and depleted, destroying her ability to nourish and heal the land.

Well of the Dead on the Elen current within the grounds of the Culloden battlefield

The male current meanwhile passes through a huge glacier boulder to the east of the battlefield next to the road to Inverness, called the 'Duke of Cumberland' Stone, on which the Duke stood to observe the battle. Perhaps subconsciously, by mounting the stone, the Hanoverian prince may have embodied the power of the male dragon and possibly influenced the way he directed the battle. Carving his name into the boulder after the battle may have had the effect of fixing the event within the psyche of the local people. Interestingly, one individual informed us that people in the area are still very sensitive about the tragic event at Drumossie Moor as if the battle had taken place only yesterday!

Duke of Cumberland Stone

Although other battles have been fought on or near the alignment, the effects of the Battle of Culloden seem to have been more powerfully felt, perhaps due to its proximity to the largest fault line in Britain near two Nodes of Elen and Belinus. We sensed that the foreboding energy here was continuing to diminish and unbalance the flow of Elen and Belinus and potentially the whole energy grid matrix of Scotland. Did the Hanoverian Kings of England know that the devastating effects of this battle would tear Scotland apart like the Great Glen Fault, or is it all just an unfortunate coincidence?

The visitor centre too provides the thousands of tourists who come to wander over the boggy ground at Culloden with a constant reminder of the gruesome battle on information boards and in numerous books and DVDs. Many are shocked by the slaughter and some leave feeling bitter towards the English. Many psychics and healers visit this place in an attempt to clear its karma and help the souls of the Highlanders still bound to this site to pass over to the light. We contributed to this by honouring the dragon currents of both Elen and Belinus, directing healing light through their flow as they journey over the key sites of the battle.

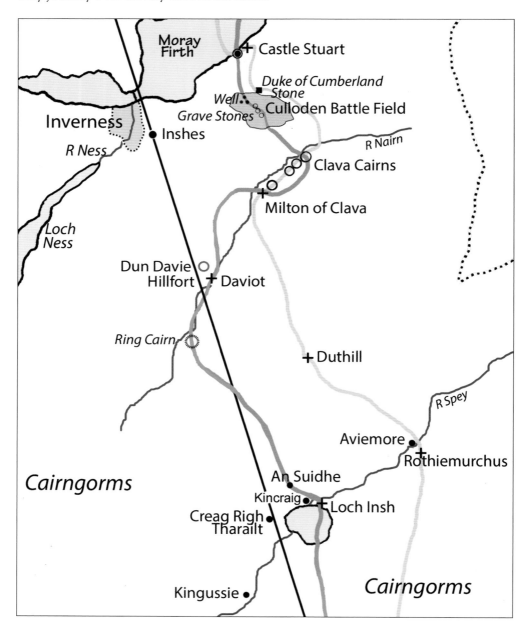

The Black Isle and Brahan the Visionary

From Culloden the currents cross the Moray Firth to the Black Isle. Although not strictly an island, its land is part of a peninsular jutting out into the North Sea, with the Moray and Beauly Firths to the south and the Cromarty Firth lapping its north shores. Compared to the rugged and often austere terrain of the Highlands, the landscape of the Black Isle has soft and undulating hills and lush wooded valleys. Some say the origin of its intriguing name stems from the black fertile soil and dense natural forest that once covered the area. Often, when the rest of Scotland is covered in snow during winter, this peninsular is untouched and appears black in contrast to the rest of the Highlands when viewed from the air. Others say the name refers to witchcraft and the dark occult practices recorded on the island for hundreds of years.

After crossing the Kessock Bridge just north of Inverness, the crop fields and wooded valleys soon come into view, reflecting the unique climate experienced in this area. As we drove east towards the town of Munlochy, I was instantly reminded of the Isle of Wight. Next to the road we spotted a holy well formerly dedicated to St Boniface or Curitan, a 7th century Bishop of Ross. Interestingly the Isle of Wight also has wells to another St Boniface, a strange coincidence. Today it is called the Clootie Well because the islanders still honour the old pagan custom of hanging pieces of cloth or 'cloot' on branches of the trees overhanging this healing spring.

The numerous chambered tombs and cairns on the Black Isle indicate a region utilised by the early cultures as a sacred burial ground. A settlement of prehistoric hut circles marks the alignment as it enters the Black Isle at the headland of Craigiehowe, which stands at the entrance to Munlochy Bay. Here by its shore is a sacred cave leading under the hill where legend says Finn MacCool and his tall warriors sleep. Although not a king, Finn MacCool has many parallels with the Celtic King Arthur as, together with his band of nine warriors known as the Fianna, he was said to protect the High King of Ireland. Many suggest his adventures form the basis of those of the Knights of the Round Table. The stories, said to originate in the 3rd century BC, probably arrived here with the Irish Scots in the 6th century.

Craigiehowe means 'rock of the cave' and inside the large grotto is a medicinal spring oozing through a huge rock said to cure ear problems. Local legend relates that in this cave Finn and his warriors lie resting on their elbows waiting for the third trumpet blast to awaken them. A herdsman wandering into the caves blew the trumpet twice but the sight of the white-haired giants scared him off before he could sound the third.

Perhaps this tale also refers to an energy that lies dormant within the cave or hill, just as we found at Alderley Edge, the Rollright Stones and Uffington. All three lie on a fault line, but Craigiehowe sits on the greatest of them all, the Great Glen Fault that formed the deep lake we know as Loch Ness. Several remains of cairns and hut circles litter the hill above the cave, constructed no doubt on the Spine of Albion to empower the bones of locals kings by harnessing the telluric energy emitted from the fault line.

I later discovered another strange tale associated with this cave, reminiscent of the German fairy tale of the Pied Piper of Hamelin. When a marriage party led by a piper entered the cave to explore its labyrinthine passages and chambers, they soon became lost and were never seen again. Farmers purportedly filled the passages with rubble to protect their sheep from wandering inside so as not to suffer the same fate as the poor unfortunate wedding party.

The alignment also visits the enigmatic Rosehaugh estate, built in Victorian times and described as 'a magnificent ornate palace of red sandstone of a highly decorated Renaissance design'. Sadly, this fairy-tale castle suffered demolition in the 1950s but the impressive grounds remain. It formed part of an ancient Pictish settlement called Pittanochtie later acquired by Sir George MacKenzie in the 17th century.

On the coast of the Moray Firth we find Belinus in the town of Fortrose, famous for its ruined cathedral dedicated to the saints of Peter and Boniface. Its stunning position on the shores of a sharp protrusion of land called Chanonry Ness overlooks the Moray Firth towards Culloden. This unusual natural feature, made up of glacial deposits and jutting out to sea like a horn, was according to local folklore built by a band of fairy workers for a wizard thought to be the infamous Michael Scott. He was said to have assembled the elementals to bridge the narrows across the Firth, but while work was in progress some unthinking passer-by shouted 'God's speed' and broke the spell, causing the little workers to flee.

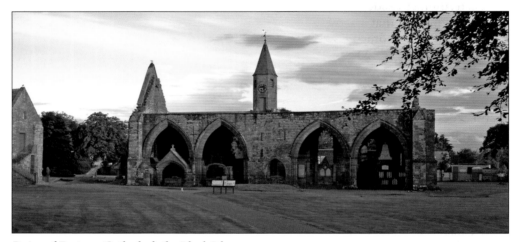

Ruins of Fortrose Cathedral, the Black Isle

As we drove into the quaint tree-lined square, we noticed the late afternoon sun highlighting the rose colour of the sandstone blocks used to build the cathedral. Only a portion of the original cathedral founded in 1126 by King David I survives, having fallen into ruin in the 17th century. Tradition blames the demise of the cathedral on Cromwell's soldiers who took many of the stones to build a great citadel in the Highland capital of Inverness. The paths that mark the old foundations reflect the colossal size of this once grand cathedral. We wandered around the grounds and soon detected the male current passing through the site of the old High Altar at its east end.

According to historical records, 'one of the purposes of the cathedral was for the clergy to sing an unbroken round of worship fit to celebrate the glory of God'. John Michell states in *The Dimensions of Paradise* (1988) that 'perpetual choirs' were established throughout Britain by the early Christian saints who came from the Holy Land. Their mystical purpose was to enchant and heal the land and spread their 'religious influence'. Michell believed this was an ancient Celtic practice from the distant past when governments 'were conducted through the influence of music rather than by a rigid code of law'. Attuned to the seasons, the choirs would also adhere to the astronomical cycle of the celestial bodies.

Belinus resides at the old south chapel and the tomb of Euphemia, Countess of Ross. Her second husband was the notorious Alexander Stuart, the Wolf of Badenoch, buried in Dunkeld Cathedral. He then takes us to another holy well dedicated to St Boniface on the outskirts of the town, now in a sad state surrounded by a housing estate. He continues through Easter Templand, thought to be a Knights Templar site, to the little hamlet of Killen meaning 'white church'. The tiny chapel here once stood on a mound above the Killen Burn, with a spring at its base called 'Bishop's Well'.

Close to the alignment are the scant and overgrown remains of St Martin's Kirk, the oldest recorded church on the Black Isle, now lying forgotten in the middle of a crop field. From here, the male current passes through the ruin of Craig Castle perched on a rock by the shore of the Cromarty Firth built around 1550 by the Urquharts of Cromarty, later becoming the summer residence of the Bishops of Ross. Throughout our journey, we have found that it was common practice for Bishops to build their so-called summer residences on the serpent energies, perhaps taking advantage of the seasonal influences that occur during this time. The ancient Chinese geomancers also channelled the earth dragons to the imperial residences of the emperors.

Returning to the Moray Firth, Elen introduces us to a memorial stone at Chanonry Point, just over a kilometre away from Fortrose, erected in memory of a 17th century local prophet known as the 'Brahan Seer' who predicted the Battle of Culloden. According to local legend the prophet, whose Gaelic name is *Coinneach Odhar Fiosache*, was burned to death at this very spot in a barrel of flaming tar having insulted the wife of the Earl of Seaforth, chief of the MacKenzie Clan. His ghastly demise was the result of a request by the Countess of Seaforth to predict the clandestine activities of her husband during a prolonged business trip to Paris. He misguidedly described his vision of the unfaithful Earl in front of a great gathering of her friends and family.

The Brahan Seer Stone, Chanonry Ness

Another story surrounding his death concerns his association with Catherine Ross from Balnagowan, just north of the Black Isle. Wishing to ensure that her husband's wealth went to her six children rather than those of his first marriage, she recruited 26 witches to do away with them. When that failed to produce the desired result she acquired a potion of poison from the Brahan Seer, who as well as a local mystic was a renowned healer. Although this solution to her problems proved largely successful, she failed to cover her tracks and was soon arrested along with 26 woman and six men for 'diabolical practices of magic, enchantment, murder, homicide and other offences'. After their trial in 1578, two of the women were burned as witches on Chanonry Point and the Brahan Seer may have been executed at the same time.

Rosemarkie, a Religious Centre of the Picts

The village of Rosemarkie lies on the northern shores of Chanonry Ness nestling next to an attractive sandy beach, the cliffs above draped with creepers and lined with trees. The beach is a haven for fossil hunters and dolphins are frequent visitors to the bay. Close by is the Fairy Glen with the Markie Burn cutting its way through its enchanted woodland of largely deciduous trees including rowan, birch and wild cherry.

Next to the beach, Elen passes through a graveyard and church, the former site of a very large Pictish settlement. The nearby Groom House Museum displays many of the Pictish stones unearthed in and around the village, one adorned with various magnificent carvings known as the 'Soul of Rosemarkie', indicating a highly articulate, artistic and cultured community. Anna Ritchie (1989) describes these monuments as unique, having baffled historians for years. Their animal designs, spirals, double discs and abstract patterns such as the Z-rod continue to intrigue historians, some possibly construed as shamanistic. The double disc and the serpent carvings may represent a Sun–Moon eclipse, the serpent symbolising the effects of such an event upon the natural earth energy. Linear lettering known as Ogham script also appears on many of the stones, a form of writing some believe was introduced to the Picts in the 7th century from Ireland.

However, no one person has truly understood their meaning, many offering rather simple explanations for what appears to be quite sophisticated designs and patterns. The crescent moon symbol, for instance, may be an adherence to the cycles of the moon or even the transit of the planet Venus. Venus is often viewed as reflecting a change in the Earth's vibration, re-aligning the Earth grids and electromagnetic forces.

This important Pictish centre attracted the attention of both St Moluag and St Boniface, who built an early Culdee Christian settlement here in the 7th century. St Moluag came from Ireland and was a contemporary of St Columba, perhaps visiting Rosemarkie while Columba was further south converting King Bridei of Fortriu. Legends say that St Boniface, also known as Curitan, was requested by the Pictish King Nechtan mac Derile to build three churches in his kingdom dedicated to St Peter, including Rosemarkie. Many of the later Pictish kings allied themselves to the Catholic Church in Rome and St Boniface was invited to the Black Isle based on his less than sympathetic views towards the teachings of the Celtic Church. Rosemarkie was the main Christian centre of the Black Isle at the time, serving ten smaller religious settlements around the island. In 1124 King David I built a larger church over this monastic centre, which eventually became the first cathedral of Ross until the cathedral at Fortrose replaced it in around 1240. A place known as Temple Croft also existed at Rosemarkie, a remnant of the Knights Templar who held property here.

From the present Victorian parish church, Elen enters the Groom House Museum before crossing the road to the magical wooded valley called the Fairy Glen. As we walked across the threshold of this enchanted realm, we sensed the elementals all around us curious at our presence as we followed the path through the rocky glen with dowsing rods in hand. The female current follows the fast-flowing river to a magnificent waterfall, where the true essence of Elen flourishes in this most beautiful of natural landscapes, such a dramatic contrast to the Culloden battlefield.

Fairy Glen, Rosemarkie

Below the waterfall, visitors over the centuries have pressed coins into the trunk of a large fallen tree as offerings to the fairies. Elizabeth Marshall recalls in *The Black Isle: A Portrait of the Past* how children used to decorate the clear pool by the waterfall with white stones and fresh wild flowers during a time when the whole area was a carpet of wood anemones, celandines and wood sorrel.

Perhaps the Fairy Glen was an important sanctuary of the goddess for the Pictish nation and the early Celtic saints who probably came to meditate by its sweet waters. The shift from the old Celtic ways of honouring the goddess energy at such places to worshipping the idols of the Catholic Church came in 1240 when the power base moved from Rosemarkie to Fortrose. The huge new cathedral, constructed over the path of the male dragon, was a massive statement by the new Roman Catholic Church during a time of great social change. The pagan culture led by the great matriarchs was soon abandoned for a new patriarchal religion introduced by Rome, when monarchs became rulers over their subjects rather than the Pictish tradition of serving the land and its people.

Within the culture of the early tribes of Scotland, woman generally had a dominant role and this continued despite the best efforts of the Catholic Church. Once the weak Abbot Colman submitted to Rome after the Synod of Whitby in AD 664 and surrendered the beliefs of the Celtic church to the Church of Rome, the practice of 'kinship', ceased and the role of women demeaned. The system of kinship as regards kings was the selection by the people of a leader based on their courage, nobility and ability to govern and defend their citizens. Kingship brought with it a feudal system, which effectively gave the monarch and the church a form of control over the rebellious Scottish tribes. However, in a letter to the Pope from the 'whole community of the realm of Scotland', kingship was essentially perceived as being 'subordinate to the community of the nation as a whole' (McHardy 2010).

After placing our own offerings at the waterfall, we continued to an area called 'the Dens' where we discovered strange pyramid-shaped mounds crowned by a pile of rocks, said to be a natural geological feature unique to this area.

Just north of here, a finger of pine forest at Mount High, on the northern edge of a wooded ridge at the centre of the island, indicated Elen's path through a hamlet appropriately called Ellenslea not far from the ruined church of St Michael near Balblair. However, Elen avoids the church, preferring a group of houses at Kirkton just to the north, before crossing the Cromarty Firth at Newall Point. Here in 1985 archaeologists unearthed human bones dating to the 11th century, believed to be from the site of an early Christian or Culdee burial ground complete with a chapel and holy well, still marked on 1880s OS maps.

After a long day touring the Black Isle, we settled down in the local Anderson's Arms in Fortrose with a well-earned drink while evaluating our findings. Looking at the map, we realised that the currents were the opposite way round to those leaving Culloden on the opposite shore to the Black Isle. Why we failed to realise this earlier was a mystery to us, but we could only put it down to the strange energy of this enigmatic region jumbling our senses. This obviously meant that either our dowsing was incorrect or there was another Node between the Culloden battlefield at Drumossie Moor and the north coast of the Moray Firth.

That night we both had disturbing dreams, which violently woke us from our slumber. An evil presence seemed to permeate the room but after projecting positive thoughts towards it the energy dispersed. When we were satisfied that all was well we eventually fell back to sleep without further incident. Over breakfast we felt compelled to ask the couple who owned the farmhouse bed and breakfast accommodation whether they had ever experienced anything paranormal in the house. They immediately looked at each other and told us that they had indeed been victims of terrifying poltergeist activity, which they thought might relate to their property being on land once owned by the Knights Templar. During the previous two days on the Black Isle, we had other disturbing experiences that we soon sensed was the result of a dark energy radiating through the energy matrix of the area, possibly through the dark occult practices said to have continued on the island for centuries. Straight after breakfast, we were on the road again but this time heading south towards Inverness and Culloden to search for a missing Node.

The Healing of Petty Mound

From the Culloden battle site, both currents pass separately through the grounds of Castle Stuart just to the east of Alturlie Point, now a five-star luxury hotel with no public access to non-residents. Just beyond the hotel, we noticed a sign indicating 'to Petty Church' which we found next to a farm. After parking our car in a lay-by, we were still mystified as to what was drawing both currents to this isolated place.

This whole region including the castle and church was once in the possession of James Stewart (Stuart), the illegitimate half-brother of Mary Queen of Scots. Mary granted him the title Earl of Moray and for a time James appeared loyal to his half-sister. However, the young Earl was quick to betray her to her enemies after the murder of her second husband Lord Darnley. He too was later assassinated, his estate transferring to his son, the Second Earl, who also met an untimely death during a feud with his neighbour, the Marquis of Huntley. The Third Earl finally completed Castle Stuart in 1625, having married Anne Gordon, the daughter of his father's murderer. The castle soon came under attack by 500 of the Macintosh Clan, in the hope of reclaiming their ancestral lands, which immediately ceased when the Stewarts paid them compensation; their family vault remains in the churchyard. The castle played host to King Charles I just before his execution and Bonnie Prince Charlie stayed here the night before the Battle of Culloden. After its abandonment, it remained in a ruinous state for 300 years until its conversion to a hotel.

The site of Petty Church has been a place of worship since the time of St Columba, previously a Culdee cell. A local legend says that in AD 565, St Columba founded a church here, having sailed into the Bay of Petty after a storm raised through the magical machinations of King Bridei's Druid. St Columba it seems upset King Bridei at his royal fort in Inverness after the saint sought permission to 'carry the light of the Gospel throughout his kingdom'. Having survived the storm, Columba apparently built the church on the spot where God had steered him to safety.

At the eastern end of this tall and imposing rectangular church are two bronzed statues of female lions, holding a flag between each paw while standing guard over the entrance to the burial vault of the Earls of Moray. Also buried here is Alexander MacGillivray of Dunmaglass, killed at the Well of the Dead, through which Elen flows at the centre of the Culloden battlefield.

Standing in the churchyard we both sensed the same atmosphere of foreboding we had previously

Petty Church, near Castle Stuart

encountered at Culloden, and had the distinct feeling we were not welcome. Putting these impressions aside, we continued dowsing the church, finding the female current arriving from the direction of the castle through the Macintosh Clan vault in the churchyard and continuing northwest avoiding the church completely. We followed her to the boundary hedge where to our surprise we could just make out an extremely overgrown mound or motte in a private garden of the neighbouring house. Belinus meanwhile travels along the east–west axis of the church to form a Node with Elen on the mound.

The mound next to Petty Church

The church itself stands on a spur of land with an inlet accessible to boats long ago. To the northwest is an enormous sand quarry, which may be another factor disrupting the local earth energies. Further dowsing revealed an anticlockwise spiral or vortex of negative energy issuing from the top of the motte or mound.

Standing between the paths of the serpents close to the mound, we meditated beneath the nurturing boughs of an old ash tree. After creating a protective force around us, we visualised golden healing light spiralling into the mound. We called upon the dragon energies of Belinus and Elen to help us clear the negative orgone that had accumulated inside it, disrupting the free-flowing chi. Suddenly we felt a shift in the atmosphere, as if a change had occurred in the frequency of the magnetic field. The gentle breeze grew into a raging wind, forcing us to cling to the tree. Enduring this sudden gale, we continued to send healing thoughts along the serpent lines, to Culloden in the south and the Black Isle in the north, dispelling any further negative charge that might still linger. As suddenly as it began, the wind ceased. The menacing atmosphere of foreboding surrounding the church was gone and we sensed harmony and balance returning to the site.

The origin of the motte is a mystery and the presence of another smaller mound nearby may indicate a sacred ceremonial place stretching back to a lost age. Many mounds similar to these have marked nodal points at other sites along the Belinus alignment including the Devil's Punch Bowl on the Isle of Wight, the mound at Kirkby Lonsdale, Skellaw Hill at Shap and the Moot Hill at Scone.

We were intrigued by the absence of a Node on the Black Isle for the Great Glen Fault runs right along its southern coast under the cathedral at Fortrose and the ancient Culdee site at Rosemarkie. Perhaps the great fault is too powerful and disruptive for the currents, preferring its secondary fissures instead. The mound at Petty Church is in an ideal place to harness the telluric energy from this geological scar.

Certainly, this little known site, together with the Clava Cairns and the countless chambered tombs that litter this region, demonstrates that the Picts and their ancient ancestors revered this sacred area. Recent historical accounts tell us that the Picts honoured the goddess in the land through their worship of Bride. We wondered if this particular mound at Petty marks the start of a sacred route to the Clava Cairns, where the early priests processed along the path of the female dragon as it passes by the sacred well on Drumossie Moor to the church of St Bride at Milton of Clava.

The Northern Highlands

With mixed feelings, we left the Black Isle to continue our journey north crossing the Moray Firth to the wilds of Easter Ross. On the coast, just west of Invergordon, we traced Elen to a ruined chapel at Rosskeen. According to the guidebook this was once a site of ancient religious significance and in a field nearby is a standing stone known as the 'Thief's Stone' which still has traces of Pictish carvings of the familiar crescent symbol and a pair of smelting tongs.

Further north, nestling behind a farm at Nonikiln, Elen arrives at yet another ruined building, believed to be one of St Ninian's churches, abandoned in 1714. A well dedicated to St Columba once existed here; some believe it was the large spring next to the church. The current disappears over a ridge lined with three stone-covered chambered cairns similar to 'Maeve's Grave' in Ireland.

Belinus is further west visiting another ruined church of St Ninian at Kiltearn near Balconie Point. A cup-marked stone at Ardoch marks his flow to Ardross Castle, once part of the Duke of Sutherland's estate. However, it was once the abode of the Picts, and traces of their roundhouses are evident in the landscape. Two carved stone slabs depicting a wolf and a deer were uncovered nearby, said to be amongst the finest surviving Pictish animal symbols ever discovered, now displayed at Inverness Museum.

Several kilometres north of Easter Ross, the serpents take us through the breathtaking scenery around the Dornoch Firth, about 1 km east of the alignment. We first locate Belinus at the Heritage Centre at Kincardine, once the local church dedicated to St

Columba, which until the 1790s was thatched with heather. It stands at the mouth of a river known as the Kyle of Sutherland just where it flows into the Dornoch Firth, south of a town called Bonar Bridge. The river once formed the natural boundary between a tribe known to the Romans as the *Decantae*, or the 'Black Isle nobles', and the *Smertae* who revered *Rosmerta*, the great goddess of fertility.

Centuries ago, the church was referred to as *Eaglais Thomhaldidh*, Thomhaldidh being a 7th century missionary from Iona sent by St Columba. According to a local legend, the Lairds of Kincardine and Tulloch were in dispute as to whose land should provide the site for a new church. The Laird of Tulloch won the day and the construction of the church duly commenced. However, the builders where constantly hindered by the stones mysteriously moving at night by some unseen hands to Kincardine. After several more occurrences of this strange phenomenon, both Lairds accepted this as a sign from God and Kincardine became the site of the new church.

Inside the Heritage Centre is an exquisitely carved stone said to be one of the finest examples of northern Pictish art. Carved in the 8th century, it includes images of David saving a lamb from the jaws of a lion with his harp nearby, the only surviving monument of this type with such scriptural imagery. A later crude carving on the stone suggests that at one time it served as a grave slab.

On the northern banks of Dornoch Loch opposite Kincardine, we find the female current at the small ruin of Creich Church mentioned in 13th century records as dedicated to St Devenic or Devenick. The saint was reputedly one of the last missionaries sent out from St Ninian's monastery at Whithorn. In a field next to the church, Elen is drawn to a pink granite standing stone incised with a Celtic cross called St Demhan's Cross. The act of carving the megalith into a preaching cross served to Christianise an already existing pagan site; even the orientation of the church honours the direction of the rising and setting sun at the solstices.

Elen continues north over Tulloch Hill through a prehistoric settlement of hut circles, chambered cairns and field systems. The site has the protection of supernatural beings, for it was from here that unseen hands at night transported stones over to Kincardine. Were the powerful spirit guardians protecting this pagan sanctity from the new religion?

In 1900, workers discovered a priceless collection of early Bronze Age jewellery during the blasting of a granite knoll near Tulloch Hill. The hoard dating from about 2000 BC includes bronze bangles, anklets, beautifully carved jet buttons, bronze hair ornaments and fragments of an elaborate bronze headdress, now in the National Museum of Scotland in Edinburgh. A large number of burial cairns also cover this area, reflecting the density of settlement during prehistoric times.

St Demhan's Cross, Creich Church

Marking the alignment and the male serpent is Carbisdale Castle standing on a commanding ridge overlooking an ancient fording of the Kyle of Sutherland. It was built by the Dowager Duchess of Sutherland between 1906 and 1917 and later purchased by the shipping magnate Theodore Salvesen in 1933. The Salvesen family gifted the castle and its contents, including marble statues and magnificent paintings, to the Scottish Youth Hostel Association in 1945. The hill behind was the site of the Battle of Carbisdale in 1650 between Royalist troops under James Graham, Marquis of Montrose, and the Covenanters, who opposed the religious reforms of King Charles I. Hundreds died, either from their wounds or by drowning in the river, the soldiers still haunting the castle to this day.

Also close to the alignment a little further north, where the Kyle of Sutherland meets the River Shin, Belinus passes through a mound surrounded by trees known as Invershin Castle. Viewing this inaccessible site from the road, we could just make out the remains of this raised earthwork and a defensive ditch encircling its base on three sides.

Ord Hill, the Centre of Sutherland

Elen follows the Shin Valley to the picturesque town of Lairg, set next to the shores of Loch Shin surrounded by romantic glens and unspoilt wilderness. On the hills surrounding the town are many prehistoric hut circles, mounds, cairns and chambered tombs the most concentrated being on Ord Hill, once an important prehistoric complex.

In the centre of Lairg, located on a high rocky mound known as the 'Knoll at Milnclairn', is the Victorian parish church. The parishioners were holding their local flower festival and a warm welcome greeted us as we entered the church. While chatting with an elderly couple, the conversation turned to the Battle of Culloden and confirmed the feelings of many Scots that the effects of the battle still reverberate throughout the Highlands. Lairg was particularly hard hit during the Highland Clearances, when in 1807, over 15,000 crofters were physically removed from their lands to make way for sheep farming, leaving the glens empty and desolate where once there were thriving townships. At the time, the area was part of the biggest estate in Europe owned by the First Duke of Sutherland, reputedly the wealthiest man in the 19th century, who saw sheep farming as more lucrative than receiving rents from crofters.

We have experienced numerous conversations like this on our journey through the Highlands of Scotland, people often using hushed and doleful tones when they speak of Culloden. But to our surprise, the wife of the couple announced that it was now time the Highland dwellers moved on from the era of 'the Clearances' and focus on the future, having been stuck in the past for far too long. Much healing is still required at Culloden to disperse the anger that has been felt since that terrible day in 1746, not only due to the mass slaughter of so many Highlanders, but also because a whole race of people were driven from their lands which their ancestors had honoured for thousands of years.

We continued to a graveyard at the northern edge of the village overlooking the loch, once the site of a Pictish settlement and an early church dedicated to St Maelrubha, patron saint of Lairg. Maelrubha was a Culdee monk who lived in a hermitage cell on an island of Loch Shin, now submerged by the dam. He arrived in Lairg in the 8th century wearing a coarse woollen garment, carrying a black cane and bible, and ringing a bell calling people to prayer. Described as fearsome, with fiery eyes gleaming beneath his long shaggy eyebrows, he wore a sharp pointed red hairy cap crowning his flowing red hair.

An old legend also refers to Loch Shin as home to a golden-haired water horse who agrees to help Maelrubha build his hermitage on the island in exchange for his soul. The horse planned to take stones from a dun, an Iron Age tower house known as a broch, on the shore and carry them across the loch on his back. Maelrubha, hearing that the fairies of the dun were enraged by the possible loss of their stones, refused to accept the monster's terms; perhaps the magnetism of the stone affected his senses too!

In 1793, the simple thatched pre-Reformation church was replaced by a grander building, which was later abandoned for the new parish church erected on the knoll in 1846. The female serpent imbues both these sites, revered as the divine goddess within the land by the early tribes.

The new visitor centre beneath Ord Hill provided the source of much of this area's history. From there, we climbed the path to the top of the hill where fabulous views of Loch Shin and the surrounding Highlands awaited us. Lairg, situated next to the River Shin that flows from the loch, was for the early tribes a strategic place to receive trade by river or over land from the north, south and west. The loch itself has a mysterious atmosphere and locals say it has a monster just like Loch Ness, perhaps the legendary golden-haired water horse.

Three large Neolithic stone-covered chambered cairns dominate Ord Hill where we find the Belinus current passing through two of them and skimming the edge of the central cairn, the largest of them measuring 27.4 m (90 ft) in diameter. Unfortunately, tall mobile phone transmitters and Tetra Communication masts also share this summit, which has the effect of distorting the energy field of this ancient site.

Cairns on the summit of Ord Hill, Lairg

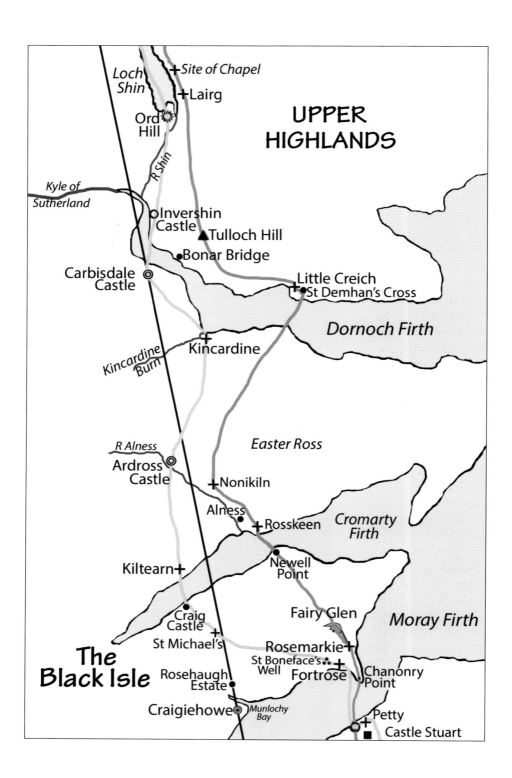

The Faraid Dragon

Realising that both currents head for the north coast of Scotland, we decided to take the A836 across the wild open moors and mountains of Sutherland's upper Highlands. We first arrived at the Dornadilla (Dornaigil) Broch, about 32 km (19.8 miles) north of Lairg, lying within metres of the alignment just to the south of Ben Hope, Scotland's most northern peak.

Now standing at half its original height, this circular Iron Age broch is a dry-stone structure with a single narrow entrance, typical of the many found throughout Scotland. The hollow walls contain a stone staircase to access the narrow galleries above, possibly used for storage. The inner courtyard would have held a thatched wooden dwelling, housing the small farming community, who archaeologists say built the broch as a fortified shelter against inter-tribal raids. However, if brochs were used as a means of defence, why were they mysteriously abandoned in the 1st or 2nd centuries AD when the Romans invaded Scotland?

The design of the Scottish broch is similar in style to the round towers found on the Balearic Islands, Sardinia and Malta, but much wider at the base. They are also reminiscent of the Irish round towers, which many researchers believe act as antennae for focusing cosmic energies to bring fertility to the land. Here, inside the broch, Elen and Belinus merge at a Node, with Belinus entering from the south and Elen from the east having passed through an ancient stone-lined well opposite. Did the ancients build this structure to contain the crossing of the male and female serpents to enhance the energies of this sacred place next to the Spine of Albion?

Ruins of Dornadilla Broch marking a Node north of Lairg

The male current continues north across the summit of Ben Hope, where many lines of the Earth's planetary grid converge. Another ruined broch on the northern-most shore of Loch Hope also attracts the current as it wanders towards the small coastal town of Durness, nestled between Loch Eriboll and the Kyle of Durness.

Elen makes an appearance high above the western shore of Loch Eriboll at a prehistoric settlement. Here we trace her entering a subterranean chamber, known

Entrance to the souterrain marking the female current in the Upper Highlands

as a souterrain, identical to the Cornish 'fogous'. Similar to the chambered long barrows, the early tribes may have used the souterrain to access the cosmic realms, communicating with the spirit world to receive ancient knowledge and wisdom. Perhaps they also served as dream chambers where, in absolute silence and darkness, the conscious mind becomes free from everyday thoughts and impressions, allowing one to obtain higher states of consciousness. Having been fortified by the natural energy in the Earth and rocks, time, space and logic give way to a fathomless connection to the divine feminine and to one's inner knowing – the oracle of the soul.

A single-track road, said by locals to lead to the 'end of the world', guided us into the town of Durness, an idyllic place that has within its bounds the tallest cliffs in Britain and gorgeous long sandy beaches. We arrived in glorious sunshine and stopped off at the visitor centre, where I spotted a book on the area's local history and archaeology. Apparently, Durness is one of those ethereal places where people visit and never want to leave, some finding a home in the abandoned buildings of the MOD early warning station, built during the Cold War in the event of a nuclear attack. Today it is a Craft Village run by gentle folk where we enjoyed a delicious mug of hot chocolate at the café. One local mentioned that great white whooper swans stop off at Balnakeil Bay on their migration from Iceland, bringing with them the snow.

Trudging up and down the moorland to the sound of eagles, we dowsed the currents heading towards the coast and a ruined church in Balnakeil Bay. The remains of the

Ruins of Balnakeil Church, near Durness, the final Node of Elen and Belinus

church and graveyard also fall exactly on the alignment as it reaches its most northerly point of the British Isles. The idyllic ruin stands next to the beach at the foot of a 3.2 km (2 miles) long spur of land or peninsular jutting out to sea called Faraid Head. As the low sun softened the evening light over the pure white sand and the grassy dunes, our eyes rested upon a rugged stone structure called Balnakeil House. According to the guidebook, this intriguing building to the right of the church was built in the 18th century over the former summer residence of the Bishops of Caithness. From 1263, it became the home of the clan chief of the MacKay's, after he acquired the land and its church through his betrothal to the Bishop's daughter and remained in the family's possession until 1829.

The ruins of Balnakeil Church date to 1619, but the guidebook informs us that Culdee priest St Maelrubha, who resided at Lairg, originally founded it in AD 720. We both independently dowsed Elen and Belinus crossing in front of a tomb set into a recess of the south wall, next to a damaged ancient font – the final Node of our journey. The tomb belonged to Donald MacMorrow, whose epitaph curiously reads 'Here lies low ... Was ill to his friends and worse to his foe ... True to his master in prosperity and woe.' Also buried here is Rob Donn Calder or Mackay, a noted Gaelic poet said to be

View from Balnakeil Church of Faraid Head

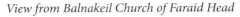

the 'Robert Burns of Gaeldom', and the aunt of John Lennon. According to locals, this famous singer/songwriter spent many of his holidays here with his aunt and cousins.

Faraid Head marks the end of the alignment in Britain and as I studied the angular outline of this peninsular, its shape seemed reminiscent of the head and shoulders of a dragon. Its open mouth, directed towards the sea, releases both the male and female dragons as they flow north towards other distant lands. As the setting sun poured its rays onto the multi-coloured ocean, we gazed across the glowing sand dunes from a standing stone that marks the eye of the Faraid dragon and the path of Elen. Beyond the dragon's snout, a distant island shaped like an Egyptian sarcophagus is the final destination of Belinus.

It was hard to believe that this long and eventful journey had finally ended. It seemed appropriate that the very last destination of the Belinus Line and its serpents is a dragon-shaped peninsular, their journey having started on the southern shores of the Isle of Wight at the head of its serpent-shaped ridge.

Our experiences of Scotland while following the alignment and currents have rewarded us with a great insight into not only its ancient history but also the psyche of its people. We were guided to the most secret places of the Neolithic, Bronze and Iron Age cultures and the lost sacred shrines of the Picts, an enigmatic people who fought endlessly for their freedom and whose sacred legacy is long forgotten. We visited long-lost sites of serpent power, ancient places of inauguration of the Scottish kings, Culdee and Christian sanctuaries, and seen the true beauty of the Scottish landscape through its mountains, river valleys, fertile plains and lochs.

We returned to the church to stand on the Node point. Here, we visualised both serpent energies as glowing beams of light, revitalising and healing the scars of the many wounded areas along the Spine of Albion. As we drove away towards a double rainbow, we wondered if this really was the end of our pilgrimage or the start of another!

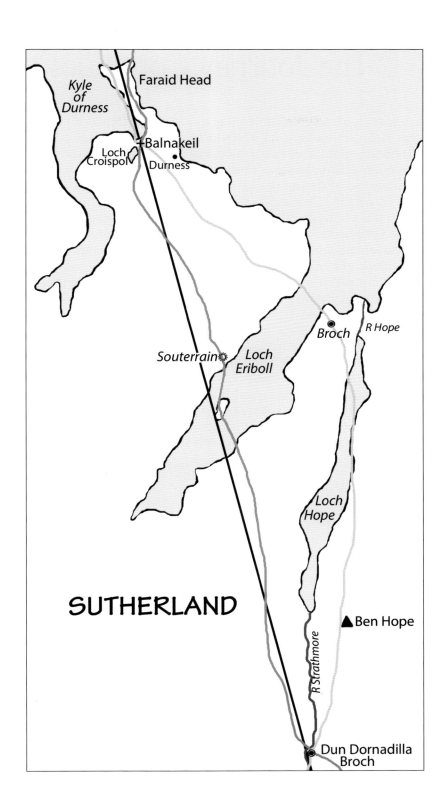

Kyle
of
Durness

Faraid Head

Loch
Croispol

Balnakeil

Durness

Broch

R Hope

Souterrain

Loch
Eriboll

Loch
Hope

SUTHERLAND

Ben Hope

R Strathmore

Dun Dornadilla
Broch

The Journey Continues

The Spine of Albion has several interesting connections to other countries after leaving the shores of Britain that has relevance to our journey (see page 501). North of the dragon-shaped peninsular of Faraid Head, the alignment targets the mysterious Faroe Islands, 370 km (230 miles) away, with their enigmatic landscape and legends of a Nordic Avalon. South of the Isle of Wight near the north coast of Normandy, the alignment passes through the suburbs of Bayeux east of its great Norman cathedral and further south it targets the royal abbey of the Plantagenet kings and queens at Fontevraud Abbey in the Loire Valley. Now a UNESCO World Heritage site, the abbey was founded around 1100 in the French province of Anjou, and contains the tombs of Henry II and Eleanor of Aquitaine, powerful characters on the Spine of Albion. This ecclesiastical institution housed a monastery for monks and an abbey for nuns, called a double monastery. Through the success of this innovative religious idea, Fontevraud became the greatest spiritual centre and largest monastic city in Europe that lasted up until the French Revolution.

The inclusion of Fontevraud on the alignment presents some interesting connections. During the reign of Henry II and Eleanor of Aquitaine, Winchester Cathedral was the spiritual centre of England and Dunfermline Abbey, founded by Henry's great-grandmother, was the spiritual centre of Scotland. Winchester was already a regional capital of England long before Henry, as was Dunfermline, but during his lifetime they became far more powerful and influential. Henry also rebuilt Carlisle in stone, solidifying its position on the Spine of Albion. Moreover, Eleanor was one of the

Fontevraud Abbey in France containing the tombs of Henry II and Eleanor of Aquitaine

key people to introduce the Grail mysteries and romances to England and perhaps rediscovered the tales of King Arthur associated with both Winchester and Carlisle.

Robert d'Arbrissel, a Breton preacher who founded Fontevraud, had the blood of Albion running through his veins. His father was a descendant of British nobles who escaped the plagues of the Dark Ages that ravaged southern England, forcing those with means to migrate to France to form a colony in Armorica. The region was especially set aside for these refugees, later becoming known as 'new Britain' or Brittany.

However, this man was unique; his vision of a mixed religious community ruled and administrated by women was extremely unusual during those times. Interestingly, the Belinus Line appears to have no traceable geomantic corridor of sites through France, certainly north of Fontevraud, which shows that d'Arbrissel must have used divine inspiration in choosing this exact location to build his community. South of Fontvraud, the alignment passes close to Poitiers, where Eleanor of Aquitaine held court with her Troubadours.

Henry II was a member of the Angevin Dynasty of which the House of Plantagenet was a branch. However, they took control of key places on the alignment and serpent energies in England long before Henry's time. This noble family, founded in the early years of the Carolingian Empire, first emerged as part of the minor feudal nobility during the 10th century in an area known then as the Kingdom of France. Their growing prominence provided them with vast power and lands including the Kingdom of Anjou in 1060. Many members went on crusade to the Holy Land with close ties to the Knights Templar, and through marriage became claimants to the Kingdom of Jerusalem in 1131.

One of the first members of this great dynasty to come to England was Ivo de Taillebois (1036–94) who created the de Radcliffe family of Radcliffe Tower and Ordsall Hall, both key sites along the Spine of Albion. After the Norman Conquest, he acquired lands in the North of England and became Baron of Kendal. He built Castle Howe on the female current at Kendal and was overseer of the building of a tower on the mound at Kirkby Lonsdale, a Node point of Elen and Belinus. He was the grandson of Fulk III, Count of Anjou (d.1040) who himself was a direct descendant of Dagobert I, the Frankish king of the Merovingian Dynasty, and one of the most remarkable figures of his time. De Taillebois was probably an initiate of the occult like Henry of Blois as, according to Hole (1977), he was associated with witches. She cites the 12th century Latin text *De Gestis Herwardi Saxonis* that recounts the deeds of the Saxon Hereward the Wake and refers to his defiance of the new Norman king William the Conqueror. The failed attempts by the king to remove him and his followers from their stronghold on the Isle of Ely in Cambridgeshire called for rather unusual measures. Although King William declared his disbelief in sorcery, he relented to the advice of his knight Ivo de Taillebois who knew a powerful witch who could cast spells over the Saxons and at the same time empower his own men.

By the early 12th century, a branch of de Taillebois' family built the tower at Radcliffe and adopted the name of the town. Nicholas de Radclyffe was born there in 1122, son of Goditha de Taillebois. His dynasty prospered during the medieval period, with branches in possession of Ordsall Hall on the alignment and Baguley Hall on the male current. They later became the Earls of Derwentwater, a descendant of which according to *Holy Blood and the Holy Grail* was Sir Charles Radcliffe, First Earl of Newburgh (1693–1746), who became a Grand Master of the Priory of Sion from 1727 until his death. He was the son of Sir Edward Radcliffe and Princess Mary Tudor, illegitimate daughter of King Charles II by Moll Davies, which also made him a cousin of Bonnie Prince Charlie.

The alignment's journey passes through southern France, Andorra, Spain and Majorca continuing to Algiers in North Africa. A few years ago, we decided to spend a few days exploring the island of Majorca, where the alignment clips Sa Dragonera, or Isle of the Dragon. Although the ancient Greeks regarded Delphi as the omphalos of the world, the Phoenicians and the later Knights Templar believed it to be Majorca. Following Belinus and Elen from the north coast of the island to the south, we visited prehistoric and Christian sacred sites and, like the Spine of Albion, we connected with some famous historical characters. Our discoveries through Europe have prompted us to continue our quest of the Belinus Line, which will be featured in a forthcoming publication (see p 501).

The Chakras

We have been asked if the Spine of Albion equates to a human spine and its energy vortices or chakras. Although it seems unlikely that the rocks of the Earth would mirror the human body, there are some interesting comparisons to be made along this alignment. The Isle of Wight, for instance, sits at the base of Britain like a coccyx on the human spine; even their shape is similar. The human Base Chakra is according to mystics the hidden force of the kundalini within, shaped like a coiled serpent. The east–west spine of hills on the Isle of Wight is like that of a serpent. Mystics also say that to achieve spiritual enlightenment we must awaken this sleeping serpent.

If there are seven chakras in the human body then could the Spine of Albion also have seven subtle energy centres radiating this vital power? In ancient Eastern traditions, the chakras were seen as a way of vitalising body, mind and spirit. They each act like a transformer, receiving and sending energy through the body to aid nourishment and connection to spirit, each one having a unique role within that process.

There are so many key places of power on the alignment that it is difficult to divide them into seven possible chakra sites. Although the Isle of Wight is a perfect representation of the Base Chakra as mentioned in the first chapter, the reader will have to formulate their own ideas as regards the others. Perhaps they are the sites associated with legends that allude to sleeping energy, such as the great prehistoric complex of Uffington, the Rollright Stones, Alderley Edge and the Black Isle. There are also the great sun hills to consider, particularly those that operate as a junction of energies, such as St Catherine's Hill in Winchester, Castle Ring on Cannock Chase, the Cloud in Cheshire, Cademuir Hill near Peebles and Ord Hill at Lairg.

The great prehistoric temples could also be included such as the Bridestones, formerly the largest chambered long barrow in Britain; Shap, the once great serpent temple of rose-coloured granite stones; Long Meg, one of the largest stone circles in England; and the Huly Hill complex near Edinburgh. Perhaps a site where two Nodes are close together could be considered a chakra site, such as Titchfield, St Catherine's Hill, Uffington, Dunfermline, Dunkeld and the Clava Cairns (see p 502).

Divine Inspiration or Collective Consciousness

The science of entangled particles may help to explain some of the extraordinary findings and experiences we encountered on our journey along the Spine of Albion. According to Quantum scientists, if the Universe was born from a small area of compressed matter, the particles expelled from the Big Bang would be entangled or related to those from the original source. The latest research suggests that entangled light particles communicate with each other and travel at light-speed, enabling them to move through time. Because we experience our reality through light particles, those within us are able to communicate information from not only the present, but also the past and future. This may explain visions, supernatural occurrences and time-slips. It might also explain how we can sense, communicate with and heal the serpent currents of Belinus and Elen locally and remotely.

Jan Wicherink describes the theory of quantum entanglement in *Souls of Distortion Awakening: A Convergence of Science and Spirituality* and writes 'our physical reality is subjective, the observer plays an active role in what nature is manifesting. In the quantum realm of subatomic particles we are co-creators of our own reality'.

The idea of non-locality, which Albert Einstein termed 'spooky actions at a distance', is also explained by quantum physics as 'the apparent ability of objects to instantaneously know about each other's state, even when separated by large distances'. It seems that 'separate' parts of the Universe are potentially connected in an intimate and immediate way, which occurs due to the phenomenon of particle entanglement. When one subatomic particle splits from another it becomes a separate particle independent of the other, and more extraordinary still is that these particles continue to communicate with each other instantaneously, even though they may be at opposite ends of the galaxy.

Furthermore, recent experimental evidence suggests that quantum non-locality occurs in the conscious and subconscious brain function whereby clusters of entangled particles in a human brain seem to communicate with clusters in other human brains, which explains the idea of telepathy. In fact, this occurs in all living things and it is believed that birds use this system of particle entanglement to migrate from one continent to the other.

Quantum physics views time as a figure of eight whereby the future, present and past all flow together in a loop. As mentioned previously, particle entanglement operates outside of time and space, moving backwards and forwards through time. This would suggest that if we have a natural resonance with the entangled masses of others, we can communicate with them whether it is in the past, present or future.

This also explains the concept of 'remote viewing', which is where the 'intentions by a viewer' in one location can focus on a target in another by interacting with the entangled particles of that target regardless of the distance between the two. However, the success of the viewer depends on whether he or she has the ability to visualise the correct images in their mind. This ability is essential for dowsing earth grids or ley lines, except for water perhaps, which we are attuned to naturally. In fact, those with a great deal of imagination will find dowsing and psychic work comes easily to them.

One can also communicate with the entangled particles of rocks, plants and trees, which is why some people pick up information from natural features, crystals and stones at ancient monuments and sacred places. We ourselves can program a crystal or imbue an object to affect future events. Some believe that the ancestors left messages in the stones to pass on knowledge for the future. Likewise we may also have a link to the future without realising, possibly explaining why some people experience premonitions.

Particle entanglement may also explain how some people can affect events remotely, as in the case of remote healing. According to renowned healer and author Deepak Chopra, our deepest thoughts and feelings play a significant role in the healing of a patient, a concept seriously underestimated in Western medical practices. The body is constantly recycling every atom in every cell. It only takes a year for the body to be completely renewed during which time every atom in every cell is replaced. So what exactly is it that keeps a cancerous tumour in its place if the whole body is rebuilt every year? Deepak explains that the blueprint for our body is the subtler 'quantum body', where diseases appear before they manifest in the physical body. If the disease fails to heal in the quantum body, our physical body will continuously reconstruct itself along with the tumour.

Andrew Collins believes that if we are conscious of the existence of entangled communication and intelligent sub-atomic particles in everything around us, then we can use meditation to help formulate that link. Once you have made that connection with other entangled clusters, events can happen instantaneously. Spells too can be created and practised using this form of communication, through intention of purpose, or through utilising the particles within a strand of hair or the blood of a victim. This might explain some of the strange coincidences we experienced along the Belinus Line. Perhaps we were in communication with the intelligent sub-atomic particles associated with those who created the Belinus Line long ago and have received information from these ancient cultures as we interact with these special sites of power along its route.

One thing is for sure, certain individuals who were born or lived on either the alignment or currents of the Spine of Albion manifested great ideas and became extremely successful, which I have no doubt was inspired through their immersion in this divine Albion energy. The creative genius of Shakespeare and Tolkien come to mind and incredible inventors and philanthropists such as Matthew Boulton and Andrew Carnegie. Furthermore, many towns established on or near the alignment and currents became major cities or religious centres. St George and King Arthur are two of the greatest characters that epitomise the soul of Albion and have inspired many over the centuries to greater things; all deeply entangled with the alignment and currents of the Spine of Albion.

The Great Rift

I believe the male and female currents are imbued with intelligent particles that react to human consciousness as well as that of the Earth, which the Chinese called chi. Moreover, the manner in which they coil around the alignment, crossing with one another at different points along the way, seems to resemble DNA or deoxyribonucleic acid, contained within every cell of all living creatures.

It also resembles the caduceus or the staff of Hermes in Greek mythology, adopted by the Romans as the rod of Mercury, messenger of the gods, guide for the dead and protector of merchants. The currents do indeed act as a guide to many sacred places of the dead and connect with many towns, now world famous for merchants such as Birmingham and Manchester.

However, the reason for the precise angle of the line is twofold. It may have been created solely as a geographically central line running from the Isle of Wight at the base of the country to correspond with ancient routes and fording places, or alternatively it was laid down to mark a cosmic axis. Perhaps it is a combination of both, where heaven and earth entangle to create a great corridor of power around the planet. Looking north from many of the important Node points along the Belinus Line towards the point where it touches the horizon, you will notice certain features marking the setting and rising of the stars of the constellation of Cygnus.

The stars of Cygnus also fall within the 'Great Rift' or Dark Rift, a black river that divides the Milky Way along its length from Cygnus to Aquila and then broadening out to Sagittarius, where it obscures the Galactic Centre. This region of the night sky was considered important to many ancient cultures as a mythological place of heaven or spiritual rebirth. According to Collins, the Inca culture believed the Milky Way was their celestial 'centre of origin', a road for the living and the dead and a pathway to the gods and their ancestors. The Canadian tribe of the Naskapi believed it to be a place where souls waited for the shaman to collect them before reincarnating on Earth.

Some authors assert that a New Age for humanity will begin at the winter solstice of 2012, the exact date the Mayan calendar runs out. Apparently, on this day the sun and the Earth for the first time in 26,000 years will be in conjunction with the centre of the Galaxy, positioned to the east of the constellation of Sagittarius. However, astronomers refute this, claiming that the sun and the Earth have been processing through the Milky Way since 1970, having reached the centre of the galaxy in 1998, where they formed a perfect alignment with its centre. In fact, they are both now moving away from this alignment, the Earth eventually passing the far edge of the Milky Way in around 2110 (see p 505).

Interestingly the New Age movement started around the 1970s, corresponding with the dawning of the Age of Aquarius. It therefore seems likely that this significant time of change has already began, but it is moving at a slower pace than expected.

The purpose of any alignment is to draw from or influence that which it targets. The Spine of Albion is both an axis mundi and a cosmic axis, targeting the horizon where once a day the Dark Rift sets, a region of the Milky Way that includes Cygnus X3. Therefore when Cygnus X3 decides to send another powerful ray of DNA-changing cosmic particles to Earth through the Dark Rift, perhaps on the day the Mayan calendar ends, the Spine of Albion and its currents may draw into themselves this cosmic energy, creating a massive shift in the Earth energies at specific sites as well as in human consciousness.

The landscape of Britain holds many secrets, but modern man has only learned to extract its great mineral wealth to produce space travel and the highest technology and in doing so has failed to respect and understand the energetic qualities of the land. We have utilised this great country solely for material gain, having lost the understanding of what it can truly provide us, such as spiritual healing and growth. The ancient peoples of this land understood and integrated themselves with the healing and inspirational power of nature. We, however, have been deprived of this knowledge through the persuasive despotic religious dogma and greedy and corrupt overlords. Nevertheless, Caroline and I feel that by following the male and female serpents along the Spine of Albion, we have exposed glimmers of this ancient knowledge and revealed some of the most enchanted landscapes and magical places that you will ever see.

Although we have helped to heal and realign many of the sites along the Belinus Line where it was needed, we strongly feel that the alignment and its corresponding serpent energies would benefit from modern pilgrims walking their paths and connecting with the special sites they visit. In doing so, the Earth serpents will respond by communicating pure rejuvenating and inspirational energy for those who are receptive. Already we have heard numerous stories and met many people who have been drawn to connect with them, some experiencing great visions, inspirational guidance or enlightenment. In the act of healing the land, we also help to heal ourselves. The Druids knew how to maintain their land by dispelling negative energies at sacred sites using words of power. The pilgrim may benefit the land by using visualisation as we have described or positive invocations or prayers.

Channelled or inspirational sources also inform us that we are experiencing a time of change, during which time higher vibrational energies directed at the Earth will rejuvenate the sacred sites and raise the consciousness of man but retain the knowledge, skills and wisdom of the ancestors. In the future, people will notice the difference in the energy and purpose of these sites; 'each will be unique but a greater power and radiance will be expressed and some sites will be reformed into their original purpose but with a different energetic and vibrational alignment. This will create a continuously flowing network of light and consciousness linking all the sacred sites into a vast network of energy' (www.omna.org). This rise in the vibration of the Earth will help humanity open their hearts as well as their minds to receiving the new consciousness and perhaps by walking the pathways of the Spine of Albion we will be helping to achieve this glorious future.

After completing the investigation of the Spine of Albion, we returned to St Catherine's Hill near Winchester and reflected on an adventure that for me began back in 1993. William Wykeham, 14th century Bishop of Winchester, owner of St Catherine's Hill and builder of Winchester College, was a key character on the Spine of Albion. Here was a man who taught his scholars the practice of connecting with the energies in the land for inspiration, summed up perfectly in an ode dedicated to him by Lord Selborne:

'Learn the old truths
Speak the old words
Walk in the ancient ways.'

Bibliography

Ainsworth W H (1899) *Guy Fawkes; or the gunpowder treason.* Routledge and Sons, London.

Aitchison N (2006) *Forteviot, A Pictish and Scottish Royal Centre.* Tempus Publishing, Stroud.

Ashe G (1968) *The Quest for Arthur's Britain.* Pall Mall Press, London.

Baigent M, Leigh R & Lincoln H (1982) *The Holy Blood and the Holy Grail.* Corgi Books, London.

Baldwin G (2004) *Most Haunted Island.* Gay Baldwin, Cowes, Isle of Wight. www.ghost-island.com.

Bergin T & Shaw S (1975) *Salford, a City and its Past.* City of Salford Cultural Services Department, Salford.

Biltcliffe G (2009) *The Spirit of Portland: Revelations of a Sacred Isle.* Roving Press, Dorchester.

Bloxham C (2005) *Folklore of Oxfordshire.* Tempus Publishing, Stroud.

Broadhurst P (2006) *The Green Man and the Dragon.* Mythos, Launceston.

Broadhurst P & Miller H (2000) *The Dance of the Dragon: An Odyssey into Earth Mysteries and Ancient Religion.* Pendragon Press, Launceston.

Bromwich R (1961) *The Welsh Triads.* University of Wales Press, Cardiff.

Burl A (1976) *The Stone Circles of the British Isles.* Yale University Press, London.

Burl A (1993) *From Carnac to Callanish: The Prehistoric Stone Rows and Avenues of Britain, Ireland and Brittany.* Yale University Press, London.

Callahan P S (1984) *Ancient Mysteries, Modern Visions.* Acres, Kansas City.

Carruthers F J (1979) *People Called Cumbri, the Heroic Age of the Cumbrian Celts.* Robert Hale, London.

Chesterton G K (1911, 2001) *Ballad of the White Horse.* Ignatius Press, San Francisco.

Child F J (1882–98) *English and Scottish Popular Ballads.* Houghton, Mifflin & Co., London.

Clare T (2007) *Prehistoric Monuments of the Lake District.* Tempus Publishing, Stroud.

Collins A (1988) *The Black Alchemist.* ABC Books, Leigh-on-Sea.

Collins A (1991) *The Seventh Sword.* Century, London.

Collins A (1992) *The Circlemakers.* ABC Books, Leigh-on-Sea.

Collins A (1993) *The Second Coming.* Century, London.

Collins A (2006) *The Cygnus Mystery.* Watkins Publishing, London.

Cooper W (1995) *After the Flood.* New Wine Press, Chichester.

Coppins P (2007) *Land of the Gods.* Frontier Publishing, Amsterdam.

Cowper A S (2003) *Historic Corstorphine and Round About.* The Corstorphine Trust, Edinburgh.

Dee Dr J (1570, 1975) *The Mathematicall Praeface to the Elements of Geometrie of Euclid of Megara.* Science History Publications, New York.

Devereux P (1990) *Places of Power, Secret Energies at Ancient Sites: A Guide to Observed or Measured Phenomena.* Blandford, London.

Dixon J (2003) *Dunsop Bridge: Bowland Forest.* Aussteiger Publications, Clitheroe.

Dixon J & Dixon P (1993) *Journeys Through Brigantia, Volume Nine: The Ribble Valley, Circular Walks 'Twixt Bowland & Pendle Where Rivers Meet.* Aussteiger Publications,

Clitheroe.

Dugdale G (1998) *Walks in Mysterious North Lakeland.* Sigma Leisure, Wilmslow.

Dugdale W (1656) *Antiquities of Warwickshire. http://archive.org/details/antiquitiesofwar00dugd.*

Dumville D (ed.), Shirley-Price L & Farmer D (translators) (2003) *Bede: Ecclesiastical History of the English People.* Penguin Classics, London.

Dunford B (2002) *The Holy Land of Scotland.* Sacred Connections, Perthshire.

Dunford B (2008) *Vision of Albion, the Key to the Holy Grail.* Sacred Connections, Perthshire.

Elder I H (1962) *Celt, Druid and Culdee.* Covenant Publishing, London.

Eliade M (1961) *Images and Symbols: Studies in Religious Symbolism.* Harvill Press, London.

Ellis R (2006) *Scota, Egyptian Queen of the Scots.* Edfu Books, Cheshire.

Evans A J (1895) The Rollright Stones and their Folklore. *Folklore,* **6** (1).

Farrah R (2008) *A Guide to the Stone Circles of Cumbria.* Hayloft Publishing, Kirkby Stephen.

Fetherstonhaugh T (1925) *Our Cumberland Village.* Chas Thurnam & Sons, Carlisle.

Fortune D (1962) *Aspects of Occultism.* Aquarian Press, Wellingborough.

Fox G (1694, 2010) *Journal of George Fox.* Friends United Press, Richmond, USA.

Furness W (1894) *The History of Penrith.* W Furness, Penrith.

Furnival B (1999) *Windsor of the North.* Ross Features, London.

Fyfe A (2010) Shakespeare and Hermetic Magic. In: *Temple Antiquities: The Templar Papers II*, O. Olsen (ed.). O Books, Winchester.

Gardner G (2008) Adventures in Dowsing, Part 6: Life, the Universe and Everything. *Dowsing Today,* **41**(301), British Society of Dowsers.

Geoffrey of Monmouth (1136, 1984) *The History of the Kings of Britain.* Folio Society, London.

Gilbert A, Wilson A & Blackett B (1998) *The Holy Kingdom: The Quest for the Real King Arthur.* Bantam Press, London.

Goodrich N (1989) *King Arthur.* Harper Collins, New York.

Gordon E O (1932) *Prehistoric London.* Covenant Publishing, London.

Graves T (1978) *Needles of Stone.* Gothic Image Publications, Glastonbury.

Grinsell L V (1977) *The Rollright Stones and Their Folklore.* Toucan Press, Guernsey.

Gunn Dr (1907) *The Book of Stobo Church. Books of the Church Series.* Peebles Press, Peebles.

Hanauer J E (2003) *Folklore of the Holy Land.* Dover Publications, New York.

Handford S A (ed.), Mattingly H (translator) (1971) *Tacitus: The Agricola and the Germania,* Penguin Classics, London.

Harpur P, Brown A & Michell J (2005) *Crooked Soley: A Crop Circle Revelation.* Roundhill Press, Brighton.

Harrison H (2009) *Crown of Stars: The Grail in the Troubadour World.* https://www.smashwords.com/books.

Hartland E S (1925) *The Science of Fairy Tales.* Methuen, London.

Henbury Society (eds) (2003) *Henbury: History of a Village.* Cambrian Press, Aberystwyth.

Henderson R W (2008/09) *The History of the Kings of the Picts.* www.thesonsofscotland.co.uk.

Hindle P (1982) *Medieval Roads and Tracks.* Shire Publications, Princes Risborough.

Hodder M (2004) *Birmingham: The Hidden History.* Tempus Publishing, Stroud.

Holder G (2006) *Guide to Mysterious Perthshire*. Tempus Publishing, Stroud.

Hole C (1977) *Witchcraft in Britain*. Paladin Books, London.

Howitt W (1840) *Visits to Remarkable Places*. Longman, Green, London.

Hutchinson W (1794) *History of the County of Cumberland*. F. Jollie, Carlisle.

Icke D (1995) *The Truth Will Set You Free*. Bridge of Love Publications, Cambridge.

Ingram J (translator) (1912) *The Anglo-Saxon Chronicle*. Everyman Press, London.

Innes B (1981) Britain's Magical Island. *The Unexplained: Mysteries of Mind, Space and Time*, **2**(14), Orbis, London.

Jones G & Jones T (translators) (1949) *The Mabinogion*. JM Dent & Sons, London.

Kaulins A (2003) *Stars, Stones and Scholars*. Trafford Publishing, Victoria, British Columbia.

Keller W (1975) *The Etruscans*. Book Club Associates, London.

Kent J (2001) *The Mysterious Double Sunset*. Witan Books, Stafford.

Langstone A (1992) *Bega and the Sacred Ring*. Lantern Press, London.

Langshaw A (1947) *The Collected Works of A. Langshaw*. Kaydee Bookshop, Clitheroe.

Liddell C (2008) *Pitlochry, a History*. Watermill Books, Aberfeldy.

Lockyer N (1906) *Stonehenge and Other British Stone Monuments Astronomically Considered*. Macmillan, London.

Lynch M (1992) *Scotland, a New History*. Pimilico, London.

Mackenzie A (1909) *The Prophecies of the Brahan Seer*. E Mackay, Stirling.

MacLellan A (1983*) The Lost World of Agharti*. Corgi Books, London.

MacLellan A (1999) *The Hollow Earth Enigma*. Souvenir Press, London.

Madden Sir F (1847) *Layamon's Brut or the Chronicle of Britain*. Society of Antiquaries of London.

Mann N & Glasson P (2010) *The Star Temple of Avalon: Glastonbury's Ancient Observatory Revealed*. Temple Publications, Wells.

Mannix D P (1961, 1970) *The Hell-Fire Club*. New English Library, London.

Marshall E (1992) *The Black Isle: A Portrait of the Past*. JC Proteroe, Fortrose.

Masterman J H B (1920) *History of the English Towns: Birmingham*. Society for Promoting Christian Knowledge, London.

Matthews S (2009) *King Arthur Lives in Merrie Carlisle*. Bookcase, Carlisle.

McHardy S (2010) *A New History of the Picts*. Luath Press, Edinburgh.

Mee A (1937) *The King's England, Staffordshire*. Hodder & Stoughton, London.

Mee A (1937) *Lake Counties*. Hodder & Stoughton, London.

Michell J (1983) *The New View Over Atlantis*. Thames & Hudson, London.

Michell J (1988) *The Dimensions of Paradise*. Thames & Hudson, London.

Michell J & Rhone C (1991) *Twelve Tribe Nations*. Thames & Hudson, London.

Miller H & Broadhurst P (1989) *The Sun and the Serpent*. Pendragon Press, Launceston.

Miller S H (transcription), Sweeting W D (translator) (1895) *De Gestis Herwardi Saxonis. The Exploits of Hereward the Saxon*. Fenland Notes & Queries, **3** (Supplements), Peterborough.

Moffat A (1999) *Arthur and the Lost Kingdoms*. Wiedenfeld & Nicholson, London.

Morton H V (2000) *In Search of England*. Methuen Publishing, London.

Oram R (2001) *The Kings & Queens of Scotland*. Tempus Publishing, Stroud.

Pearson A (1930) *Annals of Kirkby Lonsdale*. Titus Wilson & Sons, Kendal.

Peel A (1913) *The Manor of Knowlmere*. Privately published, Knowlmere.

Pennick N (1979) *The Ancient Science of Geomancy: Man in Harmony with the Earth*. Thames & Hudson, London.

Pennick N (1996) *Celtic Sacred Landscapes*. Thames & Hudson, London

Persinger M A & Lafrenière G F (1977) *Space-Time Transients and Unusual Events.* Nelson-Hall, Chicago.

Phillimore E (ed.) (1888) *The Annales Cambriae* and Old Welsh Genealogies from *Harleian* MS. 3859, *Y Cymmrodor* 9.

Phillips G & Keatman M (1984) *The Green Stone.* Grafton Books, London.

Phillips G & Keatman M (1994) *The Shakespeare Conspiracy.* Century, London.

Phillips G R (1976) *Brigantia: A Mysteriography.* Book Club Associates, London.

Pickford D (1992) *Myths and Legends of East Cheshire and the Moorlands.* Sigma Leisure, Wilmslow.

Pickford D (1994) *Staffordshire, Its Magic and Mystery.* Sigma Leisure, Wilmslow.

Pickford D (1996) *Earth Mysteries of the Three Shires.* Churnet Valley Books, Leek.

Pickford D (1998) *The Bridestones.* Bawdstone Press, Staffordshire.

Pinkham M A (1997) *The Return of the Serpents of Wisdom.* Adventures Unlimited Press, Illinois.

Probert W (1823) *The Ancient Laws of Cambria.* E Williams, London.

Queally J (2001) *The Culdees, an Ancient Religious Enigma in Scotland.* Celtic Trails, Edinburgh.

Rich D & Begg E (1991) *On the Trail of Merlin.* Aquarian Press, London.

Ritchie A (1989) *Picts: An Introduction to the Life of the Picts and the Carved Stones in the Care of Historic Scotland.* HMSO, London.

Roberts A (1975) *Atlantean Traditions in Ancient Britain.* Rider & Co, London.

Roby J (1879) *The Traditions of Lancashire Vol I.* Longman & Co, London.

Rowling M (1976) *The Folklore of the Lake District.* B T Batsford, London.

Scott D (2006) *The Clava Cairns.* For the Right Reasons Community Print, Inverness.

Screeton P (1974) *Quicksilver Heritage. The Mystic Leys: Their Legacy of Ancient Wisdom.* Thorsons, London.

Searle A (1998) *Isle of Wight Folklore.* Dovecote Press, Wimborne.

Scott Sir W (1808) *Marmion: A Tale of Flodden Field.* Archibald Constable, Edinburgh.

Skene W F (ed.) (1867) *Chronicles of the Picts, Chronicles of the Scots.* HM General Register House, Edinburgh.

Skene W F (ed.), Skene F J H (translator) (1871–72, 1993) *John of Fordun's Chronicle of the Scottish Nation*, 2 vols. Llanerch, Burnham-on-Sea.

Stebbing Shaw Revd (1801) *History and Antiquities of the County of Stafford.* EP Pub, Staffordshire County Library.

Stewart E (1926, 1979) *Dunkeld, an Ancient City.* Willian Culross & Son, Coupar Angus.

Stokes P (1996) *Craven County: The Story of Hamstead Marshall.* Penelope Stokes, Newbury.

Stukeley W (1776, 1969) *Itinerarium Curiosum: Or an Account of the Antiquities and Remarkable Curiosities in Nature or Art Observed in Travels Through Great Britain Vol II.* Greg International Publishers, Farnborough.

Sutton Revd R (1988) *A History of All Saints' Church, Church Lawton.* www.allsaintschurchlawton.co.uk.

Thacker F S (1932) *Kennet Country.* Blackwell, Oxford.

Thom A (1967) *Megalithic Sites in Britain.* Oxford University Press, Oxford.

Tolkien J R R (1937) *The Hobbit, Or There and Back Again.* George, Allen & Unwin, London.

Tolkien J R R (1954) *The Lord of the Rings.* George, Allen & Unwin, London.

Trubshaw R (1991) *The Quest for the Omphalos.* Heart of Albion Press, Loughborough.

Trubshaw R (2011) *Singing Up the Country: The Songlines of Avebury and Beyond*. Heart of Albion Press, Loughborough.

Tunstall B (1939) *The Dark Lady*. William Heinemann, London.

Warren W T (1932) *Warren's Guide to Winchester*. Warren & Son, Winchester.

Waterhouse J (1985) *The Stone Circles of Cumbria*. Phillimore, Chichester.

Watkins A (1925) *The Old Straight Track*. Methuen Publishing, London.

Watkins S (2009) *Mary Queen of Scots*. Thames & Hudson, London.

Westwood J (1986) *Albion: A Guide to Legendary Britain*. Book Club Associates, London.

Wheatley D (1998) *A New View of the Rollright Ring: The Rollright Mysteries*. Braden Press, Swindon.

Whitaker Dr T D (1872) *History of the Parish of Whalley Vol I*. George Routledge & Sons, Manchester.

Wicherink J (2005) *Souls of Distortion Awakening: A Convergence of Science and Spirituality*. www.soulsofdistortion.nl.

Wilson J M (1869) *Tales of the Borders*. William P Nimmo, Edinburgh.

Wood M (1983) The Making of King Aethelstan's Empire: An English Charlemagne? *Ideal and Reality in Frankish and Anglo-Saxon Society: Studies Presented to J.M. Wallace-Hadrill*, eds Patrick Wormald *et al*. Basil Blackwell, Oxford.

Wood M (2003) *In Search of Shakespeare*. BBC Books, London.

Wood M (2010) *In Search of Arthur*. BBC documentary. www.bbc.co.uk/history/ancient/anglo_saxons/arthur.

Worsley Sir R (1781) *History of the Isle of Wight*. www.nationalarchives.gov.uk.

Wyntoun A (1350–1420), Laing D (1793–1878) (ed.) *The Orygynale Cronykil of Scotland*. Edmonston & Douglas, Edinburgh.

Yates F (1972) *The Rosicrucian Enlightenment*. Routledge, London.

Young W S (2004) *A Spot Supremely Blessed: The History, Lore and Legends of Langholm*. Cairndhu Publishing, Langholm.

Useful Websites

www.canmore.rcahms.gov.uk (research of British archaeological sites)
www.davidfurlong.co.uk/michael_alignment.htm (St Michael alignment)
www.ian-opc.org.uk (research on Lancashire towns)
www.megalithic.co.uk (research of English archaeological sites)
www.megalthix.wordpress.com (research of megalithic sites in Northern England)
www.romanscotland.org.uk
www.scottish-places.info
www.themodernantiquarian.com (research of Europe's megalithic sites)
www.undiscoveredscotland.co.uk

Index

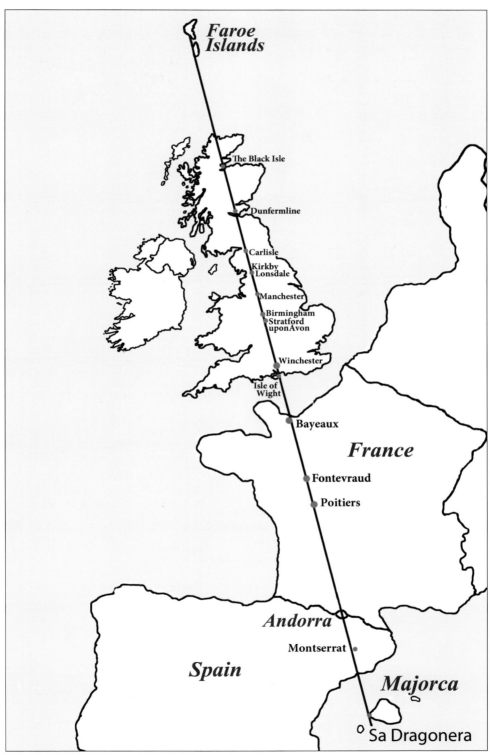

Belinus Line through Europe

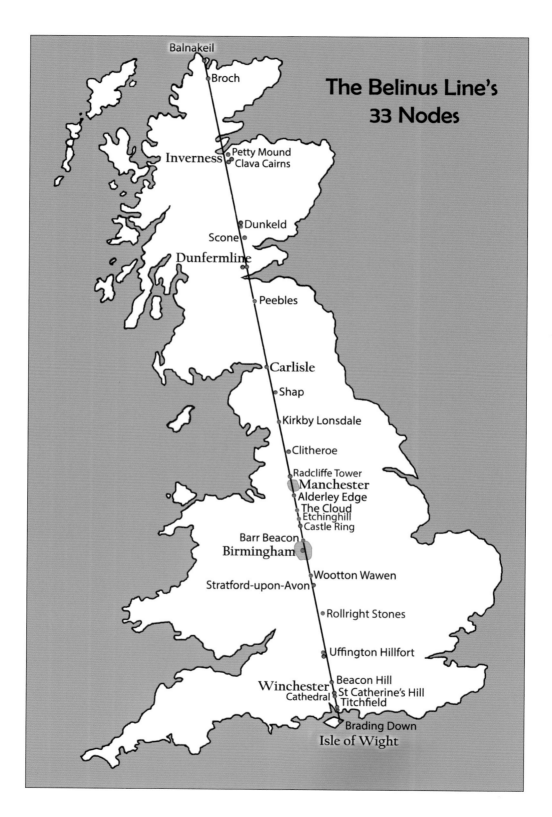

Balnakeil
Broch

The Belinus Line's 33 Nodes

Inverness Petty Mound
Clava Cairns

Dunkeld
Scone
Dunfermline

Peebles

Carlisle
Shap
Kirkby Lonsdale
Clitheroe
Radcliffe Tower
Manchester
Alderley Edge
The Cloud
Etchinghill
Castle Ring
Barr Beacon
Birmingham
Wootton Wawen
Stratford-upon-Avon
Rollright Stones
Uffington Hillfort
Beacon Hill
Winchester St Catherine's Hill
Cathedral Titchfield
Brading Down
Isle of Wight

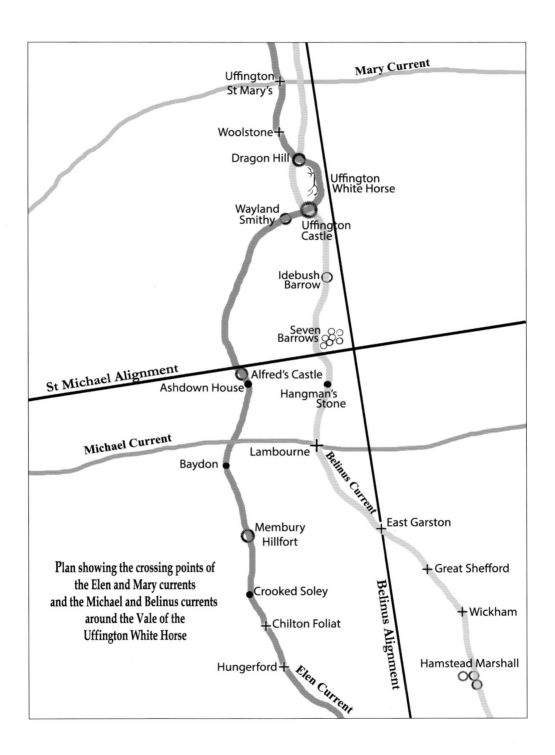

Mary Current

Uffington St Mary's ✚

Woolstone ✚

Dragon Hill ⊛

Uffington White Horse

Wayland Smithy ⊛

Uffington Castle ⊛

Idebush Barrow ○

Seven Barrows ⊛

St Michael Alignment

Alfred's Castle ⊛

Ashdown House ●

Hangman's Stone ●

Michael Current

Lambourne ✚

Baydon ●

Belinus Current

East Garston ✚

Membury Hillfort ⊛

Great Shefford ✚

Plan showing the crossing points of the Elen and Mary currents and the Michael and Belinus currents around the Vale of the Uffington White Horse

Crooked Soley ●

Chilton Foliat ✚

Wickham ✚

Belinus Alignment

Hungerford ✚

Elen Current

Hamstead Marshall ⊛

View of Winchester Cathedral with Beacon Hill beyond © Peter Trimming

The Dark Rift © Steve Jurvetson

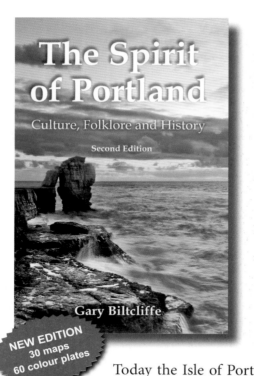

NEW EDITION
30 maps
60 colour plates

The Spirit of Portland

Culture, Folklore and History

by

Gary Biltcliffe

Priced £11.99 Plus p&p

Today the Isle of Portland in Dorset has a reputation for its stone quarrying and naval heritage, but behind this lies an island steeped in myth and legend. Why was it so important and strategic throughout Britain's history? Does Portland hold the key to an ancient Masonic secret? Was it a major centre of the Druids? Are the island families descended from Phoenicians and Jutes? This fascinating book explores the island's mysteries, its sacred geology and geometry, its ley lines, holy wells, and a giant figure formed from roads and footpaths within its landscape. The use of local traditions and archaeology helps to reveal Portland's special importance to our ancient ancestors, who built a staggering number of stone circles, standing stones and burial mounds. Discover these places and artefacts for yourself with walks that highlight Portland's hidden treasures and their significance – with surprises for both locals and visitors.

Even the sceptical must acknowledge the thorough research and considerable scholarship that have gone into the book, and it is true that Portland holds more secrets than most outsiders appreciate.

Dorset Life Magazine

Available from
www.belinusline.com